W9-DFU-565

URDU GRAMMAR AND READER

URDU
Grammar and Reader

by

ERNEST BENDER

Oriental Studies Department and South Asia Regional
Studies Department, University of Pennsylvania

Philadelphia
UNIVERSITY OF PENNSYLVANIA PRESS

HARVARD-YENCHING LIBRARY
HARVARD UNIVERSITY
2 DIVINITY AVENUE

© 1967 by the Trustees of the University of Pennsylvania

Paragon Book Gallery, Ltd.
AUG 12 1968

Library of Congress Catalogue Card Number: 66-20832

~~W 5975.07/07~~

PK 1973 .B4

Bender, Ernest, 1919-

Urdu; grammar and reader

7522
Printed in the United States of America

TO MY STUDENTS
—WHO ASKED FOR IT—

ACKNOWLEDGEMENTS

I am indebted to the following persons for help given in various ways: Professor W. Norman Brown, Dr. Anwar Hussain Syed, and Dr. Sajjad Ahmad Hashmi, and to Mrs. Regina Jaskowiak Long and Miss Gloria Gioia for their careful preparation of the typescript.

I am happy to express my gratitude for their generous support of my work to Dr. Mortimer Graves and the American Council of Learned Societies, to the Rockefeller Foundation, and to the Carnegie Corporation of New York. I extend my thanks to the United States Office of Education, Department of Health, Education and Welfare, both for its support and for making the publication of this book possible.

Philadelphia, 1963 Ernest Bender

FOREWORD

This volume is a companion volume to Professor Ernest Bender's HINDI GRAMMAR and READER. The Urdu materials were first collected in 1948 at the same time that the Hindi materials were being collected, and they have been checked and revised since then in classroom exercises. Though there is a good deal of fundamental similarity between Hindi and Urdu on the spoken level, it is nevertheless essential to differentiate between them early in their study. Hence, separate teaching materials are necessary for the two. The materials here presented have been well tested and by now are well adapted for use in American institutions. They are now being made available here in printed form.

Professor Bender's volume not only provides for instruction in the spoken language, but also introduces a student to the written language. This latter with its large amount of Persian and Arabic loanwords and idioms has so far lacked suitable teaching materials. That lack, it is hoped, will now be filled by this volume.

Philadelphia, 1964 W. Norman Brown

TABLE OF CONTENTS

Page

ACKNOWLEDGEMENTS 6

FOREWORD 7

INTRODUCTION 17

LESSON 1 25

1.1–1.13: phonology; 1.15–1.17: conversational texts.

LESSON 2 31

2.1: present tense of verb, present participle, present tense of verb "to be," **hōnā**, personal pronouns; 2.2: masculine nouns in **-ā**; 2.3: feminine nouns in **-ī**; 2.4: numbers 1 to 10; 2.5–2.6: conversational texts.

LESSON 3 37

3.1: infinitive construction with **cāhnā**; 3.2: predicate-adjective construction, adjective in **-ā**; 3.3: masculine nouns having same form for subject singular and plural; 3.4: feminine nouns ending in **-ē** in subject plural; 3.5: numbers 11 to 20; 3.6–3.7: conversational texts.

LESSON 4 43

4.2: feminine nouns in **-iyā**; 4.3: adjectives in **-ā**; 4.4: adverbs; 4.5: numerals as adjectives; 4.6: numbers 21 to 30; 4.7–4.8: conversational texts.

LESSON 5 49

5.1: direct object of personal pronoun, postposition; 5.2–5.6: direct object of noun; 5.7: numbers 31 to 40; 5.8–5.9: conversational texts.

LESSON 6 57

6.1: adjectives modifying nouns in object form; 6.2–6.3.3: demonstrative pronouns and adjectives; 6.4: numbers 41 to 60; 6.5–6.6: conversational texts.

LESSON 7 66
7.1–7.1.1: imperative; 7.2: time expressions; 7.3: numbers 61, on; 7.3.2: dates; 7.4–7.5: conversational texts.

LESSON 8 69
Review of lessons 1 to 7.

LESSON 9 78
9.1–9.4.4: postpositions (**-mẽ, -kō, -par, -sē**); 9.5: conversational text.

LESSON 10 84
10.1–10.4.3: postpositional phrases (**-kē pīchē, -kē nīcē, -kē sāth, -kē sāmnē**); 10.5–10.6: conversational texts.

LESSON 11 89
11.1–11.3: postpositional phrases (**-kē pās, -kē liyē**); 11.4: adjectives ending in consonants; 11.5–11.5.2: interrogative sentences; 11.6: conversational text.

LESSON 12 97
12.1–12.1.2: interrogative adverbs; 12.2: construction with **saknā;** 12.3–12.6: negation; 12.7–12.8: conversational texts.

LESSON 13 104
13.1: negation; 13.2–13.3: negative question; 13.4: negative of **saknā** construction; 13.5–13.5.3; pronominal possessive adjectives; 13.6: conversational text.

LESSON 14 109
14.1—14.2.1: "genitive" construction; 14.3: first and second person pronouns in compound postpositional phrases; 14.4: subjunctive; 14.5: conversational text.

LESSON 15 116
15.1–15.2.2: future; 15.3–15.3.2: **pasand karnā** construction; 15.4: conversational text.

LESSON 16 123
Review of lessons 9 to 15.

LESSON 17 134
17.1–17.2: constructions translating English "ought to, should, need, have to, must" (**cāhiyē, hai, paṛtā hai**); 17.3–17.3.4: indefinite adjective and pronoun (**kōī**); 17.4–17.4.1: **kuch;** 17.5: reading text.

LESSON 18 144
18.1–18.1.4: conditional sentences; 18.2–18.4: interrogative adjectives and pronouns (**kaun, kyā, kaun-sā, kitnā**); 18.5: reading text.

LESSON 19 154
19.1–19.1.2: "imperfect" or "past continuous"; 19.2–19.3: past of **cāhiyē** construction; 19.4: "contrary to fact" or "unreal subjunctive" construction; 19.5: ordinal numbers; 19.6: reading text.

LESSON 20 163
20.1–20.1.4: formation of past participle and perfect tense of intransitive verb; 20.2–20.2.2: **pasand hōnā** construction; 20.3–20.3.6: comparative and superlative constructions; 20.4: reading text.

LESSON 21 172
21.1–21.2.4: perfect tense of transitive verb; 21.3: reading text.

LESSON 22 180
22.1–22.1.4: past participles of **jānā, hōnā, dēnā, lēnā, karnā;** 22.2: **kaun-sā;** 22.5–22.5.5: constructions translating possession 22.6: reading text.

LESSON 23 189
23.1–23.1.1; "present progressive" or "present continuative" and "past progressive" or "past continuative"; 23.2: negative of future; 23.2.1: negative of conditional sentences; 23.2.2–23.2.3: negative of **cāhiyē** and **hai** constructions; 23.2.4: negative of "contrary to fact" construction; 23.2.5–23.4.2: negative of past tenses; 23.6: reading text.

LESSON 24 197
24.1–24.44: Review of lessons 17 to 23; 24.45–24.51: translations of reading texts of lessons 17 to 23.

LESSON 25 217
25.1–25.2: relative constructions; 25.3: reading text.

LESSON 26 224
26.1–26.4.1: relative constructions; 26.5: reading text.

LESSON 27 233
27.1–27.5: relative constructions; 27.6: and (**aur**); 27.7: reading text.

LESSON 28 240
28.1–28.7: verbal clusters (with **dēnā, lēnā, jānā, ḍālnā, paṛnā, uṭhnā, cuknā**); 28.9: reading text.

LESSON 29 248
29.1–29.2: "direct discourse"; 29.3: "indirect discourse"; 29.4: construction with **hōnā;** 29.5: reading text.

LESSON 30 255
30.1: gerund ("conjunctive participle" or "absolutive"); 30.2–30.2.3: infinitive before postpositions or postpositional phrases (i.e., infinitive as noun); 30.3: reading text.

LESSON 31 262
31.1–31.1.2: participial adjectival constructions; 31.2: **-vālā** formations; 31.3–31.4: participial adverbial constructions; 31.5: reading text.

LESSON 32 269
32.1–32.42: review of lessons 25 to 31; 32.43–32.49: translations of reading texts of lesson 25 to 31.

LESSON 33 286
33–33.1: past participial adjectival construction; 33.2: **-jaisā;** 33.3–33.3.3: temporal constructions; 33.4–33.4.1: **milnā** (= "meet, find," etc.); 33.6: gerund; 33.7: reading text.

LESSON 34 292
34.1–34.1.2: constructions with **lagnā;** 34.2: participles in adverbial phrases; 34.3: present participle + **rahnā;** 34.4–34.4.1: present participle + **jānā;** 34.5: past participle (= gerund) + **karnā;** 34.6: reading text.

LESSON 35 301
35.1: present participle as adverb; 35.2: **binā** + past participle; 35.3: possession indicating relationship; 35.4: addition, substruction, multiplication, division; 35.5–35.5.1: time expressions; 35.7: reading text.

LESSON 36 308
36.1–36.1.4: verbal stem alternations (formation of causative stems); 36.2: repetition of words; 36.3: emphatic particle (**-hī, -ī, -hī̃**); 36.4: reading text.

LESSON 37 316
37.1: "passive" construction; 37.2–37.2.1: infinitive as noun and adjective; 37.2.2: infinitive in object form without postposition; 37.2.3: infinitive with **dēnā** = "let"; 37.3: reading text.

LESSON 38 321
38.1–38.1.1: construction with **-sā;** 38.2–38.2.1: constructions with **jaisā** and **vaisā;** 38.2.2: **kaisā;** 38.3: **jitnā;** 38.4: **ḳarīb;** 38.5: **kōī ēk;** 38.6: reading text.

LESSON 39 327
Rural Economic Survey Questionnaire.

LESSON 40 334
40.1–40.30: review of lessons 33 to 38; 40.31–40.36: translations of reading texts of lessons 33 to 38.

GLOSSARY 347

INDEX 483

URDU GRAMMAR AND READER

INTRODUCTION

The area in which people speak Urdu as their mother tongue includes East and West Pakistan where, with Bengali, it functions as the official language of the land, and northern India.

The language of this course is based on the Urdu dialect of the educated classes of Pakistan. The purpose of this course is to provide an American learner with the basic grammatical equipment and vocabulary necessary to conduct his affairs in areas of Pakistan (and India) in which Urdu is the language of communication. Developed over a period of fifteen years, it is designed to be administered to students, who have little or no linguistic training, by a team consisting of a Pakistani assistant, having Urdu for his (or her) mother tongue and an American linguist, with some experience in Urdu, who provides the grammatical exegesis. The linguist conducts the language drill in English, and the Urdu assistant, in Urdu.

The organization of the course is basically simple in concept and approximates the techniques in use for progrmaming teaching machines. (In fact, with minor adjustments, it could be converted to a mechanical device.) It has a dual aim, pursued concurrently, —to provide the student with a firm comprehension of the basic grammar and indoctrinate him with the necessary linguistic habits, and to introduce him to and familiarize him with the "language in action," spoken as well as written. The first aim is represented by the grammatical sections and drill exercises of the lessons, and the second by the accompanying conversations and reading texts. In the initial stages—that is, the first sixteen lessons—the student is advised to memorize, verbatim, the simple conversations included in these lessons. To avoid the pitfalls of confronting the learner with the burden of having to deal with a number of grammatical constructions and to learn vocabulary at one and the same time, attention should not be given to identifying the individual constituents of the utterances. As he acquires the necessary grammatical comprehension and linguistic habits, the student returns periodically to the conversations and practices, manipulating the constructions he has mastered up to that time—i.e., replacing the components of certain utterances with the proper forms and words to express new ideas. From Lesson 17 on, the conversations, which are fully annotated, are longer and more complex, graduating into reading texts.

The book is arranged in five parts of eight lessons each, the last, or eighth, constituting a review. Appended are a glossary, containing all the words provided in the book, and an index. Grammar is presented through the medium of "equivalent constructions," rather than by rules to be learned by rote. The sentences of sections dealing with grammatical instruction are arranged in parallel columns—the sentences of the left-hand column exemplifying the Urdu construction to be learned, and the right-hand column providing the equivalent English translation. The accompanying grammatical discussion elucidates the constituents, formation, and usage of the construction.

The lessons start with the simplest sentence types, for example, Noun-Verb ("**[The] man walks.**"), Pronoun-Verb (**"He walks."**), Noun-Adjective (**"[The] boy is good."**), Noun-Noun (**"[The] man is [a] farmer"**). The elements of the sentence are identified and explained, and there follows drill in construction with vocabulary replacement in the example sentences to form new meaningful sentences; pronouns are replaced by other pronouns, nouns by nouns, and verbs by the different verbs learned up to this point. (The grammatical explanation need not be presented through the medium of technical terminology. For the student not versed in the terms, "noun, verb, subject, predicate, etc.," explanation can be given in terms of the equivalent words in the accompanying English translation. In the Urdu sentence **ādmī caltā hai,** the student is told that **"ādmī"** has the same functions as **"man"** in the English equivalent **"[The] man walks."** and **"caltā hai"** that of **"walks."**) Each new Urdu construction is based on constructions already mastered. The accompanying English translation functions as an identification device and the emphasis is directed to the comprehension and mastery of the Urdu construction. In the initial stages only one grammatical element is introduced in each new exercise, and this practice is followed, wherever possible, in the succeeding lessons. Thus, the student gradually learns to think in terms of Urdu and, upon completion of formal instruction, continues the refining process by relating any new construction he may encounter to those he already knows.

The initial phase of the course stresses the spoken language. Emphasis is directed to the student's acquiring "an ear for the language," that is, training him to distinguish the critical phonological features—for example, the differing qualities of vowels (see sections 1.1–1.1.1, 1.4–1.4.1, 1.8) and the characteristics which distinguish the aspirated (see section 1.9) from the non-aspirated (see sections 1.2.1, 1.5) consonants—and to utter the Urdu sounds so that the native speaker can readily recognize them The lessons are graduated, proceeding (Lesson 17) into reading exercises, which are provided in the form of romanized texts. Shortly after this the student is taught the native, or Nastālīḳ, script. (The companion volume to this will contain the Nastālīḳ transcription of all the conversations and texts contained in this book.) The postponement of reading instruction in the native script is purposeful. Experience has demonstrated the need to minimize the handicaps under which a learner labors if he has to contend with the intricacies of a new grammar, phonology and a strange alphabet, concurrently. Students as well as instructors have found the results of this arrangement gratifying. We now proceed to describe the operation of this course in detail.

Lesson 1 discusses the Urdu sounds and the symbols employed to represent them. Several short conversations with elucidatory notes follow. The conversations are designed to provide the student with practice in hearing the language as it is spoken, as well as for purposes of practice in pronunciation. The accompanying English translations are not literal renditions of the Urdu, but the English equivalents of the Urdu sentences.

The student, at this time, should not try to isolate separate words to determine their English meaning, but should memorize each Urdu sentence as a whole. Grammatical explanations are given in the lessons following. (See section 1.14.) As has been remarked before, the instructor will periodically return to the conversations and drill the student in the grammatical construction he has mastered—that is, train him to replace recognized elements or phrases with the necessary forms and words to produce new utterances. This dual approach—namely, the indoctrination of the student in the necessary grammatical comprehension and linguistic habits by means of drill in the pertinent exercises, and the memorization of the conversations and their subsequent rephrasing—will be constantly maintained throughout this and the following lessons.

Lesson 2 begins with the Urdu equivalent of the paradigms of an English verb in the present tense with the appropriate pronominal subjects. In this and the other sections which give grammatical examples the construction under examination will be included within a full utterance or sentence. (Here, for example, in section 2.1, each verb with its pronominal subject comprises a complete sentence.) In section 2.1, as in other sections dealing with grammar, the Urdu sentences are listed in the left-hand column, thus: **maĩ dēkhtā hũ, maĩ dēkhtī hũ, vo dēkhtā hai, vo dēkhtī hai, ham dēkhtē haĩ, ham dēkhtī haĩ,** etc., and the corresponding English sentences in the right-hand column read: **"I** (msc.) **see.," "I** (fm.) **see.," "He sees.," "She sees.," 'We** (msc.) **see.," We** (fm.) **see.,"** and so on. The procedure in the handling of sections of this kind is for the native speaker to pronounce the sentences to the students—first slowly, and then, at a normal rate—and to drill them in their pronunciation. After this the linguist explains the grammatical formation under consideration. Once the pronunciation of the sentences has been mastered and committed to memory, the next step is drill in the replacement of the pertinent constituent elements of the sentences to fashion new meaningful sentences. This drill is conducted, on the one hand, by the native speaker to exercise the students in aural recognition and, on the other, by the linguist to give them practice in translation from English into Urdu. New vocabulary is usually provided in sentences of the same type as the example sentences (see section 2.1.1). Since the constituent elements have been identified and their formation discussed in the grammatical section (in this case, of section 2.1), the focal point of attention is known—namely, the verb or, more precisely, the verbal stem. This is extracted from each sentence (see section 2.1.2), for the substitution exercises in which all the possible permutations are tried, using the vocabulary which is given—i.e., pronouns and verbs—to fashion meaningful sentences. This is the procedure to be followed in the subsequent lessons. (As for the translation exercises of the type given in sections 2.1.3 and 2.1.4, the instructor may assign these for work to be done out of class or in class, as he sees fit. Other teaching aids comprise tape-recordings of the Urdu example sentences, as well as of the conversations. These are supplemental to the course, to be used for drill in comprehension and pronunciation, and are to be assigned for laboratory sessions.)

The lessons which follow progressively replace and expand the constituents of the sentence type given in section 2.1. Sections 2.2 and 2.3 introduce nouns. Here the student encounters the simple substitution of the third person pronoun, singular and plural, (i.e., **vo**) with the noun forms under study—masculine nouns, with the proper participial ending and auxiliary verb, and feminine nouns with their corresponding forms. For example, section 2.2 deals with masculine nouns ending in **-ā** in the subject form, singular, which replace the **-ā** with **-ē** in the subject form, plural. Therefore, the formation of a simple sentence with a nominal subject from one with a pronominal subject is accomplished by a single substitution. (The substituted elements are underlined.) For example, **vo** of **vo caltā hai "He walks."** is replaced by **laṛkā** to fashion **laṛkā caltā hai. "The boy walks."** Similarly, **vo** of **vo caltē haĩ "They walk."** is replaced by **laṛkē** to fashion **laṛkē caltē haĩ "The boys walk."** Furthermore, in section 2.3, **vo** of **vo caltī hai. "She walks."** is replaced by **laṛkī** to form **laṛkī caltī hai. "The girl walks."**; and **vo** of **vo caltī haĩ** is replaced by **laṛkiyā̃**, resulting in **laṛkiyā̃ caltī haĩ. "The girls walk."** The drill described above is then carried out with pronouns substituted by nouns to form as many meaningful sentences as possible. Several simple conversations follow.

Lesson 3 expands the sentence type (henceforth, indicated by the symbols **(NV)**, with the infinitive. More precisely, it illustrates the use of the infinitive with the verb **cāhnā** "to want, wish." Since the verb **cāhnā** functions like the verbs already mastered, the new element is the infinitive, which is the point of concentration for drill. Observe the progression from **vo cāhtā hai "He wants."** to **laṛkā cāhtā hai "The boy wants."** to **laṛkā bōlnā cāhtā hai "The boy wants to speak."** We then continue with the exercise on the infinitive: **laṛkā bōlnā cāhtā hai "The boy wants to speak.," laṛkā dauṛnā cāhtā hai "The boy wants to run.," laṛkā khēlnā cāhtā hai "The boy wants to play.,"** and so on. Subsequent drill, both by the native speaker, as well as the linguist, is not confined to the infinitive alone, but includes all the members of each sentence—pronoun, noun and verb. For example, **vo khēlnā cāhtā hai "He wants to play.," laṛkā khēlnā cāhtā hai "The boy wants to play.," vo khēlnā cāhtē haĩ "They want to play.," laṛkē khēlnā cāhtē haĩ "The boys want to play.," vo khēlnā cāhtī hai "She wants to play.," laṛkī khēlnā cāhtī hai "The girl wants to play.," vo khēlnā cāhtī haĩ "They (fm.) want to play.," laṛkiyā̃ khēlnā cāhtī haĩ "The girls want to play.," kuttā khēlnā cāhtā hai. "The dog wants to play.," kuttā dauṛnā cāhtā hai "The dog wants to run.," kuttā khānā cāhtā hai "The dog wants to eat.," kuttā kūdnā cāhtā hai "The dog wants to jump.," vo kūdnā cāhtā hai "He wants to jump.," vo kūdnā cāhtī hai "She wants to jump.," maĩ kūdnā cāhtā hū̃ "I want to jump.," ham kūdnā cāhtē haĩ "We want to jump.," tum kūdnā cāhtē hō "You want to jump.,"** and so on, until all the possible permutations are accomplished or the time allotted exhausted. (This, of course, can not be carried out in only one or even a continuous succession of drills, but at recurring intervals, depending on how much time is allotted to the course and how it is scheduled.) The linguist, as usual, reverses this procedure, drilling from English to Urdu.

Section 3.2 introduces a new sentence type (or, as will be demonstrated shortly, a variation of the sentence type, **NV**, already learned). The new element is the predicate adjective. Here is introduced the class of adjectives whose subject form, masculine, ends in **-ā** for the singular and **ē** for the plural; and whose subject form, feminine, singular and plural, ends in **-ī**. (It may be helpful to note that the adjective occupies the same position in the sentence and functions like the participial form of the verb in the previous sentences.) Compare **laṛkā caltā hai "The boy walks."** and **laṛkā acchā hai "The boy is good.," laṛkē caltē haĩ "The boys walk."** and **laṛkē acchē haĩ "The boys are good.," laṛkī caltī hai "The girl walks.,"** and **laṛkī acchī hai "The girl is good.,"** and **laṛkiyā̃ caltī**

haĩ "The girls walk." and **laṛkiyā̃ acchī haĩ "The girls are good."**) Other noun types follow (sections 3.3, 3.4 and 4.2), drill in which follows the method discussed.

In section 4.3 we expand the subject of the sentence type, **NV**, with the adjective described in section 3.2 (i.e., which changes its form for gender, number and case): **acchā laṛkā caltā hai "The good boy walks.," acchē laṛkē caltē haĩ "The good boys walk.," acchī laṛkī caltī hai "The good girl walks.," acchī laṛkiyā̃ caltī haĩ "The good girls walk."** Section 4.4 introduces adverbs (i.e., expands the predicate), thereby increasing the scope of the drill sessions and thus furnishing the student with the means for fuller expression: **ādmī jātē haĩ "The men go.," ādmī bāhar jātē haĩ "The men go out.," ādmī andar jātē haĩ "The men go in.," ādmī vahā̃ jātē haĩ "The men go there.," ādmī āgē jātē haĩ "The men go ahead.," ādmī nīcē jātē haĩ "The men go down.," ādmī nīcē jātā hai "The man goes down.," dublā ādmī nīcē jātā hai "The lean man goes down.," dublā ādmī nīcē jānā cāhtā hai "The lean man wants to go down.," dublī laṛkī andar jānā cāhtī hai "The lean girl wants to go in.," dublī laṛkī jaldī-sē jānā cāhtī hai "The lean girl wants to go quickly.," dublī laṛkī jaldī-sē khānā cāhtī hai "The lean girl wants to eat quickly.,"** and so on.

Lesson 5 takes up the Hindi equivalent of the English "direct object," pronoun and noun, respectively, i.e., another expansion of the predicate of the sentence: **ādmi us-kō dēkhtā hai "The man sees him.,"** and **ādmī laṛkē-kō dēkhtā hai "The man sees the boy."** Here, moreover, the student experiences for the first time the function of the post-position (i.e., **-kō**). Lesson 6 demonstrates adjectives (see section 3.2) modifying nouns in the object form: **ādmī chōṭē laṛkē-kō dēkhtā hai "The man sees the little boy.,"** and **ādmī chōṭī laṛkī-kō dēkhtā hai "The man sees the little girl.";** and the demonstrative adjectives and pronouns: **ye laṛkā acchā hai "This boy is good.," vo laṛkī acchī hai "That girl is good.," ādmī is laṛkī-kō dēkhtā hai "The man sees this girl.,"** and **ādmī us laṛkē-kō dēkhtā hai "The man sees that boy."** With the mastering, in Lesson 7, of the imperative forms, the opportunities for variation in expression are further increased. Lesson 8 is, as is every subsequent eighth lesson, a review. The instructor may at this point direct the student's attention to the conversations committed to memory to further exploit the possibilities for fashioning new conversations.

During the progress of the course the student should be encouraged to maintain a vocabulary list as well as a corpus of idiomatic expressions or stereotyped phrases to be memorized for use in conversation drill. With the grammatical and lexical equipment provided up to this stage, along with the incidental information which will be treated more fully in succeeding lessons, the student can participate in simple conversations with the native speaker. (For example, the third response of the first conversation [1.3.1] is a question. The instructor will note at that point that Urdu questions are fashioned by affixing the particle **kyā** to the beginning of the sentence [11.5, ff.]. Response 8 contains a "polite" imperative and response 11 "direct discourse" [29.1, 29.2]. The fifth response of the third conversation [1.3.3] illustrates the use of **nahī̃** to express negation [cf. 23.2–23.4.2], etc.) A conversation exercise at the completion of the first four lessons may run something along these lines betweten the Urdu speaker and the student. **(The remarks contained within square brackets identify the conversation and sentence in which the construction appears. We bear in mind that by this time the student has had adequate**

drill—aural, as well as oral—in the substitution and expansion of the elements of an utterance.)

Urdu Speaker:	**salām.**	**Hello.**
Student:	**valēkum salām.**	**Hello.**
Urdu Speaker:	**āp-kā nām kyā hai?**	**What is your name?** [4.7, sentence 5.]
Student:	**mērā nām Grīn hai.**	**My name is Green.** [4.7, sentence 8 for **mērā.**]
	āp-kā nām kyā hai?	**What is your name?**
Urdu Speaker:	**mērā nām Fazal hai.**	**My name is Fazal.**
	kyā maĩ āp-sē kuch savāl pūch saktā hū̃?	**Can I ask you some questions?** [4.7, sentence 3.]
Student:	**pūchiyē.**	**(Please) ask.** [4.7, sentence 4.]
Urdu Speaker:	**āp-kē pās vaḳt hai?**	**Do you have time?** [2.6, sentence 1.]
Student:	**kahiyē?**	**Why?** [2.6, sentence 2.]
Urdu Speaker:	**mujhē madad-kī zarūrat hai.**	**I need (your help.)** [2.6, sentence 3.]
Student:	**maĩ āp-kī kyā madad kar saktā hū̃?**	**How can I help you?** [2.6, sentence 4.]
Urdu Speaker:	**maĩ muśkil-mẽ hū̃.**	**I'm in trouble.** [2.6, sentence 11.]
Student:	**kyū̃? kyā huā?**	**Why? What happened?** [2.6, sentence 12.]
Urdu Speaker:	**māmūlī bāt hai.**	**A small matter.** [1.17, sentence 11.]
	āp-kē pās mōṭar hai.	**You have an automobile.** [2.6, sentence 1.]
Student:	**jī hā̃. kyū̃?**	**Yes. Why?**
Urdu Speaker:	**mujhē mōṭar cāhiyē.**	**I need an automobile.** [2.5, sentence 5.]
Student:	**kyū̃? āp-kō mōṭar kyū̃ cāhiyē?**	**Why? Why do you need an automobile?**
Urdu Speaker:	**maĩ śahar jaldī-sē jānā cāhtā hū̃.**	**I wish to go to the city quickly.** [1.15, sentence 13.]
Student:	**bahot acchā.**	**Very well.**
	mērē sāth aiyē.	**Come with me.** [3.7, sentence 1.]
Urdu Speaker:	**bahot bahot śukriyā.**	**Thank you very much.**

The preceding conversation is an illustration of the kind of work which can be carried out with the materials of the first four lessons. We stress, as we have stressed before and will continue to stress, that proportionate attention must be given to grammatical (including vocabulary) drill; for if the student is not provided with the necessary linguistic reflexes, his progress in the colloquial—and later, the written—language will be hindered.

Lessons 9, 10 and 11 continue with the expansion of the sentence type by postpositional phrases. Sections 11.4 and 11.4.1 discuss a second type of adjective (i.e., one which has the same form for gender, number and case), and 11.5 to 11.5.1 the formation of interrogative sentences (see the remarks relating to this in the paragraph preceding the example conversation, above). A new element is introduced in 12.2, a verbal cluster, consisting of a verbal stem and a verb (see Lesson 28 for a fuller treatment). Here the verbal cluster translates the English verbal phrase comprising the verb **can (to be able)** and a second verb. For example, **laṛkā Urdū bōl saktā hai "The boy can speak Urdu."** and **laṛkī Añgrēzī samajh saktī hai "The girl can understand English."** To be exact, this is not a "new" element, but rather an expansion of the verb, for the verbal cluster functions as a unit, identical with the "simple" verbs previously encountered. In the same manner that the student has been conditioned to the utterance, **ādmī chōṭē laṛkē-kō dēkhtā hai "The man sees the little boy.,"** so he assimilates the extension with **saknā: ādmī chōṭē laṛkē-kō dēkh saktā hai "The man can see the little boy."**

Subsequent sections lead the student through the formation of negative sentences, possessive adjectives, and in Lesson 14, the equivalent to the English genitive construction — the **-kā** postpositional phrase, which again, is a substitution and extension of the adjective (see 4.3, **et passim**). Compare: **chōṭā bhāī Urdū bōltā hai. "The little brother speaks Urdu."** and **us-kā bhāī Urdū bōltā hai "His brother speaks Urdu."** or **laṛkē-kā bhāī Urdū bōltā hai "The boy's brother speaks Urdu."**; and **maĩ chōṭē bhāī-sē savāl pūchtā hū̃ "I ask the little brother questions."** and **maĩ us-kē bhāī-sē savāl pūchtā hū̃ "I ask his** brother **questions.,"** or **maĩ laṛkē-kē bhāī-sē savāl pūchtā hū̃ "I ask the boy's brother questions."** With the introduction of the subjunctive (section 14.4) and the future (section 15.1), the formation of complex sentences can be considered (sections 18.1, ff.); and thus this procedure is maintained through the succeeding lessons, with the addition of new constructions and refresher drills. Continued experience will instill a feeling for nuances and style. This, in substance, is the way the learner—or, as a matter of fact any other American—has acquired and continually augments the dialect of English he uses.

From Lesson 17 on, the texts, larger and fully annotated, are designed to acquaint the student with the flexibility and range of expression of the language—conversational, narrative, expository, etc. (At about this point the student is ready to undertake reading in the script, the instructional materials for which are contained in the companion volume, **Introductory Urdu Readings.)** English newspapers and magazine articles concerned with Indian topics have been found to be very useful in providing additional topics for exercises in advanced conversation and composition. Slides illustrating various aspects of the Indian scene may be employed for supplementary conversational materials. These may be utilized in several ways. The native speaker may use the contents of the slides (or pictures) for themes of addresses to the students, after which he questions the students about the content of his talks. Another approach is for the native speaker to record a number of discourses, which at the proper times, are played back to the students (with or without the showing of slides or pictures) for exercise in aural recognition; or the students may be asked to discourse upon the contents of the slides or pictures.

The time requirement for the completion of this course is dependent on the number of weekly hours allotted to it. A rough estimate, in terms of the course as it is described above, would be four semesters of sixteen weeks each, the first two semesters with seven hours of classes per week, and the second with four hours of classwork per week. For shorter courses, such as those offered during summer sessions, we recommend that the instructor reduce the number of example sentences to be memorized and concentrate on the student's acquiring the essentials of the grammar.

In closing it may be of interest to note that the companion Hindi grammar parallels the arrangement of this book, making it possible for the student, who so desires or whose program of work requires training in both languages, to effect a facile transition from one to the other with a minimum of investment in time and effort.

Furthermore, this book has a dual function. For the teacher it serves as a classroom text, while a researcher in Modern Indo-Aryan languages can employ it as a **Reference Grammar.** The Index and the Table of Contents offer ample guides and the examples accompanying the grammatical statements (including observations on "usage") provide the necessary clarification.

LESSON 1

1. The symbols and the Urdu sounds whch they represent. The student should read through the entire lesson carefully before returning to study the separate sections.

1.1 Vowels:

ā: has the value of the vowel in English **father, balm,** but without any trace of the diphthongization which occurs in English.

a: has the value of the vowel in English **cut, but, hut.**

ī: approximates the value of the vowel in English **meet, beat,** but without the final **y**-glide of the English sound.

i: while approximating the value of the vowel in English **bit, hit,** can be described as having the quality of the long **ī** described above, but shorter in length.

ū: has the value of the vowel in English **boot, loot, shoot,** but without the final **w**-glide of the English sound.

u: while approximating the value of the vowel of English **put,** foot, can be described as being a little shorter in length than the **ū** described above.

REMARKS: (1) Only **ī** and **ū** occur in final position—i.e., in a word.

(2) **a, ā, i, ī** are unrounded vowels. Care should be taken not to round the lips in their pronunciation.

1.1.1 In the example words which follow the consonant sounds are the same as the English:

āg fire, **gājā bājā** sound of musical instruments, **gān** singing, **gāy** cow, **jānā** to go, **jab** when, **bas!** enough! **sab** all, **gaj** elephant, **ab** now, **bīs** twenty, **bīj** seed, **īmām** belief, **jugnī** firefly, **mīn** fish, **jinis** commodity, **binā** without, **bam** bomb, **biyā** seed, **bis** poison, **misī** made of copper, **ūn** wool, **janūnī** insane, **janūb** south, **sūnā** empty, **māyūs** hopeless, **ugānā** to raise, **jānī** dear, **muzāb** melted, **muznib** sinner.

1.2 Consonants:

1.2.1 Non-aspirate stops:

t: This is not English **t.** It is a voiceless sound made with the tip of the tongue spread out against the upper teeth or slightly protruding past the teeth, as in pronouncing the English spirant, **th** of **thick, thorn.** Care must be taken not to aspirate it or to pronounce it as a fricative.

d: This is not English **d.** It is executed like the **t** described above, but it is voiced.

p: as in English **pin, put,** but without the puff of breath which follows the English sound.

b: as in English **bet, boat.**

1.2.2 Nasals:

n: as in English **neigh.**

m: as in English **meet, moat.**

1.2.3 **r:** is a voiced sound made with the tip of the tongue tapping once or twice at the base of the upper teeth.

1.2.4 **h:** is a voiced sound; never voiceless as in English.

1.3 Examples of the sounds described above are:

das ten, **ham** we, **sāt** seven, **āp** you, **is** this, **itnā** this much, **patā** address, **bīs** twenty, **pāband** fettered, **dam** less, **dām** price, **tum** you, **burā** bad, **ūn** wool, **ūpar** up, **bahā** floated, **bas!** enough! **bār** time, **bārā** twelve, **sab** all, **dabānā** to press down, **tīn** three, **tīs** thirty, **rāstā** road, **mat** not, **imārat** building, **ādmī** man, **madad** help.

1.4 Vowels:

e: has the value of the vowel in English **get, bet.**

[NOTE: **a,** when followed by **h,** has the same value. Examples are **rahnā** to stay, **nahar** canal, **sahnā** to endure.]

ē: has the value of the vowel in English **say, pay,** but without the final **y**-glide of the English sound.

REMARKS: **e, ē,** are unrounded vowels. Care should be taken not to round the lips in their pronunciation.

o: has the value of the vowel in English **bought, caught.**

ō: has the value of the vowel in English **no, hoe, toe,** but without the final **w**-glide of the English sound.

1.4.1 Diphthongs:

ai: is made by pronouncing **a** (See 1.1, above.), followed immediately by **i** (See 1.1, above.).

[NOTE: a variant pronunciation, **e** (See 1.4.), is often encountered.]

au: is made by pronouncing **a,** followed immediately by **u** (See 1.1, above.).

1.5 Non-aspirate stops:

k: as in English **coat, kite,** but without the puff of breath which follows the English **k**-sound.

g: as in English **get, goat.**

c: as in English **church, chin,** but without the puff of breath which follows the English sound.

j: as in English **joke, jam.**

1.5.1 **y:** as in English **yes, yoke.** When in final position following a vowel or between vowels, it is a glide-sound like that of the second member of the English diphthong in **say, pay.**

l: is a voiced sound made with the tip of the tongue spread out against the upper teeth.

v: is a voiced sound approximating the **w** of English **walk, wall.** In a variant pronunciation the upper teeth brush lightly against the lower lip, approximating the **v** of English **very, vat.**

1.6 Examples of the sounds described in sections 1.4 to 1.5.1 are:

behtar better, **mehmān** guest, **mehrāb** arch, **mehnat** toil, **meharbānī** kindness, **ēk** one, **lēnā** to take, **kohrā** fog, **ohdā** rank, **mohar** seal, **ōr** direction, **lōg** people, **sōnā** to sleep, **dō**

two, **jō** who, **hai** is, **aisā** such (this kind), **kaisā** what kind, **paisā** money, **tairnā** to swim, **nau** nine, **caubīs** twenty-four, **kaun** who, **kām** work, **kitnā** how much, **halkā** light, **rōknā** to stop, **sarkār** government, **carnā** to graze, **calnā** to walk, **bacānā** to save, **sac** true, **galā** throat, **gahrā** deep, **cugnā** to peck, **dēgcā** small kettle, **nāg** snake, **jānā** to go, **jūtā** shoe, **bīj** seed, **gaj** elephant, **sēb** apple, **yād** memory, **garmī** summer, **yasar** left, **gayā** gone, **liyā** taken, **gāy** cow, **girnā** to fall, **valad** son, **bōlnā** to speak, **mūl** root, **vāpas** afterwards, **havā** wind, **lōvā** fox, **basmā** dying, **vāh!** excellent!

1.7 Consonants (retroflex stops):

ṭ: is a voiceless, non-aspirate consonant made with the tip of the tongue touching the hard plate farther back than the contact-point for making English **t.**

ḍ is a voiced consonant made with the tip of the tongue touching the upper palate farther back than the contact-point for making English **d.**

[NOTE: **ḍ,** when occurring between vowels, very often has the value of **ṛ** (See following.).]

ṛ: is a voiced consonant made with the tip of the tongue turned back and flipped forward, striking the palate once at the point of contact for making Urdu **ḍ.**

1.7.1 Examples of the sounds described in section 1.7 are: **ṭukṛā** piece, **lauṭnā** to return, **taṭ** shore, **ḍagar** path, **ḍar** fear, **baḍ** banyan tree, **laṛkā** boy, **laṛnā** to fight, **baṛā** big, **dauṛnā** to run, **ciṛiyā** sparrow.

1.8 Nasalized vowels and diphthongs:

The vowels and vowel combinations described above (See sections 1.1, 1.4, 1.4.1.) can be nasalized by passing the breath through the nose while they are being pronounced. They are marked in the text by a tilde (~) written over them, thus: **ã, ā̃, ĩ, ī̃,** etc. Nasalized diphthongs are indicated by placing the tilde over the second vowel, thus: **aĩ, aũ.**

Examples are: **pā̃c** five, **ī̃ṭ** brick, **ū̃cā** high, **tē̃tīs** thirty-three, **saĩtīs** thirty-seven, **caũtīs** thirty-four, **ṭā̃ṭ** skull, **nahī̃** not, **sā̃p** snake.

1.9 Consonants (Aspirate stops):

A series of aspirate stops is made by pronouncing each of the consonants described in sections 1.2.1, 1.5 and 1.7 in conjunction with a strong aspiration or puff of breath, thus: **th, dh, ph, bh, kh, gh, ch, jh, ṭh, ḍh, ṛh.**

[NOTE: Though written with two symbols, each of these comprises a single sound.]

Examples are: **khād** dung, **rakhnā** to place, **kuch** something, **phal** fruit, **guphā** cave, **ghar** house, **sūjhnā** be visible, **jhārū** broom, **bhējnā** to send, **bhōjan** food, **lābh** gain, **thālī** dish, **cithṛā** rag, **dhūp** incense, **dūdh** milk, **idhar** hither, **bhūlnā** to forget, **dhīrē** slowly, **dēkhnā** to see, **pūchnā** to ask, **khōdnā** to dig, **ghaṛā** pot, **khaṛā** upright, **āṭh** eight, **baiṭhnā** to sit, **ṭhīk** exact, **mīṭhā** sweet, **caṛhānā** to raise, **baṛhnā** to grow, **būṛhā** old.

1.10 Other nasal consonants:

n (See 1.2.2.), before **t, th, d, dh, c, ch, j, jh, ṭ, ṭh, ḍ, ḍh,** is executed with the tongue in the same position as for making these sounds. When it occurs before the retroflex stops (**ṭ, ṭh, ḍ, ḍh**), it is written with a dot beneath it, thus: **ṇ.**

When it occurs before **k, kh, g, gh** it is pronounced like the sound **ng** in English **sing, singer, and** writen thus: **ñ.** Examples are: **ant** end, **andar** in, **andhā** blind, **uncās** forty-nine, **injan** engine, **kunjī** key, **aṇṭhlānā** to swagger, **aṇḍā** egg, **rañg** color, **sañgīn** bayonet.

1.11 Sibilants:

s: as in English **sap, singer.**

ś: is a voiceless sound made with the tongue farther back than for making the **sh** of English **shape, ship.**

ṣ: is a variant of **s** occurring before the retroflex stops, **ṭ, ṭh.** It is executed with the tip of the tongue at the contact-point for making the retroflex stops.

Examples are: **sāban** soap, **āsān** easy, **bas!** enough!, **śajā** brave, **śadīd** difficult, **muśkil** difficult, **muśār** indicated, **uṣṭra** camel, **iṣṭ** desired.

1.12 Other sounds are those occurring mainly in Perso-Arabic loan-words and in European borrowings.

f: is a bilabial voiceless fricative, often a voiceless labio-dental fricative, as in English **foot, fickle.**

Examples are: **daftar** office, **haftā** week.

z: a voiced sound as in English **zip, zing.**

Examples are: **bāzār** market, **hazār** thousand.

ḳ: is a **k**-sound made with the hump of the tongue touching the back of the soft palate.

Examples are: **haḳ** true, **huḳam** command.

ḳh: is a voiceless fricative made with the tongue in the same position as for pronouncing **ḳ**, but not touching the palate.

Examples are: **buḳhār** fever, **āḳhir** end.

g̲: is a voiced guttural fricative made with the hump of the tongue farther back than for pronouncing **ḳh.**

Examples are: **bāg̲** garden, **g̲arīb** poor.

1.13 Long or double consonants:

These are indicated by writing the symbols twice—e.g., **kk, tt, cc,** etc. They are fashioned by maintaining the articulation almost twice as long as for making the single sound.

In the case of the aspirates, when they are doubled, the aspiration comes at the end of the consonant cluster. They are written thus: **kkh, cch, tth,** etc.

Examples are: **billī** cat, **battīs** thirty-two, **unnīs** nineteen, **kuttā** dog, **ṭaṭṭī** matted shutter, **mohallā** neighborhood, **mohabbat** love, **akkhaḍ** undisciplined, rude, **acchā** good, **aṭṭhārā** eighteen, **addhā** half, **ghaṭṭhī** small landing-place, **chuṭṭhī** holiday, **jhakkī** chatterer, **tarrār** pickpocket, **patthar** stone, **nabbāz** physician, **nakkū** disgraced, **dajjāl** liar, **pillū** worm, **Dillī** Delhi, **chabbīs** twenty-six.

1.14 The conversations given here and in the lessons following are designed to provide the student with practice in hearing the language as it is spoken, as well as for purposes of practice in pronunciation. Care must be taken in pronunciation to give each symbol its proper sound value. (See discussion, above, 1.–1.13*) In groups of consonants each consonant must be given its proper value. The slurring of one into the other must be avoided.

The English sentence which accompanies each Urdu sentence is not a literal translation of the Urdu, but the English equivalent of the Urdu sentence. The student, at this time, should not try to isolate separate words to determine their English meaning, but memorize each Urdu sentence as a whole. Grammatical explanations are given in the lessons following.

[*The numerals refer to sections.]

1.15 dō musāfirō̃-kē darmiyān bāt•cīt.		Conversation Between Two Travellers.	
Jamīl Fārūḳī:	asalām alēkum.[1]	Jamīl Fārūḳī:	Hello.
Kamāl Usmānī:	valēkum asalām.	Kamāl Usmānī:	Hello.
Fārūḳī:	kyā ye basō̃-kā aḍḍā hai?	Fārūḳī:	Is this the bus depot?
Usmānī:	nahī̃. ye rēl-kā sṭēśan[2] hai.	Usmānī:	No. This is the train station.
Fārūḳī:	tō, basō̃-kā aḍḍā kahā̃ hai?	Fārūḳī:	Then where is the bus station?
Usmānī:	vo dō mīl dūr hai.	Usmānī:	That is two miles away.
Fārūḳī:	kis taraf?	Fārūḳī:	In which direction?
Usmānī:	bāī̃ taraf ēk mīl jākar, dāī̃ taraf muṛ jāiyē.	Usmānī:	Go to the left for one mile, and then turn right.
Fārūḳī:	bāī̃ taraf aur phir dāī̃?	Fārūḳī:	To the left, and then to the right?
Usmānī:	hā̃. pahilē bāī̃ aur phir dāī̃.	Usmānī:	Yes. First to the left, and then to the right.
Fārūḳī:	kyā āp-kō mālūm hai ke[3] bas kab jātī hai?	Fārūḳī:	Do you know when the bus leaves?
Usmānī:	āp kahā̃ jānā cāhtē haĩ?	Usmānī:	Where do you wish to go?
Fārūḳī:	maĩ Lāhōr jānā cāhtā hū̃.	Fārūḳī:	I wish to go to Lahore.
Usmānī:	vo bas tīn ghanṭē-kē bād[4] jāēgī.	Usmānī:	That bus leaves in three hours.
Fārūḳī:	tīn ghanṭē-kē bād?	Fārūḳī:	In three hours?
Usmānī:	hā̃. tīn ghanṭē-kē bād.	Usmānī:	Yes. In three hours.
Fārūḳī:	phir maĩ us bas-sē jāū̃gā.	Fārūḳī:	Then I will go by that bus.
Usmānī:	tab tumhẽ fauran-hī jānā cāhiyē. yād rakhiyē. pahilē bāī̃ taraf ēk mīl jāiyē, aur phir dāī̃ taraf muṛ jāiyē.	Usmānī:	Then you should go right away. Remember. First go to the left for one mile, and then turn to the right.
Fārūḳī:	bahot bahot śukriyā. Ḳhudā hāfiz.[5]	Fārūḳī:	Thank you very much. Good-by.

REMARKS: (1) A variant is **asalām-ō-alēkum.** Another term of greater respect is **ādāb arz,** the answer to which is **jītē rahō** (Long may you live.).

(2) **rēlvē sṭēśan** is also used.

(3) variant: **keh.**

(4) variant: **tīn ghanṭō̃-kē bād.**

(5) Lit.: **May God protect you.**

1:16 dō dōstō̃-kē darmiyān bāt•cīt.		Conversation Between Two Friends.	
Hādī:	asalām alēkum.	Hādī:	Hello.
Sardār:	valēkum asalām.	Sardār:	Hello.
Hādī:	āp kaisē haĩ?	Hādī:	How are you?
Sardār:	maĩ bahot acchā hū̃. āp kaisē haĩ?	Sardār:	I am very well. How are you?
Hādī:	maĩ-bhī acchā hū̃. kyā ghar-par sab ṭhīk haĩ?	Hādī:	I am well, too. Is everyone at home all right?
Sardār:	hā̃. Ḳhudā-kā śukra hai. ghar-par sab ṭhīk haĩ.	Sardār:	Yes. It is God's kindness. Everyone at home is all right.

Hādī:	māf [1] kījiyē.	Hādī:	Excuse me.
	mērī bas ā rahī hai.		My bus is coming.
	mujhē jānā hai.		I must leave.
Sardār:	mujhē āp-sē milkar bahot ḳhuśī huī.	Sardār:	I am very glad to have met you.
Hādī:	mujhē ummīd hai ke ham phir jald milẽgē.	Hādī:	I hope that we'll meet again soon.
Sardār:	Inśāllāh.	Sardār:	God willing.
Hādī:	Ḳhudā hāfiz.	Hādī:	Good-by.
Sardār:	Ḳhudā hāfiz.	Sardār:	Good-by.

REMARKS: (1) a variant is **mūāf.**

1.17 Karīm aur Fazal miltē haĩ. — **Karīm and Fazal Meet.**

Karīm:	salām, sāhab.[1]	Karīm:	Hello:
Fazal:	valēkum salām.	Fazal:	Hello.
	kahā̃ jā rahē hō?		Where are you going?
Karīm:	maĩ apnē bhāī-sē milnē jā rahā hū̃.	Karīm:	I am going to see my brother.
Fazal:	tumhārā chōṭā bhāī?	Fazal:	Your younger brother?
Karīm:	jī nahī̃. mērā baṛā bhāī.	Karīm:	No. My older brother.
Fazal:	maĩ usē nahī̃ jāntā.	Fazal:	I do not know him.
	vo kahā̃ rahtā hai?		Where does he live?
Karīm:	śahar-mẽ.	Karīm:	(He lives) in the city.
Fazal:	us-kā pēśā [2] kyā hai?	Fazal:	What does he do?
Karīm:	vo bairā hai.	Karīm:	He is a waiter.
Fazal:	kyā kōī muśkil hai?	Fazal:	Is there any problem?
Karīm:	jī nahī̃. māmūlī bāt hai.	Karīm:	No. A small matter.
Fazal:	sab ṭhīk hai na?	Fazal:	Everything is all right—isn't it?
Karīm:	jī hā̃. sab ṭhīk hai.	Karīm:	Yes. Everything is all right.
	māf kījiyē.		Excuse me.
	mērī bas ā rahī hai.		My bus is coming.
	mujhē jānā hai.		I must go, now.
	Ḳhudā hāfiz.		Good-by.
Fazal:	Ḳhudā hāfiz.	Fazal:	Good-by.

REMARKS: (1) A form of greeting to a superior from an uneducated person. Note Fazal's reply.

(2) This expression is not used in connection with women, lest a different connotation be inferred. (The literal translation is "What is his profession?") An alternate expression is **vo kyā kartā hai?** (= What does he do?)

LESSON 2

2.1

maĩ dēkhtā hū̃.	I (**msc.**) see.
maĩ dēkhtī hū̃.	I (**fm.**) see.
vo dēkhtā hai.	He sees.
vo dēkhtī hai.	She sees.
ham dēkhtē haĩ.	We (**msc.**) see.
ham dēkhtī haĩ.	We (**fm.**) see.
tum dēkhtē hō.	You (**msc.**) see
tum dēkhtī hō.	You (**fm.**) see.
āp dēkhtē haĩ.	You (**msc.**) see
āp dēkhtī haĩ.	You (**fm.**) see.
vo dēkhtē haĩ.	They (**msc.**) see.
vo dēkhtī haĩ.	They (**fm.**) see.

The sentences listed above illustrate the present tense of the Urdu verb in all three persons, singular and plural. This tense indicates an act going on in present time, or a general statement, as is expressed in such English sentences as **The children play., The women cook., Men work., Rocks fall.** It does **not** translate the Progressive Present tense of English as in **The children are playing., The rocks are falling., The woman is cooking., The men are working.** Urdu has another construction to indicate this construction (See 23.1.).

Each of the Urdu sentences, given above, consists of three words. The first word in each Urdu sentence translates the pronoun in the corresponding English sentence. The remaining two words comprise the Urdu verb. The first of the two words is a present participle and the second the present tense of the verb **to be, to exist.** The participle agrees with the subject of the verb in gender and number— **-ā** for masculine singular nouns, **-ē** for masculine plural, and **-ī** for feminine singular and plural. The present tense of the verb **to be** is: **hũ̄,** first person singular; **hai,** third person singular; **hō,** second person plural; **haĩ,** the remaining plural forms.

REMARKS: (1) Both forms given for the second person are plural. They also serve to translate into Urdu the second person singular of English. **āp** is employed as an honorific form, applied to persons to whom respect or honor is intended. **tum** is normally employed toward equals or acquaintances and to servants. The subject forms, singular and plural, of the third person pronoun are identical. The verbal form will indicate whether the form is singular or plural.

(2) The stem of the verb is obtained by dropping the final vowel and the preceding **-t-** of the particle. The stem of the verb **to see** given in the sentences above is, therefore, **dēkh.**

(3) It will be seen in the **Conversations,** following, that this tense also functions as a weak future.

4) The third person pronoun is often pronounced with a slight aspiration: **voh.**

2.1.1 More examples follow.

[NOTE: For the time being, the student should consider **kām kar** as the stem of the verb **to work.**]

maĩ kahtā hũ̄.	I (**msc.**) say.
maĩ khātā hũ̄.	I (**msc.**) eat.
maĩ pahõctā hũ̄.	I (**msc.**) arrive.
maĩ pūchtī hũ̄.	I (**fm.**) ask.
maĩ caltī hũ̄.	I (**fm.**) walk.
maĩ pītī hũ̄.	I (**fm.**) drink.
vo dauṛtā hai.	He runs.
vo khēltā hai.	He plays.
vo kūdtā hai.	He jumps (down).
vo caltī hai.	She walks.
vo bōltī hai.	She speaks.
vo pakātī hai.	She cooks.
ham lātē haĩ.	We (**msc.**) bring.
ham sōtē haĩ.	We (**msc.**) sleep.
ham pītē haĩ.	We (**msc.**) drink.
ham jātī haĩ.	We (**fm.**) go.
ham tairtī haĩ.	We (**fm.**) swim.
ham rahtī haĩ.	We (**fm.**) live.
tum mārtē hō.	You (**msc.**) beat.
tum samajhtē hō.	You (**msc.**) understand.
tum ātē hō.	You (**msc.**) come.

tum kahtī hō. — You (fm.) say.
tum bōltī hō. — You (fm.) speak.
tum khēltī hō. — You (fm.) play.

āp pūchtē haĩ. — You (msc.) ask.
āp paṛhtē haĩ. — You (msc.) read.
āp pītē haĩ. — You (msc.) drink.

āp kūdtī haĩ. — You (fm.) jump (down).
āp dauṛtī haĩ. — You (fm.) run.
āp bhējtī haĩ. — You (fm.) send.

vo pahõctē haĩ. — They (msc.) arrive.
vo kām kartē haĩ. — They (msc.) work.
vo dētē haĩ. — They (msc.) give.

vo pakātī haĩ. — They (fm.) cook.
vo samajhtī haĩ. — They (fm.) understand.
vo rahtī haĩ. — They (fm.) stay.

2.1.2 Exercise **1.** List the stems of the verbs in 2.1.1.

2.1.3 Exercise 2. **Translate into English:**

1. āp caltē haĩ. 2. vo pahõctī hai. 3. tum sōtē hō. 4. vo khēltē haĩ. 5. maĩ bōltī hū̃. 6. ham dētē haĩ. 7. tum samajhtī hō. 8. vo jātā hai. 9. vo kahtē haĩ. 10. āp lātē haĩ. 11. vo ātā hai. 12. ham kahtī haĩ. 13. tum paṛhtī hō. 14. maĩ kūdtā hū̃. 15. vo rahtī hai. 16. tum pūchtē hō. 17. vo tairtī haĩ. 18. āp dauṛtē haĩ. 19. ham khātē haĩ. 20. maĩ kām kartā hū̃.

2.1.4 Exercise 3. **Translate into Urdu:**

1. They (**msc.**) go. 2. He says. 3. You (**hon. pl. fm.**) speak. 4. I (**fm.**) understand. 5. He plays. 6. She walks. 7. They (**msc.**) speak. 8. We (**fm.**) run. 9. I (**msc.**) play. 10. You (**fm.**) jump. 11. We (**msc.**) arrive. 12. I (**msc.**) work. 13. She stays. 14. You (**msc.**) cook. 15. They (**fm.**) ask. 16. We (**msc.**) bring. 17. We (**fm.**) say. 18. I (**fm.**) read. 19. She sleeps. 20. You (**hon. pl. msc.**) drink.

2.2

laṛkā caltā hai. — The boy walks.
laṛkē caltē haĩ. — The boys walk.

bēṭā khātā hai. — The son eats.
bēṭē khātē haĩ. — The sons eat.

kuttā pītā hai. — The dog drinks.
kuttē pītē haĩ. — The dogs drink.

baccā khēltā hai. — The child plays.
baccē khētē haĩ. — The children play.

gadhā dauṛtā hai. — The donkey runs.
gadhē dauṛtē haĩ. — The donkeys run.

This section illustrates masculine nouns ending in -ā in the subject form, singular, which replace the -ā with -ē in the subject form, plural.

REMARKS: Urdu does not have an equivalent for the English article **the.**

2.2.1 Exercise 1. Fashion sentences of the type given in 2.2 with the verbs of 2.1.1 and the following nouns and verbs, both in the singular and the plural:
bakrā goat, **ghōṛā** horse, **tōtā** parrot, **bhēṛiyā** wolf, **bachṛā** calf, **nanhā** baby, **ucal-** (to) jump (See section 2.1, Remark 2, for stem of verb.), **bhāg-** (to) run swiftly, **mā̃g-** (to) demand, request.

2.2.2 Exercise 2. **Translate into English:**
1. bēṭā khātā hai. 2. baccā dauṛtā hai. 3. kuttā kūdtā hai. 4. bachṛā khātā hai. 5. gadhā rahtā hai. 6. laṛkā paṛhtā hai. 7. ghōṛā caltā hai. 8. tōtā pūchtā hai. 9. bachṛē khēltē haĩ. 10. gadhē ātē haĩ. 11. kuttē bhāgtē haĩ. 12. baccē pītē haĩ. 13. bakrē jātē haĩ. 14. ghōṛē pahõctē haĩ. 15. bhēṛiyā rahtā hai. 16. laṛkā dēkhtā hai. 17. tōtē kahtē haĩ. 18. bhēṛiyē dauṛtē haĩ. 19. bakrā khātā hai. 20. bēṭē caltē haĩ.

2.2.3 Exercise 3. **Translate into Urdu:**
1. The goat comes. 2. The calves eat. 3. The child drinks. 4. The donkey walks. 5. The dog plays. 6. The parrots sleep. 7. The wolf jumps. 8. The horse runs. 9. The children swim. 10. The goats live. 11. The boys speak. 12. The son sends. 13. The donkeys go. 14. The dogs swim. 15. The horses bring. 16. The boy asks. 17. The wolves arrive. 18. The parrot understands. 19. The sons say. 20. The calf lives.

2.3

laṛkī samajhtī hai.	The girl understands.
laṛkiyā̃ samajhtī haĩ.	The girls understand.
bēṭī pakātī hai.	The daughter cooks.
bēṭiyā̃ pakātī haĩ.	The daughters cook.
billī sōtī hai.	The cat sleeps.
billiyā̃ sōtī haĩ.	The cats sleep.
bīvī lātī hai.	The wife brings.
bīviyā̃ lātī haĩ.	The wives bring.
ghōṛī dauṛtī hai.	The mare runs.
ghōṛiyā̃ dauṛtī haĩ.	The mares run.

This section illustrates feminine nouns which end in -ī in the subject form, singular. This ī is replaced by **-iyā̃** to form the subject form, plural.

2.3.1 Exercise 1. Fashion sentences of the type given in 2.3 with the verbs of 2.1.1 and the following nouns and verbs, both in the singular and the plural:
machlī fish, **lōmṛī** fox, **murgī** hen, **makkhī** fly, **bakṛī** goat, **cug-** (to) peck and eat (e.g., of chicken).

2.3.2 Exercise 2. **Translate into English:**
1. bakrī ātī hai. 2. makkhiyā̃ jātī haĩ. 3. murgī pītī hai. 4. billī dauṛtī hai. 5. machlī

khātī hai. 6. laṛkiyā̃ paṛhtī haĩ. 7. lōmṛī kūdtī hai. 8. bīvī pakātī hai. 9. ghōṛī dēkhtī hai. 10. bēṭī samajhtī hai. 11. machliyā̃ khātī haĩ. 12. murgiyā̃ cugtī haĩ. 13. billiyā̃ khēltī haĩ. 14. makkhī caltī hai. 15. bēṭiyā̃ paṛhtī haĩ. 16. bakriyā̃ rahtī haĩ. 17. bīviyā̃ pūchtī haĩ. 18. laṛkī bhējtī hai. 19. ghōṛiyā̃ ātī haĩ. 20. lōmṛiyā̃ dauṛtī haĩ.

2.3.3 Exercise 3. **Translate into Urdu:**

1. The goats eat. 2. The cat drinks. 3. The wife arrives. 4. The fish eat. 5. The girls ask. 6. The foxes run. 7. The cats play. 8. The hen runs. 9. The daughters speak. 10. The flies go. 11. The wives cook. 12. The girl works. 13. The fox sees. 14. The hens drink. 15. The daughter reads. 16. The fly lives. 17. The daughter understands. 18. The fish lives. 19. The daughters say. 20. The goat sleeps.

2.4 The numbers 1 to 10:

ēk 1, **dō** 2, **tīn** 3, **cār** 4, **pā̃c** 5, **che** 6, **sāt** 7, **āṭh** 8, **nau** 9, **das** 10.

2.5 **mā̃ laṛkē-sē bāt kar rahī hai.** — **Mother Talking to Son.**

mā̃:	**bēṭā!**	Mother:	**Son!**
bēṭā:	**jī hā̃.**[1]	Son:	**Yes.**
mā̃:	**jaldī-sē āō!**	Mother:	**Come quickly!**
bēṭā:	**farmāiyē?**	Son:	**What do you wish?**
mā̃:	**mujhē ālū aur gōbhī cāhiyē̃.**	Mother:	**I need potatoes and cauliflower.**
bēṭā:	**kyā maĩ bāzār jāū̃?**	Son:	**Shall I go to the bazaar?**
mā̃:	**hā̃. bāzār jāō.** **ye lō paisē.**	Mother:	**Yes. Go to the bazaar.** **Take this money.**
bēṭā:	**aur kuch cāhiyē?**	Son:	**(Do you) want anything else?**
mā̃:	**agar matar tāzē hō̃, to kuch kharīd lēnā.**	Mother:	**If the peas are fresh, buy some.**
bēṭā:	**bahot acchā.**	Son:	**Very well.**
mā̃:	**ālū aur gōbhī mat bhūlnā.**	Mother:	**Do not forget the potatoes and cauliflower.**
bēṭā:	**bahot acchā. maĩ nahī̃ bhūlū̃gā.**	Son:	**All right, I'll not forget.**
mā̃:	**jald vāpas ānā.** **dēr mat karnā.** **mujhē kuē̃-sē pānī cāhiyē.**	Mother:	**Come back quickly.** **Do not lag.** **I will want water from the well.**
bēṭā:	**bahot acchā. maĩ jald vāpas āū̃gā.**	Son:	**Very well. I'll come soon.**

REMARKS: (1) This is a polite answer, indicating respect, to a person present. An alternate answer to a person within earshot, but not necessarily visible, is **jī**.

2.6 **mōṭar-kā ḳharāb hōnā.** — **Automobile Breakdown.**

mōṭar • calānēvālā:	**kyā tumhārē pās vaḳt hai?**	Motorist:	**Do you have time?**
kisān:	**kahiyē?** [1]	Farmer:	**Why?**
mōṭar • calānēvālā:	**mujhē madad-kī zarūrat hai.**	Motorist:	**I need (your) help.**
kisān:	**maĩ āp-kī kyā madad kar sakta hū̃?**	Farmer:	**How can I help you?**

mōṭar • calānēvālā:	**kyā tum Angrēzī samjhtē hō?**	Motorist:	**Do you understand English?**
kisān:	**hā̃. thōṛī Angrēzī samjhtā hū̃.**	Farmer:	**Yes. I understand a little English.**
mōṭar • calānēvālā:	**bahot acchā, tab maĩ Urdū bōlū̃gā.**	Motorist:	**All right, then I'll speak in Urdu.**
kisān:	**bahot acchā.**	Farmer:	**O.K.**
mōṭar • calānēvālā:	**mērī Urdū bahot acchī nahī̃.**	Motorist:	**My Urdu is not very good.**
kisān:	**maĩ āp-kō samajh saktā hū̃.**	Farmer:	**I can understand you.**
mōṭar • calānēvālā:	**maĩ muśkil-mē̃ hū̃.**	Motorist:	**I am in trouble.**
kisān:	**kyū̃? kyā bāt hai?**	Farmer:	**Why? What happened?**
mōṭar • calānēvālā:	**mērī mōṭar ḳharāb hō gayī hai.**	Motorist:	**My automobile has broken down.**
kisān:	**maĩ āp-kī kyā madad kar saktā hū̃?**	Farmer:	**How can I help?**
mōṭar • calānēvālā:	**kyā tum kisī mistarī [2] -kō jāntē hō?**	Motorist:	**Do you know any mechanic?**
kisān:	**hā̃. yahā̃-sē dō mīl dūr ēk mistarī hai.**	Farmer:	**Yes. There is a mechanic two miles away from here.**
mōṭar • calānēvālā:	**kis taraf?**	Motorist:	**In which direction?**
kisān:	**sīdhē [3] jāiyē. vo bahot acchā mistarī hai.**	Farmer:	**(Please go) straight ahead. He is a very good mechanic.**
mōṭar • calānēvālā:	**bahot bahot śukriyā.**	Motorist:	**Thank you very much.**

REMARKS: (1) **kahiyē** indicates that the answerer has the time. If he wished to know the reason for the question his answer would be: **kyū̃? āp kyā cāhtē haĩ?** (Why? Why do you ask?).

(2) Another term is **mikenik (ā).**

(3) An alternate expression is **sāmnē,** indicating that the farmer is pointing to the direction in which he is facing.

LESSON 3

3.1

laṛkā bōlnā cāhtā hai.	The boy wants to speak.
laṛkē khēlnā cāhtē haĩ.	The boys want to play.
laṛkī pakānā cāhtī hai.	The girl wishes to cook.
laṛkiyā̃ dēkhnā cāhtī haĩ.	The girls wish to see.
maĩ sōnā cāhtā hū̃.	I want to sleep.
tum kām karnā cāhtē hō.	You want to work.
vo dauṛnā cāhtī hai.	She wants to run.
ham lēnā cāhtī haĩ.	We wish to take.
āp dēnā cāhtē haĩ.	You wish to give.
vo sunnā cāhtī haĩ.	They want to hear.

This section illustrates the Urdu construction which translates the English phrase, **wants to, wishes to** ———. (The gap represents the verb to be translated.)

The Urdu construction consists of the verb **cāhnā to wish, want,** immediately preceded by the infinitive of the verb.

REMARKS: The infinitive of the verb is fashioned by attaching the suffix **-nā** to the verb stem. (See remark 2 of 2.1.)

3.1.1 Exercise 1. List the infinitives of the verbs of section 2.1.1.

3.1.2 Exercise 2. Fashion as many sentences as you can of the type illustrated in section 3.1, using the vocabulary (including pronouns) learned up to this point.

3.1.3 Exercise 3. **Translate into English:**

1. maĩ jānā cāhtā hū̃. 2. baccā khēlnā cāhtā hai. 3. ghōṛē ucalnā cāhtē haĩ. 4. ham paṛhnā cāhtī haĩ. 5. ghōṛī pīnā cāhtī hai. 6. kuttē ānā cāhtē haĩ. 7. vo khānā cāhtā hai. 8. laṛkī pūchnā cāhtī hai. 9. tum bhējnā cāhtē hō. 10. bīvī pakānā cāhtī hai. 11. laṛkā kām karnā cāhtā hai. 12. tōtā bōlnā cāhtā hai. 13. bēṭī rahnā cāhtī hai. 14. āp pahō̃cnā cāhtē haĩ. 15. laṛkē bhējnā cahtē haĩ. 16. bēṭiyā̃ calnā cāhtī haĩ. 17. machliyā̃ tairnā cāhtī haĩ. 18. bachṛē dauṛnā cāhtē haĩ. 19. vo dēkhnā cāhtī haĩ. 20. billiyā̃ sōnā cāhtī haĩ.

3.1.4 Exercise 4. **Translate into Urdu:**

1. I (**msc.**) want to give. 2. The child wants to eat. 3. The girls want to walk. 4. You (**msc.**) want to take. 5. The parrot wants to drink. 6. The son wants to work. 7. The wife wants to ask. 8. She wants to cook. 9. The boys want to play. 10. They (**fm.**) want to read. 11. The daughter wants to ask. 12. The cats want to go. 13. He wants to send.

14. The calf wants to run. 15. The sons want to work. 16. You (**hon. msc.**) want to arrive. 17. The dog wants to sleep. 18. The hen wants to eat. 19. The foxes want to come. 20. We (**msc.**) want to walk.

3.2

laṛkā acchā hai.	The boy is good.
laṛkē acchē haĩ.	The boys are good.
laṛkī acchī hai.	The girl is good.
laṛkiyā̃ acchī haĩ.	The girls are good.
jūtā purānā hai.	The shoe is old.
jūtē purānē haĩ.	The shoes are old.
sabzī pakkī hai.	The vegetable is ripe.
sabziyā̃ pakkī haĩ.	The vegetables are ripe.
maĩ bhūkā hū̃.	I (**msc.**) am hungry.
ham bhūkī haĩ.	We (**fm.**) are hungry.
vo pyāsā hai.	He is thirsty.
vo chōṭī haĩ.	They (**fm.**) are small.

This section illustrates the Urdu equivalent of the English predicate-adjective construction. The adjective agrees in gender and number with the subject of the verb. Adjectives modifying masculine nouns end in **-ā** for the singular and **-ē** for the plural. Adjectives modifying feminine nouns end in **-ī** for both the singular and the plural.

REMARKS: (1) Observe that the normal position of the Urdu verb is at the end of the sentence. See 2.1 for the present tense of the verb **to be.**

(2) The type of adjective given in the sentences above is identified by the subject form, singular, masculine—i.e., ends in **-ā,** which is replaced by **-ē** in the masculine plural and by **-ī** in the feminine, singular and plural.

(3) Henceforth, nouns, on their initial appearance in this book, when not otherwise identified, will be marked by an **ā** or **ī** in parentheses to indicate their gender—i.e., **jūtā (ā)** shoe, **sabzī (ī)** vegetable.

(4) **pūrānā** translates **old, ancient, of long standing,** while **būṛhā** translates **old, aged, advanced in years.**

3.2.1 Exercise 1. Fashion as many sentences as you can of the type illustrated in 3.2 with the following adjectives and nouns, and the nouns and pronouns learned up to this point: **mōṭā** fat, **jhūṭhā** false, **būṛhā** old, **burā** bad, **dublā** lean, **baṛā** large, **kēlā (ā)** banana, **tārā (ā)** star, **sabzī (ī)** vegetable.

3.2.2 Exercise 2. **Translate into English:**

1. vo bhūkī hai. 2. baccē pyāsē haĩ. 3. maĩ būṛhā hū̃. 4. billī mōṭī hai. 5. gadhē baṛē haĩ. 6. tum dublī hō. 7. bēṭiyā̃ acchī haĩ. 8. laṛkē bhūkē haĩ. 9. ham chōṭē haĩ. 10. lōmṛī dublī hai. 11. tum baṛē hō. 12. vo burē haĩ. 13. jūtā chōṭā hai. 14. bīvī acchī hai. 15. laṛkiyā̃ bhūkī haĩ. 16. āp pyāsē haĩ. 17. ghōṛā baṛā hai. 18. sabziyā̃ acchī haĩ. 19. ghōṛī mōṭī hai. 20. billī burī hai.

3.2.3 Exercise 3. **Translate into Urdu:**

1. The horses are old. 2. The wife is hungry. 3. He is lean. 4. The shoes are big. 5. The fish is small. 6. The donkeys are bad. 7. They (**fm.**) are thirsty. 8. The cat is hungry. 9. The daughters are lean. 10. The mare is small. 11. The hen is hungry. 12. I (**fm.**) am thirsty. 13. The flies are small. 14. You (**fm.**) are false. 15. She is small. 16. We (**msc.**)

are good. 17. The vegetables are big. 18. The **(female)** goat is hungry. 19. You **(msc.)** are fat. 20. She is thirsty.

3.3

ādmī kām kartā hai.	The man works.
ādmī kām kartē haĩ.	The men work.
k̤hāvind pūchtā hai.	The husband asks.
k̤hāvind pūchtē haĩ.	The husbands ask.
bhāī dētā hai.	The brother gives.
bhāī dētē haĩ.	The brothers give.
jānvar dauṛtā hai.	The animal runs.
jānvar dauṛtē haĩ.	The animals run.
bail khī̃ctā hai.	The ox drags.
bail khī̃ctē haĩ.	The oxen drag.
makān nayā hai.	The house is new.
makān nayē haĩ.	The houses are new.
phal pakkā hai.	The fruit is ripe.
phal pakkē haĩ.	The fruits are ripe.

This section illustrates masculine nouns which have the same form for the subject, singular and plural.

REMARKS: With such nouns the verb form indicates whether the subject is singular or plural.

3.3.1 Exercise 1. Fashion as many sentences as you can with the following nouns (See 3.3.) and verbs, as well as with the verbs and adjectives learned up to this point: **hāthī** elephant, **śēr** lion, **bandar** monkey, **rīch** bear, **ū̃ṭ** camel, **nahānā** to bathe, **baiṭhnā** to sit down, **ṭhaharnā** to stop, **khilānā** to feed.

3.3.2 Exercise 2. **Translate into English:**
1. hāthī khātē haĩ. 2. śēr pītā hai. 3. ū̃ṭ dauṛtā hai. 4. rīch ātē haĩ. 5. k̤hāvind kām kartā hai. 6. bandar khēltē haĩ. 7. ādmī bōltā hai. 8. hāthī sōtā hai. 9. bhāī bhējtē haĩ. 10. bail jātē haĩ. 11. makān baṛā hai. 12. śēr bhūkē haĩ. 13. k̤hāvind acchā hai. 14. bandar burā hai. 15. phal pakkā hai. 16. bhāī kām karnā cāhtē haĩ. 17. bandar khēlnā cāhtā hai. 18. jānvar khānā cāhtā hai. 19. ādmī baiṭhnā cāhtē haĩ. 20. rīch baiṭhnā cāhtā hai.

3.3.3 Exercise 3. **Translate into Urdu:**
1. The husbands bathe. 2. The bear walks. 3. The man works. 4. The brothers ask. 5. The animal sits down. 6. The elephants bathe. 7. The monkeys jump. 8. The men arrive. 9. The oxen eat. 10. The camels drag. 11. The houses are small. 12. The animals are hungry. 13. The brothers are good. 14. The fruit is ripe. 15. The lions are thirsty. 16. The husbands want to give. 17. The ox wants to stop. 18. The bears want to sit down. 19. The animals want to eat. 20. The man wants to bathe.

3.4

cīz girtī hai.	The thing falls.
cīzē̃ girtī haĩ.	The things fall.
dukān jaltī hai.	The shop burns.
dukānē̃ jaltī haĩ.	The shops burn.
fauj dauṛtī hai.	The army runs.
faujē̃ dauṛtī haĩ.	The armies run.
chat ṭūṭtī hai.	The roof breaks.
chatē̃ ṭūṭtī haĩ.	The roofs break.
gāy khātī hai.	The cow eats.
gāyē̃ khātī haĩ.	The cows eat.
aurat bōltī hai.	The woman speaks.
aurtē̃ bōltī haĩ.	The women speak.
bahan bhējtī hai.	The sister sends.
bahnē̃ bhējtī haĩ.	The sisters send.

This section illustrates feminine nouns which form their subject form, plural, by adding **-ē̃** to the subject form, singular.

REMARKS: Nouns of more than one syllable drop the vowel **-a-**, occurring within the word, when the **-ē̃** of the plural is added—provided that the **-a-** is not in the first syllable of the word. Compare **aurat: aurtē̃, bahan: bahnē̃.**

3.4.1 Exercise 1: **Translate into English:**

1. dukānē̃ girtī haĩ. 2. aurat pakātī hai. 3. gāyē̃ dauṛtī haĩ. 4. bahan pahõctī hai. 5. cīzē̃ ṭūṭtī haĩ. 6. chatē̃ jaltī haĩ. 7. faujē̃ ṭhahartī haĩ. 8. gāy khātī hai. 9. bahnē̃ nahātī haĩ. 10. fauj sōtī hai. 11. cīz baṛī hai. 12. chatē̃ nayī haĩ. 13. bahan bhūkī hai. 14. aurtē̃ pyāsī haĩ. 15. dukān chōṭī hai. 16. fauj jānā cāhtī hai. 17. gāyē̃ ṭhaharnā cāhtī haĩ. 18. aurat pakānā cāhtī hai. 19. bahnē̃ baiṭhnā cāhtī haĩ. 20. aurtē̃ lēnā cāhtī haĩ.

3.4.2 Exercise 2. **Translate into Urdu:**

1. The thing breaks. 2. The sister asks. 3. The army sits down. 4. The roof falls. 5. The cows drink. 6. The woman runs. 7. The armies walk. 8. The sisters walk. 9. The cows sleep. 10. The women cook. 11. The things are small. 12. The roofs are new. 13. The shop is big. 14. The sister is hungry. 15. The army is big. 16. The woman wants to bring. 17. The sisters want to read. 18. The army wants to sleep. 19. The cows want to eat. 20. The women want to cook.

3.5 The numbers 11 to 20:

gyārā (or **gyārah**) 11, **bārā** (or **bārah**) 12, **tērā** (or **tērah**) 13, **caudā** (or **caudah**) 14, **pandrā** (or **pandrah**) 15, **sōlā** (or **sōlah**) 16, **satrā** (or **satrah**) 17, **aṭṭhārā** (or **aṭṭhārah**) 18, **unnis** 19, **bīs.** 20.

3.6 Bandar Rōḍ-par. — On the Bandar Road.

mōṭarvālā:[1]	rāstē-sē haṭ jāō!	Motorist:	Get out of the way!
sabzīvālā:	kyā kahā, tum-nē?	Vegetable-vendor:	What did you say?
mōṭarvālā.	rāstē-sē haṭ jāō!	Motorist:	Get out of the way!
sabzīvālā:	kyū̃? [2]	Vegetable-vendor:	Why?
mōṭarvālā:	kyā! marnē-kā irādā hai?	Motorist:	What! Do you wish to die?
	tumhē̃ ṭakkar lagtē lagtē rah gayī.		You almost got hit.
sabzīvālā:	kyā kahā, tum-nē?	Vegetable-vendor:	What did you say?
	mērī samajh-mē̃ nahī̃ āyā.		I didn't understand.
mōṭarvālā:	kyā tum Urdū samjhtē hō?	Motorist:	Do you understand Urdu?
sabzīvālā:	hā̃. samajhtā hū̃.	Vegetable-vendor:	Yes. (I can) understand (Urdu).
	lēkin tumhārī Urdū nahī̃.		But not your Urdu.
mōṭarvālā:	bahot acchā. maĩ aur āhistā bōlū̃gā.	Motorist:	All right, I'll speak more slowly.
	rāstē-sē haṭ jāō!		Get out of the way!
	ab samjhē?		Understand now?
sabzīvālā:	acchā.	Vegetable-vendor:	All right.

REMARKS: (1) Note this is a variant for moṭar•calānēvālā.
(2) A variant is kyȭ.

3.7 guftagū. — Conversation.

Nasīm:	mērē sāth āō.	Nasīm:	Come with me.
Anvār:	kyā bāt hai?	Anvār:	What's the matter?
Nasīm:	kōī ḳhās bāt nahī̃. aisē-hī.	Nasīm:	Nothing special. Just (for the heck of it).
Anvār:	tum kahā̃ jā rahē hō?	Anvār:	Where are you going?
Nasīm:	zarā bāzār-mē̃ ghumē̃gē.	Nasīm:	We're just going to roam about in in the market.
Anvār:	bāzār kaisē jāōgē?	Anvār:	How are you going to the market?
Nasīm:	paidal jāū̃gā.	Nasīm:	I will walk.
	idhar āō.		Come this way.
Anvār:	kidhar?	Anvār:	Where?
Nasīm:	sunō.	Nasīm:	Listen.
	dāyī̃ taraf calō.		Go to the right.
Anvār:	us taraf?	Anvār:	In that direction?
Nasīm:	hā̃. us taraf.	Nasīm:	Yes. That way.
	dhyān-sē.		Take care.
Anvār:	kyū̃?	Anvār:	Why?
Nasīm:	saṛak ḳhatarnāk hai.	Nasīm:	The street is dangerous.
Anvār:	ye ḳhatarnāk kyū̃ hai?	Anvār:	Why is it dangerous?

Nasīm:	ye saṛak bahot cauṛī hai. gāṛiyā̃ aur mōṭrē̃ bahot tēz jātī haĩ.	Nasīm:	This street is very wide. The carts and automobiles go very fast.
Anvār:	ō kē. maĩ ḳhayāl rakhū̃gā.	Anvār:	O.K. I'll be careful.
Nasīm:	zarā tēz calō.	Nasīm:	Walk a little faster.

LESSON 4

4.1 Additional vocabulary.

4.1.1 Feminine nouns of the type described in 3.4 (See the remarks of that section for a note relating to the dropping of the vowel **-a-** within a word.):
mēz table, **rāt** night, **kitāb** book, **tasvīr** picture, **saṛak** street, road, **imārat** building, **jagah** place, **davā** medicine, **havā** wind.

4.1.2 Adjectives of the type described in 3.2:
ṭhanḍā cold, **cauṛā** broad, **lambā** long, tall, **ū̃cā** high, **mailā** dirty, **sūkhā** dry, **mīṭhā** sweet, **patlā** thin, **saccā** true, truthful, **andhērā** dark, **karvā** bitter, **kālā** dark.

4.1.3 Exercise 1. Fashion as many sentences as possible with the words of the preceding two paragraphs, together with the vocabulary learned up to this point.

4.1.4 Exercise 2. **Translate into English:**
1. imārat jaltī hai. 2. mēzẽ girtī haĩ. 3. tasvīr ṭūṭtī hai. 4. saṛak jātī hai. 5. havāẽ ātī haĩ. 6. kitābẽ girtī haĩ. 7. rāt ātī hai. 8. tasvīrẽ girtī haĩ. 9. imārtẽ jaltī haĩ. 10. mēz ṭūṭtī hai. 11. kitābẽ baṛī haĩ. 12. saṛkẽ cauṛī haĩ. 13. jagah baṛī hai. 14. davāẽ nayī haĩ. 15. mēz nayī hai. 16. jaghẽ chōṭī haĩ. 17. imārtẽ purānī haĩ. 18. rāt lambī hai. 19. mēz cauṛī hai. 20. kitāb acchī hai.

4.1.5 Exercise 3. **Translate into Urdu:**
1. The table breaks. 2. The building falls. 3. The picture burns. 4. The winds go. 5. The night comes. 6. The roads go. 7. The pictures fall. 8. The tables fall. 9. The building burns. 10. The picture breaks. 11. The place is new. 12. The book is old 13. The medicines are good. 14. The tables are old. 15. The roads are wide. 16. The buildings are small. 17. The place is good. 18. The medicine is new. 19. The books are big. 20. The building is old.

4.2

buṛhiyā sōtī hai.	The (**little**) old woman sleeps.
buṛhiyā̃ sōtī haĩ.	The (**little**) old women sleep.
ciṛiyā uṛtī hai.	The sparrow flies.
ciṛiyā̃ uṛtī haĩ.	The sparrows fly.
hanḍiyā nayī hai.	The cooking-pot is new.
hanḍiyā̃ nayī haĩ.	The cooking-pots are new.

cuhiyā chōṭī hai.	The mouse is small.
cuhiyā̃ chōṭī haĩ.	The mice are small.

This section illustrates feminine nouns whose ending in the subject form, singular, is- **iyā**. The final **-ā** is nasalized to form the subject form, plural (i.e., **ā̃**).

REMARKS: The greater number of nouns of this class are diminutives or terms of endearment.

4.2.1 Exercise 1. **Translate into English:**

1. ciṛiyā jātī hai. 2. buṛhiyā̃ caltī haĩ. 3. cuhiyā̃ dauṛtī haĩ. 4. buṛhiyā sōnā cāhtī hai. 5. cuhiyā khānā cāhtī hai. 6. buṛhiyā pyāsī hai. 7. ciṛiyā̃ chōṭī haĩ. 8. haṇḍiyā purānī hai. 9. ciṛiyā dublī hai. 10. cuhiyā̃ bhūkī haĩ.

4.2.2 Exercise 2. **Translate into Urdu:**

1. The mouse comes. 2. The (**little**) old woman sleeps. 3. The sparrows fly. 4. The mice want to eat. 5. The sparrow wants to fly. 6. The (**little**) old women are hungry. 7. The mice are thirsty. 8. The cooking-pots are good. 9. The sparrows are hungry. 10. The cooking-pot is old.

4.3

acchā laṛkā kām kartā hai.	The good boy works.
acchē laṛkē kām kartē haĩ.	The good boys work.
acchī aurat kām kartī hai.	The good woman works.
acchī aurtē̃ kām kartī haĩ.	The good women work.
pyāsā ghōṛā pītā hai.	The thirsty horse drinks.
pyāsē ghōṛē pītē haĩ.	The thirsty horses drink.
pyāsī billī pītī hai.	The thirsty cat drinks.
pyāsī billiyā̃ pītī haĩ.	The thirsty cats drink.
dublā jānvar dauṛtā hai.	The lean animal runs.
dublē jānvar dauṛtē haĩ.	The lean animals run.
dublī bahan dauṛtī hai.	The lean sister runs.
dublī bahnē̃ dauṛtī haĩ.	The lean sisters run.

This section is concerned with adjectives whose subject form, singular, masculine, ends in **-ā** (See 3.2, Remarks.) modifying masculine and feminine nouns in the subject form, singular and plural. The adjective agrees in gender, number and form with the noun. Adjectives modifying masculine nouns in the subject form, singular, end in **-ā,** and end in **-ē** when modifying nouns in the subject form, plural. Adjectives modifying feminine nouns end in **-ī** for both the singular and plural, subject form.

REMARKS: **dublā** can also be translated into English as **skinny** or **emaciated.**

4.3.1 Exercise 1. With the vocabulary learned up to this point construct as many sentences as possible of the type illustrated in 4.1.

4.3.2 Exercise 2. Translate into English:

1. bhūkī billī khātī hai. 2. burē kuttē dauṛtē haĩ. 3. pyāsī laṛkiyā̃ pītī haĩ. 4. baṛā ādmī kām kartā hai. 5. acchā laṛkā paṛhtā hai. 6. mōṭā kuttā sōtā hai. 7. dublī laṛkī khēltī hai. 8. purānā makān jaltā hai. 9. pakkē phal girtē haĩ. 10. būṛhā gadhā khī̃ctā hai. 11. acchē

laṛkē khēlnā cāhtē haĩ. 12. chōṭī billī khānā cāhtī hai. 13. dublē bakrē ṭhaharnā cāhtē haĩ. 14. bhūkī aurtē̃ pakānā cāhtī haĩ. 15. pyāsē ghōṛē pīnā cāhtē haĩ. 16. chōṭā laṛkā bhūkā hai. 17. bhūkī laṛkī dublī hai. 18. baṛē ādmī būṛhē haĩ. 19. purānē jūtē chōṭē haĩ. 20. baṛī gāyē̃ mōṭī haĩ.

4.3.3 Exercise 3. **Translate into Urdu:**

1. The fat goats eat. 2. The thirsty girls drink. 3. The small women cook. 4. The big shop burns. 5. The hungry armies stop. 6. The bad monkeys play. 7. The old roof breaks. 8. The new building falls. 9. The hungry men work. 10. The little girls run. 11. The good sisters want to cook. 12. The little horse wants to stop. 13. The thirsty cows want to drink. 14. The hungry camel wants to drag. 15. The old man wants to sleep. 16. The little child is hungry. 17. The big shop is new. 18. The small fruits are ripe. 19. The wide road is long. 20. The new books are big.

4.4

ādmī bāhar jātē haĩ.	The men go out.
ādmī andar ātē haĩ.	The men come in.
ham yahā̃ rahtē haĩ.	We live here.
vo vahā̃ dauṛtē haĩ.	They run there.
laṛkā āgē jātā hai.	The boy goes ahead.
kuttā pīchē jātā hai.	The dog goes behind.
laṛkī pās jātī hai.	The girl goes near.
ghōṛā pās-sē jātā hai.	The horse goes by.
bandar nīcē ātā hai.	The monkey comes down.
bīvī fauran jātī hai.	The wife leaves immediately.
baccā jaldī-sē ātā hai.	The child comes quickly.
laṛkē āhistā caltē haĩ.	The boys walk slowly.
ādmī āhistā āhistā bōltā hai.	The man speaks slowly.
vo kabhī kabhī kām kartē haĩ.	They work sometimes.
laṛkē ēk-sāth khātē haĩ.	The boys eat together.
vo zyāda khātā hai.	He eats (too) much.
vo bahot zyādā khātā hai.	He eats very much.
ādmī bahot kām kartā hai.	The man works very much.
laṛkā bahot acchā hai.	The boy is very good.
laṛkī bahot acchī hai.	The girl is very good.
jānvar bahot burā hai.	The animal is very bad.
jānvar bahot burē haĩ.	The animals are very bad.
ghōṛī tēzī-sē dauṛtī hai.	The mare runs swiftly.

This section is concerned with the adverbs. The student should encounter little difficulty in identifying the adverbs in the sentences above. All he need do is identify the noun (or pronoun) subject of each sentence and then the verb. The form or forms which remain are the adverbs.

REMARKS: (1) Several of the adverbs consist of two words connected by a hyphen. These are to be considered a single form.

(2) In two sentences the adverb is repeated. The repetition of the adverb indicates that the action modified by the adverb progresses at a uniform pace.

(3) **bahot** modifies both adjectives and adverbs; **jaldī-sē quickly** is used to describe

a sudden action as contrasted with **tēzī-sē swiftly, fast,** describing an action in progress over a period of time.

(4) **kabhī** also translates **ever** in the phrase **kabhī nahī.**

(5) A variant of **bāhar** is **bāhir.**

4.4.1 Exercise 1. **Translate into English:**

1. jānvar jaldī-sē daurṭē haĩ. 2. ādmī andar kām kartā hai. 3. ham yahā̃ rahtē haĩ. 4. aurat āhistā āhistā bōltī hai. 5. tum bāhar jātē hō. 6. bhāī bahot kām kartē haĩ. 7. aurtē̃ andar pakātī haĩ. 8. hāthī bahot zyādā khātē haĩ. 9. vo vahā̃ jātē hai. 10. laṛkiyā̃ kabhī kabhī khēltī haĩ. 11. pyāsā ghōṛā jaldī-sē pītā hai. 12. bhūkē bandar nīcē jātē haĩ. 13. chōṭā baccā pīchē ātā hai. 14. baṛē hāthī vahā̃ rahtē haĩ. 15. acchī laṛkiyā̃ ēk-sāth khēltī haĩ. 16. chōṭē baccē bāhar jānā cāhtē haĩ. 17. bhūkī ghōṛī jaldī-sē khānā cāhtī hai. 18. bāṛā ādmī bahot kām karnā cāhtā hai. 19. pyāsē bail kabhī kabhī ṭhaharnā cāhtē haĩ. 20. dublī aurtē̃ fauran khānā cāhtī haĩ.

4.4.2 Exercise 2. **Translate into Urdu:**

1. The brothers eat together. 2. The girl goes out. 3. The woman comes in. 4. The children go behind. 5. The husband goes ahead. 6. The boy speaks slowly. 7. We **(fm.)** play sometimes. 8. The animals are very hungry. 9. They **(fm.)** eat too much. 10. I **(fm.)** walk slowly. 11. The hungry child eats quickly. 12. The thirsty horse drinks too much. 13. The bad monkey goes down. 14. The little boys play together. 15. The fat man goes by. 16. The big boys want to play outside. 17. The big girls want to cook inside. 18. The hungry animals want to come here. 19. The big elephant wants to come here. 20. The thirsty horse wants to drink quickly.

4.5

ēk ādmī sōtā hai.	One man sleeps.
dō ādmī kām kartē haĩ.	Two men work.
tīn aurtē̃ daurṭī haĩ.	Three women run.
cār aurtē̃ ṭhahartī haĩ.	Four women stop.
pā̃c ādmī khēltē haĩ.	Five men play.
che ādmī baiṭhtē haĩ.	Six men sit down.
sāt aurtē̃ nāctī haĩ.	Seven women dance.
āṭh aurtē̃ likhtī haĩ.	Eight women write.
nau ādmī dhōtē haĩ.	Nine men wash.
das ādmī khōdtē haĩ.	Ten men dig.
gyārā aurtē̃ laṛtī haĩ.	Eleven women fight.
bārā ghōṛiyā̃ lēṭtī haĩ.	Twelve mares lie down.

This section illustrates the numerals functioning as adjectives. Their forms do not change for gender, number, subject, or object.

4.6 The numbers 21 to 30:

ikkīs 21, **bāīs** 22, **tēīs** 23, **caubīs** 24, **paccīs** 25, **chabbīs** 26, **sattāīs** 27, **aṭṭhāīs** 28, **untīs (unattīs)** 29, **tīs** 30.

4.7 **ēk dihātī-sē guftagū.** — **Conversation with a Villager.**

sarkārī afsar:	**salām alēkum.**	Government officer:	**Hello.**
dihātī:	**salām sāhab.**	Villager:	**Hello.**

sarkārī afsar:	maĩ tum-sē kuch savāl pūchnā cāhtā hū̃.	Government officer:	I wish to ask you some questions.
dihātī:	pūchiyē.	Villager:	(Please) ask.
sarkārī afsar:	is gā̃v-ka nām kyā hai?	Government officer:	What is the name of this village?
dihātī:	is gā̃v-kā nām Śāhpur hai.	Villager:	The name of this village is Shahpur.
sarkārī afsar:	kyā ye tumhārā ghar [1] hai?	Government officer:	Is this your house?
dihātī:	jī hā̃. ye mērā ghar hai.	Villager:	Yes. This is my house.
sarkārī afsar:	tumhārā pēśā kyā hai?	Government officer:	What is your occupation?
dihātī:	kisān hū̃.	Villager:	I am a farmer.
sarkārī afsar:	kyā kōī dūsrā kām-bhī kartē hō?	Government officer:	Do you do any other work?
dihātī:	jī hā̃. aur kām-bhī kartā hū̃.	Villager:	Yes. I do other work, too.
sarkārī afsar:	aur kyā kām kartē hō?	Government officer:	What other work do you do?
dihātī:	fasal-kē bād maĩ śahar-mē̃ kām kartā hū̃.	Villager:	After the harvest I work in the city.
sarkārī afsar:	tum śahar-mē̃ kahā̃ kām kartē hō?	Government officer:	Where do you work in in the city?
dihātī:	maĩ kapṛē-kē kārḳhānē-mē̃ kām kartā hū̃.	Villager:	I work in the cloth mill.
sarkārī afsar:	kyā sārē ḳhāndān-mē̃-sē sirf tum-hī kapṛē-kē kārḳhānē-mē̃ kām kartē hō?	Government officer:	Are you the only one in the entire family who works in the cloth mill?
dihātī:	nahī̃. mērē dō bhāī aur cacā-bhī vahā̃ kām kartē haĩ.	Villager:	No. My two brothers and my uncle work there, too.
sarkārī afsar:	tum śahar-mē̃ kitnē arsē ṭhahartē hō?	Government officer:	How long do you stay in the city?
dihātī:	cār mahīnē.	Villager:	Four months.
sarkārī afsar:	phir tum gā̃v vāpas a jātē ho?	Government officer:	Then you return to the village?
dihātī:	jī hā̃.	Villager:	Yes.

REMARKS: (1) ghar (ā) translates **home** as contrasted with makān (ā) building. It can also translate **household**.

4.8 mā̃ aur bēṭē-kī guftagū. — Conversation Between Mother and Son.

mā̃:	bēṭē![1]	Mother:	Son!
bēṭā:	jī.	Son:	Yes.
mā̃:	idhar āō!	Mother:	Come here!
bēṭā:	kyū̃?	Son:	Why?
mā̃:	maĩ tumhē̃ [2] nahlānā cāhtī hū̃.	Mother:	I want to bathe you.

bēṭā:	pā̃c minaṭ-mē̃ ātā hū̃.[3]	Son:	**I'll come in five minutes.**
mā̃:	fauran āō!	Mother:	**Come at once!**
	maĩ tumhē̃ nahlānā aur phir khānā dēnā cāhtī hū̃.		**I want to bathe you and then give you food.**
bēṭā:	tīn minaṭ-mē̃.	Son:	**In three minutes.**
mā̃:	maĩ kahtī hū̃: fauran āō!	Mother:	**I'm telling (you): come at once!**
bēṭā:	ṭhōṛī dēr-mē̃.	Son:	**In a little while.**
mā̃:	parēśān mat karō!	Mother:	**Don't bother me!**
	fauran āō!		**Come immediately!**
bēṭā:	bahot acchā. ātā hū̃.[3]	Son:	**Very well. I'm coming.**
mā̃:	apnē kapṛē utārō.	Mother:	**Take off your clothes.**
bēṭā:	kyū̃?	Son:	**Why?**
mā̃:	maĩ tumhē̃ nahlānā cahtī hū̃.	Mother:	**I want to bathe you.**
bēṭā:	pānī bahot ṭhaṇḍā hai.	Son:	**The water is very cold.**
mā̃:	cup rahō!	Mother:	**Keep quiet!**
bēṭā:	mujhē ṭhaṇḍā pānī pasand nahī̃.	Son:	**I do not like cold water.**
mā̃:	ḳhāmōś!	Mother:	**Keep quiet!**
	mērē pās vaḳt nahī̃ hai.		**I don't have time.**

REMARKS: (1) **bēṭē,** voc., sg. (pl.**bēṭō**).

(2) **tujhē,** the alternate is applied to children and servants and to God.

(3) The present term is employed to indicate an action taking place in the immediate future.

LESSON 5

5.1

ādmī mujhē dēkhtā hai.	The man sees me (**msc.**)
ādmī mujhē dēkhtī hai.	The man sees me (**fm.**).
ādmī us-kō dēkhtā hai.	The man sees him.
ādmī us-kō dēkhtā hai.	The man sees her.
ādmī hamẽ dēkhtā hai.	The man sees us (**msc.**).
ādmī hamẽ dēkhtā hai.	The man sees us (**fm.**).
ādmī tumhẽ dēkhtā hai.	The man sees you (**msc.**).
ādmī tumhẽ dēkhtā hai.	The man sees you (**fm.**).
ādmī āp-kō dēkhtā hai.	The man sees you (**msc.**).
ādmī āp-kō dēkhtā hai.	The man see you (**fm.**).
ādmī un-kō dēkhtā hai.	The man sees them (**msc.**).
ādmī un-kō dēkhtā hai.	The man sees them (**fm.**).

This section introduces the direct object constructions, singular and plural, of the personal pronouns. With the exception of **mujhē, hamẽ** and **tumhẽ,** the direct object forms, respectively, of the first and second personal pronouns, which are single words, the direct object constructions consist of two forms linked by a hyphen. In each of these hyphenated forms the second is the form, **-kō,** which will henceforth be referred to as a **postposition.** A function of the postposition **-kō** is to mark the direct object. Words occurring before postpositions have a form designated "the object form." The object form of **vō,** singular, is **us;** of **vo,** plural, **un;** of the remaining pronoun, **āp,** the same as the subject.

REMARKS: Note these variant forms: **usē** for **us-kō, unhẽ** for **un-kō, ham-kō** for **hamẽ** and **tum-kō** for **tumhẽ.**

5.1.1 More examples are:

mā̃ us-kō bulātī hai.	The mother calls him.
ādmī hamẽ paṛhātā hai.	The man makes us read.

dōst mujhē jāntā hai.	The friend knows me.
naukar āp-kō māntā hai.	The servant obeys you.
ustād•sāhab un-kō samajhtē haĩ.	The teacher understands them.
bahan tumhẽ nahlātī hai.	Sister bathes you.
ghōṛē mujhē khĩctē haĩ.	The horses drag me.
bāp hamẽ cūmtā hai.	Father kisses us.
aurtẽ un-kō ghurtī haĩ.	The women stare at them.
bahnẽ tumhẽ pātī haĩ.	The sisters find you.

REMARKS: (1) **paṛhānā** can be translated into English **to make read** or **to teach; cūmnā** translates **to kiss** or **to lick; nahlānā** translates **to bathe (someone).** A variant of **khĩcnā** is **khẽcnā.**

(2) The plural form of the verb is used with **ustād•sāhab, teacher,** to indicate respect or honor.

(3) **dōst (msc.** and **fm.), naukar (ā), ustād•sāhab (ē), bāp (ā), sunnā** to hear.

5.1.2 Exercise 1. **Translate into English:**

1. dōst usē suntē haĩ. 2. ādmī āp-kō pātē haĩ. 3. mā̃ hamẽ nahlātī hai. 4. laṛkā us-kō ghurtā hai. 5. ustād•sāhab mujhē suntē haĩ. 6. ghōṛī tumhẽ jāntī hai. 7. bāp āp-kō bulātā hai. 8. naukar mujhē samajhtē haĩ. 9. māẽ hamẽ bulātī haĩ. 10. bahan un-kō cūmtī hai.

5.1.3 Exercise 2. **Translate into Urdu:**

1. The man calls us. 2. The servant understands me. 3. Mother bathes them. 4. The women know her. 5. Sisters pull you. 6. You (**hon.**) make him read. 7. Father kisses me. 8. They (**msc.**) obey you (**hon.**). **9.** The friends call them. 10. The horse pulls you.

5.2

maĩ laṛkē-kō dēkhtā hū̃.	I see the boy.
maĩ laṛkõ-kō dēkhtā hū̃.	I see the boys.
maĩ kapṛē-kō dēkhtā hū̃.	I see the cloth.
maĩ kapṛõ-kō dēkhtā hū̃.	I see the clothes.
vo baccē-kō bulātī hai.	She calls the child.
vo baccõ-kō bulātī hai.	She calls the children.
ham kuttē-kō khilātē haĩ.	We feed the dog.
ham kuttõ-kō khilātē haĩ.	We feed the dogs.
bāp tōtē-kō ḳharīdtā hai.	Father buys the parrot.
bāp tōtõ-kō ḳharīdtā hai.	Father buys the parrots.

Sections 5.2 to 5.6.2 are concerned with the direct object constructions, singular and plural, of the nouns discussed in sections 2.2, 2.3, 3.3, 3.4, 4.1.1, and 4.2. See 5.1 for remarks on the postposition **-kō,** and note that the forms preceding it are the object forms of the pronouns when they occur before the other postpositions.

This section, 5.2, discusses nouns, the subject form, singular, of which ends in **-ā,** which is replaced by **-ē** in the subject form, plural. (Compare 2.2.) This **-ā** is replaced by **-ē** in the object singular and **-ō̃** in the object plural forms.

REMARKS: Added vocabulary. **cāṭnā to lick.**

5.2.1 Exercise 1. **Translate into English:**

1. laṛkē gadhō̃-kō khilātē haĩ. 2. ādmī bakrē-kō ḳharīdtā hai. 3. ham bachṛō̃-kō khĩctē haĩ. 4. aurat ghōṛē-kō bulātī hai. 5. ādmī bhēṛiyō̃-kō dēkhtā hai. 6. mā̃ laṛkō-kō̃ khilātī hai. 7. vo tōtē-kō pātī haĩ. 8. bāp bēṭē-kō cūmtā hai. 9. gadhā laṛkē-kō khĩctā hai. 10. ustad •sāhab laṛkō̃-kō paṛhātē haĩ. 11. maĩ ghōṛō̃-kō khilānā cāhtā hū̃. 12. laṛkē kuttē-kō khĩcnā cāhtē haĩ. 13. mā̃ bēṭō-kō khilānā cāhtī hai. 14. ham tōtō̃-kō ḳharīdnā cāhtē haĩ. 15. ādmī bhēṛiyō̃-kō dēkhnā cāhtā hai. 16. chōṭī bahan kuttē-kō khilātī hai. 17. chōṭā laṛkā bachṛē-kō bulātā hai. 18. mōṭē ghōṛē laṛkō̃-kō khĩctē haĩ. 19. baṛā ādmī gadhē-kō pātā hai. 20. pyāsā hāthī kuttē-kō khĩctā hai. 21. kuttā baccē-kō bāhar khĩctā hai. 22. bhāī tōtē-kō vahā̃ pātā hai. 23. mā̃ laṛkō̃-kō andar bulātī hai. 24. gāy bachṛē-kō jaldī-sē khilātī hai. 25. ustād•sāhab bētō̃-kō kabhī kabhī paṛhātē haĩ.

5.2.2 Exercise 2. **Translate into Urdu:**

1. The mother feeds the children. 2. We (**msc.**) pull the dog. 3. The teacher makes the boys read. 4. You (**fm.**) understand the child. 5. They (**msc.**) know the son. 6. I (**fm.**) hear the parrots. 7. The man calls the sons. 8. Mother bathes the child. 9. The men buy horses. 10. Mother kisses the boy. 11. Mother wants to feed the goats. 12. The horse wants to pull the boys. 13. We (**msc.**) want to hear the parrots. 14. Sister wants to bathe the child. 15. Brother wants to call the horse. 16. The old man teaches the boy. 17. The hungry wife calls the boys. 18. The little child pulls the dog. 19. The fat servant calls the children. 20. The good dog licks the child. 21. Mother calls the children in. 22. Sister bathes the child there. 23. The boy feeds the horses quickly. 24. Teacher makes us read here. 25. Fathers understand children sometimes.

5.3

maĩ laṛkī-kō dēkhtā hū̃.	I see the girl.
maĩ laṛkiyō̃-kō dēkhtā hū̃.	I see the girls.
mā̃ bēṭī-kō sikhātī hai.	Mother teaches the daughter.
mā̃ bēṭiyō̃-kō sikhātī hai.	Mother teaches the daughters.
ādmī bīvī-kō bulātā hai.	The man calls (**his**) wife.
ādmī bīviyō̃-kō bulātē haĩ.	The men call (**their**) wives.
baccā billī-kō pakaṛtā hai.	The child grabs the cat.
baccā billiyō̃-kō pakaṛtā hai.	The child grabs the cats.
ham murgī-kō khilātē haĩ.	We feed the hen.
ham murgiyō̃-kō khilātē haĩ.	We feed the hens.

This section takes up the direct object constructions of feminine nouns, the subject form, singular, of which ends in **-ī.** (See 2.3.) The object singular form is the same as the subject singular. The object plural form is made by replacing the **-ī** of the subject singular (or the **-iyā̃** of the subject plural) with **-iyō̃.**

5.3.1 Exercise 1. **Translate into English:**

1. aurat bēṭiyō̃-kō sikhātī hai. 2. ādmī bīvī-kō suntā hai. 3. laṛkē murgiyō̃-kō khilātē haī̃. 4. baccā billī-kō pakaṛtā hai. 5. bāp bēṭī-kō cūmtā hai. 6. ham machliyō̃-kō ḳharīdtī haī̃. 7. vo makkhiyō̃-kō pātē haī̃. 8. mā̃ laṛkī-kō bhējtī hai. 9. laṛkē machlī-kō pakaṛtē haī̃. 10. maĩ billī-kō lātā hū̃. 11. ādmī machliyō̃-kō pakaṛnā cāhtā hai. 12. vo murgī-kō lēnā cāhtī haī̃. 13. mā̃ bēṭiyō̃-kō cūmnā cāhtī hai. 14. bāp laṛkī-kō dēkhnā cāhtā hai. 15. vo ghōṛī-kō pānā cāhtā hai. 16. būṛhā ādmī ghōṛī-kō pakaṛtā hai. 17. chōṭī aurat murgiyō̃-kō khilātī hai. 18. baṛā laṛkā billī-kō khī̃ctā hai. 19. bhūkī aurat murgī-kō pakaṛtī hai. 20. būṛhā śēr bakriyō̃-kō dēkhtā hai. 21. ham bēṭiyō̃-kō yahā̃ bulātē haī̃. 22. rīch murgiyō̃-kō vahā̃ khī̃ctē haī̃. 23. bāp laṛkī-kō kabhī kabhī sikhātā hai. 24. billī machlī-kō āhistā khātī hai. 25. mā̃ bēṭiyō̃-kō zyādā khilātī hai.

5.3.2 Exercise 2. **Translate into Urdu.**

1. The child feeds the cat. 2. Mother calls the hens. 3. The father calls the daughters. 4. You (**hon. msc.**) teach the girls. 5. The lion seizes the hens. 6. The woman catches the flies. 7. We (**msc.**) catch the fish. 8. The monkeys see the fox. 9. The mother kisses the girl. 10. The woman catches the hens. 11. We (**msc.**) want to catch the fish. 12. Mother wants to catch the hen. 13. You (**fm.**) want to teach the girls. 14. The lion wants to seize the goats. 15. The child wants to feed the mare. 16. The hungry man wants to catch the fish. 17. The big lion wants to see the goat. 18. The little boy feeds the hens. 19. The good sister teaches the girl. 20. The old woman calls the daughters. 21. The hungry lion wants to eat the goat quickly. 22. The boy wants to catch the fish here. 23. The mother feeds the daughter too much. 24. Father buys chickens there. 25. You (**fm.**) call the girls in.

5.4

maĩ ādmī-kō dēkhtā hū̃.	I see the man.
maĩ ādmiyō̃-kō dēkhtā hū̃.	I see the men.
kuttā bhāī-kō kāṭtā hai.	The dog bites the brother.
kuttā bhāiyō̃-kō kāṭtā hai.	The dog bites the brothers.
kisān jānvar-kō bā̃dhtā hai.	The farmer ties the animal.
kisān us-kō bā̃dhtā hai.	The farmer ties it (**the animal**).
kisān jānvarō̃-kō bā̃dhtā hai.	The farmer ties the animals.
kisān un-kō bā̃dhtā hai.	The farmer ties them (**the animals**).
bandar phal-kō curātā hai.	The monkey steals the fruit.
bandar us-kō curātā hai.	The monkey steals it (**the fruit.**)
bandar phalō̃-kō curātā hai.	The monkey steals the fruits.
bandar un-kō curātā hai.	The monkey steals them (**the fruits**).
ādmī makān-kō ḳharīdtā hai.	The man buys the house.
ādmī us-kō ḳharīdtā hai.	The man buys it (**the house**).
ādmī makānō̃-kō ḳharīdtā hai.	The man buys the houses.
ādmī un-kō ḳharīdtā hai.	The man buys them (**the houses**).

This section describes the formation of the direct object construction of the nouns described in section 3.3. The object singular form is the same as the subject singular. In the plural nouns, ending in **-ī**, replace this with **-iyō̃** to make the object form; nouns, ending in a consonant add **-ō̃**, to the subject form to make the object plural.

REMARKS: The third person pronoun indicates things and animals, as well as human beings. (Compare 5.1.)

5.4.1 Exercise 1. **Translate into English:**

1. kuttā bail-kō kāṭtā hai. 2. bandar phalō̃-kō khātā hai. 3. bāp makān-kō k̤harīdtā hai. 4. bīvī k̤hāvind-kō bulātī hai. 5. ham makānō̃-kō dēkhtī haī̃. 6. śēr jānvar-kō pakaṛtā hai. 7. mā̃ bhāiyō̃-kō bhējtī hai. 8. kisān ādmiyō̃-kō khilātā hai. 9. bandar bhāī-kō kāṭtā hai. 10. ādmī hāthī-kō nahlātā hai. 11. ham phalō̃-kō khānā cāhtē haī̃. 12. ādmī makān-kō k̤harīdnā cāhtā hai. 13. kuttā bandar-kō kāṭnā cāhtā hai. 14. mā̃ bhāiyō̃-kō khilānā cāhtī hai. 15. baccā hāthī-kō dēkhnā cāhtā hai. 16. būṛhā ādmī hāthī-kō nahlātā hai. 17. chōṭā kisān bailō̃-kō bā̃dhtā hai. 18. baṛā śēr jānvar-kō pakaṛnā cāhtā hai. 19. burē bandar phalō̃-kō khātē haī̃. 20. bhūkā kuttā bail-kō kāṭtā hai. 21. bail kisān-kō yahā̃ khī̃ctā hai. 22. mā̃ bhāiyō̃-kō ēk-sāth bhējnā cāhtī hai. 23. bāp ādmiyō̃-kō andar bulātā hai. 24. ham kisānō̃-kō kabhī kabhī dēkhtē haī̃. 25. bandar phal-kō vahā̃ khātā hai.

5.4.2 Exercise 2. **Translate into Urdu:**

1. The boy takes the fruit. 2. The dog bites the men. 3. The farmer ties the oxen. 4. The man buys the elephant. 5. The wives feed the husbands. 6. The sister kisses the brother. 7. The bear bites the man. 8. The oxen drag the farmer. 9. The boy sees the elephants. 10. The monkey grabs the fruits. 11. I (**msc.**) want to see the lions. 12. The dog wants to bite the men. 13. The farmer wants to tie the oxen. 14. The horses want to drag the men. 15. We (**fm.**) want to eat the fruits. 16. The bad monkeys steal the fruits. 17. The old lion wants to grab the goat. 18. The hungry oxen pull the farmers. 19. The big bear bites the man. 20. The black wolf steals the chickens. 21. Father buys a house here. 22. The monkeys take the fruits there. 23. The horses pull the farmers quickly. 24. We (**msc.**) see animals sometimes. 25. The hungry oxen pull the man slowly.

5.5

maĩ aurat-kō dēkhtā hū̃.	I see the woman.
maĩ aurtō̃-kō dēkhtā hū̃.	I see the women.
bhāī bahan-kō bulātā hai.	The brother calls the sister.
bhāī bahnō̃-kō bulātā hai.	The brother calls the sisters.
aurat gāy-kō bā̃dhtī hai.	The woman ties the cow.
aurat us-kō bā̃dhtī hai.	The woman ties it (**the cow**).
aurat gayō̃-kō bā̃dhtī hai.	The woman ties the cows.
aurat un-kō bā̃dhtī hai.	The woman ties them (**the cows**).
laṛkā kitāb-kō paṛhtā hai.	The boy reads the book.
laṛkā us-kō paṛhtā hai.	The boy reads it (**the book**).
laṛkā kitābō̃-kō paṛhtā hai.	The boy reads the books.
laṛkā un-kō paṛhtā hai.	The boy reads them (**the books**).

This section takes up the formation of the direct object construction of the feminine nouns described in 3.4 and 4.1.1. The object singular is the same as the subject form; to form the object plural **-ō̃** is added to the subject singular form.

REMARKS: See 3.4, Remarks, for the dropping of the vowel **-ā-** within a word.

5.5.1 Exercise 1. **Translate into English:**

1. mā̃ bahnō̃-kō bulātī hai. 2. ustād•sāhab kitābō̃-kō paṛhtē haĩ. 3. kisān gāyō̃-kō bā̃dhtē haĩ. 4. aurat cīz-kō ḳharīdtī hai. 5. ādmī mēz-kō ḳharīdtā hai. 6. baccā davā-kō pītā hai. 7. ham tasvīrō̃-kō dēkhtē haĩ. 8. laṛkī kitāb-kō ḳharīdtī hai. 9. mā̃ bahnō̃-kō sikhātī hai. 10. baccā tasvīr-kō pakaṛtā hai. 11. ham rāt-kō dēkhnā cāhtē haĩ. 12. ustād•sāhab kitāb-kō paṛhnā cāhtē haĩ. 13. aurat cīzō̃-kō ḳharīdnā cāhtī hai. 14. vo tasvīr-kō dēkhnā cāhtī hai. 15. kisān gāyō̃-kō bā̃dhnā cāhtē haĩ. 16. acchā baccā davā-kō pītā hai. 17. bhūkī aurat cīzō̃-kō ḳharīdtī hai. 18. chōṭā laṛkā kitāb-kō paṛhtā hai. 19. būṛhī aurat gāyō̃-kō bā̃dhnā cāhtī hai. 20. baṛā ādmī imārtō̃-kō ḳharīdnā cāhtā hai. 21. būṛhā kisān gāyō̃-kō yahā̃ bā̃dhnā cāhtā hai. 22. aurtē̃ cīzō̃-kō vahā̃ ḳharīdnā cāhtī haĩ. 23. ham tasvīrō̃-kō kabhī kabhī dēkhtē haĩ. 24. ustād•sāhab kitābō̃-kō tēzī-sē paṛhtē haĩ. 25. acchē baccē davā-kō kabhī kabhī pītē haĩ.

5.5.2 Exercise 2. **Translate into Urdu:**

1. The woman buys the table. 2. The boys read the books. 3. The father brings the picture. 4. The farmers tie the cows. 5. Father buys the buildings. 6. Mother brings the medicine. 7. The wife calls the women. 8. Sister brings the table. 9. We (**msc.**) feed the cows. 10. The child drinks the medicine. 11. We (**fm.**) want to see the night. 12. The farmer wants to tie the cows. 13. I (**fm.**) want to buy the pictures. 14. She wants to read the books. 15. Mother wants to send the women. 16. The good boys bring the table. 17. The little woman calls the cows. 18. The old farmer ties the cows. 19. The big man buys the buildings. 20. The fat dog bites the sisters. 21. The small cat bites the woman there. 22. The good child brings the books quickly. 23. The farmers bring the oxen slowly. 24. We (**msc.**) read books sometimes. 25. The little boy wants to read the book here.

5.6

laṛkī ciṛiyā̃-kō khilātī hai.	The girl feeds the sparrow.
laṛkī ciṛiyō̃-kō khilātī hai.	The girl feeds the sparrows.
billī cuhiyā̃-kō pakaṛtī hai.	The cat catches the mouse.
billī cuhiyō̃-kō pakaṛtī hai.	The cat catches the mice.

This section illustrates the formation of the direct object constructions of the feminine nouns given in 4.2. The object singular is identical in form with the subject singular; the object plural is formed by replacing the final **-ā̃** of the subject plural with **-ō̃.**

5.6.1 Exercise 1. **Translate into English:**

1. billī ciṛiyā-kō pakaṛtī hai. 2. aurat buṛhiyā-kō bulātī hai. 3. ham cuhiyō̃-kō dēkhtē haĩ. 4. aurtē̃ haṇḍiyā-kō ḳharīdtī haĩ. 5. vo ciṛiyō̃-kō khilātē haĩ 6. laṛkā haṇḍiyō̃-kō lātā hai. 7. acchī aurat būṛhiyō-kō̃ khilātī hai. 8. chōṭī cuhiyā būṛhiyā-kō kāṭtī hai. 9. ham haṇḍiyō̃-kō ḳharīdnā cāhtē haĩ. 10. tum cuhiyā-kō dēkhtē hō.

5.6.2 Exercise 2. **Translate into Urdu:**

1. The woman catches the mouse. 2. The man calls the (**little**) old woman. 3. The girl

feeds the sparrows. 4. The cat sees the mice. 5. We (**msc.**) bring the cooking-pots. 6. I (**fm.**) want to catch the mouse. 7. The boys want to bring the sparrows here. 8. You (**fm.**) feed the (**little**) old woman. 9. The boys catch the mouse there. 10. The little girl brings the cooking-pot quickly.

5.7 The numbers 31 to 40:
iktīs (ikattīs) 31, **battīs** 32, **tẽtīs** 33, **caũtīs** 34, **paĩtīs** 35, **chattīs** 36, **saĩtīs** 37, **aṛtīs** 38, **untālīs** 39, **cālīs** 40.

	5.8 **mā̃ bēṭē-sē bāt kar rahī hai.**		**Conversation Between Mother and Son.**
bēṭā:	**maĩ bhūkā hū̃.**	Son:	**I'm hungry.**
mā̃:	**ghar-mē̃ āō!**	Mother:	**Come into the house!**
	maĩ tumhē̃ khānē-kē liyē kuch dū̃gī.		**I'll give you something to eat.**
bēṭā:	**khānē-kē liyē kyā hai?**	Son:	**What is there to eat?**
mā̃:	**cāval.**	Mother:	**Rice.**
bēṭā:	**kyā khīr hai?**	Son:	**Is there khīr?**
mā̃:	**nahī̃. khīr nahī̃ hai.**	Mother:	**No. (There is) no khīr.**
bēṭā:	**mujhē khīr cāhiyē.**	Son:	**I want khīr.**
mā̃:	**ham amīr nahī̃ haĩ.**	Mother:	**We are not rich.**
	tum khīr har rōz nahī̃ khā saktē.		**You cannot eat khīr everyday.**
	har rōz Īd nīst, keh halvā k̤hurad kasē.[1]		**Everyday is not a feast day, so that you can have sweets.**
bēṭā:	**mujhē ye khānā pasand nahī̃.**	Son:	**I don't like this food.**
mā̃:	**kōī bāt nahī̃.**	Mother:	**No matter.**
	khāō aur jākar sō jāō.		**Eat and go to sleep.**
bēṭā:	**kyā vak̤t hai?**	Son:	**What time is it?**
mā̃:	**che bajē haĩ.**	Mother:	**It is six o'clock.**
	tērā [2] **bāp khēt-sē ā rahā hai.**		**Your father is coming from the field.**
	mujhē us-kō khānā dēnā hai.		**I must give him (his) dinner.**
bēṭā:	**maĩ abbā** [3]**-kē sāth khānā khāū̃gā.**	Son:	**I'll eat with father.**
mā̃:	**tum abbā-kē sāth nahī̃ khā saktē.**	Mother:	**You cannot eat with daddy.**
	jaldī khāō aur jākar sō jāō.		**Eat your food quickly and go to bed.**

REMARKS: (1) A Persian proverb. Lit.: **Every day is not Īd that you will get pudding.**

Ramzān is the ninth month of the Muhammadan calendar, during which Muslims are required to observe fasts. The close of this period is marked by **Īd,** the festivities of which are in sharp contrast with the austerities of the preceding month.

(2) **tērā** is the possessive adjective corresponding to the 2nd personal pronoun, **tū**.
(3) **abbā** (ā) = **daddy.**

	5.9 **rāstā mālūm karnā.**		**Asking Directions.**
musāfir:	**māf kījiyē.**	Traveller:	**Excuse me.**
	maĩ kuch pūchnā cāhtā hū̃.		**I want to ask (you) something.**

dihātī:	pūchiyē.	Villager:	(Please) ask.
musāfir:	kyā ye saṛak Rāvalpindī jātī hai?	Traveller:	Does this road go to Rawalpindi?
dihātī:	nahī̃. ye saṛak Rāvalpindī nahī̃ jātī.	Villager:	No. This road does not go to Rawalpindi.
	kyā āp Rāvalpindī jānā cāhtē haĩ?		Do you wish to go to Rawalpindi?
musāfir:	hā̃. maĩ kaisē Rāvalpindī jā saktā hū̃?	Traveller:	Yes. How can I get to Rawalpindi?
dihātī:	kyā āp bas-sē jā rahē haĩ?	Villager:	Are you going by bus?
musāfir:	nahī̃. maĩ mōṭar-sē jā rahā hū̃.	Traveller:	No. I am going by automobile.
dihātī:	is saṛak-par sāmnē [1] jāiyē aur ēk mīl-kē bād bāyī̃ taraf muṛ jāiyē.	Villager:	Go on this road and after one mile turn to the left.
musāfir:	bāyī̃ taraf?	Traveller:	To the left?
dihātī:	hā̃. bāyī̃ taraf.	Villager:	Yes. To the left.
musāfir:	phir?	Traveller:	(And) then?
dihātī:	vahā̃ tumhẽ ēk cauṛī saṛak milēgī. vo Rāvalpindi jātī hai.	Villager:	You will find a wide road. It goes to Rawalpindi.
musāfir:	maĩ is saṛak-par kis taraf jāū̃?	Traveller:	In which direction should I go on this road?
dihātī:	pahilē sāmnē [1] jāiyē aur bāyī̃ taraf muṛ jāiyē.	Villager:	First go straight ahead and then turn left.
musāfir:	bahot bahot śukriyā.	Traveller:	Thank you very much.

REMARKS: (1) See 2.6, note 3.

LESSON 6

6.1

ham būṛhē dānā-kō suntē haĩ.	We listen to the old wise man.
ham būṛhē dānāō̃-kō suntē haĩ.	We listen to the old wise men.
maĩ dublē ghōṛē-kō calātā hū̃.	I drive the lean horse.
maĩ dublē ghōṛō̃-kō calātā hū̃.	I drive the lean horses.
tum lambē bāzār-kō dikhātē hō.	You point out the long bazaar.
tum lambē bāzārō̃-kō dikhātē hō.	You point out the long bazaars.
vo būṛhē śer-kō mārtā hai.	He kills the old lion.
vo būṛhē śērō̃-kō mārtā hai.	He kills the old lions.
vo pakkē phal-kō tōṛtī hai.	She plucks the ripe fruit.
vo pakkē phalō̃-kō tōṛtī hai.	She plucks the ripe fruits.
vo pyāsī laṛkī-kō pilātī haĩ.	They cause the thirsty girl to drink.
vo pyāsī laṛkiyō̃-kō pilātī haĩ.	They cause the thirsty girls to drink.
tum chōṭī bēṭī-kō batātē hō.	You tell the little daughter.
tum chōṭī bēṭiyō̃-kō batātē hō.	You tell the little daughters.
vo kaccī sabzī-kō bēctī hai.	She sells the raw vegetable.
vo kaccī sabziyō̃-kō bēctī hai.	She sells the raw vegetables.
maĩ ū̃cī imārat-kō pātā hū̃.	I find the high building.
maĩ ū̃cī imārtō̃-kō pātā hū̃.	I find the high buildings.
vo purānī kitāb-kō girātā hai.	He drops the old book.
vo purānī kitābō̃-kō girātā hai.	He drops the old books.

This section is concerned with adjectives modifying nouns in the object form.—i.e., nouns before postpositions. (See also 3.2, Remarks.)

Before masculine nouns, both singular and plural, the adjective replaces **-ā** with **-ē**; before feminine nouns it replaces **-ā** with **-ī**, in both numbers.

REMARKS: **pilānā** means **to give to drink** or **to cause to drink; batānā** means **to tell, to point out** or **to inform; calānā** means **to drive, to cause to move.**

6.1.1 Exercise 1. **Translate into English:**

1. ādmī kaccī sabziyõ-kō khātā hai. 2. aurtẽ chōṭē baccõ-kō bulātī haĩ. 3. kisān pyāsē bailõ-kō pilātā hai. 4. ustād•sāhab acchē laṛkē-kō batātē haĩ. 5. ham ũcī imārtõ-kō dēkhtē haĩ. 6. laṛkē pakkē phalõ-kō tōṛtē haĩ. 7. vo lambī saṛak-kō jāntī haĩ. 8. kisān baṛē bail-kō calātā hai. 9. mā̃ kaccī sabziyõ-kō pakātī hai. 10. ādmī nayī tasvīrõ-kō bēctā hai. 11. lambā ādmī pakkē phalõ-kō tōṛtā hai. 12. chōṭē laṛkē purānī kitāb-kō paṛhtē haĩ. 13. acchī bahan pyāsē bhāiyõ-kō pilātī hai. 14. chōṭī laṛkī nayī tasvīr-kō girātī hai. 15. dublā ādmī saccē dōst-kō jāntā hai. 16. bandar pakkē phalõ-kō khānā cāhtē haĩ. 17. aurat kaccī sabziyõ-kō pakānā cāhtī hai. 18. ham baṛē jānvarõ-kō dēkhnā cāhtē haĩ. 19. laṛkā chōṭī kitāb-kō paṛhnā cāhtā hai. 20. vo nayī tasvīrõ-kō dēkhnā cāhtī haĩ. 21. baccā pakkē phal-kō āhistā khātā hai. 22. mā̃ chōṭī laṛkiyõ-kō andar bulātī hai. 23. bāp ũcē makānõ-kō vahā̃ dikhātā hai. 24. ghōṛī kaccī sabziyõ-kō jaldī-sē khātī hai. 25. vo purānī tasvīr-kō yahā̃ ḳharīdtī haĩ.

6.1.2 Exercise 2. **Translate into Urdu:**

1. We (**fm.**) feed the hungry men. 2. The boy points out the wide street. 3. The child grabs the raw vegetable. 4. The monkeys steal the ripe fruits. 5. They (**msc.**) call the tall man. 6. The farmer drives the fat oxen. 7. The woman buys the new picture. 8. She knows the long street. 9. Mother calls the hungry daughters. 10. The girl drops the new book. 11. The good woman makes the thirsty cow drink. 12. The hungry monkeys eat the small fruits. 13. The old farmer drives the big horses. 14. The lean fathers eat the raw vegetables. 15. The thirsty dogs find true friends. 16. We (**msc.**) want to find the high building. 17. The farmer wants to feed the hungry goats. 18. The woman wants to make the thirsty cow drink. 19. The boy wants to read the little book. 20. The farmer wants to sell the raw vegetables. 21. I (**msc.**) want to drive the big horses. 22. Mother wants to call the hungry children here. 23. The good woman feeds the little children too much. 24. The very good boy reads the new books sometimes. 25. The hungry monkey eats the ripe fruits immediately.

6.2

ye ādmī mōṭā hai.	This man is fat.
ye mōṭā hai.	This (**one**) is fat.
ye aurat bhūkī hai.	This woman is hungry.
ye bhūkī hai.	This (**one**) is hungry.
ye kuttā burā hai.	This dog is bad.
ye burā hai.	This (**one**) is bad.
ye billī gussīlī hai.	This cat is bad-tempered.
ye gussīlī hai.	This (**one**) is bad-tempered.
ye phūl baṛā hai.	This flower is big.
ye bāṛā hai.	This (**one**) is big.

ye ādmī mōṭē haĩ.	These men are fat.
ye mōṭē haĩ.	These are fat.
ye aurtẽ bhūkī haĩ.	These woman are hungry.
ye bhūkī haĩ.	These are hungry.
ye kuttē burē haĩ.	These dogs are bad.
ye burē haĩ.	These are bad.
ye billiyā̃ gussīlī haĩ.	These cats are bad-tempered.
ye gussīlī haĩ.	These are bad-tempered.
ye daraḳht baṛē haĩ.	These trees are big.
ye baṛē haĩ.	These are big.

Sections 6.2 to 6.3.5 are concerned with the demonstrative pronouns and adjectives. The first sentence in each of the groups of two, above, illustrates the subject form of the demonstrative adjective; the second, that of the demonstrative pronoun.

Sections 6.2 to 6.2.5 take up **ye,** the demonstrative pronoun and adjective indicating beings and things nearer to the person talking as contrasted with beings and things at a distance from him (Compare **vo** in 6.3 to 6.3.5, following.).

ye serves for the subject form, singular and plural. Note that the forms for the pronoun and adjective are the same. **(ye** is often pronounced with a final aspiration: **yeh.)**

REMARKS: (1) **ye** can function as a personal pronoun, translating "he, she, it, and they."

(2) **phūl (ā)** flower, **daraḳht (ā)** tree.

6.2.1 Exercise 1. **Translate into English:**

1. ye khēltā hai. 2. ye tōtā bōltā hai. 3. ye sōtī haĩ. 4. ye bēṭī pakātī hai. 5. ye jānvar dauṛtē haĩ. 6. ye sabzī pakkī hai. 7. ye mēz nayī hai. 8. ye pītē haĩ. 9. ye lambī hai. 10. ye dukān jaltī hai. 11. ye bēṭiyā̃ jānnā cāhtī haĩ. 12. ye purānā makān jaltā hai. 13. ye aurtẽ āhistā āhistā bōltī haĩ. 14. ye sōnā cāhtā hai. 15. ye kabhī kabhī khēltī haĩ. 16. ye bhūkī ghōṛī jaldī-sē khānā cāhtī hai. 17. ye pakkē phal girtē haĩ. 18. ye kisān bahot kām kartā hai. 19. ye pyāsā bail kabhī kabhī ṭhaharnā cāhtā hai. 20. ye chōṭē baccē bāhar jānā cāhtē haĩ.

6.2.2 Exercise 2. **Translate into Urdu:**

1. These (**msc.**) run. 2. This goat jumps. 3. These girls understand. 4. This wife cooks. 5. These (**msc.**) drink. 6. This (**one** [**msc.**]) works. 7. These dogs run. 8. These cows drink. 9. These fish eat. 10. This (**one [fm.]**) reads. 11. This boy wants to read. 12. These (**msc.**) want to drink. 13. This big building burns. 14. This monkey wants to play. 15. These small books fall. 16. These dogs want to play. 17. This little horse wants to drink. 18. These (**fm.**) want to eat. 19. These big men work. 20. This old woman wants to sleep.

6.2.3

maĩ is ādmī-kō jāntā hū̃.	I know this man.
maĩ is-kō jāntā hū̃.	I know this (**one**).
maĩ is mōṭē ādmī-kō jāntā hū̃.	I know this fat man.

vo is aurat-kō dēkhtī hai.	She sees this woman.
vo is-kō dēkhtī hai.	She sees this (**one**).
vo is bhūkī aurat-kō dēkhtī hai.	She sees this hungry woman.
vo is kuttē-kō mārtā hai.	He beats this dog.
vo is-kō mārtā hai.	He beats this (**one**).
vo is burē kuttē-kō mārtā hai.	He beats this bad dog.
vo is billī-kō pakaṛtē haī̃.	They grab this cat.
vo is-kō pakaṛtē haī̃.	They grab this (**one**).
vo is g̱ussīlī billī-kō pakaṛtē haī̃.	They grab this bad-tempered cat.
ham is daraḳht-kō kāṭtē haī̃.	We cut this tree.
ham is-kō kāṭtē haī̃.	We cut this (**one**).
ham is baṛē daraḳht-kō kāṭtē haī̃.	We cut this big tree.
vo in ādmiyō̃-kō dikhātā hai.	He points out these men.
vo in-kō dikhātā hai.	He points out these.
vo in mōṭē ādmiyō̃-kō dikhātā hai.	He points out these fat men.
ham in aurtō̃-kō suntē haī̃.	We hear these women.
ham in-kō suntē haī̃.	We hear these.
ham in bhūkī aurtō̃-kō suntē haī̃.	We hear these hungry women.
tum in kuttō̃-kō khilātē hō.	You feed these dogs.
tum in-kō khilātē hō.	You feed these.
tum in burē kuttō̃-kō khilātē hō.	You feed these bad dogs.
vo in billiyō̃-kō lātī hai.	She brings these cats.
vo in-kō lātī hai.	She brings these.
vo in g̱ussīlī billiyō̃-kō lātī hai.	She brings these bad-tempered cats.
vo in daraḳhtō̃-kō kāṭtā hai.	He cuts these trees.
vo in-kō kāṭtā hai.	He cuts these.
vo in baṛē daraḳhtō̃-kō kāṭtā hai.	He cuts these big trees.

This section gives the object forms of **ye,** pronoun and adjective. As in 6.2, the first sentence in each group of three, above, illustrates the adjective and the second, the pronoun (See 6.2, Remarks.). The third sentence illustrates the demonstrative adjective modifying a noun modified by another adjective.

6.2.4 Exercise 1. **Translate into English:**

1. maī̃ is laṛkē-kō dēkhtā hū̃. 2. kisān in jānvarō̃-kō bā̃dhtā hai. 3. ādmī is-kō bulātā hai. 4. mā̃ is bēṭī-kō sikhātī hai. 5. ham in kuttō̃-kō khilātē haī̃. 6. kuttā is bhāī-kō kāṭtā hai. 7. baccē in-kō pakaṛtē haī̃. 8. vo in-kō khilātī haī̃. 9. aurat is-kō pakātī hai. 10. bāp in tōtō̃-kō ḳharīdtē haī̃. 11. laṛkī in chōṭī kitābō̃-kō paṛhtī hai. 12. kuttā is baccē-kō bāhar

khĩctā hai. 13. mā̃ in-kō andar bulātī hai. 14. bāp is bēṭē-kō cūmnā cāhtā hai. 15. aurat is bhūkī gāy-kō bā̃dhnā cāhtī hai. 16. kisān in bakrō̃-kō ḳharīdtā hai. 17. ustād·sāhab in-kō kabhī kabhī paṛhtē haĩ. 18. bhāī is chōṭē tōtē-kō yahā̃ pātā hai. 19. gāy in bhūkē bachṛō̃-kō jaldī-sē khilātī hai. 20. aurat is-kō khilātī hai.

6.2.5 Exercise 2. **Translate into Urdu:**

1. The mother feeds these children. 2. We (**msc.**) pull this (**one**). 3. I (**msc.**) hear these parrots. 4. Sister bathes this child. 5. We (**fm.**) buy this (**one**). 6. The man buys these horses. 7. The boy brings these quickly. 8. The woman cooks these vegetables. 9. They (**fm.**) want to hear these. 10. We (**msc.**) buy this picture. 11. The good woman feeds these hungry children too much. 12. The mokeys eat these fruits quickly. 13. The woman feeds these fat cows. 14. The child wants to eat this raw vegetable. 15. The very good girl reads the news books sometimes. 16. We (**fm.**) know this long street. 17. The woman buys this new picture. 18. The hungry boys eat these ripe fruits. 19. She drops this raw vegetable. 20. The boy wants to read this little book here.

6.3

vo ādmī mōṭā hai.	That man is fat.
vo mōṭā hai.	That (**one**) is fat.
vo aurat bhūkī hai.	That woman is hungry.
vo bhūkī hai.	That (**one**) is hungry.
vo kuttā burā hai.	That dog is bad.
vo burā hai.	That (**one**) is bad.
vo billī ġussīlī hai.	That cat is bad-tempered.
vo ġussīlī hai.	That (**one**) is bad-tempered.
vo daraḳht baṛā hai.	That tree is big.
vo baṛā hai.	That (**one**) is big.
vo ādmī mōṭē haĩ.	Those men are fat.
vo mōṭē haĩ.	Those are fat.
vo aurtē̃ bhūkī haĩ.	Those women are hungry.
vo bhūkī haĩ.	Those are hungry.
vo kuttē burē haĩ.	Those dogs are bad.
vo burē haĩ.	Those are bad.
vo billiyā̃ ġussīlī haĩ.	Those cats are bad-tempered.
vo ġussīlī haĩ.	Those are bad-tempered.
vo daraḳht baṛē haĩ.	Those trees are big.
vo baṛē haĩ	Those are big.

Sections 6.3 to 6.3.5 are concerned with the demonstrative pronouns and adjectives which indicate beings and things at a distance from the speaker (Compare 6.2, above.).

This section illustrates the subject forms of the pronouns and adjectives.

REMARKS: Note that the demonstrative pronouns function also as the third person pronoun. (See 2.1 and 5.1.)

6.3.1 Exercise 1. **Translate into English:**

1. vo paṛhtā hai. 2. vo tōtē bōltē haĩ. 3. vo gāy pītī hai. 4. vo dukānẽ jaltī haĩ. 5. vo khēltī haĩ. 6. vo phal pakkā hai. 7. vo khātē haĩ. 8. vo aurat pakātī hai. 9. vo ādmī kām kartē haĩ. 10. vo lambī hai. 11. vo bēṭiyā̃ khēlnā cāhtī haĩ. 12. vo pyāsī laṛkī paṛhtī hai. 13. vo laṛkī jānā cāhtī hai. 14. vo pakkā phal girtā hai. 15. vo purānē makān jaltē haĩ. 16. vo pyāsē bakrē yahā̃ pītē haĩ. 17. vo bhūkē ghōṛē jaldī-sē khānā cāhtē haĩ. 18. vo imārat ū̃cī hai. 19. vo būṛhā kisān bahot kām kartā hai. 20. vo tasvīrẽ cauṛī haĩ.

6.3.2 Exercise 2. **Translate into Urdu:**

1. She cooks. 2. That boy walks. 3. Those cows eat. 4. Those (**msc.**) go there. 5. That farmer buys. 6. That (**one** [**fm.**]) runs. 7. Those vegetables are new. 8. That (**one** [**msc.**]) teaches. 9. Those buildings are high. 10. They (**msc.**) work there. 11. That boy feeds the horse quickly. 12. That little girl pulls the cat. 13. Those farmers buy the oxen. 14. Those women want to bathe the children. 15. That teacher lives here. 16. Those parrots want to speak. 17. That big horse wants to pull the man. 18. Those little children are hungry. 19. Those hens want to eat. 20. That hungry man wants to catch the fish.

6.3.3

maĩ us ādmī-kō jāntā hū̃.	I know that man.
maĩ us-kō jāntā hū̃.	I know that (**one**).
maĩ us mōṭē ādmī-kō jāntā hū̃.	I know that fat man.
vo us aurat-kō samajhtē haĩ.	They understand that woman.
vo us-kō samajhtē haĩ.	They understand that (**one**).
vo us bhūkī aurat-kō samajhtē haĩ.	They understand that hungry woman.
vo us kuttē-kō khilātī hai.	She feeds that dog.
vo us-kō khilātī hai.	She feeds that (**one**).
vo us burē kuttē-kō khilātī hai.	She feeds that bad dog.
vo us billī-kō bulātā hai.	He calls that cat.
vo us-kō bulātā hai.	He calls that (**one**).
vo us gussīlī billī-kō bulātā hai.	He calls that bad-tempered cat.
vo us daraḳht-kō kāṭtē haĩ.	They cut that tree.
vo us-kō kāṭtē haĩ.	They cut that (**one**).
vo us baṛē daraḳht-kō kāṭtē haĩ.	They cut that big tree.
vo un ādmiyō̃-kō lātā hai.	He brings those men.
vo un-kō lātā hai.	He brings those.
vo un mōṭē ādmiyō̃-kō lātā hai.	He brings those fat men.

āp un aurtō̃-kō bacātē haĩ.	You save those women.
āp un-kō bacātē haĩ.	You save those.
āp un bhūkī aurtō̃-kō bacātā haĩ.	You save those hungry women.
vo un kuttō̃-kō khĩctā hai.	He drags those dogs.
vo un-kō khĩctā hai.	He drags those.
vo un burē kuttō̃-kō khĩctā hai.	He drags those bad dogs.
vo un billiyō̃-kō pilātī hai.	She makes those cats drink.
vo un-kō pilātī hai.	She makes those drink.
vo un g̠ussīlī billiyō̃-ko pilātī hai.	She makes those bad-tempered cats drink.
tum un darak̤htō̃-kō pātē hō.	You find those trees.
tum un-kō pātē hō.	You find those.
tum un baṛē darak̤htō̃-kō pātē hō.	You find those big trees.

This section illustrates object forms of **vo,** demonstrative pronoun and adjective.

6.3.4 Exercise 1. **Translate into English:**

1. vo us-kō jāntē haĩ. 2. aurat un gāyō̃-kō khilātī hai. 3. kuttā us ādmī-kō kāṭtā hai. 4. mā̃ us-kō nahlātī hai. 5. ham us saṛak-kō jāntē haĩ. 6. kisān un phalō̃-kō tōṛtē haĩ. 7. bāp un-kō bulātē haĩ. 8. tum un sabziyō̃-kō k̤harīdtī hō. 9. bēṭī us billī-kō pātī hai. 10. laṛkā us-kō pakaṛtā hai. 11. tum un bailō̃-kō calātē hō. 12. ham un baṛē jānvarō̃-kō dēkhnā cāhtē hai. 13. aurtē̃ un kaccē phalō̃-kō pakānā cāhtī haĩ. 14. vo un kaccī sabziyō̃-kō bēctē haĩ. 15. ādmī un nayī tasvirō̃-kō bēctā hai. 16. bahan un bhūkē laṛkō̃-kō andar bulānā cāhtī hai. 17. laṛkā us lambī saṛak-kō dikhātā hai. 18. bāp un ū̃cī imārtō̃-kō dikhānā cāhtā hai. 19. ham un pakkē phalō̃-ko khānā cāhtē haĩ. 20. vo us purānī kitāb-kō girātī hai.

6.3.5 Exercise 2. **Translate into Urdu:**

1. I (**msc.**) point out that high building. 2. The little boy pulls that cat. 3. The horse eats those. 4. They (**msc.**) call those tall men. 5. We (**fm.**) feed them. 6. Father buys that big house. 7. You (**msc.**) know those friends. 8. That fox seizes those fat hens. 9. She sees her. 10. The good woman makes those thirsty cows drink. 11. We (**msc.**) want to find that big house. 12. The boy brings those little books. 13. The hungry monkeys want to steal those fruits. 14. Father feeds those little boys too much. 15. The woman buys that new cooking-pot. 16. The cat catches that little mouse. 17. The farmer kills that old fox. 18. I (**msc.**) drive that big horse sometimes. 19. The hungry dog bites that bad boy. 20. The farmer wants to find that (**one**).

6.4 The numbers 41 to 60:

iktālīs 41, **bayālīs** 42, **tē̃tālīs** 43, **cauvālīs (cavālīs)** 44, **paĩtālīs** 45, **chiyālīs** 46, **saĩtālīs** 47, **aṛtālīs** 48, **uncās** 49, **pacās** 50, **ikyāvan** 51, **bāvan** 52, **trēpan** 53, **cauvan** 54, **pacpan** 55, **chappan** 56, **sattāvan** 57, **aṭṭhāvan** 58, **unsaṭh** 59, **sāṭh** 60.

6.5 ēk g̠airmulkī aur Pākistānī-mē̃ bātcīt	**Conversation Between a Pakistani and a Foreigner.**
K̤hurśīd: **helō.**	K̤hurśīd: **Hello.**
Smith: **helō.**	Smith: **Hello.**

Khurśīd:	kyā maĩ āp-kī madad kar saktā hũ?	Khurśīd:	Can I help you?
Smith:	hā̃. āp mērī madad kar saktē haĩ. maĩ ajnabī hũ aur makāmī zabān acchī tarah nahī̃ bōl saktā.	Smith:	Yes. You can help me. I am a stranger and cannot speak the local language well.
Khurśīd:	āp kahā̃-sē haĩ?	Khurśīd.	Where do you come from?
Smith:	maĩ Amrīkā[1]-sē hũ. kyā āp Urdū bōltē haĩ?	Smith:	I come from America. Do you speak Urdu?
Khurśīd:	hā̃. maĩ Urdū bōltā hũ.	Khurśīd:	Yes. I speak Urdu.
Smith:	kyā ap mērī Urdū samajh saktē haĩ?	Smith	Can you understand my Urdu?
Khurśīd:	hā̃. maĩ āp-kō acchī tarah samajh saktā hũ.	Khurśīd:	Yes. I can understand you (very) well.
Smith:	śukriyā. lēkin zarā aur āhistā bōliyē. maĩ āp-kō nahī̃ samajh saktā.	Smith:	Thank you. But (please) speak a little more slowly. I cannot understand you.
Khurśīd:	maĩ aur āhistā bolū̃gā. kyā āp ab mujhē samajh saktē haĩ?	Khurśīd:	I'll speak more slowly. Can you understand me now?
Smith:	hā̃. maĩ ab samajh saktā hũ.	Smith:	Yes. I can understand (you) now.
Khurśīd:	āiyē. apnē apnē mulk-kē bārē-mē̃ bāt karē̃. maĩ āp-kō Pākistan-kē bārē-mē̃ batāū̃gā.	Khurśīd:	Come. Let us talk about our countries. I shall tell you about Pakistan.
Smith:	khuśī-sē. maĩ Amrīkā-kē bārē-mē̃ batāū̃gā.	Smith:	With pleasure. I shall tell you about America.

REMARKS: (1) A variant of this is **Amerikā.**

6.6 dō dōst bātcīt kartē haĩ — **Conversation Between Two Friends.**

Hudā:	tum kahā̃ ṭhahrē hō?	Hudā:	Where are you staying?
Grīn:	Grenḍ Hōṭal-mē̃.	Green:	(I am staying) at the Grand Hotel.
Hudā:	kyā vo bahot mahēgā hai?	Hudā:	Is it very expensive?
Grīn:	hā̃. vo bahot mahēgā hai. maĩ zyādā munāsib jagah-kī talāś-mē̃ hũ. kyā tum mērī madad kar saktē hō?	Green:	Yes. It is very expensive. I am looking for a more suitable place. Can you help me?
Hudā:	hā̃. zarūr.	Hudā:	Yes. Certainly.
Grīn:	bahot bahot śukriyā. mujhē ab jānā hai.	Green:	Thank you very much. I must go now.
Hudā:	tum kahā̃ jā rahē hō?	Hudā:	Where are you going?
Grīn:	maĩ apnē hōṭal vāpas jā rahā hũ.	Green:	I'm going back to my hotel.
Hudā:	vo bahot nazdīk hai. kyā maĩ tumhārē sāth cal saktā hũ?	Hudā:	It is quite near. Can I come with you?
Grīn:	hā̃. zarūr.	Green:	Yes. Certainly.
Hudā:	ye hai, tumhārā hōṭal.	Hudā:	Here is your hotel.

Grīn:	kyā tum andar āōgē?	Green:	**Will you come in?**
Hudā:	mujhē afsōs hai ke maĩ tumhārē sāth andar nahī̃ ā saktā.	Hudā:	**I'm sorry that I cannot come in with you.**
	mujhē kahī̃ aur jānā hai.		**I have to go somewhere else.**
Grīn:	mujhē afsōs hai.	Green:	**I am very sorry.**
	kyā tum mujh-sē kal mil saktē hō?		**Can you meet me tomorrow?**
Hudā:	hā̃. maĩ tum-sē kal mil saktā hū̃.	Hudā:	**Yes. I can meet you tomorrow.**
Grīn:	kyā das bajē ṭhīk rahēgā?	Green:	**Will ten o'clock be all right?**
Hudā:	hā̃. das bajē ṭhīk hai.	Hudā:	**Yes. ten o'clock is all right.**
Grīn:	tab maĩ das bajē milū̃gā.	Green:	**Then I'll meet (you) at ten o'clock.**
Hudā:	acchā. phir milēgē.	Hudā:	**Good. We'll meet again.**

LESSON 7

7.1

baiṭhiyē.	**(Please)** sit down.
āhistā caliyē.	**(Please)** walk slowly.
Urdū bōliyē.	**(Please)** speak Urdu.
andar āiyē.	**(Please)** come in.
ye phal khāiyē.	**(Please)** eat these friuts.

Sections 7.1 and 7.1.1 illustrate the imperative forms of the verb. 7.1 illustrates the "polite" imperative, or the form employed to address a person to whom respect or honor is intended. (Compare **āp** and 2.1, Remarks.) It is formed by attaching **-iyē** to the stem of the verb.

7.1.1

baiṭhō!	Sit down!
āhistā calō!	Walk slowly!
Urdū bōlō!	Speak Urdu!
andar āō!	Come in!
ye phal khāō!	Eat these fruits!

This section illustrates the imperative form employed towards persons who are equals or close friends of the speaker and to servants. (Compare **tum** and 2.1, Remarks.)

REMARKS: Nouns indicating things, when occurring as objects of transitive verbs, need not be placed in the object form before the postposition **-kō.** The nominative form suffices. (See in the last sentence **ye phal.**) More examples of this construction will be given later.

7.2 Telling time:

ēk bajā hai.	It is one o'clock.
dō bajē haĩ.	It is two o'clock.
tīn bajē haĩ.	It is three o'clock.
cār bajē haĩ.	It is four o'clock.
pā̃c bajē haĩ.	It is five o'clock.

7.3 The numbers from 61 on:

iksaṭh 61, **bāsaṭh** 62, **trēsaṭh** 63, **caũsaṭh** 64, **paĩsaṭh** 65, **chiyāsaṭh** 66, **sarsaṭh** 67, **arsaṭh**

68, **unhattar** 69, **sattar** 70, **ik·hattar** 71, **bahattar** 72, **tihattar** 73, **cauhattar** 74, **pāc·hattar** 75, **chihattar** 76, **satattar** 77, **aṭh·hattar** 78, **unāsī** 79, **assī** 80, **ikkāsī** 81, **bayāsī** 82, **tirāsī** 83, **curāsī** 84, **pacāsī** 85, **cheyāsī** 86, **sattāsī** 87, **aṭṭhāsī** 88, **navāsī** 89, **navvē** 90, **ikkānvē** 91, **bānvē** 92, **tirānvē** 93, **curānvē** 94, **paccānvē** 95, **chiyānvē** 96, **sattānvē** 97, **aṭṭhānvē** 98, **ninnānvē** 99, **sau** 100, **ēk sau ēk** 101, **ēk sau das** 110, **dō sau** 200, **tīn sau** 300, **cār sau** 400, **pā̃c sau** 500, **hazār** 1,000, **lākh** 100,000, **das lākh** 1,000,000, **karōṛ** 10,000,000.

REMARKS: The raised dot in the words for 71, 75 and 78 is employed to distinguish what otherwise might be considered aspirate stops.

7.3.1 Reading numbers:

ēk hazār nau sau iksaṭh	one thousand, nine hundred and sixty-one (1,961)
ēk hazār nau sau bāsaṭh	one thousand, nine hundred and sixty-two (1,962)
ēk hazār nau sau trēsaṭh	one thousand, nine hundred and sixty-three (1,963)
ēk hazār nau sau caũsaṭh	one thousand, nine hundred and sixty-four (1,964)
ēk hazār nau sau paĩsaṭh	one thousand, nine hundred and sixty-five (1,965)

7.3.2 Reading dates:

unnīs sau iksaṭh	nineteen hundred and sixty-one (1961)
unnīs sau bāsaṭh	nineteen hundred and sixty-two (1962)
unnīs sau trēsaṭh	nineteen hundred and sixty-three (1963)
unnīs sau caũsaṭh	nineteen hundred and sixty-four (1964)
unnīs sau paĩsaṭh	nineteen hundred and sixty-five (1965)

7.4 **dō aurtō̃-kē darmiyān bātcīt.**	**Conversation Between Two Women.**
Rānā: **salām ālēkum.**	Rānā: **Hello.**
Nargis: **vālēkum salām.**	Nargis: **Hello.**
Rānā: **kyā mujhē dēr hō gayī?**	Rānā: **Am I late?**
Nargis: **nahī̃. tumhē̃ der nahī̃ huī. andar ā jāō.**	Nargis: **No. You are not late. Come in.**
Rānā: **āj bahot garmī hai.**	Rānā: **It is very warm today.**
Nargis: **hā̃. bahot garmī hai. yahā̃ khiṛkī-kē pās baiṭhō. kyā piyōgī?**	Nargis: **Yes. It is very warm. Sit here by the window. What will you drink?**
Rānā: **sirf ṭhaṇḍē pānī-kā ēk glās.**	Rānā: **Just a glass of cold water.**
Nargis: **kam-az-kam sharbat-kā ēk glās tō piyō.**	Nargis: **At least have a glass of sherbet.**
Rānā: **acchā.**	Rānā: **Fine.**
Nargis: **Kalū!**	Nargis: **Kalū!**
Kalū: **ji begam sāhibā.**[1]	Kalū: **Yes, madam.**

Nargis: sharbat-kē dō glās lāō.	Nargis: Bring two glasses of sherbet.
Kalū: bahot acchā.	Kalū: Very good.
abhī lātā hū̃.	I'm bringing (them) right away.
kahā̃ rakhū̃?	Where should I place them?
Nargis: is mēz-par rakh dō.	Nargis: Place (them) on this table.
Kalū: bahot acchā.	Kalū: Very good.
aur kuch?	(Should I bring) anything else?
Nargis: nahī. abhī nahī.	Nargis: No. Not now.
Kalū: bahot acchā.	Kalū: Very good.

REMARKS: (1) Variant is sāhabā.

7.5 dō musāfirō̃-mē̃ bātcīt.	Conversation of Two Travellers.
Karīm: salām ālēkum.	Karīm: Hello.
Umar: vālēkum salām.	Umar: Hello.
Karīm: āp-kā nām kyā hai?	Karīm: What is your name?
Umar: mērā nām Umar hai.	Umar: My name is Umar.
āp-kā nām kyā hai?	What is your name?
Karīm: mērā nām Karīm hai.	Karīm: My name is Karīm.
Umar: āp kahā̃-sē haĩ?	Umar: Where do you come from?
Karīm: maĩ Farīdpur-sē hū̃.	Karīm: I am from Faridpur.
Umar: maĩ Farīdpur-sē vākif nahī̃.	Umar: I am not acquainted with Faridpur.
kyā vo kisī baṛē śahar-kē nazdīk hai?	Is it near any large town?
Karīm: hā̃. vo baṛē śahar-kē nazdīk hai.	Karīm: Yes. It is near a large town.
Umar: śahar-kā nām kyā hai?	Umar: What is the name of the town?
Karīm: us-kā nām Multān hai.	Karīm: Its name is Multān.
Umar: maĩ us śahar-sē ḳhūb vāḳif hū̃.	Umar: I know that town very well.
mēra gā̃v bārā mīl us-kē śumāl-mē̃ hai.	My village is twelve miles to the north of it.
Karīm: mērā gā̃v nau mīl us-kē maśriḳ-mē̃ hai.	Karīm: My village is nine miles east of it.
Umar: mujhē āp-sē milkar baṛī ḳhuśī huī.	Umar: I am very glad to have met you.
Karīm: mujhē-bhī āp-sē milkar bahot ḳhuśī huī.	Karīm: I, too, am very glad to have met you.
mērā sṭāp ā gayā hai.	Here is my stop.
mujhē ab jānā hai.	I must go now.
Umar: phir milẽgē. Ḳhudā hāfiz.	Umar: We'll meet again. Good-by.
Karīm: Ḳhudā hāfiz.	Karīm: Good-by.

LESSON 8

8. REVIEW. The numbers in brackets refer to the exercises in the previous lessons.

8.1 [2.1.3] **Translate into Urdu:**

1. You (**hon. msc.**) walk. 2. She arrives. 3. You (**msc.**) sleep. 4. They (**msc.**) play. 5. I (**fm.**) speak. 6. We (**msc.**) give. 7. You (**fm.**) understand. 8. He goes. 9. They (**msc.**) say. 10. You (**hon. msc.**) bring. 11. He comes. 12. We (**fm.**) say. 13. You (**fm.**) read. 14. I (**msc.**) jump. 15. She lives. 16. You (**msc.**) ask. 17. They (**fm.**) swim. 18. You (**hon. msc.**) run. 19. We (**msc.**) eat. 20. I (**msc.**) work.

8.2 [2.1.4] **Translate into English:**

1. vo jātē haĩ. 2. vo kahtā hai. 3. āp bōltī haĩ. 4. maĩ samajhtī hū̃. 5. vo khēltā hai. 6. vo caltī hai. 7. vo bōltē haĩ. 8. ham dauṛtī haĩ. 9. maĩ khēltā hū̃. 10. tum kūdtī hō. 11. ham pahõctē haĩ. 12. maĩ kām kartā hū̃. 13. vo rahtī hai. 14. tum pakātē hō. 15. vo pūchtī haĩ. 16. ham lātē haĩ. 17. ham kahtī haĩ. 18. maĩ paṛhtī hū̃. 19. vo sōtī hai. 20. āp pītē hai.

8.3 [2.2.2] **Translate into Urdu:**

1. The son eats. 2. The child runs. 3. The dog jumps. 4. The calf eats. 5. The donkey lives. 6. The boy reads. 7. The horse walks. 8. The parrot asks. 9. The calves play. 10. The donkeys come. 11. The dogs flee. 12. The children drink. 13. The goats go. 14. The horses arrive. 15. The wolf stays. 16. The boy sees. 17. The parrots say. 18. The wolves run. 19. The goat eats. 20. The sons walk.

8.4 [2.2.3] **Translate into English:**

1. bakrā ātā hai. 2. bachṛē khātē haĩ. 3. baccā pītā hai. 4. gadhā caltā hai. 5. kuttā khēltā hai. 6. tōtē sōtē haĩ. 7. bhēṛiyā ucaltā hai. 8. ghōṛā dauṛtā hai. 9. baccē tairtē haĩ. 10. bakrē rahtē haĩ. 11. laṛkē bōltē haĩ. 12. bēṭā bhējtā hai. 13. gadhē jātē haĩ. 14. kuttē tairtē haĩ. 15. ghōṛē lātē haĩ. 16. laṛkā pūchtā hai. 17. bhēriyē pahõctē haĩ. 18. tōtā samajhtā hai. 19. bēṭē kahtē haĩ. 20. bachṛā rahtā hai.

8.5 [2.3.2] **Translate into Urdu:**

1. The (**female**) goat comes. 2. The flies go. 3. The hen drinks. 4. The cat runs. 5. The fish eats. 6. The girls read. 7. The fox jumps. 8. The wife cooks. 9. The mare sees. 10. The daughter understands. 11. The fish eat. 12. The hens eat. 13. The cats play. 14. The fly walks. 15. The daughters read. 16. The (**female**) goats live. 17. The wives ask. 18. The girl sends. 19. The mares come. 20. The foxes run.

8.6 [2.3.3] **Translate into English:**

1. bakriyā̃ khātī haĩ. 2. billī pītī hai. 3. bīvī pahõctī hai. 4. machliyā̃ khātī haĩ. 5. laṛkiyā̃

pūchtī haī̃. 6. lōmṛiyā̃ dauṛtī haī̃. 7. billiyā̃ khēltī haī̃. 8. murgī dauṛtī hai. 9. bēṭiyā̃ bōltī haī̃. 10. makkhiyā̃ jātī haī̃. 11. bīviyā̃ pakātī haī̃. 12. laṛkī kām kartī hai. 13. lōmṛī dēkhtī hai. 14. murgiyā̃ pītī haī̃. 15. bēṭī paṛhtī hai. 16. makkhī rahtī hai. 17. bēṭī samajhtī hai. 18. machlī rahtī hai. 19. bēṭiyā̃ kahtī haī̃. 20. bakrī sōtī hai.

8.7 [3.1.3] **Translate into Urdu:**

1. I (**msc.**) want to go. 2. The child wants to play. 3. The horses want to jump. 4. We (**fm.**) want to read. 5. The mare wants to drink. 6. The dogs want to come. 7. He wants to eat. 8. The girl wants to ask. 9. You (**msc.**) want to send. 10. The wife wants to cook. 11. The boy wants to work. 12. The parrot wants to speak. 13. The daughter wants to stay. 14. You (**hon. msc.**) want to arrive. 15. The boys want to send. 16. The daughters want to walk. 17. The fish want to swim. 18. The calves want to run. 19. They (**fm.**) want to see. 20. The cats want to sleep.

8.8 [3.1.4] **Translate into English:**

1. maī̃ dēnā cāhtā hū̃. 2. baccā khānā cāhtā hai. 3. laṛkiyā̃ calnā cāhtī haī̃. 4. tum lēnā cāhtē hō. 5. tōtā pīnā cāhtā hai. 6. bēṭā kam karnā cāhtā hai. 7. bīvī pūchnā cāhtī hai. 8. vo pakānā cāhtī hai. 9. laṛkē khēlnā cāhtē haī̃. 10. vo paṛhnā cāhtī haī̃. 11. bēṭī pūchnā cāhtī hai. 12. billiyā̃ jānā cāhtī haī̃. 13. vo bhējnā cāhtā hai. 14. bachṛā dauṛnā cāhtā hai. 15. bēṭē kām karnā cāhtē haī̃. 16. āp pahõ̃cnā cāhtē haī̃. 17. kuttā sōnā cāhtā hai. 18. murgī khānā cāhtī hai. 19. lōmṛiyā̃ ānā cāhtī haī̃. 20. ham calnā cāhtē haī̃.

8.9 [3.2.2] **Translate into Urdu:**

1. She is hungry. 2. The children are thirsty. 3. I (**msc.**) am old. 4. The cat is fat. 5. The donkeys are big. 6. You (**fm.**) are lean. 7. The daughters are good. 8. The boys are hungry. 9. We (**msc.**) are small. 10. The fox is lean. 11. You (**msc.**) are big. 12. They (**msc.**) are bad. 13. The shoe is small. 14. The wife is good. 15. The girls are hungry. 16. You (**hon. msc.**) are thirsty. 17. The horse is big. 18. The vegetables are good. 19. The mare is fat. 20. The cat is bad.

8.10 [3.2.3] **Translate into English:**

1. ghōṛē būṛhē haī̃. 2. bīvī bhūkī hai. 3. vo dublā hai. 4. jūtē baṛē haī̃. 5. machlī chōṭī hai. 6. gadhē burē haī̃. 7. vo pyāsī haī̃. 8. billī bhūkī hai. 9. bēṭiyā̃ dublī haī̃. 10. ghōṛī chōṭī hai. 11. murgī bhūkī hai. 12. maī̃ pyāsī hū̃. 13. makkhiyā̃ chōṭī haī̃. 14. tum jhūṭhī hō. 15. vo chōṭī hai. 16. ham acchē haī̃. 17. sabziyā̃ baṛī haī̃. 18. bakrī bhūkī hai. 19. tum mōṭē hō. 20. vo pyāsī hai.

8.11 [3.3.2] **Translate into Urdu:**

1. The elephants eat. 2. The lion drinks. 3. The camel runs. 4. The bears come. 5. The husband works. 6. The monkeys play. 7. The man speaks. 8. The elephant sleeps. 9. The brothers send. 10. The oxen go. 11. The house is big. 12. The lions are hungry. 13. The husband is good. 14. The monkey is bad. 15. The fruit is ripe. 16. The brothers want to work. 17. The monkey wants to play. 18. The animal wants to eat. 19. The men want to sit. 20. The bear wants to sit.

8.12 [3.3.3] **Translate into English:**

1. ḳhāvind nahātē haī̃. 2. rīch caltā hai. 3. ādmī kām kartā hai. 4. bhāī pūchtē haī̃. 5. jānvar baiṭhtā hai. 6. hāthī nahātē haī̃. 7. bandar kūdtē haī̃. 8. ādmī pahõ̃ctē haī̃. 9. bail khātē haī̃. 10. ū̃ṭ khī̃ctē haī̃. 11. makān chōṭē haī̃. 12. jānvar bhūkē haī̃. 13. bhāī acchē haī̃. 14. phal pakkā hai. 15. śēr pyāsē haī̃. 16. ḳhāvind dēnā cāhtē haī̃. 17. bail ṭhaharnā cāhtā hai. 18. rīch baiṭhnā cāhtē haī̃. 19. jānvar khānā cāhtē haī̃. 20. ādmī nahānā cāhtā hai.

8.13 [3.4.1] **Translate into Urdu:**
1. The shops fall. 2. The woman cooks. 3. The cows run. 4. The sister arrives. 5. The things break. 6. The roofs burn. 7. The armies stop. 8. The cow eats. 9. The sisters bathe. 10. The army sleeps. 11. The thing is big. 12. The roofs are new 13. The sister is hungry. 14. The women are thirsty. 15. The shop is small. 16. The army wants to go. 17. The cows want to stop. 18. The woman wants to cook. 19. The sisters want to sit. 20. The women want to cook.

8.14 [3.4.2] **Translate into English:**
1. cīz ṭūṭtī hai. 2. bahan pūchtī hai. 3. fauj baiṭhtī hai. 4. chat girtī hai. 5. gāyẽ pītī haĩ. 6. aurat dauṛtī hai. 7. faujẽ caltī haĩ. 8. bahnẽ caltī haĩ. 9. gāyẽ sōtī haĩ. 10. aurtẽ pakātī haĩ. 11. cīzẽ chōṭī haĩ. 12. chatẽ nayī haĩ. 13. dukān baṛī hai. 14. bahan bhūkī hai. 15. fauj baṛī hai. 16. aurat lānā cāhtī hai. 17. bahnẽ paṛhnā cāhtī haĩ. 18. fauj sōnā cāhtī hai. 19. gāyẽ khānā cāhtī haĩ. 20. aurtẽ pakānā cāhtī haĩ.

8.15 [4.1.4] **Translate into Urdu:**
1. The building burns. 2. The tables fall. 3. The picture breaks. 4. The street goes. 5. The winds come. 6. The books fall. 7. The night comes. 8. Th pictures fall. 9. The buildings burn. 10. The table breaks. 11. The books are big. 12. The roads are broad. 13. The place is big. 14. The medicines are new. 15. The table is new. 16. The places are small. 17. The buildings are old. 18. The night is long. 19. The table is broad. 20. The book is good.

8.16 [4.1.5] **Translate into English:**
1. mēz ṭūṭtī hai. 2. imārat girtī hai. 3. tasvīr jaltī hai. 4. havāẽ jātī haĩ. 5. rāt ātī hai. 6. saṛkẽ jātī haĩ. 7. tasvīrẽ girtī haĩ. 8. mēzẽ girtī haĩ. 9. imārat jaltī hai. 10. tasvīr ṭūṭtī hai. 11. jagah nayī hai. 12. kitāb purānī hai. 13. davāẽ acchī haĩ. 14. mēzẽ purānī haĩ. 15. saṛkẽ cauṛī haĩ. 16. imārtẽ chōṭī haĩ. 17. jagah acchī hai. 18. davā nayī hai. 19. kitābẽ baṛī haĩ. 20. imārat purānī hai.

8.17 [4.2.1] **Translate into Urdu:**
1. The sparrow goes. 2. The (**little**) old women walk. 3. The mice run. 4. The (**little**) old woman wants to sleep. 5. The mouse wants to eat. 6. The (**little**) old woman is thirsty. 7. The sparrows are small. 8. The cooking-pot is old. 9. The sparrow is thin. 10. The mice are hungry.

8.18 [4.2.2] **Translate into English:**
1. cuhiyā ātī hai. 2. buṛhiyā sōtī hai. 3. ciṛiyā̃ uṛtī haĩ. 4. cuhiyā̃ khānā cāhtī haĩ. 5. ciṛiyā uṛnā cāhtī hai. 6. buṛhiyā́ bhūkī haĩ. 7. cuhiyā̃ pyāsī haĩ. 8. hanḍiyā̃ acchī haĩ. 9. ciṛiyā̃ bhūkī haĩ. 10. hanḍiyā purānī hai.

8.19 [4.3.2] **Translate into Urdu:**
1. The hungry cat eats. 2. The bad dogs run. 3. The thirsty girls drink. 4. The big man works. 5. The good boy reads. 6. The fat dog sleeps. 7. The lean girl plays. 8. The old house burns. 9. The ripe fruits fall. 10. The old donkey pulls. 11. The good boys want to play. 12. The little cat wants to eat. 13. The lean goats want to stop. 14. The hungry women want to cook. 15. The thirsty horses want to drink. 16. The little boy is hungry. 17. The hungry girl is lean. 18. The big men are old. 19. The old shoes are small. 20. The big cows are fat.

8.20 [4.3.3] **Translate into English:**
1. mōṭē bakrē khātē haĩ. 2. pyāsī laṛkiyā̃ pītī haĩ. 3. chōṭī aurtẽ pakātī haĩ. 4. baṛī dukān

jaltī hai. 5. bhūkī faujē̃ ṭhahartī haĩ. 6. burē bandar khēltē haĩ. 7. purānī chat ṭuṭtī hai. 8. nayī imārat girtī hai. 9. bhukē ādmī kām kartē haĩ. 10. chōṭī laṛkiyā̃ dauṛtī haĩ. 11. acchī bahnē̃ pakānā cāhtī haĩ. 12. chōṭā ghōṛā ṭhaharnā cāhtā hai. 13. pyāsī gāyē̃ pīnā cāhtī haĩ. 14. bhūkā ū̃ṭ khī̃cnā cāhtā hai. 15. būṛhā ādmī sōnā cāhtā hai. 16. chōṭā baccā bhūkā hai. 17. baṛī dukān nayī hai. 18. chōṭē phal pakkē haĩ. 19. cauṛī saṛak lambī hai. 20. nayī kitābē̃ baṛī haĩ.

8.21 [4.4.1] **Translate into Urdu:**

1. The animals run quickly. 2. The man works inside. 3. We (**msc.**) live here. 4. The woman speaks slowly. 5. You (**msc.**) go out. 6. The brothers work a lot. 7. The women cook inside. 8. Elephants eat a lot. 9. They (**msc.**) go there. 10. The girls play sometimes. 11. The thirsty horse drinks quickly. 12. The hungry monkeys go down. 13. The little child comes behind. 14. The big elephants live there. 15. The good girls play together. 16. The little children want to go out. 17. The hungry mare wants to eat quickly. 18. The big man wants to work a lot. 19. The thirsty oxen want to stop sometimes. 20. The thin women want to eat immediately.

8.22 [4.4.2] **Translate into English:**

1. bhāī ēk-sath khātē haĩ. 2. laṛkī bāhar jātī hai. 3. aurat andar ātī hai. 4. baccē pīchē jātē haĩ. 5. ḳhāvind āgē jātā hai. 6. laṛkā āhistā āhistā bōltā hai. 7. ham kabhī kabhī khēltī haĩ. 8. jānvar bahot bhūkē haĩ. 9. vo zyādā khātī haĩ. 10. maĩ āhistā caltī hū̃. 11. bhūkā baccā jaldī-sē khātā hai. 12. pyāsā ghōṛā zyādā pītā hai. 13. burā bandar nīcē jātā hai. 14. chōṭē laṛkē ēk-sāth khēltē haĩ. 15. mōṭā ādmī pās-sē jātā hai. 16. baṛē laṛkē bāhar khēlnā cāhtē haĩ. 17. baṛī laṛkiyā̃ andar pakānā cāhtī haĩ. 18. bhūkē jānvar yahā̃ ānā cāhtē haĩ. 19. baṛā hāthī yahā̃ ānā cāhtā hai. 20. pyāsā ghōṛā jaldī-sē pīnā cāhtā hai.

8.23 [5.1.2] **Translate into Urdu:**

1. The friends hear him. 2. The men find you (**hon.**). 3. Mother bathes us. 4. The boy stares at him. 5. The teacher hears me. 6. The mare knows you. 7. Father calls you (**hon.**). 8. The servants understand me. 9. The mothers call us. 10. Sister kisses them.

8.24 [5.1.3] **Translate into English:**

1. ādmī hamē̃ bulātā hai. 2. naukar mujhē samajhtā hai. 3. mā̃ un-kō nahlātī hai. 4. aurtē̃ us-kō jāntī haĩ. 5. bahnē̃ tumhē̃ khī̃ctī haĩ. 6. āp us-kō paṛhātē haĩ. 7. vālid mujhē cūmtē haĩ. 8. vo āp-kō māntē haĩ. 9. dōst un-kō bulātē haĩ. 10. ghōṛā tumhē̃ khī̃ctā hai.

8.25 [5.2.1] **Translate into Urdu:**

1. The boys feed the donkeys. 2. The man buys the goat. 3. We (**msc.**) pull the calves. 4. The woman calls the horse. 5. The man sees the wolves. 6. Mother feeds the boys. 7. They (**fm.**) find the parrot. 8. The father kisses the boy. 9. The donkey pulls the boy. 10. The teacher makes the boys read. 11. I want to feed the horses. 12. The boys want to pull the dog. 13. The mother wants to feed the sons. 14. We (**msc.**) want to buy the parrots. 15. The man wants to see the wolves. 16. The small sister feeds the dog. 17. The little boy calls the calf. 18. The fat horses pull the boys. 19. The big man finds the donkey. 20. The thirsty elephant pulls the dog. 21. The dog pulls the child out. 22. The brother finds the parrot there. 23. The mother calls the boys in. 24. The cow feeds the calf quickly. 25. The teacher makes the boys read sometimes.

8.26 [5.2.2] **Translate into English:**

1. mā̃ baccō̃-kō khilātī hai. 2. ham kuttē-kō khī̃ctē haĩ. 3. ustād·sāhab laṛkō̃-kō paṛhātē haĩ. 4. tum baccē-kō samajhtī hō. 5. vo bēṭē-kō jāntē haĩ. 6. maĩ tōtō̃-kō suntī hū̃. 7. ādmī

bēṭō-kō bulātā hai. 8. mā̃ baccē-kō nahlātī hai. 9. ādmī ghōṛō̃-kō k͟harīdtē haĩ. 10. mā̃ laṛkē-kō cūmtī hai. 11. mā̃ bakrō̃-kō khilānā cāhtī hai. 12. ghōṛā laṛkō̃-kō khī̃cnā cāhtā hai. 13. ham tōtō̃-kō sunnā cāhtē haĩ. 14. bahan baccē-kō nahlānā cāhtī hai. 15. bhāī ghōṛē-kō bulānā cāhtā hai. 16. būṛhā ādmī laṛkē-kō parhātā hai. 17. bhūkī bīvī laṛkō̃-kō bulātī hai. 18. chōṭā baccā kuttē-kō khī̃ctā hai. 19. mōṭā naukar baccō̃-kō bulātā hai. 20. acchā kuttā baccē-kō cāṭtā hai. 21. mā̃ baccō̃-kō andar bulātī hai. 22. bahan baccē-kō vahā̃ nahlātī hai. 23. laṛkā ghōṛō̃-kō jaldī-sē khilātā hai. 24. ustād•sāhab hamē̃ yahā̃ paṛhātē haĩ. 25. bāp baccō̃-kō kabhī kabhī samajhtē haĩ.

8.27 [5.3.1] **Translate into Urdu:**

1. The woman teaches the daughters. 2. The man hears (**his**) wife. 3. The boys feed the hens. 4. The child seizes the cat. 5. The father kisses the daughter. 6. We (**fm.**) buy the fish (**pl.**) 7. They (**msc.**) find the flies. 8. The mother sends the girl. 9. The boys grab the fish (**sg.**). 10. I bring the cat. 11. The man wants to catch the fish (**pl.**). 12. They (**fm.**) want to take the hen. 13. The mother wants to kiss the daughters. 14. The father wants to see the girl. 15. He wants to find the mare. 16. The old man seizes the mare. 17. The little woman feeds the hens. 18. The big boy drags the cat. 19. The hungry woman seizes the hen. 20. The old lion sees the (**female**) goats. 21. We (**msc.**) call the daughters here. 22. The bears drag the hens there. 23. The father teaches the girl sometimes. 24. The cat eats the fish (**sg.**) slowly. 25. The mother feeds the daughters too much.

8.28 [5.3.2] **Translate into English:**

1. baccā billī-kō khilātā hai. 2. mā̃ murgiyō̃-kō bulātī hai. 3. bāp bēṭiyō̃-kō bulātā hai. 4. āp laṛkiyō̃-kō sikhātē haĩ. 5. śēr murg͟iyō̃-kō pakaṛtā hai. 6. aurat makkhiyō̃-kō pakaṛtī hai. 7. ham machliyō̃-kō pakaṛtē haĩ. 8. bandar lōmṛī-kō ḍēkhtē haĩ. 9. mā̃ laṛkī-kō cūmtī hai. 10. aurat murgiyō̃-kō pakaṛtī hai. 11. ham machliyō̃-kō pakaṛnā cāhtē haĩ. 12. mā̃ murg͟ī-kō pakaṛnā cāhtī hai. 13. tum laṛkiyō̃-kō sikhānā cāhtī hō. 14. śēr bakriyō̃-kō pakaṛnā cāhtā hai. 15. baccā ghōṛī-kō khilānā cāhtā hai. 16. bhūkā ādmī machliyō̃-kō pakaṛnā cāhtā hai. 17. baṛā śēr bakrī-kō dēkhnā cāhtā hai. 18. chōṭā laṛkā murg͟iyō̃-kō khilātā hai. 19. acchī bahan laṛkī-kō sikhātī hai. 20. būṛhī aurat bēṭiyō̃-kō bulātī hai. 21. bhūkā śēr bakrī-kō jaldī-sē khānā cāhtā hai. 22. laṛkā machliyō̃-kō yahā̃ pakaṛnā cāhtā hai. 23. mā̃ bēṭī-kō zyādā khilātī hai. 24. bāp murg͟iyō̃-kō vahā̃ k͟harīdtā hai. 25. tum laṛkiyō̃-kō andar bulātī hō.

8.29 [5.4.1] **Translate into Urdu:**

1. The dog bites the ox. 2. The monkey eats the fruits. 3. The father buys the house. 4. The wife calls the husband. 5. We (**fm.**) see the houses. 6. The lion seizes the animal. 7. The mother sends the brothers. 8. The farmer feeds the men. 9. The monkey bites the brother. 10. The man bathes the elephant. 11. We (**msc.**) want to eat fruits. 12. The man wants to buy the house. 13. The dog wants to bite the monkey. 14. Mother wants to feed the brothers. 15. The child wants to see the elephant. 16. The old man bathes the elephant. 17. The little farmer ties the oxen. 18. The big lion wants to seize the animal. 19. The bad monkeys eat the fruits. 20. The hungry dog bites the ox. 21. The ox drags the farmer here. 22. Mother wants to send the brothers together. 23. Father calls the men in. 24. We (**msc.**) see the farmers sometimes. 25. The monkey eats the fruit there.

8.30 [5.4.2] **Translate into English:**

1. laṛkā phal-kō lētā hai. 2. kuttā ādmiyō̃-kō kāṭtā hai. 3. kisān bailō̃-kō bā̃dhtā hai. 4.

ādmī hāthī-kō ḳharīdtā hai. 5. bīviyā̃ ḳhāvindō̃-kō khilātī haī. 6. bahan bhāī-kō cūmtī hai. 7. rīch ādmī-kō kāṭtā hai. 8. bail kisān-kō khī̃ctē haī. 9. laṛkā hāthiyō̃-kō dēkhtā hai. 10. bandar phalō̃-kō pakaṛtā hai. 11. maī śērō̃-kō dēkhnā cāhtā hū̃. 12. kuttā ādmiyō̃-kō kāṭnā cāhtā hai. 13. kisān bailō̃-kō bā̃dhnā cāhtā hai. 14. ghōṛē ādmiyō̃-kō khī̃cnā cāhtē haī. 15. ham phalō̃-kō khānā cāhtī haī. 16. burē bandar phalō̃-kō curānā cāhtē haī. 17. būṛhā śēr bakrē-kō pakaṛnā cāhtā hai. 18. bhūkē bail kisānō̃-kō khī̃ctē haī. 19. baṛā rīch ādmī-kō kāṭtā hai. 20. kālā bhēṛiyā murgiyō̃-kō curātā hai. 21. bāp yahā̃ makān-kō ḳharīdtā hai. 22. bandar phalō̃-kō vahā̃ lētē haī. 23. ghōṛē kisanō̃-kō jaldī-sē khī̃ctē haī. 24. ham jānvarō̃-kō kabhī kabhī dēkhtē haī. 25. bhūkē bail ādmī-kō āhistā khī̃ctē haī.

8.31 [5.5.1] **Translate into Urdu:**

1. The mother calls the sisters. 2. The teacher reads the books. 3. The farmers tie the cows. 4. The woman buys the thing. 5. The man buys the table. 6. The child drinks the medicine. 7. We see the pictures. 8. The girl buys the book. 9. Mother teaches the sisters. 10. The child grabs the picture. 11. We want to see the night. 12. The teacher wants to read the book. 13. The woman wants to buy the things. 14. She wants to see the picture. 15. The farmers want to tie the cows. 16. The good child drinks the medicine. 17. The hungry woman buys the things. 18. The little boy reads the book. 19. The old woman wants to tie the cows. 20. The big man wants to buy the buildings. 21. The old farmer wants to tie the cows here. 22. The women want to buy things there. 23. We (**msc.**) see the pictures sometimes. 24. The teacher reads the books quickly. 25. The good children drink the medicine sometimes.

8.32 [5.5.2] **Translate into English:**

1.aurat mēz-kō ḳharīdtī hai. 2. laṛkē kitābō̃-kō paṛhtē haī. 3. bāp tasvīr-kō lātā hai. 4.kisān gāyō̃-kō bā̃dhtē haī. 5. bāp imārtō̃-kō ḳharīdtā hai. 6. mā̃ davā-kō lātī hai. 7. bīvī aurtō̃-kō bulātī hai. 8. bahan mēz-kō lātī hai. 9. ham gāyō̃-kō khilātē haī. 10. baccā davā-kō pītā hai. 11. ham rāt-kō dēkhnā cāhtī haī. 12. kisān gāyō̃-kō bā̃dhnā cāhtā hai. 13. maī tasvīrō̃-kō ḳharīdnā cāhtī hū̃. 14. vo kitābō̃-kō paṛhnā cāhtī hai. 15. mā̃ aurtō̃-kō bhējnā cāhtī hai. 16. acchē laṛkē mēz-kō lātē haī. 17. chōṭī aurat gāyō̃-kō bulātī hai. 18. būṛhā kisān gāyō̃-kō bā̃dhtā hai. 19. baṛā ādmī imārtō̃-kō ḳharīdtā hai. 20. mōṭā kuttā bahnō̃-kō kāṭtā hai. 21. chōṭī billī aurat-kō vahā̃ kāṭtī hai. 22. acchā baccā kitābō̃-kō jaldī-sē lātā hai. 23. kisān bailō̃-kō āhistā lātē haī. 24. ham kitābō̃-kō kabhī kabhī paṛhtē haī. 25. chōṭā laṛkā kitāb-kō yahā̃ paṛhnā cāhtā hai.

8.33 [5.6.1] **Translate into Urdu:**

1. The cat grabs the sparrow. 2. The woman calls the (little) old woman. 3. We (**msc.**) see the mice. 4. The women buy the cooking-pot. 5. They (**msc.**) feed the sparrows. 6. The boy brings the cooking-pots. 7. The good woman feeds the (**little**) old women. 8. The little mouse bites the (**little**) old woman. 9. We (**msc.**) want to buy the cooking-pots. 10. You (**msc.**) see the mouse.

8.34 [5.6.2] **Translate into English:**

1. aurat cuhiyā-kō pakaṛtī hai. 2. ādmī būṛhiyā-kō bulātā hai. 3. laṛkī ciṛiyō̃-kō khilātī hai. 4. billī cuhiyō̃-kō dēkhtī hai. 5. ham haṇḍiyō̃-kō lātē haī. 6. maī cuhiyā-kō pakaṛnā cāhtī hū̃. 7. laṛkē ciṛiyō̃-kō yahā̃ lānā cāhtē haī. 8. tum būṛhiyā-kō khilātī hō. 9. larkē cuhiyā-kō vahā̃ pakaṛtē haī. 10. chōṭī laṛkī haṇḍiyā-kō jaldī-sē lātī hai.

8.35 [6.1.1] **Translate into Urdu:**

1. The man eats raw vegetables. 2. The women call the little children. 3. The farmer

makes the thirsty oxen drink. 4. The teacher tells the good boy. 5. We (**msc.**) see the high buildings. 6. The boys pluck the ripe fruits. 7. They (**fm.**) know the long street. 8. The farmer drives the big ox. 9. Mother cooks the raw vegetables. 10. The man sells the new pictures. 11. The tall man plucks the ripe fruits. 12. The little boys read the old book. 13. The good sister makes the thirsty brothers drink. 14. The little girl drops the new picture. 15. The thin man knows the true friend. 16. The monkeys want to eat the ripe fruits. 17. The woman wants to cook the raw vegetables. 18. We (**msc.**) want to see the big animals. 19. The boy wants to read the little book. 20. They (**fm.**) want to see the new pictures. 21. The child eats the ripe fruit slowly. 22. The mother calls the little girls inside. 23. Father points out the high houses there. 24. The mare eats the raw vegetables quickly. 25. They (**fm.**) buy the old picture here.

8.36 [6.1.2] **Translate into English:**

1. ham bhūkē ādmiyō̃-kō khilātī haĩ. 2. laṛkā cauṛī saṛak-kō dikhātā hai. 3. baccā kaccī sabzī-kō pakaṛtā hai. 4. bandar pakkē phalō̃-kō curātē haĩ. 5. vo lambē ādmī-kō bulātē haĩ. 6. kisān mōṭē bailō̃-kō calātā hai. 7. aurat nayī tasvīr-kō ḳharīdtī hai. 8. vo lambī saṛak-kō jāntī hai. 9. mā̃ bhūkī bēṭiyō̃-kō bulātī hai. 10. laṛkī nayī kitāb-kō girātī hai. 11. acchī aurat pyāsī gāy-kō pilātī hai. 12. bhūkē bandar chōṭē phalō̃-kō khātē haĩ. 13. būṛhā kisān baṛē ghōṛō̃-kō calātā hai. 14. dublē bāp kaccī sabziyō̃-kō khātē haĩ. 15. pyāsē kuttē saccē dōstō̃-kō pātē haĩ. 16. ham ū̃cī imārat-kō pānā cāhtē haĩ. 17. kisān bhūkē bakrō̃-kō khilānā cāhtā hai. 18. aurat pyāsī gāy-kō pilānā cāhtī hai. 19. laṛkā chōṭī kitāb-kō paṛhnā cāhtā hai. 20. kisān kaccī sabziyō̃-kō bēcnā cāhtā hai. 21. maĩ baṛē ghōṛō̃-kō calānā cāhtā hū̃. 22. mā bhūkē baccō̃-kō yahā̃ bulānā cāhtī hai. 23. acchī aurat chōṭē baccō̃-kō zyādā khilātī hai. 24. bahot acchā laṛkā nayī kitābō̃-kō kabhī kabhī paṛhtā hai. 25. bhūkā bandar pakkē phalō̃-kō fauran khātā hai.

8.37 [6.2.1] **Translate into Urdu:**

1. This (**one** [**msc.**]) plays. 2. This parrot speaks. 3. These (**fm.**) sleep. 4. This daughter cooks. 5. These animals run. 6. This vegetable is ripe. 7. This table is new. 8. These (**msc.**) drink. 9. This (**fm.**) is long. 10. This shop burns. 11. These daughters want to know. 12. This old house burns. 13. These women speak slowly. 14. This (**one** [**msc.**]) wants to sleep. 15. These (**fm.**) play sometimes. 16. This hungry mare wants to eat quickly. 17. These ripe fruits fall. 18. This farmer works a lot. 19. This thirsty ox wants to stop sometimes. 20. These small children want to go out.

8.38 [6.2.2] **Translate into English:**

1. ye dauṛtē haĩ. 2. ye bakrā ucaltā hai. 3. ye laṛkiyā̃ samajhī haĩ. 4. ye bīvī pakātī hai. 5. ye pitē haĩ. 6. ye kām kartā hai. 7. ye kuttē dauṛtē haĩ. 8. ye gāyē̃ pītī haĩ. 9. ye machliyā̃ khātī haĩ. 10. ye paṛhtī hai. 11. ye laṛkā paṛhnā cāhtā hai. 12. ye pīnā cāhtē haĩ. 13. ye baṛī imārat jaltī hai. 14. ye bandar khēlnā cāhtā hai. 15. ye chōṭī kitābē̃ girtī haĩ. 16. ye kuttē khēlnā cāhtē haĩ. 17. ye chōṭā ghōṛā pīnā cāhtā hai. 18. ye khānā cāhtī haĩ. 19. ye baṛē ādmī kām kartē haĩ. 20. ye būṛhī aurat sōnā cāhtī hai.

8.39 [6.2.4] **Translate into Urdu:**

1. I see this boy. 2. The farmer ties these animals. 3. The man calls this (**one**). 4. The mother teaches this daughter. 5. We feed these dogs. 6. The dog bites this brother. 7. The children seize these. 8. They (**fm.**) feed these. 9. The woman cooks this. 10. The fathers buy these parrots. 11. The girl reads these small books. 12. The dog pulls this child out. 13. Mother calls these in. 14. The father wants to kiss this son. 15. The woman

wants to tie this hungry cow. 16. The farmer buys these goats. 17. The teacher reads these sometimes. 18. The brother finds this small parrot here. 19. The cow feeds these hungry calves quickly. 20. The woman feeds this (**one**).

8.40 [6.2.5] **Translate into English:**

1. mā̃ in baccõ-kō khilātī hai. 2. ham is-kō khĩctē haĩ. 3. maĩ in tōtõ-kō suntā hū̃. 4. bahan is baccē-kō nahlātī hai. 5. ham is-kō ḳharīdtī haĩ. 6. ādmī in ghōṛõ-kō ḳharīdtā hai. 7. laṛkā in-kō jaldī-sē lātā hai. 8. aurat in sabziyõ-kō pakātī haĩ. 9. vo in-kō sunnā cāhtī haĩ. 10. ham is tasvīr-kō ḳharīdtē haĩ. 11. acchī aurat in bhūkē baccõ-kō zyādā khilātī hai. 12. bandar in phalõ-kō jaldī-sē khātē haĩ. 13. aurat in mōṭī gāyõ-kō khilātī hai. 14. baccā is kaccī sabzī-kō khānā cāhtā hai. 15. bahot acchī laṛkī nayī kitābõ-kō kabhī kabhī paṛhtī hai. 16. ham is lambī saṛak-kō jāntī haĩ. 17. aurat is nayī tasvīr-kō ḳharīdtī hai. 18. bhūkē laṛkē in pakkē phalõ-kō khātē haĩ. 19. vo is kaccī sabzī-kō girātī hai. 20. laṛkā is chōṭī kitāb-kō yahā̃ paṛhnā cāhtā hai.

8.41 [6.3.1] **Translate into Urdu:**

1. That (**one** [**msc.**]) reads. 2. Those parrots speak. 3. That cow drinks. 4. Those shops burn. 5. They (**fm.**) play. 6. That fruit is ripe. 7. They (**msc.**) eat. 8. That woman cooks. 9. Those men work. 10. That (**one** [**fm.**] is tall. 11. Those daughters want to play. 12. That thirsty girl reads. 13. That girl wants to go. 14. That ripe fruit falls. 15. Those old houses burn. 16. Those thirsty goats drink here. 17. Those hungry horses want to eat quickly. 18. That building is high. 19. That old farmer works a lot. 20. Those pictures are wide.

8.42 [6.3.2] **Translate into English:**

1. vo pakātī hai. 2. vo laṛkā caltā hai. 3. vo gāyẽ khātī haĩ. 4. vo vahā̃ jātē haĩ. 5. vo kisān ḳharīdtā hai. 6. vo dauṛtī hai. 7. vo sabziyā̃ nayī haĩ. 8. vo sikhātā hai. 9. vo imārtẽ ū̃cī haĩ. 10. vo vahā̃ kām kartē haĩ. 11. vo laṛkā ghōṛē-kō jaldī-sē khilātā hai. 12. vo chōṭī laṛkī billī-kō khĩctī hai. 13. vo kisān bailõ-kō ḳharīdtē haĩ. 14. vo aurtẽ baccõ-kō nahlānā cāhtī haĩ. 15. vo ustād•sāhab yahā̃ rahtē haĩ. 16. vo tōtē bōlnā cāhtē haĩ. 17. vo baṛā ghōṛā ādmī-kō khĩcnā cāhtā hai. 18. vo chōṭē baccē bhūkē haĩ. 19. vo murgiyā̃ khānā cāhtī haĩ. 20. vo bhūkā ādmī machliyõ-kō pakaṛnā cāhtā hai.

8.43 [6.3.4] **Translate into Urdu:**

1. They (**msc.**) know that (**one**). 2. The woman feeds those cows. 3. The dog bites that man. 4. Mother bathes that (**one**). 5. We (**msc.**) know that road. 6. The farmers pluck those fruits. 7. The father calls them. 8. You (**fm.**) buy those vegetables. 9. The daughter finds that cat. 10. The boy seizes that (**one**). 11. You (**msc.**) drive those oxen. 12. We (**msc.**) want to see those big animals. 13. The women want to cook those raw fruits. 14. They (**msc.**) sell those raw vegetables. 15. The man sells those new pictures. 16. The sister wants to call in those hungry boys. 17. The boy points out that long road. 18. Father wants to point out those high buildings. 19. We (**msc.**) want to eat those ripe fruits. 20. She drops that old book.

8.44 [6.3.5] **Translate into English:**

1. maĩ us ū̃cī imārat-kō dikhātā hū̃. 2. chōṭā laṛkā us billī-kō khĩctā hai. 3. ghōṛā un-kō khātā hai. 4. vo un lambē ādmiyõ-kō bulātē haĩ. 5. ham un-kō khilātī haĩ. 6. vālid us baṛē makān-kō ḳharīdtē haĩ. 7. tum un dōstõ-kō jāntē hō. 8. vo lōmṛī un mōṭī murgiyõ-kō pakaṛtī hai. 9. vo us-kō dēkhtī hai. 10. acchī aurat un pyāsī gāyõ-kō pilātī hai. 11. ham us baṛē makān-kō pānā cāhtē haĩ. 12. laṛkā un chōṭī kitābõ-kō lātā hai. 13. bhūkē

bandar un phalõ-kō curānā cāhtē haĩ. 14. bāp un chōṭē laṛkõ-kō zyādā khilātā hai. 15. aurat us nayī haṇḍiyā-kō ḳharīdtī hai. 16. billī us chōṭī cuhiyā-kō pakaṛtī hai. 17. kisān us būṛhī lōmṛī-kō mārtā hai. 18. maĩ us baṛē ghōrē-kō kabhī kabhī calātā hū̃. 19. bhūkā kuttā us burē laṛkē-kō kāṭtā hai. 20. kisān us-kō pānā cāhtā hai.

LESSON 9

9.1.

ādmī kamrē-mẽ hai.	The man is in the room.
ū̃cī imārtẽ śahar-mẽ haĩ.	The high buildings are in the city.
is divār-mẽ ēk khiṛkī hai.	There is one window in this wall.
us divār-mẽ dō khiṛkiyā̃ haĩ.	There are two windows in that wall.

Sections 9.1 to 9.4.4 are concerned with postposition constructions. The Urdu postpositions correspond in function to the English prepositions. The postpositions of Urdu, however, are placed AFTER the words they govern and the prepositions of English are placed before the words they govern.

Words governed by postpositions have the object form (See discussion in 5.1 and 5.2). In the system of transliteration employed in these lessons the postposition is linked to the word it governs by a hyphen. This section illustrates the postposition **-mẽ** in.

REMARKS: See the two English sentences above beginning with the phrases **There is. . . . , There are. . . .** Urdu expresses this English construction by taking the postpositional phrase out of its normal order in the sentence and placing it first. Compare **ādmī kamrē-mẽ hai.** A man is in the room. and **kamrē-mẽ ādmī hai.** There is a man in the room.; **ū̃cī imārtẽ śahar-mẽ haĩ.** The high buildings are in the city. and **śahar-mẽ ū̃cī imārtẽ haĩ.** There are high buildings in the city.

9.1.1 More examples are:

zamīn-mẽ kōēlā hai.	There is coal in the ground.
vo āg-mẽ kāṭh ḍāltī hai.	She throws wood in the fire.
śikārī ū̃cē darakhtõ-mẽ parindē dēkhtā hai.	The hunter sees birds in the tall trees.
mā̃ haṇḍiyõ-mẽ sabziyā̃ ḍāltī hai.	Mother puts vegetables in the cooking-pots.
tārē ākāś-mẽ haĩ.	Stars are in the sky.
chōṭē thālõ-mẽ khānā rakhiyē.	(**Please**) place the food on the small dishes.
ghanē jaṅgalõ-mẽ jānvar haĩ.	There are animals in the thick jungles.
baccē bāg-mẽ ēk-sāth khēltē haĩ.	The children play together in the garden.
kisān abhī khēt-mẽ kām kartā hai.	The farmer works now in the field.
gahrē samundar-mẽ machliyā̃ haĩ.	There are fish in the deep sea.

REMARKS: (1) Nouns denoting non-human beings and things need not, when placed in the direct object form, take the postposition **-kō.** (See the second and third sentences, above.) When the direct object form does not occur before the postposition

-kō, it has the same form as that of the subject. In the majority of occurrences nouns denoting things will not take **-kō** in the direct object form. Nouns denoting non-human beings tend to take the **-kō,** especially when the reference is to a specific or individual being. Compare **śikārī ū̃cē daraḳhtō̃-mē̃ parindē dēkhtā hai.** The hunter sees birds in the tall trees. and **śikārī ū̃cē daraḳhtō̃-mē̃ parindō̃-kō dēkhtā hai.** The hunter sees the birds in the tall trees.

(2) Remember that adjectives modifying nouns in the object form are placed in the corresponding object form (See 6.1.).

(3) When more than one adverb occurs in an utterance, the adverb of time will normally precede that of manner and the adverb of manner will precede that of place. (See the eighth and ninth sentences, above.) When emphasis is placed on an adverb in such a sequence, the adverb is taken out of its position in the normal order and placed first. Postpositional phrases, with the exception of those of the direct and indirect object, can be considered to function as adverbs.

9.1.2 Vocabulary Notes:

āsmān (ā) sky, **āg** (ī) fire, **kōēlā** (ā) coal, **kapṛā** (ā) cloth [in **pl.** clothes], **kāṭh** (ā) wood, timber, **khōdnā** to dig, **jañgal** (ā) jungle, **zamīn** (ī) ground, soil, **tārā** (ā) star, **thālā** (ā) dish, plate, **divār** (ī) wall, **daryā** (ā) river, **bāg** (ā) garden, **śikārī** (ā) hunter, **samundar** [variant: **samandar**] (ā) ocean, sea, **parindā** (ā) bird, **daraḳht** (ā) tree.

9.1.3 Exercise 1. **Translate into English:**

1. śikārī jañgalō̃-mē̃ jānvar mārtē haĩ. 2. bandar ū̃cē daraḳhtō̃-mē̃ jaldī-sē dauṛtē haĩ. 3. baṛī machliyā̃ gahrē samundar-mē̃ tairtī haĩ. 4. ham śahar-mē̃ kām kartī haĩ. 5. chōṭē laṛkē gahrē daryā-mē̃ tairnā cāhtē haĩ. 6. bhūkī aurat nayī haṇḍiyō̃-mē̃ khānā pakātī hai. 7. ādmī ghar-mē̃ āhistā jātā hai. 8. ham baṛē bāg-mē̃ vo phal tōṛnā cāhtē haĩ. 9. kisān chōṭē daryā-mē̃ hāthī nahlātē haĩ. 10. ādmī abhī chōṭē khētō̃-mē̃ jānā cāhtē haĩ.

9.1.4 Exercise 2. **Translate into Urdu:**

1. The farmer digs in the garden. 2. The little child wants to see the fish in the river. 3. There are two tables in the large room. 4. The old man cuts wood in the thick jungle. 5. The women want to buy cloth in the shop. 6. There are many fish in the deep ocean. 7. The little boys want to play together in the garden. 8. There is a hungry cow in the field. 9. The woman wants to cook the vegetables in the new cooking-pot. 10. There are small shops in the bazaar.

9.2

ustād laṛkē-kō kitāb dētē haĩ.	The teacher gives the book to the boy.
ustād us-kō kitāb dētē haĩ.	The teacher gives the book to him.
abbā baccē-kō phal dētā hai.	The father gives the fruit to the child.
laṛkā aurtō̃-kō lakṛī dētā hai.	The boy gives the wood to the women.

This section illustrates the Urdu equivalent of the English indirect object construction. In the Urdu construction the noun indicating the indirect object is placed in the object form before the postposition **-kō.** The normal order of sequence will be indirect object phrase before direct object phrase, therefore there will not arise occasion for confusion between this construction and that of the direct object when the two constructions occur in the same sentence. (Compare 5.1 and 5.2 to 5.6.).

9.2.1 More examples are:

mā̃ baccō̃-kō kahāniyā̃ sunātī hai.	The mother tells the children stories.

laṛkī bahan-kō nayī sāṛī dikhātī hai.	The girl shows (**her**) sister the new sari.
aurat bhūkī gāy-kō ghās dētī hai.	The woman gives grass to the hungry cow.
acchā laṛkā pyāsē ādmī-kō pānī dētā hai.	The good boy gives water to the thirsty man.
ham musāfir-kō daryā dikhātē haĩ.	We point out the river to the traveller.
naukar mālik-kō ṭhaṇḍā pānī lātā hai.	The servant brings cold water to the master.
mā̃ naukar-kō nayē rakābiyā̃ dētī hai.	Mother gives the new dishes to the servant.
ādmī bīvī-kō ciṭṭhī paṛhtā hai.	The man reads the letter to (**his**) wife.
dhōbī ādmī-kō kapṛē bhējtā hai.	The washerman sends the clothes to the man.
aurat dōst-kō nayī cūṛiyā̃ dikhātī hai.	The woman shows (**her**) new bangles to (**her**) friend.

9.2.2 Vocabulary Notes:
kahānī (ī) story, tale, **ghās** (ī) grass, fodder, **ciṭṭhī** (ī) letter, **cūṛī** (ī) bangle, **dhōbī** (ā) washerman, **naukar** (ā) servant, **sāṛī** (ī) sari, **phūl** (ā) flower, **musāfir** (ā) traveller, **mālik** (ā) master, **rakābī** (ī) dish, **ustād** (ā) teacher, **abbā** (ā) father, daddy, **chīnnā** to snatch.

9.2.3 Exercise 1. **Translate into English:**
1. acchā laṛkā mā̃-kō kāṭh lātā hai. 2. abbā chōṭē baccõ-kō kitāb sunātē haĩ. 3. ham ādmī-kō lambī saṛak dikhātē haĩ. 4. bīvī bhūkē kisān-kō khānā bhējtī hai. 5. mā̃ abbā-kō burē laṛkē-kō dikhātī hai. 6. laṛkiyā̃ mā̃-kō pānī dētī haĩ. 7. chōṭī laṛkī abbā-kō phūl dētī hai. 8. khāvind bīvī-kō tārē dikhātā hai. 9. aurat baccõ-kō pakkē phal bāhar bhējtī hai. 10. kisān chōṭē khēt-kō gāyẽ calānā cāhtā hai.

9.2.4 Exercise 2. **Translate into Urdu:**
1. The little girl wants to bring water to (**her**) mother. 2. The boys point out the high building to the old man. 3. We (**msc.**) want to give food to the hungry man. 4. The men point out the city to the farmers. 5. The father gives the small parrot to (**his**) daughter. 6. The hungry farmer brings vegetables to (**his**) wife. 7. The mother sends the bad son to (**his**) father. 8. The boy gives flowers to (**his**) teacher. 9. The men point out the lion to the hunter. 10. The sister brings the little brother to (**their**) mother.

9.3

kursī-par ṭōpī hai.	There is a cap on the chair.
is divār-par tīn tasvīrẽ haĩ.	There are three pictures on this wall.
kitābẽ mēzõ-par haĩ.	The books are on the tables.
kalam kitābõ-par hai.	The pen is on the books.

This section illustrates constructions with the postposition **-par** on, upon.

9.3.1 More examples are:

baccē chat-par khēltē haĩ.	The children play on the roof.
naukar zamīn-par pānī ḍāltā hai.	The servant pours water on the ground.
laṛkā mēz-par rakābī rakhtā hai.	The boy places the dish on the table.
vo palaṅg-par kapṛē rakhtī hai.	She places clothes on the bed.
aurat divārõ-par tasvīrẽ laṭkātī hai.	The woman hangs pictures on the walls.
chōṭē parindē chat-par baiṭhtē haĩ.	The little birds sit down on the roof.
mālī paudē-par pānī ḍāltā hai.	The gardener pours water on the plant.
aurat sar-par bōjh rakhtī hai.	The woman places the burden on (**her**) head.
bandar śākhõ-par baiṭhtē haĩ.	The monkeys sit on the branches.
ādmī kursī-par haiṭ rakhtā hai.	The man places (**his**) hat on the chair.

9.3.2 Vocabulary Notes:
ḳalam (ā and ī) pen, **kursī** (ī) chair, **chat** (ī) roof, **ṭōpī** (ī) cap, **tasvīr** (ī) picture, **palañg** (ā) bed, bedstead, **paudā** (ā) plant, sapling, **bōjh** (ā) weight, load, **mālī** (ā) gardener, **śāḳh** (ī) branch, **sar** (ā) head, **haiṭ** (ā) hat.

9.3.3 Exercise 1. **Translate into English:**
1. laṛkā kitābõ-par ḳalam rakhtā hai. 2. naukar zamīn-par bōjh rakhtā hai. 3. burā laṛkā bahan-par pānī ḍāltā hai. 4. chōṭē baccē chat-par khēlnā cāhtē haĩ. 5. naukar mēz-par rakābiyā̃ rakhtā hai. 6. laṛkā śāḳh-par baiṭhnā cāhtā hai. 7. ādmī saṛak-par bōjh girātā hai. 8. dhōbī zamīn-par kapṛē rakhnā cāhtā hai. 9. aurat paudõ-par pānī ḍāltī hai. 10. ādmī palañg-par sōnā cāhtā hai.

9.3.4 Exercise 2... **Translate into Urdu:**
1. We (**msc.**) want to play on the roof. 2. The birds want to sit on the branch. 3. The man places the bed on the roof. 4. The servant hangs the picture on the wall. 5. The woman places the ripe fruits on the table. 6. There are two houses on the road. 7. The boy places the grass on the ground. 8. The dog sleeps on the ground. 9. There is a monkey on the roof. 10. The woman places the dishes on the table.

9.4

macherā śahar-sē ātā hai.	The fisherman comes from the city.
laṛkī laṛkē-sē pānī lētī hai.	The girl takes water from the boy.
ustād laṛkiyõ-sē savāl pūchtē haĩ.	The teacher asks the girls questions.
ustād un-sē savāl pūchtē haĩ.	The teacher asks them questions.
laṛkā chaṛī-sē ghōṛē-kō mārtā hai.	The boy strikes the horse with the stick.
laṛkā us-sē ghōṛē-kō mārtā hai.	The boy strikes the horse with it.

This section illustrates the postposition **-sē** which translates English **from** and **with, by means of which.**

9.4.1 More examples are:

aurat mujh-sē lakṛī lētī hai.	The woman takes the wood from me.
macherā daryā-sē machliyā̃ pakaṛtā hai.	The fisherman catches fish from the river.
laṛkā kitāb-sē ēk varaḳ phāṛtā hai.	The boy tears a leaf from the book.
laṛkī jhāṛī-sē phūl tōṛtī hai.	The girl plucks flowers from the bush.
ādmī ḳalam-sē ēk ciṭṭhī likhtā hai.	The man writes a letter with the pen.
aurat rassē-sē gāy-kō bā̃dhtī hai.	The woman ties the cow with a rope.
pyāsā ādmī mujh-sē pānī lētā hai.	The thirsty man takes water from me.
laṛkī kuē̃-sē pānī lātī hai.	The girl brings water from the well.
bandar baccē-sē khānā curātā hai.	The monkey steals the food from the child.
kisān hal-sē khēt-mē̃ kām kartā hai.	The farmer works in the field with the plow.

REMARKS: (1) The object form of the first person singular pronoun, when occurring before the simple postpositions, is **mujh** (See Remarks of 5.1.).

(2) Observe the use of the postposition **-sē** with the verb **pūchnā** to ask.

9.4.2 Vocabulary Notes:
kuā̃ (ā) well, **chaṛī** (ī) stick, **varaḳ** (ā) leaf, page, **bandar** (ā) monkey, **macherā** (ā) fisherman, **rassā** (ā) rope, **savāl** (ā) question, **hal** (ā) plow, **jhāṛī** (ī) bush.

9.4.3 Exercise 1. **Translate into English:**
1. ham un-sē savāl pūchtē haĩ. 2. vo baccõ-sē phal lēnā cāhtē haĩ. 3. dhōbī daryā-sē kapṛē

lātā hai. 4. gāy paudō̃-sē phal khātī hai. 5. kisān chaṛī-sē bandarō̃-kō mārnā cāhtā hai. 6. pyāsā ā̃dmī acchē laṛkē-sē pānī lētā hai. 7. musāfir śahar-sē ātā hai. 8. aurat khēt-sē sabziyā̃ lātī hai. 9. ādmī rassē-sē ghās bā̃dhtā hai. 10. ustād mujh-sē savāl pūchnā cāhtē haĩ.

9.4.4 Exercise 2. **Translate into Urdu:**

1. The teacher asks the boy a question. 2. The small farmer strikes the big ox with a stick. 3. The man ties the wood with a rope. 4. The thirsty traveller takes water from me. 5. The woman calls the cow from the garden. 6. We (**fm.**) bring water from the well. 7. The hungry farmer comes from the field. 8. They (**msc.**) want to tie the bad goat with a rope. 9. Mother asks me questions. 10. The hungry dog steals food from the child.

9.5 ēk Amrīkī aur Pākistānī-mē̃ mulāḳāt. **An American Meets a Pakistani.**

Jān:	**helō.**	John:	**Hello.**
Hamīd:	**helō.**	Hamīd:	**Hello.**
Jān:	**kyā āp mērī madad kar saktē haĩ?**	John:	**Can you help me?**
Hamīd:	**mujhē mālūm nahī̃. kyā bāt hai?**	Hamīd:	**I do not know. What's the matter?**
Jān:	**maĩ yahā̃ ajnabī hū̃.**	John:	**I am a stranger here.**
Hamīd:	**kyā āp Urdū bōl saktē haĩ?**	Hamīd:	**Can you speak Urdu?**
Jān:	**hā̃. maĩ Urdū bōl saktā hū̃, magar bahot acchī nahī̃.**	John:	**Yes. I can speak Urdu, but not very well.**
Hamīd:	**maĩ āp-kī kyā madad kar saktā hū̃?**	Hamīd:	**What can I do for you?**
Jān:	**maĩ Urdū-kā ustād cāhtā hū̃.**	John:	**I need an Urdu tutor.**
Hamīd:	**āp Urdū-kā ustād kyō̃ cāhtē haĩ?**	Hamīd.	**Why do you need an Urdu teacher?**
Jān:	**maĩ Urdū acchī bōlnā sīkhnā cāhtā hū̃.**	John:	**I wish to learn to speak Urdu well.**
Hamīd:	**āp Urdū acchī bōltē haĩ. āp-kō ustād-kī zarūrat nahī̃.**	Hamīd:	**You speak Urdu well. You do not need a teacher.**
Jān:	**lēkin jab lōg bahot tēz bōltē haĩ, tab maĩ unhē̃ nahī̃ samajh saktā.**	John:	**But when people speak too fast, I cannot understand them.**
Hamīd:	**kyā āp mujhē samajh saktē haĩ?**	Hamīd:	**Can you understand me?**
Jān:	**zarā aur āhistā bōliyē, tab maĩ āp-kō samajh sakū̃gā.**	John:	**Please speak more slowly, then I can understand you.**
Hamīd:	**mērā bhāī āp-kī madad kar saktā hai.**	Hamīd:	**My brother can help you.**
Jān:	**āp-kā bhāī kyā kartā hai?**	John:	**What does your brother do?**
Hamīd:	**mērā bhāī yunivarsiṭī-mē̃ paṛhtā hai.**	Hamīd:	**My brother studies in the university.**
Jān:	**vo kyā paṛhtā hai?**	John.	**What does he study?**
Hamīd:	**vo bahot-sē mazāmīn paṛhtā hai.**	Hamīd:	**He studies many subjects.**
Jān:	**us-kā baṛā mazmūn kyā hai?**	John:	**What is his chief subject?**
Hamīd:	**us-kā baṛā mazmūn sāins hai. vo sāinsdān bannā cāhtā hai.**	Hamīd:	**His chief subject is science. He wants to be a scientist.**
Jān:	**ye tō bahot acchī bāt hai.**	John:	**That is very nice.**

Hamīd:	mērā-bhī yehī ḳhayāl hai.	Hamīd:	That is my understanding, too.
Jān:	kyā āp apnē bhāī-kō mērē pās bhēj saktē haĩ?	John:	Can you send your brother to me?
Hamīd:	kab bhējū̃?	Hamīd:	When should I send (him)?
Jān:	kal bād dopahar cār bajē.	John:	Tomorrow afternoon at four o'clock.
Hamīd:	ṭhik hai. āp kahā̃ ṭhahrē haĩ?	Hamīd:	All right. Where are you staying?
Jān:	maĩ Impīriyal Hōṭel-mẽ ṭhahrā hū̃.	John:	I am staying at the Imperial Hotel.
Hamīd:	bahot acchā. vo ā jāẽgā.	Hamīd:	Very well. He will come.
Jān:	bahot bahot śukriyā. Ḳhudā hāfiz.	John:	Thank you very much. Good-by.
Hamīd:	Ḳhudā hāfiz.	Hamīd:	Good-by.

LESSON 10

10.1

darakht makān-kē pīchē hai. The tree is behind the house.
us-kē pīchē darakht hai. There is a tree behind it.
ādmī gāṛī-kē pīchē caltā hai. The man walks behind the cart.
ādmī us-kē pīchē caltā hai. The man walks behind it.
baccē ghōṛē-kē pīchē dauṛtē haĩ. The children run behind the horse.
baccē us-kē pīchē dauṛtē haĩ. The children run behind it.

Sections 10.1 to 10.4.3 are concerned with compound postpositions. These consist of two forms, the first of which is **-kē** and the second a form which in many instances can be recognized as an adverb. Compare these adverbs: **pīchē** "behind" of **-kē pīchē** in section 10.1; **nīcē** "down" of **-kē nīcē** in 10.2; **pās** "near" of **-kē pās** in 11.1. (See 4.4 for remarks on the adverbs.) Other such compound postpositions will be introduced in the lessons following.

This section introduces the compound postposition **-kē pīchē** behind, after.

REMARKS: Of the pronominal forms only the following occur before the compound postpositions: **us, un, āp.** Constructions involving the other pronouns will be introduced shortly. (See 14.3.)

10.1.1 More Examples are:

śahar-kē pīchē jaṅgal hai. There is a jungle behind the city
kitāb mēz-kē pīchē girtī hai. The book falls behind the table.
baccē bhāiyõ-kē pīchē caltē haĩ. The children walk behind (**their**) brothers
kisān bailõ-kē pīchē dauṛtā hai. The farmer runs after the oxen.
darvāzē-kē pīchē bāg̱ hai. There is a garden behind the door.
dhōbī gadhē-kē pīchē caltā hai. The washerman walks behind the donkey.

10.1.2 Vocabulary Notes:

gāṛī (ī) cart, wagon, **darvāzā** (ā) door, **bhāī** (ā) brother.

10.1.3 Exercise 1. **Translate into English:**

1. baccā darvāzē-kē pīchē hai. 2. aurtẽ kuẽ-kē pīchē ēk-sāth bōltī haĩ. 3. mā̃ chōṭē baccē-kē pīchē dauṛtī hai. 4. billī laṛkī-kē pīchē jātī hai. 5. bīvī khāvind-kē pīchē caltī hai. 6. ham un-kē pīchē jātē haĩ. 7. musāfir us darakht-kē pīchē baiṭhtā hai. 8. lōmṛī kuẽ-kē pīchē murgī pakaṛtī hai. 9. kisān hal-kē pīchē jātā hai. 10. bhūkā kuttā chōṭē baccē-kē pīchē caltā hai.

10.1.4 Exercise 2. **Translate into Urdu:**
1. There is a cow behind the tree. 2. The woman bathes behind the well. 3. The river is behind the city. 4. The little boy walks behind (**his**) father. 5. We (**fm.**) sit behind the tall tree. 6. The gardener works behind the house. 7. The woman puts the picture behind the door. 8. The son walks behind (**his**) father. 9. The servant digs the ground behind the garden. 10. There is a garden behind the house.

10.2

gāy daraḳht-kē nīcē hai.	The cow is under the tree.
kuttē mēzõ-kē nīcē haĩ.	The dogs are under the tables.
kuttē un-kē nīcē haĩ.	The dogs are under them.
sā̃p makān-kē nīcē hai.	The snake is under the house.
us-kē nīcē sā̃p hai.	There is a snake under it.

This section deals with the compound postposition **-kē nīcē** under.

10.2.1 More Examples are:

sā̃p ghar-kē nīcē jātā hai.	The snake goes under the house.
jūtē palaṅg-kē nīcē haĩ.	The shoes are under the bed.
faḳīr daraḳht-kē nīcē baiṭhtā hai.	The beggar sits under the tree.
machērā pul-kē nīcē machliyā̃ pakaṛtā hai.	The fisherman catches fish under the bridge.
bāp daraḳht-kē nīcē ārām kartā hai.	The father rests under the tree.
kārīgar mōṭargāṛī-kē nīcē kām kartā hai.	The mechanic works under the car.

REMARKS: **ārām karnā** corresponds to the English verb to **rest, to repose; faḳīr** (ā) translates **beggar.**

10.2.2 Exercise 1. **Translate into English:**
1. aurat gāy-kō daraḳht-kē nīcē bā̃dhtī hai. 2. billī makān-kē nīcē dauṛtī hai. 3. śēr chōṭē gadhē-kō pul-kē nīcē khī̃ctā hai. 4. naukar jūtē palaṅg-kē nīcē rakhtā hai. 5. ghar-kē nīcē baṛā sā̃p rahtā hai. 6. kisān bhūkē bailõ-kō daraḳhtõ-kē nīcē bā̃dhtā hai. 7. baccā mēz-kē nīcē khēltā hai. 8. kisān daraḳht-kē nīcē sōnā cāhtā hai. 9. lambā sā̃p makān-kē nīcē jātā hai. 10. pul-kē nīcē mōṭī gāy hai.

10.2.3 Exercise 2. **Translate into Urdu:**
1. The oxen stop under the tree. 2. The boy drops the book under the table. 3. We (**msc.**) see the big animals under the bridge. 4. The oxen drag the farmer under the tree. 5. The dog wants to sleep under the tall tree. 6. The hungry cat eats the food under the table. 7. The lean cow rests under the tree. 8. There are ripe fruits under the tree. 9. The fisherman wants to catch fish under the bridge. 10. The little girls want to play under the tree.

10.3

mā̃ baccē-kē sāth śahar-kō jātī hai.	The mother goes to the city with the child.
mā̃ us-kē sāth śahar-kō jātī hai.	The mother goes to the city with it.
laṛkā chōṭī laṛkī-kē sāth khēltā hai.	The boy plays with the little girl.
bachṛā baṛī gāy-kē sāth dauṛtā hai.	The calf runs with the large cow.

This section illustrates constructions with the compound postposition **-kē sāth, with, in the company of, together with.**

REMARKS: The postposition **-kō** is used to indicate the place towards which an action is directed. (Compare 9.2.) When the general direction of an action is indicated, rather than the specific, the **-kō** is dropped. Compare: **aurat śahar-kō jātī hai.** The woman goes to the city, and **aurat śahar jātī hai.** The woman goes to town.

10.3.1 More Examples are:

kisān laṛkō̃-kē sāth khēt-kō jātā hai.	The farmer goes to the field with the boys.
ādmī bēṭī-kē sāth bāg̱-mē̃ ātā hai.	The man comes into the garden with (**his**) daughter.
laṛkā bhāī-kē sāth mā̃-kō pānī lātā hai.	The boy brings water to (**his**) mother with (**his**) brother.
baccē bēṭiyō̃-kē sāth chat-par khēltē haī̃.	The children play on the roof with the daughters.
laṛkā aurtō̃-kē sāth bōltā hai.	The boy speaks with the women.
ammā̃ abbā-kē sāth bāzār-kō jānā cāhtī hai.	Mother wants to go to the bazaar with father.

10.3.2 Exercise 1. **Translate into English:**

1. abbā baccō̃-kē sāth khēltā hai. 2. ammā̃ bēṭiyō̃-kē sāth bōltī hai. 3. laṛkā būṛhī mā̃-kē sāth chōṭē makān-mē̃ rahtā hai. 4. bēṭī bhāiyō̃-kē sāth ghar dauṛtī hai. 5. aurat naukar-kē sāth bāzār jātī hai. 6. laṛkā dōstō̃-kē sāth chat-par baiṭhtā hai. 7. ādmī naukar-kē sāth śahar-kō jātā hai. 8. laṛkā bāp-kē sāth khēt-kō jātā hai. 9. baṛā laṛkā dōstō̃-kē sāth daryā-mē̃ tairtā hai. 10. mā̃ aurtō̃-kē sāth bāzār-sē ātī hai.

10.3.3 Exercise 2. **Translate into Urdu:**

1. The boy goes with (**his**) brother to the field. 2. The farmer goes to the city with (**his**) sons. 3. The children play on the roof with (**their**) friends. 4. The woman cooks in the house with (**her**) daughter. 5. The gardener goes into the garden with the children. 6. The mother plays with the child. 7. The daughter works with (**her**) mother in the house. 8. The servant goes to the bazaar with the woman. 9. The little girl plays in the garden with (**her**) sister. 10. The girl goes to the bazaar with (**her**) friends.

10.4

ādmī makān-kē sāmnē hai.	The man is in front of the house.
us-kē sāmnē ādmī hai.	There is a man in front of it.
makān daraḳhtō̃-kē sāmnē hai.	The house is in front of the trees.
daryā masjid-kē sāmnē hai.	The river is in front of the mosque.

This section illustrates the compound postposition **-kē sāmnē, in front of.**

REMARKS: (1) The being or thing represented by the subject of the verb is in a position facing the being or thing represented by the noun placed before **-kē sāmnē.**

(2) Vocabulary notes: **masjid** (ī) mosque, **pīr** (ā) holy man, **murīd** (ā) disciple.

10.4.1 More Examples are:

imārat-kē sāmnē ēk dukān hai.	There is a shop in front of the building.
gāṛī makān-kē sāmnē ruktī hai.	The cart stops in front of the house.
pīr murīdō̃-kē sāmnē baiṭhtē haī̃.	The holy man sits in front of his disciples.
mālī ghar-kē sāmnē khōdtā hai.	The gardener digs in front of the house.
makān-kē sāmnē bāg̱ hai.	There is a garden in front of the house.
bīvī ḳhāvind-kē sāmnē khānā rakhtī hai.	The wife puts food in front of (**her**) husband.

10.4.2 Exercise 1. **Translate into English:**

1. ādmī dukān-kē sāmnē bahot cīzē̃ bēctā hai. 2. daryā-kē sāmnē khēt hai. 3. aurat

pīr-kē sāmnē phūl rakhtī hai. 4. mōṭargāṛī imārat-kē sāmnē ruktī hai. 5. chōṭā laṛkā abbā-kē sāmnē dauṛtā hai. 6. mālī makān-kē sāmnē kām kartā hai. 7. śikārī jañgal-kē sāmnē bhēṛiyē-kō mārtā hai. 8. bhūkī aurat bāg̲-kē sāmnē murgī-kō pakaṛtī hai. 9. makān-kē sāmnē ēk ū̃cā darak̲ht hai. 10. laṛkī ghar-kē sāmnē khēlnā cāhtī hai.

10.4.3 Exercise 2. **Translate into Urdu:**

1. The beggar sits down in front of the river. 2. The woman is in front of the well. 3. The mother places fruit in front of the child. 4. The little girl plays in front of the house. 5. We (msc.) want to play in front of the mosque. 6. There is a small shop in front of the high building. 7. The servants sit in front of the house. 8. The boy sits in front of the teacher. 9. There is a thick jungle in front of the city. 10. The gardener wants to rest in front of the house.

10.5	**hōṭal-kē daftar-mē̃.**		**In the Hotel Office**
klark:	**farmāiyē?**	Clerk:	**What can I do for you?**
Jāvēd:	**maĩ Jōnz • sāhab-sē milnā cāhtā hū̃.**	Jāvēd:	**I wish to see Mr. Jones.**
klark:	**kyā Misṭar Jōnz āp-kō jāntē haĩ?**	Clerk:	**Does Mr. Jones know you?**
Jāvēd:	**hā̃. Jōnz • sāhab mujhē jāntē haĩ. unhō̃-nē mujhē bulāyā hai.**	Jāvēd:	**Yes. Mr. Jones knows me. He has called me.**
klark:	**bahot acchā. un-kā kamrā nambar sāt sau das hai.**	Clerk:	**Very well. His room number is 710.**
Jāvēd:	**maĩ vahā̃ kaisē jāū̃?**	Jāvēd:	**How do I go there?**
klark:	**lifṭ istēmāl kījiyē.**	Clerk:	**Please use the elevator.**
Jāvēd:	**lifṭ kahā̃ hai?**	Jāvēd:	**Where is the elevator?**
klark:	**āp-kī dāyī̃ taraf.**	Clerk:	(It is) **to your right.**
Jāvēd:	**mērī dāyī̃ taraf?**	Jāvēd:	**To my right?**
klark:	**hā̃. āp-kī dāyī̃ taraf. mulāzim āp-kō batā dēgā.**	Clerk:	**Yes. To your right. The attendant will direct you.**
Jāvēd:	**bahot bahot śukriyā.**	Jāvēd:	**Thank you very much.**

10.6	**Jōnz • sāhab-kē kamrē-mē̃.**		**In Mr. Jones' Room.**
Jāvēd:	**kyā Jōnz • sāhab andar haĩ?**	Jāvēd:	**Is Mr. Jones in?**
sekreṭarī:	**hā̃. Jōnz • sāhab andar haĩ.**	Secretary:	**Yes. Mr. Jones is in.**
Jāvēd:	**Jōnz • sāhab-nē mujhē bulāyā hai.**	Jāvēd:	**Mr. Jones has called me.**
sekreṭarī:	**āp-kā nām kyā hai?**	Secretary:	**What is your name?**
Jāvēd:	**mērā nām Jāvēd hai.**	Jāvēd:	**My name is Jāvēd.**
sekreṭarī:	**taśrīf rakhiyē.**[1] **maĩ Jōnz • sāhab-kō ittalā dētā hū̃.**	Secretary:	**Please sit down. I shall inform Mr. Jones** (that you are here).
Jāvēd:	**śukriyā.**	Jāvēd:	**Thank you.**
sekreṭarī:	**Jōnz • sāhab ṭēlifōn-par bāt kar rahē haĩ. vo pā̃c minaṭ-mē̃ ā jāẽgē. kyā āp kuch piyẽgē?**	Secretary:	**Mr. Jones is speaking on the telephone. He will come in five minutes. Will you take something to drink?**
Jāvēd:	**sirf ēk glās pānī.**	Jāvēd:	**Only a glass of water.**

sekreṭarī:	**aur kuch nahī̃?**	Secretary:	**Nothing else?**
Jāvēd:	**nahī̃. sirf ṭhanḍā pānī.**	Jāvēd:	**No. Just cold water.**
	āj bahot garmī hai.		**It is very warm today.**
sekreṭarī:	**ye lījiyē.**	Secretary:	**Here it is.**
	Jōnz • sāhab abhī ātē haĩ.		**Mr. Jones will be in shortly.**
Jāvēd:	**śukriyā.**	Jāvēd:	**Thank you.**

REMARKS: (1) Graceful expression for **baiṭhiyē.**

LESSON 11

11.1

baṛā jānvar bāg-kē pās hai.	The large animal is near the garden.
us-kē pās baṛā jānvar hai.	There is a large animal near it.
bandar khānē-kē pās hai.	The monkey is near the food.
kuā̃ khēt-kē pās hai.	The well is near the fields.

This section illustrates the compound postposition **-kē pās, near, near-by.** Another phrase translating "near" is **-kē nazdīk.**

11.1.1 More Examples are:

dukāndār dukān-kē pās hai.	The shop-keeper is near the shop.
ṭrām masjid-kē pās ruktī hai.	The trolley stops near the mosque.
ghar-kē pās kuā̃ hai.	There is a well near the house.
aurat kuē̃-kē pās dōstō̃-kē sāth bāt kartī hai.	The woman talks with (**her**) friends near the well.
arḍalī daftar-kē pās hai.	The orderly is near the office.
saṛak-kē pās chōṭā makān hai.	There is a small house near the road.

Vocabulary Notes: **dukāndār** (ā) shopkeeper, **ṭrām** (ī) trolley, **arḍalī** (ā) orderly, attendant, messenger, **nadī** (ī) stream, river.

11.1.2 Exercise 1. **Translate into English:**

1. aurat dukān-kē pās dukāndār-sē bāt kartī hai. 2. naukar daftar-kē pās ṭhahartā hai. 3. pyāsā bail kuē̃-kē pās ruktā hai. 4. laṛkā pul-kē pās tairtā hai. 5. ādmī daryā-kē pās baṛē hāthī-kō nahlātā hai. 6. chōṭī laṛkiyā̃ ēk-sāth ghar-kē pās khēltī haĩ. 7. saṛak-kē pās gahrā kuā̃ hai. 8. ham ēk-sāth masjid-kē pās khēlnā cāhtē haĩ. 9. ṭrām pul-kē pās ruktī hai. 10. pyāsī gāy nadī-kē pās ṭhahartī hai.

11.1.3 Exercise 2. **Translate into Urdu:**

1. The gardener works near the well. 2. The woman stops near the shop. 3. The little boys play near the mosque. 4. The thirsty dog is near the well. 5. There is a beggar near the mosque. 6. We (**msc.**) want to play with (**our**) friends near the bridge. 7. The little girls want to sleep near (**their**) mother. 8. The big camel wants to sleep near the tall tree. 9. Mother speaks with (**her**) friends near the river. 10. The hungry horse wants to stop near the grass.

11.2

laṛkē-kē pās kuttā hai.	The boy has a dog.
us-kē pās kuttā hai.	He has a dog.

chōṭī laṛkiyō̃-kē pās nayē rūmāl haĩ.	The little girls have new handkerchiefs.
un-kē pās nayē rūmāl haĩ.	They have new handkerchiefs.
būṛhē ādmī-kē pās kitābē̃ haĩ.	The old man has books.
us-kē pās kitābē̃ haĩ.	He has books.

This section illustrates the construction with the compound postposition **-kē pās,** indicating one way of expressing possession in Urdu. (Note that this construction refers to physical possession of non-human beings or things, the ownership of which can be transferred from one person to another.) The noun indicating the English "possessor" is placed in the object form before **-kē pās** and the being or thing possessed is made the subject of the verb **hōnā, to be, exist.** The **-kē pās** postpositional phrase occurs in initial position in the sentence.

11.2.1 More Examples are:

kuttē-kē pās haḍḍī hai.	The dog has a bone.
us-kē pās chōṭā kabūtar hai.	He has a little pigeon.
tālibilm-kē pās nayā kāgaz hai.	The student has new paper.
un-kē pās tāzē ām haĩ.	They have fresh mangoes.
machērē-kē pās baṛā jāl hai.	The fisherman has a big net.
aurat-kē pās nayī garārā hai.	The woman has new trousers.
chōtē laṛkē-ke pās baṛī gē̃d hai.	The little boy has a big ball.
śikārī-kē pās chōṭā phandā hai.	The hunter has a small snare.
ḳhātūn-kē pās baṛī gāṛī hai.	The lady has a large carriage.
ustād-kē pās aḳhbār hai.	The teacher has a newspaper.

REMARKS: **garārā** (ā) are very wide-bottomed trousers worn by women.

11.2.2 Vocabulary Notes:

ustād (ā) teacher, **ām** (ā) mango, **kabūtar** (ā) pigeon, **gē̃d** (ī) ball, **jāl** (ā) net, **phandā** (ā) snare, **ḳhātūn** (ī) lady, **rūmāl** (ī) handkerchief, **tālibilm** (ā and ī) student, **haḍḍī** (ī) bone, **aḳhbār** (ā) newspaper.

11.2.3 Exercise 1. **Translate into English:**

1. aurat-kē pās rūmāl hai. 2. tālibilm-kē pās dō kitābē̃ haĩ. 3. dukāndār-kē pās bahot tāzē ām haĩ. 4. bēṭiyō̃-kē pās nayī sāṛiyā̃ haĩ. 5. ustād-kē pās chōṭā ghar hai. 6. kisānō̃-kē pās hal haĩ. 7. bāp-kē pās aḳhbār hai. 8. aurat-kē pās nayī hanḍiyā̃ haĩ. 9. ādmī-kē pās mōṭargāṛī hai. 10. kisān-kē pās dō bail haĩ.

11.2.4 Exercise 2. **Translate into Urdu:**

1. The woman has ten chickens. 2. The child has a new ball. 3. The man has a new automobile. 4. They have a large house. 5. The woman has a cow. 6. The washerman has a donkey. 7. He has a new plow. 8. The girls have many bangles. 9. The shopkeeper has many things. 10. The lady has many saris.

11.3

ādmī baṛē kunbē-kē liyē kām kartā hai.	The man works for the large family.
laṛkā aurtō̃-kē liyē pānī lātā hai.	The boy brings water for the women.
laṛkā ēk kitāb paṛhnē-kē liyē ḳharīdtā hai.	The boy buys a book to read.
baccā khēlnē-kē liyē bāhar jātā hai.	The child goes out to play.
ādmī pīnē-kē liyē pānī mā̃gtā hai.	The man asks for water to drink.

This section illustrates the compound postposition **-kē liyē, for, for the benefit of, in order to.**

REMARKS: The infinitive, when occurring before a postposition, is placed in the object form, i.e., the final **-ā** is replaced by **-ē**.

11.3.1

musāfir nahānē-kē liyē pānī m̃āgtā hai.	The traveller asks for water to bathe.
aurat pakānē-kē liyē sabziyā̃ ḳharīdtī hai.	The woman buys vegetables to cook.
mālī zamīn khōdnē-kē liyē nayā phāvṛā lātā hai.	The gardener brings a new spade to dig the ground.
laṛkā baṛē tālāb-sē pīnē-kē liyē pānī lātā hai.	The boy brings water to drink from the big tank.
aurat kuttē-kē liyē khānā bāhar lātī hai.	The woman brings out food for the dog.
bāp baccē-kē liyē nayē khilaunē ḳharīdtā hai..	The father buys new toys for the child.

11.3.2 Vocabulary Notes:

kunbā (ā) family, **khilaunā** (ā) top, **tālāb** (ā) tank, pool, **phāvṛā** (ā) spade, **m̃āgnā** to request, to ask for.

11.3.3 Exercise 1. **Translate into English:**

1. naukar musāfir-kō nahānē-kē liyē pānī lātā hai. 2. ustād tālibilm-kō paṛhnē-kē liyē kitāb dētē haĩ. 3. laṛkā mā̃-kē liyē lakṛī kāṭtā hai. 4. kisān pyāsē bailō̃-kē liyē pānī khĩctā hai. 5. mā̃ bēṭiyō-kē liyē cūṛiyā̃ ḳharīdtī hai. 6. admī bēṭō̃-kē sāth nahānē-kē liyē tālāb-kō jātā hai. 7. aurat kunbē-kē liyē khānā pakātī hai. 8. ḳhātūn bēṭiyō̃-kē sāth sāṛiyā̃ ḳharīdnē-kē liyē bāzār-kō jātī hai. 9. bēṭī pānī lānē-kē liyē kuē̃-kō dauṛtī hai. 10. ham khānē-kē liyē khānā m̃āgnā cāhtē haĩ.

11.3.4 Exercise 2. **Translate into Urdu:**

1. The boys go out to play with their friends. 2. The hungry children want to come in to eat. 3. The monkeys want to go into the garden to pluck fruit from the trees. 4. We (**fm.**) ask for a new book to read. 5. Mother buys a toy for the little boy. 6. The farmer gives the two oxen grass to eat. 7. The washerman throws the clothes in the tank to wash (**them**). 8. The messenger buys the master a book to read. 9. The man works in the city for (**his**) family. 10. The woman brings vegetables to cook from the field.

11.4

gīlī saṛak ḳhatarnāk hai.	The wet road is dangerous.
ḳhū̃ḳhār śēr jaṅgal-mē̃ rahtā hai.	The dreadful tiger lives in the jungle.
mā̃ bēṭī-kē liyē lāl jūtē ḳharīdtī hai.	The mother buys red shoes for (**her**) daughter.
aurat ḳhāvind-kō sāf ḳamīz dētī hai.	The woman gives (**her**) husband a clean shirt.
safēd gāy daraḳht-kē nīcē sōtī hai.	The white cow sleeps under the tree.
gōl mēz kōnē-mē̃ rakhiyē.	(**Please**) place the round table in the corner.
nahānē-kē liyē garm pānī lāiyē.	(**Please**) bring warm water for bathing.
mazbūt ghōṛā sūkhī ghās-kō khātā haī.	The strong horse eats the dry grass.
ḳhūbsūrat laṛkī kapṛē ḳharīdnē-kē liyē bāzār-kō jātī hai.	The beautiful girl goes to the bazaar to buy clothes.
amīr ādmī-kē pās mōṭargāṛī hai.	The rich man has an automobile.

This section is concerned with adjectives ending in consonants. All adjectives ending in consonents and some ending in vowels (See 11.4.1 following.) do not change their form for gender, number, subject or object.

REMARKS: (1) **gīlā** wet, agrees in gender, number, and form with the noun it modifies. (See 3.2.)

(2) Vocabulary Notes: **ḳamīz** (ī) shirt, **kōnā** (ā) corner, **śēr** (ā) (also **bāgh** [ā]) tiger.

(3) Added Vocabulary: **badmāś** wicked, **meharbān** kind, **bīmār** sick, **udās** sad, **amīr** rich, **ḳhuś** happy, **jōtnā** to till, **rōnā** to weep.

11.4.1

haṇḍiyā ḳhālī hai.	The cooking-pot is empty.
mā̃ ḳhābīdā baccē-kō palaṅg-par liṭātī hai.	The mother places the sleepy child on the bed.
laṛkā bhārī lakṛī lātā hai.	The boy brings the heavy wood.
mehantī tālibilm har rōz paṛhtā hai.	The industrious student studies daily.

This section illustrates adjectives ending in vowels which do not change for gender and number. (See 11.4, above.)

11.4.2 Exercise 1. **Translate into English:**

1. kuā̃ miṭhā hai. 2. mazbūt kisān chōṭē gadhē-kō khī̃ctā hai. 3. ḳhuś aurat ḳhāvind-kē sāmnē khānā rakhtī hai. 4. śikārī ḳhū̃ḳhār jānvar-kō mārtā hai. 5. bāp ḳhūbsūrat bēṭī-kē liyē lāl sāṛī ḳharīdtā hai. 6. bahan bīmār baccē-kō palaṅg-par liṭātī hai. 7. ḳhābīdā naukar kōnē-mē̃ sōtā hai. 8. laṛkā aurtō̃-kē liyē bhārī lakṛī lātā hai. 9. amīr ādmī udās laṛkē-kō khānā dētā hai. 10. maĩ garm pānī mā̃gtā hū̃. 11. ḳhūbsūrat laṛkī sāf ḳamīz lātī hai. 12. aurat safēd gāy-kō daraḳht-kē nīcē bā̃dhtī hai. 13. kōnē-mē̃ gōl mēz hai. 14. meharbān aurat bhūkē bail-kō ghās khilātī hai. 15. amīr ādmī-kē pās bahot makān haĩ.

11.4.3 Exercise 2. **Translate into Urdu:**

1. The farmer wants to kill the dreadful tiger. 2. The happy girl buys a red sari. 3. The mother wants to feed the red chicken. 4. The white cow is in the garden. 5. (**Please**) bring out that round table. 6. There is warm water in the cooking-pot. 7. The friend (**fm.**) brings food to the sick woman. 8. The sad girl weeps beside the deep well. 9. The boys point out the wicked thief. 10. The washerman brings clean clothes. 11. The woman puts the heavy wood on (**her**) head. 12. The little man walks behind the strong donkey. 13. There is a white horse near the river. 14. The kind woman gives the hungry man food. 15. The rich man has many friends.

11.5

kyā laṛkā māntā hai?	Does the boy obey?
kyā billiyā̃ khātī haĩ?	Do the cats eat?
kyā ādmī laṛkē-kō dēkhtā hai?	Does the man see the boy?
kyā aurtē̃ sabziyō̃-kō dēkhtī haĩ?	Do the women see the vegetables?
kyā āp būṛhē ādmī-kō dēkhtē haĩ?	Do you see the old man?

Sections 11.5 to 11.5.4 illustrate the formation of questions. Any one of the sentences given in the lessons preceding can be made into a question by placing the particle **kyā** at the beginning of it.

11.5.1

kyā ādmī mōṭā hai?	Is the man fat?
kyā ādmī mōṭē haĩ?	Are the men fat?

kyā aurat bhūkī hai?	Is the woman hungry?
kyā aurtē̃ bhūkī haī?	Are the women hungry?
kyā ye darakht baṛā hai?	Is this tree big?
kyā ye darakht baṛē haī?	Are these trees big?
kyā vo kuttā burā hai?	Is that dog bad?
kyā vo kuttē burē haī?	Are those dogs bad?

11.5.2

kyā laṛkā bōlnā cāhtā hai?	Does the boy want to speak?
kyā laṛkē bōlnā cāhtē haī?	Do the boys want to speak?
kyā aurat pakānā cāhtī hai?	Does the woman want to cook?
kyā aurtē̃ pakānā cāhtī haī?	Do the women want to cook?
kyā vo paṛhnā cāhtī hai?	Does she want to read?
kyā vo paṛhnā cāhtī haī?	Do they want to read?

11.5.3 Exercise 1. **Translate into English:**

1. kyā billī us chōṭī cuhiyā-kō pakaṛtī hai? 2. kyā bhūkē bandar un phalō̃-kō curānā cāhtē haī? 3. kyā vo chōṭē baccē bhūkē haī? 4. kyā vo aurtē̃ baccō̃-kō nahlānā cāhtī haī? 5. kyā aurat in sabziyō̃-kō pakātī hai? 6. kyā ye chōṭā ghōṛā pīnā cāhtā hai? 7. kyā aurat pyāsī gāy-kō pilānā cāhtī hai? 8. kyā acchī aurat chōṭē baccō̃-kō zyādā khilātī hai? 9. kyā gussīlī billī aurat-kō vahā̃ kāṭtī hai? 10. kyā kisān bailō̃-kō bā̃dhtā hai? 11. kyā tum laṛkiyō̃-kō andar bulātī hō? 12. kyā abbā baccō̃-kō kabhī kabhī samajhtē haī? 13. kyā naukar mujhē samjhtā hai? 14. kyā haṇḍiyā̃ acchī haī? 15. kyā ghōṛā baṛā hai? 16. kyā zamīn-mē̃ kōēlā hai? 17. kyā jaṅgalō̃-mē̃ jānvar haī? 18. kyā chōṭē laṛkē gahrē daryā-mē̃ tairnā cāhtē haī? 19. kyā dhōbī ādmī-kō kapṛē bhējtā hai? 20. kyā mālī paudē-par pānī ḍāltā hai? 21. kyā kisān hal-sē khēt jōttā hai? 22. kyā ghar-kē pīchē bāg hai? 23. kyā kisān darakht-kē nīcē ārām kartā hai? 24. kyā laṛkā aurtō̃-sē bāt kartā hai? 25. kyā śikārī khū̃khār jānvar-kō mārtā hai?

11.5.4 Exercise 2. **Translate into Urdu:**

1. Are the girls happy? 2. Are the vegetables good? 3. Are the places small? 4. Do the thirsty horses want to drink? 5. Does the man work inside? 6. Do the little children want to go out? 7. Does the boy obey him? 8. Does the teacher make the boy read? 9. Does the fisherman want to catch fish? 10. Does the mother feed the daughters too much? 11. Does the man want to bathe the elephant? 12. Does the monkey eat the fruit there? 13. Does the woman want to buy things in the shop? 14. Does the mare eat the raw vegetables quickly? 15. Does this thirsty ox want to stop sometimes? 16. Does the dog pull this child out? 17. Is this building high? 18. Is this the high building? 19. Are there stars in the sky? 20. Are there fish in the deep sea? 21. Does the mother tell the children stories? 22. Does the gardener pour water on the plants? 23. Does the fisherman catch fish near the bridge? 24. Is there a jungle behind the city? 25. Do the hungry children want to come in to eat?

11.6 Jōnz·sāhab kamrē-mē̃ dākhil hōtē haī. — **Mr. Jones Enters the Room.**

Jōnz·sāhab:	**helō.**	Mr. Jones:	**Hello.**
Jāvēd:	**helō.**	Jāvēd:	**Hello.**
Jōnz·sāhab:	**kyā āp Hamīd·sāhab-kē bhāī haī?**	Mr. Jones:	**Are you Hamīd's brother?**

Jāvēd:	hā̃. maĩ Hāmīd • sāhab-kā bhāī hū̃.	Jāvēd:	Yes. I am Hamīd's brother.
	unhō̃-nē mujhē āp-kē pās bhējā hai.		He sent me to you.
Jōnz • sāhab:	maĩ Urdū sīkhnā cāhtā hū̃. kyā āp mērī madad kar saktē haĩ?	Mr. Jones:	I wish to learn Urdu. Can you help me?
Jāvēd:	hā̃. mērē bhāī • sāhab [1] -nē mujhē is-kē bārē-mē̃ batāyā hai.	Jāvēd:	Yes. My brother has told me about this.
	maĩ āp-kī kyā madad kar saktā hū̃?		How can I help you?
Jōnz • sāhab:	maĩ Urdū bōlnā sīkhnā cāhtā hū̃.	Mr. Jones:	I wish to learn to speak Urdu.
	maĩ-nē kuch Urdū Amrīkā-mē̃ paṛhī hai.		I have studied some Urdu in America.
	lēkin mērī Urdū acchī nahī̃.		But my Urdu is not good.
Jāvēd:	āp-kī Urdū bahot acchī hai.	Jāvēd:	Your Urdu is very good.
Jōnz • sāhab:	jab lōg bahot tēz bōltē haĩ, tab maĩ āsānī-sē nahī̃ samajh saktā.	Mr. Jones:	I cannot understand easily when people talk too fast.
Jāvēd:	kyā maĩ bahot tēz bōl rahā hū̃?	Jāvēd:	Am I talking too fast?
Jōnz • sāhab:	hā̃. aur āhistā bōliyē.	Mr. Jones:	Yes. Please speak more slowly.
Jāvēd:	kyā āp ab samajh saktē haĩ?	Jāvēd:	Can you understand (me) now?
Jōnz • sāhab:	hā̃. maĩ ab samajh saktā hū̃.	Mr. Jones:	Yes. I can understand (you) now.
Jāvēd:	ab ham kis-kē bārē-mē̃ bāt karē̃?	Jāvēd:	What shall we talk about now?
Jōnz • sāhab:	pahilē, kuch alfāz [2] sīkhnā cāhtā hū̃.	Mr. Jones:	First, I wish to learn some words.
Jāvēd:	pūchiyē.	Jāvēd:	Please ask.
Jōnz • sāhab:	"house" -kō Urdū-mē̃ kyā kahtē haĩ?	Mr. Jones:	How do (they) say "house" in Urdū?
Jāvēd:	"house" -kō Urdū-mē̃ "ghar" kahtē haĩ.	Jāvēd:	They say "ghar" for "house" in Urdu.
Jōnz • sāhab:	"room" -kō Urdū-mē̃ kyā kahtē haĩ?	Mr. Jones:	How do (they) say "room" in Urdu?
Jāvēd:	"room" -kō Urdū-mē̃ "kamrā" kahtē haĩ.	Jāvēd:	They say "kamrā" for "room" in Urdu.
Jōnz • sāhab:	"water" -kō Urdū-mē̃ kyā kahtē haĩ?	Mr. Jones:	How do (they) say "water" in Urdu?
Jāvēd:	"water" -kō Urdū-mē̃ "pānī" kahtē haĩ.	Jāvēd:	They say "pānī" for "water" in Urdu.
Jōnz • sāhab:	"to the left" -kō Urdū-mē̃ kyā kahtē haĩ?	Mr. Jones:	How do (they) say "to the left" in Urdu?

Jāvēd:	"bāyī̃ taraf" **kahtē haī.**	Jāvēd:	**They say** "bāyī̃ taraf."
Jōnz • sāhab:	"straight ahead" **-kō kyā kahtē haī?**	Mr. Jones:	**How do** (they) **say** "straight ahead"?
Jāvēd:	"straight ahead" **-kō** "sīdhē āgē-kō" **yā** "sāmnē" **kahtē haī.**	Jāvēd:	**For** "straight ahead" **they say** "sīdhē āgē-kō" **or** "sāmnē."
Jōnz • sāhab:	"what time is it" **-kō kyā kahtē haī?**	Mr. Jones:	**How will** (you) **say** "what time is it"?
Jāvēd:	"what time is it" **-kō** "kitnē bajē haī" **kahtē haī.**	Jāvēd:	**For** "what time is it" (we'll) **say** "kitnē bajē haī."
Jōnz • sāhab:	**ab ham kisī aur cīz-kē bārē-mē̃ bāt karē̃gē.**	Mr. Jones:	**Now we will talk about something else.**
Jāvēd:	**kyā bāt karē̃?**	Jāvēd:	**What should we talk about?**
Jōnz • sāhab:	**mujhē Pākistān-sē bahot dilcaspī hai.**	Mr. Jones:	**I am very interested in Pakistan.**
	mujhē is-kē bārē-mē̃ kuch batāiyē.		**Tell me something about it.**
Jāvēd:	**ḳhuśī-sē.**	Jāvēd:	**With pleasure.**
Jōnz • sāhab:	**maī āp-sē bāt karnā pasand kartā hū̃.**	Mr. Jones:	**I like to talk with you.**
Jāvēd:	**bahot bahot śukriyā.**	Jāvēd:	**Thank you very much.**
Jōnz • sāhab:	**maī āp-sē har rōz thōṛī dēr-kē liyē milnā cāhtā hū̃.**	Mr. Jones:	**I wish to meet you for a little while every day.**
Jāvēd:	**agar mujhē kāfī paisē milē̃, tō maī ḳhuśī-sē āū̃gā.**	Jāvēd:	**If I get enough money, I'll come gladly.**
Jōnz • sāhab:	**kyā āp har rōz ēk ghanṭē-kē liyē ā saktē haī?**	Mr. Jones:	**Can you come every day for one hour?**
Jāvēd:	**subah-kō yā bād dōpahar?**	Jāvēd:	**In the morning or in the afternoon?**
Jōnz • sāhab:	**āp-kō kaun-sā vaḳt zyādā pasand hai?**	Mr. Jones:	**Which time would you prefer?**
Jāvēd:	**bād dōpahar.**	Jāvēd:	**The afternoon.**
Jōnz • sāhab:	**āp bād dōpahar kyū̃ zyādā pasand kartē haī?**	Mr. Jones:	**Why do you prefer the afternoon?**
Jāvēd:	**kyū̃-ke maī subah-kō kālēj jātā hū̃.**	Jāvēd:	**Because I go to college in the morning.**
Jōnz • sāhab:	**tab bād dōpahar ṭhīk rahēgā.**	Mr. Jones:	**Then the afternoon will be all right.**
	kyā āp-kō ēk ghanṭē-kē kām-kē tīn rūpayē manzūr haī?		**Will you take three rupees for each hour's work?**
Jāvēd:	**tīn rūpayē ṭhīk rahē̃gē.**	Jāvēd:	**Three rupees will be fine.**
Jōnz • sāhab:	**kyā āp kal ā sakē̃gē?**	Mr. Jones:	**Will you be able to come tomorrow?**
Jāvēd:	**hā̃. mai kal ā sakū̃gā.**	Jāvēd:	**Yes. I will be able to come tomorrow.**

Jōnz • sāhab:	**cār bajē?**	Mr. Jones:	**At four o'clock?**
Jāvēd:	**ṭhīk cār bajē.**	Jāvēd:	**Precisely at four.**
Jōnz • sāhab:	**bahot acchā.**	Mr. Jones:	**Very good.**
Jāvēd:	**maĩ kal āū̃gā.**	Jāvēd:	**I'll come tomorrow.**
Jōnz • sāhab:	**guḍbāī.**	Mr. Jones:	**Good-by.**
Jāvēd:	**guḍbāī.**	Jāvēd:	**Good-by.**

REMARKS: (1) Note the term applied to the elder brother.

(2) The singular of **alfāz** is **lafz** (ā).

LESSON 12

12.1

ādmī kahā̃ rahtā hai?	Where does the man live?
baccā kahā̃ khēltā hai?	Where does the child play?
baṛā daryā kahā̃ hai?	Where is the big river?
ādmī kahā̃-sē ātā hai?	Where does the man come from?
kuttā kahā̃-sē dauṛtā hai?	Where does the dog run from?
baccē kahā̃-sē caltē haĩ?	Where do the children walk from?

This section and the following, 12.1 to 12.1.4. are concerned with interrogative adverbs. (See 4.4 and notes.)

12.1.1

laṛkā Urdū kyū̃ bōltā hai?	Why does the boy speak Urdu?
kuttā bhūkā kyū̃ hai?	Why is the dog hungry?
ādmī śahar-kō kyū̃ jātā hai?	Why does the man go to the city?
ustād kahānī kyū̃ paṛhtā haĩ?	Why does the teacher read the story?
daryā cauṛā kyū̃ hai?	Why is the river broad?
ghōṛā pyāsā kyū̃ hai?	Why is the horse thirsty?

REMARKS: A variant is **kyō̃.**

12.1.2

śēr jaṅgal-mē̃ kab rahtā hai?	When does the lion stay in the jungle?
gāṛī kab jātī hai?	When does the train leave?
gāṛī kab vāpas ātī hai?	When does the train return?
dūsrī bas śahar-sē kab vāpas ātī hai?	When does the other bus return from the city?

12.1.3 Exercise 1. **Translate into English:**

1. vo kahā̃-sē ātē haĩ? 2. baccē dūsrē baccō̃-kē sāth kab khēltē haĩ? 3. mā̃ bēṭī-kē liyē lāl jūtē kyū̃ ḳharīdtī hai? 4. burā laṛkā bahan-par pānī kyū̃ ḍāltā hai? 5. śikārī ḳhū̃ḳhār jānvar-kō kab mārtā hai? 6. kisān chaṛī-sē bandarō̃-kō kyū̃ mārnā cāhtā hai? 7. ustād sāhab tālibilm-kō paṛhnē-kē liyē kitāb kyū̃ dētē haĩ? 8. bandar pakkē phalō̃-kō kahā̃-sē curātē haĩ? 9. aurat paudō̃-par pānī kab ḍāltī hai? 10. musāfir śahar-sē kab ātā hai? 11. kōēlā kahā̃ hai? 12. musāfir kyū̃ pānī mā̃gtā hai? 13. dhōbī ādmī-kō kapṛē kab bhējtā hai? 14. aḳhbār kahā̃ hai? 15. bail kuē̃-kē pās kyū̃ ruktā hai? 16. naukar kahā̃ raḳābiyā̃ rakhtā hai? 17. dhōbī kahā̃-sē kapṛē lātā hai? 18. mazbūt kisān chōṭē gadhē-kō kyū̃ khī̃ctā hai? 19. naukar mālik-kō ṭhaṇḍā pānī kab lātā hai? 20. ḳhū̃ḳhār śēr kahā̃ rahtā hai?

12.1.4 Exercise 2. **Translate into Urdu:**

1. When does the man work? 2. Why is the boy hungry? 3. When do animals come from the jungle? 4. From where do the boys bring wood for (their) mother? 5. Where does the woman want to cook? 6. Why does the man bring water for the automobile? 7. When does the fisherman catch fish? 8. Why do you (msc.) want to study? 9. Where does the trolley stop? 10. Why does the ox stop under the tree? 11. When does mother cook? 12. Why does the woman weep near the river? 13. Where does the washerman wash the clothes? 14. Why does the train stop? 15. When does the holy man sit under the tree? 16. When does the cow want to eat grass? 17. From where does the animal come? 18. Why does father come back from the city? 19. When does the kind woman give beggars food? 20. From where does the servant bring water for the traveller?

12.2

laṛkā Urdū bōl saktā hai.	The boy can speak Urdu.
laṛkē Urdū bōl saktē haī̃.	The boys can speak Urdu.
laṛkī Añgrēzī samajh saktī hai.	The girl can understand English.
laṛkiyā̃ Añgrēzī samajh saktī haī̃.	The girls can understand English.
aurat pakā saktī hai.	The woman can cook.
bēṭē dēkh saktē haī̃.	The sons can see.
vo paṛh saktē haī̃.	They can read.
laṛkī sī saktī hai.	The girl can sew.
baccē gā saktē haī̃.	The boys can sing.
chōṭī laṛkiyā̃ ēk-sāth ghar-kē pās khēl saktī haī̃.	The little girls can play together near the house.
laṛkā bhārī lakṛī lā saktā hai.	The boy can carry the heavy wood.
kyā dhōbī ādmī-kō kapṛē bhēj saktā hai?	Can the washerman send the clothes to the man?
śikārī ḳhū̃ḳhār bāgh-kō kab mār saktā hai?	When can the hunter kill the dreadful tiger?
naukar kahā̃ raḳābiyā̃ rakh saktā hai?	Where can the servant place the plates?

This section introduces the Urdu construction which corresponds to the English construction comprising the verb **can** or **to be able to** followed by another verb. The Urdu construction consists of the verb **saknā, can, to be able to,** immediately preceded by the stem of the verb translating the second verb of the English phrase. This sequence consisting of **verbal stem + saknā** can be considered to function as a single verb (See 2.1, Remarks.). No other forms can intrude between the verbal stem and the form of **saknā.**

12.2.1 Exercise 1. **Translate into English:**

1. kyā ādmī baṛē kunbē-kē liyē kām kar saktā hai? 2. aurat pakānē-kē liyē sabziyā̃ ḳharīd saktī hai. 3. laṛkā mā̃-kē liyē lakṛī kāṭ saktā hai. 4. kyā musāfir ādmī-kē sāth Urdū bōl saktā hai? 5. ham ādmī-kō daryā dikhā saktē haī̃. 6. mālī paudō̃-par pānī ḍāl saktā hai. 7. machērā daryā-sē māchliyā̃ pakaṛ saktā hai. 8. kisān hal-sē khēt jōt saktā hai. 9. laṛkī haṇḍiyā-kō jaldī-sē lā saktī hai. 10. kārīgar mōṭargārī-kē nīcē kām kar saktā hai.

12.2.2 Exercise 2. **Translate into Urdu:**

1. Where can the washerman wash clothes? 2. When can the boy bring wood for the woman? 3. Can the fisherman catch fish to sell in the bazaar? 4. The boys can point

out the wicked thief. 5. The kind woman can give the hungry man food. 6. The happy girl can buy a new red sari. 7. We (**msc.**) are able to read Urdu. 8. The girls can go out to play with (**their**) friends. 9. The woman can buy vegetables to cook from the man. 10. The boy can swim under the bridge.

12.3

laṛkā nahī̃ caltā.	The boy does not walk.
laṛkē nahī̃ caltē.	The boys do not walk.
bēṭā nahī̃ khātā.	The son does not eat.
bēṭē nahī̃ khātē.	The sons do not eat.
laṛkī nahī̃ samajhtī.	The girl does not understand.
laṛkiyā̃ nahī̃ samajhtī̃.	The girls do not understand.
bēṭī nahī̃ pakātī.	The daughter does not cook.
bēṭiyā̃ nahī̃ pakātī̃.	The daughters do not cook.

This section and the following illustrate the negative of the verbal constructions given in the preceding lessons. Section 12.3 illustrates the formation of the negative of the present tense of the Urdu verb. The particle **nahī** is placed directly before the present participle, the verb **hōnā, to be, to exist,** not being expressed. The participle agrees in gender and number with the subject of the sentence. (Compare 2.1 and Remarks.) Note that the final vowel of the feminine of the participle is nasalized in the plural. (See the sixth and eighth sentences, above.)

12.3.1 Exercise **1. Translate into English:**

1. maī nahī̃ khātā. 2. vo nahī̃ kūdtī̃. 3. tum nahī̃ samajhtī̃. 4. ham nahī̃ pītē. 5. āp nahī̃ paṛhtē. 6. maī nahī̃ kahtā. 7. ham nahī̃ tairtī̃. 8. vo nahī̃ khēltī. 9. tum nahī̃ bōltē. 10. āp nahī̃ dauṛtī̃. 11. kuttā nahī̃ pītā. 12. bachṛē nahī̃ khātē. 13. baccā nahī̃ dauṛtā. 14. bīviyā̃ nahī̃ lātī̃. 15. murgī nahī̃ khātī 16. bhāī nahī̃ dētā. 17. hāthī nahī̃ nahātē. 18. fauj nahī̃ dauṛtī. 19. gāy nahī̃ khātī. 20. ciṛiyā̃ nahī̃ uṛtī̃.

12.3.2 Exercise 2. **Translate into Urdu:**

1. We (**msc.**) do not eat. 2. You (**msc.**) do not play. 3. He does not run. 4. You (**hon. msc.**) do not understand. 5. I (**fm.**) do not go. 6. You (**hon. msc.**) do not cook. 7. She does not dig. 8. They (**msc.**) do not speak. 9. They (**fm.**) do not see. 10. I (**msc.**) do not read. 11. The man does not walk. 12. The boys do not play. 13. The cat does not drink. 14. The girls do not talk. 15. The (**little**) old women do not sleep. 16. The women do not speak. 17. The men do not see. 18. The wife does not understand. 19. The daughters do not sleep. 20. The child does not eat.

12.4

laṛkā bōlnā nahī̃ cāhtā.	The boy does not want to speak.
laṛkī calnā nahī̃ cāhtī.	The girl does not want to walk.
ādmī dēnā nahī̃ cāhtē.	The men do not want to give.
ham lēnā nahī̃ cāhtē.	We do not want to take.
aurtē̃ ḳharīdnā nahī̃ cāhtī̃.	The women do not want to buy.

This section illustrates the negative of the **cāhnā** construction. The particle **nahī̃** is normally placed between the infinitive and the present participle. (See 3.1 and Remarks.)

12.4.1 Exercise 1. **Translate into English:**

1. vo khānā nahī̃ cāhtā. 2. laṛkē bhējnā nahī̃ cāhtē. 3. ghōṛī pīnā nahī̃ cāhtī. 4. maī jānā nahī̃ cāhtī. 5. tōtē bōlnā nahī̃ cāhtē. 6. vo khānā nahī̃ cāhtī̃. 7. bīvī pakānā nahī̃ cāhtī.

8. ham paṛhnā nahī̃ cāhtē. 9. machliyā̃ khānā nahī̃ cāhtī̃. 10. tum bhējnā nahī̃ cāhtē.

12.4.2 Exercise 2. **Translate into Urdu:**

1. The children do not want to play. 2. We (**msc.**) do not want to read. 3. The girls do not want to talk. 4. The dog does not want to eat. 5. The woman does not want to cook. 6. I (**fm.**) do not want to play. 7. The man does not want to dig. 8. The father does not want to hear. 9. She does not want to speak. 10. You (**msc.**) do not want to give.

12.5

laṛkā acchā nahī̃ hai.	The boy is not good.
laṛkē acchē nahī̃ haĩ.	The boys are not good.
laṛkī bhūkī nahī̃ hai.	The girl is not hungry.
laṛkiyā̃ bhūkī nahī̃ haĩ.	The girls are not hungry.
ghōṛā pyāsā nahī̃.	The horse is not thirsty.
pānī garm nahī̃.	The water is not warm.
sāmān halkā nahī̃.	The baggage is not light.
galī tañg nahī̃.	The street is not narrow.
javāb ṭhīk nahī̃.	The answer is not exact.
savāl muśkil nahī̃.	The question is not difficult.

This section illustrates the negative of the predicate-adjective construction taken up in section 3.2 (See Remarks.). Note that here the verb **hōnā, to be, to exist,** may be expressed with **nahī̃** placed directly before it; otherwise **nahī̃** is final in the utterance.

Vocabulary Notes: **galī** (ī) street, lane, **javāb** (ā) answer, **sāmān** (ā) baggage, **makkar** (adj., n.c.) cunning, **chīnnā** to snatch.

12.5.1 Exercise 1. **Translate into English:**

1. vo bhūkī nahī̃. 2. bēṭiyā̃ acchī nahī̃ haĩ. 3. jūtā chōṭā nahī̃ hai. 4. maĩ būṛhā nahī̃. 5. ghōṛā baṛā nahī̃. 6. billī burī nahī̃. 7. tum baṛē nahī̃ hō. 8. lōmṛī makkar nahī̃. 9. baccē pyāsē nahī̃. 10. āp pyāsī nahī̃ haĩ.

12.5.2 Exercise 2. **Translate into Urdu:**

1. The horses are not old. 2. I (**msc.**) am not lean. 3. The fish are not small. 4. They (**fm.**) are not thirsty. 5. The donkeys are not bad. 6. She is not thirsty. 7. The girl is not happy. 8. The flies are not small. 9. The daughters are not hungry. 10. I (**msc.**) am not sleepy.

12.6

ādmī bāhar nahī̃ jātē.	The men do not go out.
bīvī fauran nahī̃ jātī.	The wife does not leave immediately.
laṛkā bahot kām nahī̃ kartā.	The boy does not work very much.
ghōṛā pās-sē nahī̃ jātā.	The horse does not go by.
vo vahā̃ nahī̃ dauṛtē.	They do not run there.

This section illustrates the negative of the construction taken up in section 4.4. Note that the negative particle **nahī̃** is placed directly before the present participle—no other word should intervene between **nahī̃** and the participle.

12.6.1 Exercise 1. **Translate into English:**

1. ham yāhā̃ nahī̃ rahtē. 2. aurat āhistā āhistā nahī̃ bōltī. 3. tum bāhar nahī̃ jātē. 4. aurtē̃ andar nahī̃ pakātī̃. 5. hāthī bahot zyādā nahī̃ khātā. 6. chōṭā baccā pīchē nahī̃ ātā.

7. bhūkī ghōṛī ṭhaharnā nahī̃ cāhtī. 8. dublī aurtē̃ fauran ḵhānā nahī̃ cāhtī̃. 9. baṛā ādmī jaldī-sē ḵhānā nahī̃ cāhtā. 10. chōṭē baccē bāhar jānā nahī̃ cāhtē.

12.6.2 Exercise 2. **Translate into Urdu:**

1. The brothers do not eat together. 2. The woman does not come in. 3. The boys do not speak slowly. 4. The cows are not very happy. 5. The good girls do not go outside. 6. The hungry women do not eat slowly. 7. They (**fm.**) do not want to come here. 8. The big boys do not want to play inside. 9. I (**fm.**) do not want to play sometimes. 10. The thirsty mare does not want to drink slowly.

12.7	**bāzār-mē̃.**		**At the Bazaar.**
dukāndār:	**farmāiyē, bēgam·sāhibā?** [1]	Shopkeeper:	**What do you wish, madam?**
bēgam:	**maĩ sāṛī ḵharīdnā cāhtī hū̃.**	Lady:	**I wish to buy a sari.**
dukāndār:	**bahot acchā, bēgam·sāhibā. hamārē pās har ḳism-kī sāriyā̃ haĩ.**	Shopkeeper:	**Very good, madam. We have all kinds of saris.**
bēgam:	**kyā tumhārē pās Banārsī sāṛiyā̃ haĩ?**	Lady:	**Do you have saris from Banaras?**
dukāndār:	**hā̃. hamārē pās bahot ḵhubsūrat Banārsī sāṛiyā̃ haĩ.**	Shopkeeper:	**Yes. We have many beautiful saris from Banaras.**
bēgam:	**mujhē dikhāiyē.**	Lady:	**Please show** (them) **to me.**
dukāndār:	**bahot acchā.**	Shopkeeper:	**Very well.**
bēgam:	**mujhē ye tīn sāṛiyā̃ pasand haĩ. in-kē kitnē paisē lōgē?**	Lady:	**I like these three saris. How much will you take for them?**
dukāndār:	**lāl sāṛī che sau rupayē-kī hai. nīlī pā̃c sau-kī, aur sabz cār sau rupayē-kī.**	Shopkeeper:	**The red sari is 600 rupees. The blue is 500, and the green 400.**
bēgam:	**ye bahot mahẽgī haĩ. kyā tumhārē pās sastī-bhī haĩ?**	Lady:	**These are very expensive. Do you have something cheaper?**
dukāndār:	**bēgam·sāhibā, Banārsī sāṛiyā̃ mahẽgī hōtī haĩ. śāyad āp sādī rēśmī sāṛī pasand karẽ. vō itnī mahẽgī nahī̃.**	Shopkeeper:	**Madam, Banaras saris are expensive. Perhaps you may like a plain silk sari. They do not cost so much.**
bēgam:	**nahī̃. mērī sab dōstō̃-kē pās sādī rēśmī sāṛiyā̃ haĩ. maĩ kōī nayī cīz cāhtī hū̃.**	Lady:	**No. All my friends have plain silk saris. I wish to have something new.**
dukāndār:	**kyā maĩ āp-kō kuch aur dikhā saktā hū̃?**	Shopkeeper:	**Can I show you something else?**
bēgam:	**nahī̃. āj nahī̃. ab mujhē jānā hai.**	Lady:	**No. Not today. I must go now.**
dukāndār:	**phir taśrīf lāiyē.**	Shopkeeper:	**Please come again.**

REMARKS: (1) A variant is **sāhabā.**

	12.8 Jamīlā Surayyā-sē miltī hai.		Jamīlā Meets Surayyā.
Jamīlā:	salām alēkum.	Jamīlā:	Hello.
Surayyā:	valēkam salām.	Surayyā:	Hello.
Jamīlā:	tum tō Id-kā c͡ād hō gayī hō.[1] kahā̃ hō āj • kal?	Jamīlā:	I have not seen you for a long time. Where are you now?
Surayyā:	maī ab Karācī-mē̃ rahtī hū̃.	Surayyā:	I live in Karachi now.
Jamīlā:	kahtē haī, Karācī māḍarn śahar hai.	Jamīlā:	They say Karachi is a modern city.
Surayyā:	hā̃. Karācī māḍarn śahar hai.	Surayyā:	Yes. Karachi is a modern city.
Jamīlā:	kyā us-mē̃ bahot-sī nayī imārtē̃ haī?	Jamīlā:	Does it have many new buildings?
Surayyā:	hā̃. us-mē̃ bahot-sē nayē sarkārī dafātir[2] aur kuch nayē hōṭal haī.	Surayyā:	Yes. It has very many new government offices and several new hotels.
Jamīlā:	ēk jagah-sē dusrī jagah jānā tō muśkil hōgā.	Jamīlā:	It must be difficult to go from one place to another.
Surayyā:	nahī, bahot muśkil nahī̃. ānē jānē-kē bahot-sē zarīyē[3] haī.	Surayyā:	No, it is not very difficult. There are different means of transportation.
Jamīlā:	lōg ēk jagah-sē dusrī jagah kaisē jātē haī?	Jamīlā:	How do people go from one place to another?
Surayyā:	kuch lōg ṭaiksiyā̃ • istēmāl kartē haī.	Surayyā:	Some people ride in taxis.
Jamīlā:	ṭaiksiyā̃ tō mahē̃gī hō̃gī.	Jamīlā:	Taxis must be expensive.
Surayyā:	kuch lōg paidal jātē haī.	Surayyā:	Some people go on foot.
Jamīlā:	kyā kuch lōg sāikal • istēmāl kartē haī?	Jamīlā:	Do any use bicycles?
Surayyā:	zyādatar, sarkāri mulāzmīn[4] aur tulābā[5] sāikil • istēmāl kartē haī.	Surayyā:	Mostly government office people and students ride bicycles.
Jamīlā:	tumhārē śōhar daftar kaisē jātē haī?	Jamīlā:	How does your husband go to (his) office?
Surayyā:	hamārē pās kār hai.	Surayyā:	We have a car.
Jamīlā:	tab tō tumhārā kārōbār acchā hōgā.	Jamīlā:	Your business must be good, then.
Surayyā:	hā̃. ham ḳhūś • hāl haī.	Surayyā:	Yes. We are comfortable.
Jamīlā:	jab-bhī tum ā sakō, mujh-sē milnē-kē liyē āō.	Jamīlā:	Please come to see me whenever you can.
Surayyā:	bahot acchā. maī kabhī ā̃ūgī.	Surayyā:	Very well. I'll come sometime.
Jamīlā:	phir milē̃gē. fī-amānillāh.[6]	Jamīlā:	We'll meet again. May God protect you.
Surayyā:	Ḳhudā hāfiz.	Surayyā:	Good-by.

REMARKS: (1) Lit. You have become the moon of Id. = It's been (almost) an eternity since I've seen you.

(2) Plural of daftar (ā).

(3) A variant of this is **zarāē.**

(4) Plural of **mulāzim** (ā) servant.

(5) Plural of **tālibilm, tālib-ē-ilm** (ā) student, which also functions as plural.

(6) An Arabic expression directed to a person on his or her departure for some length of time.

LESSON 13

13.1

ādmī mujhē nahī̃ dēkhtā.	The man does not see me.
maĩ laṛkē-kō nahī̃ dēkhtā.	I do not see the boy.
vo lambē ādmī-kō nahī̃ dēkhtā.	He does not see the tall man.
maĩ is burē kuttē-kō nahī̃ mārtā.	I do not beat this bad dog.
ādmī kamrē-mē̃ nahī̃ hai.	The man is not in the room.
śahar-mē̃ kōī ū̃cī imārtē̃ nahī̃ haĩ.	There are no high buildings in the city.
laṛkā aurtō̃-kō lakṛī nahī̃ dētā.	The boy does not give wood to the women.
kitābē̃ mēzō̃-par nahī̃ haĩ.	The books are not on the tables.
ustād • sāhab un-sē savāl nahī̃ pūchtē.	The teacher does not ask them questions.

This section is concerned with the negative of sentences illustrating the object forms of nouns and pronouns. (See 5.1 to 5.6, 6.1 to 6.3, 9.1 to 9.4, and 10.1 to 10.4.)

13.1.1 Exercise 1. **Translate into English:**
1. ādmī un-kō nahī̃ dēkhtā. 2. aurtē̃ us-kō nahī̃ suntī̃. 3. māē̃ ham-kō nahī̃ bulātī̃. 4. gadhā laṛkī-kō nahī̃ khī̃ctā. 5. maĩ ghōṛō̃-kō khilānā nahī̃ cāhtā. 6. gāy bachṛō̃-kō jaldī-sē nahī̃ khilātī. 7. baccā billī-kō nahī̃ pakaṛtā. 8. ham machliyā̃ nahī̃ ḳharīdtī̃. 9. maĩ khānā nahī̃ lātī. 10. chōṭī aurat murgiyā̃ nahī̃ khilātī. 11. billī machlī-kō āhistā nahī̃ khātī. 12. bhūkā kuttā bail-kō nahī̃ kāṭtā. 13. būṛhā kisān gāyō̃-kō yahā̃ bā̃dhnā nahī̃ cāhtā. 14. bandar pakkē phal khānā nahī̃ cāhtē. 15. vo pūrānī tasvīr yahā̃ nahī̃ ḳharīdtī̃. 16. bahan bhūkē laṛkō̃-kō andar bulānā nahī̃ cāhtī. 17. vo āg-mē̃ lakṛī nahī̃ ḍāltā. 18. ham śahar-mē̃ kām nahī̃ kartē. 19. naukar musāfir-kō saṛak nahī̃ dikhātā. 20. aurat divārō̃-par tasvīrē̃ nahī̃ laṭkātī.

13.1.2 Exercise 2. **Translate into Urdu:**
1. We (**msc.**) do not feed the hungry dog. 2. The monkey does not eat the ripe fruits. 3. The old farmer does not drive the big horses. 4. Mother does not want to call the hungry children here. 5. The good woman does not feed the little boys too much. 6. The happy man does not want to catch fish. 7. The farmer does not dig in the ground. 8. The woman does not want to cook vegetables in the new cooking-pot. 9. The men do not point out the tiger to the hunter. 10. The servant does not hang the pictures on the wall. 11. The hungry dog does not snatch food from the big child. 12. The gardener does not work behind the house. 13. The fisherman does not want to catch fish under the bridge. 14. The servant does not go to the bazaar with the woman. 15. The beggar does not

sit in front of the house. 16. There isn't a well near the house. 17. The washerman does not have a donkey. 18. The man does not work in the city for (**his**) family. 19. The farmer does not have a plow. 20. The children are not in front of the house.

13.2

kyā laṛkā nahī̃ caltā?	Doesn't the boy walk?
kyā aurtẽ sabziyõ-kō nahī̃ pakātī̃?	Don't the women cook the vegetables?
kyā pānī ṭhaṇḍā nahī̃?	Isn't the water cold?
kyā daryā gahrā nahī̃?	Isn't the river deep?
kyā aurat pakānā nahī̃ cāhtī?	Doesn't the woman want to cook?

This section illustrates the negative of the interrogative sentences taken up in 11.5.

13.2.1 Exercise 1. **Translate into English:**

1. kyā ye chōṭā ghōṛā pīnā nahī̃ cāhtā? 2. kyā billī us cuhiyā-kō nahī̃ pakaṛtī? 3. kyā kisān bailõ-kō nahī̃ bā̃dhtā? 4. kyā bāp baccõ-kō kabhī nahī̃ samajhtā? 5. kyā śikārī ḳhū̃ḳhār jānvar-kō nahī̃ mārtā? 6. kyā ghar-kē pīchē bāg nahī̃? 7. kyā kisān hal-sē khēt nahī̃ jōttā? 8. kyā dhōbī ādmī-kō kapṛē nahī̃ bhējtā? 9. kyā jaṅgal-mẽ jānvar nahī̃? 10. kyā aurat ye sabziyā̃ nahī̃ pakātī?

13.2.2 Exercise 2. **Translate into Urdu:**

1. Aren't the vegetables good? 2. Doesn't the man work inside? 3. Aren't there fish in the river? 4. Doesn't the horse want to drink? 5. Aren't there stars in the sky? 6. Doesn't the mother tell the children stories? 7. Doesn't the woman want to buy things in the bazaar? 8. Doesn't the fisherman bring fish from the river? 9. Isn't there a book on the table? 10. Isn't the child hungry?

13.3

laṛkā Urdū kyū̃ nahī̃ bōltā?	Why doesn't the boy speak Urdu?
gāṛī vāpas kyū̃ nahī̃ ātī?	Why doesn't the train return?
kuttā bhūkā kyū̃ nahī̃?	Why isn't the dog hungry?

This section illustrates the negative of sentences containing interrogative adverbs. (See 12.1 to 12.1.2.)

13.3.1 Exercise 1. **Translate into English.**

1. baccā dusrē baccõ-kē sāth kab nahī̃ khēltā? 2. musāfir pānī kyū̃ nahī̃ mā̃gtā? 3. abbā baccõ-kō kab nahī̃ cūmtā? 4. mālī paudõ-par pānī kyū̃ nahī̃ ḍāltā? 5. śikārī ḳhūḳhār jānvar-kō kyū̃ nahī̃ mārtā? 6. bandar pakkē phal kahā̃-sē nahī̃ curātā? 7. kisān khēt-sē kyū̃ nahī̃ ātā? 8. kuttā kab nahī̃ sōtā? 9. dhōbī ādmī-kē liyē kapṛē kyū̃ nahī̃ dhōtā? 10. ustād sāhab tālibilm-kō paṛhnē-kē liyē kab kitāb nahī̃ dētē?

13.3.2 Exercise 2. **Translate into Urdu:**

1. Why doesn't the man bring water for the automobile? 2. When isn't the child hungry? 3. Where doesn't a bullock sleep? 4. When doesn't a kind woman give a beggar food? 5. Why doesn't the washerman bring the clothes? 6. When doesn't the camel stop to eat grass? 7. Why doesn't the train stop? 8. Why doesn't the boy come back from the well? 9. Why aren't the children in the house? 10. Why isn't the cow near the tree?

13.4

ādmī Urdū nahī̃ bōl saktē.	The men cannot speak Urdu.
laṛkī Aṅgrēzī nahī̃ samajh saktī.	The girl cannot understand English.
ham nahī̃ sun saktē.	We cannot hear.
baccā nahī̃ sīkh saktā.	The child cannot learn.

This section illustrates the negative of sentences containing the construction with the verb **saknā** (See 12.2.).

REMARKS: The phrase comprising **the stem of the verb + saknā** functions as a unit. The particle **nahī̃** is placed directly before it (i.e., before the verb-stem). It does not intrude between the stem and **saknā.**

13.4.1 Exercise 1. **Translate into English:**
1. laṛkā bhārī lakṛī nahī̃ lā saktā. 2. kyā dhōbī ādmī-kō kapṛē nahī̃ bhēj saktā? 3. śikārī ḳhū̃ḳhār jānvar-kō kyū̃ nahī̃ mār saktā? 4. naukar aurat-kē liyē lakṛī nahī̃ kāṭ saktā. 5. mālī paudō̃-par pānī nahī̃ ḍāl saktā. 6. kārīgar mōṭargāṛī-kē nīcē kām nahī̃ kar saktā. 7. machērā daryā-sē machliyā̃ nahī̃ pakaṛ saktā. 8. kyā aurat Urdū nahī̃ bōl saktī? 9. bandar pakkē phal nahī̃ pakaṛ saktā. 10. aurat divārō̃-par tasvīrē̃ nahī̃ laṭkā sāktī.

13.4.2 Exercise 2. **Translate into Urdu:**
1. The woman can't cook food for the family. 2. The fisherman can't bring fish to the city. 3. The man can't bring water for the automobile. 4. Why can't you (**msc.**) point out the road to the traveller? 5. The farmer can't dig the ground with the little plow. 6. I (**fm.**) cannot go to the bazaar with you (**hon.**). 7. The mother cannot tell the children stories. 8. The woman cannot take the clothes to the tank to wash (**them**). 9. The thief cannot steal the calf. 10. Why can't the washerman wash the clothes for the man?

13.5

mērā makān tālāb-kē pās hai.	My house is near the tank.
mērē kapṛē nayē haī.	My clothes are new.
mērī ṭōpī mēz-par hai.	My cap is on the table.
mērī imartē̃ śahar-mē̃ haī.	My buildings are in the city.

Sections 13.5 to 13.5.3 present the possessive adjectives of the first and second person pronouns. **mērā** is the possessive adjective of **maī; hamārā** that of **ham;** and **tumhārā** that of **tum.** These adjectives function in the same way as the adjectives described in 3.2, 4.3 and 6.1, agreeing with the nouns they modify in gender, number and form. The possessive constructions involving **vo** and **āp** follow. (See 14.1.)

13.5.1

hamārā bail nadī-kē pās cartā hai.	Our ox grazes by the river.
hamārē bail nadī-sē pānī pītē haī.	Our oxen drink water from the river.
hamārī bahan badsūrat nahī̃.	Our sister is not ugly.
hamārī bahnē̃ ghar-mē̃ nahī̃.	Our sisters are not at home.

13.5.2

tumhārī bailgāṛī pul-kē nīcē hai.	Your oxcart is under the bridge.
tumhārē bhāī Hindī acchī nahī̃ bōl saktē.	Your brothers cannot speak Hindi well.

13.5.3 More Examples are:

mērē bāl lambē haī.	My hair is long.
tumhārā gīt bahot mīṭhā hai.	Your song is very sweet.
ye mērē bail haī.	These are my oxen.
vo aurat hamārī mā̃ hai.	That woman is our mother.
vo ṭōpī tumhārī hai.	That cap is yours.
mōṭarsāikul hamārī hai.	The motorcycle is ours.
ye chātā mērā hai.	This umbrella is mine.

ghōṛā tumhārā nahī̃.	The horse is not yours.
mā̃ mērī bahnō̃-kō bulātī hai.	Mother calls my sisters.
acchī aurat tumhārī pyāsī gāy-kō pilātī hai.	The good woman makes your thirsty cow drink.
bhūkē bandar hamārē phal khātē haĩ.	The hungry monkeys eat our fruit.
aurat mērī sabziyā̃ ḳharīdnā cāhtī hai.	The woman wants to buy my vegetables.
tumhārā sāmān halkā nahī̃.	Your baggage is not light.
vo hamārī tañg galī dikhātē haĩ.	They point out our narrow street.
ustād • sāhab mērā javāb nahī̃ suntē.	The teacher doesn't hear my answer.
naukar tumhārē pyāsē baccē-kō dūdh pilānā cāhtā hai.	The servant wants to feed your thirsty child milk.
kisān hamārē bailō̃-kō pakaṛtā hai.	The farmer seizes our oxen.
tumhārē savāl muśkil haĩ.	Your questions are difficult.
mērā naukar Añgrēzī bōl saktā hai.	My servant can speak English.
maĩ tumhārē dōstō̃-kē sāth Urdū bōlnā cāhtā hū̃.	I want to speak Urdu with your friends.

Vocabulary Notes: **bāl** (ā) hair, **gīt** (ī) song, **chātā** (ā), **chatrī** (ī) umbrella, **nadī** (ī) river, stream, **mōṭarsāikul** (ī) motorcycle, **badsūrat** (adj., n.c.) ugly.

13.5.4 Exercise 1. **Translate into English:**

1. tumhārī mōṭarsāikul kahā̃ hai? 2. hamārā bāp kisān hai. 3. baccē tumhārī bailgāṛī-mē̃ khēltē haĩ. 4. mērī bahnē̃ tālāb-kē pās khēlnā cāhtī haĩ. 5. kyā ye ghar tumhārā hai? 6. tumhārē javāb ṭhīk nahī̃. 7. naukar mērē dōst-kō nahī̃ jāntā. 8. mērē bhāī galī-mē̃ khēltē haĩ. 9. tumhārē ustād muśkil savāl kyū̃ pūchtē haĩ? 10. hamārī billī garm dūdh pīnā cāhtī hai. 11. kārīgar mērī mōṭargāṛī-kē nīcē kām nahī̃ kartā. 12. kuttā tumhārē bhāī-kō kāṭnā cāhtā hai. 13. ye mērā ghar nahī̃. 14. kyā tumhārē bāp ghar-mē̃ haĩ? 15. maĩ tumhārī mā̃-kē sāth Urdū-mē̃ nahī̃ bōl saktā. 16. tumhārā bail mērē bāg-mē̃ cartā hai. 17. kyā vo laṛkā tumhārā bhāī hai? 18. mērī ṭōpī lāiyē. 19. āp mērē vālid-kē sāth kyū̃ bōlnā cāhtē haĩ? 20. acchā laṛkā hamārē bhāiyō̃-kō phal dētā hai.

13.5.5 Exercise 2. **Translate into Urdu:**

1. Our house is in that street. 2. Please bring water for my car. 3. Why does your cow graze in our field? 4. Your sisters want to talk with my sister. 5. This is my house. 6. This house is mine. 7. Does your father know our father? 8. Please bring my cap. 9. Is my automobile in front of the house? 10. Your servant does not know me. 11. I (**msc.**) cannot speak with your friends. 12. Our oxen graze under the new bridge. 13. The kind woman gives your hungry cow grass. 14. That is not your field. 15. Sister brings back water from our well. 16. That shop is mine. 17. The mechanic does not want to work under your car. 18. When does your father come to the city? 19. My brother does not want to go out to play. 20. Is your father the shopkeeper?

13.6 **ṭūṭī huī ghaṛī.** — **The Broken Watch.**

Āzād:	**kitnē bajē haĩ?**	Āzād:	**What time is it?**
Manzūr:	**mujhē mālūm nahī̃.**	Manzūr:	**I do not know.**
Āzād:	**āp-kō kyū̃ mālūm nahī̃?**	Āzād:	**Why don't you know?**
Manzūr:	**kyū̃-ke mērē pās ghaṛī nahī̃.**	Manzūr:	**Because I do not have a watch.**
Āzād:	**āp-kī ghaṛī-kō kyā huā?**	Āzād:	**What happened to your watch?**
Manzūr:	**ṭūṭ gayī hai.**	Manzūr:	(It) **is broken.**

Āzād:	kaisē?	Āzād:	How (did it break)?
Manzūr:	mujh-sē gir gayī.	Manzūr:	I dropped it.
Āzād:	gir gayī?	Āzād:	(You) dropped it?
Manzūr:	hā̃. maĩ-nē usē mēz-kē kinārē-kē bahot nazdīk rakh diyā thā.	Manzūr:	Yes. I placed it too near the edge of the table.
	vahā̃-sē gir gayī.		It fell off from there.
Āzād:	kyā āp usē ṭhīk karā saktē haĩ?	Āzād:	Can you have it fixed?
Manzūr:	hā̃. maĩ usē ṭhīk karā saktā hū̃.	Manzūr:	Yes. I can have it repaired.
Āzād:	maĩ āp-kō acchē ghaṛīsāz-kā nām dē saktā hū̃.	Āzād:	I can give (you) the name of a good watchrepairman.
Manzūr:	mujhē us-kā nām dījiyē.	Manzūr:	Please give me his name.
Āzād:	us-kā nām Ahmad hai.	Āzād:	His name is Ahmad.
Manzūr:	Ahmad?	Manzūr:	Ahmad?
Āzād:	hā̃.	Āzād:	Yes.
Manzūr:	kyā maĩ usē jāntā hū̃?	Manzūr:	Do I know him?
Āzād:	hā̃. āp usē jāntē haĩ.	Āzād:	Yes. You know him.
Manzūr:	vo kaun hai?	Manzūr:	Who is he?
Āzād:	vo mērā sālā[1] hai.	Āzād:	He is my wife's brother.
Manzūr:	vohī jō dō sāl huē Sargōdhā gayā thā?	Manzūr:	The one who went to Sargodha two years ago?
Āzād:	hā̃. che mahīnē huē vo vāpas ā gayā.	Āzād:	Yes. He came back six months ago.
Manzūr:	vo vāpas kyū̃ āyā?	Manzūr:	Why did he come back?
Āzād:	use chōṭā śahar pasand nahī̃.	Āzād:	He did not like a little city.
Manzūr:	vo kahā̃ rahtā hai?	Manzūr:	Where does he live?
	maĩ us-kē pās jāū̃gā.		I'll go to him.
Āzād:	us-kī dukān Vikṭōriyā Rōḍ-par hai.	Āzād:	His shop is on Victoria Road.
	āp vahā̃ āsānī-sē pahõc saktē haĩ.		You can get there easily.
Manzūr:	acchā. śukriyā.	Manzūr:	Good. Thanks.
Āzād:	kōī bāt nahī̃.	Āzād:	Don't mention it.

REMARKS: (1) sālā (ā) wife's brother.

LESSON 14

14.1

us-kā bhāī kārḳhānē-mē̃ kām kartā hai.	**His brother** works in the factory.
un-kē bhāī kārḳhānē-mē̃ kām kartē haĩ	**Their brothers** work in the factory.
us-kā bhāī kārḳhānē-mē̃ kām kartā hai.	**Her brother** works in the factory.
un-kē bhāī kārḳhānē-mē̃ kām kartē haĩ	**Their (fm.) brothers** work in the factory.

Sections 14.1 to 14.2.3 are concerned with the Urdu equivalent to the English genitive construction—i.e., English **the man's hat, the woman's house, the son of the man, the brother of the girl.** The Urdu construction under consideration is underlined in each of the example sentences ḡiven in 14.1, 14.1.1 and 14.2. Each of the underlined sequences consists of a pronoun (See 10.1, Remarks.) or noun in the **object** form before the forms, **-kā**, **-kē** or **-kī**, followed by a noun. The noun or pronoun (in the object form) and the postposition constitute the Urdu equivalent to the English genitive construction. (Compare the underlined portions of the English example phrases, above.) The postposition **-kā** functions simultaneously both as a postposition, taking the noun or pronoun governed by it in the object form (Compare 5.1 and 9.1 to 9.4.), and as an adjective ending in **-ā** (See 3.2, 4.3 and 6.1.), agreeing with the noun it modifies in gender, number and form.

Compare:

us-kā bhāī	**his** brother
us-kē bhāī	**his** brothers
laṛkē-kī bahan	the **boy's** sister **or** the sister **of the boy**
laṛkē-kī bahnē̃	the **boy's** sisters **or** the sisters **of the boy**

More examples are:

maĩ laṛkē-kē bhāī-kō dēkhtā hū̃.	I see the **boy's** brother.
maĩ baccē-kī bahan-kē sāth bāt kartā hū̃.	I speak with the **child's** sister.
vo laṛkō̃-kī mā̃-kē liyē pānī lātē haĩ.	They bring water for the **boy's** mother.
ham baccō̃-kē bhāī-kō lakṛī lātē haĩ.	We bring the wood to the brother **of the children.**
ustād • sāhab laṛkē-kē bhāī-sē savāl pūchtē haĩ.	The teacher asks the **boy's** brother questions.

Note that the phrase consisting of the noun or pronoun and **-kā** can be considered to function as a unit equal to an adjective, the masculine singular nominative of which ends in **-ā** (See 4.3 and 6.1), agreeing in gender, number and form with the noun it modifies.

14.1.1

āp-kā pyālā bahot chōṭā hai.	**Your cup** is very small.
āp-kē bistar taiyār haĩ.	**Your beds** are ready.
āp-kī bahan kahā̃ hai?	Where is **your sister?**

14.2

laṛkē-kā bhāī śahar-mẽ kām kartā hai.	**The boy's brother** works in the city.
laṛkē-kā bhāī śahar-mẽ kām kartē haĩ.	**The boy's brothers** work in the city.
laṛkō̃-kā bhāī śahar-mẽ kām kartā hai.	**The brother of the boys** works in the city.
laṛkō̃-kē bhāī śahar-mẽ kām kartē haĩ.	**The brothers of the boys** work in the city.
laṛkī-kā bhāī śahar-mẽ kām kartā hai.	**The girl's brother** works in the city.
laṛkī-kē bhāī śahar-mẽ kām kartē haĩ.	**The girl's brothers** work in the city.
laṛkiyō̃-kā bhāī śahar-mẽ kām kartā hai.	**The brother of the girls** works in the city.
laṛkiyō̃-kē bhāī śahar-mẽ kām kartē haĩ.	**The brothers of the girls** work in the city.
laṛkē-kī mā̃ kuē̃-kō jātī hai.	**The boy's mother** goes to the well.
laṛkō̃-kī māẽ kuē̃-kō jātī haĩ.	**The boys' mothers** go to the well.
laṛkī-kī mā̃ kuē̃-kō jātī hai.	**The girl's mother** goes to the well.
laṛkiyō̃-kī māẽ kuē̃-kō jātī haĩ.	**The girls' mothers** go to the well.

14.2.1 More examples are:

ādmī-kā ghar saṛak-par hai.	The man's house is along the road.
us-kā kām kyā hai?	What is his business?
us-kā pēśā kyā hai?	What is his profession?
us-kī dukān śahar-mẽ hai.	His shop is in the city.
vo har tarah-kī cīzẽ bēctā hai.	He sells all kinds of things.
laṛkā daraḳht-kī cōṭī-par caṛhnā cāhtā hai.	The boy wants to climb to the top of the tree.
maĩ hōṭal-kē mainējar-sē milnā cāhtā hū̃.	I want to see the manager of the hotel.
vālid • sāhab pīnē-kā pānī cāhtē haĩ.	The father wants drinking water.
nāī-kī dukān sṭēśan-kē pās hai.	The barbershop is near the station.

REMARKS: (1) **har** means **each, every; tarah** (ī) means **kind, sort.**

(2) Bear in mind that the infinitive, when governed by a postposition, is placed in the **object** form. Compare **pīnē-kā pānī, drinking water,** and **pinē-kē liyē pānī, water for drinking.**

(3) Vocabulary Notes: **kām** (ā) work, occupation, **cōṭī** (ī) top, summit, **nāī** (ā) barber, **pēśā** (ā) trade, profession, **mainējar** (ā) manager, **sṭēśan** (ā) station, railroad station.

14.2.2 Exercise 1. **Translate into English:**

1. us-kī mōṭargāṛī ghar-kē sāmnē hai. 2. vālid • sāhab laṛkē-kē bhāī-kō phal dētē haĩ. 3. baccē dhōbī-kē gadhē-kē pīchē caltē haĩ. 4. laṛkā āp-kī mōṭargāṛī-kē liyē pānī lātā hai. 5. aurat har tarah-kī cīzẽ ḳharīdnā cāhtī hai. 6. kyā us-kā bāp kārīgar hai? 7. laṛkā kisān-kē ghōṛē-kō chaṛī-sē kyū̃ mārtā hai? 8. mā̃ chōṭē laṛkē-kī bahan-kē sāth śahar-kō jātī hai. 9. ye us-kī ṭōpī hai. 10. baṛī gāy būṛhē kisān-kē khēt-mẽ sabziyā̃ khātī hai. 11. kyā ādmī bhāī-kē baṛē kunbē-kē liyē kām kar saktā hai? 12. musāfir āp-kē naukar-kē sāth Urdū-mẽ kyū̃ bōlnā cāhtā hai? 13. un-kē bail khēt-kē pās haĩ. 14. amīr ādmī-kī nayī mōṭargāṛī sṭēśan-kē pās hai. 15. kārīgar āp-kē bāp-kē mōṭargāṛī-kē nīcē kām kartā hai. 16. maĩ āp-kē savālō̃-kē javāb nahī̃ dē saktā. 17. musāfir-kā sāmān halkā hai. 18. mālī

bāg-kē paudō̃-par pānī kyū̃ nahī̃ ḍāltā? 19. āp-kā laṛkā būṛhī aurat-kē liyē bhārī lakṛī lātā hai. 20. naukar un-kī ṭōpiyā̃ nahī̃ lā saktā. 21. bhūkē ādmī-kē rakābī-par khānā rakhiyē. 22. aurat būṛhē ādmī-kī bhūkī gāy-kō ghās dētī hai. 23. dhōbī ādmī-kē pūrānē kapṛē kyū̃ nahī̃ dhōtā? 24. āp-kā pēśā kyā hai? 25. naukar hamārē abbā-kē ghar-mē̃ cōr-kō pakaṛtā hai.

14.2.3 Exercise 2. **Translate into Urdu:**
1. His father works in the city. 2. The boy brings wood for the traveller's fire. 3. The woman buys all kinds of things in the bazaar. 4. Their brother ties the ox under the tree. 5. The child wants to climb to the top of the tree. 6. We (**msc.**) catch the thief in (**our**) hotel room. 7. Where is your automobile? 8. The servant places the bed on the roof of the house. 9. The boy goes slowly to the barbershop. 10. Can your servant bring wood for the fire? 11. The monkeys play on the roof of the hotel. 12. The boy sits on the branch of the tree. 13. I (**msc.**) want to drink well-water. 14. The children run behind the washerman's donkey. 15. What is your business? 16. Please place the traveller's baggage in the room. 17. The trees of the garden have very ripe fruits. 18. There are all kinds of things to buy in the shops of the bazaar. 19. The holy man sits under a tree near the mosque. 20. From where can the boy bring water for your automobile? 21. There are all kinds of animals in the jungle. 22. What is that man's profession? 23. Where is your house? 24. The man drinks water from the mosque well. 25. Why don't they (**fm.**) bring wood for your mother?

14.3

ādmī mērē pīchē caltā hai.	The man walks behind me.
kuttā hamārē pīchē dauṛtā hai.	The dog runs behind us.
mērē sāth āiyē.	(**Please**) come with me.
laṛkē hamārē sāth bōltē haī̃.	The boys speak with us.
mērē pās cābī hai.	I have the key.
tumhārē pās paisē haī̃.	You have the money.
mērē liyē pānī lāiyē.	(**Please**) bring water for me.
us-kē vālid hamārē liyē sēb lātē haī̃.	His father brings apples for us.

This section is concerned with the construction for the first and second person pronouns corresponding to the construction in which nouns are governed by compound postpositions. (See 10.1 to 10.4, and 11.1 to 11.3, and 10.1, Remarks.)

In 13.5 to 13.5.3, above, have been presented the possessive adjectives of the first and second person pronouns—i.e., **mērā, hamārā, tumhārā.** Constructions involving the first and second person pronouns are rendered into Urdu by placing the object singular masculine form of the possessive adjectives of these pronouns before the second member of the postpositional compound—that is, the **-kē** is dropped.

REMARKS: (1) It has been pointed out in 10.1 that the compound postpositions consist of **-kē** (now recognizable as the object form, masculine singular, of the **-kā** postposition) and a form which in many instances can be identified as an adverb.

In 14.1, above, the construction consisting of noun (in object form) and the postposition **-kā** has been described to function as an adjective like any of the other adjectives ending in **-ā,** which agree with the noun they modify in gender, number and form.

It can now be shown that the constructions with the possessive adjectives taken up in this section, 14.3, comprise an adjective in the object form—i.e., equivalent to the noun (in object form) and **-kē** of the other postpositional phrases—before an adverbial form (which can be considered to function as a noun in the object form).

(2) Vocabulary Notes: **cābī** (ī) key, **sēb** (ā) apple, **kāfī** enough.

14.3.1 Exercise 1. **Translate into English:**

1. baccē tumhārē pīchē dauṛnā cāhtē haĩ. 2. naukar mērē sāmnē khānā rakhtā hai. 3. kyā vo tumhārē sāth Urdū-mē̃ bōl saktā hai? 4. mōṭargāṛī mērē sāmnē ruktī hai. 5. ādmī mērē pīchē caltā hai. 6. mērē pās kāfī paisē nahĩ haĩ. 7. acchā laṛkā pīnē-kā pānī hamārē liyē lātā hai. 8. musāfir hamārē sāth Aṅgrēzī bōlnā cāhtā hai. 9. laṛkī tumhārē liyē bāg-sē sēb lātī hai. 10. chōṭē bandar mērē pās haĩ.

14.3.2 Exercise 2. **Translate into Urdu:**

1. The washerman washes the clothes for us. 2. The boy brings drinking-water from the well for us. 3. Do you have a car? 4. The holy man stops in front of us. 5. Can he speak Urdu with you? 6. The dog runs behind me. 7. Do you have enough money to buy food? 8. Can you (**fm.**) go to the city with me? 9. I do not have a horse. 10. Please bring food from the hotel for us.

14.4

śāyad maĩ likhū̃.	I (**msc.**) may write.
śāyad maĩ likhū̃.	I (**fm.**) may write.
śāyad vo likhē.	He may write.
śāyad vo likhē.	She may write.
śāyad ham likhē̃.	We (**msc.**) may write.
śāyad ham likhē̃.	We (**fm.**) may write.
śāyad tum likhō.	You (**msc.**) may write.
śāyad tum likhō.	You (**fm.**) may write.
śāyad āp likhē̃.	You (**msc.**) may write.
śāyad āp likhē̃.	You (**fm.**) may write.
śāyad vo likhē̃.	They (**msc.**) may write.
śāyad vo likhē̃.	They (**fm.**) may write.

This section introduces the Urdu subjunctive. This mood indicates that the act described by the verb has the possibility of being fulfilled. (The **may** of the English sentences is not the verb **may** denoting permission.)

The Urdu subjunctive is made by attaching to the stem of the verb the following verbal suffixes: **-ū̃** for the first person singular; **-ē** for the third person singular; **-ō** for the **tum** form of the second person; and **-ē̃** for the remaining plural forms.

There is no distinction for gender.

REMARKS: **śāyad** translates English **perhaps.** It is not an indispensable part of the subjunctive construction and need not be expressed.

14.4.1 More examples are:

śāyad ādmī itvār-kō śahar jāē̃.	The man may go to the city on Sunday.
śāyad baccē āj skūl jāē̃.	The children may go to school today.
śāyad kuttā pīr-kō vāpas āē.	The dog may come back on Monday.
śāyad dukāndār mañgal-kō cīzē̃ bēcē.	The shopkeeper may sell the things on Tuesday.
śāyad baccē din-mē̃ sōē̃.	The children may sleep in the morning.
śāyad vāldain budh-kō rēsṭōrenṭ-mē̃ khāē̃.	The parents may eat in a restaurant on Wednesday.
śāyad baṛhaī jumērāt-kō darakht kāṭē.	The carpenter may cut the tree on Thursday.
śāyad tum jumē-kē din kitābē̃ paṛhō.	You may read the books on Friday.
śāyad maĩ haftē-kō āp-sē milnē-kē liyē āū̃.	I may come to see you on Saturday.

REMARKS: (1) The names of the days of the week are: **itvār** Sunday; **pīr** Monday; **mañgal** Tuesday; **budh** Wednesday; **jumērāt** Thursday; **jumā** Friday; **haftā** Saturday. With the exception of **jumērāt** Thursday, which is feminine, the names for the days of the week are masculine.

(2) **din-mē̃** (See sentence 5.) can also be translated "during the day."

(3) Vocabulary Notes: **baṛhaī** (ā) carpenter, **vāldain** (ē) parents, **cītā** (ā) cheetah.

14.4.2 Exercise 1. **Translate into English:**

1. śāyad mālī makān-kē sāmnē kām karē. 2. śāyad śikārī jañgal-mē̃ jānvar mārē. 3. sāyad ham mañgal-kō śahar jāē̃. 4. śāyad maĩ baccō̃-kō kahāniyā̃ sunāū̃. 5. śāyad dhōbī pīr-kō ādmī-kē liyē kapṛē dhōē. 6. śāyad chōṭē baccē itvār-kō chat-par khēlnā cāhē̃. 7. śāyad aurat rassē-sē gāy-kō bā̃dhē. 8. śāyad machērā budh-kō hamārē liyē machliyā̃ lāē. 9. śāyad tum darakht-kē nīcē ārām karō. 10. śāyad fakīr masjid-kē sāmnē baiṭhē̃. 11. śāyad naukar jumērāt-kō aurat-kē sāth bāzār jāē. 12. śāyad vo tumhārē sāth Urdū-mē̃ bōl sakē. 13. śāyad tumhārē ustād muśkil savāl pūchē̃. 14. śāyad maĩ mōṭargāṛī calā sakū̃. 15. sāyad ādmī musāfir-kō pīnē-kā pānī lāē.

14.4.3 Exercise 2. **Translate into Urdu:**

1. The old fisherman may be able to catch fish. 2. The teacher may want to speak Urdu with you. 3. The carpenter may bring wood from the jungle. 4. I may go to the city with you (**hon. msc.**) on Monday. 5. The washerman may be able to bring the clothes on Thursday. 6. The hunter may be able to kill the dreadful cheetah. 7. The student may want to come on Friday to speak with you in English. 8. The gardener may pour water on the plants. 9. We may go with you on Saturday to eat in the hotel's restaurant. 10. The mechanic may be able to work under the automobile. 11. The shopkeeper may sell all kinds of things. 12. The farmer may work in the field on Tuesday. 13. The woman may buy vegetables from the old man. 14. The servant may bring food from the restaurant for us. 15. We may bring wood from the jungle for you on Wednesday.

14.5 **tā̃gēvālā.** **Tongawala.**

bēōpārī:[1] **ō! tā̃gēvālē.**	Businessman: **Hey! Tongawala.**
tā̃gēvālā: **jī, janāb?**	Tongawala: **Yes, Sir?**
bēōpārī: **maĩ Saddar Bāzār jānā cāhtā hū̃.**	Businessman: **I wish to go to the Saddar Bazaar.**

tā̃gēvālā:	maĩ āp-kō vahā̃ lē ja saktā hū̃.	Tongawala:	I can take you there.
bēōpārī:	kitnē paisē lōgē?	Businessman:	How much will you take?
tā̃gēvālā:	tīn rūpayē.	Tongawala:	Three rupees.
bēōpārī:	tīn rūpayē?	Businessman:	Three rupees?
tā̃gēvālā:	jī hā̃. tīn rūpayē.	Tongawala:	Yes, sir. Three rupees.
bēōpārī:	tīn rūpayē bahot zyādā haĩ. maĩ tumhẽ ēk rūpayā dū̃gā.	Businessman:	Three rupees is too much. I'll give you one rupee.
tā̃gēvālā:	ēk rūpayā? ēk rūpayā kāfī nahī̃. mērē iḳhrājāt [2] bahot haĩ.	Tongawala:	One rupee? One rupee is no enough. My expenses are great.
bēōpārī:	tumhārē iḳhrājāt bahot haĩ? kaisē?	Businessman:	Your expenses are great? How?
tā̃gēvālā:	ēk tō mujhē apnē kunbē-kō khilānā paṛtā hai, aur dusrē ghōṛē-kō.	Tongawala:	First, I have to feed my fam ily, and secondly, my horse.
bēōpārī:	kyā tumhārā kunbā baṛā hai?	Businessman:	Is your family large?
tā̃gēvālā:	hā̃. mērī bīvī aur dō baccē.	Tongawala:	Yes. My wife and two chil dren.
bēōpārī:	tab tō tumhārā kunbā baṛā nahī̃.	Businessman:	Then your family is not large
tā̃gēvālā:	ghar-mẽ aur lōg-bhī haĩ.	Tongawala:	There are more people, too, i the house.
bēōpārī:	kaun kaun? [3]	Businessman:	Who?
tā̃gēvālā:	mērā bhāī, us-kī bīvī aur dō baccē.	Tongawala:	My brother, his wife and tw children.
bēōpārī:	kyā tumhẽ un-kā ḳhayāl-bhī rakhnā paṛtā hai?	Businessman:	Do you have to look afte them, too?
tā̃gēvālā:	mērā bhāī bīmār hai aur kām nahī̃ kar saktā.	Tongawala:	My brother is ill and canno work.
bēōpārī:	afsōs-kī bāt hai.	Businessman:	That's too bad.
tā̃gēvālā:	mērī mā̃-bhī hamārē sāth rahtī hai.	Tongawala:	My mother also lives with us
bēōpārī:	maĩ tumhẽ ḍēṛh rūpayā dū̃gā.	Businessman:	I will give you one and one half rupees.
tā̃gēvālā:	ye kāfī nahī̃, janāb. ḍhāī rūpayē dījiyē aur maĩ āp-kō fauran vahā̃ lē jāū̃gā.	Tongawala:	This is not enough, sir. Give (me) two and one-hal rupees and I will take yo there immediately.
bēōpārī:	ḍhāī rūpayē bahot haĩ. maĩ tumhẽ dō rūpayē dū̃gā. bas!	Businessman:	Two and one-half rupees is to much. I'll give you two rupees. That's all!
tā̃gēvālā:	bahot acchā, janāb. baiṭhiyē.	Tongawala:	Very well, sir. Please get in.
bēōpārī:	dihān dō! ehtiyāṭ-sē calāō.	Businessman:	Pay attention! Drive carefully.

REMARKS: (1) Variants are **kārōbārī, biznasmain** and **tājir.** (**tājir** also means **trader.**)

(2) Plural of ḳharj (ā). (cf. ḳharac (ā) **expenses.**)

(3) i.e., **which specific people.**

LESSON 15

15.1

maĩ likhū̃gā.	I (msc.) will write.
maĩ likhū̃gī.	I (fm.) will write.
vo likhēgā.	He will write.
vo likhēgī.	She will write.
ham likhē̃gē.	We (msc.) will write.
ham likhē̃gī.	We (fm.) will write.
tum likhōgē.	You (msc.) will write.
tum likhōgī.	You (fm.) will write.
āp likhē̃gē.	You (msc.) will write.
āp likhē̃gī.	You (fm.) will write.
vo likhē̃gē.	They (msc.) will write.
vo likhē̃gī.	They (fm.) will write.

This section is concerned with the formation of the future tense of the Urdu verb. This tense is made by attaching to the SUBJUNCTIVE forms the following suffixes: **-gā** for the masculine singular, **-gē** for the masculine plural, and **-gī** for the feminine singular and plural.

15.1.1 More examples are:

ādmī śahar-kō jāēgā.	The man will go to the city.
baccē āj iskūl jāē̃gē.	The children will go to school today.
kuttā vāpas āēgā.	The dog will come back.
laṛkī sāf karēgī.	The girl will clean.
aurtē̃ baccō̃-kō dēkhē̃gī.	The women will see the children.
laṛkā Hindī bōlnā cāhēgā.	The boy will want to speak Hindi.
kamzōr ādmī kōśiś karnā cāhē̃gē.	The weak men will want to try.
laṛkī Aṅgrēzī samajhnā cāhēgī.	The girl will want to understand English.

bīviyā̃ savāl pūchnā cāhē̃gī.	The wives will want to ask questions.
laṛkā Urdū bōl sakēgā.	The boy will be able to speak Urdu.
ādmī āj • rāt kām kar sakē̃gē.	The men will be able to work tonight.
laṛkī kal gā sakēgī.	The girl will be able to sing tomorrow.
aurtē̃ sabziyā̃ bēc sakē̃gī.	The women will be able to sell vegetables.
maĩ nastālīḳ paṛh sakū̃gā.	I will be able to read Nastalik.
machērā machliyā̃ bēcnē-kē liyē bāzār-kō jāēgā.	The fisherman will go to the bazaar to sell fish.
laṛkā aurtō̃-kē liyē pānī lāēgā.	The boy will bring water for the women.
laṛkī paudē-sē phūl tōṛēgī.	The girl will pluck flowers from the plant.
aurtē̃ pakānē-kē liyē sabziyā̃ ḳharīdē̃gī.	The women will buy vegetables to cook.
kyā laṛkā tālāb-kō calēgā?	Will the boy walk to the pond?
kyā aurat dukān-mē̃ kapṛā ḳharīdēgī?	Will the woman buy cloth in the shop?
kyā ādmī aḳhbār paṛhnā cāhēgā?	Will the man want to read the newspaper?
kyā baccā khēlnā cāhēgā?	Will the child want to play?
kyā sipāhī cōr-kō pakaṛ sakēgā?	Will the policeman be able to catch the thief?
kyā aurtē̃ khānā taiyār kar sakē̃gī?	Will the women be able to prepare the food?

Vocabulary Notes: **kamzōr** (adj.) weak, **kōśiś karnā** to try, to attempt, **kōśiś** (ī) attempt, **cōr** (ā) thief, **taiyār** (adj.) ready, prepared, **taiyār karnā** to prepare, **taiyār hōnā** to be prepared, **nastālīḳ** (ī) the Nastalik script, **sāf** (adj.) clean, clear, **sāf karnā** to clean, **sāf hōnā** to be clean, **sipāhī** (ā) policeman, **iskūl** (ā) school.

15.1.2 Exercise 1. **Translate into English:**

1. śikārī jaṅgal-mē̃ bahot jānvar mārē̃gē. 2. ham āp-kē sāth śahar-kō jāē̃gē. 3. machērā us daryā-mē̃ baṛī machliyā̃ pakaṛ sakēgā. 4. naukar musāfir-kē liyē ṭhaṇḍā pānī lāēgā. 5. mā̃ baccō̃-kō acchī kahāniyā̃ sunāēgī. 6. kisān daraḳht-kē nīcē kām kab karēgā? 7. kyā faḳīr āj masjid-kē sāmnē baiṭhē̃gē? 8. dhōbī ādmī-kē purānē kapṛē dhōnā cāhēgā. 9. laṛkā būṛhī aurat-kē liyē bhārī lakṛī lāēgā. 10. kyā vo tumhārē sāth Urdū-mē̃ bōl sakēgī? 11. maĩ āj • rāt tumhārē sāth bāzār jā sakū̃gā. 12. aurat har tarah-kī cīzē̃ ḳharīdnā cāhēgī. 13. bāp śahar-sē kab vāpas āēgā? 14. gāy daryā-kē pās carēgī. 15. kyā naukar Aṅgrēzī samajh sakē̃gē?

15.1.3 Exercise 2. **Translate into Urdu:**

1. I (**msc.**) will not be able to study tonight. 2. Will the student be able to read Nastalik? 3. My parents will eat in the restaurant on Tuesday. 4. Will you be able to work in the garden today? 5. The carpenter will want to cut the tree on Thursday. 6. Will you (**hon. msc.**) come to see us on Friday? 7. I (**msc.**) will speak in Urdu with the men. 8. When will the hunters kill the dreadful cheetah? 9. The servant will be able to understand English. 10. Will the weak farmer be able to work in the large field with the small plow? 11. The teacher will ask us difficult questions today. 12. The washerman will walk behind the donkey. 13. Will the washerman bring the clothes tonight? 14. The elephant will drag the heavy wood from the jungle to the river. 15. The fisherman will want to take the fish to sell (**them**) in the city.

15.2

maĩ āj iskūl-mē̃ hū̃gā.	I will be in school today.
vo makān-kē pīchē hōgā.	He will be behind the house.

vo us-mē̃ hōgī.	She will be in it.
ham un-kē pīchē hō̃gē.	We will be behind them.
tum śahar-mē̃ hōgē.	You will be in the city.
āp daftar-mē̃ hō̃gē.	You will be in the office.
vo bāg̲-mē̃ hō̃gī.	They will be in the garden.

This section presents the future of the verb **hōnā,** to become, to be, to exist, the subjunctive of which is obtained by dropping the future suffixes (**-gā, -gē, -gī**). Note that the subjunctive of the first person singular is **hōū̃,** which is replaced by **hū̃** in forming the future.

15.2.1

maī g̲arīb ādmī-kō paisē dū̃gā.	I will give money to the poor man.
vo ustād-kō javāb dēgā.	He will answer the teacher.
vo baccē-kō miṭhāī dēgī.	She will give candy to the child.
ham bhūkī aurat-kō rōṭī dē̃gē.	We will give bread to the hungry woman.
tum bāp-kō ak̲hbār dōgī.	You will give father the newspaper.
āp naukar-kō hukam dē̃gē.	You will give commands to the servant.
vo gāy-kō ghās dē̃gī.	They will give the cow grass.

This section presents the future tense of the verb **dēnā,** to give, which is formed by adding the future suffixes to the subjunctive.

15.2.2

maī mēz-sē nayā kāg̲az lū̃gā.	I will take fresh paper from the table.
vo baccē-sē śakkar lēgī.	She will take the sugar from the child.
vo laṛkī-sē pānī lēgā.	He will take water from the girl.
ham gāy-sē dūdh lē̃gē.	We will take milk from the cow.
tum bail-kī gardan-sē chōṭī ghaṇṭī lōgē.	You will take the little bell from the ox's neck.
āp ham-sē phūl lē̃gē.	You will take flowers from us.
vo cōr-sē nayī ghaṛī vāpas lē̃gī.	They will take back the new watch from the thief.

This section presents the future tense of the verb **lēnā,** to take, which is formed by adding the future suffixes to the subjunctive.

15.2.3 Vocabulary Notes:

kāg̲az (ā) paper, **gardan** (ī) neck, **g̲arīb** (adj.) poor, **ghaṛī** (ī) watch, **ghaṇṭī** (ī) bell, **miṭhāī** (ī) candy, sweets, **rōṭī** (ī) [unleavened] bread, **śakkar** (ā) sugar, **hukam** (ā) command, order, **hukam dēnā** to command, order, **hukam mānnā** to obey.

15.2.4 Exercise 1. **Translate into English:**

1. bāp miṭhāī k̲harīdnē-kē liyē paisē dēgā. 2. śāyad gāy darak̲ht-kē nīcē hō. 3. aurat acchē laṛkē-sē lakṛī-sē lakṛī lēgī. 4. sipāhī cōr-sē har tarah-kī cīzē̃ lēgā. 5. śāyad maī āj daftar-mē̃ hōū̃. 6. kuā̃ khētō̃-kē pās hōgā. 7. dōst mujhē kitābē̃ kab vāpas dēgā? 8. śāyad meharbān aurat g̲arīb ādmī-kō khānā dē. 9. cōr amīr ādmī-sē ghaṛī lēgā. 10. dhōbī naukar-sē kapṛē lēgā. 11. mā̃ baccē-kō garm dūdh dēgī. 12. būṛhē ādmī-kē pās kitābē̃ hō̃gī. 13. śāyad dhōbī āj dhōnē-kē liyē kapṛē lē. 14. tum mērē savāl-kē javāb kab dōgī? 15. aurat bēṭī-sē phūl lēgī. 16. ādmī chōṭē baccō̃-sē miṭhāī kyū̃ lēgā? 17. śāyad maī tum-kō ak̲hbār dū̃. 18. mā̃ bhūkē musāfir-kō rōṭī dēgī. 19. kyā laṛkē-kē pās ēk kuttā hōgā? 20. śāyad maī āj rāt āp-sē kitāb lū̃.

15.2.5 Exercise 2. **Translate into Urdu:**

1. There will be a bell on my ox's neck. 2. When will you (**msc.**) give back the candy to the child? 3. I may give you the newspaper. 4. The father will give the girl a handkerchief. 5. The child will take the cup of milk from the mother. 6. The dog may take the candy from the child. 7. The policeman will give back the watch to the rich man. 8. When will he be in the office? 9. He may be in the city tonight. 10. The carpenter will take the wood from the jungle. 11. The little girl will give the flowers to the father. 12. I may take the plates from the table. 13. The policeman will give orders to the servants. 14. The servant will take the sugar from the child. 15. The boy will give a cup of cold water to the thirsty traveller. 16. I may be in the house tomorrow. 17. The servant will show the man a room in the hotel. 18. The father will give all sorts of things to the children. 19. You may give the paper to the student. 20. The boy will take drinking water from the well.

15.3

laṛkā Urdū bōlnā pasand kartā hai.	The boy likes to speak Urdu.
bandar daraḳhtō̃-par caṛhnā pasand kartā hai.	The monkey likes to climb trees.
baccē tālāb-mē̃ tairnā pasand kartē haĩ.	The children like to swim in the tank.
maĩ safar karnā pasand kartā hū̃.	I like to travel.
vo kitābē̃ paṛhnā pasand kartā hai.	He likes to read books.
laṛkiyā̃ nayē kapṛē sīnā pasand kartī haĩ.	Girls like to sew new clothes.
baccē miṭhāī pasand kartē haĩ.	Children like candy.
laṛkā Urdū pasand kartā hai.	The boy likes Urdu.
billī dūdh pasand kartī hai.	The cat likes milk.
baccā billiyā̃ pasand kartā hai.	The child likes cats.
laṛkā bhāī-kō pasand kartā hai.	The boy likes his brother.

This section illustrates the Urdu equivalent of the English construction consisting of the words **like to** followed by a verb, or **like** followed by a noun. **pasand karnā** translates the English verb **to like.** These two words can be considered to function as a single verb with the second verb of the first English phrase placed in the infinitive form before it, or the noun of the second English phrase placed in the object form (before **-kō** when it indicates a rational being or animal).

Vocabulary Notes: **safar** (ā) journey, travel, **safar karnā** to travel.

15.3.1

laṛkā Urdū bōlnā zyādā pasand kartā hai.	The boy prefers to speak Urdu.
bandar daraḳhtō̃-par caṛhnā zyādā pasand kartā hai.	The monkey prefers to climb trees.
baccē tālāb-mē̃ tairnā zyādā pasand kartē haĩ.	The children prefer to swim in the tank.
maĩ safar karnā zyādā pasand kartā hū̃.	I prefer to travel.
vo kitābē̃ paṛhnā zyādā pasand kartā hai.	He prefers to read books.
laṛkiyā̃ nayē kapṛē sīnā zyādā pasand kartī haĩ.	Girls prefer sewing new clothes.
baccē miṭhāī zyādā pasand kartē haĩ.	Children prefer candy.
laṛkā Urdū zyādā pasand kartā hai.	The boy prefers Urdu.

billī dūdh zyādā pasand kartī hai.	The cat prefers milk.
baccā billiyā̃ zyādā pasand kartā hai.	The child prefers cats.

This section illustrates the Urdu equivalent of the English construction consisting of the words **prefer to** followed by a verb or noun. This construction is identical with that in 15.3, above, with one addition—the adverb **zyādā, more** is placed before **pasand karnā.**

15.3.2

laṛkā Angrēzī bōlnē-sē Urdū bōlnā zyādā pasand kartā hai.	The boy prefers speaking Urdu to speaking English.
bandar tālāb-mē̃ tairnē-sē daraḳhtō̃-par caṛhnā zyādā pasand kartā hai.	The monkey prefers climbing trees to swimming in the tank.
baccē ghar-mē̃ nahānē-sē tālāb-mē̃ tairnā zyādā pasand kartē haĩ.	The children prefer swimming in the tank to bathing at home.
maĩ ghar-mē̃ rahnē-sē safar karnā zyādā pasand kartā hū̃.	I prefer travelling to remaining at home.
laṛkiyā̃ pūrānē kapṛē sīnē-sē nayē kapṛē sīnā zyādā pasand kartī haĩ.	Girls prefer sewing new clothes to sewing old clothes.
baccē dūdh-sē miṭhāī zyādā pasand kartē haĩ.	Children prefer candy to milk.
laṛkā Angrēzī-sē Urdū zyādā pasand kartā hai.	The boy prefers Urdu to English.
baccā kuttō̃-sē billiyā̃ zyādā pasand kartā hai.	The child prefers cats to dogs.

This section illustrates the Urdu translation of the English construction indicating preference for one being, thing or action to another. This construction is identical with that described in 15.3.1, above, with one addition. Compare: **laṛkā Urdū bōlnā zyādā pasand kartā hai. The boy prefers to speak Urdu.** (or **The boy prefers speaking Urdu.**) and **laṛkā Angrēzī bōlnē-sē Urdū bōlnā zyādā pasand kartā hai. The boy prefers speaking Urdu to speaking English.** Note that the word or words introduced in the English phrase by the preposition **to** are placed in Urdu in the object form before the postposition **-sē.** The phrase indicating the thing not preferred (i.e., the **-sē** postpositional phrase) is normally placed in the utterance before the phrase indicating the thing preferred (i.e., before **Urdu bōlnā** in the example sentence).

15.3.3 Exercise 1. **Translate into English:**

1. maĩ ām pasand kartā hū̃. 2. naukar sōnā zyādā pasand kartā hai. 3. baccē kuttō̃-sē billiyā̃ zyādā pasand kartē haĩ. 4. kuttē haḍḍī zyādā pasand kartē haĩ. 5. ādmī kārḳhānē-mē̃ kām karnā zyādā pasand kartā hai. 6. ham sēbō̃-sē ām zyādā pasand kartē haĩ. 7. āp restorent-mē̃ khānā kyū̃ zyādā pasand karē̃gē? 8. gāyē̃ ghās zyādā pasand kartī haĩ. 9. musāfir pīnē-kā pānī zyādā pasand kartā hai. 10. maĩ nahānē-kē liyē ṭhaṇḍē pānī-sē garm pānī zyādā pasand kartā hū̃. 11. bāp kunbē-kē liyē kām karnā pasand kartē haĩ. 12. aurat mōṭargāṛī-sē śahar-kō jānā zyādā pasand kartī hai. 13. bandar miṭhē phal khānā pasand kartī haĩ. 14. āp Urdū-mē̃ bōlnā kyū̃ zyādā pasand kartē haĩ? 15. ham kām karnē-sē khēlnā zyādā pasand kartē haĩ. 16. billiyā̃ dūdh pīnā pasand kartī haĩ. 17. tālibilm Angrēzī paṛhnē-sē Urdū paṛhnā zyādā pasand kartā hai. 18. vo śahar jānē-sē hōṭel-mē̃ rahnā zyādā pasand kartē haĩ. 19. chōṭē baccē bāp-kē sāth śahar-kō jānā pasand kartē haĩ. 20. musāfir ghar-mē̃ rahnē-sē safar karnā zyādā pasand karēgā.

15.3.4 Exercise 2. **Translate into Urdu:**

1. The child likes dogs. 2. The father prefers to read the newspaper. 3. The traveller will prefer a large hotel room to a small room. 4. We (**msc.**) like food. 5. Mother prefers to stay at home. 6. The old farmer will prefer resting under the tree to working in the field. 7. Fish like water. 8. I (**fm.**) prefer resting in the hotel to swimming in the river. 9. The girl prefers to talk with (**her**) friends. 10. The boys like to swim. 11. The good student will prefer studying to playing with (**his**) friends. 12. The cow prefers to graze near the river. 13. We (**msc.**) like travelling by automobile. 14. The girls like to sew. 15. Mother prefers staying at home to travelling. 16. The fisherman prefers to sell the fish in the city. 17. I (**msc.**) will prefer to drink well-water. 18. The dog likes to swim with (**his**) master. 19. The gardener prefers sitting under the tree to watering the plants. 20. Snakes like milk.

15.4	**hōṭal-mẽ̄.**		**In the Hotel.**
musāfir:	**mujhē kamrā cāhiyē.**	Traveller:	**I wish to have a room.**
klark:	**kyā āp-kī rizarvēśan hai?**	Clerk:	**Do you have a reservation?**
musāfir:	**hā̃. mērī rizarvēśan hai.**	Traveller:	**Yes. I have a reservation.**
klark:	**āp-kā nām kyā hai?**	Clerk:	**What is your name?**
musāfir:	**mērā nām Mumtāz hai.**	Traveller:	**My name is Mumtāz.**
	maĩ-nē dō haftē huē likhā thā.		**I had written two weeks ago.**
klark:	**hā̃. ye hai āp-kā ḳhat.**	Clerk:	**Yes. Here is your letter.**
musāfir:	**kyā kamrā acchā hai?**	Traveller:	**Is the room good?**
klark:	**hā. kamrā acchā hai.**	Clerk:	**Yes. The room is good.**
	hamārē sab kamrē acchē haĩ.		**All our rooms are good.**
musāfir:	**kyā kamrē-mẽ̄ g̱usalḳhānā-bhī hai?**	Traveller:	**Does the room have a bath?**
klark:	**hā̃. kamrē-mẽ̄ g̱usalḳhānā hai.**	Clerk:	**Yes. The room has a bath.**
	sab kamrȭ-mẽ̄ g̱usalḳhānē haĩ.		**All the rooms have baths.**
	ye nayā hōṭal hai.		**This is a new hotel.**
musāfir:	**mērē kamrē-kā nambar kyā hai?**	Traveller:	**What is the number of my room?**
klark:	**āp-kē kamrē-kā nambar sāt sau caudā hai.**	Clerk:	**Your room number is 714.**
	naukar āp-kā sāmān vahā̃ lē jāẽgā.		**The servant will take your luggage there.**
	Jumman!		**Jumman!**
Jumman:	**jī, janāb.**	Jumman:	**Yes, sir.**
klark:	**in sāhab-kā sāmān kamrā nambar sāt sau caudā-mẽ̄ lē jāō.**	Clerk:	**Take the gentleman's luggage to 714.**
Jumman:	**bahot acchā.**	Jumman:	**Yes, sir.**
	[musāfir-sē] **mērē sāth āiyē, janāb.**		[to traveller] **Please come with me, sir.**
	[kamrē-kē pās] **ye hai āp-kā kamrā, janāb.**		[Near the room] **This is your room, sir.**
	andar ā jāiyē.		**Please come in.**
musāfir:	**mērā sāmān palañg-kē pās rakh dō.**	Traveller:	**Place my luggage near the bed.**

Jumman:	**bahot acchā. aur kuch?**	Jumman:	**Very well. Anything else?**
musāfir:	**hā̃. yahā̃ tauliyē nahī̃.**	Traveller:	**Yes. There are no towels here.**
	maī nahānā cāhtā hū̃.		**I wish to take a bath.**
Jumman:	**maī abhī lātā hū̃.**	Jumman:	**I'll bring** (towels) **immediately.**
	aur kuch?		**Anything else?**
musāfir:	**hā̃. ṭhaṇḍā pānī-bhī lānā.**	Traveller:	**Yes. Bring** (me) **cold water.**
Jumman:	**bahot acchā.**	Jumman:	**Very well.**
	[dō minaṭ-kē bād vāpas ātā hai.]		[He returns after two minutes.]
	yē lījiyē, tauliyē aur ṭhaṇḍā pānī.		**Here are the towels and the cold water.**
musāfir:	**bahot acchā. pānī mēz-par rakh dō.**	Traveller:	**Very good. Place the water on the table.**
Jumman:	**kyā maī khiṛkī khōl dū̃?**	Jumman:	**Shall I open the window?**
musāfir:	**hā̃. khiṛkī khōl dō.**	Traveller:	**Yes. Open the window.**
	yahā̃ bahot garmī hai.		**It is very warm in here.**
Jumman:	**bahot acchā. aur kuch?**	Jumman:	**Very good. Anything else?**
musāfir:	**nahī̃. abhī nahī̃.**	Traveller:	**No. Not now.**
Jumman:	**bahot acchā.**	Jumman:	**Very good.**
musāfir:	**ye lō.**	Traveller:	**Take this** (money).
Jumman:	**bahot bahot śukriyā, janāb.**	Jumman:	**Thank you very much, sir.**

LESSON 16

16.1 [9.1.3] **Translate into Urdu:**

1. The hunters kill animals in the jungles. 2. The monkeys run quickly in the high trees. 3. Big fish swim in the deep ocean. 4. We (**fm.**) work in the city. 5. The little boys want to swim in the deep river. 6. The hungry woman cooks food in the new pots. 7. The man goes slowly in the house. 8. We (**msc.**) want to pluck those fruits in the large garden. 9. The farmers bathe the elephant in the little river. 10. The men want to go into the small fields now.

16.2 [9.1.4] **Translate into English:**

1. kisān bāg-mē̃ khōdtā hai. 2. chōṭā laṛkā daryā-mē̃ machliyā̃ dēkhnā cāhtā hai. 3. baṛē kamrē-mē̃ dō mēzē̃ haĩ. 4. būṛhā ādmī ghanē jaṅgal-mē̃ lakṛī kāṭtā hai. 5. aurtē̃ dukān-mē̃ kapṛā kharīdnā cāhtī haĩ. 6. gahrē samundar-mē̃ bahot machliyā̃ haĩ. 7. chōṭē laṛkē ēk-sāth bāg-mē̃ khēlnā cāhtē haĩ. 8. khēt-mē̃ bhūkī gāy hai. 9. aurat sabziyā̃ nayī haṇḍiyā-mē̃ pakānā cāhtī hai. 10. bāzār-mē̃ choṭī dukānē̃ haĩ.

16.3 [9.2.3] **Translate into Urdu:**

1. The good boy brings wood to (**his**) mother. 2. Father reads (aloud) the book to the small children. 3. We (**msc.**) point out the long road to the man. 4. The wife sends food to the hungry farmer. 5. Mother points out the bad boy to father. 6. The girls give water to the mother. 7. The little girl gives flowers to (**her**) father. 8. The husband points out the stars to (**his**) wife. 9. The woman sends out ripe fruits to the children. 10. The farmer wants to drive the cows to the small field.

16.4 [9.2.4] **Translate into English:**

1. chōṭī laṛkī mā̃-kō pānī lānā cāhtī hai. 2. laṛkē būṛhē ādmī-kō ū̃cī imārat dikhātē haĩ. 3. ham bhūkē ādmī-kō khānā dēnā cāhtē haĩ. 4. ādmī kisānõ-kō śahar dikhātē haĩ. 5. bāp bēṭī-kō chōṭā tōtā dētā hai. 6. bhūkā kisān bīvī-kō sabziyā̃ lātā hai. 7. mā̃ bāp-kō burē bēṭē-kō bhējtī hai. 8. laṛkā ustād • sāhab-kō phūl dētā hai. 9. ādmī śikārī-kō śēr dikhātē haĩ. 10. bahan mā̃-kō chōṭē bhāī-kō lātī hai.

16.5 [9.3.3] **Translate into Urdu:**

1. The boy places the pen on the books. 2. The servant places the load on the ground. 3. The bad boy pours water on (**his**) sister. 4. The little children want to play on the roof. 5. The servant places the plates on the table. 6. The boy wants to sit on the branch. 7. The man drops the load on the road. 8. The washerman wants to place the clothes on the ground. 9. The woman pours water on the plants. 10. The man wants to sleep on the bed.

16.6 [9.3.4] **Translate into English:**

1. ham chat-par khēlnā cāhtē haĩ. 2. parindē śākḥ-par baiṭhnā cāhtē haĩ. 3. ādmī chat-par palañg rakhtā hai. 4. naukar tasvīr divār-par laṭkātā hai. 5. aurat pakkē phal mēz-pār rakhtī hai. 6. saṛak-par dō makān haĩ. 7. laṛkā zamīn-par ghās rakhtā hai. 8. kuttā zamīn-par sōtā hai. 9. chat-par bandar hai. 10. aurat rakābiyā̃ mēz-par rakhtī hai.

16.7 [9.4.3] **Translate into Urdu:**

1. We (**msc.**) ask them questions. 2. They (**msc.**) want to take the fruit from the children. 3. The washerman brings the clothes from the river. 4. The cow eats the fruit from the bushes. 5. The farmer wants to strike the monkeys with a stick. 6. The thirsty man takes water from the good boy. 7. The traveller comes from the city. 8. The woman brings vegetables from the field. 9. The man ties the grass with a rope. 10. The teacher wants to ask me questions.

16.8 [9.4.4] **Translate into English:**

1. ustād • sāhab laṛkē-sē savāl pūchtē haĩ. 2. chōṭā kisān baṛē bail-kō chaṛī-sē mārtā hai. 3. ādmī lakṛī rassē-sē bā̃dhtā hai. 4. pyāsā musāfir mujh-sē pānī lētā hai. 5. aurat gāy bāg-sē bulātī hai. 6. ham kuē̃-sē pānī lētī haĩ. 7. bhūkā kisān khēt-sē ātā hai. 8. vo burē bakrē-kō rassē-sē bā̃dhnā cāhtē haĩ. 9. mā̃ mujh-sē savāl pūchtī hai. 10. bhūkā kuttā baccē-sē khānā chīntā hai.

16.9 [10.1.3] **Translate into Urdu:**

1. The child is behind the door. 2. The women speak together behind the well. 3. The mother runs after the little child. 4. The cat goes after the girl. 5. The wife walks behind the husband. 6. We (**msc.**) go after them. 7. The traveller sits behind that tree. 8. The fox seizes the hen behind the well. 9. The farmer goes behind the plow. 10. The hungry dog walks behind the little child.

16.10 [10.1.4] **Translate into English:**

1. darakht-kē pīchē gāy hai. 2. aurat kuē̃-kē pīchē nahātī hai. 3. daryā śahar-kē pīchē hai. 4. chōṭā laṛkā bāp-kē pīchē caltā hai. 5. ham ū̃cē darakht-kē pīchē baiṭhtī haĩ. 6. mālī makān-kē pīchē kām kartā hai. 7. aurat tasvīr darvāzē-kē pīchē rakhtī hai. 8. bēṭā bāp-kē pīchē caltā hai. 9. naukar bāg-kē pīchē zamīn khōdtā hai. 10. ghar-kē pīchē bāg hai.

16.11 [10.2.2] **Translate into Urdu:**

1. The woman ties the cow under the tree. 2. The cat runs under the house. 3. The lion drags the little donkey under the bridge. 4. The servant places the shoes under the bed. 5. Under the house lives a big snake. 6. The farmer ties the hungry oxen under the trees. 7. The child plays under the table. 8. The farmer wants to sleep under the tree. 9. The long snake goes under the house. 10. There is a fat cow under the bridge.

16.12 [10.2.3] **Translate into English:**

1. bail darakht-kē nīcē ṭhahartē haĩ. 2. laṛkā mēz-kē nīcē kitāb girātā hai. 3. ham baṛē jānvar pul-kē nīcē dēkhtē haĩ. 4. bail kisān-kō darakht-kē nīcē khī̃ctē haĩ. 5. kuttā ū̃cē darakht-kē nīcē sōnā cāhtā hai. 6. bhūkī billī mēz-kē nīcē khānā khātī hai. 7. dublī gāy darakht-kē nīcē ārām kartī hai. 8. darakht-kē nīcē pakkē phal haĩ. 9. machērā pul-kē nīcē machliyā̃ pakaṛnā cāhtā hai. 10. chōṭī laṛkiyā̃ darakht-kē nīcē khēlnā cāhtī haĩ.

16.13 [10.3.2] **Translate into Urdu:**

1. The father plays with the children. 2. The mother speaks with (**her**) daughters. 3. The boy lives in the small house with (**his**) old mother. 4. The daughter runs home with (**her**) brothers. 5. The woman goes to the bazaar with the servant. 6. The boy sits on the roof with (**his**) friends. 7. The man goes to the city with the servant. 8. The boy

goes to the field with (**his**) father. 9. The big boy swims in the river with (**his**) friends. 10. Mother comes from the bazaar with the women.

16.14 [10.3.3] **Translate into English:**

1. laṛkā bhāī-kē sāth khēt-kō jātā hai. 2. kisān bēṭō̃-kē sāth śahar-kō jātā hai. 3. baccē dōstō̃-kē sāth chat-par khēltē haĩ. 4. aurat bēṭī-kē sāth ghar-mẽ pakātī hai. 5. mālī baccō̃-kē sāth bāg-mẽ jātā hai. 6. mā̃ baccē-kē sāth khēltī hai. 7. bēṭī mā̃-kē sāth ghar-mẽ kām kartī hai. 8. naukar aurat-kē sāth bāzār jātā hai. 9. chōṭī laṛkī bahan-kē sāth bāg-mẽ khēltī hai. 10. laṛkī dōstō̃-kē sāth bāzār jātī hai.

16.15 [10.4.2] **Translate into Urdu:**

1. The man sells many things in front of the shop. 2. There is a field in front of the river. 2. The woman places flowers in front of the holy man. 4. The automobile stops in front of the building. 5. The little boy runs in front of (**his**) father. 6. The gardener works in front of the house. 7. The hunter kills the wolf in front of the jungle. 8. The hungry woman grabs the chicken in front of the garden. 9. In front of the house there is a high tree. 10. The girl wants to play in front of the house.

16.16 [10.4.3] **Translate into English:**

1. fakīr daryā-kē sāmnē baiṭhtā hai. 2. aurat kuẽ-kē sāmnē hai. 3. mā̃ baccē-kē sāmnē phal rakhtī hai. 4. chōṭī laṛkī ghar-kē sāmnē khēltī hai. 5. ham masjid-kē sāmnē khēlnā cāhtē haĩ. 6. ū̃cī imārat-kē sāmnē chōṭī dukān hai. 7. naukar ghar-kē sāmnē baiṭhtē haĩ. 8. laṛkā ustād-kē sāmnē baiṭhtā hai. 9. śahar-kē sāmnē ghanā jaṅgal hai. 10. mālī makān-kē sāmnē ārām karnā cāhtā hai.

16.17 [11.1.2] **Translate into Urdu:**

1. The woman speaks with the shopkeeper near the shop. 2. The servant waits near the office. 3. The thirsty ox stops near the well. 4. The boy swims near the bridge. 5. The man bathes the big elephant near the river. 6. The little girls play together near the house. 7. There is a deep well near the road. 8. We (**msc.**) want to play together near the mosque 9. The trolley stops near the bridge. 10. The thirsty cow waits near the river.

16.18 [11.1.3] **Translate into English:**

1. mālī kuẽ-kē pās kām kartā hai. 2. aurat dukān-kē pās ṭhahartī hai. 3. chōṭē laṛkē masjid-kē pās khēltē haĩ. 4. pyāsā kuttā kuẽ-kē pās hai. 5. masjid-kē pās fakīr hai. 6. ham dōstō̃-kē sāth pul-kē pās khēlnā cāhtē haĩ. 7. chōṭī laṛkiyā̃ mā̃-kē pās sōnā cāhtī haĩ. 8. baṛā ū̃ṭ ū̃cē darakht-kē pās sōnā cāhtā hai. 9. mā̃ dōstō̃-kē sāth daryā-kē pās bōltī hai. 10. bhūkā ghōṛā ghās-kē pās ruknā cāhtā hai.

16.19 [11.2.3] **Translate into Urdu:**

1. The woman has a handkerchief. 2. The student has two books. 3. The shopkeeper has very fresh mangoes. 4. The daughters have new saris. 5. The teacher has a small house. 6. The farmers have plows. 7. Father has a newspaper. 8. The woman has new cooking-pots. 9. The man has an automobile. 10. The farmer has two oxen.

16.20 [11.2.4] **Translate into English:**

1. aurat-kē pās das murgiyā̃ haĩ. 2. baccē-kē pās nayī gẽd hai. 3. ādmī-kē pās nayī mōṭargāṛī hai. 4. un-kē pās baṛā makān hai. 5. aurat-kē pās gāy hai. 6. dhōbī-kē pās gadhā hai. 7. us-kē pās nayā hal hai. 8. laṛkiyō̃-kē pās bahot cūṛiyā̃ haĩ. 9. dukāndār-kē pās bahot cīzẽ haĩ. 10. khātūn-kē pās bahot sāṛiyā̃ haĩ.

16.21 [11.3.3] **Translate into Urdu:**

1. The servant brings water for bathing to the traveller. 2. The teacher gives the student a book to read. 3. The boy cuts wood for the mother. 4. The farmer draws water for the

thirsty oxen. 5. The mother buys bangles for (**her**) daughters. 6. The man goes to the tank to bathe with (**his**) sons. 7. The woman cooks food for the family. 8. The lady goes to the bazaar with (**her**) daughters to buy saris. 9. The daughter runs to the well to bring water. 10. We (**msc.**) want to ask for food (**to eat**).

16.22 [11.3.4] **Translate into English:**

1. laṛkē dōstõ-kē sāth khēlnē-kē liyē bāhar jātē haĩ. 2. bhūkē baccē khānē-kē liyē andar ānā cāhtē haĩ. 3. bandar daraḳhtõ-sē phal tōṛnē-kē liyē bāg-mẽ jānā cāhtē haĩ. 4. ham paṛhnē-kē liyē ēk nayī kitāb mā̃gtī haĩ. 5. mā̃ chōṭē laṛkē-kē liyē khilaunā ḳharīdtī hai. 6. kisān dō bailõ-kō khānē-kē liyē ghās dētā hai. 7. dhōbī dhōnē-kē liyē tālāb-mẽ kapṛē ḍāltā hai. 8. arḍalī sāhab-kē paṛhnē-kē kitāb ḳharīdtā hai. 9. ādmī śahar-mẽ kunbē-kē liyē kām kartā hai. 10. aurat khēt-sē pakānē-kē liyē sabziyā̃ lātī hai.

16.23 [11.4.2] **Translate into Urdu:**

1. The well is sweet. (lit: = **The water of the well is sweet.**) 2. The strong farmer pulls the small donkey. 3. The happy woman places food in front of (**her**) husband. 4. The hunter kills the dreadful animal. 5. The farmer buys a red sari for the beautiful daughter. 6. The sister places the sick child on the bed. 7. The sleepy servant sleeps in the corner. 8. The boy brings the heavy wood for the women. 9. The rich man gives food to the sad boy. 10. I (**msc.**) ask for warm water. 11. The beautiful girl brings the clean shirt. 12. The woman ties the white cow under the tree. 13. There is a round table in the corner. 14. The kind woman feeds grass to the hungry ox. 15. The rich man has many houses.

16.24 [11.4.3] **Translate into English:**

1. kisān ḳhũḳhār bāgh-kō mārnā cāhtā hai. 2. ḳhuś laṛkī lāl sāṛī ḳharīdtī hai. 3. mā̃ lāl murgī-kō khilānā cāhtī hai. 4. safēd gāy bāg-mẽ hai. 5. us gōl mēz-kō bāhar lāiyē. 6. hanḍiyā-mẽ garm pānī hai. 7. dōst bīmār aurat-kō khānā lātī hai. 8. udās laṛkī gahrē kuẽ-kē pās rōtī hai. 9. laṛkē badmāś cōr-kō dikhātē haĩ. 10. dhōbī sāf kapṛē lātā hai. 11. aurat sar-par bhārī lakṛī rakhtī hai. 12. chōṭā ādmī mazbūt gadhē-kē pīchē caltā hai. 13. daryā-kē pās safēd ghōṛā hai. 14. meharbān aurat bhūkē ādmī-kō khānā dētī hai. 15. amīr ādmī-kē pās bahot dōst haĩ.

16.25 [11.5.3] **Translate into Urdu:**

1. Does the cat catch that small mouse? 2. Do the hungry monkeys want to steal those fruits? 3. Are those small children hungry? 4. Do those women want to bathe the children? 5. Does the woman cook these vegetables? 6. Does this small horse want to drink? 7. Does the woman want to make the thirsty cow drink? 8. Does the good woman feed the small children too much? 9. Does the bad-tempered cat bite the woman there? 10. Does the farmer tie the oxen? 11. Do you (**fm.**) call the girls in? 12. Do fathers understand children sometimes? 13. Does the servant understand me? 14. Are the cooking-pots good? 15. Is the horse big? 16. Is there coal in the ground? 17. Are there animals in the jungles? 18. Do the small boys want to swim in the deep river? 19. Does the washerman send the man the clothes? 20. Does the gardener pour water on the plant? 21. Does the farmer till the field with the plow? 22. Is there a garden behind the house? 23. Does the farmer rest under the tree? 24. Does the boy speak with the women? 25. Does the hunter kill the dreadful animal?

16.26 [11.5.4] **Translate into English:**

1. kyā laṛkiyā̃ ḳhuś haĩ? 2. kyā sabziyā̃ acchī haĩ? 3. kyā jaghẽ chōṭī haĩ? 4. kyā pyāsē

ghōṛē pīnā cāhtē haī? 5. kyā ādmī andar kām kartā hai? 6. kyā chōṭē baccē bāhar jānā cāhtē haī? 7. kyā laṛkā us-kō māntā hai? 8. kyā ustād laṛkē-kō paṛhātē haī? 9. kyā machērā machliyā̃ pakaṛnā cāhtā hai? 10. kyā mā̃ bēṭiyō̃-kō zyādā khilātī hai? 11. kyā ādmī hāthī nahlānā cāhtā hai?. 12. kyā bandar vahā̃ phal khātā hai? 13. kyā aurat dukān-mẽ cīzẽ k̤harīdnā cāhtī hai? 14. kyā ghōṛī kaccī sabziyā̃ jaldī-sē khātī hai? 15. kyā ye pyāsā bail kabhī kabhī ṭhaharnā cāhtā hai? 16. kyā kuttā is baccē-kō bāhar khī̃ctā hai? 17. kyā ye imārat ū̃cī hai? 18. kyā ye ū̃cī imārat hai? 19. kyā āsmān-mẽ tārē haī? 20. kyā gahrē samundar-mẽ machliyā̃ haī? 21. kyā mā̃ baccō̃-kō kahāniyā̃ sunātī hai? 22. kyā mālī paudō̃-par pānī ḍāltā hai? 23. kyā machērā pul-kē pās machliyā̃ pakaṛtā hai? 24. kyā śahar-kē pīchē jaṅgal hai? 25. kyā bhūkē baccē khānē-kē liyē andar ānā cāhtē haī?

16.27 [12.1.3] **Translate into Urdu:**

1. Where do they (**msc.**) come from? 2. When do the children play with other children? 3. Why does the mother buy red shoes for (**her**) daughter? 4. Why does the bad boy pour water on (**his**) sister? 5. When does the hunter kill the dreadful animal? 6. Why does the farmer want to beat the monkeys with a stick? 7. Why does the teacher give the student a book to read? 8. From where do the monkeys steal ripe fruits? 9. When does the woman pour water on the plants? 10. When does the traveller come from the city? 11. Where is the coal? 12. Why does the traveller ask for water? 13. When does the washerman send the clothes to the man? 14. Where is the newspaper? 15. Why does the ox stop near the well? 16. Where does the servant place the dishes? 17. From where does the washerman bring the clothes? 18. Why does the strong farmer drag the small donkey? 19. When does the servant bring cold water to (**his**) master? 20. Where does the dreadful tiger live?

16.28 [12.1.4] **Translate into English:**

1. ādmī kām kab kartā hai? 2. laṛkā bhūkā kyū̃ hai? 3. jānvar jaṅgal-sē kab ātē haī? 4. laṛkē mā̃-kē liyē lakṛī kahā̃-sē lātē haī? 5. aurat kahā̃ pakānā cāhtī hai? 6. ādmī mōṭargāṛī-kē liyē pānī kyū̃ lātā hai? 7. machērā machliyā̃ kab pakaṛtā hai? 8. tum paṛhnā kyū̃ cāhtē hō? 9. ṭrām kahā̃ ruktī hai? 10. bail darak̤t-kē nīcē kyū̃ ṭhahartā hai? 11. mā̃ kab pakātī hai? 12. aurat daryā-kē pās kyū̃ rōtī hai? 13. dhōbī kapṛē kahā̃ dhōtā hai? 14. gāṛī kyū̃ ruktī hai? 15. pīr darak̤ht-kē nīcē kab baiṭhtē haī? 16. gāy ghās kab khānā cāhtī hai? 17. jānvar kahā̃-sē ātā hai? 18. abbā śahar-sē vāpas kyū̃ ātā hai? 19. meharbān aurat fak̤īrō̃-kō khānā kab dētī hai? 20. naukar musāfir-kē liyē pānī kahā̃-sē lātā hai?

16.29 [12.2.1] **Translate into Urdu:**

1. Can the man work for the large family? 2. The woman can buy vegetables to cook. 3. The boy can cut wood for the mother. 4. Can the traveller speak Urdu with the man? 5. We (**msc.**) can show the man the river. 6. The gardener can pour water on the plants. 7. The fisherman can catch fish from the river. 8. The farmer can till the field with the plow. 9. The girl can bring the cooking-pot quickly. 10. The mechanic can work under the automobile.

16.30 [12.2.2] **Translate into English:**

1. dhōbī kapṛē kahā̃ dhō saktā hai? 2. laṛkā aurat-kē liyē lakṛī kab lā saktā hai? 3. kyā machērā bāzār-mẽ bēcnē-kē liyē machliyā̃ pakaṛ saktā hai? 4. laṛkē badmāś cōr-kō dikhā saktē haī. 5. meharbān aurat bhūkē ādmī-kō khānā dē saktī hai. 6. k̤huś laṛkī nayī lāl sāṛī k̤harīd saktī hai. 7. ham Urdū paṛh saktē haī. 8. laṛkiyā̃ dōstō̃-kē sāth khēlnē-kē

liyē bāhar jā saktī haī. 9. aurat pakānē-kē liyē sabziyā̃ ādmī-sē ḳharīd saktī hai. 10. laṛkā pul-kē nīcē tair saktā hai.

16.31 [12.3.1] **Translate into Urdu:**

1. I (**msc.**) do not eat. 2. They (**fm.**) do not jump. 3. You (**fm.**) do not understand. 4. We (**msc.**) do not drink. 5. You (**msc. hon.**) do not read. 6. I (**msc.**) do not say. 7. We (**fm.**) do not swim. 8. She does not play. 9. You (**msc.**) do not speak. 10. You (**hon. fm.**) do not run. 11. The dog does not drink. 12. The calves do not eat. 13. The child does not run. 14. The wives do not bring. 15. The hen does not eat. 16. The brother does not give. 17. The elephants do not bathe. 18. The army does not run. 19. The cow does not eat. 20. The sparrows do not fly.

16.32 [12.3.2] **Translate into English:**

1. ham nahī̃ khātē. 2. tum nahī̃ khēltē. 3. vo nahī̃ dauṛtā. 4. āp nahī̃ samajhtē. 5. maī nahī̃ jātī. 6. āp nahī̃ pakātē. 7. vo nahī̃ khōdtī. 8. vo nahī̃ bōltē. 9. vo nahī̃ dēkhtī̃. 10. maī nahī̃ paṛhtā. 11. ādmī nahī̃ caltā. 12. laṛkē nahī̃ khēltē. 13. billī nahī̃ pītī. 14. laṛkiyā̃ nahī̃ bōltī̃. 15. buṛhiyā̃ nahī̃ sōtī̃. 16. aurtē̃ nahī̃ bōltī̃. 17. ādmī nahī̃ dēkhtē. 18. bīvī nahī̃ samajhtī. 19. bēṭiyā̃ nahī̃ sōtī̃. 20. baccā nahī̃ khātā.

16.33 [12.4.1] **Translate into Urdu:**

1. He does not want to eat. 2. The boys do not want to send. 3. The mare does not want to drink. 4. I (**fm.**) do not want to go. 5. The parrots do not want to speak. 6. They (**fm.**) do not want to eat. 7. The wife does not want to cook. 8. We (**msc.**) do not want to study. 9. The fish do not want to eat. 10. You (**msc.**) do not want to send.

16.34 [12.4.2] **Translate into English:**

1. baccē khēlnā nahī̃ cāhtē. 2. ham paṛhnā nahī̃ cāhtē. 3. laṛkiyā̃ bōlnā nahī̃ cāhtī̃. 4. kuttā khānā nahī̃ cāhtā. 5. aurat pakānā nahī̃ cāhtī. 6. maī khēlnā nahī̃ cāhtī. 7. ādmī khōdnā nahī̃ cāhtā. 8. abbā sunnā nahī̃ cāhtā. 9. vo bōlnā nahī̃ cāhtī. 10. tum dēnā nahī̃ cāhtā.

16.35 [12.5.1] **Translate into Urdu:**

1. She is not hungry. 2. The daughters are not good. 3. The shoe is not small. 4. I (**msc.**) am not old. 5. The horse is not big. 6. The cat is not bad. 7. You (**msc.**) are not big. 8. The fox is not cunning. 9. The children are not thirsty. 10. You (**hon. fm.**) are not thirsty.

16.36 [12.5.2] **Translate into English:**

1. ghōṛē būṛhē nahī̃ haī. 2. maī dublā nahī̃ hū̃. 3. machliyā̃ chōṭī nahī̃. 4. vo pyāsī nahī̃. 5. gadhē burē nahī̃. 6. vo pyāsī nahī̃ hai. 7. laṛkī ḳhuś nahī̃ hai. 8. makkhiyā̃ chōṭī nahī̃. 9. bēṭiyā̃ bhūkī nahī̃. 10. maī ḳhābīdā nahī̃ hū̃.

16.37 [12.6.1] **Translate into Urdu:**

1. We (**msc.**) do not live here. 2. The woman does not speak slowly. 3. You (**msc.**) do not go out. 4. The women do not cook inside. 5. The elephant does not eat too much. 6. The little child does not come after. 7. The hungry mare does not want to stop. 8. The lean women do not want to eat immediately. 9. The big man does not want to eat quickly. 10. The small children do not want to go out.

16.38 [12.6.2] **Translate into English:**

1. bhāī ēk-sāth nahī̃ khātē. 2. aurat andar nahī̃ ātī. 3. laṛkē āhistā āhistā nahī̃ bōltē. 4. gāyē̃ bahot ḳhuś nahī̃. 5. acchī laṛkiyā̃ bāhar nahī̃ jātī̃. 6. bhūkī aurtē̃ āhistā nahī̃ khātī̃. 7. vo yahā̃ ānā nahī̃ cāhtī̃. 8. baṛē laṛkē andar khēlnā nahī̃ cāhtē. 9. maī kabhī kabhī khēlnā nahī̃ cāhtī. 10. pyāsī ghōṛī āhistā pīnā nahī̃ cāhtī.

16.39 [13.1.1] **Translate into Urdu:**

1. The man does not see them. 2. The women do not hear him. 3. The mothers do not call us. 4. The donkey does not drag the girl. 5. I do not want to feed the horses. 6. The cow does not feed the calves quickly. 7. The child does not seize the cat. 8. We (**fm.**) do not buy fish. 9. I (**fm.**) do not bring food. 10. The little woman does not feed the hens. 11. The cat does not eat the fish slowly. 12. The hungry dog does not bite the bullock. 13. The old farmer does not want to tie the cows here. 14. The monkeys do not want to eat ripe fruit. 15. They (**fm.**) do not buy an old picture here. 16. The sister does not want to call in these hungry boys. 17. He does not throw the wood in the fire. 18. We (**msc.**) do not work in the city. 19. The servant does not point out the road to the traveller. 20. The woman does not hang pictures on the walls.

16.40 [13.1.2] **Translate into English:**

1. ham bhūkē kuttē-kō nahī̃ khilātē. 2. bandar pakkē phal nahī̃ khātā. 3. būṛhā kisān baṛē ghōṛō̃-kō nahī̃ calātā. 4. mā̃ bhūkē baccō̃-kō yahā̃ bulānā nahī̃ cāhtī. 5. acchī aurat chōṭē laṛkō̃-kō zyādā nahī̃ khilātī. 6. ḳhuś ādmī machliyā̃ pakaṛnā nahī̃ cāhtā. 7. kisān zamīn-mē̃ nahī̃ khōdtā. 8. aurat nayī haṇḍiyā-mē̃ sabziyā̃ pakānā nahī̃ cāhtī. 9. ādmī śikārī-kō śēr nahī̃ dikhātē. 10. naukar divār-par tasvīrē̃ nahī̃ laṭkātā. 11. bhūkā kuttā baṛē baccē-sē khānā nahī̃ chīntā. 12. mālī makān-kē pīchē kām nahī̃ kartā. 13. machērā pul-kē nīcē machliyā̃ pakaṛnā nahī̃ cāhtā. 14. naukar aurat-kē sāth bāzār nahī̃ jātā. 15. faḳīr ghar-kē sāmnē nahī̃ baiṭhtā. 16. ghar-kē pās kuā̃ nahī̃. 17. dhōbī-kē pās gadhā nahī̃. 18. ādmī kunbē-kē liyē śahar-mē̃ kām nahī̃ kartā. 19. kisān-kē pās hal nahī̃. 20. baccē makān-kē sāmnē nahī̃ haī.

16.41 [13.2.1] **Translate into Urdu:**

1. Doesn't this small horse want to drink? 2. Doesn't the cat catch that mouse? 3. Doesn't the farmer tie the oxen? 4. Doesn't a father ever understand children? 5. Doesn't the hunter kill the dreadful animal? 6. Isn't there a garden behind the house? 7. Doesn't the farmer till the field with the plow? 8. Doesn't the washerman send the clothes to the man? 9. Aren't there animals in the jungle? 10. Doesn't the woman cook these vegetables?

16.42 [13.2.2] **Translate into English:**

1. kyā sabziyā̃ acchī nahī̃? 2. kyā ādmī andar kām nahī̃ kartā? 3. kyā daryā-mē̃ machliyā̃ nahī̃ haī? 4. kyā ghōṛā pīnā nahī̃ cāhtā? 5. kyā āsmān-mē̃ tārē nahī̃? 6. kyā mā̃ baccō̃-kō kahāniyā̃ nahī̃ sunātī? 7. kyā aurat bāzār-mē̃ cīzē̃ ḳharīdnā nahī̃ cāhtī? 8. kyā machērā daryā-sē machliyā̃ nahī̃ lātā? 9. kyā mēz-par kitāb nahī̃? 10. kyā baccā bhūkā nahī̃?

16.43 [13.3.1] **Translate into Urdu:**

1. When doesn't a child play with other children? 2. Why doesn't the traveller ask for water? 3. When doesn't a father kiss (**his**) children? 4. Why doesn't the gardener pour water on the plants? 5. Why doesn't the hunter kill the dreadful animal? 6. From where doesn't the monkey steal ripe fruit? 7. Why doesn't the farmer come from the field? 8. When doesn't a dog sleep? 9. Why doesn't the washerman wash the clothes for the man? 10. When doesn't the teacher give the student a book to read?

16.44 [13.3.2] **Translate into English:**

1. ādmī mōṭargāṛī-kē liyē pānī kyū̃ nahī̃ lātā? 2. baccā bhūkā kab nahī̃? 3. bail kahā̃ nahī̃ sōtā? 4. meharbān aurat faḳīr-kō khānā kab nahī̃ dētī? 5. dhōbī kapṛē kyū̃ nahī̃ lātā?

6. ũṭ ghās khānē-kē liyē nahī̃ ṭhahartā? 7. gāṛī kyũ nahī̃ ruktī? 8. laṛkā kuē̃-sē kyũ vāpas nahī̃ ātā? 9. baccē ghar-mē̃ kyũ nahī̃ haī? 10. gāy daraḳht-kē pās kyũ nahī̃ hai?

16.45 [13.4.1] **Translate into Urdu:**

1. The boy cannot bring the heavy wood. 2. Can't the washerman send the man the clothes? 3. Why can't the hunter kill the dreadful animal? 4. The servant cannot cut the wood for the woman. 5. The gardener cannot pour water on the plants. 6. The mechanic cannot work under the automobile. 7. The fisherman cannot catch fish from the river. 8. Can't the woman speak Urdu? 9. The monkey cannot seize the ripe fruit. 10. The woman cannot hang pictures on the walls.

16.46 [13.4.2] **Translate into English:**

1. aurat kunbē-kē liyē nahī̃ pakā saktī. 2. macherā śahar-kō machliyā̃ nahī̃ lā saktā. 3. ādmī mōṭargāṛī-kē liyē pānī nahī̃ lā saktā. 4. tum musāfir-kō saṛak kyũ nahī̃ dikhā saktē? 5. kisān chōṭē hal-sē zamīn-mē̃ nahī̃ khōd saktā. 6. maī āp-kē sāth bāzār nahī̃ jā saktī. 7. mā̃ baccō̃-kō kahāniyā̃ nahī̃ sunā saktī. 8. aurat dhōnē-kē liyē kapṛē tālāb-kō nahī̃ lē saktī. 9. cōr bachṛē-kō nahī̃ curā saktā. 10. dhōbī ādmī-kē liyē kapṛē kyũ nahī̃ dhō saktā?

16.47 [13.5.4] **Translate into Urdu:**

1. Where is your motorcycle? 2. Our father is a farmer. 3. The children play in your oxcart. 4. My sisters want to play near the tank. 5. Is this house yours? 6. Your answers are not exact. 7. The servant does not know my friend. 8. My brothers play in the street. 9. Why does your teacher ask difficult questions? 10. Our cat wants to drink warm milk. 11. The mechanic does not work under my automobile. 12. The dog wants to bite your brother. 13. This is not my house. 14. Is your father at home? 15. I cannot speak Urdu with your mother. 16. Your ox grazes in my garden. 17. Is that boy your brother.? 18. Please bring my cap. 19. Why do you (**hon. msc.**) want to speak with my father? 20. The good boy gives our brothers fruit.

16.48 [13.5.5] **Translate into English:**

1. hamārā ghar us galī-mē̃ hai. 2. mērī mōṭargāṛī-kē liyē pānī lāiyē. 3. tumhārī gāy hamārē khēt-mē̃ kyũ cartī hai? 4. tumhārī bahnē̃ mērī bahan-kē sāth bāt karnā cāhtī haī. 5. ye mērā makān hai. 6. ye makān mērā hai. 7. kyā tumhārē abbā hamārē abbā-kō jāntē haī? 8. mērī ṭōpī lāiyē. 9. kyā mērī mōṭargāṛī ghar-kē sāmnē hai? 10. tumhārā naukar mujhē nahī̃ jāntā. 11. maī tumhārē dōstō̃-kē sāth nahī̃ bōl saktā. 12. hamārē bail nayē pul-kē nīcē cartē haī. 13. meharbān aurat tumhārī bhūkī gāy-kō ghās dētī hai. 14. vo tumhārā khēt nahī̃ hai. 15. bahan hamārē kuē̃-sē pānī vāpas lātī hai. 16. vo dukān mērī hai. 17. kārīgar tumhārī mōṭargāṛī-kē nīcē kām karnā nahī̃ cāhtā. 18. tumhārē abbā śahar-kō kab ātē haī. 19. mērā bhāī khēlnē-kē liyē bāhar jānā nahī̃ cāhtā. 20. kyā tumhārā bāp dukāndār hai?

16.49 [14.2.2] **Translate into Urdu:**

1. His automobile is in front of the house. 2. The father gives fruit to the boy's brother. 3. The children walk behind the washerman's donkey. 4. The boy brings water for your automobile. 5. The woman wants to buy all kinds of things. 6. Is his father a mechanic? 7. Why does the boy beat the farmer's horse with a stick? 8. Mother goes to the city with the little boy's sister. 9. This is his cap. 10. The big cow eats vegetables in the old farmer's field. 11. Can the man work for (**his**) brother's big family? 12. Why does the traveller want to speak in Urdu with your servant? 13. Their oxen are near the field. 14. The rich man's new automobile is near the station. 15. The mechanic works under

your father's automobile. 16. I (msc.) cannot answer your question. 17. The traveller's baggage is light. 18. Why doesn't the gardener pour water on the garden's plants? 19. Your boy brings heavy wood for the old woman. 20. The servant cannot bring their caps. 21. Please place food on the hungry man's plate. 22. The woman gives grass to the old man's hungry cow. 23. Why doesn't the washerman wash the man's old clothes? 24. What's your profession? 25. The servant catches the thief in our father's house.

16.50 [14.2.3] **Translate into English:**

1. us-kē vālid śahar-mē̃ kām kartē haĩ. 2. laṛkā musāfir-kī āg-kē liyē lakṛī lātā hai. 3. aurat bāzār-mē̃ har tarah-kī cīzē̃ ḳharīdtī hai. 4. un-kā bhāī bail-kō daraḳht-kē nīcē bā̃dhtā hai. 5. baccā darḳht-kī cōṭī-par caṛhnā cāhtā hai. 6. ham hōṭal-kē kamrē-mē̃ cōr-kō pakaṛtē haĩ. 7. āp-kī mōṭargāṛī kahā̃ hai? 8. naukar ghar-kī chat-par palang rakhtā hai. 9. laṛkā nāī-kī dukān-kō āhistā āhistā jātā hai. 10. kyā āp-kā naukar āg-kē liyē lakṛī la saktā hai?. 11. bandar hōṭal-kī chat-par khēltē haĩ. 12. laṛkā daraḳht-kī śāḳh-par baiṭhtā hai. 13. maĩ kuē̃-kā pānī pīnā cāhtā hū̃. 14. baccē dhōbī-kē gadhē-kē pīchē dauṛtē haĩ. 15. āp-kā pēśā kyā hai? 16. musāfir-kā sāmān kamrē-mē̃ rakhiyē. 17. bāġ-kē daraḳhtō̃-kē bahot pakkē phal haĩ. 18. bāzār-kī dukānō̃-mē̃ ḳharīdnē-kē liyē har tarah-kī cīzē̃ haĩ. 19. pīr masjid-kē daraḳht-kē nīcē baiṭhtē haĩ. 20. laṛkā tumhārī mōṭargāṛī-kē liyē kahā̃-sē pānī lā saktā hai? 21. jangal-mē̃ har tarah-kē jānvar haĩ. 22. us ādmī-kā pēśā kyā hai? 23. āp-kā ghar kahā̃ hai? 24. ādmī masjid-kē kuē̃-sē pānī pītā hai. 25. vo tumhārī mā̃-kē liyē lakṛī kyū̃ nahī̃ lātī?

16.51 [14.3.1] **Translate into Urdu:**

1. The children want to run after you. 2. The servant places food in front of me. 3. Can he speak Urdu with you? 4. The automobile stops in front of me. 5. The man walks after me. 6. I don't have enough money. 7. The good boy brings drinking water for us. 8. The traveller wants to speak English with us. 9. The girl brings apples for you from the garden. 10. The little monkeys are near me.

16.52 [14.3.2] **Translate into English:**

1. dhōbī hamārē liyē kapṛē dhōtā hai. 2. laṛkā kuē̃-sē pīnē-kā pānī hamārē liyē lātā hai. 3. kyā tumhārē pās mōṭargāṛī hai? 4. pīr hamārē sāmnē ṭhahartē haĩ. 5. kyā vo tumhārē sāth Urdū bōl saktā hai? 6. kuttā mērē pīchē dauṛtā hai. 7. kyā tumhārē pās khānā ḳharīdnē-kē liyē kāfī paisē haĩ? 8. kyā āp mērē sāth śahar-kō jā saktī haĩ? 9. mērē pās ghōṛā nahī̃ hai. 10. hamārē liyē hōṭal-sē khānā lāiyē.

16.53 [14.4.2] **Translate into Urdu:**

1. The gardener may work in front of the house. 2. The hunter may kill the animal in the jungle. 3. We may go to the city on Tuesday. 4. I may tell stories to the children. 5. The washerman may wash the clothes for the man on Monday. 6. The little children may want to play on the roof on Sunday. 7. The woman may tie the cow with the rope. 8. The fisherman may bring fish for us on Wednesday. 9. You may rest under the tree. 10. The beggars may sit in front of the mosque. 11. The servant may go to the bazaar with the woman on Thursday. 12. He may be able to speak in Urdu with you. 13. Your teacher may ask difficult questions. 14. I may be able to drive the automobile. 15. The man may bring drinking water to the traveller.

16.54 [14.4.3] **Translate into English:**

1. śāyad būṛhā machērā machliyā̃ pakaṛ sakē. 2. śāyad ustād tumhārē sāth Urdū bōlnā cāhē̃. 3. śāyad baṛhaī jangal-sē lakṛī lāē. 4. śāyad maĩ pīr-kō āp-kē sāth śahar jāū̃. 5. śāyad

dhōbī jūmērāt-kō kapṛē lā sakē. 6. śāyad śikārī ḳhū̃ḳhār cītē-kō mār sakē. 7. śāyad tālibilm tumhārē sāth Añgrēzī-mẽ bōlnē-kē liyē jūmē-kō ānā cāhē. 8. śāyad mālī paudõ-par pānī ḍālē. 9. śāyad ham hōṭal-kē resṭōrenṭ-mẽ khānē-kē liyē āp-kē sāth haftē-kō jāẽ. 10. śāyad kārīgar mōṭargāṛī-kē nīcē kām kar sakē. 11. śāyad dukāndār har tarah-kī cīzẽ bēcē. 12. śāyad kisān mañgal-kō khēt-mẽ kām karē. 13. śāyad aurat būṛhē ādmī-sē sabziyā̃ ḳharīdē. 14. śāyad naukar resṭōrenṭ-sē hamārē liyē khānā lāē. 15. śāyad ham budh-kō jañgal-sē āp-kē liyē lakṛī lāẽ.

16.55 [15.1.2] **Translate into Urdu:**

1. The hunters will kill many animals in the jungle. 2. We (**msc.**) will go to the city with you. 3. The fisherman will be able to catch big fish in that river. 4. The servant will bring cold water for the traveller. 5. The mother will tell the children good stories. 6. When will the farmer work under the tree? 7. Will the beggars sit in front of the mosque today? 8. The washerman will want to wash the man's old clothes. 9. The boy will bring the heavy wood for the old woman. 10. Will she be able to speak in Urdu with you? 11. I (**msc.**) will be able to go to the bazaar with you tonight. 12. The woman will want to buy all kinds of things. 13. When will father come back from the city? 14. The cow will graze near the river. 15. Will the servants be able to understand English?

16.56 [15.1.3] **Translate into English:**

1. maĩ āj • rāt nahĩ paṛh sakū̃gā. 2. kyā tālibilm nastālīḳ paṛh sakēgā? 3. mērē vāldain mañgal-kō resṭōrenṭ-mẽ khāẽgē. 4. kyā tum āj bāg̱-mẽ kām kar sakōgē? 5. baṛhaī jūmērāt-kō daraḳht kāṭnā cahēgā. 6. kyā āp jūmē-kō ham-sē milnē-kē liyē āẽgē? 7. maĩ ādmiyõ-sē Urdū-mẽ bōlū̃gā. 8. śikārī ḳhū̃ḳhār cītē-kō kab mārẽgē? 9. naukar Añgrēzī samajh sakēgā. 10. kyā kamzōr kisān chōṭē hal-sē baṛē khēt-kō kām kar sakēgā? 11. ustād āj ham-sē muśkil savāl pūchẽgē. 12. dhōbī gadhē-kē pīchē calēgā. 13. kyā dhōbī āj • rāt kapṛē lāēgā? 14. hāthī jañgal-sē daryā-kī taraf bhārī lakṛī khī̃cēgā. 15. machērā śahar-mẽ bēcnē-kē liyē machliyā̃ lēnā cāhēgā.

16.57 [15.2.4] **Translate into Urdu:**

1. Father will give money to buy candy. 2. The cow may be under the tree. 3. The woman will take the wood from the good boy. 4. The policeman will take all kinds of things from the thief. 5. I may be in the office today. 6. The well will be near the fields. 7. When will (**my**) friend return my books? 8. The kind woman may give food to the poor man. 9. The thief will take the watch from the rich man. 10. The washerman will take the clothes from the servant. 11. The mother will give warm milk to the child. 12. The old man will have books. 13. The washerman may take the clothes to wash today. 14. When will you (**fm.**) answer my questions? 15. The woman will take the flower from her daughter. 16. Why will the man take candy from little children? 17. I may give you the newspaper. 18. Mother will give the hungry traveller bread. 19. Will the boy have a dog? 20. I may take a book from you tonight.

16.58 [15.2.5] **Translate into English:**

1. mērē bail-kī gardan-par ēk ghanṭī hōgī. 2. tum baccē-kō miṭhāī kab vāpas dōgē. 3. śāyad maĩ āp-kō aḳhbār dū̃. 4. abbā laṛkī-kō ēk rumāl dēgā. 5. baccā mā̃-sē dūdh-kā pyālā lēgā. 6. śāyad kuttā baccē-sē miṭhāī lē. 7. sipāhī amīr ādmī-kō ghaṛī vāpas dēgā. 8. vo daftar-mẽ kab hōgā? 9. śāyad vo āj • rāt śahar-mẽ hō. 10. baṛhaī jañgal-sē lakṛī lēgā. 11. chōṭī laṛkī abbā-kō phūl dēgī. 12. śāyad maĩ mēz-sē raḳābiyā̃ lū̃. 13. sipāhī

naukarõ̃-kō hukam dēgā. 14. naukar baccē-sē śakkar lēgā. 15. laṛkā pyāsē musāfir-kō ṭhaṇḍē pānī-kā pyālā dēgā. 16. śāyad maĩ kal ghar-mẽ hōū̃. 17. naukar ādmī-kō hōṭal-mẽ kamrā dikhāēgā. 18. abbā baccõ-kō har tarah-kī cīzẽ dēgā. 19. śāyad tum tālibilm-kō kāg̲az dōgē. 20. laṛkā kuẽ-sē pīnē-kā pānī lēgā.

16.59 [15.3.3] **Translate into Urdu:**

1. I (**msc.**) like mangoes. 2. The servant prefers to sleep. 3. The children prefer cats to dogs. 4. Dogs prefer bones. 5. The man prefers to work in the factory. 6. We (**msc.**) prefer mangoes to apples. 7. Why will you (**hon. msc.**) prefer to eat in a restaurant? 8. Cows prefer grass. 9. The traveller prefers drinking water. 10. I (**msc.**) prefer warm water to cold water for bathing. 11. The father likes to work for (**his**) family. 12. The woman prefers to go to the city by automobile. 13. Monkeys like to eat sweet fruits. 14. Why do you (**hon. msc.**) prefer to speak in Urdu? 15. We (**msc.**) prefer playing to working. 16. Cats like to drink milk. 17. The student prefers studying Urdu to studying English. 18. They (**msc.**) prefer to stay in the hotel to going to the city. 19. The little children like to go to the city with (**their**) father. 20. The traveller will prefer travelling to remaining at home.

16.60 [15.3.4] **Translate into English:**

1. baccā kuttõ-kō pasand kartā hai. 2. bāp ak̲hbār paṛhnā zyādā pasand kartā hai. 3. musāfir chōṭē kamrē-sē hōṭal-kā baṛā kamrā zyādā pasand karēgā. 4. ham khānā pasand kartē haĩ. 5. mā̃ ghar-mẽ rahnā zyādā pasand kartī hai. 6. būṛhā kisān khēt-mẽ kām karnē-sē darak̲ht-kē nīcē ārām karnā zyādā pasand karēgā. 7. machliyā̃ pānī pasand kartī haĩ. 8. maĩ daryā-mẽ tairnē-sē hōṭal-mẽ ārām karnā zyādā pasand kartī hū̃. 9. laṛkī dōstõ-kē sāth bōlnā zyādā pasand kartī hai. 10. laṛkē tairnā pasand kartē haĩ. 11. acchā tālibilm dōstõ-kē sāth khēlnē-sē paṛhnā zyādā pasand karēgā. 12. gāy daryā-kē pās carnā zyādā pasand kartī hai. 13. ham mōṭargāṛī-sē safar karnā pasand kartē haĩ. 14. laṛkiyā̃ sīnā pasand kartī haĩ. 15. mā̃ safar karnē-sē ghar-mẽ rahnā zyādā pasand kartī hai. 16. machērā śahar-mẽ machliyā̃ bēcnā zyādā pasand kartā hai. 17. maĩ kuẽ-kā pānī pīnā zyādā pasand karū̃gā. 18. kuttā mālik-kē sāth tairnā pasand kartā hai. 19. mālī paudõ-par pānī ḍālnē-sē darak̲ht-kē nīcē baiṭhnā zyādā pasand kartā hai. 20. sā̃p dūdh pasand kartē haĩ.

LESSON 17

17.1

mujhē jānā cāhiyē.	I need to go.
tālibilm-kō paṛhnā cāhiyē.	The student needs to study.
naukar-kō hamārē jānē-kē liyē sab kuch taiyār karnā cāhiyē.	The servant ought to prepare everything for our departure.
aurat-kō bāvarcīḳhānē-mẽ pakānā cāhiyē.	The woman should cook in the kitchen.
laṛkī-kō kuẽ-sē pānī lānā cāhiyē.	The girl ought to bring water from the well.
mehmān-kō Urdū bōlnā cāhiyē.	The guest should speak Urdu.

This section illustrates the Urdu equivalent to the English verbal phrases introduced by the words **ought to, should** or **needs to** followed by a verb. These phrases are translated into Urdu by placing the subject of the English sentence in the OBJECT FORM before the postposition **-kō** and the verb in the infinitive form before **cāhiyē.**

Vocabulary Notes: **bāvarcīḳhānā** (ā) kitchen, **mehmān** (ā or ī) guest.

17.1.1

mujhē jānā hai.	I have to go.
tālibilm-kō paṛhnā hai.	The student has to study.
naukar-kō hamārē jānē-kē liyē sab kuch taiyār karnā hai.	The servant has to prepare everything for our departure.
aurat-kō bāvarcīḳhānē-mẽ pakānā hai.	The woman has to cook in the kitchen.
laṛkī-kō kuẽ-sē pānī lānā hai.	The girl must bring water from the well.
marīz-kō davāī pīnā hai.	The patient has to take medicine.

This section illustrates the Urdu equivalent to the English verbal phrases introduced by the words **have to, has to** or **must** followed by a verb. The construction is identical with the one described in section 17.1 above, with the exception that **cāhiyē** is replaced by the third person, singular, present tense of **hōnā, hai,** which remains unchanged.

The construction indicates an inner compulsion upon the actor to perform the action expressed by the infinitive. Compare the construction described in the following section.

Vocabulary Notes: **marīz** (ā) patient, **davāī** (ī) medicine.

17.1.2

mujhē jānā paṛtā hai.	I have to go.
tālibilm-kō paṛhnā paṛtā hai.	The student has to study.
ḳhānsāmē-kō hamārē jānē-kē liyē sab kuch taiyār karnā paṛtā hai.	The cook has to prepare everything for our departure.

bāvarcī-kō bāvarcīḳhānē-mē̃ pakānā paṛtā hai.	The cook must cook in the kitchen.
klark-kō daftar-mē̃ kām karnā paṛtā hai.	The clerk has to work in the office.

The construction illustrated in this section is identical with that described in section 17.1.1, above, with the exception that **hai** is replaced by the third person, singular present tense of **paṛnā,** fall, **paṛtā hai,** which remains unchanged.

This section indicates a compulsion from without on the actor to perform the action expressed by the infinitive. Compare 17.1.1, above.

Compare 17.1.1, above.

REMARKS: **ḳhānsāmā** (ā) cook, butler, **bāvarcī** (ā) cook, **klark** (ā) clerk.

17.1.3 Exercise 1. **Translate into English:**

1. naukar-kō musāfir-kō pānī dēnā cāhiyē. 2. śikārī-kō ḳhū̃ḳhār jānvar mārnā hai. 3. hamē̃ bāzār jānā paṛtā hai. 4. dhōbī-kō kapṛē dhōnā cāhiyē. 5. bāp-kō bāzār-sē laṛkī-kē liyē ām lānā hai. 6. naukar-kō hamārē liyē bistar taiyār karnā paṛtā hai. 7. laṛkē-kō aurat-kē liyē lakṛī lānā cāhiyē. 8. tālibilmō̃-kō kitāb paṛhnā hai. 9. dhōbī-kō kapṛē sāf karnā hai. 10. hamē̃ Urdū-mē̃ bōlnā cāhiyē. 11. baṛhaī-kō lakṛī kāṭnā hai. 12. pyāsē bail-kō pānī pīnā paṛtā hai. 13. baccō̃-kō nahānā cāhiyē. 14. ādmī-kō kunbē-kē liyē kām karnā hai. 15. kisān-kō āj khēt-mē̃ kām karnā paṛtā hai. 16. naukar-kō ṭhaṇḍā pānī lānā cāhiyē. 17. kyā tumhē̃ jānā hai? 18. bhūkē machērē-kō āj machliyā̃ pakaṛnā paṛtā hai. 19. ādmī-kō paisē vāpas dēnā paṛtā hai. 20. mālī-kō paudō̃-par pānī ḍālnā cāhiyē.

17.1.4 Exercise 2. **Translate into Urdu:**

(**Note:** Translate the sentences containing "must" or "have to" with either one of the constructions described in 17.1.1 and 17.1.2.)

1. I should eat this apple. 2. Do you have to work today? 3. Must you go? 4. The thirsty child needs to drink milk. 5. The washerman must bring back the clothes tonight. 6. The woman has to go to the well to bring back water. 7. We ought to stay in the house. 8. Does mother have to cook in the kitchen? 9. You must come to see us tomorrow. 10. The poor man needs to work. 11. Why must you go to the office? 12. The men have to work in the factory. 13. The old farmer needs to rest under the wide tree. 14. The woman must take the food to (**her**) husband. 15. You should rest today. 16. You should speak in Urdu with me. 17. The thirsty traveller needs to drink cold water. 18. When do you have to come back from the bazaar? 19. Why do you need to go? 20. The traveller needs hot water for bathing.

17.2

āp-kō kyā cāhiyē?	What do you need?
mujhē ēk ādmī madad dēnē-kē liyē cāhiyē.	I need a man to help (**me.**)
aurat-kō tāzā pānī cāhiyē.	The woman needs fresh water.
āp-kō kitnē paisē cāhiyē̃?	How much money do you need?
kisān-kō mazdūrō̃-kī madad cāhiyē.	The farmer needs the help of workers.
bāp-kō ārām karnē-kē liyē thōṛā vaḳt cāhiyē.	The father needs a little time for rest.
mā̃-kō khānā pakānē-kē liyē āg cāhiyē.	The mother needs fire to cook the food.
baccē-kē nayē jūtē cāhiyē̃.	The child needs new shoes.

tālibilm-kō bahot kitābẽ cāhiyẽ.	The student needs many books.
chōṭī laṛkī-kō khēlnē-kē liyē guṛiyā̃ cāhiyẽ.	The little girl needs dolls to play with.

Compare this construction with that described in section 17.1. Here, instead of an infinitive, a noun is the subject of **cāhiyē.** When the noun is plural, the final vowel of **cāhiyē** is nasalized—e.g., **cāhiyẽ.**

REMARKS: (1) This construction also corresponds to the English **to want,** meaning **to need, to lack, to require.**

(2) Vocabulary notes: **ārām** (ā) rest, **ārām karnā** to rest (trans.), **guṛī** (ī) doll, **madad** (ī) help, assistance, **[-kō] madad dēnā** to help, **[-kī] madad karnā** to help, **mazdūr** (ā) worker, laborer.

17.2.1 Exercise 1. **Translate into English:**

1. aurat-kō āg-kē liyē lakṛī cāhiyē. 2. hamẽ āj mazdūr-kī madad cāhiyē. 3. kisān-kō khēt jōtnē-kē liyē baṛā hal cāhiyē. 4. kyā āp-kō mērī madad cāhiyē? 5. mujhē mōṭargāṛī calānē-kē liyē ādmī cāhiyē. 6. musāfir-kō saṛak dikhānē-kē liyē ādmī cāhiyē. 7. kyā āp-kō kuch cāhiyē? 8. tumhẽ mērī madad kyũ cāhiyē? 9. naukar-kō āj mujh-sē milnā kyũ cāhiyē? 10. aurat-kō bāzār-mẽ khānā ḳharīdnē-kē liyē paisē cāhiyẽ.

17.2.2 Exercise 2. **Translate into Urdu:**

1. When does a man need friends? 2. We need fresh water. 3. I need this ox-cart today. 4. Why do you need the newspaper now? 5. Do you need anything for your travel? 6. The woman needs wood for the fire this morning. 7. Do you need the clean clothes now? 8. Why do you need to see me tomorrow? 9. I need four gardeners for two days. 10. The traveller needs warm water for (**his**) bath.

17.3

kōī ādmī makān-kē pīchē hai.	Some man is behind the house.
kōī makān-kē pīchē hai.	Someone is behind the house.
kōī baccā daraḳht-kē nīcē hai.	Some child is under the tree.
kōī daraḳht-kē nīcē hai.	Someone is under the tree.
kōī laṛkā pānī lāēgā.	Some boy will bring water.
kōī pānī lāēgā.	Someone will bring water.
kōī kuttā andar ānā cāhtā hai.	Some dog wants to come in.
kōī andar ānā cāhtā hai.	Someone wants to come in.
kōī aurat kuẽ-kē pās hai.	Some woman is beside the well.
kōī kuẽ-kē pās hai.	Someone is beside the well.
kōī laṛkī kapṛē dhōēgī.	Some girl will wash the clothes.
kōī kapṛē dhōēgī.	Someone will wash the clothes.
kyā kōī aurat pakānā cāhtī hai?	Does any woman want to cook?
kyā kōī pakānā cāhtī hai?	Does anyone want to cook?

kyā kōī bēṭī ghar-mē̃ rahnā cāhtī hai?	Does any daughter want to remain at home?
kyā kōī ghar-mē̃ rahnā cāhtī hai?	Does anyone want to remain at home?
kōī kitāb mēz-par hai.	Some book is on the table.
kōī cīz mēz-par hai.	Something is on the table.
kōī mēz kōnē-mē̃ hai.	Some table is in the corner.
kōī cīz kōnē-mē̃ hai.	Something is in the corner.
kyā kōī gāṛī sṭēśan-mē̃ hai?	Is any train in the station?
kyā kōī cīz sṭēśan-mē̃ hai?	Is anything in the station?
kyā kōī makān saṛak-par hai?	Is any house along the road?
kyā kōī cīz saṛak-par hai?	Is anything along the road?

Sections 17.3 to 17.3.3 are concerned with the indefinite adjectives and pronouns.

This section, 17.3, illustrates the nominative singular of the indefinite adjective, **some, any,** and the indefinitive pronouns, **someone, anyone.** In each of the pairs of sentences given the first illustrates the adjective and the second the pronoun. The form, **kōī,** serves to translate both adjective and pronoun, masculine and feminine.

REMARKS: **kōī cīz** translates English **something.**

17.3.1

maĩ kisī ādmī-kī āvāz suntā hū̃.	I hear some man's voice.
maĩ kisī-kī āvāz suntā hū̃.	I hear someone's voice.
maĩ kisī baccē-kō daraḳht-kē nīcē dēkhtā hū̃.	I see some child under the tree.
maĩ kisī-kō daraḳht-kē nīcē dēkhtā hū̃.	I see someone under the tree.
maĩ kisī laṛkē-sē pānī lū̃gā.	I will take water from some boy.
maĩ kisī-sē pānī lū̃gā.	I will take water from someone.
maĩ kisī kuttē-kō khānā dū̃gā.	I will give food to some dog.
maĩ kisī-kō khānā dū̃gā.	I will give food to someone.
maĩ kisī aurat-sē sabziyā̃ ḳharīdtā hū̃.	I buy vegetables from some woman.
maĩ kisī-sē sabziyā̃ ḳharīdtā hū̃.	I buy vegetables from someone.
maĩ kisī laṛkī-kō batāū̃gā.	I will tell some girl.
maĩ kisī-kō batāū̃gā.	I will tell someone.
laṛkā kisī laṛkī-kē sāth khēlnā nahī̃ cāhtā.	The boy does not want to play with any girl.
laṛkā kisī-kē sāth khēlnā nahī̃ cāhtā.	The boy does not want to play with anyone.

kuttā kisī billī-kā dūdh pītā hai.	The dog drinks some cat's milk.
kuttā kisī-kā dūdh pītā hai.	The dog drinks someone's milk.
laṛkī kisī mēz-par khānā rakhtī hai.	The girl places the food on some table.
laṛkī kisī cīz-par khānā rakhtī hai.	The girl places the food on something.
maĩ kōī kitāb paṛhtā hū̃.	I read some book.
maĩ kōī cīz paṛhtā hū̃.	I read something.

This section illustrates the object singular form, **kisī,** of the indefinite adjective and pronoun.

REMARKS: (1) See sentences 19 and 20 and note that, when the noun modified by the adjective is not governed by a postposition and has, therefore, the subject form, the indefinite adjective also has the subject form.

(2) āvāz (ī) voice, sound.

17.3.2

kuch ādmī makān-kē pīchē haĩ.	Some men are behind the house.
kuch lōg makān-kē pīchē haĩ.	Some people are behind the house.
kuch baccē daraḳht-kē nīcē haĩ.	Some children are under the tree.
kuch lōg daraḳht-kē nīcē haĩ.	Some people are under the tree.
kuch laṛkiyā̃ pānī lāẽgī.	Some girls will bring water.
kuch lōg pānī lāẽgī.	Some people will bring water.
kuch aurtẽ kuẽ-kē pās haĩ.	Some women are beside the well.
kuch laṛkiyā̃ kapṛē dhōẽgī.	Some girls will wash the clothes.
kuch aurtẽ pakānā cāhtī haĩ.	Some women want to cook.
kuch gāṛiyā̃ sṭēśan-mẽ haĩ.	Some trains are in the station.
kyā saṛak-par kuch makān haĩ?	Are there any houses along the road?

This section and the following illustrate the subject and object plural forms of the indefinitive adjective. The form employed here is **kuch.** To translate the plural of the indefinitive pronoun a word such as **lōg** people is used with the adjective. See the second sentence in each of the first three sets of sentences.

17.3.3

maĩ kuch baccõ-kō daraḳht-kē nīcē dēkhtā hū̃.	I see some children under the tree.
maĩ kuch lōgõ-kō daraḳht-kē nīcē dēkhtā hū̃.	I see some people under the tree.
maĩ kuch laṛkõ-sē pānī lū̃gā.	I will take water from some boys.
maĩ kuch lōgõ-sē pānī lū̃gā.	I will take water from some people.
maĩ kuch kuttõ-kō khānā dū̃gā.	I will give food to some dogs.
maĩ kuch aurtõ-sē sabziyā̃ ḳharīdū̃gā.	I will buy vegetables from some women.
laṛkā kuch laṛkiyõ-kē sāth khēlnā nahī̃ cāhtā.	The boy does not want to play with some girls.

maī kuch kitābē̃ paṛhtā hū̃.	I read some books.
laṛkī kuch mēzō̃-par khānā rakhtī hai.	The girl places the food on some tables.
musāfir kuch gāṛiyō̃-mē̃ jātē haī.	The travellers go into some trains.

17.3.4

makān-kē pīchē kōī ādmī nahī̃ hai.	There isn't any man behind the house.
makān-kē pīchē kōī nahī̃ hai.	There's no one behind the house.
mēz-par kōī kitāb nahī̃ hai.	There isn't any book on the table.
mēz-par kōī cīz nahī̃ hai.	There isn't anything on the table.
kōī cīz mēz-par nahī̃.	Nothing's on the table.
maī kisī ādmī-kī āvāz nahī̃ suntā.	I do not hear any man's voice.
maī kisī-kī āvāz nahī̃ suntā.	I do not hear anyone's voice.
maī kōī kitāb nahī̃ paṛhtā.	I do not read any book.
maī kōī cīz nahī̃ paṛhtā.	I do not read anything.

This section illustrates the negative of the constructions given in sections 17.3 to 17.3.3, translating English **no, not any.**

Urdu ordinarily does not employ the negative of this construction in the plural. For example, English **There aren't any men behind the house.** is translated into Urdu either by **ghar-kē pīchē kōī ādmī nahī̃ (hai)** (lit., **There is no man behind the house.**) or **ghar-kē pīchē ādmī nahī̃ (haī)** (lit., **There aren't [any] men behind the house.**) Similarly, **I will not buy vegetables from any woman,** is translated either by **maī kisī-bhī aurat-sē sabziyā̃ nahī̃ ḳharīdū̃gā** (lit., **I will not buy vegetables from any woman.**) or **maī aurtō̃-sē sabziyā̃ nahī̃ ḳharīdū̃gā.** (lit., **I will not buy vegetables from [any] women).**

17.4

kuch ādmī makān-kē pīchē haī.	Some men are behind the house.
kuch baccē sabaḳ yād kartē haī.	Some children remember the lesson.
kuch mazdūr sāmān uṭhāẽ̄gē.	Several laborers will pick up the baggage.
kuch aurtē̃ kuē̃-kē pās haī.	Some women are beside the well.
kuch dhōbnē̃ kapṛē dhōẽ̄gī.	Some washerwoman will wash the clothes.
kuch aurtē̃ pakānā cāhtī haī.	Several women want to cook.
kuch kitābē̃ mēz-kē nīcē haī.	Several books are under the table.
kuch basē̃ sṭēśan-mē̃ haī.	Some buses are in the station.
kyā saṛak-par kuch kōṭhiyā̃ haī?	Are there several bungalows along the road?

This section and 17.4.1, following, illustrate **kuch,** functioning as an adjective modifying a plural to translate English **some, several.**

REMARKS: **kuch,** when employed in the singular as an indefinite pronoun, referring to an inanimate thing, or as an adjective, translates English **something, anything, some, any.** The subject and object forms are identical. **kuch** in its function as a pronoun never appears before a postposition.

COMPARE:

kyā mēz-par kuch hai?	Is there anything on the table?
tālibilm kuch jāntā hai.	The student knows something.
kuē̃-mē̃ kuch hai.	There is something in the well.

maĩ kuch garm dūdh pīnā cāhtā hū̃.	I want to drink some warm milk.
kyā ghar-mẽ kuch khānā hai?	Is there any food in the house?

REMARKS: (1) **cand** also translates **several.**

(2) **sabaḳ** (ā) lesson, **yād karnā** to remember, memorize, **dhōban** (ī) washerwoman, **bas** (ī) bus, **nadī** (ī) stream, **hājī** (ā) traveller.

17.4.1

maĩ kuch baccõ-kō nadī-kē kinārē-par dēkhtā hū̃.	I see some children on the bank of the stream.
maĩ kuch laṛkõ-sē pānī lū̃gā.	I will take water from several boys.
maĩ kuch kuttõ-kō khānā dū̃gā.	I will give food to several dogs.
maĩ kuch aurtõ-sē sabziyā̃ ḳharīdū̃gā.	I will buy vegetables from some women.
maĩ kuch kitābẽ paṛhtā hū̃.	I read several books.
laṛkī kuch mēzõ-par khānā rakhtī hai.	The girl places the food on some tables.
hājī kuch gāṛiyõ-mẽ jātē haĩ.	The travellers go into several trains.

17.4.2 Exercise 1. **Translate into English.**

1. kyā aurtẽ kisī dukān-mẽ kapṛā ḳharīdnā cāhtī haĩ? 2. kuch parindē śāḳh-par baiṭhtē haĩ. 3. kuch parindē śāḳh-par baiṭhtē haĩ. 4. saṛak-par kuch makān haĩ. 5. ustād mujh-sē kuch savāl pūchtē haĩ. 6. ham kuch baṛē jānvar pul-kē nīcē dēkhtā haĩ. 7. kuch dublī gāyẽ daraḳht-kē nīcē ārām kartī haĩ. 8. daraḳht-kē nīcē kuch pakkē phal haĩ. 9. kyā khēt-mẽ kuch kisān haĩ? 10. kōī pīr daryā-kē sāmnē haĩ. 11. kisān bailõ-kō khānē-kē liyē kuch ghās dētā hai. 12. śikārī kisī jānvar-kō jaṅgal-mẽ mārtā hai. 13. kisī mēz-kō bāhar lāiyē. 14. ū̃cī imārat-kē sāmnē kuch chōṭī dukānẽ haĩ. 15. bāzār-mẽ kuch chōṭī dukānẽ haĩ.

17.4.3 Exercise 2. **Translate into Urdu:**

1. Is anyone at home? 2. Can the traveller speak English with anyone? 3. There are several good rooms in the hotel. 4. Please bring some water for my automobile. 5. Some farmer will rest under the tree. 6. Is there any coal in the ground? 7. The big dog may bite someone. 8. Is there any well near here? 9. Please bring me some well-water. 10. Someone is outside. 11. The thirsty bullock does not want to eat anything. 12. Something is behind the door. 13. Several newspapers are on the table. 14. Some newspaper is on the table. 15. Can anyone speak in Urdu with me?

17.5 Text 1: **Sair.**[1]

Translate into English. Answer the questions in Urdu:

[Khurśīd Ahmad Karācī [2] -mẽ kaī [3] sālõ [4] -sē rahtā hai. āj itvār hai aur daftar [5] band [6] haĩ. is liyē Khurśīd āj kām-par nahī̃ jāēgā. us-kā irādā [7] hai ke [8] āj apnī bīvī-kō apnē sāth sair [9] kē liyē lē jāē.[10] us-kī bīvī-kā nām Najmā [11] hai. Najma ēk paṛhī likhī [12] laṛkī hai. Khurśīd aur Najma dōnõ [13] em ē [14] pās [15] haĩ. Khurśīd laṛkõ-kē kālaj [16] -mẽ paṛhātā hai [17] aur Najma laṛkiyõ-kē kālaj-mẽ. āj Najma-kō -bhī [18] chuṭṭī [19] hai. un-kā ḳhayāl [20] hai ke [21] āj Kliftān Bīc [22] -par piknik [23] -kē liyē jāẽ. Najma is vakt [24] bāvarcīḳhānē-mẽ gōśt [25] bhūn rahī [26] hai. thōṛī dēr-mẽ [27] naukar nānbaī [28] -kī dukān-sē nān [29] lēkar āēgā. [30] bhūnē huē [31] gōśt-kē sāth nān bahot mazēdār [32] hōtē haĩ.[33] Khurśīd-kī mōṭargāṛī āj us-kē ēk dōst-kē pās hai. dōnõ miyā̃ • bīvī [34] sōctē [35] haĩ kē [8] piknik-par kaisē [36] jāẽ. Khurśīd-kā ḳhayāl hai ke [8] ṭaiksī [37] kirāyē [38] -par lē lẽ.[39] lēkin Najma kahtī hai ke [40] kōī [41] ḳhūbsūrat-sā tā̃gā [42] lēnā cāhiyē. ab [43] sab sāmān [44] taiyār hai. abhī naukar tā̃gā bulānē [45] jāēgā. lō! [46] tā̃gā-bhī ā gayā.[47] bilkul [48] nayā hai. ghōṛā ḳhūb [49] javān [50] aur tāḳatvar [51] hai.]

Ḳhurśīd: kyū̃,[52] bhāī [53] tā̃gēvālē! [54] Kliftan Bīc calōgē?

Tā̃gēvālā: hā̃, janāb,[55] kyū̃ nahī̃.

Ḳhurśīd: kitnē paisē lōgē?

Tā̃gēvālā: siraf [56] jānē-kē yā [57] ānē • jānē [58] -kē?

Ḳhurśīd: ānē • jānē-kē.

Tā̃gēvālā: bābū-jī,[59] āp pandrā rūpayē dījiyē.

Ḳhurśīd: pandrā rūpayē! miyā̃,[60] hōś [61] -mē̃ āō.

Tā̃gēvālā: sāhab,[62] maĩ tō hōś-mē̃-hī [63] hū̃. pandrā rūpayē kōī zyādā [64] tō [65] nahī̃.

Ḳhurśīd: kyā kahā? [66] zyādā nahī̃! hamārē pās kōī harām-kā [67] paisā tō nahī̃. kām kartē haĩ tumhārī tarāh.[68]

Tā̃gēvālā: bābū • sāhab,[69] zarā [70] mērē ghōṛē-kō tō dēkhō. havā [71] -kī tarāh caltā hai. das rūpayē-kā dānā [72] rōz [73] isē khilātā [74] hū̃, aur tā̃gā-bhī tō dēkhiyē. bilkul nayā hai. mazā [75] ā jāēgā, savārī [76] karnē-kā. mērā tā̃gā mōṭargāṛī-kō māt kartā [77] hai.

Ḳhurśīd: kyū̃, bēgam! [78] kyā ḳhayāl hai?

Najma: tā̃gā tō acchā hai, lēkin pandrā rūpayē bahot zyādā haĩ. tā̃gēvālē! kirāyā kam karō.[79]

Tā̃gēvālā: bībī-jī! [80] maĩ kyā araz [81] karū̃? āp ḳhud [82] -hī insāf [83] kījiyē. ghar-mē̃ bīvī hai aur sāt baccī haĩ. un sab-kā ḳharc [84] isī [85] tā̃gē-sē nikāltā [86] hū̃.

Najma: tum ṭhīk [87] kahtē hō, lēkin ham-bhī kōī sēṭh [88] tō nahī̃. kuch kam karō.

Tā̃gēvālā: ab āp-sē kyā jhagṛā [89] karū̃? āp tō rōz-kē gāhak [90] haĩ. caliyē! āp ēk rūpayā kam dījiyē.

Ḳhurśīd: dēkhō, bhāī! ēk bāt karō. ham das rūpayē dē̃gē. zyādā nahī̃.

Tā̃gēlāvā: jī nahī̃,[91] das rūpayē tō bahot thōṛē haĩ. āp aur [92] tā̃gā bulvā lījiyē.[93] (āhistā āhistā ghōṛē-kō calānē [94] lagtā hai.)

Ḳhurśīd: acchā, gyārā rūpayē lē lō.[39]

Tā̃gēvālā: maĩ-nē tō āp-sē caudā rūpayē mā̃gē [95] haĩ. caliyē! tērā dījiyē.

Ḳhurśīd: nahī̃, tērā zyādā haĩ. acchā, bārā rūpayē dē dē̃gē.[96]

Tā̃gēvālā: āp bīc [97] -par kitnī dēr ṭharē̃gē?

Ḳhurśīd: zyādā dēr nahī̃. yehī kōī [98] cār ghanṭē.[99]

Tā̃gēvālā: acchā, baiṭhiyē.

[Ḳhurśīd aur Najma tā̃gē-kī pichlī [100] sīṭ [101] -par baiṭh jātē [102] haĩ. naukar un-kā sāmān [103] sīṭ-kē nīcē rakh dētā [104] hai. tā̃gā pahilē [105] āhistā aur phir [106] tēz [107] caltā hai. thōṛī dēr-mē̃ ēk cauk[108] ātā hai. tā̃gēvālā sipāhī [109] -kā iśārā [110] nahī̃ dēkhtā aur guzar jātā [111] hai. sipāhī sīṭī [112] bajātā [113] hai aur tā̃gēvālē-kō ruknā paṛtā hai. ṭrēfik pōlīs [114] -kā sipāhī us-kī taraf ātā hai.]

Tā̃gēvālā: kyā bāt hai, janāb?

Sipāhī: bāt kyā hai! apnā lāisens [115] nikālō. cālān [116] hōgā tumhārā!

Tā̃gēvālā: janāb, mērā ḳasūr [117] kyā hai?

Sipāhī: baṛē lāṭ • sāhab [118] bankar [119] tā̃gā calātē hō. sipāhī-kā hāth [120] -bhī nahī̃ dēkhtē. agar [121] takkar [122] hō jāē,[123] tō kaun [124] zimmēdār [125] hai?

Tā̃gēvālā: janāb, galtī [126] hō gayī,[127] ab muāf kar dījiyē.[128] agar [121] āp cālān [129] karē̃gē, mujhē jurmānā [130] hō jāẽgā. janāb, garīb ādmī hū̃. ghar-mē bīvī hai aur sāt bacce haĩ. vo bhūkē mar jāẽgē.[131] phir, aisā nahī̃ hōgā.

Sipāhī: ab bātẽ banātē [132] hō. maĩ kyā kar saktā hū̃. sarkārī [133] ḳānūn [134] hai ke,[8] jō[135] sipāhī-kā iśārā na [136] mānē, us-kā cālān kar dō. lāisens nikālō. jaldī karō.[137]

Tā̃gēvālā: jī,[138] sarkār [139] tō āp-hī haĩ. (ēk rūpayā nikālkar [140] sipāhī-kō dētā hai.) ye āp-kē śarbat • pānī [141] -kē liyē hai.

Sipāhī: tum hamẽ harāmḳhōr [142] samajhtē [143] hō! ham riśvat [144] nahī lētē. bas,[145] ab tō zarūr [146] tumhārā cālān karẽgē!

Tā̃gēvālā: (Ḳhurśīd-sē) bābū • jī, āp in-sē mērī sifāriś kījiyē.[147]

Ḳhurśīd: (sipāhī [148] -sē) is-nē galtī kī [149] hai. lēkin, ab śarmindā [150] hai. mērē ḳhayāl-mẽ tum isē is dafā [151] jānē dō.[152]

Najma: hā̃, hā̃. jānē-bhī dō. garīb ādmī hai. tum cālān karōgē, tō bēcārē [153] -kē bīvī • baccē [154] bhūkē mar jāẽgē.

Sipāhī: acchā, sāhab, (agar [121]) āp kahtē haĩ, tō is badmāś [155] -kō is dafā jānē dētā hū̃. (tā̃gēvālē-kī taraf dēkhkar [156]) dēkhō! ab muāf kartā hū̃. lēkin agar [121] phir ḳānūn-kē ḳhilāf [157] kām karōgē, tō bilkul nahī̃ chōṛū̃gā.

Tā̃gēvālā: bahot acchā, janāb. āp-kī bahot meharbānī.[158] Ḳhudā āp-kē bāl • baccõ [159] -kō ḳhuś [160] rakhē.[161]

savālāt:

1. tā̃gēvālē-nē Ḳhurśīd-sē kitnē paisē mā̃gē? [95] 2. Ḳhurśīd aur Najma kyā kām kartē haĩ? 3. Najma bāvarcīḳhānē-mẽ kyā kartī thī? 4. sipāhī-nē tā̃gēvālē-sē kyā kahā? [162] 5. kyā tā̃gēvālē-kā cālān huā? [163]

NOTES: 1. excursion, stroll, short walk (ī); 2. city of Karachi (ā); 3. many (**adj., n.c.**); 4. year (ā); 5. office (ā); 6. closed; 7. plan, intention (ā); 8. = that, see 29.2, Remarks 1 and 2; 9. a ride, drive, promenade, outing, trip (ī); 10. **lē jānā** to take, for such verbal clusters, see lesson 28; 11. name of woman; 12. **paṛhā • likhā** educated (**adj.**); 13. both (**adv.**); 14. M.A. (degree); 15. **pās hōnā** to pass; 16. college (ā); 17. **paṛhānā** to teach, for causative stems, see 36.1 to 36.1.4; 18. also, too (**emph. pt.**); 19. holiday, leave of absence (ī); 20. thought, idea (ā); 21. = **that,** for the construction with **ke,** see 29.2, Remarks 1 and 2; 22. Clifton Beach (ī); 23. picnic (ī); 24. **is vakt** at this time, now (**adv.**); 25. meat (ā); 26. **bhūn rahnā** to roast (int.); 27. **thōṛī dēr-mē** in a little while; 28. baker (ā); 29. kind of bread (ā); 30. **lēkar ānā** to bring, for the construction see 30.1; 31. **bhūnā huā** roasted, for the construction, see 33.1; 32. tasty (**adj., n.c.**); 33. **hōtē hai,** see 29.4; 34. **miyā̃ • bīvī** husband and wife (ē); 35. **sōcnā** to wonder, think, see 29.2, Remark 2; 36. how (**interr. adv.**); 37. taxi (ī); 38. **kirāyā** (ā) rent, hire; 39. **lē lēnā** to take, see lesson 28; 40. see fn. 8; 41. some (**indef. adj.**); 42. tonga (a two-wheeled, horse-driven carriage) (ā); 43. now (**adv.**); 44. luggage, necessary things (ā); 45. = **bulānē-kē liyē** to fetch; 46. there! (=**excl.**); 47. **ā jānā** to come, arrive, see lesson 28; 48. completely (**adv.**); 49. very (**adv.**); 50. young (**adj., n.c.**); 51. strong, powerful (**adj., n.c.**); 52. well! (=**excl.**); 53. compare use of "Brother" in American English; 54. **tā̃gevālā** tonga-driver, coachman (here **vocative**) (ā); 55. sir; 56. only (**adv.**); 57. or (**conj.**); 58. **ānā • jānā** coming and going, both ways (ā); 59. sir; 60. dear (**friend, fellow**) (term of polite address); 61. **hōś** senses (ā), **hōś-mẽ ānā** be sensible; 62. sir; 63. **emph. pt.**; 64. **kōī zyādā** too much; 65. **emph. pt.**; 66. heard, for the simple perfect of transitive verbs see 21.1. (Here the "subject," **tum-nē,** has been omitted.); 67. **harām-kā** improper, illegal, black-market (= adj.); 68. **tarāh** (ī) like, manner, sort; 69. sir; 70. just, a little (adv.); 71. wind (ī); 72. grams (ā); 73. every day (**adv.**); 74. **khilānā** to feed, see 36.1-36.1.4; 75. pleasure, enjoyment (ā); 76. trip, journey, ride (ī); 77. **māt karnā** to excel; 78. dear (term of endearment to a lady); 79. **kam karnā** to reduce; 80. lady, madame (ī); 81. **araz karnā** to say, submit; 82. **ḳhud** self (**refl. pron., n.c.**); 83. justice (ā); 84. expenses (ā); 85. ī (**emph. pt.**); 86. **nikālnā** to take out, get out, see 36.1-36.1.4; 87. exact, true, right; 88. rich person, millionaire (ā); 89. dispute, haggling (ā); 90. customer (ā);

91. no; 92. **aur tā̃gā** another tonga; 93. **bulvā lēnā** to send for, call, see lesson 28; 94. **calānā** to move, see 36.1-36.1.4, for the causative, and 34.1.2, for the construction with **lagnā**; 95. asked, (**mā̃gnā**). (For the present perfect construction with transitive verbs see 21.1.2); 96. **dē dēnā** to give, see lesson 28; 97. beach (ī); 98. **yehī kōī** just about, around; 99. hour (ā); 100. **pichlā** back (**adj.**); 101. seat (ī); 102. **baiṭh jānā** to sit, see lesson 28; 103. things, baggage (ā); 104. **rakh dēnā** to place, see lesson 28; 105. at first (**adv.**); 106. then (**conj.**); 107. swiftly (**adv.**); 108. (street-) crossing (ā); 109 (police-) officer (ā); 110. signal, gesture (ā); 111. **guzar jānā** to go on, pass along, see lesson 28; 112. whistle (ī); 113. to blow, sound, see 36.1-36.1.4; 114. traffic-policeman (ā); 115. license (ā); 116. ticket, summons (ā); 117. fault (ā); 118. governor (ā); 119. **baṛē lāṭ • sāhab bankar** like a big-shot; 120. = signal; 121. if (See lesson 18 for conditional constructions.); 122. accident, collision (ī); 123. **hō jānā** = **hōnā**, see lesson 28; 124. who (**interr. pron.**), see 18.2; 125. responsible (**adj., n.c.**); 126. mistake (ī); 127. was (For perfect tense of intransitive verb see 20.1 and following sections.); 128. **mūāf karnā** to excuse (**tr.**), see lesson 28 (a variant is māf); 129. **cālān karnā** to give a ticket, summons (**tr.**) (**cālān** (a)); 130. fine (ā); 131. **bhūkē marnā** to die of hunger (**int.**), for **mar jānā**, see lesson 28; 132. **bātẽ banānā** to talk (**tr.**); 133. official, governmental (**adj., n.c.**); 134. law (ā); 135. which (**rel. adj.**), for the construction see 25.1; 136. not; 137. **jaldī karnā** to be quick (**tr.**); 138. sir; 139 government (ī); 140. taking out, see 30.1; 141. refreshments (ā); 142. grafter (ā); 143. to take for, consider; 144. bribe (ī); 145. enough! finish! (**excl.**); 146. certainly; 147. **sifāriś karnā** to recommend (**tr.**), **sifāriś** (ī); 148. sentry, policeman (ā); 149. done, for the perfect participle of **karnā**, see 22.1.4, and 21.1, ff., for perfect tense; 150. repentent (**adj., n.c.**); 151. **is dafā** this time; 152. **jānē dēnā** to let go, see 37.2.3; 153. **bēcārā** wretch (ā); 154. wife and children (ē); 155. rascal (ā); 156. looking, see 30.1; 157. **-kē k͟hilāf** against (**postpos.**); 158. thanks (ī); 159. **bāl • baccē** family (ē); 160. happy (**adj., n.c.**); 161. keep, see 14.4 for subjunctive; 162. said, see 21.1, ff., for construction; 163. was, see 22.1.1 and 20.1, ff., for perfect tense of intransitive verb.

17.6

The learning of the Nastalik script can be undertaken at this point. For a description of the Nastalik script, see **Selections in Urdu Readings,** the companion volume to this book. The student will find his learning of the script expedited by the fact that the book consists of Nastalik transcriptions of the romanized conversations and texts that he has previously encountered and mastered in this book. He therefore can devote his undivided attention to the mastery of the script without the distraction of dealing with grammatical constructions, vocabulary, and subject matter that unfamiliar texts would present.

LESSON 18

18.1

agar āp hukam dētē haī, tō acchā naukar us-kō māntā hai.	If you order (**him**), (**then**) the good servant obeys it.
agar laṛkē-kē pās miṭhāī hai, tō vo dōstō̃-kō us-kō dētā hai.	If the boy has candy, (**then**) he gives it to (**his**) friends.
agar bail bhūkā hai, tō vo ghās khānē-kē liyē ruktā hai.	If the bullock is hungry, (**then**) he stops to eat grass.
agar baccā pyāsā hai, tō vo rōtā hai.	If the child is thirsty, (**then**) he cries.
agar aurat sust hai, tō vo gap mārnē-kē liyē ruktī hai.	If the woman is lazy, (**then**) she stops to gossip.
agar tālibilm paṛhtā hai, tō vo savāl-kē javāb jāntā hai.	If the student studies, (**then**) he knows the answers to the questions.
agar mērā bhāī ghar-mē̃ rahtā hai, tō maī āsānī-sē sinēmā-kō jā saktā hū̃.	If my brother stays at home, (**then**) I can easily go to the movies.
agar abbā vaḳt-par vāpas ātē haī, tō ham khānā khātē haī.	If father comes back in time, (**then**) we eat dinner.
agar mā̃ bāzār jātī hai, tō vo dukānō̃-mē̃ bahot cīzē̃ ḳharīdnā cāhtī hai.	If mother goes to the bazaar, (**then**) she wants to buy many things in the shops.
agar āp holē holē bōltē haī, tō maī samajh saktā hū̃.	If you speak softly, (**then**) I can understand.

This section introduces the Urdu conditional construction, the verb of each clause being in the present tense. (Compare 2.1) The "if" clause of English is introduced in Urdu by the word **agar, if,** and the second clause by the word **tō** (lit., **then**).

REMARKS: **tō** is often not expressed in Urdu.

18.1.1

agar āp thakē haī, tō baiṭhiyē.	If you are tired, (**then**) sit down.
agar musāfir pyāsā hai, tō us-kō pānī dījiyē.	If the traveller is thirsty, (**then**) give him water.
agar tumhē̃ Urdū-mē̃ bōlnā hai, tō āhistā bōlō!	If you must speak Urdu, (**then**) speak slowly!

agar tum javāb jāntē hō, tō us-kō mujhē batāō!	If you know the answer, (**then**) tell it to me!
agar āp cāhtē haĩ, tō andar āiyē.	If you wish, (**then**) come in.
agar tum ṭhahar saktē hō, tō baiṭhō!	If you can stay, (**then**) sit down!
agar tum bhūkē hō, tō mēz-sē ēk phal lō!	If you are hungry, (**then**) take a fruit from the table!
agar āp jānnā cāhtē haĩ, tō us-sē pūchiyē.	If you want to know, (**then**) ask him.
agar tum-kō mērē sāth ānā paṛtā hai, tō āhistā āhistā calō!	If you must come with me, (**then**) walk slowly!
agar āp ḳhat paṛhnā cāhtē haĩ, tō ye lījiyē.	If you wish to read the letter, (**then**) take it.

This section illustrates the conditional sentence, the "if" clause of which contains a verb in the present tense, and the second clause an imperative. (see 7.1 and 7.1.1)

REMARKS: The polite imperatives of **dēnā, lēnā,** and **karnā** are **dījiyē, lījiyē,** and **kījiyē,** respectively. The **tum** imperatives (see 7.1.1) of these are **dō, lō,** and **karō,** respectively.

18.1.2

agar āp us-kō hukam dē̃, tō (śāyad) acchā naukar us-kō mānē.	If you (**should**) give him an order, (**then**) the good servant may obey it.
agar bail bhūkā hō, tō vo (śāyad) ghās khānē-kē liyē rukē.	If the ox (**should**) be hungry, (**then**) he may stop to eat grass.
agar baccā pyāsā hō, tō (śāyad) vo rōē.	If the child (**should**) be thirsty, (**then**) he may cry.
agar aurat thakī hō, tō vo ārām karnē-kē liyē rukē.	If the woman (**should**) be tired, (**then**) she may stop to rest.
agar āp mērē ānē-tak vahā̃ ṭhaharē̃, tō (śāyad) maĩ āp-kē liyē aḳhbar lā sakū̃.	If you (**should**) wait there until I arrive, (**then**) I may be able to bring you the newspaper.
agar khānā ḳharāb hō, tō (śāyad) āp bīmār hō jāē̃.	If the food (**should**) be bad, (**then**) you may get sick.
agar vo pakāē, tō ham khāē̃.	If she (**should**) cook, (**then**) we may eat.
agar āp āhistā bōlē̃, tō maĩ samajh sakū̃.	If you (**should**) speak slowly, (**then**) I may be able to understand.
agar āp gandā pānī piyē̃, tō (śāyad) āp bīmār hō jaē̃.	If you (**should**) drink dirty water, (**then**) you may become sick.
agar mā̃ bāzār jāē, tō vo dukānō̃-mē̃ bahot cīzē̃ ḳharīdnā cāhē.	If mother goes to the bazaar, (**then**) she may want to buy many things in the shops.

This section illustrates conditional sentences, both clauses of which contain verbs in the subjunctive—indicating the possibility of fulfillment of the condition or act expressed by the verbs. (The word **should,** which is not necessarily expressed in English, is, therefore, placed in parentheses in the English sentences.)

REMARKS: (1) **hō jānā, become,** functions as a single verb, **hōnā.** The construction will be discussed later.

(2) The verb **pīnā** replaces its stem **pī** with a secondary stem, **piy,** before suffixes starting with vowels other than **ī.** (See sentence 9, above.)

(3) **śāyad, perhaps,** is often not expressed.

18.1.3

agar āp cāhē̃, tō maī āp-kē sāth jāū̃gā.	If you (**should**) wish, (**then**) I will go with you.
agar mērā bhāī yahā̃ rahē, tō maī āj • rāt sinēmā-kō jā sakū̃gā.	If my brother (**should**) remain here, (**then**) I will be able to go to the movies tonight.
agar āp mērē ānē-tak vahā̃ ṭharē̃, tō maī āp-kē liyē akhbār lā sakū̃gā.	If you (**should**) wait there until I arrive, (**then**) I will be able to bring you the newspaper.
agar khānā ḳharāb hō, tō āp bīmār hō jāē̃gē.	If the food (**should**) be bad, (**then**) you will get sick.
agar vo pakāē, tō ham zarūr khāē̃gē.	If she (**should**) cook, (**then**) we surely will eat.

This section illustrates conditional sentences, the "if" clauses of which have verbs in the subjunctive, and the second clauses verbs in the future.

18.1.4

agar āp cāhē̃, tō maī āp-kē sāth jāū̃gā.	If you (**will**) wish, (**then**) I will go with you.
agar mērā bhāī yahā̃ rahē, tō maī āj • rāt sinēmā-kō jā sakū̃gā.	If my brother will remain here, (**then**) I will be able to go to the movies tonight.
agar āp mērē ānē-tak vahā̃ ṭharē̃, tō maī āp-kē liyē akhbār lā sakū̃gā.	If you will remain there until I arrive, (**then**) I will be able to bring the newspaper for you.
agar āp āhistā bōlē̃, tō maī samajh sakū̃gā.	If you will speak slowly, (**then**) I will be able to understand.
agar āp vaqt-par āē̃, tō ham vaqt-par khānā khā sakē̃gē.	If you will come on time, (**then**) we will be able to eat dinner on time.

This section illustrates conditional sentences, both clauses of which contain in English verbs in the future tense. Note that the verb of the first clause usually is placed in the subjunctive in sentences of this type.

REMARKS: In the English translation of such sentences the verb of the first clause is often in the present indicative (functioning as a future).

18.1.5 Exercise 1. **Translate into English:**

1. agar baccā acchā hai, tō maī us-kō cumtā hū̃. 2. agar mōṭargāṛī dēr-sē āē, tō maī āp-kē liyē ṭharū̃. 3. agar āp bōl saktē haī, tō Urdū-mē̃ āhistā bōliyē. 4. agar daryā gahrā hō, tō maī us-mē̃ tairū̃. 5. agar pānī acchā hōgā, tō musāfir us-kō piyēgā. 6. agar daryā-mē̃ machliyā̃ haī, tō machērā un-kō pakaṛtā hai. 7. agar phal pakkē hō̃, tō maī un-kō khāū̃. 8. agar tum cāhtē hō, tō mujhē ṭhaṇḍā pānī dō! 9. agar mālik cāhē̃gē, tō naukar un-kē liyē khānā taiyār karēgā. 10. agar tum Urdū paṛhō, tō śāyad tum bōl sakō. 11. agar mērā

dōst k̤hat likhēgā, tō maĩ us-sē milnē-kē liyē safar karū̃gā. 12. agar darak̤ht-kē nīcē ghās hai, tō gāy usē khātī hai. 13. agar ādmī kām karēgā, tō maĩ us-kō paisē dū̃gā. 14. agar bāzār nazdīk hō, tō maĩ us-kō dēkhnē-kē liyē jāū̃. 15. agar mērī ṭōpī kursī-par hai, tō usē lāiyē. 16. agar mā̃ cāhē, tō vo laṛkē-kē sāth bāzār jāē. 17. agar kuttā vāpas āēgā, tō laṛkī us-kō khānā dēgī. 18. agar hōṭal-kā kamrā acchā hai, tō musāfir k̤huś hai. 19. agar aurat dukān-mẽ bahot cīzẽ k̤harīdēgī, tō dukāndār k̤huś hōgā. 20. agar tumhẽ bāzār jānā hai, tō mērē sāth āō! 21. agar tum bīmār hō, tō ham tumhārē ghar-kō āj • rāt jāẽ. 22. agar āp hukam dẽ, tō maĩ āp-sē milnē-kē liyē āū̃. 23. agar dhōbī acchā hai, tō maĩ dhōnē-kē liyē us-kō kapṛē dētā hū̃. 24. agar din acchā hō, tō mālī bāg-mẽ khōdē. 25. agar baccā daryā-kī taraf dauṛtā hai, tō us-kō vāpas lāō.

18.1.6 Exercise 2. **Translate into Urdu:**

1. If I (**msc.**) run, I fall. 2. If the policeman will catch the thief, he will beat him. 3. If you (**msc.**) (**should**) want to go to the river, I (**fm.**) may be able to go with you. 4. If you (**fm. hon.**) are tired, please sit in that chair. 5. If the bullocks stop, the farmer beats them. 6. If the water will be cold, we (**msc.**) will drink it. 7. If I (**msc.**) (**should**) run, I may fall. 8. If you (**fm.**) come back on time, please stop to talk with me. 9. If my friend (**msc.**) will buy the Urdu newspapers, he will read them for me. 10. If there are fruits on the tree, the monkey will steal them. 11. If you (**msc.**) want to talk with me, don't talk fast! 12. If the newspaper is on the table, please give (**it**) to me. 13. If the family is poor, the man has to go to the city to work in the factory. 14. If the road is long, the traveller will become tired. 15. If you (**msc.**) can, stop to see me on your return. 16. If the river water will be warm, we will want to swim in it. 17. If there (**should**) be ripe fruits on the tree, the monkeys may steal them. 18. If you (**msc.**)must come, come on time. 19. If the place is beautiful, the woman will want to stop to rest there. 20. If the servant is good, the master is happy. 21. If you (**fm.**) are tired, do not work! 22. If the manager can, he will give us a good room. 23. If the clothes are clean, the woman will take them from the washerman. 24. If the servant wants to talk to the master in Urdu, he should talk slowly. 25. If your house is near-by, I will go there with you.

18.2

kaun laṛkā śarārat kartā hai?	Which boy makes mischief?
vo kaun hai?	Who is he?
laṛkā kis ādmī-kō dēkhtā hai?	Which man does the boy see?
laṛkā kis-kō dēkhtā hai?	Whom does the boy see?
kaun ādmī parindõ-kō pakaṛtē haĩ?	Which men catch the birds?
vo kaun haĩ?	Who are they?
laṛkā kin ādmiyõ-kō dēkhtā hai?	Which men does the boy see?
laṛkā kin-kō dēkhtā hai?	Whom does the boy see?
kaun aurat daryā-kē pās hai?	Which women is by the river
vo kaun hai?	Who is she?

laṛkā kis aurat-kō miltā hai?	Which woman does the boy meet?
laṛkā kis-kō miltā hai?	Whom does the boy meet?
kaun aurtē̃ gātī haī̃?	Which women sing?
vo kaun haī̃?	Who are they?
javān ādmī kin aurtō̃-kō ghurtā hai?	At which women does the young man stare?
javān ādmī kin-kō ghurtā hai?	At whom does the young man stare?

This section is concerned with the interrogative pronouns and adjectives. In each of the pairs of sentences, above, the first sentence illustrates the interrogative adjective and the second the interrogative pronoun. The forms for pronoun and adjective are identical. There is no distinction between masculine and feminine forms.

The forms for pronoun and adjective are: **kaun** subject form, singular and plural; **kis** object, singular; and **kin** object, plural.

REMARKS: **śarārat** (ī) mischief, **parindā** (ā) bird, **javān (adj., n.c.)** young, **ghurnā** to stare at.

18.2.1

vo kyā cīz hai?	What thing is that?
vo kyā hai?	What is that?
laṛkā kyā cīz paṛhtā hai?	What thing does the boy read?
laṛkā kyā paṛhtā hai?	What does the boy read?
vo kyā cīzē̃ haī̃?	What things are those?
vo kyā haī̃?	What are they?
laṛkā kyā cīzē̃ cāhtā hai?	What things does the boy want?
laṛkā kyā cāhtā hai?	What does the boy want?

This section illustrates the interrogative adjective and pronoun, **kyā,** which modifies or refers to inanimate objects. The form is the same for case, number, and gender. **kis** and **kin,** singular and plural, respectively, are the forms which appear before postpositions.

REMARKS: **kyā,** in its function as an adjective, appears only with **cīz, thing.**

18.2.2 Exercise 1. **Translate into English:**

1. kaun ādmī Añgrēzī samajh sakēgā? 2. ye kyā hai? 3. maī̃ Kalkattā kis tarah jā saktā hū̃? 4. kyā bāt hai? 5. agar āp śahar jāē̃, tō āp kis-kē sāth jāē̃gē? 6. vo kaun kitābē̃ paṛhnā zyādā pasand kartā hai? 7. machērā hamē̃ kaun machliyā̃ bēcēgā? 8. maī̃ Kalkattā kis saṛak-sē jā saktā hū̃? 9. laṛkā kis aurat-kē liyē pānī lātā hai? 10 vo aurat kaun hai? 11. kaun aurtē̃ khānā taiyār kar sakē̃gī? 12. āp kin ādmiyō̃-kē sāth bōlnā zyādā pasand kartē haī̃? 13. kaun bailgāṛī tumhārī hai? 14. maī̃ kis-kē sāth Urdū bōlū̃? 15. kis

tālibilm-kō kitāb paṛhnā hai? 16. vo ādmī kaun haĩ? 17. baccā kis kamrē-mẽ hai? 18. maĩ kis-kō paisē dũ? 19. kaun ādmī pīnē-kā pānī cāhtā hai? 20. āp Urdū-mẽ **"train"**-kō kyā kahtē haĩ?

18.2.3 Exercise 2. **Translate into Urdu:**

1. What's the matter? 2. How do you (**hon., msc.**) say 'book" in Urdu? 3. How can I (**fm.**) go to Calcutta? 4. Who is the hunter? 5. For whom should I (**msc.**) bring back a newspaper? 6. With which man will I (**fm.**) be able to speak Bengali? 7. Who understands English? 8. For whose arrival are you (**hon. msc.**) waiting? 9. If you (**msc.**) can, with which plow will you till the field? 10. Which men are farmers? 11. From which tree do the monkeys steal the ripe fruits? 12. Whom will the teacher ask questions? 13. By what road can I (**msc.**) go to Calcutta? 14. What is that thing? 15. In front of which house is your automobile? 16. With what will the policeman strike the thief? 17. Which woman is your wife? 18. To which holy-man will you (**hon., fm.**) give the flowers? 19. What is his business? 20. What kinds of things does the shopkeeper sell?

18.3

kaun-sā ādmī bāg̠-mẽ hai?	Which man is in the garden?
kaun-sē ādmī bāg̠-mẽ haĩ?	Which men are in the garden?
laṛkā kis ādmī-kē liyē kām kartā hai?	For which man does the boy work?
laṛkā kin ādmiyõ-kē liyē kām kartā hai?	For which men does the boy work?
kaun-sī aurat galī-mẽ hai?	Which woman is in the street?
kaun-sī aurtẽ galī-mẽ haĩ?	Which women are in the street?
laṛkā kis aurat-kē liyē kām kartā hai?	For which woman does the boy work?
laṛkā kin aurtõ-kē liyē kām kartā hai?	For which women does the boy work?
kaun-sī kitāb mēz-par hai?	Which book is on the table?
kaun-sī kitābẽ mēz-par haĩ?	Which books are on the table?
laṛkā kis kitāb-sē varaḳ phāṛtā hai?	From which book does the boy tear pages?
laṛkā kin kitābõ-sē varaḳ phāṛtā hai?	From which books does the boy tear pages?

Compare the interrogative adjective forms in the first two sentences of each of the three groups of four sentences, above, and the interrogative adjective, **kaun**, of section 18.2. To the subject form of **kaun** is attached the particle **-sā** which agrees with the noun modified in gender and number. The resultant interrogative adjective, **kaun-sā**, is employed to refer to a specific being or thing as contrasted with **kaun** which refers to a being or thing generally unspecified. (See 38.1.1) Compare: **vo ādmī kaun hai? Who is that man?** and **vo ādmī kaun-sā hai? Who is that** (particular) **man** (i.e., **of the men mentioned or known).**

REMARKS: (1) The object forms are normally the same as those for **kaun. (kaun-sē** and **kaun-sī** often occur as the object forms, masculine and feminine, respectively.

(2) **galī** (ī) street, **varaḳ** (ā) page.

18.4

āp kitnā pānī cāhtē haĩ?	How much water do you want?
mālī kitnī lakṛī jãngal-sē lāēgā?	How much wood will the gardener bring from the jungle?
baccā kitnā dūdh piyēgā?	How much milk will the child drink?
kitnē ādmī khēt-mẽ haĩ?	How many men are in the field?
āp kitnē ādmiyõ-kō paisē dētē haĩ?	To how many men do you give money?
ghar-mẽ kitnē mehmān haĩ?	How many guests are there in the house?
laṛkī kitnī ustāniyõ-kē liyē tohfē lātī hai?	For how many instructresses does the girl bring gifts?
gāõ-mē kitnē mazdūr haĩ?	How many workers are in the village?

This section illustrates the interrogative adjective, **kitnā**, which indicates quantity. It functions like the adjectives described in sections 3.2, 4.3, and 6.1.

REMARKS: **ustānī** (ī) instructress, **tohfā** (ā) gift, **marīz** (ā) patient, sick person.

18.4.1 Exercise 1. **Translate into English:**

1. kitnē bajē haĩ? 2. maĩ āp-kē liyē kitnē lakṛī vāpas lāũ? 3. kitnē paisē lōgē? 4. kitnē ādmī is śahar-mẽ rahtē haĩ? 5. is hōṭal-mẽ kitnē ādmī Aṅgrēzī bōl saktē haĩ? 6. kitnī aurtẽ sī saktī haĩ? 7. āp in sabziyõ-kē liyē kitnē paisē lẽgē? 8. kitnē marīz davāī pītē haĩ? 9. musāfir kitnē dinõ-kē liyē yahā̃ rahẽgē? 10. aurat kitnī laṛkiyõ-kē liyē pakātī hai?

18.4.2 Exercise 2. **Translate into Urdu:**

1. What time is it? 2. How many days do you have to stay here? 3. How many rooms are in this house? 4. How many newspapers do you (**hon., fm.**) read? 5. How big is it? 6. How many children does the man have? 7. How much money will you (**msc.**) take for these fruits? 8. How much milk does your cow give? 9. How many oxen does the farmer have? 10. How many wells are there in the village?

18.5 Text 2: **Bātcīt.**[1]

Translate into English. Answer the questions in Urdu:

[Karam Dīn [2] aur Mohammad Būtā [2] Śālimār-kē mēlē [3] -mẽ ēk dūsrē-sē miltē haĩ. ye dōnõ kisān haĩ aur ēk chōṭē gāõ-mẽ rahtē haĩ. dōnõ pahilī dafā [4] Lāhōr [5] -mẽ haĩ.]

Karam Dīn: caudharī [6] Būtā! salām-ō-alēkum.[7]

Mohammad Būtā: valēkum-asalām, caudharī. kyā hal • cāl [8] haĩ? bāl • baccē rāzī • ḳhuśī [9] haĩ.

Karam Dīn: Allah-kā fazal [10] hai. sab ḳheriyyat [11] hai. sunāō, mēlā dēkhtē hō?

Mohammad Būtā: hā̃, bhāī. is dafā tō mēlē-mẽ bahot cahal • pahal [12] hai. hazārõ [13] ādmī aur aurtẽ haĩ. aur sẽkrõ [14] dukānẽ haĩ. mērā tō jī [15] cāhtā hai ke [16] bīvī •baccõ-kē liyē bahot-sī [17] cīzẽ ḳharīd lũ,[18] lēkin kafī [19] paisē nahĩ haĩ. tum bōlō, śahar-kī sair kab karōgē?

Karam Dīn: Lāhōr tō bahot-hī baṛā śahar hai. kuch lōg kahtē haĩ ke [16] jis [20] -nē Lāhōr nahĩ dēkhā,[21] vo paidā [22] -hī nahĩ huā.[23] mērā-bhī aisā-hī ḳhayāl hai. maĩ aur mērā ēk sāthī [24] Śāhī Masjid [25] dēkhkar [26] āyē haĩ. maĩ tumhẽ kyā batāũ, baṛī-hī ḳhūbsūrat imārat hai.

Mohammad Būtā: acchā, ye tō batāō ke [27] is masjid-kā banānēvālā [28] kaun hai?

Karam Dīn: ēk bābū [29] -kē kahnē-kē mutābiḳ [30] mugal [31] bādśāh [32] Auraṅgzēb is masjid-kā banvānēvālā [33] hai. ye sārē Pākistān-mē̃ avval • nambar [34] masjid hai.

Mohammad Būtā: bhalā! [35] ēk vaḳt-mē̃ kitnē ādmī masjid-mē̃ namāz [36] paṛh saktē haĩ?

Karam Dīn: mērā ḳhayāl hai ke [27] kam-az-kam [37] ēk lākh [38] ādmī ēk • sāth [39] us masjid-mē̃ namāz paṛh saktē haĩ.

Mohammad Būtā: acchā, ye tō batāō [40] tum mēlē-mē̃ kyā kuch ḳharīdōgē?

Karam Dīn: maĩ kaī cīzē̃ ḳharīdū̃gā—chōṭī laṛkī-kē liyē kā̃c [41] -kī cūṛiyā̃,[42] bīvī-kē liyē ḳhuśbūdār [43] tēl [44] aur sāban,[45] aur bāp-kē liyē ēk ḳamīz [46] ḳharīdū̃gā.

Mohammad Būtā: yār,[47] tumhārē pās tō phir bahot paisē hō̃gē.

Karam Dīn: arē,[48] bhāī, kapās [49] -kī fasal [50] bēcnē-sē mērē pās kuch paisē haĩ. vo [51] ḳharc kartā [52] hū̃. kyā tumhārē pās fasal-kē paisē nahī̃ haĩ?

Mohammad Būtā: hā̃, mērē pās-bhī kuch hai. maĩ āhistā āhistā ḳharc kartā hū̃. tum jānō agar [53] is vāḳt zyādā paisē ḳharc kar dū̃,[54] tō phir bāḳī [55] sārā sāl kyā karū̃.

Karam Dīn: bhāī Būtā, tum tō dūr-kī [56] sōctē hō. hamārā tō ye īmān [57] hai ke [27] jis [58] Ḳhudā-nē paidā kiyā [59] hai, vo rōṭī-bhī dēgā. kyā maulvī • sāhab [60] masjid-mē̃ har jumē nahī̃ kahtē ke [27] Allah-hī sab-kō rōzī [61] dētā hai?

Mohammad Būtā: bēśak [62] Allah sab-kā mālik hai. lēkin mērī rāy [63] ye hai ke [16] Allah un-kī madad kartā hai jō apnī madad āp kartē haĩ. hamārē gāõ-mē̃ ēk skūl hai. us-mē̃ tō ustād • sāhab yehī sikhātē [64] haĩ.

Karam Dīn: (gussē-mē̃) tō kyā tumhārā matlab [65] ye hai ke [16] hamārē maulvī • sāhab jhūṭ bōltē [66] haĩ?

Mohammad Būtā: nahī̃, caudharī, mērā ye matlab nahī̃. lēkin tum jāntē hō ke [16] maulvī • sāhab-bhī hamārē tumhārē-jaise [67] ādmī haĩ. vo galtī-bhī kar saktē haĩ. ye-bhī yād rakhō [68] ke [16] hamārē skūl-kē māsṭar • sāhab-bhī bahot paṛhē • likhē aur syānē [69] ādmī haĩ.

Karam Dīn: hō saktā hai ke [16] tum ṭhīk kahtē hō. tumhārē ḳhayāl-mē̃ mujhē āpnē paisō̃-kō kyā karnā cāhiyē?

Mohammad Būtā: mērī rāy-mē tō tumhē̃ apnē fāltū [70] paisē baink [71] -mē̃ jamā karvā dēnā [72] cāhiyē̃. tumhārē gāõ-kē pās-hī anjuman-ē-imdād-ē-bāhmī [73] -kā baink hai. agar tum apnē paisē vahā̃ jamā karvāō,[74] tō tumhē̃ sau rūpayē-par tīn rūpayē sūd [75] ēk sāl-mē̃ milēgā. mazē-kī bāt ye hai ke [16] jab [76] tum cāhō, apnē paisē nikalvā [77] saktē hō.

Karam Dīn: caudharī! tumhārē is ḳīmtī [78] maśvarē [79] -kā bahot śukriyā.[80] maĩ is-kē bārē-mē̃ [81] sōcū̃gā. hā, ye batāō ke [16] tumhārē gāõ-mē̃ faslō̃-kā kyā hāl [82] haĩ?

Mohammad Būtā: Ḳhudā-kī meharbānī [83] -sē faslē̃ is sāl [84] tō baṛī acchī haĩ. bāriś vaḳt-par hō gayī. kisānō̃-kī mehnat [85] -kā natījā [86] ye hai ke [16] fasal bahot acchī hai.

Karam Dīn: is sāl kapās-kā bhāō [87] bahot ū̃cā hai. agar [88] hamēśā [89] aisā [90] rahē, tō zamindār • lōg [91] ḳhuś • hāl [92] hō jāē̃.[93]

Mohammad Būtā: aisā [90] hōnā tō muśkil [94] hai. hamārē māsṭar • sāhab kahtē haī ke [16] Kōryā [95] -kī jañg [96] -kī vajāh-sē [97] kapās-kā bhāō tēz [98] hai. jū-hī [99] jañg ḳhatam [100] hōgī, bhāō gir jāēgā.[101]

Karam Dīn: ye tō tum burī ḳhabar sunātē hō.

Mohammad Būtā: nahī̃, caudharī, aisā [90] na kahō. agar [88] Kōryā-kī jañg ḳhatah hō jāē, tō dunyā [102] -mẽ aman [103] hō jāē. yād rakhō ke [16] jañg Kōryā-sē hamārē mulk [104] -mẽ-bhī ā saktī hai.

Karam Dīn: yār Mohammad Būtā tum tō baṛē syānē ādmī mālūm [105] hōtē hō. maī ḳhud [106] tō paṛhā • likhā nahī hū̃. lēkin mērā laṛkā ab baṛā hō rahā [107] hai. mērā ḳhayāl hai kē [16] usē skūl-mẽ bhēj dū̃.[108]

Mohammad Būtā: bhāī Karam Dīn, tum laṛkē-kō hamārē skūl-mẽ kyū̃ nahī̃ bhējtē? vahā̃ ustād • sāhab baccõ-kō har ḳisam [109] -kī tālīm [110] dētē haī.

Karam Dīn: mērē pās itnē [111] paisē nahī̃ ke [112] laṛkē-kō bōrḍing • haus [113] -mẽ rakhū̃.

Mohammad Būtā: is-kā tum fikr [114] na karō. tumhārā laṛkā mērē pās ṭhahar saktā hai. hamārē ghar-mẽ us-kē liyē jagāh hai. maī us-par nazar rakhū̃gā.[115]

Karam Dīn: caudharī, tumhārī baṛī meharbānī. maī inśā-Allah laṛkē-kō jald tumhārē pās bhēj dū̃gā. mujhē yaḳīn [116] hai ke [16] tum usē apnē bēṭõ-kī tarāh [117] samjhōgē.

Mohammad Būtā: zarūr, zarūr. acchā, phir milẽgē. Ḳhudā hāfiz.[118]

Karam Dīn: Ḳhudā hāfiz.

[ab dōnõ dōst mēlē-kī sair-mẽ maśgūl [119] haī.]

savālāt:

1. Karam Dīn aur Mohammad Būtā ēk dūsrē-kō kahā̃ milē? [120] 2. Karam Dīn-kī Lāhōr-kē bārē-mẽ kyā rāy thī? 3. Śāhī Masjid kis-nē banvāyī thī? 4. Mohammad Būtā-kē gāõ-mẽ jō [121] skūl thā, us-kē māsṭar • sāhab baccõ-kō kyā sikhātē thē? 5. Mohammad Būtā-nē Karam Dīn-kō fāltū paisõ-kē bārē-mẽ kyā maśvarā diyā? [122]

NOTES: 1. conversation (ī); 2. name of man; 3. **mēlā** fair (ā); 4. **pahilī dafā** for the first time (= **adv.**); 5. city of Lahore; 6. title of respect among farmers; 7. cf. variant: **asalām-alēkum;** 8. conditions, state of things (ā); 9. comfortable, all right (**adj., n.c.**); 10. kindness (ā); 11. well-being (ī); 12. hub-bub, to-do (ī); 13. thousands (**adv.**); 14. hundreds (**adv.**); 15. heart (ā); 16. see 29.2 and Remarks; 17. **bahot-sā** many, see 38.1; 18. **ḳharīd lēnā** to buy (**tr.**), see lesson 28; 19. enough; 20. by whom (**rel. pron.**), see 25.1 for construction; 21. seen, **pst. part.** of **dēkhnā,** (for construction see 21.1, ff.); 22. born; 23. **pst. part.** of **hōnā,** see 22.1.1; 24. friend, companion (ā); 25. Śāhī Mosque (ī); 26. having seen, see 30.1; 27. see fn. 16; 28. builder (ā), see 31.2; 29. educated man (ā); 30. **-kē mutābiḳ** according to (**postpos. phrase**); 31. Mogul (**adj., n.c.**); 32. king (ā); 33. builder (ā), see 36.1–36.1.4 for verbal stem formation and 31.2; 34. **avval • nambar** number one; 35. well! (**intj.**); 36. **namāz** prayer (ī), **namāz paṛhnā** to pray (**tr.**); 37. **kam-az-kam** at least (**adv.**); 38. one-hundred thousand; 39. all together (**adj.**); 40. **batānā** to tell (**tr.**); 41. glass (ā); 42. **cūṛī bangle** (ī); 43. scented (**adj., n.c.**); 44. oil (ā); 45. soap (ā), **sābun** is a variant; 46. shirt (ī); 47. dear friend (ā); 48. oh! (**vocative pt.**); 49. cotton (ā); 50. crop (ī); 51. The subject form is employed for the direct object form, when referring to things (and sometimes irrational beings).; 52. **ḳharc karnā** to spend (**tr.**); 53. For conditional constructions see 18.1–18.1.4; 54. **ḳharc kar dēnā** to spend, see lesson 28; 55. remaining (**adj., n.c.**); 56. **dūr-kā** far ahead (= **adj.**); 57. belief, idea, faith (ā); 58. see 25.1; 59. created, see 21.1, ff., for perfect tense constructions; 60. Muslim religious leader (ā); 61. livelihood, every day's provisions (ī); 62. doubtless (**adv.**); 63. opinion (ī); 64. **sikhānā** teach, see 36.1, ff., for verbal stem formations; 65. meaning (ā); 66. **jhūṭ bōlnā** to lie (**tr.**),**jhūṭ** lie (ā); 67. like, see 33.2;

68. **yād rakhnā** to remember, keep in mind (**tr.**), **yād** memory (ī); 69. **syānā** wise (**adj.**); 70. spare, extra (**adj., n.c.**); 71. bank (ā); 72. **jamā karvā dēnā** to deposit, accumulate (**tr.**), see lesson 28 and 36.1, ff.; 73. **anjuman-ē-imdād-ē-bāhmī** cooperative society (ī); 74. **jamā karvāna** to deposit, save (**tr.**), see 36.1, ff.; 75. interest (ā); 76. when (**rel. adv.**), see 26.3 and Remarks, 1; 77. **nikalvānā** to take out, withdraw (**tr.**), see 36.1, ff.; 78. valuable (**adj., n.c.**); 79. **maśvarā** advice (ā); 80. thanks (ā); 81. **-kē bārē-mē̃** about, concerning (**postpos. phrase**); 82. condition, state (ā); 83. grace, kindness (ī); 83. **is sāl** this year (= **adv.**); 85. hard work, toil (ī); 86. result (ā); 87. rate (ā); 88. see 18.1.2; 89. always (**adv.**); 90. like this (**adv.**); 91. farmers, land-owners (ē), note use of **lōg** as a plural particle; 92. well-to-do (**adj., n.c.**); 93. **hō jānā** to become (**int.**), see lesson 28; 94. difficult (**adj., n.c.**); 95. Korea (ā); 96. war (ī); 97. **-kī vajāh-sē** on account of; 98. = high (i.e., **in price**) (**adj., n.c.**); 99. as soon as (**adv.**); 100. **k̤hatam hōnā** to end, finish (**int.**); 101. **gir jānā** to fall (**int.**); see lesson 28; 102. world (ī); 103. peace (ā); 104. country, land (ā); 105. **mālūm hōnā** to appear, seem; 106. self (**reflex. pt.**); 107. **baṛā hō rahnā** to be growing up (**int.**); 108. **bhēj dēnā** to send (**tr.**), see lesson 28; 109. **har k̤isam** every kind of, all kinds of; 110. instruction (ī); 111. **itnā** this much (**adj.**); 112. see fn. 16; 113. boarding-house (ā); 114. worry, concern (ā); 115. **nazar** sight (ī), **nazar rakhnā** to keep an eye on (**tr.**); 116. certainty (ā); 117. **-kī tarāh** like (= **postpos. phrase**); 118. God be with you; 119. **maśgūl hōnā** to be busy, engaged in (**int.**); 120. met, **pst. part.** of **milnā**, see 20.1, ff.; 121. see 25.1; 122. gave, **pst. part.** of **dēnā**; see 22.1.2 and 21.1, ff.

LESSON 19

19.1

maĩ khātā thā.	I (**msc.**) was eating.
maĩ khātī thī.	I (**fm.**) was eating.
vo khātā thā.	He was eating.
vo khātī thī.	She was eating.
ham khātē thē.	We (**msc.**) were eating.
ham khātī thī̃.	We (**fm.**) were eating.
tum khātē thē.	You (**msc.**) were eating.
tum khātī thī̃.	You (**fm.**) were eating.
āp khātē thē.	You (**msc.**) were eating.
āp khātī thī̃.	You (**fm.**) were eating.
vo khātē thē.	They (**msc.**) were eating.
vo khātī thī̃.	They (**fm.**) were eating.

This section illustrates the past of the tense described in section 2.1. (This is termed the "Imperfect" or "Past Continuous" by grammarians.)

The construction consists of the present participle, which agrees with the subject of the sentence in gender and number, and the imperfect of **hōnā, thā** (for the masculine singular), **thē** (for the masculine plural), **thī** (for the feminine singular), and **thī** (for the feminine plural).

19.1.1 More examples are:

ādmī lēṭtā thā.	The man was lying down.
ādmī lēṭtē thē.	The men were lying down.
aurat phē̃ktī thī.	The woman was throwing.
aurtē̃ phē̃ktī thī̃.	The women were throwing.

bahādur ādmī laṛtā thā.	The brave man was fighting.
bahādur aurtẽ laṛtī thī̃.	The brave women were fighting.
ḳhofzadā aurat laṛtī thī.	The frightened woman was fighting.
ḳhofzadā aurtẽ laṛtī thī̃.	The frightened women were fighting.
mohtāt laṛkī kām kartī thī.	The careful girl was working.
mohtāt laṛkiyā̃ kām kartī thī̃.	The careful girls were working.
hōśiyār tālibilm skūl jātā thā.	The clever student was going to school.
hōśiyār tālibilm skūl jātē thē.	The clever students were going to school.
mehantī laṛkī skūl jātī thī.	The industrious girl was going to school.
mehantī laṛkiyā̃ skūl jātī thī̃.	The industrious girls were going to school.
ḳhuś klark daftar-mẽ gātā thā.	The happy clerk was singing in the office.
imāndār laṛkā paisē vāpas dētā thā.	The honest boy was giving back the money.
garīb ādmī mandar-kē sāmnē phūl bēctā thā.	The poor man was selling flowers in front of the temple.
cupcap cōr taṅg galī-mẽ intazār kartā thā.	The quiet thief was waiting in the narrow street.
ḳhūbsūrat laṛkī gātī thī.	The beautiful girl was singing.
udās baccā ḳhālis dūdh pītā thā.	The sad child was drinking the pure milk.
amīr ādmī kyā kartā thā?	What was the rich man doing?
gairmulkī ādmī ēk tēz ustarā chupātā thā.	The foreign man was hiding a sharp razor.
kamzōr ādmī mazbūt rassā mā̃gtā thā.	The weak man was asking for a strong rope.
akalmand bāp baccē-kō miṭhāī dētē thē.	The wise father was giving candy to the child.
ajnabī javān ādmī ēk sigrēṭ pītā thā.	The young stranger was smoking a cigarette.
naukarānī sāf jūtē lātī thī.	The maidservant was bringing clean shoes.
naukar sāf pyālē lātā thā.	The servant was bringing clean cups.
laṛkī ēk āsān sabaḳ paṛhtī thī.	The girl was reading an easy lesson.
kisān saḳht zamīn khōdtā thā.	The farmer was digging the hard ground.
ādmī bhārī bōjh tōltā thā.	The man was weighing the heavy load.
aurat ḳhūbsūrat tasvīr ḳharīdtī thī.	The woman was buying the beautiful picture.
laṛkiyā̃ bīmār ādmī-kō ēk phal dētī thī̃.	The girls were giving a fruit to the sick man.
baṛhaī ēk gōl mēz banātā thā.	The carpenter was making a round table.
laṛkī ghar-sē garm dūdh lātī thī.	The girl was bringing warm milk from the house.
aurtẽ muḳaddas jagah jātī thī̃.	The women were going to a sacred place.
aurtẽ numāēśgāh-kō jātī thī̃.	The women were going to the exhibition place.

REMARKS: (1) The adjectives occurring in this section are of the type described in section 11.4.

(2) [-kā] **intazar karnā** translates English **to wait for.**

(3) Vocabulary notes: **ustarā** (ā) razor, **muḳaddas jagah** (ī) sacred place, pilgrimage spot, **pyālā** (ā) cup, **bōjh** (ā) load, burden, **sabaḳ** (ā) lesson, **sigrēṭ** (ī) cigarette, **naukarānī** (ī) maidservant, **numāēśgāh** (ā) exhibition place, **g̱airmulkī** (**adj., n.c.**) foreign, **ajnabī** (**adj., n.c.**) unknown, strange, **ardalī** (ā) orderly, **g̱amgīn** (**adj.**) sad.

19.1.2

klark ḳhuś thā.	The clerk was happy.
klark ḳhuś thē.	The clerks were happy.
ādmī g̱arīb thā.	The man was poor.
ādmī g̱arīb thē.	The men were poor.
aurat kamzōr thī.	The woman was weak.
aurtē̃ kamzōr thī̃.	The women were weak.
mēz gōl thī.	The table was round.
mēzē̃ gōl thī̃.	The tables were round.

This section illustrates the "Imperfect" of the Urdu verb **to be, to exist.** The form agrees in gender and number with the subject of the sentence - **thā** for the masculine singular; **thē** for the masculine plural; **thī** for the feminine singular; **thī** for the feminine plural. (See 19.1 above.)

19.1.3 Exercise 1. **Translate into English:**
1. ham kamzōr ādmiyō̃-kō khilātē thē. 2. baccā garm dūdh pītā thā. 3. kisān-kē pās hal thā. 4. ḳhuś laṛkiyā̃ khēlnē-kē liyē bāhar jātī thī̃. 5. naukar musāfir-kē liyē pānī lātā thā. 6. hōśiyār ardalī daftar-kē pās thā. 7. ustād • sāhab āsān kahānī kyū̃ paṛhtē thē? 8. aurat bīmār ādmī-kē liyē garm pānī lātī thī. 9. mōṭarbas muḳaddas jagah-sē kab vāpas ātī thī? 10. mālī saḳht zamīn khōdtā thā. 11. kyā aurtē̃ sāf pyālē lātī thī̃? 12. saṛak-kē pās ḳhūbsūrat imārtē̃ thī̃. 13. ustād • sāhab hōśiyār laṛkō̃-sē āsān savāl kyū̃ pūchtē thē? 14. āmīr ādmī ēk sigrēṭ pītā thā. 15. kyā naukar imāndār thā? 16. aurat-kē pās nayī sāṛiyā̃ thī̃. 17. javān ādmī daftar-mē̃ gātā thā. 18. laṛkī mēz-kē nīcē garm dūdh chupātī thī. 19. cupcāp faḳīr mandar-kē sāmnē baiṭhtē thē. 20. bīmār ādmī udās thā.

19.1.4 Exercise 2. **Translate into Urdu:**
1. The boy was bringing the heavy wood for the woman. 2. The boy had a book. 3. Were the women going to a sacred place? 4. The stranger was asking the servant for water. 5. Was the boy honest? 6. Father was smoking a cigarette. 7. The young woman was giving candy to the child. 8. Why were the farmers digging the hard ground? 9. Why was the child sad? 10. The poor woman was wanting to sell flowers in front of the temple. 11. The weak man was sad. 12. The round house was near the narrow street. 13. The young women were beautiful. 14. For whom was the man buying the razor? 15. The happy girls were singing together near the well. 16. The weak man was weighing the heavy wood. 17. The clever girls were reading the easy lesson. 18. The women were

waiting for (**their**) friends near the well. 19. He was bringing a clean cup for the sick man. 20. The mother was bringing a cup of warm milk for the happy child.

19.2

mujhē śahar jānā cāhiyē thā.	I ought to have gone to town.
tālibilm-kō paṛhnā cāhiyē thā.	The student ought to have studied.
naukar-kō hamārē jānā-kē liyē sab kuch taiyār karnā cāhiyē thā.	The servant should have prepared everything for our departure.
laṛkī-kō kuē̃-sē pānī lānā cāhiyē thā.	The girl ought to have brought water from the well.
aurat-kō bāvarcīḳhānē-mē̃ pānī ubālnā cāhiyē thā.	The woman should have boiled water in the kitchen.

This section illustrates the past tense of the **cāhiyē** construction described in section 17.1. **thā** remains unchanged.

19.2.1 Exercise 1. **Translate into English:**

1. dhōbī-kō kapṛē dhōnā cāhiyē thā. 2. laṛkē-kō āg-kē liyē lakṛī lānā cāhiyē thā. 3. tumhē̃ Urdū-mē̃ bōlnā cāhiyē thā. 4. mālī-kō paudō̃-par pānī ḍālnā cāhiyē thā. 5. śikārī-kō ḳhū̃ḳhār jānvar mārnā cāhiyē thā. 6. kisān-kō saḳht zamīn khōdnā cāhiyē thā. 7. āp-kō Urdū samajh saknā cāhiyē thā. 8. baccē-kō bīmār ādmī-kō ēk phal dēnā cāhiyē thā. 9. ādmiyō̃-kō muḳaddas jagah jānā cāhiyē thā. 10. hamē̃ dāyī̃ taraf jānā cāhiyē thā.

19.2.2 Exercise 2. **Translate into Urdu:**

1. You should have drunk the milk. 2. Should the children have stayed at home? 3. We ought to have given the poor man money. 4. You should have rested today. 5. The weak gardener needed to rest beside the well. 6. The washerman should have brought back the clothes today. 7. They should have come to see us yesterday. 8. The poor man needed to work. 9. Ought you to have gone to the office today? 10. Should we have gone to the movies tonight?

19.3

aurat-kō tāzā pānī cāhiyē thā.	The woman needed fresh water.
āp-kō kitnē paisē cāhiyē̃ thē?	How much money did you need?
kisān-kō mazdūrō̃-kī madad cāhiyē thī.	The farmer needed the help of workers.
baccē-kō nayē jūtē cāhiyē̃ thē.	The child needed new shoes.
tālibilm-kō bahot kitābē̃ cāhiyē̃ thī̃.	The student needed many books.
āp-kō kyā cāhiyē thā?	What did you need?
bāp-kō ārām karnē-kē liyē thōṛā vaḳt cāhiyē thā.	Father needed a little time for rest.
mā̃-kō khānā pakānē-kē liyē āg cāhiyē thī.	Mother needed fire to cook the food.
chōṭī laṛkī-kō khēlnē-kē liyē guṛiyā̃ cāhiyē̃ thī̃.	The little girl needed dolls to play with.

These sentences illustrate the past of the construction described in 17.2. Here **thā** agrees in gender and number with the subject. The final vowel of **cāhiyē** is nasalized (i.e., **cāhiyē̃**), when the noun is plural.

19.3.1 Exercise 1. **Translate into English:**

1. aurat-kō āg-kē liyē lakṛī cāhiyē thī. 2. hamē̃ kal mazdūr-kī madad cāhiyē thī. 3. kisān-kō khēt-mē̃ khōdnē-kē liyē baṛā hal cāhiyē thā. 4. kyā āp-kō mērī madad cāhiyē thī? 5. mujhē mōṭargāṛī calānē-kē liyē ādmī cāhiyē thā. 6. musāfir-kō saṛak dikhānē-kē liyē

ādmī cāhiyē thā. 7. kyā āp-kō kuch cāhiyē thā? 8. tumhẽ mērī madad kyũ cāhiyē thī? 9. naukar-kō kal mujhē milnā kyũ cāhiyē thā? 10. aurat-kō bāzār-mẽ khānā ḳharīdnē-kē liyē paisē cāhiyẽ thē.

19.3.2 Exercise 2. **Translate into Urdu:**

1. When did a man need friends? 2. We needed fresh water. 3. I needed this ox-cart yesterday. 4. Why did you need to go to the office yesterday? 5. Did you need anything for your travel? 6. The woman needed wood for the fire this morning. 7. Did you need the clean clothes yesterday? 8. Why did you need to see me yesterday? 9. I needed a gardener for two days. 10. The traveller needed warm water for (**his**) bath.

19.4

agar vo āj śahar-mẽ hōtā, tō maĩ us-kē sāth hōtā.	If he were in town today, I would be with him.
agar āp vaḳt-par ātē, tō ham vaḳt-par khānā khā saktē.	If you had come on time, we would have been able to have dinner on time.
agar maĩ ghar-mẽ hōtā, tō maĩ palaṅg-par sōtā.	If I were home, I would sleep in bed.
agar maĩ skūl-mẽ hōtā, tō maĩ paṛhtā.	If I had been in school, I would have studied.
agar aurat bāzar-kō jātī, tō vo dukānõ-mẽ cīzẽ ḳharīdtī̃.	If the woman had gone to the bazaar, she would have bought things in the shops.
agar āp-kī bahan savērē uṭhtī, tō vo hamārē sāth khātī.	If your sister had gotten up early in the morning, she would have eaten with us.
agar maĩ paṛh saktā, tō bahot kuch sīkhtā.	If I could have read, I would have learned a lot.
agar baccā cal saktā, tō vo ghar-kē bāhar khēltā.	If the child could walk, it would play outside the house.
agar tālibilm kuch jāntā, tō vo ustād • sāhab-kō batātā.	If the student knew anything, he would tell the teacher.
agar mērī mā̃ pakātī, tō ham zarūr khātē.	If my mother would cook, (**then**) we surely would eat.

This section illustrates another conditional construction. In sentences of this type the verb of the "if" clause indicates an act or action which was incapable of being carried out and, hence, the act or action described by the verb of the following clause did not take place. This conditional construction is termed in some grammars "Contrary to Fact" or "Unreal Subjunctive." (Compare the conditional construction discussed in 18.1 to 18.1.4. In those the verbs of the "if" clauses indicated acts capable of completion, and, therefore, the verbs of the following clauses indicated acts carried out or being carried out or about to be carried out.)

Consider the following: In the first sentence, above, **If we were in town today, I would be with him.**, the person referred to by the pronoun, **he,** is **not** or was **not** in town and I, therefore, am not with him. In the third sentence, **If I were home, I would sleep in bed.**, I am **not** home and, therefore, I am **not** sleeping in bed. In the fourth sentence, **If I had been in school, I would have studied.**, I was **not** in school; I, therefore, did **not** study. In the seventh sentence, **If I could have read, I would have learned a lot.**, I could **not** read and I, therefore, did **not** learn a lot. The **significant feature** of this construction is that the verb of each clause is rendered into Urdu by the **present participle, alone,** which agrees in gender and number with the subject.

REMARKS: (1) This construction is to be distinguished from the conditional constructions having verbs in the subjunctive. (See 18.1.2 and 18.1.3 where the verbs of the "if" clauses describe acts capable of completion.)

(2) The compound postposition **-kē bāhar, outside of,** functions like the compound postpositions discussed in sections 11.1 to 11.3.

19.4.1 Exercise 1. **Translate into English:**

1. agar aurat thakī hōtī, tō vo ārām karnē-kē liyē ruktī. 2. agar āp mērē ānē-tak vahā̃ ṭhahartē, tō maĩ āp-kē liyē aḳhbār lā saktā. 3. agar khānā ḳharāb hōtā, tō ham bīmār hō jātē. 4. agar āp āhistā bōltē, tō maĩ samajh saktī. 5. agar tum cāhtē, tō ham tumhārē sāth śahar-kē bāhar jātē. 6. agar laṛkī Urdū paṛhtī, tō vo āp-kē sāth bōl saktī. 7. agar daraḳht-kē nīcē ghās hōtī, tō gāy us-kō khātī. 8. agar bāzār nazdīk hōtā, tō aurat us-kō dēkhnē-kē liyē jātī. 9. agar hōṭal-kā kamrā acchā hōtā, tō musāfir ḳhuś hōtā. 10. agar tumhẽ śahar jānā hōtā, tō maĩ tumhārē sāth ātā. 11. agar dhōbī acchā hōtā, tō ham us-kō dhōnē-kē liyē kapṛē dētē. 12. agar ādmī Urdū bōl saktā, tō vo āp-kē sāth bōltā. 13. agar pānī mīṭhā hōtā, tō laṛkā us-kō pītā. 14. agar mērī bahan gātī, tō maĩ ghar-kē bāhar jātā. 15. agar phal pakkē hōtē, tō bandar un-kō curātē.

19.4.2 Exercise 2. **Translate into Urdu:**

1. If the policeman would catch the thief, he would beat him. 2. If the oxen had stopped, the farmer would have driven them. 3. If the water were cold, we would drink it. 4. If my friend would buy the newspaper, we would be able to read it. 5. If you (**hon., fm.**) had wanted to say anything, you would have talked. 6. If there had been ripe fruits on the tree, the monkeys would have plucked them. 7. If you (**msc.**) were tired, you would have rested. 8. If the servant were good, the master would be happy. 9. If the water had been hot, we (**msc.**) would have washed with it. 10. If your house had been nearby, I (**msc.**) could have gone there with you. 11. If the child were to run, he would fall. 12. If the road were long, the traveller would become tired. 13. If you (**hon., msc.**) had to come to see me, you should have come on time. 14. If the road had been long, the traveller would have become tired. 15. If you (**hon., fm.**) could get up early, you could go with us to the city.

19.5

pahilā laṛkā kitāb paṛhtā hai.	The first boy reads the book.
dūsrā laṛkā us-kī bāt suntā hai.	The second boy listens to him.
tisrā laṛkā kamrē-sē bāhar jātā hai.	The third boy goes out of the room.
cauthī laṛkī kuē̃-kē pās ruktī hai.	The fourth girl stops near the well.
pā̃cvī̃ laṛkī us-kī madad kartī hai.	The fifth girl helps her.
chaṭhī laṛkī bālṭī kuē̃-mē̃ ḍāltī hai.	The sixth girl drops the bucket in the well.
sātvā̃ ādmī khēt-mē̃ khōdtā hai.	The seventh man digs in the field.
āṭhvā̃ ādmī us-kā hukam māntā hai.	The eighth man obeys his command.
navā̃ ādmī paudō̃-par pānī ḍāltā hai.	The ninth man pours water on the plants.
dasvī̃ aurat miṭhāī banātī hai.	The tenth woman makes sweets.
gyārvī̃ aurat baccē-kē pīchē bhāgtī hai.	The eleventh woman runs after the child.
bārhvī̃ aurat un-par hā̃stī hai.	The twelfth woman laughs at them.

This section illustrates the ordinal numbers. Observe that **pā̃cvā̃, fifth,** and the adjectives from **sātvā̃, seventh,** on, are formed by adding the suffix -vā̃ to the cardinal numbers. The ordinals function like the adjectives described in sections 4.3 and 6.1. The adjectives whose final vowels are nasalized keep this nasalization when the final vowels are changed to agree in gender, number, and form with the nouns they modify.

REMARKS: (1) **bāt sunnā** means **to listen** (lit., **to hear the account** or **saying**); **madad karnā** translates English **to help.** It functions like **kām karnā,** to work.

(2) **dūsrā** also translates **other, another;** e.g., **laṛkā dūsrē laṛkō-kē sāth khēltā hai. The boy plays with other boys.; ye dūsrā dōst hai. This is another** (= a second) **friend.**

19.5.1 Exercise 1. **Translate into English:**

1. mā̃ baccō̃-kō tisrī kahānī paṛhēgī. 2. pā̃cvā̃ laṛkā būṛhī aurat-kē liyē bhārī lakṛī lāēgā. 3. tum mērē bārhvẽ savāl-kā javāb kab dōgē? 4. kisān dūsrē daraḳht-kē nīcē ārām kartā hai. 5. dōst mujhē āṭhvī̃ kitāb vāpas dētā hai. 6. chaṭhī ṭrēn kab pahõcēgī. 7. vo cauthē makān-kē pīchē hai. 8. navī̃ laṛkī gyārvẽ laṛkē-kī bāt suntī hai. 9. pahilī laṛkī bālṭī kuẽ-mẽ ḍālnē-kē liyē jātī hai. 10. naukar dasvẽ musāfir-kē liyē ṭhaṇḍā pānī lātā hai.

19.5.2 Exercise 2. **Translate into Urdu:**

1. The carpenter cuts the fifth tree. 2. The traveller stays in the third room. 3. You (**hon. msc.**) can take water from the second well. 4. When will the seventh train come into the station? 5. The eleventh man may be in the office today. 6. The first man will be able to speak Urdu with you. 7. Father prefers to read the tenth newspaper. 8. You should take the fourth fruit. 9. The fourth servant will pick up the plates from the table. 10. The eleventh pilgrim prefers to rest.

19.6. Text 3: **Skūl.**

Translate into English. Answer the questions in Urdu:

[Śarīf Husain [1] aur Jamīl [1] hāi • skūl [2] -kī sātvī̃ [3] jamāat [4] -mẽ paṛhtē haĩ. āj jumē-kā din hai. nau bajē haĩ. skūl-kī ghaṇṭī bajtī [5] hai. sab laṛkē skūl-kē maidān [6] -mẽ jamā [7] hōtē haĩ. har jumē-kō hēḍ • māsṭar • sāhab [8] taḳrīr [9] kartē haĩ. us-kē bād klāsẽ śurū [10] hōtī haĩ. sātvī̃ jamāat-kē laṛkē pahilē pīryaḍ [11] -mẽ hisāb [12] paṛhẽgē. māsṭar Śēr Ahmad [13] • Sāhab hisāb paṛhātē [14] haĩ. vo baṛē [15] saḳht [16] ādmī haĩ. ghar-kā kām [17] bahot dētē haĩ. jō [18] laṛkā kām nahī̃ kartā, usē jurmānā [19] hōtā hai. aur us-kē valdain [20] -kō rīpōrṭ [21] -bhī jātī hai. āj Śarīf Husain-kā ghar-kā kām taiyār nahī̃ hai. is liyē vo bahot parēśān [22] hai. vo daṛtā [23] hai ke,[24] agar [25] us-kē ghar ripōrṭ jāēgī, tō abbā [26] bahot ḳhafā [27] hõgē. śāyad vo us-kā jēb • ḳharc [28] ēk mahīnē [29] -kē liyē band kar dẽ.[30]]

Śarīf Husain: yār Jamīl, āj māsṭar Śēr Ahmad-kī klās hai—na? [31]

Jamīl: bēśak.[32] aur dēkhō! māsṭar • sāhab-kā mūḍ [33] -bhī āj kuch ḳharāb mālūm hōtā hai. ḳhayāl hai ke [24] śāyad vo āj bīvī-sē laṛē [34] haĩ.

Śarīf: acchā![35] tumhẽ kaisē [36] mālūm [37] hai?

Jamīl: mujhē pakkī tarāh [38] tō mālūm nahī̃. yū̃-hī [39] mērā ḳayās [40] hai. hō saktā hai ke [24] ġalat [41] hō. dasvī̃ [42] jamāat-kē laṛkē kahtē haĩ ke [24] māsṭar • sāhab būṛhē haĩ. in-kō acchī tarāh [43] nī̃d [44] nahī̃ ātī. subah • savērē [45] uṭh baiṭhtē [46] haĩ aur cāy mā̃gtē haĩ. in-kī bīvī hai javān. dūsrī śādī [47] hai—na? [31] pahilī bīvī-kē marnē-kē bād dō • bārā [48] śādī-kī hai. ḳhair [49] tō bāt ye hai ke [24] māsṭar • sāhab-kī bīvī-kō sab javān lōgō̃-kī tarāh subah-kī nī̃d pasand [50] hai. us-kō subah • subah [51] uṭhkar [52] cāy banānā pasand [50] nahī̃. is liyē [53] laṛāī [54] hōtī hai.

Śarīf: hmmm. mujhē māsṭar • sāhab-kī ḳhāñgī [55] siyāsat [56] -sē tō kōī dilcaspī [57] nahī̃. lēkin un-kē mūḍ-kā āj ḳharāb hōnā [58] tō mērē liyē burā hōgā.

Jamīl: tumhārā matlab hai ke [24] tum un-kē savālō̃-kā javāb nahī̃ dē sakōgē?

Śarīf: nahī̃. mērā ye matlab nahī̃. un-kē savālō̃-kā mujhē fikr nahī̃ hai. lēkin mērā ghar-kā kām taiyār nahī̃.

Jamīl: tō phir kyā irādē haī? maī ēk āsān [59] tarīḳ [60] batāū̃?

Śarīf: kyā?

Jamīl: bas,[61] gāib hō [62] jāō un-kī klās-sē. maī kahū̃gā ke [24] tum bīmār hō.

Śarīf: tumhārā matlab hai ke [24] ēk gunāh [63] ḳhud karū̃ aur ēk tum-sē karvāū̃? [64]

Jamīl: mērē ḳhayāl-mē̃ tō ye kōī gunāh nahī̃. aur agar hai-bhī, tō kyā ḍar [65] hai? jab [66] bahot-sē [67] gunāh jamā hō jāẽgē, tō buṛhāpē [68] -mē̃ haj [69] karẽgē.

Śarīf: agar tum aisā ḳhayāl kartē hō, tō bahot baṛī galtī kartē hō. haj karnā acchī bāt [70] hai lēkin is liyē ke [71] sārī dunyā-kē musalmān [72] sāl-mē̃ ēk dafā [73] ēk jagah [74] jamā hō̃, ēk dusrē-sē milẽ, ēk dusrē-kē hālāt jānẽ, aur ēk dusrē-kī madad karẽ. haj is liyē farz [75] nahī̃ ke [76] ādmī sārī umar [77] mazē-sē gunāh karẽ aur marnē-sē pahilē Makkē [78] jākar [79] un-kō muāf karvāẽ.[80]

Jamīl: acchā, maulvī • sāhab,[81] ab tum zyādā vaz [82] na karō. klās lagnēvālī [83] hai. āō calẽ.[84] maī śām [85] -kō tumhārē ghar āū̃gā. phir is mōzū [86] -par bātcīt karẽgē.

[dōnō̃ klās-mē̃ jātē haī aur apnī apnī [87] jagah-par baiṭhtē haī. ēk • dō [88] minaṭ-kē bād māsṭar • sāhab-bhī ātē haī. sab laṛkē adab [89] -sē khaṛē [90] hōtē haī. māsṭar • sāhab un-kō baiṭhnē-kē liyē kahtē haī aur apnā rejisṭar [91] nikālkar [92] hāzrī [93] lētē haī. jō [94] laṛkē gairhāzir [95] haī, un-kī hēḍ • māsṭar-kē pās ripōrṭ hōgī.]

Māsṭar: kyā sab laṛkō̃-kē pās ghar-kā kām ṭhīk • ṭhāk taiyār [96] hai? jin [97] -kē pās nahī̃, vo hāth khaṛā karẽ.[98]

[Śarīf Husain, Jamīl aur kuch aur [99] laṛkē hāth khaṛā kartē haī.]

Māsṭar: Jamīl, tumhārē kām na karnē-kī kyā vajah [100] hai?

Jamīl: māsṭar • sahab, mērī kāpī [101] gum hō [102] gayī hai.

Māsṭar: tum har dafā kōī na kōī [103] bahānā [104] banātē hō. kām kuch nahī̃ kartē. mērē ḳhayāl-mē̃ tō tum apnā vaḳt aur apnē mā̃ • bāp [105] -kā paisā bēkār [106] zāē [107] kartē hō. tumhẽ agar paṛhnē-kā śauk [108] nahī̃ hai, tō skūl chōṛ dō [109] aur kisī kārḳhānē-mē̃ naukrī kar lō.[110]

[Jamīl sar [111] jhukākar [112] muskarātā [113] hai, lēkin kōī javāb nahī̃ dētā.]

Māsṭar: Śarīf Husain, tumhārī kāpī-bhī gum [114] hai?

Śarīf: janāb, mērī kāpī tō gum nahī̃. mērē pās kōī bahānā nahī̃. mujhē muāf kar dījiyē. āindā [115] aisā nahī̃ hōgā.

Māsṭar: is dafā tumhẽ muāf kartā hū̃. lēkin phir kabhī aisā na hōnā cāhiyē. maī bahot ḳhuś hū̃ ke [24] tum jhūṭē bahānē nahī̃ banātē.

savālāt:

1. māsṭar aur un-kī bīvī-mē̃ kyū̃ laṛāī hōtī thī? 2. Jamīl-nē Śarīf Husain-kō kyā maśvarah diyā? 3. Śarīf Husain-nē is maśvarē-kō kyū̃ na mānā? 4. hēḍ • māsṭar kis din taḳrīr kartē thē? 5. jō laṛkā ghar-kā kām nahī̃ kartā thā, usē kyā sazā [116] miltī thī?

NOTES: 1. man's name; 2. high-school (ā); 3. **sātvā̃** seventh (**adj.**); 4. grade, class (ī); 5. to sound, ring (**int.**); 6. ground, yard (ā); 7. **jamā hōnā** to be collected (**int.**); 8. head-master (ā); 9. speech (ī); 10. **śurū hōnā** to begin (**int.**); 11. period (ā); 12. arithmetic (ā); 13. man's name; 14. **paṛhānā** to teach (**tr.**), see 36.1, ff.; 15. = very; 16. strict (**adj., n.c.**); 17. **ghar-kā kām** home-work (ā); 18. which (**rel. adj.**), see 25.1; 19. fine (ā); 20. parents (ē); 21. report (ī); 22. worried (**adj., n.c.**); 23. **ḍarnā** to fear, be afraid (**int.**); 24. see 29.2; 25. see 18.1.4 and 18.1; 26. father (ā); 27. angry (**adj., n.c.**); 28. pocket-money (ā); 29. month (ā); 30. **band kar dēnā** to stop (**tr.**), see lesson 28; 31. = is this not so?; 32. sure! certainly!; 33. mood (ā); 34. fought, **pst. part** of **laṛnā** (For construction see 20.1.2); 35. = is that so!; 36. how (**interr. adv.**); 37. **-kō mālūm hōnā** to know; 38. **pakkī tarāh** for certain (=**adv.**); 39. just, only (**adv.**); 40. **ḳayās** guess (ā); 41. wrong (**adj., n.c.**); 42. **dasvā̃** tenth (**adj.**); 43. **acchī tarāh** well, in a good manner (=**adv.**); 44. sleep (ī); 45. early in the morning (= **adv.**); 46. **uṭh baiṭhnā** to get up, rise (**int.**), see lesson 28; 47. marriage, wedding (ī); 48. second (time) (**adj., n.c.**); 49. anyway; 50. **pasand hōnā** to like, see 20.2; 51. early in the morning (= **adv.**); 52. having gotten up, see 30.1; 53. **is liyē** therefore; 54. quarrel, fight (ī); 55. domestic (**adj., n.c.**); 56. politics (ī); 57. interest (ī); 58. **ḳharāb hōnā** being bad; 59. easy (**adj., n.c.**); 60. method, device (ā); 61. just; 62. **g̲aib hō jānā** to disappear (**int.**), see lesson 28; 63. sin (ā); 64. **karvānā** to cause to do, see 36.1, ff.; 65. fear (ā); 66. when (**rel. adv.**), see 26.3; 67. many, for **-sā** see 38.1; 68. old age (ā); 69. pilgrimage (ā); 70. = thing (ī); 71. **is liyē ke** so that; 72. Muslim (ā); 73. at one time (**adv.**); 74. in one place (**adv.**); 75. duty (ā); 76. so that; 77. life (ī); 78. (city of) Mecca (ā); 79. having gone, see 30.1; 80. **muāf karvānā** to get forgiveness, see 36.1, ff.; 81. Mister Priest (jokingly;) 82. sermon (ā); 83. about to begin, see 31.2; 84. let's go!; 85. evening (ī); 86. subject (ā); 87. each in his own, see 36.2 for the repetition; 88. one or two; 89. respect (ā); 90. **khaṛā hōnā** to stand up (**int.**); 91. register (ā); 92. taking out, see 30.1; 93. roll, list (ī); 94. which (**rel. adj.**), see 25.1; 95. absent (**adj., n.c.**); 96. all set, all ready (**adj., n.c.**); 97. who (**rel. pron.**), see 25.2; 98. **hāth khaṛā karnā** to raise hands (**tr.**); 99. **kuch aur** some other; 100. reason (ī); 101. copy-book (ī); 102. **gum hō jānā** to be lost (**int.**); 103. **kōī na kōī** some one or another; 104. excuse (ā); 105. parents (ē); 106. uselessly (**adv.**); 107. **zāē karnā** to waste (**tr.**); 108. interest (ā); 109. **chōṛ dēnā** to leave (**tr.**), see lesson 28; 110. employment (ī), **naukrī kar lēnā** to take job (**tr.**), see lesson 28; 111. head (ā); 112. hanging, see 30.1; 113. **muskarānā** to smile (**tr.**); 114. **gum hōnā** to be lost (**int.**); 115. in the future (**adv.**); 116. punishment (ī).

LESSON 20

20.1

maĩ calā.	I (**msc.**) walked.
maĩ calī.	I (**fm.**) walked.
vo calā.	He walked.
vo calī.	She walked.
ham calē.	We (**msc.**) walked.
ham calī̃.	We (**fm.**) walked.
tum calē.	You (**msc.**) walked.
tum calī̃.	You (**fm.**) walked.
āp calē.	You (**msc.**) walked.
āp calī̃.	You (**fm.**) walked.
vo calē.	They (**msc.**) walked.
vo calī̃.	They (**fm.**) walked.

This section introduces the Urdu equivalent of the English "Simple Perfect" tense. The Urdu construction consists of the past participle of the verb which, in the case of intransitive verbs (i.e., verbs which cannot take a direct object), agrees in gender and number with the subject of the sentence.

The past participle of a verb is formed by attaching to the verbal stem the following suffixes; **-ā** for the masculine singular; **-ē** for the masculine plural; **-ī** for the feminine singular; and **-ī̃** for the feminine plural. (Compare the "Imperfect" of **hōnā** in 19.1.)

20.1.1 More examples are:

baccē ghar ṭharē.	The children remained at home.
musāfir āj subah pahō̃cā.	The traveller arrived this morning.
daryā samandar-mē̃ gayī.	The river flowed into the sea.
laṛkī dukān-mē̃ das minaṭ ṭharī.	The girl waited in the shop for ten minutes.
billī kuē̃-mē̃ girī.	The cat fell into the well.

sabziyā̃ khēt-mē̃ ugī̃.	The vegetables grew in the field.
ādmī dō ghaṇṭē calē.	The man walked (**for**) two hours.
ādmī kamrē-mē̃ āyā.	The man came into the room.
ādmī kamrē-mē̃ āyē.	The men came into the room.
aurat kamrē-mē̃ āyī.	The woman came into the room.
aurtē̃ kamrē-mē̃ āyī̃.	The women came into the room.
laṛkā daraḳht-kē nīcē sōyā.	The boy slept under the tree.
laṛkē daraḳht-kē nīcē sōyē.	The boys slept under the tree.
laṛkī daraḳht-kē nīcē sōyī.	The girl slept under the tree.
laṛkiyā̃ daraḳht-kē nīcē sōyī̃.	The girls slept under the tree.

REMARKS: (1) Verbal stems ending in a vowel add **-y-** before the suffixes are attached. See sentences 3 and 8 to 15, above. **jānā, to go,** replaces the stem **jā** with **ga** to form the past participle. See section 2.1, remarks (2) for the stem and section 22.1 for the past participle of **jānā.**

20.1.2

baccē ghar ṭharē haĩ.	The children have remained at home.
hājī āj subah pahō̃cā hai.	The traveller has arrived this morning.
daryā samandar-mē̃ gayā hai.	The river has flowed into the sea.
laṛkī dukan-mē̃ das minaṭ ṭharī hai.	The girl has waited in the shop for ten minutes.
billī kuē̃-mē̃ girī hai.	The cat has fallen into the well.
sabziyā̃ khēt-mē̃ ugī haĩ.	The vegetables have grown in the field.
jalūs dō ghaṇṭē calā hai.	The procession has walked (**for**) two hours.
jaj adālat-mē̃ āyā hai.	The judge has come into the court.
laṛkī daraḳht-kē nīcē sōyī hai.	The girl has slept under the tree.

This section illustrates the Urdu equivalent of the English "Present Perfect" tense. This consists of the past participle of the construction described in section 20.1, above, plus the present tense of the verb **hōnā.**

REMARKS: (1) Here the past partciple suffix is not nasalized for the feminine plural.

(2) **baiṭhā hai** translates, is seated, **jalūs** (ā) procession, **jaj** (ā) judge, **adālat** (ī) court.

20.1.3

śarārtī baccē ghar-mē̃ ṭharē thē.	The mischievous children had remained at home.
hājī āj subah Makkē pahō̃cā thā.	The pilgrim had arrived in Mecca this morning.
daryā samandar-mē̃ gayē thē.	The rivers had flowed into the sea.
laṛkī dukān-mē̃ das minaṭ ṭharī thī.	The girl had waited in the shop for ten minutes.

faslẽ khēt-mẽ ugī thī̃.	The crops had grown in the field.
vakīl kamrẽ-mē āyē thē.	The lawyers had come into the room.
laṛkiyā̃ daraḳht-kē nīcē sōyī thī̃.	The girls had slept under the tree.

This section illustrates the Urdu equivalent of the English "Past Perfect" tense. This consists of the past participle plus the imperfect construction of the verb **hōnā, thā** (See 19.1), which, with the past participle, agrees with the subject of the sentence in gender and number.

20.1.4

baccē ghar ṭhaharē hõgē.	The children will have remained at home.
samandarī • jahāz āj subah pahõcā hōgā.	The ocean liner will have arrived this morning.
laṛkī dukān-mẽ das minaṭ ṭhaharī hōgī.	The girl will have waited in the shop for ten minutes.
mullā masjid-mẽ āyē hõgē.	The religious leader will have come into the mosque.
maĩ cār ghaṇṭē sōyā hū̃gā.	I will have slept four hours.

This section illustrates the Urdu equivalent of the English "Future Perfect" tense. This consists of the past participle plus the future of the verb **hōnā** (See 15.2), the suffix of which with the past participle agrees in gender and number with the subject of the sentence.

REMARKS: (1) This construction also translates English **must have** (expressing the possibility of an act having taken place). E.g., the first sentence can be translated: **The children must have remained at home.** and the second sentence: **The traveller must have arrived this morning.**

(2) **mullā** (hon. pl.) religious leader, **śarārtī (adj., n.c.)** mischievous.

20.1.5 Exercise 1. **Translate into English:**

1. laṛkē dō ghaṇṭõ-kē liyē chōṭē daryā-mẽ tairē. 2. mā̃ aurtõ-kē sāth bāzār-sē āyī thī. 3. musāfir śahar-sē āyā hai. 4. laṛkā būṛhī mā̃-kē sāth chōṭē makān-mẽ rahā thā. 5. hamārā bail daryā-kē pās carā hōgā. 6. bandar ū̃cē daraḳht-par jaldī-sē dauṛē. 7. gāṛī makān-kē sāmnē rukī thī. 8. baccē dhōbī-kē gadhē-kē pīchē calē hõgē. 9. bhūkā kuttā chōṭē baccē-kē pīchē calā hai. 10. mōṭargāṛī mērē sāmnē rukī hōgī. 11. gāy chōṭē bachṛē-kē sāth dauṛī hai. 12. ādmī ghar-kē sāmnē baiṭhē. 13. naukar daftar-kē pās bīs minaṭ ṭhaharē thē. 14. bāp śahar-sē vāpas āyē hōgē. 15. kisān daraḳht-kē nīcē sōyā. 16. pīr tālāb-kē pās baiṭhē haĩ. 17. ġamgīn laṛkā daryā-kē pās rōyā thā. 18. bēṭī bāp-kē sāth śahar-kō āyī hai. 19. musāfir hōṭal-mẽ das din rahā hōgā. 20. bāp baccõ-kē sāth khēlē.

20.1.6 Exercise 2. **Translate into Urdu:**

1. The dog slept on the ground. 2. My friend had come to the city to see me. 3. The barber has come into the house. 4. The washerman had walked behind the donkey. 5. The boy will have swum under the bridge. 6. The thirsty pilgrim went to the well. 7. The child will have slept in the garden. 8. The beggar is seated beside the road. 9. The animals had come from the jungle at night. 10. The camel will have stopped beside the river to drink. 11. The servant walked behind **(his)** master. 12. The women have stopped near the shop. 13. Why had the train stopped near the bridge? 14. Your cow will have grazed in our field. 15. The trolley stopped in front of the temple. 16. The

hungry horse has stopped near the grass. 17. Why had the man come back from the city? 18. Will the boy have come back from the well with water? 19. The little girls played under the tree. 20. The servants are seated in front of the office.

20.2

naukar-kō kām karnā pasand hai.	The servant likes to work.
baccē-kō sōnā pasand hai.	The child likes to sleep.
mujhē khēlnā pasand hai.	I like to play.
mujhē ye kitāb pasand hai.	I like this book.
laṛkē-kō ye mulk pasand hai.	The boy likes this country.
billī-kō dūdh pasand hai.	The cat likes milk.
afsar-kō kuttē pasand haī.	The officer likes dogs.
laṛkī-kō ḳhūbsūrat kapṛē pasand haī.	The girl likes beautiful clothes.
mujhē khaṭṭē āmlē pasand nahī̃ haī.	I don't like sour olives.
mujhē mahẽgī cīzẽ pasand nahī̃ haī.	I don't like expensive things.
mujhē mīṭhē ām pasand haī.	I like sweet mangoes.
kyā āp-kō sardī pasand hai?	Do you like the cold?
kyā āp-kō garmī-kā mausam pasand hai?	Do you like hot weather?

This section illustrates another way of translating into Urdu the English construction consisting of **likes** (**to**) followed by another verb or noun. (Compare 15.3)

The English subject is placed in Urdu in the object form before the postposition **-kō;** the English object is made the subject of **pasand hōnā, to be liked.**

REMARKS: **amlā** (ā) olive, **garmī** (ī) warm weather, summer, **mulk** (ā) country, **sardī** (ī) cold weather, winter, **afsar** (ā) officer.

20.2.1

naukar-kō kām karnā pasand hai.	The servant prefers to work.
baccē-kō sōnā zyādā pasand hai.	The child prefers to sleep.
mujhē khēlnā zyādā pasand hai.	I prefer to play.
mujhē ye kitāb zyādā pasand hai.	I prefer this book.
laṛkē-kō ye mulk zyādā pasand hai.	The boy prefers this country.
billī-kō dūdh pīnā zyādā pasand hai.	The cat prefers to drink milk.
vazīr-kō daftar zyādā pasand hai.	The minister prefers (**his**) office.
laṛkī-kō ḳhūbsūrat kapṛē ḳharīdnā zyādā pasand hai.	The girl prefers to buy beautiful clothes.

This section illustrates another way of translating into Urdu the English phrase beginning with the word **prefers** (**to**). (See 15.3.1) The construction is identical with that described in section 20.2 with one addition—the adverb **zyādā, more,** is placed before **pasand hōnā.**

REMARKS: **vazīr** (ā) minister.

20.2.2

naukar-kō khēt-mẽ khōdnē-sē ghar-mẽ kam karnā zyādā pasand hai.	The servant prefers working in the house to digging in the field.
mujhē paṛhnē-sē khēlnā zyādā pasand hai.	I prefer playing to studying.

mujhē us kitāb-sē ye kitāb zyādā pasand hai.	I prefer this book to that book.
laṛkē-kō kisī aur mulk-sē ye mulk dēkhnā zyādā pasand hai.	The boy prefers seeing this country to some other country.
baccē-kō billiyō̃-sē kuttē zyādā pasand haĩ.	The child prefers dogs to cats.
laṛkī-kō badsūrat kapṛō̃-sē k̲h̲ūbsūrat kapṛē zyādā pasand haĩ.	The girl prefers beautiful clothes to ugly clothes.

This section illustrates another way of translating into Urdu the English construction indicating preference for one being or thing over another. (Compare 15.3.2) This construction is identical with that described in section 20.2.1 with one addition. Compare: **mujhē ye kitāb zyādā pasand hai. I prefer this book.**; and **mujhē us kitāb-sē ye kitāb zyādā pasand hai. I prefer this book to that book.** Observe that the words introduced in the English phrase by the preposition **to** are placed in Urdu in the object form before the postposition **-sē.**

20.2.3 Exercise 1. **Translate into English:**
1. musāfir-kō pīnē-kē liyē ṭhaṇḍā pānī pasand hai. 2. hamẽ mōṭargāṛī-sē safar karnā zyādā pasand hai. 3. kyā tumhẽ sardī-sē garmī-kā mausam zyādā pasand hai? 4. mujhē kamrē-mẽ ārām karnā zyādā pasand hai. 5. baccō̃-kō mīṭhē ām pasand haĩ. 6. āj-kō mujh-sē vo ādmī kyũ zyādā pasand hai? 7. us-kō ak̲h̲bār paṛhnā zyādā pasand hai. 8. kyā tum-kō bailgāṛī-sē ṭrām-mẽ safar karnā zyādā pasand hai? 9. hamẽ sardī-kā mausam pasand hai. 10. ādmī-kō kām karnē-sē ghar-mẽ ārām karnā zyādā pasand hai. 11. mujhē nahānē-kē liyē garm pānī zyādā pasand hai. 12. āp-kō garmī-kā mausam kyũ pasand nahĩ? 13. mujhē paṛhnē-sē sōnā zyādā pasand hai. 14. laṛkē-kō ghar-mẽ rahnā zyādā pasand nahĩ. 15. kyā āp-kō safar karnā pasand hai?

20.2.4 Exercise 2. **Translate into Urdu:**
1. Do you like working? 2. Why do you prefer travelling? 3. The pilgrim prefers cold weather to hot weather for travelling. 4. The boy likes to swim. 5. Does the child prefer sour things? 6. I prefer automobiles to ox-carts. 7. Why do you prefer this book to that newspaper? 8. I like to rest. 9. Does anyone prefer to walk? 10. Some people prefer walking to going by automobile. 11. The girl likes to sew. 12. Some people prefer sweet things. 13. We will prefer mangoes to sour olives. 14. Will anyone prefer that country to this country? 15. The cow likes to eat grass.

20.3

ādmī laṛkē-sē baṛā hai.	The man is bigger than the boy.
darak̲h̲t makān-sē ũcā hai.	The tree is higher than the house.
daryā kuẽ-sē gahrā hai.	The river is deeper than the well.
saṛak galī-sē lambī hai.	The road is longer than the street.
laṛkī aurat-sē chōṭī hai.	The girl is smaller than the woman.
bahan bhāī-sē acchī hai.	The sister is better than the brother.

Sections 20.3 to 20.3.8 deal with the Urdu constructions equivalent to the comparative and superlative of English adjectives. This section illustrates the comparative construction. It can be seen that this is based on the Predicate-Adjective construction described in section 3.2, with one addition—the word or words introduced in the English sentence by **than** are placed in Urdu in the object form before the postposition

-sē. Compare: ādmī baṛā hai. The man is big. and ādmī laṛkē-sē baṛā hai. The man is bigger than the boy.; daraḳht ū̃cā hai. The tree is high. and daraḳht makān-sē ū̃cā hai. The tree is higher than the house.; daryā gahrā hai. The river is deep. and daryā kuē̃-sē gahrā hai. The river is deeper than the well.; ye ū̃cā daraḳht hai. This is a high tree. and ye us-sē ū̃cā daraḳht hai. This is a higher tree than that.; ye gahrā daryā hai. This is a deep river. and ye us daryā-sē gahrā daryā hai. This is a deeper river than that river.

20.3.1

ye tasvīr us tasvīr-sē zyādā ḳhūbsūrat hai.	This picture is more beautiful than that picture.
ye laṛkā us laṛkē-sē zyādā hośiyār hai.	This boy is cleverer than that boy.
hiran gīdar-sē zyādā buzdil hai.	The deer is more cowardly than the jackel.
naram zamīn saḳht zamīn-sē zyādā zarḳhēz hai.	Soft ground is more fertile than hard ground.
billī kuttē-sē zyādā pyāsī hai.	The cat is thirstier than the dog.

The comparative construction illustrated in this section is identical with that described in section 20.3 with the addition of the adverb **zyādā, more,** which is used with certain adjectives.

REMARKS: (1) It is difficult to formulate a rule indicating when **zyādā** is required for the comparative construction and when it is not. In many instances adjectives describing quality require **zyādā** and those describing quantity (See 20.3) do not require it. It seems, too, that adjectives which do not change their form for gender and number (See 11.4) require **zyādā** in this construction.

(2) gīdar (ā) jackal, hiran (ā) deer.

20.3.2

ādmī sab-sē baṛā hai.	The man is the biggest (**of all**).
daraḳht sab-sē ū̃cā hai.	The tree is the tallest (**of all**).
saṛak sab-sē lambī hai.	The road is the longest (**of all**).
laṛkī sab-sē chōṭī hai.	The girl is the smallest (**of all**).
tasvīr sab-sē zyādā ḳhūbsūrat hai.	The picture is the most beautiful (**of all**).
laṛkā sab-sē zyādā hośiyār hai.	The boy is the most clever (**of all**).
hiran sab-sē zyādā buzdil hai.	The deer is the most cowardly (**of all**).

This section deals with the superlative construction. Like the comparative constructions described above, the superlative is based on the "Predicate-Adjective" construction described in section 3.2 with one addition—the phrase sab-sē (lit., of all).

Compare: ādmī baṛā hai. The man is big. and ādmī sab-sē baṛā hai. The man is the biggest (of all).; daraḳht ū̃cā hai. The tree is tall. and daraḳht sab-sē ū̃cā hai. The tree is the tallest (of all).; saṛak lambī hai. The road is long. and saṛak sab-sē lambī hai. The street is longest (of all). (Note the sentence with zyādā and see section 20.3.1 above.)

20.3.3 Exercise 1. Translate into English:

1. ye mazdūr us mazdūr-sē zyādā kamzōr nahī̃ hai. 2. ham sab-sē mīṭhē phal khānā cāhtē haī̃. 3. kyā kuā̃ daryā-sē gahrā hai? 4. galī saṛak-sē zyādā tang hai. 5. ye chōṭī mēz us gōl mēz-sē cauṛī hai. 6. mujhē sab-sē lambā rassā cāhiyē. 7. laṛkā dōst-sē zyādā javān hai. 8. ye mandar sab-sē zyādā ḳhūbsūrat hai. 9. us-kā bōjh mērē bōjh-sē zyādā bhārī nahī̃. 10. mā̃ baccē-kō sab-sē mīṭhā sēb dētī hai. 11. mērē liyē sab-sē lambī charī lāiyē. 12. kuē̃-kā pānī daryā-kē pānī-sē ṭhanḍā hai. 13. hāthī sab jānvarō̃-sē baṛā hai. 14. mujhē sab-sē zyādā mazbūt mazdūr bhējiyē. 15. galī sab-sē zyādā ḳhatarnāk hai.

20.3.4 Exercise 2. **Translate into Urdu:**

1. For travelling an automobile is better than an ox-cart. 2. I need a stronger man than you. 3. Why do you (**fm.**) want the biggest apple? 4. Do you have a longer rope than this? 5. Is your ox-cart the best? 6. For this work I need a stronger man than you. 7. He is the happiest of all. 8. Isn't well water better to drink than tank water? 9. I need the driest wood for the fire. 10. This room is not better than that room. 11. His automobile is smaller than yours. 12. Did the woman need to buy the best sari in the shop? 13. This road is longer than the other road. 14. I (**msc.**) want to drink colder water than this. 15. This is not the prettiest flower.

20.3.5

ye tasvīr us tasvīr-sē kam k̲hūbsūrat hai.	This picture is less beautiful than that picture.
ye laṛkā us laṛkē-sē kam hōśiyār hai.	This boy is less clever than that boy.
gīdaṛ hiran-sē kam buzdil hai.	The jackal is less cowardly than the deer.
sak̲ht zamīn naram zamīn-sē kam zark̲hēz hai.	Hard ground is less fertile than soft ground.

The construction illustrated in this section is identical with that described in section 20.3.1. Here **kam, less,** replaces **zyādā, more.**

20.3.6

ye tasvīr sab-sē kam k̲hūbsūrat hai.	This picture is the least beautiful (**of all**).
ye vazīr sab-sē kam hōśiyār hai.	This minister is the least clever (**of all**).
ye śēr sab-sē kam buzdil hai.	This lion is the least cowardly (**of all**).
sak̲ht zamīn sab-sē kam zark̲hēz hai.	Hard ground is the least fertile (**of all**).

The construction illustrated in this section is identical with the sentences with **zyādā** described in section 20.3.2. Here **kam** replaces **zyādā.**

20.3.7 Exercise 1. **Translate into English:**

1. ye khēt us khēt-sē kam zark̲hēz hai. 2. vo sab-sē kam mehantī mazdūr hai. 3. kyā tumhẽ is-sē kam lambā rassā cāhiyē? 4. āp-kē bail kyū̃ sab-sē kam chōṭē haĩ? 5. vo zamīn is zamīn-sē kam sak̲ht hai. 6. kyā tum is-sē kam mahẽgī haṇḍiyā k̲harīdnā cāhtī hō? 7. āp-kā khēt kyū̃ sab-sē kam zark̲hēz hai? 8. kyā us-kā kūā̃ sab-sē kam gahrā hai? 9. kisān-kō is-sē kyū̃ kam baṛā hal cāhiyē? 10. ye śahar-kī sab-sē kam ū̃cī imārat hai.

20.3.8 Exercise 2. **Translate into Urdu:**

1. Why is your field less fertile than his? 2. This ox is less strong than that ox. 3. Is this road less long than that road? 4. Which is the least difficult of these questions? 5. Is the hard ground the least fertile of all? 6. The man is bringing a less heavy load than (**his**) servant. 7. This road is the least dangerous of all. 8. The servant is less thirsty than the gardener. 9. Call in the least sleepy servant to help me. 10. He is the least careful of all.

20.4 Text 4: **Lahōr-kā Safar.**

Translate into English. Answer the questions in Urdu:

[Śamśād Alī [1] Nārōvāl [2] -sē Lahōr jānā cāhtā hai. us-kī bīvī-bhī us-kē sāth jānā cāhtī hai. dōnõ āpas-mẽ [3] maśvarā [4] kartē haĩ ke [5] kyā kyā [6] cīzẽ sāth [7] lēkar [8] jāẽ. Śamśād Alī-kā k̲hayāl hai ke [5] zyādā sāmān sāth nahĩ lē jānā [9] cāhiyē.]

Śamśād: maĩ-nē kahā,[10] suntī hō? (kōī javāb nahĩ ātā.) ajī,[11] kahā̃ hō tum?

Kalsūm: (us-kī bīvī): miyā̃, tum tō yū̃-hī har vak̲t śōr macātē [12] hō. bāvarcīk̲hānē-mẽ. tumhārē liyē khānā pakātī hū̃. khāōgē nahĩ āj?

Śamśād: hā̃, hā̃. khāẽgē—kyū̃ nahī̃. magar[13] maĩ kahtā hū̃ ke[5] gāṛī chūṭnē[14] -mẽ zyādā vaḳt nahī̃ hai. sāmān-bhī tō bā̃dhnā[15] hai! agar tum mujhē batāō ke[5] kyā kyā[6] cīzẽ sāth jāẽgī, tō maĩ un-kō ēk jagah jamā kar dū̃.[16]

Kalsūm: ajī, maĩ kyā batāū̃? tumhẽ ḳhud mālūm nahī̃ kyā? āḳhir[17] dō mahinē Lahōr ṭhaharōgē. sardī[18] -kā mausam[19] hai. garm kapṛē tō sāth jāẽgē. tumhārā kōṭ,[20] ōvarkōṭ,[21] patlunẽ,[22] mērē kōṭ, śāl,[23] jurābẽ,[24] jūtē[25] vag̠airā.[26] ye sab kuch-bhī lē jānā paṛēgā. hā̃, aur bistar[27] -bhī tō. āḳhir riśtēdārō̃[28] -kō zyādā taklīf[29] dēnā-bhī tō munāsab[30] nahī̃. un-kī meharbānī hai ke[31] hamẽ rahnē-kē liyē dō kamrē dẽgē.

Śamśād: ye sab tō ṭhīk hai. lēkin itnā sāmān lēkar[8] jānē-kē liyē tō ēk ṭrak[32] cāhiyē.

Kalsūm: acchā![33] kyū̃ ḳhāh•maḳhāh[34] mujhē ḍarātē[35] hō? ṭrak-kī kyā zarūrat hai? gāṛī-mẽ jāēgā ye sab sāmān. aur itnā zyādā kahā̃ hai?

Śamśād: jī hā̃, zarūr. (tanz-sē[36]) āp-kō mālūm hai ke[5] ēk ṭikaṭ-par siraf ēk man[37] sāmān jā saktā hai. aur hazūr[38] -kā sāmān tō kōī bīs[39] man hōgā.

Kalsūm: kyū̃ mujhē is tarah ḍarātē hō. agar bīs man hōgā, tō zyādā paisē dẽgē.

Śamśād: bēśak. tum tō sēṭhānī[40] hō na? kyā tumhārī ammā̃ kōī das bīs hazār rūpāyē martē vaḳt[41] tumhẽ dē gayī thī̃?[42]

Kalsūm: dēkhō-jī,[43] ḳhabardār![44] agar mērī marhūm[45] mā̃-kē bārē-mẽ aisī bātẽ karōgē, tō phir laṛāī hōgī.

Śamśād: hā̃, hā̃. tumhẽ apnī marhūm mā̃ mujh-sē zyādā pyārī[46] hai. yehī tō rōnā hai. tumhẽ mērē paisē-kā tō kuch ḳhayāl-hī nahī̃. pānī-kī tarah ḳharc kartī[47] hō. agar kamānā[48] paṛē, tō mālūm hō ke[8] paisā kitnī muśkil[49] -sē ātā hai. tum mazē-sē ghar-mẽ baiṭhtī hō. kām tō maĩ kartā hū̃.

Kalsūm: acchā. maĩ būrī hū̃, fazūl•ḳharc[50] hū̃, mērī mā̃-bhī būrī thī, śādī-sē pahilē maĩ friśtā[51] thī, mujh-mẽ sab ḳhubiyā̃[52] thī̃. ab dō sāl bād[53] mujh-mẽ sārē jahā̃[54] -kī burāiyā̃[55] ā gayī̃.[56] tum idhar udhar-kī[57] bātẽ kyū̃ kartē hō. sāf sāf[58] kyū̃ nahī̃ kahtē ke[5] tumhẽ mujh-sē muhabbat[59] nahī̃ hai? tum mujhē talāḳ[60] dē dō[61] aur āzād[62] hō jāō. phir mazē karō.[63] apnē paisē āp sambhālō.[64] kanjūś makkhī cūs![65]

[Kalsūm-kā mūh[66] g̠ussē-sē lāl[67] hai aur us-kī ā̃khō̃-sē ā̃sū[68] bahtē[69] haĩ. Śamśād Alī apnī bīvī-kō rōtē dēkhkar[70] bahot ghabrātā[71] hai aur us-kō manānē[72] -kī kōśiś kartā hai.]

Śamśād: bēgam,[73] tum tō yū̃-hī ḳhafā hōtī hō. kaun kahtā hai ke[5] mujhē tum-sē muhabbat nahī̃. maĩ tō tumhẽ pahilē-sē bhī zyādā pyār kartā[74] hū̃. maĩ āḳhir insān[75] hū. kabhī g̠ussā ā jātā hai aur fazūl[76] bāt mūh-sē nikal jātā[77] hai. tum mujhē muāf kar dō.[78]

Kalsūm: jī nahī̃. ab hamārā tumhārā kōī vāstā[79] nahī̃. maĩ kal apnē bāp-kē ghar jāū̃gī. tum kōī aur[80] bīvī ḍhū̃ṛhō[81] ab.

[Śamśād Alī Kalsūm-kē bālō̃[82] -mẽ ū̃gliyā̃[83] phērtā[84] hai aur us-kā mūh cūmtā[85] hai. lēkin Kalsūm usē parē[86] dhakēltī[87] hai. Śamśād Alī bahot udās[88] hō jātā hai. us-kī ā̃khō̃-mẽ ā̃sū ā jātē haĩ. ye dēkhkar[70] Kalsūm-kā dil[89] naram[90] hō jātā hai aur us-kā g̠ussā-bhī g̠āib hō jātā hai. dōnō̃ miyā̃•bīvī[91] ēk dūsrē-kī taraf dēkhkar[70] muskarātē haĩ.]

Śamśād: mujhē muāf kar dō, bēgam.

Kalsūm: nahī̃, tum mujhē muāf kar dō. g̠altī tō mērī hai.

[ēk * dam bāvarcīkhānē-mē̃ kisī cīz-kē jalnē ⁹² -kī bū ⁹³ ātī hai.|

Kalsūm: hāē, hāē! ⁹⁴ ab maĩ kyā karũ! handiyā-mē̃ gōśt tō jal gayā.⁹⁵

(Śamśād Alī-kī taraf dēkhkar ⁷⁰) ab kyā hōgā?

Śamśād: kōī bāt nahī̃.⁹⁶ hōṭal-mē̃ khānā khā lē̃gē.⁹⁷ ye sab āpas-mē̃ laṛāī karnē-kā natījā hai. phir laṛāī karōgī hamārē sāth?

Kalsūm: (muskarākar ⁹⁸) nahī̃, kabhī nahī̃. lēkin laṛāī śurū tō tum-nē kī thī. tum bōlō, karōgē phir?

Śamśād: nahī̃, kabhī nahī̃.

savālāt:

1. Kalsūm kyā kyā cīzē̃ sāth lē jānā cāhtī thī? 2. Śamśād-nē apnī sās ⁹⁹ -kē bārē-mē̃ kyā kahā? 3. Kalsūm aur Śamśād-mē̃ laṛāī kyũ huī? 4. ēk ṭikāṭ-par kitnā sāmān rēlgāṛī-mē̃ lē jā saktē haĩ? 5. bāvarcīkhānē-mē̃ kyā cīz jalī?

NOTES: 1. man's name; 2. town of Naroval; 3. with one another (**adv.**); 4. **maśvarā karnā** to consult (**tr.**); 5. see 29.2; 6. what different, for the repetition see 36.2; 7. along (**adv.**); 8. taking, see 30.1; 9. **lē jānā** to take (**tr.**), see lesson 28; 10. **maĩ-nē kahā** = I say; 11. expression employed at times between husband and wife to attract attention. 12. **śōr macānā** to make noise (**tr.**); 13. but (**conj.**); 14. leave (**inf.**); 15. to be tied (= **adj.**); 16. **jamā kar dēnā** to put together (**tr.**); 17. after all (**adv.**); 18. cold, winter (ī); 19. season (ā); 20. coat (ā); 21. overcoat (ā)); 22. trousers (ī); 23. shawl (ā); 24. socks (ī); 25. shoes (ā); 26. et cetera; 27. bedding (ā); 28. **riśtēdār** relative (ā); 29. trouble (ī); 30. proper, suitable, fitting; 31. see fn. 5; 32. truck (ī); 33. well!; 34. without reasons; 35. **daṛānā** to frighten (**tr.**), see 36.1, ff.; 36. **tanz-sē** ironically (**adv.**); 37. maund (= 82 lbs.) (ā); 38. your honor; 39. some twenty; 40. rich man's wife (ī); 41. **martē vaḳt** at time of death (= **adv.**); 42. **dē jānā** to give, see lesson 28; 43. look, now!; 44. careful! take care! (**adj., n.c.**); 45. deceased (**adj., n.c.**); 46. **pyārā** dear (**adj.**); 47. **ḳharc karnā** to spend (**tr.**); 48. to earn (**tr.**); 49. difficulty (ī); 50. extravagant (**adj., n.c.**); 51. angel (ā); 52. **ḳhubī** virtue (ī); 53. two years afterward (**adv.**); 54. world (ā); 55. **burī** evil (ī); 56. **ā jānā** to come, see lesson 28; 57. **idhar udhar-kā** irrelevant (= **adj.**); 58. plainly, clearly, see 36.2 for the repetition; 59. love (ī); 60. divorce (ī); 61. **dē dēnā** to give (**tr.**), see lesson 28; 62. free (**adj., n.c.**); 63. **mazē karnā** to enjoy, have fun (**tr.**); 64. **sambhālnā** to take care, watch over; 65. miser of misers; 66. face (ā); 67. red (**adj., n.c.**); 68. tear (ā); 69. **bahnā** to flow (**int.**); 70. seeing, see 30.1; 71. **ghabrānā** to be upset (**int.**); 72. **manānā** to conciliate; 73. lady, wife (ī) 74. **pyār karnā** to love (**tr.**); 75. **insān** human-being (ā); 76. unless (**adj., n.c.**); 77. **nikal jānā** to come out (**int.**), see lesson 28. 78. **muāf kar dēnā** to forgive (**tr.**), see lesson 28; 79. **vāstā** connection (ā); 80. **kōī aur** some other; 81. **ḍhū̃ṛhnā** (also **ḍhū̃ḍhnā**) to look for, seek; 82. **bāl** hair (ā); 83. **ū̃glī** finger (ī); 84. **phērnā** to stroke (**tr.**); 85. to kiss (**tr.**); 86. away, apart (**adv.**); 87. **dhakēlnā** to push (**tr.**); 88. sad (**adj., n.c.**); 89. heart (ā); 90. soft (**adj., n.c.**); 91. husband and wife (ē); 92. **jalnā** to burn (**int.**); 93. smell (ī); 94. Alas!; 95. **jal jānā** to become burned (**int.**), see lesson 28; 96. **kōī bāt nahī̃** it's all right; 97. **khā lēnā** to eat (**tr.**), see lesson 28; 98. smiling, see 30.1; 99. mother-in-law (ī).

LESSON 21

21.1

maĩ-nē dēkhā.	I (**msc.**) saw.
maĩ-nē dēkhā.	I (**fm.**) saw.
us-nē dēkhā.	He saw.
us-nē dēkhā.	She saw.
ham-nē dēkhā.	We (**msc.**) saw.
ham-nē dēkhā.	We (**fm.**) saw.
tum-nē dēkhā.	You (**msc.**) saw.
tum-nē dēkhā.	You (**fm.**) saw.
āp-nē dēkhā.	You (**msc.**) saw.
āp-nē dēkhā.	You (**fm.**) saw.
unhō̃-nē dēkhā.	They (**msc.**) saw.
unhō̃-nē dēkhā.	They (**fm.**) saw.

This section illustrates the Urdu construction which translates English constructions involving the Simple Perfect tense of transitive verbs (i.e., verbs which can take a direct object). The Urdu construction consists of the English subject placed in the OBJECT FORM before the postposition **-nē**, and the past participle of the verb, bearing the subject singular masculine suffix, **-ā**. These sentences illustrate transitive verbs without direct objects. Here the past participle will bear the subject singular masculine suffix, **-ā**, no matter what the gender of the noun placed before the postposition **-nē** may be.
REMARKS: The form of the first person pronoun when placed before the postposition **-nē** is **maĩ**; the form of the third person plural pronoun is **unhō̃**- (Similarly, the plural form of the **ye** pronoun will be **inhō̃-**; and that of **kaun, kinhō̃**-).

21.1.1

bēṭē-nē laṛkē-kō dēkhā.	The son saw the boy.
bēṭē-nē laṛkō̃-kō dēkhā.	The son saw the boys.
bēṭō̃-nē laṛkō̃-kō dēkhā.	The sons saw the boys.

bēṭē-nē laṛkī-kō dēkhā.	The son saw the girl.
bēṭē-nē laṛkiyō̃-kō dēkhā.	The son saw the girls.
bēṭō̃-nē laṛkiyō̃-kō dēkhā.	The sons saw the girls.
bēṭī-nē laṛkī-kō dēkhā.	The daughter saw the girl.
bēṭī-nē laṛkiyō̃-kō dēkhā.	The daughter saw the girls.
bēṭiyō̃-nē laṛkiyō̃-kō dēkhā.	The daughters saw the girls.
bēṭī-nē laṛkē-kō dēkhā.	The daughter saw the boy.
bēṭī-nē laṛkō̃-kō dēkhā.	The daughter saw the boys.
bēṭiyō̃-nē laṛkō̃-kō dēkhā.	The daughters saw the boys.

This section is concerned with the translation into Urdu of the direct objects of English transitive verbs in the Simple Perfect tense.

The direct object of the English sentence is translated into Urdu by the object form of the noun or pronoun which is placed before the postposition **-kō.** The verbal construction is the same as that described in 21.1, with the particle having only one form—that bearing the subject singular masculine suffix, **-ā.**

REMARKS: It has been noted before (See 9.1.1, Remarks 1) that in connection with nominal forms denoting things (and, sometimes, animals), when the postposition **-kō** is not employed, the noun is placed in the subject form. In such cases the past construction used will be that described in section 21.2, following.

It can further be said that when a particular or specific thing (or animal) is indicated the postposition **-kō** is used, and, therefore, the construction described in this section would apply.

21.1.2

bēṭē-nē laṛkē-kō dēkhā hai.	The son has seen the boy.
bēṭē-nē laṛkō̃-kō dēkhā hai.	The son has seen the boys.
bēṭō̃-nē laṛkō̃-kō dēkhā hai.	The sons have seen the boys.
bēṭē-nē laṛkī-kō dēkhā hai.	The son has seen the girl.
bēṭē-nē laṛkiyō̃-kō dēkhā hai.	The son has seen the girls.
bēṭō̃-nē laṛkiyō̃-kō dēkhā hai.	The sons have seen the girls.
bēṭī-nē laṛkī-kō dēkhā hai.	The daughter has seen the girl.
bēṭī-nē laṛkiyō̃-kō dēkhā hai.	The daughter has seen the girls.
bēṭiyō̃-nē laṛkiyō̃-kō dēkhā hai.	The daughters have seen the girls.
bēṭī-nē laṛkē-kō dēkhā hai.	The daughter has seen the boy.
bēṭī-nē laṛkō̃-kō dēkhā hai.	The daughter has seen the boys.
bēṭiyō̃-nē laṛkō̃-kō dēkhā hai.	The daughters have seen the boys.

This section illustrates the Urdu equivalent of English constructions containing the Present Perfect of transitive verbs. It consists of the past participle of the construction described in section 21.1.1 plus the present third person singular of **hōnā, hai.**

21.1.3

bēṭē-nē laṛkī-kō dēkhā thā.	The son had seen the boy.
bēṭē-nē laṛkō̃-kō dēkhā thā.	The son had seen the boys.
bēṭō̃-nē laṛkō̃-kō dēkhā thā.	The sons had seen the boys.
bēṭē-nē laṛkī-kō dēkhā thā.	The son had seen the girl.
bēṭē-nē laṛkiyō̃-kō dēkhā thā.	The son had seen the girls.
bēṭō̃-nē laṛkiyō̃-kō dēkhā thā.	The sons had seen the girls.
bēṭī-nē laṛkī-kō dēkhā thā.	The daughter had seen the girl.
bēṭī-nē laṛkiyō̃-kō dēkhā thā.	The daughter had seen the girls.
bēṭiyō̃-nē laṛkiyō̃-kō dēkhā thā.	The daughters had seen the girls.
bēṭī-nē laṛkē-kō dēkhā thā.	The daughter had seen the boy.
bēṭī-nē laṛkō̃-kō dēkhā thā.	The daughter had seen the boys.
bēṭiyō̃-nē laṛkō̃-kō dēkhā thā.	The daughters had seen the boys.

This section illustrates the Urdu equivalent of English constructions containing the Past Perfect of transitive verbs. It consists of the past participle of the construction described in section 21.1.1 plus **thā,** the imperfect of **hōnā,** which bears the subject singular masculine suffix, **-ā.**

21.1.4

bēṭē-nē laṛkē-kō dēkhā hōgā.	The son will have seen the boy.
bēṭē-nē laṛkō̃-kō dēkhā hōgā.	The son will have seen the boys.
bēṭō̃-nē laṛkō̃-kō dēkhā hōgā.	The sons will have seen the boys.
bēṭē-nē laṛkī-kō dēkhā hōgā.	The son will have seen the girl.
bēṭē-nē laṛkiyō̃-kō dēkhā hōgā.	The son will have seen the girls.
bēṭō̃-nē laṛkiyō̃-kō dēkhā hōgā.	The sons will have seen the girls.
bēṭī-nē laṛkī-kō dēkhā hōgā.	The daughter will have seen the girl.
bēṭī-nē laṛkiyō̃-kō dēkhā hōgā.	The daughter will have seen the girls.
bēṭiyō̃-nē laṛkiyō̃-kō dēkhā hōgā.	The daughters will have seen the girls.
bēṭī-nē laṛkē-kō dēkhā hōgā.	The daughter will have seen the boy.
bēṭī-nē laṛkō̃-kō dēkhā hōgā.	The daughter will have seen the boys.
bēṭiyō̃-nē laṛkō̃-kō dēkhā hōgā.	The daughters will have seen the boys.

This section illustrates the Urdu equivalent of English constructions containing the Future Perfect tense of transitive verbs. To the past participle of the construction described in section 21.1.1 is added the future third person, singular, of the verb **hōnā,** the future suffix of which bears the masculine singular suffix, **-ā.** (See Remarks of 20.1.4)

21.1.5 Exercise 1. **Translate into English:**

1. mā̃-nē baccō̃-kō ghar-mē̃ bulāyā. 2. śikārī-nē ḳhū̃ḳhār jānvar-kō sunā. 3. naukar-nē

pul-kē nīcē gāyō̃-kō bā̃dhā. 4. kisānō̃-nē bailō̃-kō khilāyā thā. 5. aurat-nē ghar-kē pās gāy-kō sunā hai. 6. musāfir-nē naukar-kō bulāyā thā. 7. naukar-nē mālik-kō samjhā. 8. ham-nē khēt-kē nazdīk kisān-kō dēkhā. 9. gadhē-nē dhōbī-kō khī̃cā. 10. gāy-nē kuē̃-kē pās bachṛē-kō khilāyā hōgā. 11. ustād-nē tālibilmō̃-kō paṛhāyā hai. 12. ḳhāvind-nē ghar-mē̃ bīvī-kō sunā thā. 13. kisān-nē bēṭē-kō bulāyā hai. 14. ham-nē us-kō samjhā hai. 15. śikārī-nē jaṅgal-mē̃ hāthiyō̃-kō dēkhā hai. 16. sipāhī-nē dukān-mē̃ cōr-kō pakṛā hōgā. 17. aurtō̃-nē bāzār-mē̃ har tarah-kī cīzō̃-kō ḳharīdā thā. 18. ham-nē dhōbī-kō bulāyā hōgā. 19. śikārī-nē śēr-kō mārā hōgā. 20. unhō̃-nē sṭēśan-mē̃ gāṛī-kō sunā hōgā.

REMARKS: Verbal stems of two syllables or more drop the vowel, **-a-** when the suffixes of the past participle are attached—provided that the vowel **-a-** is not in the first syllable of the stem. (Compare 3.4, Remarks) For example, the past participle of **samajhnā** is **samjhā**, and that of **pakaṛnā** is **pakṛā.**

21.1.6 Exercise 2. **Translate into Urdu:**

1. The man bathed the elephant. 2. We had seen the woman near the well. 3. The oxen had dragged the plow for two hours. 4. The woman has fed the hens. 5. The bear will have dragged the little goat into the jungle. 6. The traveller bought (a) horse in the city. 7. The cat had seized the mouse. 8. The servant cut wood from the tree. 9. I had sent the orderly into the office. 10. The gardener has tied our cow near the well. 11. The woman will have bought the fish from the fisherman. 12. The cat will have grabbed the fat sparrow. 13. When had you seen that man? 14. The hunter killed the animal in the jungle. 15. Mother has cooked food for us. 16. The servant pointed out the road. 17. Mother has sent the servant to the bazaar to buy vegetables. 18. The dog will have bitten the old man. 19. Have you bought a house for me? 20. The boy drew cold water from the well for the traveller.

21.2

bēṭē-nē laṛkā dēkhā.	The son saw the boy.
bēṭē-nē laṛkē dēkhē.	The son saw the boys.
bēṭō̃-nē laṛkē dēkhē.	The sons saw the boys.
bēṭē-nē laṛkī dēkhī.	The son saw the girl.
bēṭē-nē laṛkiyā̃ dēkhī̃.	The son saw the girls.
bēṭō̃-nē laṛkiyā̃ dēkhī̃.	The sons saw the girls.
bēṭī-nē laṛkī dēkhī.	The daughter saw the girl.
bēṭī-nē laṛkiyā̃ dēkhī̃.	The daughter saw the girls.
bēṭiyō̃-nē laṛkiyā̃ dēkhī̃.	The daughters saw the girls.
bēṭī-nē laṛkā dēkhā.	The daughter saw the boy.
bēṭī-nē laṛkē dēkhē.	The daughter saw the boys.
bēṭiyō̃-nē laṛkē dēkhē.	The daughters saw the boys.

This section presents an alternative Urdu equivalent for English constructions containing transitive verbs in the Simple Perfect tense. (See 21.1.1)

The English subject is placed in the Urdu construction in the OBJECT FORM before the postposition **-nē** (See 21.1, Remarks); the English direct object is placed in the SUBJECT FORM; and the past participle is made to agree with this subject in gender, number and form.

REMARKS: (1) The suffix **-ī** of the feminine plural is nasalized when the participle is final in the utterance. (Compare the following constructions where the participle is not final and, therefore, not nasalized.)

(2) See Remarks of section 2.1.1.

21.2.1

bēṭē-nē laṛkā dēkhā hai.	The son has seen the boy.
bēṭē-nē laṛkē dēkhē haĩ.	The son has seen the boys.
bēṭō̃-nē laṛkē dēkhē haĩ.	The sons have seen the boys.
bēṭē-nē laṛkī dēkhī hai.	The son has seen the girl.
bēṭē-nē laṛkiyā̃ dēkhī haĩ.	The son has seen the girls.
bēṭō̃-nē laṛkiyā̃ dēkhī haĩ.	The sons have seen the girls.

This section presents an alternative Urdu equivalent for English constructions containing transitive verbs in the Present Perfect tense. (Compare 21.1.2)

This construction is identical with that described in section 21.2 with the addition of the present tense of **hōnā.**

21.2.2

bēṭē-nē laṛkā dēkhā thā.	The son had seen the boy.
bēṭē-nē laṛkē dēkhē thē.	The son had seen the boys.
bēṭō̃-nē laṛkē dēkhē thē.	The sons had seen the boys.
bēṭē-nē laṛkī dēkhī thī.	The son had seen the girl.
bēṭē-nē laṛkiyā̃ dēkhī thī̃.	The son had seen the girls.
bēṭō̃-nē laṛkiyā̃ dēkhī thī̃.	The sons had seen the girls.

This section presents an alternative Urdu equivalent for constructions containing transitive verbs in the Past Perfect tense. (Compare 21.1.3)

This construction is identical with that described in section 21.2 with the addition of **thā,** the imperfect of the verb **hōnā,** which along with the past participle agrees in gender, number, and form with the subject of the sentence. The **-ī,** of the feminine plural of **thā** is nasalized.

21.2.3

bēṭē-nē laṛkā dēkhā hōgā.	The son will have seen the boy.
bēṭē-nē laṛkē dēkhē hō̃gē.	The son will have seen the boys.
bēṭō̃-nē laṛkē dēkhē hō̃gē.	The sons will have seen the boys.
bēṭē-nē laṛkī dēkhī hōgī.	The son will have seen the girl.
bēṭē-nē laṛkiyā̃ dēkhī hō̃gī.	The son will have seen the girls.
bēṭō̃-nē laṛkiyā̃ dēkhī hō̃gī.	The sons will have seen the girls.

This section presents an alternative Urdu equivalent for English constructions containing transitive verbs in the Future Perfect tense. (Compare 21.1.4)

This construction is identical with that described in section 21.2 with the addition of the future of **hōnā,** which agrees with the subject of the sentence in gender and number.

REMARKS: See remarks of 20.1.4 and 21.1.4.

21.2.4 More examples of the constructions described in sections 21.2 to 21.2.3 are:

aḳhbārnavīs-nē safīr-sē savāl pūchē.	The newspaperman asked the ambassador questions.
kyā āp-nē kabhī Kalkattā dēkhā hai?	Have you ever seen Calcutta?
ādmī-nē ēk ḳhat likhā thā.	The man had written a letter.
ḳulī-nē mērā sāmān uṭhāyā.	The coolie picked up my luggage.
naukar-nē cār bajē cāy banāyī thī.	The servant had made the tea at four o'clock.
kuttē-nē laṛkē-kā hāth cāṭā.	The dog licked the boy's hand.
ādmī-nē dōstō̃-kō kahānī sunāyī hōgī.	The man will have told (**his**) friends the story.
naukar-nē mālik-kā hukam kyū̃ g̲alat samjhā thā?	Why had the servant misunderstood the master's order?
kyā unhō̃-nē Hindī ṭhīk bōlī?	Did they speak Hindi correctly?
maĩ-nē dukān-mẽ ḳalam ḳharīdā thā.	I had bought the pen in the shop.
ham-nē chat-sē nahar dēkhī.	We saw the canal from the roof.
laṛkō̃-nē surāḳh-mẽ patthar ḍālē.	The boys threw rocks into the hole.
kisān-nē bail-par chaṛī phẽkī.	The farmer threw the stick at the bullock.
śām-kō aurtō̃-nē gīt gāyē thē.	In the evening the women had sung songs.
unhō̃-nē baṛē śahar-kē pās nahrẽ dēkhī thī̃.	They had seen the canals near the large city.
ḍrāivar-nē ṭrām rōkī.	The driver stopped the trolley.

REMARKS: **g̲alat** (adj.) incorrect, wrong, **g̲alat samajhnā** to misunderstand, **surāḳh** (ā) hole, **nahar** (ī) canal, **patthar** (ā) stone, **hāth** (ā) hand, **aḳhbārnavīs** (ā) newspaperman, **safīr** (ā) ambassador, **ḳulī** (ā) coolie.

21.2.5 Exercise 1. **Translate into English:**

1. kyā naukar-nē khānā pakāyā hai? 2. maĩ-nē būṛhē ādmī-kē liyē ḳhat paṛhā. 3. aurat-nē bāzār-mẽ ye tasvīr ḳharīdī hōgī. 4. kisān-nē bail khilāyē. 5. dukāndār-nē hamẽ phal bēcē thē. 6. āp-nē garm pānī kyū̃ piyā thā? 7. kyā naukar-nē cār bajē cāy banāyī? 8. bandarō̃-nē daraḳht-kē pakkē phal khāyē hō̃gē. 9. us-nē musāfir-kō Kalkattē-kī saṛak batāyī. 10. maĩ-nē āp-kā hukam g̲alat samjhā. 11. unhō̃-nē hamārē ḳhat kal paṛhē thē. 12. kyā us-nē Angrēzī ṭhīk samjhī? 13. laṛkē-nē nahar-sē pānī khīcā hai. 14. baccō̃-nē bailō̃-par kyū̃ patthar phẽkē thē? 15. śikārī-nē jānvar kahā̃ mārā hai? 16. ādmiyō̃-nē chōṭī daryā-mẽ hāthī nahlāyā hōgā. 17. kyā mālī-nē paudō̃-par pānī ḍālā? 18. ham-nē bhūkē ādmiyō̃-kō khānā bhējā. 19. laṛkē-nē gāṛī-mẽ bhārī bōjh rakhā hai. 20. maĩ-nē us-kā ḳalam mēz-par rakhā thā.

21.2.6 Exercise 2. **Translate into Urdu:**

1. Why did you eat the candy? 2. The man had placed the light luggage on the bed. 3. Had he read your book? 4. Will he have seen Calcutta? 5. When had he watered the plants in the garden? 6. They threw stones at the oxen. 7. Has the servant placed the

plates on the table? 8. Who had written this letter? 9. When did you hear their song? 10. They misunderstood my orders. 11. To whom had the woman sent the food? 12. Who sent me this letter? 13. This man tied the grass with a rope. 14. Why did the dog bite the horse? 15. He understood my Urdu exactly. 16. Who picked up my luggage? 17. Will he have heard your story? 18. Where did the tiger drag the goat? 19. Why did you stop the automobile near the canal? 20. Where had the servant placed the shoes?

21.3. Text 5: **Bātcīt.**[1]

Translate into English. Answer the questions in Urdu:

[Hamīd[2] aur Jalāl[2] bacpan[3]-kē sāthī[4] haĩ. lēkin[5] vo kaī[6] sālō̃[7]-sē ēk dūsrē-sē[8] nahī̃ milē.[9] kuch din huē[10] Jalāl śahar-mē̃ saudā • sulaf[11] ḳharīdnē[12] gayā. vahā̃ purānē[13] dōst phir[14] ēk dūsrē-sē milē. (āō,[15] ham-bhī un-kī bātcīt sunē̃.)]

Hamīd: arē, Jalāl bhāī! ye tum hō. salām-ō-alēkum.

Jalāl: ō[16] mērē yār[17] Hamīd. miyā̃,[18] tum kahā̃?[19] bahot dēr-kē bād mulāḳāt[20] huī. sunāō, acchē tō[21] hō na?

Hamīd: hā̃, sab ṭhīk • ṭhāk[22] hai. Allah[23]-kā śukar[24] hai. tum śahar kaisē[25] āyā?

Jalāl: bhāī,[26] laṛkī-kī śādī kar rahā hū̃.[27] tum-nē tō dēkhā nahī̃. ab javān hō gayī hai.[28]

Hamīd: śādī kab hai?

Jalāl: aglē[29] mahinē-kī pandrā tārīḳh-kō.

Hamīd: kyā sab sāmān mukammal[30] hai?

Jalāl: hā̃, zēvar[31] sab taiyār haĩ. aur dulhan[32]-kē kapṛē-bhī ban gayē[33] haĩ. lēkin bārāt[34]-kē khānē-kē liyē paisō̃-kā bandōbast[35] abhī nahī̃.

Hamīd: tō is bārē-mē̃[36] tumhārā kyā ḳhayāl hai?

Jalāl: pahilē mērā ḳhayāl thā ke[37] apnē kisī riśtēdār yā dōst-sē ḳarz mā̃g lū̃.[38] tā-kē[39] sūd na dēnā paṛē. lēkin mērī bīvī-kā ḳhayāl hai ke[37] riśtēdārō̃-kā ahsān[40] lēnā acchā nahī̃. ab ye ḳhayāl[41] hai ke[37] kisī sāhūkār[42]-sē ḳarz lē lū̃.[43]

Hamīd: sāhūkārō̃-sē ḳarz lēnē-mē̃ ēk muśkil[44] hai. vo sūd bahot zyādā lētē haĩ aur hisāb • kitāb[45]-mē̃ bēīmānī[46]-bhī kartē haĩ. tum mērē purānē dōst hō. mērā maśvarā tō ye hai ke[37] anjuman-ē-imdād-ē-bāhmī-sē ḳarz lēnē-kī kōśiś karō.

Jalāl: yār, vo tō maĩ kar cukā hū̃.[47] anjuman-ē-imdād-ē-bāhmī-kē inspekṭār[48]-sē milā thā. vo mērē bēṭē-kā ham • jamāat[49] thā aur hamārē kunbē-kā dōst-bhī hai. us-nē kahā ke[37] bīj[50] yā hal[51] yā jānvar ḳharīdnē-kē liyē tō anjuman[52]-sē ḳarz[53] mil saktā hai, lēkin śādī-kē liyē nahī̃. sarkārī ḳānūn is-kī ijāzat[54] nahī̃ dētā.

Hamīd: ye kām[55] tō phir ḳharāb hai. aisī sūrat[56]-mē̃ tō sāhūkār-kē pās-hī jānā paṛēgā. mērī bāt sunō. hamārē gāō̃-mē ēk nayā sāhūkār āyā hai. usē kār-ō-bār[57]-mē̃ zyādā dēr[58] nahī̃ huī. is liyē vo abhī-tak[59] īmāndār hai. mērī salāh[60] hai ke[37] tumhē̃ us-kē pās jānā cāhiyē.

Jalāl: bhāī, tumhārā bahot bahot śukriyā. maĩ zarūr us-kē pās jāū̃gā. hā̃ aur sab-sē zarūrī[61] bāt tō maĩ bhūl-hī gayā[62] thā. tum tō laṛkī-kē cacā huē—na?[63] śādī-par zarūr ānā aur bīvī • baccō̃-kō-bhī sāth lānā. mērī bīvī tumhārē bīvī • baccō̃-sē milkar[64] bahot ḳhuś hōgī.

Hamīd: kyū̃ nahī! zarūr āū̃gā aur bīvī • baccō̃-kō-bhī sāth lāū̃gā. ab mujhē ijāzat dō. mērī chōṭī laṛkī bīmār hai. ḍākṭar[65]-sē davāī[66] lēkar[67] vāpas ghar jāū̃gā aur bīmār-kō davāī dū̃gā.

Jalāl: āp-kī laṛkī-kī bīmārī[68]-kā tō mujhē patā[69]-hī nahī̃ thā. baṛā afsōs hai. usē kyā bīmārī hai?

Hamīd: miyā̃, kyā batāū̃? pahilē tō māmūlī[70] zukām[71] thā, lēkin āhistā āhistā khā̃sī[72]-bhī ānē lagī.[73] chōṭē ḍākṭar-kē ilāj[74]-sē kōī faidā nahī huā. ab baṛē ḍākṭar • sāhab-kā ilāj kartā hū̃.

Jalāl: kyā ab pahilē-sē laṛkī-kī sēhat[75] acchī hai?

Hamīd: hā̃, kuch farḳ[76] hai. lēkin bahot zyādā nahī̃. tum jānō, agar marīz[77] jaldī acchē hō jāē, tō ḍākṭar paisē kaisē kamāē̃? vo-bhī saccē haī.

Jalāl: mērē ḳhayāl-mē̃ tō sarkār-kō sab bīmārō̃-kā muft[78] ilāj karnē-kē liyē haspatāl[79] khōlnē[80] cāhiyē̃.

Hamīd: bēśak, tum ṭhīk kahtē hō. alekśan[81]-kē vaḳt tō sarkār lōgō̃-sē hamēśā yehī vādā[82] kartī hai. mērā ḳhayāl hai ke[37] is dafā maī aur mērē kunbē-kē lōg kisī aur pārṭī[83]-kō apnē vōṭ[84] dē̃gē.

Jalāl: mērē ḳhayāl-mē̃ tō sab pārṭiyā̃ ēk jaisī[85] haī. vādē karnē-mē̃ sab tēz haī, lēkin vādā pūrā karnē[86]-mē̃ sab sust[87] haī. ēk tarāh[88] sarkār-bhī ṭhīk kahtī hai. sarkār-kē pās itnē paisē kahā̃ hai ke[89] sab-kē liyē ēk • dam[90] haspatāl khōl dē.[91] ye kām tō āhistā āhistā hō̃gē.

Hamīd: acchā, dōst. maī ab tumhārā zyādā vaḳt nahī̃ zāē[92] karnā cāhtā. ab ijāzat dō.[93] inśā Allah, phir mulāḳāt hōgī.

Jalāl: bahot acchā. Ḳhudā hāfiz.

Hamīd: Ḳhudā hāfiz.

savālāt:

1. Jalāl śahar-mē̃ kyā karnē[94] gayā aur vahā̃ usē kaun milā? 2. Jalāl-kō kis liyē paisō̃-kī zarūrat thī? 3. Jalāl-kī bīvī-kā riśtēdārō̃-sē paisē lēnē-kē barē-mē̃ kyā ḳhayāl thā? 4. anjuman-ē-imdād-ē-bāhmī-nē Jalāl-kō kyā batāyā? 5. Hamid-kī laṛkī-kō kyā bīmārī thī?

NOTES: 1. conversation (ī); 2. name of man; 3. childhood (ā); 4. friend (ā); 5. but; 6. some, several; 7. year (?); 8. **ēk dūsrē-sē** one another; 9. **milnā** to meet (**int.**); 10. **kuch din huē** some days ago (**adv.**); 11. provisions (groceries, etc.) (ā); 12. = **ḳharīdnē-kē liyē;** 13. old (**adj.**); 14. again (**adv.**); 15. come! 16. oh!; 17. friend, buddy (ā); 18. dear (friend); 19. **tum kahā̃** = Where have you been?; 20. meeting (ī); 21. then (**emph. pt.**); 22. all right (**adj., n.c.**); 23. God (ā); 24. thanks (ā); 25. for what reason (**interr. adv.**); 26. = brother, buddy, pal; 27. **kar rahā hū̃** I am doing, see 23.1; 28. She is now of marriageable age; 29. coming, approaching (adj.); 30. completed (**adj., n.c.**); 31. ornaments, jewelry (ā); 32. bride (ī); 33. **ban jānā** to be made, see lesson 28; 34. bridegroom's party (ī); 35. **bandōbast** arrangement (ā); 36. **is bārē-mē̃** about this; 37. see 29.2; 38. **ḳarz mā̃g lēnā** to borrow (**tr.**), see lesson 28; 39. so that; 40. obligation (ā); 41. idea (ā) 42. money-lender (ā); 43. **ḳarz lē lēna** to borrow, see lesson 28; 44. difficulty (ī); 45. account, bookkeeping (ā); 46. dishonesty (ī); 47. I have already done . . . , see 28.7; 48. inspector (ā); 49. classmate (ā); 50. seed (ā); 51. plow (ā); 52. society (ī); 53. loan (ā); 54. permission (ī); 55. = thing, matter; 56. condition, look of things (ī); 57. business (ā); 58. long (=**adv.**); 59. up till now; 60. advice (ī); 61. important, necessary (**adj., n.c.**); 62. **bhūl jānā** to forget (**int.**), see lesson 28, note the function of the emphatic particle, **hī**; 63. =aren't you?; 64. having met, see 30.1; 65. doctor (ā); 66. medicine (ī); 67. taking = with, see 30.1; 68. sickness (ī); 69. knowledge, information, sign (ā); 70. ordinary (**adj. n.c.**); 71. cold (ā); 72. cough (ī); 73. began to come, see 34.1.2; 74. treatment (ā); 75. health (ī); 76. difference (ā); 77. patient, sick person (ā); 78. free (**adj. n.c.**); 79. hospital (ā); 80. This illustrates the infinitive functioning as an adjective—i.e., agreeing with the noun modified (here, **haspatāl**) in gender, number and case; 81. election (ā); 82. promise (ā); 83. (political) party (ī); 84. vote (ā); 85. **ēk jaisā** all alike; 86. **pūrā karnā** to fulfill (**tr.**); 87. slow, lazy (**adj., n.c.**); 88. **ēk tarāh** in one way; 89. that (**conj.**); 90. immediately (**adv.**); 91. **khōl dēnā** to open (**tr.**), see lesson 28; 92. **zāē karnā** to waste (**tr.**); 93. **ab ijāzat dō** = now excuse me; 94. = **karnē-kē liyē,** see 37.2.2.

LESSON 22

22.1

ādmī śahar gayā.	The man went to the city.
ādmī śahar gayē.	The men went to the city.
aurat śahar gayī.	The woman went to the city.
aurtē̃ śahar gayī̃.	The women went to the city.

This section illustrates the formation of the past participle of **jānā,** to go, to express the simple perfect.

22.1.1

ādmī ḳhuś huā.	The man became happy.
ādmī ḳhuś huē.	The men became happy.
aurat ḳhuś huī.	The woman became happy.
aurtē̃ ḳhuś huī̃.	The women became happy.

This section illustrates the formation of the past participle of **hōnā,** to be, to become, to express the simple perfect.

22.1.2

laṛkē-nē savāl-kā javāb diyā.	The boy answered the question.
laṛkē-nē savālō̃-kē javāb diyē.	The boy answered the questions.
maĩ-nē laṛkē-kō ēk kitāb dī.	I gave the boy a book.
maĩ-nē laṛkē-kō kitābē̃ dī̃.	I gave the boy books.

This section illustrates the formation of the past participle of **dēnā,** to give, to express the simple perfect.

22.1.3

ādmī-nē naukar-sē pyālā liyā.	The man took the cup from the servant.
ādmiyō̃-nē naukarō̃-sē pyālē liyē.	The men took the cups from the servants.
laṛkē-nē laṛkī-sē bālṭī lī.	The boy took the bucket from the girl.
laṛkō̃-nē laṛkiyō̃-sē bālṭiyā̃ lī̃.	The boys took the buckets from the girls.

This section illustrates the formation of the past participle of **lēnā,** to take, to express the simple perfect.

REMARKS: **bālṭī** (ī) bucket.

22.1.4

maĩ-nē Pākistān-kō safar kiyā.	I travelled to Pakistan.
unhō̃-nē pardēs-mē̃ bahot safar kiyē.	They travelled a lot abroad.
ādmī-nē samandar-kī sair kī.	The man strolled along the sea.
ādmiyō̃-nē samandar-kī sairē̃ kī̃.	The men strolled along the sea (i.e., **a number of times).**

This section illustrates the formation of the past participle of **karnā,** to do, to make, to express the simple perfect.

REMARKS: **samandar** (ā) ocean, sea, **sair** (ī) stroll, walk.

22.1.5

kārīgar-nē mōṭargāṛī-kī marammat kī.	The mechanic repaired the car.
vo hamārē sāth gāō̃-kō gayē.	They went to the village with us.
mōcī-nē mērē hare jūtō̃-kē marammat kī thī.	The shoemaker had repaired my green shoes.
ham-nē ġarīb ādmī-kō paisē diyē.	We gave money to the poor man.
ādmiyō̃-nē kārk͟hānē-mē̃ kām kiyā thā.	The men had worked in the factory.
naukar-nē kursī-sē bhūrī ṭōpī lī.	The servant took the brown cap from the chair.
maĩ-nē naukar-sē rakābī lī thī.	I had taken the plate from the servant.
laṛkō̃-nē paṛhnē-kī kōśiśē̃ kī̃.	The boys made attempts to read.
mālik-nē tum-kō kyā diyā?	What did the master give you?
laṛkē baṛē jahāzō-kō̃ dēkhnē-kē liyē bandargāh gayē.	The boys went to the harbor to see the big ships.
naukar-nē darvāzā band kiyā hai.	The servant has closed the door.
us-nē kis paudē-sē zard phūl tōṛē?	From which plant did he pluck the yellow flowers?
kyā āp-nē kabhī jahāz-sē safar kiyā thā?	Had you ever travelled by ship?
maĩ havāī·jahāz dēkhnē-kē liyē bāhar gayī.	I went out to see the airplane.
tum-nē mujhē ēk gandā glās diyā hai.	You have given me a dirty glass.

REMARKS: (1) Many English verbs are translated into Urdu by a phrase consisting of a **noun** + **karnā.** Compare **kām karnā** to work; **safar karnā** to journey, to travel; **kōśiś karnā** to attempt, to try; **marammat karnā** to repair, to fix.

If the English verb, translated into Urdu by a **noun** + **karnā** phrase, takes a direct object, this when translated into Urdu is placed in the **object** form before the postposition **-kā** which agrees in gender, number and form with the noun of the **noun** + **karnā** phrase. For example, see in the first sentence, **kārīgar-nē mōṭargāṛī-kī marammat**

kī., literally, **The mechanic made the repair of the automobile.**, and in the eighth sentence, **laṛkō̃-nē paṛhnē-kē kōśiśē̃ kī.**, literally, **The boys made attempts at reading.**
(2) **jahāz** (ā) ship, band (**adj.**) closed, **band karnā** to close, **band hōnā** to be closed, **bandargāh** (ā) harbor, port, **marammat** (ī) repair, **[-kī] marammat karnā** to repair, **mōcī** (ā) shoemker, **[-kī] kōśiś karnā** to attempt, try, **glās** (ā) glass, **zard (adj., n.c.)** yellow.

22.2

kaun-sē ādmī-nē ye kiyā?	Which (particular) man did this?
kis ādmī-nē ye kiyā?	Which man did this?
kis-nē ye kiyā?	Who did this?
kaun-sī aurat-nē ye kiyā?	Which (particular) woman did this?
kis aurat-nē ye kiyā?	Which woman did this?
kis-nē ye kiyā?	Who did this?
kaun-sē ādmiyō̃-nē ye kiyā?	Which (particular) men did this?
kin ādmiyō̃-nē ye kiyā?	Which men did this?
kinhō̃-nē ye kiyā?	Who did this?
kaun-sī aurtō̃-nē ye kiyā?	Which (particular) women did this?
kin aurtō̃-nē ye kiyā?	Which women did this?
kinhō̃-nē ye kiyā?	Who did this?

This section illustrates the use of the interrogative adjectives and pronouns in constructions with the past participles of transitive verbs. For **kaun-sā** see sections 18.3 and 38.1.1.

Note the plural form **kinhō̃-** before the postposition **-nē.**

22.2.1

is ādmī-nē vo kiyā.	This man did that.
is-nē vo kiyā.	This (**one**) did that.
is aurat-nē vo kiyā.	This woman did that.
is-nē vo kiyā.	This (**one**) did that.
in ādmiyō̃-nē vo kiyā.	These men did that.
inhō̃-nē vo kiyā.	These did that.
in aurtō̃-nē vo kiyā.	These women did that.
inhō̃-nē vo kiyā.	These did that.

This section illustrates the use of the demonstrative pronoun and adjective **vo** in constructions with the past participles of transitive verbs. Note the plural form **inhō̃-** before the postposition **-nē.**

22.2.2

us ādmī-nē ye kiyā.	That man did this.
us-nē ye kiyā.	That (**one**) did this. **or** He did this.
us aurat-nē ye kiyā.	That woman did this.
us-nē ye kiyā.	That (**one**) did this. **or** She did this.
un ādmiyō̃-nē ye kiyā.	Those men did this.
unhō̃-nē ye kiyā.	Those did this. **or** They did this.
un aurtō̃-nē ye kiyā.	Those women did this.
unhō̃-nē ye kiyā.	Those did this. **or** They did this.

This section illustrates the use of the demonstrative adjective and pronoun **vo** in constructions with the past participle of transitive verbs. Note the plural form **unhō̃-** before the postposition **-nē.**

22.3 Exercise 1. **Translate into English:**
1. mālik-nē naukar-kō kyā hukam diyā? 2. kyā āp-nē machliyā̃ pakaṛnē-kī kōśiś kī thī? 3. ham mōcī-kī dukān-kō gayē thē. 4. musāfir-nē pardēs-mē̃ safar kiyā. 5. naukar gāõ-kō kyū̃ vāpas gayā? 6. mā̃-nē bēṭī-kō nayē harē jutē diyē. 7. kārīgar-nē kab āp-kī mōṭar-gāṛī-kī marammat kī? 8. pyāsē ādmī-nē laṛkē-sē ṭhaṇḍē pānī-kā pyālā liyā. 9. jahāz kab bandargāh-mē̃ gayā thā? 10. aurtē̃ pānī vāpas lānē-kē liyē kuē̃-kō gayī̃. 11. tālibilmō̃-nē ustād-kē savālō̃-kē ṭhik javāb diyē thē. 12. g̲arīb ādmī-nē meharbān aurat-sē khānā liyā. 13. kyā mōcī-nē jutō̃-kī marammat-kī kōśiś kī? 14. bāp-nē bēṭī-kō cūṛiyā̃ dī̃. 15. naukar-nē mērē kamrē-kē darvāzā band kiyā. 16. kaun-sā ādmī kal vahā̃ gayā? 17. maī-nē daryā-mē̃ tairnā pasand kiyā. 18. kinhō̃-nē pīr-kō phul diyē thē? 19. naukar-nē mērē jūtē sāf kiyē thē. 20. kyā āp-nē havāī • jahāz-sē kabhī safar kiyā?

22.3.1 Exercise 2. **Translate into Urdu:**
1. Did the servant clean my shoes? 2. What did the mechanic do under the automobile? 3. The happy man took the food from the woman. 4. The women made journeys to many sacred places. 5. Did you like to travel abroad? 6. The carpenter has repaired the round table. 7. The student had tried to study the easy lesson. 8. Who closed the door? 9. We gave the poor woman money to buy food. 10. The servant had tried to pick up the heavy load. 11. I preferred to eat in the hotel's restaurant. 12. The woman became very happy. 13. When did the mechanic repair the automobile? 14. The washerman had taken the clothes from the servant to wash (**them**). 15. The student preferred speaking Urdu to speaking English. 16. Which (**particular**) servant took your cap? 17. The little girl had tried to prepare the tea for us. 18. They had gone to Calcutta by train. 19. Did you try to speak Urdu? 20. When did they go back to the village?

22.4

mujhē jānā paṛā.	I had to go.
tālibilm-kō paṛhnā paṛā.	The student had to study.

naukar-kō hamārē jānē-kē liyē sab kuch taiyār karnā paṛā.	The servant had to prepare everything for our departure.
aurat-kō bāvarcīkhānē-mē̃ pakānā paṛā.	The woman had to cook in the kitchen.
laṛkī-kō kuē̃-sē pānī lānā paṛā.	The girl had to bring water from the well.

The construction of the sentences in this section is identical with that of section 17.1.2, with one change: here the verb of the English sentence is in the past tense, which is translated into Urdu by the subject singular, masculine, of the past participle of the verb paṛnā, paṛā.

22.4.1

mujhē jānā paṛēgā.	I will have to go.
tālibilm-kō paṛhnā paṛēgā.	The student will have to study.
naukar-kō hamārē jānē-kē liyē sab kuch taiyār karnā paṛēgā.	The servant will have to prepare everything for our departure.
aurat-kō bāvarcīkhānē-mē̃ pakānā paṛēgā.	The woman will have to cook in the kitchen.
laṛkī-kō kuē̃-sē pānī lānā paṛēgā.	The girl will have to bring water from the well.

The construction of the sentences in this section is identical with that of section 17.1.2, with one change: here the verb paṛnā is in the future tense, the suffix always being that of the subject form, singular, masculine.

22.4.2

mujhē jānā hōgā.	I will have to go.
tālibilm-kō paṛhnā hōgā.	The student will have to study.
naukar-kō hamārē jānē-kē liyē sab kuch taiyār karnā hōgā.	The servant will have to prepare everything for our departure.
aurat-kō bāvarcīkhānē-mē̃ pakānā hōgā.	The woman will have to cook in the kitchen.
laṛkī-kō kuē̃-sē pānī lānā hōgā.	The girl will have to bring water from the well.

The construction of the sentences in this section is identical with that of section 17.1.1, with one change: the future of hōnā is used with the suffix always in the subject form, singular, masculine.

22.4.3 Exercise 1. **Translate into English:**

1. hamē̃ bāzār jānā paṛā. 2. āp-kō Pākistān-mē̃ Urdū bōlnā hōgā. 3. dhōbī-kō kapṛē sāf karnā paṛā. 4. naukar-kō hamārē liyē bistar taiyār karnā paṛēgā. 5. machērē-kō machliyā̃ pakaṛnā paṛā. 6. hamē̃ Urdū bōlnē-kī kōśiś karnā hōgā. 7. kārīgar-kō mōṭargāṛī-kī marammat karnā paṛā. 8. naukar-kō hamārē nahānē-kē liyē garm pānī lānā paṛēgā. 9. tumhē̃ mērā darvāzā band karnā hōgā. 10. kyā unhē̃ gā̃ō vāpas jānā paṛā?

22.4.4 Exercise 2. **Translate into Urdu:**

1. Will you have to work today? 2. Who had to repair the chair? 3. I will have to go to the well for water. 4. We will have to stay at home tonight. 5. Who will have to prepare the tea for us? 6. The shoemaker had to repair my new green shoes. 7. Why did he have to go to the village? 8. Did you have to buy fish from that fisherman? 9. Who will have to cut wood for the fire? 10. I had to go to the city to see him.

22.5

ādmī-kē ēk bēṭā hai.	The man has a son.
ādmī-kē dō bēṭē haĩ.	The man has two sons.
ādmī-kē ēk bēṭī hai.	The man has a daughter.
ādmī-kē dō bēṭiyā̃ haĩ.	The man has two daughters.

Sections 22.5 to 22.5.7 illustrate ways of translating into Urdu English phrases indicating possession.

The construction of the above sentences involves human relationship, usually family relationship.

REMARKS: (1) The postposition **-kē** remains unchanged.

(2) An alternate and preferred construction is one in which the postposition **-kā** is made to agree with the subject of the verb **hōnā** in gender, number and case. Compare section 14.1 and 14.2.

22.5.1

mērā ēk bhāī hai.	I have a brother.
mērē dō bhāī haĩ.	I have two brothers.
mērī ēk bahan hai.	I have a sister.
mērī dō bahnẽ haĩ.	I have two sisters.
hamārā ēk bhāī hai.	We have a brother.
hamārē dō bhāī haĩ.	We have two brothers.
mērī ēk bahan śahar-mẽ rahtī hai.	One of my sisters lives in the city.
maĩ tumhārē ēk bhāī-kō jāntā hū̃.	I know one of your brothers.

This section illustrates the construction indicating human relationship, usually family relationship, with the pronouns of the first and second person (i.e., **maĩ, ham, tum**). Compare sections 13.5, 13.5.1 and 13.5.2.

22.5.2

ādmī-kē pās dō makān haĩ.	The man has two houses.
tālibilm-kē pās ēk pensil hai.	The student has a pencil.
kisān-kē pās ēk hal hai.	The farmer has a plow.
kuttē-kē pās ēk haḍḍī hai.	The dog has a bone.
mērē pās siyāhī hai.	I have ink.
āp-kē pās ēk cābī hai.	You have a key.
hamārē pās dō bhūrē kambal haĩ.	We have two brown blankets.
aurat-kē pās chūrī hai.	The woman has a knife.
naukar-kē pās āp-kī jurābẽ nahī̃ haĩ.	The servant does not have your socks.
musāfir-kē pās kāfī paisē nahī̃ haĩ.	The traveller does not have enough money.

These sentences illustrate the construction indicating the physical possession of beings or things, the ownership of which can be transferred. Compare section 11.2.

REMARKS: **kambal** (ā) blanket, **cābī** (ī) key, **chūrī** (ī) knife, **pensil** (ī) pencil, **jurāb** (ī) sock, **siyāhī** (ī) ink, **rōśnāī** (ī) ink, **bhūrā** (**adj.**) brown.

22.5.3

kuttē-kē cār pāō̃ haĩ.	The dog has four feet.
ādmī-kī bāhẽ lambī haĩ.	The man has long arms.
baccē-kē dā̃t safēd haĩ.	The child has white teeth. (= **The child's teeth are white.**)
kuttē-kē dā̃t pīlē haĩ.	The dog has yellow teeth.
mērī ā̃khē nīlī haĩ.	I have blue eyes.
tumhārē dā̃t tēz haĩ.	You have sharp teeth.

This section illustrates the construction indicating possession with reference to parts of the body. Compare section 14.2 for the construction with the postposition **-kā.**

REMARKS: **ā̃kh** (ī) eye, **dā̃t** (ā) tooth, **pā̃v** (ā),(pl. **pāō̃**) foot, **bāh** (ī) arm, **pīlā** (adj.) yellow, **nīlā (adj.)** blue.

22.5.4

makān-mẽ bahot kamrē haĩ.	The house has many rooms.
kamrē-mẽ cār khiṛkiyā̃ haĩ.	The room has four windows.
thailē-mẽ bahot surāḳh haĩ.	The bag has many holes.

For the postpositional construction in these sentences see section 9.1.

REMARKS: **surāḳh** (ā) hole.

22.5.5

daraḳht-kī bahot śāḳhẽ haĩ.	The tree has many branches.
mōṭar-kē cār pahiyē haĩ.	The automobile has four wheels.
palaṅg-kē cār pāyē haĩ.	The bed has four legs.

For the postpositional construction in these sentences see section 14.2.

REMARKS: **śāḳh** (ī) branch, **pahiyā** (ā) wheel, **pāyā** (ā) leg.

22.5.6 Exercise 1. **Translate into English:**

1. kyā kisān-kē pās ēk hal hai? 2. kyā aurat-kē baccē haĩ? 3. aurat-kī ēk bēṭī hai. 4. maĩ-nē kal tumhārē ēk bhāī-kō dēkhā. 5. jaṅgal-mẽ bahot daraḳht haĩ. 6. billī-kē dā̃t tēz haĩ. 7. mērē ēk bhāī-nē pardēs-mẽ safar kiyā. 8. bāg-mẽ bahot paudē haĩ. 9. mērē pās kāfī paisē nahĩ. 10. hāthī-kē dō lambē dā̃t haĩ.

22.5.7 Exercise 2. **Translate into Urdu:**

1. Does the man have a son? 2. Who has ink? 3. I travelled with one of your brothers. 4. The room has two doors. 5. The garden has many trees. 6. Does the carpenter have wood? 7. The girl has new shoes. 8. One of your servants tried to repair the cart. 9. This garden has no gardener. 10. She has long hair.

22.6. Text 6: **Musāfir-kā Vāpas Ānā.**

Translate into English. Answer the questions in Urdu:

[Ahmad Alī [1] pā̃c sāl huē [2] Pākistān-sē Amrīkā-mẽ tālīm hāsil karnē [3] -kē liyē āyā thā apnā kām ḳhatam karnē-kē bād aur kaī chōṭī baṛī ḍigriyā̃ lēkar [4] vo vāpas gayā. Nyū Yārk [5] -sē Karācī [6] -tak havāī•jahāz [7] -kā safar thā. Karācī-sē Lāhōr [8] jānē-kē liyē vo rēlgāṛī-mẽ baiṭhā. gāṛī subah nau bajē calkar [9] aglē din [10] subah āṭh bajē Lāhor pahõcī sṭēśan-par us-kē mā̃ • bāp, bahan • bhāī, dōst • yār,[11] sab usē lēnē-kē liyē āyē huē thē. jab vo gāṛī-sē utrā,[12] tō sab-lōg us-kī taraf dauṛē. unhō̃-nē us-kē galē[13] -mē̃ phulō̃-kē hār[14] ḍālē. dōstō̃-nē us-kē sāth hāth milāyē.[15] bhāiyō̃-nē galē lagāyā.[16] mā̃ • bāp-nē us-kā māthā[17] cūmā. sab-lōg us-kē vāpas ānē-par bahot k͟huś thē. thōṛī dēr-mē̃ Ahmad Alī aur bāḳī[18] sab-lōg sṭēśan-sē bāhar āyē aur mōṭargāṛiyō̃-mē̃ baiṭhkar[19] ghar pahō̃cē. Ahmad Alī-kō bhūk lagī thī.[20] sab-nē milkar[21] nāśtā[22] kiyā. kaī sālō̃-kē bād ye pahilā mauḳā[23] thā ke[24] Ahmad Alī-nē apnē ghar-mē̃ apnē mā̃ • bāp, bahan • bhāiyō̃-kē sāth baiṭhkar[19] khānā khāyā.]

Ammī: Ahmad Alī, bēṭā! maĩ aur tumhārē abbā tō tumhārē intazār-mē̃ bahōt bēcain[25] rahē.

Ahmad: Ammī • jān,[26] maĩ-bhī āp-kō dēkhnē-kē liyē bahot mētāb[27] thā.

Ammī: mērē bēṭē-kō pardēs-mē̃[28] kōī taklīf tō nahĩ huī?

Ahmad: nahĩ, Ammī • jān, K͟hudā-kī meharbānī-sē sab ṭhīk • ṭhāk rahā.

Chōṭī Bahan: Bhāī • jān,[29] āp mērē liyē Amrīkā-sē kyā kyā cīzē̃ lāyē haĩ?

Nanhā[30] (Ahmad-kā bhatījā[31]): Cacā • jān,[32] āp mērē liyē kyā lāyē haĩ? [sab baccē śōr macātē haĩ: bhāī • jān, cacā • jān, māmū̃ • jān,[33] āp hamārē liyē kyā lāyē haĩ?]

Ammī: dēkhō, baccō̃![34] śōr na karō. mērē bēṭē-kō mat[35] satāō![36]

Ahmad: dēkhō, bhāī, Amrīkā-mē̃ tō cīzē̃ bahot mahãgī[37] haĩ. is liyē maĩ-nē sōcā ke[38] Lāhōr-sē tumhārē liyē lakṛī-kē ghōṛē aur pisṭōl[39] vagairā[40] k͟harīdū̃gā.

[sab baccē ye sunkar[41] udās hō jātē haĩ.]

Ahmad: dēkhō, baccō̃! rōnā nahĩ.[42] maĩ tō yū̃-hī jhūṭ • mūṭ kahtā[43] thā. maĩ tumhārē liyē bahot khilaunē[44] layā hū̃. vo sab samandrī • jahāz[45] -mē̃ ā rahē haĩ.[46]

Nanhā: Cacā • jān! āp mērē liyē pisṭōl layē haĩ na?

Ahmad: hā̃, bēṭē.[47]

Nanhā: aur havāī • jahāz-bhī?

Ahmad: hā̃.

Nanhā: Cacā • jān! āp mērē liyē ēk bahot baṛī guṛiyā[48] lāyā haĩ na?

Abbā: ō baccō̃![49] ab zyādā śōr na karō.

[sab baccē cup[50] hō jātē haĩ. har • ēk dādā • jān[51] -sē ḍartā hai.]

Abbā: Ahmad, bēṭā! tum śāyad is lambē safar-kē bād thak gayē[52] hō. mērē k͟hayāl-mē̃ tō tumhē̃ thōṛī dēr ārām karnā[53] cāhiyē.

Ahmad: nahĩ, Abbā • jān, maĩ tō bilkul ṭhīk • ṭhāk hū̃. Ammī • jān! āp-kī sēhat kaisī hai?

Ammī: bēṭā, maĩ acchī hū̃. kabhī kabhī kamar[54] -mē̃ dard[55] hōnē lagtā[56] hai. tumhē̃ yād hai ēk dafā maĩ sīṛhiyō̃[57] -sē gir paṛī[58] thī. tab-sē jab-bhī sardī zyādā paṛtī hai mērī kamar-mē̃ dard hōnē lagtā[56] hai.

Ahmad: ḍākṭar kyā kahtē haĩ?

Ammī: bēṭā, sab-sē baṛā maraz[59] tō buṛhāpā[60] hai.

[Jamīlā,[61] Ahmad-kī māmū̃zād bahan,[62] milnē-kē liyē ātī hai. Ahmad aur Jamīlā bacpan[63] -kē dōst haĩ. Jamīlā ab śādī • śūdā[64] hai.]

Ahmad: vāh, vāh![65] ye tō Jamīlā haĩ.!

Jamīlā: Khudā-kā śukr hai. tum sahī • salāmat [66] hō.

Ahmad: bhāī,[67] tum tō ab śādī • śūdā hō nā? sunāō, tumhārā miyā̃ [68] kaisā hai? (cupkē-sē [69] Jamīlā-kē kān [70] -mē̃: tumhē̃ pasand hai na? Jamīlā muskrākar [71] "hā̃" kahtī hai.[72])

Jamīlā: miyā̃ acchā hai. (Ammī-kī taraf dēkhkar [73]) aur in-kō dēkhā, satāīs sāl-kē hō gayē. abhī-tak kāvārē [74] haī. in-kī śādī karō-jī.[75]

Ahmad: lō aur sunā.[76] ab ye hamārī śādī-bhī tay karnē lagī̃! [56]

Ammī: bhāī, ham tō is bāt-mē̃ dakhal [77] nahī̃ dētē. Ahmad, māśā • Allah,[78] javān hai, samajhdār [79] hai. jab cāhē, jis-kē sāth cāhē, śādī kar lē.[80] (Ahmad-kē abbā-kī taraf dēkhkar [73]) kyū̃-jī,[81] ṭhīk hai na?

Abbā: bēśak, bēśak! (abbā bahot-sī [82] bātō̃-kō siraf "bēśak" kahkar [63] hī tāl dētē [84] haī.)

Ammī: ajī,[85] tum "bēśak" -kē ilāvā [86] -bhī tō kabhī kuch kahā karō.[87]

Abbā: bēgam! tum tō khāh • makhāh khafā hōtī hō. mērā matlab hai ke [88] tumhārā khayāl darust [89] hai.

[darvāzē-kī ghaṇṭī bajtī hai. Ahmad-kē dōst us-sē milnē [90] āyē haī. Ahmad ḍrāingrūm [91] -mē dōstō-sē milnē [90] jātā hai.]

savālāt:

1. Ahmad Alī Amrīkā-mē̃ kis liyē āyā thā aur us-nē yahā̃ kyā kiyā? 2. Lāhōr-kē sṭēśan-par kaun lōg us-sē milnē āyē thē? 3. chōṭē baccē Ahmad Alī-kō kyā kahtē thē? 4. Jamīlā kaun thī? 5. Ahmad Alī-kī śādī-kē bārē-mē̃ us-kī ammī-kā kyā khayāl thā?

NOTES: 1. man's name; 2. five years ago, see 33.3.2; 3. **hāsil karnā** to get, obtain (**tr.**); 4. having taken, see 30.1; 5. New York; 6. city of Karachi; 7. air-plane (ā); 8. city of Lahore; 9. starting, see 30.1; 10. next day (**adv.**); 11. friends and cronies; 12. **utarnā** to get off (**int.**); 13. **galā** neck (ā); 14. garland (ā); 15. **hāth milānā** to shake hands (**tr.**); 16. **galē lagānā** to embrace (**tr.**); 17. forehead (ā); 18. remaining (**adj., n.c.**); 19. sitting, taking seats, see 30.1; 20. Ahmad Alī was hungry, cf. 34.1.1; 21. = together; 22. **nāśtā karnā** to take breakfast (**tr.**); 23. occasion (ā); 24. that, see 29.2; 25. restless, = eager (**adj., n.c.**); 26. mother dear; 27. restless, = eager; 28. abroad, in foreign countries; 29. brother dear; 30. baby boy (ā); [**nanhī** baby girl (ī)]; 31. nephew, brother's son (ā); 32. (paternal) uncle dear (ā); 33. (maternal) uncle dear (ā); 34. children, kiddies (**voc. pl.**); 35. not, negative particle used with imperative; 36. **satānā** to bother (**tr.**); 37. **mahã̄gā** expensive (**adj.**); 38. see fn. 24; 39. pistol (ā); 40. et cetera; 41. having heard, see 30.1; 42. Don't cry!, the infinitive can be employed as a weak or polite imperative; 43. **jhūṭ • mūṭ kahnā** to spoof, kid (**tr.**); 44. toy (ā); 45. ocean vessel, ship (ā); 46. **ā rahē haī** are coming, see 23.1; 47. sonny (**voc. s. msc.**); 48. doll (ī); 49. kiddies (**voc. pl. msc.**); 50. **cup hōnā** to be still (**int.**); 51. grandfather (ā); 52. **thak jānā** to become tired (**int.**); 53. **ārām karnā** to rest (**tr.**); 54. back (ī); 55. pain (ā); 56. see 34.1.2; 57. **sīṛhī** stairs (ī); 58. **gir paṛnā** to fall (**int.**), see lesson 28; 59. disease (ā); 60. old age (ā); 61. girl's name; 62. **māmū̃zād bahan** maternal cousin (ī); 63. childhood (ā); 64. married (**adj., n.c.**); 65. oh, ho!; 66. hale and hearty (**adj., n.c.**); 67. well! 68. husband (ā); 69. quietly (**adv.**); 70. ear (ā); 71. smiling, see 30.1; 72. see 29.1; 73. looking, see 30.1; 74. **kū̃vārā** bachelor (ā); 75. **honorific particle of address;** 76. Just listen to her!; 77. **dakhal dēnā** to interfere (**tr.**); 78. with God's grace; 79. wise (**adj., n.c.**); 80. **śādī kar lēnā** to marry (**tr.**); see lesson 28; 81. eh?; 82. many, for **-sā**, see 38.1; 83. saying, see 30.1; 84. **tāl dēnā** to dispose of, dismiss (**tr.**); 85. expression employed between husband and wife to attract attention; 86. **-kē ilāvā** besides (**postpos. phrase**); 87. **kahā karnā** to say, speak (**tr.**); 88. see fm. 24; 89. correct (**adj., n.c.**); 90. = **milnē-kē liyē;** 91. living-room.

LESSON 23

23.1

laṛkā Panjābī bōl rahā hai.	The boy is speaking Panjabi.
laṛkē Panjābī bōl rahē haĩ.	The boys are speaking Panjabi.
laṛkī pānī pī rahī hai.	The girl is drinking water.
laṛkiyā̃ pānī pī rahī haĩ.	The girls are drinking water.
laṛkā Baṅgālī bōl rahā thā.	The boy was speaking Bengali.
laṛkē Baṅgālī bōl rahē thē.	The boys were speaking Bengali.
laṛkī śarbat pī rahī thī.	The girl was drinking a sweet drink.
laṛkiyā śarbat pī rahī thī̃.	The girls were drinking a sweet drink.
vālid • sāhab sigreṭ pī rahē haĩ.	Father is smoking a cigarette.
vālid • sāhab sigreṭ pī rahē thē.	Father was smoking a cigarette.
aurat ḳamīz sī rahī hai.	The woman is sewing the shirt.
aurat ḳamīz sī rahī thī̃.	The woman was sewing the shirt.
kīṛā pēṛ-par caṛh rahā hai.	The insect is climbing up the plant.
kīṛā pēṛ-par caṛh rahā thā.	The insect was climbing up the plant.
billī farś-par sō rahī hai.	The cat is sleeping on the floor.
billī farś-par sō rahī thī.	The cat was sleeping on the floor.
lōg Paśtū-mē̃ bōl rahē haĩ.	The people are speaking in Pashtu.
lōg Paśtū-mē̃ bōl rahē thē.	The people were speaking in Pashtu.

This section introduces the constructions equivalent to the Present Progressive (or President Continuative) and the Past Progressive (or Past Continuative) of English. Compare the construction discussed in section 2.1.

The present tense is expressed in Urdu by a phrase consisting of the **stem of the**

verb, translating the English verb, **plus rahā** (the past participle of **rahnā**) which agrees with the subject of the sentence in gender and number, and the present of **hōnā** which agrees with the subject in number.

The past tense is expressed in Urdu by an identical construction, except that the present of **hōnā** is replaced by **thā,** which agrees with the subject in gender and number.

REMARKS: (1) This tense describes an act going on at a specific time—at the same time that another act is taking place. For example, see the first sentence, **The boy is speaking Panjabi.** (i.e., at the same time as I walk into the room); or the eleventh sentence, **The woman is sewing the shirt.** (i.e., while I am waiting for it).

For the past of this construction see sentence ten, **Father was smoking a cigarette.** (i.e., while he was reading the newspaper) or sentence fourteen, **The insect was climbing up the plant.** (i.e., at the moment when I came into the garden).

(2) The verb **rahnā to stay, to live** does not occur as the stem member of this construction. See, for example, **lōg śahar-mē̃ rahtē thē. The people were living in the city.**

(3) **farś** (ā) floor, **śarbat** (ā) a cold, sweet beverage, **kīṛā** (ā) insect, **pēṛ** (ā) plant, **Panjābī** (ā) Panjabi language, **Baṅgāli** (6) Bengali language, **Paśtū** (ī) Pashtu language.

23.1.1 More examples are:

aurtē̃ pakā rahī haī̃.	The women are cooking.
is vaḳt bāriś hō rahī hai.	It is raining now.
kisān is vaḳt mehnat kar rahā hai.	The farmer is working hard now.
āp mērā intazār kab-sē kar rahē haī̃?	How long have you been waiting for me?
tālibilm kitāb paṛh rahā hai.	The student is reading a book.
ustād tālibilmō̃-kē javāb sun rahē haī̃.	The teacher is listening to the answers of the students.
bail hal khī̃c rahē haī̃.	The oxen are pulling the plow.
ādmī kaṅghē-kā istēmāl kar rahā hai.	The man is using the comb.
mehtar ghar-kē sāmnē baiṭh rahā hai.	The sweeper is seated in front of the house.
musāfir hōṭal-mē̃ tīn rātō̃-kē liyē ṭhahar rahā hai.	The traveller is staying in the hotel for three nights.
baccē gẽd-sē khēl rahē haī̃.	The children are playing with the ball.
bābū ēk purānē ustarē-sē hajāmat banā rahā hai.	The clerk is shaving with an old razor.
murgiyā̃ ṭīlē-par sō rahī haī̃.	The chickens are sleeping on the mound.
bairā jahāziyō̃-sē bātē̃ kar rahā hai.	The bearer is talking with the sailors.
laṛkē daraḳht-kē nīcē khēl rahē thē.	The boys were playing under the tree.
laṛkiyā̃ māō̃-kī madad kar rahī thī̃.	The girls were helping (**their**) mothers.
kisān khētō̃-mē̃ kām kar rahē thē.	The farmers were working in the fields.
aurtē̃ kuē̃-kē pās bātē̃ kar rahī thī̃.	The women were talking near the well.
us vaḳt bāriś hō rahī thī.	It was raining at that time.
āp mērā intazār kab-sē kar rahē thē?	How long were you waiting for me?
tālibilm kitāb paṛh rahā thā.	The student was reading a book.
ustād tālibilmō̃-kē javāb sun rahē thē.	The teacher was listening to the answers of the students.

REMARKS: (1) See section 22.1.5, Remarks (1), and in the sixteenth sentence, above, **to help,** translated by the phrase **-kī madad karnā;** in the fourth sentence **to wait** and the Urdu phrase **-kā intazār karnā;** in the eighth sentence **to use** and the Urdu phrase **-kā istēmāl karnā.**

(2) **istēmāl** (ā) use, **[-kā] istēmāl karnā** to use, **kañghā** (ā) comb, **ṭilā** (ā) heap, mound, **bairā** (ā) bearer, **bāriś** (ī) rain, **bāriś hōnā** to rain, **mehtar** (ā) sweeper, **mehnat** (ā) hard work, toil, **mehnat karnā** to toil, **hajāmat** (ī) shaving, **hajāmat banānā** to shave, **bābū** (ā) clerk.

23.1.2 Exercise 1. **Translate into English:**

1. āp-kē sāth Añgrēzī-mē̃ kaun bātē̃ kar rahē thē? 2. maī bairē-kē śahar-sē vāpas ānē-kā intazār kar rahā hū̃. 3. ādmī purānē ustarē-sē kyū̃ hajāmat banā rahā hai? 4. laṛkī ṭīlē-par ṭhahar rahī thī. 5. naukar mālik-kī madad kar rahā hai. 6. aurtē̃ dōstō̃-kē sāth bātē̃ kar rahī thī̃. 7. jahāzī kab-sē pardēs-mē̃ safar kar rahā hai? 8. vo mērī sigreṭ kyū̃ pī rahī hai? 9. kisān us vaḳt khēt-mē̃ mehnat kar rahā thā. 10. vo farś-par baiṭh rahī thī̃. 11. tum kis-kē liyē pānī lā rahē hō? 12. bāriś hō rahī hai. 13. hājī muḳaddas • jaghō̃-kō safar kar rahā hai. 14. kaun mērī kañghē-kā istēmāl kar rahā thā? 15. mālī paudō̃-sē zard phūl tōṛ rahā hai. 16. baṛhaī kursī-kī marammat kar rahā hai. 17. vo is vaḳt kis-kē sāth bātē̃ kar rahī hai? 18. mōcī mērē jūtē lā rahā hai. 19. meharbān ādmī mērī madad-kī kōśiś kar rahē haī. 20. aurat gandā pyālā sāf karnē-kī kōśiś kar rahī thī.

23.1.3 Exercise 2. **Translate into Urdu:**

1. I (**msc.**) am trying to learn Hindi. 2. Who (**fm. sing.**) was trying to come in? 3. We (**msc.**) are going back to the village. 4. What were they (**fm.**) trying to say to you? 5. The little boy is using the sharp razor. 6. The ship is coming into the harbor now. 7. Why is he travelling by airplane? 8. The gardener is working hard in the garden. 9. The sweeper is pouring water on the floor. 10. What are the bearers eating under the tree? 11. How long have you been working in this factory? 12. The mechanic is repairing my car. 13. The sweeper was going to the village to see (**his**) family. 14. The girl was buying green cloth in the shop. 15. For whom are you (**fm.**) waiting? 16. We (**msc.**) are going to see the temple. 17. With whom were you (**msc.**) staying in the village? 18. How long have you (**msc. hon.**) been sitting here? 19. She is preparing tea for us. 20. How long had he been trying to see me?

23.2

ādmī śahar nahī̃ jāēgā.	The man will not go to the city.
baccē skūl nahī̃ jāē̃gē.	The children will not go to school.
kuttā vāpas nahī̃ āēgā.	The dog will not come back.
laṛkī nahī̃ pakāēgī.	The girl will not cook.
aurtē̃ baccō̃-kō nahī̃ dēkhē̃gī.	The women will not see the children.
ādmī kām karnā nahī̃ cāhē̃gē.	The men will not want to work.
laṛkē savāl pūchnā nahī̃ cāhē̃gē.	The boys will not want to ask questions.
ādmī āj • rāt kām nahī̃ kar sakē̃gē.	The men will not be able to work tonight.
laṛkī kal nahī̃ gā sakēgī.	The girl will not be able to sing tomorrow.

This section illustrates the negative of the future construction. (See 15.1) The particle **nahī̃** is placed **before** the verb or verbal phrase consisting of verbal stem plus verb.

REMARKS: **skūl** is a variant of **iskūl** (ā) school.

23.2.1

agar tālibilm na paṛhē, tō vo savālō̃-kē javāb nahī̃ jānēgā.	If a student should not study, he will not know the answers to the questions.
agar āp dēr-sē na āē̃, tō ham vaḳt-par khānā khā sakē̃gē.	If you do not come late, we will be able to have dinner on time.
agar āp āhistā na bōlē̃, tō maĩ nahī̃ samajh sakū̃gā.	If you do not speak slowly, I will not be able to understand.

This section illustrates the negative of conditional constructions, the verbs of which are in the subjunctive or future tenses. (See 18.1.2, 18.1.3 and 18.1.4) The particle **na** is used with the subjunctive and **nahī̃** with the future. (See 23.2, above)

23.2.2

mujhē nahī̃ jānā cāhiyē.	I need not go.
tālibilm-kō nahī̃ paṛhnā cāhiyē.	The student need not study.
aurat-kō nahī̃ pakānā cāhiyē.	The woman need not cook.

This section illustrates the negative of the construction with **cāhiyē.** (See 17.1 and 19.2 for the past tense.) The particle **nahī̃** is placed before the infinitive.

23.2.3

mujhē nahī̃ jānā hai.	I do not have to go.
tālibilm-kō nahī̃ paṛhnā hai.	The student does not have to study.
aurat-kō nahī̃ pakānā hai.	The woman does not have to cook.

This section illustrates the negative of the construction illustrated in section 17.1.1. The particle **nahī̃** is placed before the infinitive.

23.2.4

agar vo āj śahar-mē̃ na hōtā, tō maĩ us-kē sāth na hōtā.	If he were not in town today, I would not be with him.
agar tālibilm kuch na jāntā, tō vo ghar-mē̃ rahtā.	If the student didn't know anything, he would stay at home.
agar maĩ skūl-mē̃ na hōtā, tō maĩ sōtā.	If I were not in school, I would sleep.

This section illustrates the negative of the Contrary to Fact construction described in section 19.4. The particle **na** is placed before the present participle.

23.2.5

imāndār bairā paisē vāpas nahī̃ dētā thā.	The honest bearer was not giving back the money.
aurat rēśam nahī̃ ḳharīdtī thī.	The woman was not buying the silk.
ādmī śarāb nahī̃ pītā thā.	The man was not drinking the wine.

This section illustrates the negative of the past construction described in section 19.1. **nahī̃** is placed before the verb.

REMARKS: **rēśam** (ā) silk, **śarāb** (ī) wine.

23.3

mehtar nahī̃ pahõcā.	The sweeper did not arrive.
laṛkā ḍākḳhānē-mẽ nahī̃ gayā.	The boy did not go into the post office.
kyā ādmī Iñglistān-sē nahī̃ āyā?	Didn't the man come from England?

Sections 23.3 to 23.3.2 illustrate the negative of the past tense construction described in sections 20.1 to 20.1.4. The particle **nahī̃** is placed before the past participle.

REMARKS: **ḍākḳhānā** (ā) post office, **Iñglistān** (ā) England.

23.3.1

tār nahī̃ pahõcā hai.	The telegram has not arrived.
baccē ghar-mẽ nahī̃ rahē haĩ.	The children have not remained at home.
laṛkā tārghar-kē bāhar nahī̃ āyā hai.	The boy has not come out of the telegraph office.

REMARKS: **tār** (ā) telegram, **tārghar** (ā) telegraph office.

23.3.2

ḍākgāṛī nahī̃ pahõcī thī.	The mail train had not arrived.
baccē ghar-mē nahī̃ rahē thē.	The children had not remained at home.
jahāzī kiśtī-mẽ nahī̃ kūdā thā.	The sailor had not jumped into the boat.

REMARKS: **ḍākgāṛī** (ī) mail train, **kiśtī** (ī) boat.

23.4

ādmī-nē ḳhat nahī̃ likhā.	The man did not write the letter.
mā̃-nē baccõ-kō ēk kahānī nahī̃ sunāyī.	The mother did not tell the children a story.
naukar-nē mālik-kā hukam nahī̃ samjhā.	The servant did not understand the master's order.

Sections 23.4 to 23.4.2 illustrate the negative of the past tense construction described in sections 21.1 to 21.1.4. The particle **nahī̃** is placed before the past participle.

REMARKS: **mālik** (ā) master, owner.

23.4.1

naukar-nē bistar taiyār nahī̃ kiyā hai.	The servant has not prepared the bed.
bairē-nē gusalḳhānē-mẽ pānī nahī̃ liyā hai.	The bearer has not taken water into the bathroom.
kyā āp-nē ghōṛē-par savārī kabhī nahī̃ kī hai?	Haven't you ever ridden a horse?

REMARKS: bistar (ā) bed, bedding, gusalk̲h̲ānā (ā) bathroom, savārī (ī) riding, savārī karnā to ride.

23.4.2

kisān-nē zamīndār-kō kirāyā nahī̃ diyā thā.	The farmer had not paid the landlord the rent.
ham-nē kiśtī kirāyē-par nahī̃ lī thī.	We had not hired the boat.
kyā āp-nē k̲h̲at d̤āk-mē̃ nahī̃ d̤ālā thā?	Hadn't you posted the letter?

REMARKS: zamīndār (ā) landlord, kirāyā (ā) rent, kirāyē-par dēnā to rent out, kirāyē-par lēnā to hire.

23.5 Exercise 1. Translate into English:

1. mehtar āj • rāt kām nahī̃ kar sakēgā. 2. naukar-kō tālāb-sē pānī nahī̃ lānā hai. 3. ustād āsān kahānī kyū̃ nahī̃ par̤htē thē? 4. agar bail bhūkā na hō, tō vo ghās khānē-kē liyē na rukē. 5. mālī sak̲h̲t zamīn-mē̃ nahī̃ khōdtā thā. 6. kisānõ-kō āj khēt-mē̃ kām karnā nahī̃ hai. 7. musāfir śahar-sē nahī̃ āyā hai. 8. agar bāzār pās na hō, tō maī̃ us-kō dēkhnē-kē liyē na jāū̃. 9. śikārī jaṅgal-mē̃ bahot jānvar nahī̃ mārēgē. 10. agar bābū āhistā na bōltā, tō maī̃ na samajh saktā. 11. d̤āk-gāṛī st̤ēśan-mē̃ nahī̃ rukī. 12. mehtar-kō Aṅgrēzī-mē̃ nahī̃ bōlnā cāhiyē. 13. bairē-nē mālik-kā hukam nahī̃ samjhā. 14. tālibilm-kō āj • rāt nahī̃ par̤hnā hai. 15. agar hōt̤al-kā kamrā acchā na hōtā, tō musāfir k̲h̲uś na hōtā. 16. kyā dhōbī ādmī-kē purānē kapṛē dhōnā nahī̃ cāhēgā? 17. pīr tālāb-kē pās nahī̃ baiṭhē thē. 18. agar ādmī Panjābī-mē̃ na bōl saktā, tō vo āp-kē sāth na bōltā. 19. laṛkõ-kō gahrī nadī-mē̃ nahī̃ tairnā cāhiyē. 20. klārk k̲h̲uś nahī̃ thā. 21. sipāhī-nē dukān-mē̃ cōr-kō nahī̃ pakṛā hai. 22. agar mehtar kām nahī̃ karēgā, tō maī̃ us-kō paisē nahī̃ dū̃gā. 23. kisān-kē pās hal nahī̃ thā. 24. unhõ-nē bandargāh-mē̃ kiśtiyā̃ nahī̃ dēkhī̃. 25. mālī-kō āj paudõ-par pānī nahī̃ d̤ālnā cāhiyē.

23.5.1 Exercise 2. Translate into Urdu:

1. I (fm.) will not be able to speak with anyone today. 2. If the road had not been long, the traveller would not have become tired. 3. If you (msc.) should not become tired, you will not have to stop to rest. 4. If the water were not cold, we would not drink it. 5. You need not go to the post office. 6. Why weren't the men in the telegraph office? 7. Won't the washerman bring the clothes today? 8. The sweeper is not seated in front of the house. 9. Who does not have to eat? 10. Didn't the mail train arrive on time? 11. If you (msc.) cannot, do not stop to see me on your return. 12. The bearer had not drawn water for my bath. 13. Why doesn't the clerk have to wait outside the office? 14. Who hadn't hired this automobile? 15. Won't you (msc.) repair the door? 16. Why didn't you (fm.) post the letter? 17. Didn't you need the clean clothes today? 18. If we (fm.) had not become tired, we would not have rested. 19. We didn't ride out to the fields on horses. 20. If your house should not be near-by, I (msc.) will not go there with you. 21. The servant was not preparing the bed for the traveller. 22. When didn't he become tired? 23. Didn't you need hot water for shaving? 24. Why didn't the traveller have money? 25. I didn't have to pay the rent today to the landlord.

23.6. Text 7: Guzrē Huē [1] Zamānē [2] -kī Yād.

Translate into English. Answer the questions in Urdu.

[Ikrām Ullāh [3] kamiśnar [4] -kē daftar-mē̃ hed̤ • klark [5] hai. vo adhēṛ • umr-kā [6] k̲h̲uś śakal [7] ādmī hai. us-kē cahrē [8] -par ilm [9] aur tajrubē [10] -kē niśān [11] haī̃. kamiśnar • sāhab abhī-tak daftar nahī̃ āyē. is liyē Ikrām Ullāh-kō kōī k̤hās [12] kām nahī̃. vo apnē kamrē-mē̃ apnī kursī [13] -par baiṭhā [14] sigrēṭ pī rahā hai. usē guzrē huē zamānē-kī yād ā rahī hai. vo soctā hai ke [15] ēk zamānē-mē̃ vo chōṭā-sā [16] laṛkā thā. us-kē abbā pansārī-kī dukān [17] kartē thē.[18] dukān k̤hūb caltī thī.[19] munāfā [20] acchā • k̤hāsā [21] hōtā thā. Ikrām Ullāh-kē mā̃ • bāp k̤huś • hāl [22] thē. un-kō apnē bēṭē-kī tālīm-kā bahot k̤hayāl rahtā thā. jab vo pā̃c sāl-kā huā us-kē abbā-nē skūl-mē̃ dāk̤hil karvā diyā.[23] skūl-mē̃ us-kī umr-kē aur-bhī haĩ [24] laṛkē • laṛkiyā̃ thī. Ikrām Ullāh bacpan-sē-hī bahot hōśiyār [25] thā. skūl-kā kām mehnat-sē kartā thā. māsṭar • sāhab us-par meharbān thē. vo ēk ēk [26] sāl-mē̃ dō dō jamāatē̃ pās kartā huā [27] jald-hī chaṭī jamāat-mē̃ pahō̃c gayā.[28] chaṭī jamāat-kō Māsṭar Narindar Nāth [3] jugrāfiyā [29] paṛhātē thē. ye māsṭar • sāhab bahot zālim [30] thē. jō laṛkā sabak̤ [31] yād nahī̃ kartā thā, usē mār paṛtī [32] thī. māsṭar-kē pās ēk kālē [33] rañg [34] -kī chaṛī thī. vo us-sē tālibilmō̃-kō mārtē thē. ēk din Ikrām Ullāh-nē jugrāfiyē-kā sabak̤ yād na kiyā aur us-kō baṛī sak̤ht mār paṛī. us-kē hāth zak̤hmī [35] hō gayē, aur us-kī paslī [36] -mē̃ dard hōnē lagā.[37] klās-mē̃ jitnē laṛkē thē, sab-kē sab pahlē tō ḍar gayē.[38] lēkin, jab kuch vak̤t guzrā, un-kō ġussā ānē lagā.[37] thōṛī dēr-kē bād ghanṭī bajī aur māsṭar • sāhab bāhar calē gayē.[39] skūl-mē̃ chuṭṭī hō gayī.[40] sab laṛkē Ikrām-kī taraf dauṛē.]

Mansūr: yār, ye māsṭar tō baṛā-hī zālim hai. dēkhō, mār mārkar [41] Ikrām-kē hāth zak̤hmī kar diyē.[42]

Indar: [3] yārō,[43] maĩ kahtā hū̃ is māsṭar-kī aisī-kī taisī.[44] hamē̃ is-kā kōī bandōbast [45] karnā cāhiyē.

Majīd: [3] [Majīd bahot lambā ū̃cā aur mazbūt laṛkā hai aur pahalvānī[46] kartā hai.] bandōbast kyā? bas ēk phaĩṭā lagāō [47] māsṭar • sāhab-kō. jab taubā karē,[48] tab chōṛō.

Karīm: [3] hā̃, hā̃! bātē̃ banānē-mē̃ tō sab śēr [49] haĩ. āgē baṛhkar [50] māsṭar • sāhab-kō pakṛēgā kaun?

Majīd: jī, Karīm • sāhab, bātē̃ banānā tō āp-kō ātā hai, ham tō kām kartē haĩ. āp-kī zabān [51] caltī hai, hamārā hāth caltā hai. agar tum sab-lōg mērē sāth rahō, tō maĩ māsṭar Narindar Nāth-kō vo phaĩṭā lagāū̃ ke [52] un-kō āṭē [53] • dāl [54] -kā bhāō mālūm hō jāē.[55] bōlō! rahōgē mērē sāth?

Zuhrā: [56] nahī̃, bhāī. hamē̃ ḍar lagtā hai. agar tum māsṭar-kō mārōgē, tō hēḍ • māsṭar-kē pās ripōrṭ jāēgī. phir ham-sab skūl-sē nikālē jāē̃gē.[57]

Majīd: yār in laṛkiyō̃-nē hamē̃ baṛī musībat [58] ḍālī hai. patā nahī̃ ye laṛkō̃-kē skūl-mē̃ kyū̃ ā gayī. apnē laṛkiyō̃-kē skūl-mē̃ rahtī. buzdil! [59]

Āsiyā: [56] dēkhō, Majīd • sāhab. ham buzdil nahī̃ haĩ. hamē̃-bhī Ikrām-sē utnī-hī ham • dardī [60] hai jitnī ke tumhē hai. ham tō siraf ye kahtē haĩ ke k̤ānūnī bāt karō. ġussē-mē̃ aisā kam na karō jis-mē̃ sab-ka nuksān [61] hō aur bād-mē̃ paśemān [62] hōnā paṛē.

Majīd: acchā, baṛī bī.[63] bahot acchā. lēkin tumhārā matlab ye hai ke [64] ham kuch na karē̃. āj Ikrām-kō mār paṛī hai, kal isī tarāh kisī aur-kō paṛēgī. tum tō laṛkī hō na? [65] is liyē tumhē̃ kōī kuch kah nahī̃ saktā. śamat [66] tō ham-laṛkō̃-kī hai.

Āsiyā: maĩ ēk tarkīb [67] batātī hū̃. hēḍ • māsṭar • sāhab-kē pās ripōrṭ karō. vo Māsṭar Narindar Nāth-kō ṭhīk kar dē̃gē.[68]

Indar: [56] hā̃, hā̃, ṭhīk hai. arē, Jamīl, tum klās-kē mauniṭar [69] hō. tum hēḍ • māsṭar-kē pas cār • pā̃c [70] laṛkō̃-kā vafad [71] lēkar [72] jāō. un-kō kahō ke Māsṭar Narindar Nāth-kī jagah hamē̃ kōī aur [73] māsṭar dē̃, varna [74] ham-sab dūsrē skūl-mē̃ calē jāē̃gē. agar hēḍ • māsṭar • sāhab kōī kārrvāī [75] na karē̃, tō Ikrām-kē abbā skūl-par mukadmā [76] kar saktē haĩ.

[sab laṛkē tajvīz [77] -kō pasand kartē haĩ. unhō̃-nē cār laṛkē aur dō laṛkiyā̃ hēḍ • māsṭar-kē pās jānē-kē liyē cunē.[78] ye che lōg Ikrām-kō sāth lēkar heḍ • māsṭar-kē ghar gayē. ittafāk-sē [79] vahā̃ Māsṭar Narindar Nāth-bhī maujūd [80] thē. laṛkō̃ aur laṛkiyō̃-nē hēḍ • māsṭar-kō sārā kissā [81] sunāyā. jū̃ jū̃ [82] ye lōg apnī kahānī sunātē thē, Māsṭar Narindar Nāth-kā rang uṛtā jātā thā.[83] hēḍ • māsṭar kabhī laṛkō-kō dēkhtē thē aur kabhī Māsṭar Narindar Nāth-kī taraf. jab unhō̃-nē Ikrām-kē hāthō̃-par zakhm [84] dēkhē tō unhē̃ bahot gussā āyā. unhō̃-nē vādā kiyā ke [85] Māsṭar Narindar Nāth-kō kisī aur [86] jagah tabdīl karā dē̃gē.[87]]

[Ikrām Ullāh ye vākēā [88] yād karkē [89] muskrā rahā hai. us-kā sigrēṭ aiś • ṭrē [90] -mē̃ paṛā paṛā [91] jal gayā [92] hai. caprāsī [93] andar ākar [94] kahtā hai ke [95] kamiśnar • sāhab ā gayē haĩ aur Ikrām-kō bulātē haĩ.]

savālāt:

1. Ikrām Ullāh kahā̃ kām kartā thā? 2. Ikrām-kē abbā kyā kām kartē thē? 3. Māsṭar Narindar Nāth-kē bārē-mē̃ tum kyā jāntē hō? 4. jab Ikrām Ullāh-kō mār paṛī, tō Majīd-nē kyā maśvarāh diyā? 5. hēḍ • māsṭar • sāhab-nē kyā kārrvāī [96] kī?

NOTES: 1. past, see 33.1; 2. **zamānā** time (ā); 3. man's name; 4. commissioner (ā); 5. head-clerk (ā); 6. **aḍhēr • umr-kā** middle-aged (= **adj.**); 7. good-looking (**adj., n.c.**); 8. **cahrā** face (ā); 9. knowledge (ā); 10. experience (ā), variant: **tajarbē;** 11. look, mien (ā); 12. special (**adj., n.c.**); 13. chair (ī); 14. seated, see 33.1 for the past participle functioning as an adjective; 15. that (**conj.**), 16. rather small, see 38.1 for **-sā;** 17. grocery shop; 18. **dukān karnā** to run shop (tr.); 19. The shop had good business; 20. profit (ā); 21. considerable (**adj.**); 22. prosperous (**adj., n.c.**); 23. **ḍākhil karvā dēnā** to enroll, see lesson 28 and 36.1, ff.; 24. several other; 25. clever (**adj., n.c.**); 26. only one; 27. **pās karnā** to pass (**tr.**), for the participle functioning as an adverb see 34.2; 28. **pahōc jānā** to arrive (**int.**), see lesson 28; 29. geography (ā); 30. cruel (**adj., n.c.**); 31. lesson (ī); 32. **mār paṛnā** to beat, thrash (**int.**), see lesson 28; 33. **kālā** black (**adj.**); 34. color (ā); 35. hurt, wounded (**adj., n.c.**); 36. rib (ī); 37. see 34.1.2; 38. **ḍar jānā** to become afraid (**int.**), see lesson 28; 39. **calā jānā** to go away (**int.**); 40. School was closed; 41. beating, see 33.6; 42. **zakhmī kar dēnā** to hurt (**tr.**), see lesson 28; 43. friends (**voc. pl., msc.**); 44. is **māsṭar-kī aisī-kī taisī** damn this master!; 45. arrangement (ā); 46. wrestling (ī); 47. **phaĩṭā lagānā** to thrash, beat up (**tr.**); 48. **taubā karnā** to ask forgiveness (**tr.**); 49. lion (ā); 50. stepping forward, see 30.1; 51. tongue (ī); 52. so (that); 53. **āṭā** flour (ā); 54. pulse (ī); 55. **un-kō āṭē • dāl-kā bhāō malūm hō jāē** He'll come to his senses, He'll know what's what; 56. girl's name; 57. **nikālā jānā** to be expelled (**int.**), see 37.1; 58. difficulty (ī); 59. coward (**adj., n.c.**); 60. sympathy (ī); 61. harm, loss (ā); 62. repentent (**adj., n.c.**); 63. lady (ī); 64. see fn. 15; 65. = after all; 66. misery (ī); 67. plan, scheme (ī); 68. **ṭhīk karnā** to fix up (**tr.**); 69. monitor (ā); 70. four or five; 71. delegation (ā); 72. taking, see 30.1; 73. some other; 74. otherwise; 75. action (ī); 76. lawsuit (ā); 77. suggestion (ī); 78. **cunnā** to select, elect (**tr.**); 79. by chance (**adv.**); 80. present (**adj., n.c.**); 81. story (ā); 82. as; 83. Master Narindar Nath paled, see 34.4; 84. wound (ā); 85. see fn. 15; 86. some other; 87. **tabdīl karā dēnā** to transfer (**tr.**), see lesson 28; 88. incident (ā); 89. remembering, see 30.1; 90. ash tray (ī); 91. lying, for the participle functioning as an adverb cf. 34.2 and cf. 33.6 for the repetition; 92. **jal jānā** to burn out (**int.**), see lesson 28; 93. office boy (ā); 94. coming, see 30.1; 95. see fn. 15; 96. **kārrvāī karnā** to take action (**tr.**).

LESSON 24

24.1 [17.1.3] **Translate into Urdu:**

1. The servant should give the traveller water. 2. The hunter must kill the dreadful animal. 3. We have to go to the bazaar. 4. The washerman needs to wash the clothes. 5. The father has to bring mangoes from the bazaar for the girl. 6. The servant has to prepare the bed for us. 7. The boy should bring wood for the woman. 8. The students have to read the book. 9. The washerman has to clean the clothes. 10. We need to speak in Urdu. 11. The carpenter has to cut wood. 12. The thirsty bullock has to drink water. 13. The children should bathe. 14. The man has to work for the family. 15. The farmer has to work in the field today. 16. The servant should bring cold water. 17. Do you have to go? 18. The hungry fisherman has to catch fish today. 19. The man has to give back the money. 20. The gardener needs to water the plants.

24.2 [17.1.4] **Translate into English:**

1. mujhē ye sēb khānā cāhiyē. 2. kyā āp-kō āj kām karnā hai? 3. kyā tumhē jā̃nā hai? 4. pyāsē baccē-kō dūdh pīnā cāhiyē. 5. dhōbī-kō āj • rat kapṛē vāpas lānā hai. 6. aurat-kō pānī vāpas lānē-kē liyē kuẽ-kō jānā paṛtā hai. 7. hamẽ ghar-mẽ rahnā cāhiyē. 8. kyā mā̃-kō bāvarcīḳhānē-mẽ pakānā paṛtā hai? 9. āp-kō ham-sē milnē-kē liyē ānā hai. 10. garīb ādmī-kō kām karnā cāhiyē. 11. āp-kō daftar-kō kyũ jānā hai? 12. ādmiyõ-kō kārḳhānē-mẽ kām karnā hai. 13. būṛhē kisān-kō cauṛē daraḳht-kē nīcē ārām karnā cāhiyē. 14. aurat-kō ḳhāvind-kē liyē khānā lānā paṛtā hai. 15. tumhẽ āj ārām karnā cāhiyē. 16. āp-kō mujh-sē Urdū-mẽ bōlnā cāhiyē. 17. pyāsē musāfir-kō pīnē-kē liyē ṭhaṇḍā pānē cāhiyē. 18. āp-kō bāzār-sē kāb vāpas ānā hai? 19. tumhẽ kyũ jānā cāhiyē? 20. musāfir-kō nahānē-kē liyē garm pānī cāhiyē.

24.3 [17.2.1] **Translate into Urdu:**

1. The woman needs wood for the fire. 2. We need the help of a laborer today. 3. The farmer needs a big plow to till the field. 4. Do you need my help? 5. I need a man to drive the automobile. 6. The traveller needs a man to point out the road. 7. Do you need anything? 8. Why do you need my help? 9. Why does the servant need to see me today? 10. The woman needs money to buy food in the bazaar.

24.4 [17.2.2] **Translate into English:**

1. ādmī-kō kab dōst cāhiyẽ? 2. hamẽ tāzā pānī cāhiyē. 3. mujhē āj ye bailgāṛī cāhiyē. 4. āp-kō ab kyũ aḳhbār cāhiyē? 5. kyā āp-kō safar karnē-kē liyē kuch cāhiyē? 6. aurat-kō āj • subah āg-kē liyē lakṛī cāhiyē. 7. kyā āp-kō abhī sāf kapṛē cāhiyẽ? 8. āp-kō kal kyũ

mujhē milnā cāhiyē. 9. mujhē dō dinõ-kē liyē cār mālī cāhiyẽ. 10. musafir-kō nahānē-kē liyē garm pānī cāhiyē.

24.5 [17.4.2] **Translate into Urdu:**

1. Do the women want to buy cloth in any shop? 2. Some birds sit on the branch. 3. Several birds sit on the branch. 4. There are several houses along the road. 5. The teacher asks me several questions. 6. We see several large animals under the bridge. 7. Some thin cows rest under the tree. 8. There are several ripe fruits under the tree. 9. Are there any farmers in the field? 10. Some holy man is in front of the river. 11. The farmer gives the oxen some grass to eat. 12. The hunter kills some animal in the jungle. 13. Please bring some table out. 14. There are some small shops in front of the high building. 15. There are several small shops in the bazaar.

24.6 [17.4.3] **Translate into English:**

1. kyā kōī ghar-mẽ hai? 2. kyā musāfir kisī-sē Añgrēzī bōl saktā hai? 3. hōṭal-mẽ kuch acchē kamrē haĩ. 4. mērī mōṭargāṛī-kē liyē kuch pānī lāiyē. 5. kōī kisān daraḳht-kē nīcē ārām karēgā. 6. kyā zamīn-mẽ kuch kōēlā hai? 7. śayad baṛā kuttā kisī-kō kāṭē. 8. kyā yahā̃ kōī kuā̃ pās hai? 9. mērē liyē kuẽ-kā kuch pānī lāiyē. 10. kōī bāhar hai. 11. pyāsā bail kuch khānā nahī̃ cāhtā. 12. kōī cīz darvāzē-kē pīchē hai. 13. kuch aḳhbār mēz-par haĩ. 14. kōī aḳhbār mēz-par haĩ. 15. kyā kōī mujh-sē Urdū-mẽ bōl saktā hai?

24.7 [18.1.5] **Translate into Urdu:**

1. If the child is good, I kiss him. 2. If the automobile should come late, I may wait for you. 3. If you (**hon., msc.**) can, please speak slowly in Urdu. 4. If the river should be deep, I (**msc.**) may swim in it. 5. If the water will be good, the traveller will drink it. 6. If there are fish in the river, the fisherman catches them. 7. If the fruits are ripe, I may eat them. 8. If you (**msc.**) wish, give me cold water. 9. If the master will wish, the servant will prepare food for him. 10. If you should study Urdu, you may be able to speak. 11. If my friend (**msc.**) will write a letter, then I (**msc.**) will take a trip to see him. 12. If there is grass under the tree, the cow eats it. 13. If the man will work, I (**msc.**) will give him money. 14. If the bazaar should be near, I may go to see it. 15. If my cap is on the chair, please bring it. 16. If the mother should wish, she may go to the bazaar with the boy. 17. If the dog will come back, the girl will give it food. 18. If the hotel room is good, the traveller is happy. 19. If the woman will buy many things in the shop, the shopkeeper will be happy. 20. If you have to go to the bazaar, then come with me. 21. If you should be sick, we may go tonight to your house. 22. If you should order, I may come to see you. 23. If the washerman is good, I give him clothes to wash. 24. If the day should be nice, the gardener may dig in the garden. 25. If the child runs to the river, bring him back!

24.8 [18.1.6] **Translate into English:**

1. agar maĩ dauṛtā hū̃, tō girtā hū̃. 2. agar sipāhī cōr-kō pakāṛēgā, tō vo us-kō mārēgā. 3. agar tum daryā-kō jānā cāhō, tō śāyad maĩ tumhārē sāth jā sakū̃. 4. agar āp thakī haĩ, tō us kursī-par baiṭhiyē. 5. agar bail ṭhahartē haĩ, tō kisān un-kō mārtā hai. 6. agar pānī ṭhaṇḍā hōgā, tō ham us-kō piyẽgē. 7. agar maĩ dauṛū̃, tō śāyad girū̃. 8. agar āp vaḳt-par vāpas āẽ, tō mujh-sē bāt karnē-kē liyē ṭhahariyē. 9. agar mērā dōst Urdū aḳhbār ḳharīdēgā, tō vo unhẽ mērē liyē paṛhēgā. 10. agar daraḳht-par phal hõgē, tō bandar un-kō curāēgā. 11. agar tum mujh-sē bāt karnā cāhtē hō, tō jald jald na bōlō. 12. agar aḳhbār mēz-par hai, tō mujhē dījiyē. 13. agar kunbā g̱arīb hai, tō ādmī-kō kārḳhānē-mẽ kām

karnē-kē liyē śahar jānā paṛtā hai. 14. agar saṛak lambī hai, tō musāfir thakā hōgā. 15. agar tum ṭhahar saktē hō, tō mujh-sē milnē-kē liyē vāpas ānē-par ṭhaharō. 16. agar daryā-kā pānī garm hōgā, tō ham us-mẽ tairnā cāhẽgē. 17. agar daraḳht-par pakkē phal hõ, tō śāyad bandar un-kō cūrāẽ. 18. agar āp-kō ānā hai, tō vaḳt-par āiyē. 19. agar jagah ḳhūb-sūrat hai, tō aurat ārām karnē-kē liyē vahā̃ ṭhaharnā cāhēgī. 20. agar naukar acchā hai, tō mālik ḳhuś hai. 21. agar āp thakī haĩ, tō kām na kījiyē! 22. agar mainejar dē saktā hai, tō vo ham-kō accha kamrā dēgā. 23. agar kapṛē sāf haĩ, tō aurat dhōbī-sē un-kō lēgī. 24. agar naukar mālik-sē Urdū-mẽ bōlnā cāhtā hai, tō us-kō āhistā āhistā bōlnā cāhiyē. 25. agar āp-kā ghar nazdīk hai, tō maĩ āp-kē sāth vahā̃ jāū̃gā.

24.9 [18.2.2] **Translate into Urdu:**

1. Which man will be able to understand English? 2. What is this? 3. How can I go to Calcutta? 4. What's the matter? 5. If you should go to the city, with whom will you go? 6. Which books does he prefer to read? 7. Which fish will the fisherman sell to us? 8. By which road can I (**msc.**) go to Calcutta? 9. For which woman does the boy bring water? 10. Who is that woman? 11. Which women will be able to prepare food? 12. With which men do you (**hon., msc.**) prefer to speak? 13. Which oxcart is yours? 14. With whom should I speak Urdu? 15. Which student has to read the book? 16. Who are those men? 17. In which room is the child? 18. To whom should I give money? 19. Which man wants drinking water? 20. How do you (**hon., msc.**) say "train" in Urdu?

24.10 [18.2.3] **Translate into English:**

1. kyā bāt hai? 2. āp Urdū-mẽ "book"-kō kyā kahtē haĩ? 3. maĩ Kalkattē kis tarah jā saktī hū̃? 4. śikārī kaun hai? 5. maĩ kis-kē liyē aḳhbār vāpas lāū̃? 6. maĩ kis ādmī-sē Baṅgālī bōl sakū̃gī? 7. Aṅgrēzī kaun samajhtā hai? 8. āp kis-kē ānē-kā intazār kar rahē haĩ? 9. agar tum jōt sakō, tō kis hal-sē khēt-mẽ khōdōgē? 10. kaun ādmī kisān hai? 11. bandar kis daraḳht-sē pakkē phal curātē haĩ? 12. ustād kis-sē savāl pūchẽgē? 13. maĩ kis saṛak-sē Kalkattē jā saktā hū̃. 14. vo cīz kyā hai? 15. āp-kī mōṭargāṛī kis makān-kē sāmnē hai? 16. sipāhī cōr-kō kis-sē mārēgā? 17. kaun aurat āp-kī bīvī hai? 18. āp kis pīr-kō phūl dẽgī? 19. us-kā kām kyā hai? 20. dukāndār kis tarah-kī cīzẽ bēctā hai?

24.11 [18.4.1] **Translate into Urdu:**

1. What time is it? 2. How much wood should I (**msc.**) bring back for you? 3. How much money will (you) take? 4. How many men live in this city? 5. How many men in this hotel can speak English? 6. How many women can sew? 7. How much money will you (**hon., msc.**) take for these vegetables? 8. How many patients take the medicine? 9. How many days will the travellers stay here? 10. How many girls does the woman cook for?

24.12 [18.4.2] **Translate into English:**

1. kitnē bajē haĩ? 2. āp-kō kitnē dinõ-kē liyē yahā̃ rahnā paṛēgā? 3. is ghar-mẽ kitnē kamrē haĩ? 4. āp kitnē aḳhbār paṛhtī haĩ? 5. vo kitnā baṛā hai? 6. ādmī-kē kitnē baccē haĩ? 7. tum in phalõ-kē liyē kitnē paisē lōgē? 8. āp-kī gāy kitnā dūdh dētī hai? 9. kisān-kē pās kitnē bail haĩ? 10. gāõ-mē kitnē kuẽ haĩ?

24.13 [19.1.3] **Translate into Urdu:**

1. We (**msc.**) were feeding the weak men. 2. The child was drinking (**the**) warm milk. 3. The farmer had a plow. 4. The happy girls were going out to play. 5. The servant was bringing water for the traveller. 6. The clever orderly was near the office. 7. Why

was the teacher reading the easy story? 8. The woman was bringing warm water for the sick man. 9. When was the bus coming back from the holy place? 10. The gardener was digging the hard ground. 11. Were the women bringing clean cups? 12. There were beautiful buildings near the road. 13. Why was the teacher asking easy questions of the clever boys? 14. The rich man was smoking a cigarette. 15. Was the servant honest? 16. The woman had new saris. 17. The young man was singing in the office. 18. The girl was hiding the warm milk under the table. 19. The quiet beggars were sitting in front of the temple. 20. The sick man was sad.

24.14 [19.1.4] **Translate into English:**

1. laṛkā aurat-kē liyē bhārī lakṛī lātā thā. 2. laṛkē-kē pās kitāb thī. 3. kyā aurtẽ mukaddas jagah jātī thī̃? 4. ajnabī ādmī naukar-sē pānī mā̃gtā thā. 5. kyā laṛkā imāndār thā? 6. bāp sigrēṭ pītā thā. 7. javān aurat baccē-kō miṭhāī dētī thī. 8. kisān sakht zamīn kyū̃ khōdtē thē? 9. baccā kyū̃ gamgīn thā? 10. garīb aurat mandar-kē sāmnē phūl bēcnā cāhtī thī. 11. kamzōr ādmī udās thā. 12. gōl makān tañg galī-kē pās thā. 13. javān aurtẽ khūbsūrat thī. 14. ādmī kis-kē liyē ustarā kharīdtā thā? 15. khuś laṛkiyā̃ ēk-sāth kuẽ-kē pas gātī thī. 16. kamzōr ādmī bhārī lakṛī tōltā thā. 17. hōśiyār laṛkiyā̃ āsān sabak paṛhtī thī̃. 18. aurtẽ kuẽ-kē pās dōstõ-kā intazār kartī thī. 19. vo bīmār ādmī-kē liyē sāf pyālā lātā thā. 20. mā̃ khuś baccē-kē liyē garm dūdh-kā pyālā lātī thī.

24.15 [19.2.1] **Translate into Urdu:**

1. The washerman should have washed the clothes. 2. The boy ought to have brought wood for the fire. 3. You should have spoken in Urdu. 4. The gardener ought to have watered the plants. 5. The hunter ought to have killed the dreadful animal. 6. The farmer ought to have dug the hard ground. 7. You ought to have been able to understand Urdu. 8. The child should have given the sick man a fruit. 9. The men ought to have gone to the holy place. 10. We should have gone towards the right.

24.16 [19.2.2] **Translate into English:**

1. āp-kō dūdh pīnā cāhiyē thā. 2. kyā baccõ-kō ghar-mẽ rahnā cāhiyē thā? 3. hamẽ garīb ādmī-kō paisē dēnā cāhiyē thā. 4. tumhẽ āj ārām karnā cāhiyē thā. 5. kamzōr mālī-kō kuẽ-kē pās ārām karnā cāhiyē thā. 6. dhōbī-kō āj kapṛē vāpas lānā cāhiyē thā. 7. unhẽ ham-sē milnē-kē liyē kal ānā cāhiyē thā. 8. garīb ādmī-kō kām karnā cāhiyē thā. 9. kyā tumhẽ āj daftar jānā cāhiyē thā? 10. kyā hamẽ āj • rāt sinēmā jānā cāhiyē thā?

24.17 [19.3.1] **Translate into Urdu:**

1. The woman needed wood for the fire. 2. We needed the help of a laborer yesterday. 3. The farmer needed a big plow to till the field. 4. Did you need my help? 5. I needed a man to drive the autombile. 6. The traveller needed a man to point out the road. 7. Did you need anything? 8. Why did you need my help? 9. Why did the servant need to see me yesterday? 10. The woman needed money to buy food in the bazaar.

24.18 [19.3.2] **Translate into English:**

1. ādmī-kō kab dōst cāhiyẽ thē? 2. hamẽ tāzā pānī cāhiyē thā. 3. mujhē kal ye bailgāṛī cāhiyē thī. 4. āp-kō kal kyū̃ daftar jānā cāhiyē thā? 5. kyā āp-kō safar karnē-kē liyē kuch cāhiyē thā? 6. aurat-kō āj • subah āg-kē liyē lakṛī cāhiyē thī. 7. kyā āp-kō kal sāf kapṛē cāhiyẽ thē? 8. āp-kō kal kyū̃ mujhē milnā cāhiyē thā? 9. mujhē dō dinõ-kē liyē mālī cāhiyē thā. 10. musāfir-kō nahānē-kē liyē garm pānī cāhiyē thā.

24.19 [19.4.1] **Translate into Urdu:**

1. If the woman had become tired, she would have stopped to rest. 2. If you had waited

there until my arrival, I would have been able to bring you the newspaper. 3. If the food were bad, we would get sick. 4. If you spoke slowly, I (**fm.**) would be able to understand. 5. If you wished, we would go out of the city with you. 6. If the girl studied Urdu, she would be able to speak with you. 7. If there would be grass under the tree, the cow would eat it. 8. If the bazaar had been near, the woman would have gone to see it. 9. If the hotel room were good, the traveller would be happy. 10. If you had had to go to the city, I would have come with you. 11. If the washerman were good, we would give him clothes to wash. 12. If the man could speak Urdu, he would speak with you. 13. If the water had been sweet, the boy would have drunk it. 14. If my sister were to sing, I would go out of the house. 15. If the fruits had been ripe, the monkeys would have stolen them.

24.20 [19.4.2] **Translate into English:**

1. agar sipāhī cōr-kō pakaṛtā, tō vo us-kō mārtā. 2. agar bail ṭhahartē, tō kisān un-kō calātā. 3. agar pānī ṭhaṇḍā hōtā, tō ham us-kō pītē. 4. agar mērā dōst aḳhbār ḳharīdtā, tō ham us-kō paṛh saktē. 5. agar āp kuch kahnā cāhtī, tō bōltī. 6. agar daraḳht-par pakkē phal hōtē, tō bandar un-kō tōṛtē. 7. agar tum thakē hōtē, tō ārām kartē. 8. agar naukar acchā hōtā, tō mālik ḳhuś hōtā. 9. agar pānī garm hōtā, tō ham us-sē dhōtē. 10. agar tumhārā ghar pās hōtā, tō maĩ tumhārē sāth vahā̃ jā saktā. 11. agar baccā dauṛtā, tō vo girtā. 12. agar saṛak lambī hōtī, tō musāfir thak jātā. 13. agar āp-kō mujh-sē milnē-kē liyē ānā paṛtā, tō vaḳt-par ānā cāhiyē hōtā. 14. agar saṛak lambī hōtī, tō musāfir thak jātā. 15. agar āp savērē uṭh saktī̃, tō hamārē sāth śahar jā saktī̃.

24.21 [19.5.1] **Translate into Urdu:**

1. The mother will read the children the third story. 2. The fifth boy will bring the heavy wood for the old woman. 3. When will you (**msc.**) answer my twelfth question? 4. The farmer rests under the second tree. 5. The friend gives me back the eighth book. 6. When will the sixth train arrive? 7. He is behind the fourth house. 8. The ninth girl listens to the eleventh boy. 9. The first girl goes to drop the bucket in the well. 10. The servant brings cold water for the tenth traveller.

24.22 [19.5.2] **Translate into English:**

1. baṛhaī pā̃cvē̃ daraḳht-kō kāṭtā hai. 2. musāfir tisrē kamrē-mē̃ rahtā hai. 3. āp dusrē kuē̃-sē pānī lā saktē haĩ. 4. sātvī̃ gāṛī sṭēśan-mē̃ kab āēgī? 5. śāyad gyārvā̃ ādmī āj daftar-mē̃ hō. 6. pahilā ādmī āp-kē sāth Urdu bōl sakēgā. 7. bāp dasvā̃ aḳhbār paṛhnā zyādā pasand kartā hai. 8. āp-kō cauthā phal lēnā cāhiyē. 9. cauthā naukar mēz-sē raḳābiyā̃ ūṭhāēgā. 10. gyārvā̃ hājī ārām karnā zyādā pasand kartā hai.

24.23 [20.1.5] **Translate into Urdu:**

1. The boys swam for two hours in the little river. 2. Mother had come from the bazaar with the women. 3. The traveller has come from the city. 4. The boy had stayed with the old mother in the little house. 5. Our bullock will have grazed near the river. 6. The monkeys ran quickly up the high tree. 7. The cart had stopped in front of the house. 8. The children will have walked behind the washerman's donkey. 9. The hungry dog has walked behind the little child. 10. The automobile will have stopped in front of me. 11. The cow has run with the little calf. 12. The men sat in front of the house. 13. The servants had waited twenty minutes near the office. 14. Father will have come back from the city. 15. The farmer slept under the tree. 16. The holy man is seated near the tank. 17. The sad boy had wept near the river. 18. The daughter has come with (**her**)

father to the city. 19. The traveller will have stayed ten days in the hotel. 20. The father played with the children.

24.24 [20.1.6] Translate into English:

1. kuttā zamīn-par sōyā. 2. mērā dōst mujh-sē milnē-kē liyē śahar-kō āyā thā. 3. nāī ghar-mē̃ āyā hai. 4. dhōbī gadhē-kē pīchē cālā thā. 5. laṛkā pul-kē nīcē tairā hōgā. 6. pyāsā hājī kuē̃-kō gayā. 7. baccā bāg-mē̃ sōyā hōgā. 8. fakīr saṛak-par baiṭhā hai. 9. jānvar rāt-kō jaṅgal-sē āyē thē. 10. ūṭ daryā-kē pās pānī pīnē-kē liyē ṭhaharā hōgā. 11. naukar mālik-kē pīchē cālā. 12. aurtē̃ dukān-kē pās rukī haĩ. 13. rēlgāṛī pul-kē pās kyũ rukī thī? 14. āp-kī gāy hamārē khēt-mē̃ carī hōgī. 15. ṭrām mandar-kē samnē rukī. 16. bhūkā ghōṛā ghās-kē pās rukā hai. 17. ādmī śahar-sē kyũ vāpas āyā tha? 18. kyā laṛkā kuē̃-sē pānī-kē sāth vāpas āyā hōgā? 19. chōṭī laṛkiyā̃ darakht-kē nīcē khēlĩ. 20. naukar daftar-kē sāmnē baiṭhē haĩ.

24.25 [20.2.3] Translate into Urdu:

1. The traveller likes cold water for drinking. 2. We prefer to travel by automobile. 3. Do you prefer the warm weather to cold weather? 4. I prefer to rest in the room. 5. Children like sweet mangoes. 6. Why do you prefer that man to me? 7. He prefers to read the newspaper. 8. Do you prefer travelling by trolley to (**travelling by**) ox-cart? 9. We like the cold weather. 10. The man prefers resting at home to working. 11. I prefer warm water for bathing. 12. Why don't you like the warm weather? 13. I prefer sleeping to studying. 14. The boy does not prefer to stay at home. 15. **Do you like to travel?**

24.26 [20.2.4] Translate into English:

1. kyā āp-kō kām karnā pasand hai? 2. tumhē̃ safar karnā kyũ zyādā pasand hai? 3. hājī-kō safar karnē-kē liyē garmī-kē mausam-sē sardī-kā mausam zyādā pasand hai. 4. laṛkē-kō tairnā pasand hai. 5. kyā baccē-kō khaṭṭī cīzē̃ zyādā pasand haĩ? 6. mujhē bailgāṛiyō̃-sē mōṭargāṛiyā̃ zyādā pasand haĩ. 7. āp-kō us akhbār-sē ye kitāb kyũ zyādā pasand hai? 8. mujhē ārām karnā pasand hai. 9. kyā kīsī-kō calnā zyādā pasand hai? 10. kuch lōgō̃-kō mōṭargāṛī-mē̃ jānē-sē calnā zyādā pasand hai. 11. laṛkī-kō sīnā pasand hai. 12. kuch lōgō̃-kō mīṭhē cīzē̃ zyādā pasand haĩ? 13. hamē̃ khaṭṭē amlō̃-sē ām zyādā pasand hōgē. 14. kyā kisī-kō is mulk-sē vo mulk zyādā pasand hōgā? 15. gāy-kō ghās khānā pasand hai.

24.27 [20.3.3] Translate into Urdu:

1. This laborer is not weaker than that laborer. 2. We (**msc.**) want to eat the sweetest fruits. 3. Is the well deeper than the river? 4. The street is narrower than the road. 5. This small table is broader than that round table. 6. I need the longest rope. 7. The boy is younger than (**his**) friend. 8. This temple is the most beautiful. 9. His load is not heavier than my load. 10. The mother gives the child the sweetest apple. 11. Please bring me the longest stick. 12. The well water is colder than the river water. 13. The elephant is the biggest of all animals. 14. Please send me the strongest worker. 15. The street is the most dangerous of all.

24.28 [20.3.4] Translate into English:

1. safar karnē-kē liyē bailgāṛī-sē mōṭargāṛī acchī hai. 2. mujhē āp-sē zyādā maⁿbūt ādmī cāhiyē. 3. tum sab-sē baṛā sēb kyũ cāhtī hō? 4. kyā āp-kē pās is-sē lambā rassā hai? 5. kyā āp-kī bailgāṛī sab-sē acchī hai? 6. is kām-kē liyē mujhē āp-sē zyādā mazbūt ādmī cāhiyē. 7. vo sab-sē zyādā khuś hai. kyā kuē̃-kā pānī tālāb-kē pānī-sē pīnē-kē liyē acchā nahĩ hai? 9. mujhē āg-kē liyē sab-sē sūkhī lakṛī cāhiyē. 10. ye kamrā us kamrē-sē acchā

nahī̃ hai. 11. us-kī mōṭargāṛī tumhārī mōṭargāṛī-sē chōṭī hai. 12. kyā aurat-kō dukān-mē̃ sab-sē acchī sāṛī ḳharīdnā cāhiyē thā? 13. ye saṛak dusrī saṛak-sē lambī hai. 14. maĩ is-sē zyādā ṭhaṇḍā pānī pīnā cāhtī hū̃. 15. ye sab-sē zyādā ḳhūbsūrat phūl nahī̃.

24.29 [20.3.7] **Translate into Urdu:**

1. This field is less fertile than that field. 2. He is the least industrious laborer. 3. Do you need a less long rope than this? 4. Why are your bullocks the smallest (lit., **least small**) of all? 5. That ground is less hard than this ground. 6. Do you (**fm.**) want to buy a less expensive cooking-pot than this? 7. Why is your field the least fertile of all? 8. Is his well the least deep of all? 9. Why does the farmer need a smaller (lit. **less big**) plow than this? 10. This is the lowest (lit., **least high**) building in the city.

24.30 [20.3.8] **Translate into English:**

1. āp-kā khēt us-kē khēt-sē kyū̃ kam zarḳhēz hai? 2. ye bail us bail-sē kam mazbūt hai. 3. kyā ye saṛak us saṛak-sē kam lambī hai? 4. in sab-mē̃-sē kaun savāl kam muśkil hai? 5. kyā saḳht zamīn sab-sē kam zarḳhēz hai? 6. ādmī naukar-sē kam bhārī bōjh lātā hai. 7. ye saṛak sab-sē kam ḳhatarnāk hai. 8. naukar mālī-sē kam pyāsā hai. 9. mujhē madad dēnē-kē liyē sab-sē kam ḳhābīdā naukar bulāō! 10. vo sab-sē kam mohtāt hai.

24.31 [21.1.5] **Translate into Urdu:**

1. The mother called the children into the house. 2. The hunter heard the dreadful animal. 3. The servant tied the cows under the bridge. 4. The farmers had fed the bullocks. 5. The woman has heard the cow near the house. 6. The traveller had called the servant. 7. The servant understood the master. 8. We saw the farmer near the field. 9. The donkey dragged the washerman. 10. The cow will have fed the calf near the well. 11. The teacher has made the students read. 12. The husband had heard (**his**) wife in the house. 13. The farmer has summoned the son. 14. We have understood him. 15. The hunter has seen the elephants in the jungle. 16. The policeman will have seized the thief in the shop. 17. The women had bought all sorts of things in the bazaar. 18. We will have called the washerman. 19. The hunter will have killed the tiger. 20. They will have heard the train in the station.

24.32 [21.1.6] **Translate into English:**

1. ādmī-nē hāthī-kō nahlāyā. 2. ham-nē kuē̃-kē pās aurat-kō dēkhā thā. 3. bailō̃-nē dō ghanṭē-kē liyē hal-kō khī̃cā thā. 4. aurat-nē murgiyō̃-kō khilāyā hai. 5. rīch-nē jañgal-mē̃ chōṭē bakrē-kō khī̃ca hōgā. 6. musāfir-nē śahar-mē̃ ghōṛē-kō ḳharīdā. 7. billī-nē cuhiyā-kō pakṛā thā. 8. naukar-nē daraḳht-sē lakṛī-kō kāṭā. 9. maĩ-nē daftar-mē ardalī-kō bhējā thā. 10. mālī-nē kuē̃-kē pās hamārī gāy-kō bā̃dhā hai. 11. aurat-nē machērē-sē machliyō̃-kō ḳharīdā hōgā. 12. billī-nē mōṭī cīṛiyā-kō pakṛā hōgā. 13. āp-nē us ādmī-kō kab dēkhā thā? 14. śikārī-nē jañgal-mē̃ jānvar-kō mārā. 15. mā̃-nē hamārē liyē khānā pakāyā hai. 16. naukar-nē saṛak-kō dikhāyā. 17. mā̃-nē sabziyā̃ ḳharīdnē-kē liyē naukar-kō bāzār bhējā hai. 18. kuttē-nē būṛhē ādmī-kō kāṭā hōgā. 19. kyā āp-nē mērē liyē makān-kō ḳharīdā hai? 20. laṛkē-nē musāfir-kē liyē kuē̃-sē ṭhaṇḍā pānī khī̃cā.

24.33 [21.2.5] **Translate into Urdu:**

1. Has the servant cooked the food? 2. I read the letter for the old man. 3. The woman will have bought this picture in the bazaar. 4. The farmer fed the bullocks. 5. The shopkeeper had sold us the fruit. 6. Why had you drunk warm water? 7. Did the servant prepare the tea at four o'clock? 8. The monkeys will have eaten the tree's ripe fruits. 9. He showed the traveller the road to Calcutta. 10. I misunderstood your order.

11. They had read our letters yesterday. 12. Did he understand English correctly? 13. The boy has brought water from the canal. 14. Why had the children thrown stones at the bullocks? 15. Where has the hunter killed the animal? 16. The men will have washed the elephant in the little river. 17. Did the gardener water the plants? 18. We sent food to the hungry men. 19. The boy has placed the heavy load in the train. 20. I had placed his pen on the table.

24.34 [21.2.6] **Translate into English:**

1. āp-nē miṭhāī kyũ khāyī? 2. ādmī-nē palang-par halkā sāmān rākhā thā. 3. kyā us-nē āp-kī kitāb paṛhī thī? 4. kyā us-nē Kalkattā dēkhā hōgā? 5. us-nē bāg-kē paudõ-par pānī kab ḍālā thā? 6. unhõ-nē bailõ-par patthar phẽkē. 7. kyā naukar-nē mēz-par rakābiyā̃ rakhī haĩ? 8. kis-nē ye ḳhat likhā thā? 9. āp-nē un-kā gānā kab sunā? 10. unhõ-nē mērē hukam galat samjhē. 11. aurat-nē kis-kō khānā bhējā thā? 12. kis-nē mujhē ye ḳhat bhējā? 13. is ādmī-nē rassē-sē ghās bā̃dhī. 14. kuttē-nē ghōṛē-kō kyũ kāṭā? 15. us-nē mērī Urdū ṭhīk samjhī. 16. kis-nē mērā sāmān uṭhāyā? 17. kyā us-nē āp-kī kahānī sunī hōgī? 18. śēr-nē bakrā kahā̃ khĩcā? 19. āp-nē nahar-kē pās mōṭargāṛī kyũ rōkī? 20. naukar-nē jūtē kahā̃ rakhē thē?

24.35 [22.3] **Translate into Urdu:**

1. What did the master order the servant? 2. Had you tried to catch fish? 3. We had gone to the shoemaker's shop. 4. The traveller travelled abroad. 5. Why did the servant go back to the village? 6. The mother gave the daughter new green shoes. 7. When did the mechanic repair your automobile? 8. The thirsty man took a cup of cold water from the boy. 9. When had the ship gone into the harbor? 10. The women went to the well to bring back water. 11. The students had answered the teacher's questions correctly. 12. The poor man took food from the kind woman. 13. Did the shoemaker try to mend the shoes? 14. The father gave (**his**) daughter bangles. 15. The servant closed the door to my room. 16. Which (**particular**) man went there yesterday? 17. I liked to swim in the river. 18. Who had given flowers to the holy man? 19. The servant had cleaned my shoes. 20. Did you ever travel by airplane?

24.36 [22.3.1] **Translate into English:**

1. kyā naukar-nē mērē jūtē sāf kiyē? 2. kārīgar-nē mōṭargāṛī-kē nīcē kyā kiyā? 3. ḳhuś ādmī-nē aurat-sē khānā liyā. 4. aurtõ-nē bahot muḳaddas•jaghõ-kō safar kiyē. 5. kyā āp-nē pardēs-mẽ safar karnā pasand kiyā? 6. baṛhaī-nē gōl mēz-kī marammat kī hai. 7. tālibilm-nē āsān sabaḳ paṛhnē-kī kōśiś kī thī. 8. kis-nē darvāzā band kiyā? 9. ham-nē garīb aurat-kō khānā ḳharīdnē-kē liyē paisē diyē. 10. naukar-nē bhārī bōjh uṭhānē-kī kōśiś kī thī. 11. maĩ-nē hōṭal-kē restōranṭ-mẽ khānā zyādā pasand kiyā. 12. aurat bahot ḳhuś huī. 13. kārīgar-nē mōṭargāṛī-kī marammat kab kī? 14. dhōbī-nē naukar-sē dhōnē-kē liyē kapṛē liyē thē. 15. tālibilm-nē Angrēzī bōlnē-sē Urdū bōlnā zyādā pasand kiyā. 16. kaun-sē naukar-nē āp-kī ṭōpī lī? 17. chōṭī laṛkī-nē hamārē liyē cāy banānē-kī kōśiś kī thī. 18. vō rēlgāṛī-sē Kalkattē gayē thē. 19. kyā āp-nē Urdū bōlnē-kī kōśiś kī? 20. vō gāõ kab vāpas gayē?

24.37 [22.4.3] **Translate into Urdu:**

1. We had to go to the bazaar. 2. You will have to speak Urdu in Pakistan. 3. The washerman had to clean the clothes. 4. The servant will have to prepare the bed for us. 5. The fisherman had to catch fish. 6. We will have to try to speak Urdu. 7. The mechanic had to repair the automobile. 8. The servant will have to bring warm water for our

bath. 9. You will have to close my door. 10. Did they have to go back to the village?

24.38 [22.4.4] **Translate into English:**

1. kyā āp-kō āj kām karnā hōgā? 2. kis-kō kursī-kī marammat karnā paṛā? 3. mujhē pānī-kē liyē kuẽ-kō jānā paṛēgā. 4. hamẽ āj • rāt ghar-mẽ rahnā hōgā. 5. kis-kō hamārē liyē cāy banānā hōgā? 6. mōcī-kō mērē nayē harē jūtē-kī marammat karnā paṛā. 7. us-kō gāõ kyũ jānā paṛā? 8. kyā āp-kō us machērē-sē machliyā̃ k̲harīdnā paṛā? 9. āg-kē liyē kis-kō lakṛī kāṭnā paṛēgā? 10. mujhē us-sē milnē-kē liyē śahar jānā paṛā.

24.39 [22.5.6] **Translate into Urdu:**

1. Does the farmer have a plow? 2. Does the woman have children? 3. The woman has a daughter. 4. I saw a brother of yours yesterday. 5. The jungle has many trees. 6. The cat has sharp teeth. 7. One of my brothers travelled abroad. 8. The garden has many plants. 9. I don't have enough money. 10. The elephant has two long teeth.

24.40 [22.5.7] **Translate into English:**

1. kyā ādmī-kē ēk bēṭā hai? 2. kis-kē pās siyāhī hai? 3. maĩ-nē āp-kē ēk bhāī-kē sāth safar kiyā. 4. kamrē-kē dō darvāzē haĩ. 5. bāg̲-mẽ bahot darak̲ht haĩ. 6. kyā baṛhaī-kē pās lakṛī hai? 7. laṛkī-kē pās nayē jūtē haĩ. 8. tumhārē ēk naukar-nē gāṛī-kī marammat karnē-kī kōśiś kī. 9. is bāg̲-kā kōī malī nahī̃. 10. us-kē bāl lambē haĩ.

24.41 [23.1.2] **Translate into Urdu:**

1. Who (**msc. pl.**) was talking with you in English? 2. I (**msc.**) am waiting for the bearer to come back from the city. 3. Why is the man shaving with an old razor? 4. The girl was stopping on the mound. 5. The servant is helping the master. 6. The women were speaking with their friends. 7. Since when has the sailor been travelling abroad? 8. Why is she smoking my cigarette? 9. The farmer was working hard in the field at that time. 10. They (**fm.**) were sitting on the floor. 11. For whom are you bringing the water? 12. It is raining. 13. The pilgrim is making trips to holy places. 14. Who (**msc. sg.**) was using my comb? 15. The gardener is plucking yellow flowers from plants. 16. The carpenter is repairing the chair. 17. With whom is she talking now? 18. The shoemaker is bringing my shoes. 19. The kind men are trying to help me. 20. The woman was trying to clean the dirty cup.

24.42 [23.1.3] **Translate into English:**

1. maĩ Hindī sikhnē-kī kōśiś kar rahā hũ. 2. kaun andar ānē-kē kōśiś kar rahī thē? 3. ham gāõ-kō vāpas jā rahē haĩ. 4. vo tum-sē kyā kahnē-kī kōśiś kar rahī thī? 5. chōṭā laṛkā tēz ustarē-kā istēmāl kar rahā hai. 6. jahāz is vak̲t bandargāh-mẽ ā rahā hai. 7. vo havāī • jahāz-sē safar kyũ kar rahā hai? 8. mālī bāg̲-mẽ mehnat kar rahā hai. 9. mehtar farś-par pānī ḍāl rahā hai. 10. bairē darak̲ht-kē nīcē kyā khā rahē haĩ? 11. tum kab-sē is kārk̲hānē-mẽ kām kar rahē hō? 12. kārīgar mērī mōṭargāṛī-kī marammat kar rahā hai. 13. mehtar kunbē-sē milnē-kē liyē gāõ-kō jā rahā thā. 14. laṛkī dukān-mẽ harā kapṛā k̲harīd rahī thī. 15. tum kis-kā intazār kar rahī hō? 16. ham mandar dēkhnē-kē liyē jā rahē haĩ. 17. āp kis-kē sāth gāõ-mẽ rahē thē? 18. āp kab-sē yahā̃ baiṭhē haĩ? 19. vo hamārē liyē cāy taiyār kar rahī hai. 20. vo kab-sē mujh-sē milnē-kī k̲ōśiś kar rahā thā?

24.43 [23.5] **Translate into Urdu:**

1. The sweeper will not be able to work tonight. 2. The servant does not have to bring water from the tank. 3. Why wasn't the teacher reading an easy story? 4. If the bullock should not become hungry, then he may not stop to eat grass. 5. The gardener was not digging in the hard ground. 6. The farmers do not have to work in the field today. 7.

The traveller has not come from the city. 8. If the bazaar should not be near, I may not go to see it. 9. The hunters will not kill many animals in the jungle. 10. If the clerk had not spoken slowly, I would not have been able to understand. 11. The mail train did not stop in the station. 12. The sweeper needn't speak in English. 13. The bearer did not understand (**his**) master's order. 14. The student does not have to study tonight. 15. If the hotel-room would not be good, the traveller would not be happy. 16. Won't the washerman want to wash the man's old clothes? 17. The holy man was not sitting near the tank. 18. If the man could not speak in Panjābī, he would not speak with you. 19. The boys shouldn't swim in the deep river. 20. The clerk was not happy. 21. The officer has not caught the thief in the shop. 22. If the sweeper will not work, I will not pay him. 23. The farmer did not have a plow. 24. They did not see boats in the harbor. 25. The gardener need not water the plants today.

24.44 [23.5.1] **Translate into English:**

1. maĩ āj kisī-sē nahī̃ bōl sakū̃gī. 2. agar saṛak lambī na hōtī, tō musāfir thakā na hōtā. 3. agar āp thakē na hō̃, tō āp-kō ārām karnē-kē liyē ṭhaharnā nahī̃ paṛēgā. 4. agar pānī ṭhaṇḍā na hōtā, tō ham us-kō na pītē. 5. āp-kō ḍākḳhānē nahī̃ jānā cāhiyē. 6. ādmī tārghar-mē̃ kyū̃ nahī̃ thē? 7. kyā dhōbī kapṛē āj nahī̃ lāēgā? 8. mehtar ghar-kē sāmnē nahī̃ baiṭhā hai. 9. kis-kō nahī̃ khānā paṛtā hai? 10. kyā ḍākgāṛī vaḳt-par nahī̃ pahō̃cī? 11. agar tum nahī̃ ṭhahar saktē, tō vāpas ānē-par mujh-sē milnē-kē liyē na ṭhaharō. 12. bairē-nē mērē nahānē-kē liyē pānī nahī̃ khī̃cā thā. 13. bābū-kō daftar-kē bāhar kyū̃ nahī̃ ṭhaharnā hai? 14. kis-nē yah mōṭargāṛī kirāyē-par nahī̃ lī thī? 15. kyā āp darvāzē-kī marammat nahī̃ karē̃gē? 16. āp-nē ḳhat ḍāk-mē̃ kyū̃ nahī̃ ḍālā? 17. kyā āp-kō āj sāf kapṛē nahī̃ cāhiyē thē? 18. agar ham thakī na hōtī̃, tō ham ārām na kartī̃. 19. ham-nē khētō̃-mē̃ ghōṛē-par savārī nahī̃ kī. 20. agar āp-kā ghar pās na hō, tō maĩ āp-kē sāth vahā̃ nahī̃ jāū̃gā. 21. naukar musāfir-kē liyē bistar taiyār nahī̃ kartā thā. 22. vo kab nahī̃ thakā? 23. kyā āp-kō hajāmat banānē-kē liyē garm pānī nahī̃ cāhiyē thā? 24. musāfir-kē pās paisē kyū̃ nahī̃ thē? 25. mujhē āj zamindār-kō kirāyā nahī̃ dēnā hai.

Following are translations of texts given in lessons 17 to 23. They can be employed for practice in translating English texts into Urdu. [It should be noted that the English translations in a number of places tend toward a literal or, perhaps, inelegant rendition. This could not be avoided because the primary purpose of these is to direct the student's attention to the Urdu constructions. These remarks apply to the translated texts in the Review Lessons following.]

24.45 [17.5] **An Excursion.**

[Khurśid Ahmad has been living in Karachi for many years. Today is Sunday and the office is closed. Therefore, Khurśid will not go to work today. He plans to take his wife along for a ride. His wife's name is Najma. Najma is an educated girl. Khurśid and Najma both have Master's degrees. Khurśid teaches at a boy's college and Najma teaches at a girl's college. Today, Najma is also off from work. They are thinking of going to Clifton Beach for a picnic. Najma is roasting meat in the kitchen at this time. In a short while the servant will bring bread from the baker's shop. This bread tastes very good with roast meat. Khurśid's automobile is with one of his friends today. Both the husband and wife wonder how they should go on the picnic. Khurśid thinks that they should hire a taxi. But Najma says they should take a pretty tonga. Now everything is ready. (Soon) the servant will go to fetch a tonga. Oh! There is the tonga! It's completely new. The horse is very young and strong.]

Khurśid: Hey, tongawala, will you take us to Clifton Beach?

Tongawala: Yes sir! Why not!

Khurśid: How much will you charge?

Tongawala: Only one way or both ways?

Khurśid: Both ways.

Tongawala: Sir, I'll charge you only fifteen rupees.

Khurśid: Fifteen rupees! Dear fellow, be sensible.

Tongawala: Sir, I know what I am talking about. Fifteen rupees are not too much.

Khurśid: What did you say? Aren't much? We don't have illegal money. We work just like you.

Tongawala: Sir, just look at my horse. He goes like the wind. I feed him daily on ten rupees worth of grams. And, please, look at my tonga, too. It is brand new. You will enjoy the ride. My tonga is better than an automobile.

Khurśid: Well, darling, what do you say?

Najma: The tonga is good—yes. But fifteen rupees is too much. Tongawala, reduce the fare.

Tongawala: Madame, what shall I say? Please be just and fair. I have a wife and seven children. All their expenses are met by what I earn through this tonga.

Najma: You are right. But we aren't rich, either. Reduce (**your fare**) a little.

Tongawala: (**Why**) should I haggle with you. You are a daily customer. All right, you can have it at a rupee less.

Khurśid: Look, brother. Say one thing. We will pay ten rupees. Not more than that.

Tongawala: No sir. Ten rupees are too little. You can send for some other tonga. (**Begins to move the horse slowly.**)

Khurśid: All right. Take eleven rupees.

Tongawala: I have asked you for fourteen rupees. O.K., come along. Give me thirteen.

Khurśid: No, thirteen is too much. All right, we will give you twelve rupees.

Tongawala: How long will you stay at the beach?

Khurśid: Oh, not too long. Just about four hours.

Tongawala: O.K., please sit down.

[Khurśid and Najma get into the back seat of the tonga. The servant puts their things under the seat. The tonga at first moves slowly and then swiftly. After a short time, they come to a crossing. The tongawala does not notice the signal of the policeman and passes through. The policeman blows his whistle and the tongawala has to stop. The traffic-policeman comes towards him.]

Tongawala: Sir, what's the matter?

Policeman: What's the matter! Let's see your license. We will give you a ticket.

Tongawala: Sir, what's my fault?

Policeman: You drive your tonga as if you were the governor. You don't even care for the policeman's signal. Who would be responsible if there were a collision?

Tongawala: Sir, it was a mistake. Now forgive me. If you give me a ticket, I will get fined. Sir, I am a poor man. I have a wife and seven children. They will starve to death. Sir, this will not happen again.

Policeman: Now you talk. What can I do? It's just regulations that anyone who disregards the policeman's signal should be given a ticket. Now, take out your license. Quick.

Tongawala: Sir you are the government. (**Takes out a rupee and offers it to the policeman.**) This is for your refreshments.

Policeman: You take me for a grafter. I don't take bribes. Now I certainly will give give you a ticket.

Tongawala: (**Addressing Khurśid**) Please, sir, speak to the policeman in my behalf.

Khurśid: (**To the policeman:**) He has made a mistake. But now he is sorry. I think you should let him off this time.

Najma: Yes, yes, policeman, let him off. He is a poor man. If you give him a ticket, the poor man's wife and children will starve to death.

Policeman: All right, sir, if you say so, I'll let this fellow off this time. (**To the Tongawala:**) I forgive you this time. But if you go against the law again, then I will certainly not spare you.

Tongawala: Very well, sir. Thank you very much. May God keep you and your family happy.

24.46 [18.5] **A Conversation.**

[Karam Din and Mohammad Buta meet each other at the Shalimar Fair. Both of them are farmers and live in a small village. The two are in Lahore for the first time.]

Karam Din: Caudhari Buta! Greetings.

Mohammad Buta: Greetings, Caudhari. How are things? Your family is well?

Karam Din: God is kind to us. Everything's all right. Tell me, are you seeing the fair?

Mohammad Buta: Yes, brother. There's lot of to-do in the fair at this time. There are thousands of men and women and hundreds of shops. I feel like buying many things for my wife and children, but I don't have enough money. Tell me, when will you stroll about the city?

Karam Din: Lahore is a very big city. Some people say that anyone who has not seen Lahore is as (**ignorant and inexperienced**) as if he were never born. I think so, too. A friend of mine and I have come after seeing the Śahi Mosque. What shall I tell you—. It is a very beautiful building.

Mohammad Buta: Well tell me; who is the builder of this mosque?

Karam Din: According to an educated man, the Mogul king, Aurangzeb, is the builder of this mosque. This is the Number One mosque in the whole of Pakistan.

Mohammad Buta: Well! How many people can pray in the Mosque at one time?

Karam Din: My impression is that, at least, a hundred thousand people can pray in that mosque at one time.

Mohammad Buta: Well, tell me, what will you buy at the fair?

Karam Din: I'll buy several things. I'll buy glass bangles for (**my**) little girl, scented oil and soap for (**my**) wife, and a shirt for my father.

Mohammad Buta: Friend, you must have a lot of money, then.

Karam Din: Oh brother, I have some money from selling (**my**) cotton crop. I'm spending that. Don't you have money from your crop?

Mohammad Buta: Yes, I have some, too. I'm spending (**it**) slowly. You know, if I spend a lot at this time, then what will I do (**during**) the remaining entire year?

Karam Din: Brother Buta, you think far ahead. Our faith is that the God who has created us will also provide bread. Doesn't the Maulvi-Sahab say every Friday in the mosque that God provides the livelihood for all?

Mohammad Buta: Undoubtedly, God is the lord and master of all. But my opinion is that God helps those who help themselves. There is a school in our village. This is what the teacher teaches there.

Karam Din: (**Angrily**) Then do you mean that our Maulvi-Sahab tells lies?

Mohammad Buta: No, caudhari. This is not my meaning. But you know that Maulvi-Sahab is a man like you and me. He can make a mistake too. Remember this, too, that our school-master is also very well read and wise.

Karam Din: Perhaps you are right. In your opinion, what should I do with my money?

Mohammad Buta: In my opinion, you should deposit your spare money in the bank. The Cooperative Society Bank is right near your village. If you deposit your money there, you will receive an interest of three rupees per hundred rupees per year. The good thing (**about it**) is that you can withdraw your money whenever you like.

Karam Din: Caudhari, thank you very much for this valuable advice. I will think about it. Yes, tell me, what is the condition of the crops in your village?

Mohammad Buta: With God's grace, the crops are very good this year. It rained on time The result of the farmers' hard work is that the crop is very good.

Karam Din: The price of cotton is very high this year. If it remains like this always, then farmers will become well-to-do.

Mohammad Buta: It is difficult (**for things**) to be like this. Our school-master says that the rate of cotton is high because of the Korean war. The rate will fall as soon as the war ends.

Karam Din: This is bad news you tell.

Mohammad Buta: No, caudhari. Don't talk like that. If the Korean war ends, there will be peace in the world. Remember that the war can also come to our country from Korea.

Karam Din: Friend Mohammad Buta, you seem to be a very wise man. I am not educated myself, but my boy is now growing up. I plan to send him to school.

Mohammad Buta: Brother Karam Din, why don't you send the boy to our school? The teacher there imparts all kinds of instruction to the children.

Karam Din: I don't think I have enough money to keep the boy in a boarding house.

Mohammad Buta: Don't worry about this. Your boy can stay with me. There is room for him in our house. I will keep an eye on him.

Karam Din: Caudhari! Thank you very much! God willing, I will send the boy to you soon. I am sure that you will treat him like your sons.

Mohammad Buta: Certainly. Certainly. All right, we will meet again. God be with you.

Karam Din: God be with you.

[Now both friends busy themselves seeing the fair.]

24.47 [19.6] **School.**

[Sharif Husain and Jamil study in the seventh grade of the high-school. Today is Friday. It's nine o'clock. The school-bell rings. All the boys gather in the school-ground. Every Friday, the headmaster makes a speech. After that, the classes begin. The seventh grade boys will study arithmetic in the first period. Master Sher Ahmad teaches arithmetic. He is a very strict man. He gives a lot of homework. The boy who doesn't do his homework is fined and a report is also sent to his parents. Today, Sharif Husain's homework is not prepared. He is, therefore, very upset. He is afraid that, if a report goes to his home, his daddy will be very cross with him. He may stop his pocket money for a month.]

Sharif Husain: Friend Jamil, Master Sher Ahmad's class is today, isn't it.

Jamil: Certainly, and look! The master's mood seems bad today. My idea is that he's quarrelled with his wife today.

Sharif Husain: Is that so? How do you know?

Jamil: I don't know for sure. It's just my guess. Perhaps it's wrong. The tenth-grade boys say that the master is old and doesn't sleep well. He gets up early in the morning and asks for tea. His wife is young. It is the second marriage, you see. He married again after the death of his first wife. Anyway, the thing is that the master's wife, like all young people, likes (her) morning sleep. She doesn't like to get up early in the morning and make tea. So they quarrel.

Sharif Husain: Hmmm. I'm not interested in the teacher's domestic politics. But his mood will mean trouble for me today.

Jamil: You mean, you will not be able to answer his questions?

Sharif Husain: No, that's not what I mean. I'm not worried about his questions, but my homework is not ready.

Jamil: Then, what are your plans? Shall I tell you an easy way out?

Sharif Husain: What?

Jamil: Just disappear from his class. I'll tell him you are sick.

Sharif Husain: You mean that I should commit a sin myself and make you commit one, too?

Jamil: In my opinion, this is no sin. And what's the fear, even if it is? When we accumulate too many sins, we'll make a pilgrimage (**to Mecca**) in (**our**) old-age.

Sharif Husain: If you think so, you make a great mistake. It's good to make a pilgrimage, so that all Muslims of the world may assemble at one place once a year, meet one another, learn one another's circumstances, and help one another. A pilgrimage is a duty—not that a man may commit sins all his life without fear and then earn atonement by going to Mecca before death.

Jamil: All right, Mister Priest! No more of this sermon, now. The class is about to start. Let's go. I'll come to your place in the evening. Then we'll talk on this subject.

[Both go to class and sit down in their places. After one or two minutes, the teacher comes. All boys stand up as a token of respect. The teacher asks them to sit down and, taking out his register, calls the roll. The boys who are absent will be reported to the headmaster.]

Master: Do all the boys have their homework all set? Those who do not should raise their hands.

[Sharif Husain and Jamil and some other boys raise their hands.]

Master: Jamil! What's the reason for your not doing the work?

Jamil: Sir, I lost my notebook.

Master: You're always making some one excuse or another. You don't do a thing. I think you're wasting your time and your parents' money uselessly. If you don't like studying, leave school and take a job in a factory. (**Jamil hangs his head and smiles, but does not answer.**)

Master: Sarif Husain! Is your notebook also lost?

Sharif Husain: No sir, my notebook isn't lost. I have no excuse to offer. Please forgive me. This will not happen in the future.

Master: I forgive you this time. But it must never happen again. I am very happy to see that you do not make false excuses.

24.48 [20.4] **Trip to Lahore.**

[Shamshad Ali wants to go to Lahore from Naroval. His wife wants to go along with him. They consult each other about what things they should take along. Shamshad Ali thinks that they shouldn't take too much baggage.]

Shamshad: I say, do you hear (**me**)? (**No answer comes.**)
Ajī, where are you?

Kalsum (his wife): Miyā̃, you're screaming all the time. I am here in the kitchen. I'm cooking dinner for you. Won't you eat today?

Shamshad: Yes, yes, why not? But I say, there isn't too much time for the train to leave. We have to pack, too! If you tell me what things you are taking along, I'll put them together.

Kalsum: Ajī, what can I say? Don't you know, yourself? After all, you will stay in Lahore for two months. It's winter-time. We will have to take the woolen clothes—your coat, overcoat, trousers, my coat, shawls, socks and shoes, etc. All this, too, will have to be carried. And, yes, the bedding, too. After all, it isn't proper to inconvenience (**your**) relatives too much. Isn't it kind of them to give us two rooms to live in?

Shamshad: All this is fine. But you need a truck to carry all this luggage along.

Kalsum: Why do you scare me for nothing? What's the need of a truck? All this will go by train. And, it is not too much.

Shamshad: Sure, sure. (**Ironically**) Do you know that only one maund of luggage is allowed on one ticket? And your luggage would be about 20 maunds.

Kalsum: Why do you frighten me like that? If it is 20 maunds, then we'll pay some extra money.

Shamshad: Sure, you are a millionaire's wife, aren't you? Did your mother leave you a legacy of ten, twenty-thousand rupees?

Kalsum: Look here! Be careful! If you talk like that about my dead mother, then the result will be a quarrel.

Shamshad: Yes, yes, (**I know**) you love your dead mother more than you love me. This is the whole trouble. You don't care how my money is earned. You spend it like water. You would know how difficult it is if you were to earn, yourself. You sit at home comfortably. It's I who do the work.

Kalsum: All right. I am no good. I am extravagant. My mother was no good, too. Before our marriage, I was an angel. I had all the virtues. Now, after two years, you see all the vices of the world in me. Why do you beat about the bush? Why don't you say it plainly that you don't love me (**anymore**)? Divorce me and be free. Then you'll be happy. And take care of your money, yourself. Miser of Misers!!

[Kalsum's face is red with anger and tears flow from her eyes. Shamshad Ali is very upset to see his wife crying and tries to make up.]

Shamshad: Begam, you are angry with me without reason. Who says I don't love you? I love you more than ever before. After all, I am human. Sometimes I get angry and some meaningless words escape me. Please forgive me.

Kalsum: No sir. Now there is nothing between us. I will go to my father's house tomorrow. You look for another wife now.

[Shamshad runs his fingers through Kalsum's hair and kisses her. But Kalsum pushes him away. Shamshad Ali becomes very sad. Tears come into his eyes. Seeing this, Kalsum's heart melts and her anger too, disappears. The husband and wife smile at each other.]

Shamshad: Forgive me darling.

Kalsum: No, you forgive me. The fault was mine.

[**Suddenly something burns in the kitchen.**]

Kalsum: Alas! Now, what shall I do! The meat has burnt in the pot. (**Looking at Shamshad**) What will happen now?

Shamshad: It's all right. We will eat in a hotel. All this is the result of fighting with each other. Now, will you ever quarrel with me again?

Kalsum: (**Smiling**) No, never. But you started it. Now you speak. Will you do it again?

Shamshad: No, never again.

24.49 [21.3] **Conversation.**

[Hamid and Jalal are childhood friends. But they have not met each other for some years. Several days ago, Jalal went to town to buy provisions. The old friends met each other again there.]

(**Come, let's listen to their conversation.**)

Hamid: Hey! Brother Jalal, it's you! Greetings.

Jalal: Oh! My buddy, Hamid! Where have you been dear (**friend**)? We meet after a long time. Tell me, you're all right, aren't you?

Hamid: Yes, everything is all right. Thank God. Why have you come to town?

Jalal: Brother, I'm arranging my daughter's wedding. You haven't seen her. She's grown to marriageable age now.

Hamid: When is the wedding?

Jalal: On the fifteenth of the next month.

Hamid: Are all the arrangements completed?

Jalal: Yes, the jewelry is all ready and the bride's costumes are also prepared. But there's no arrangement yet for the money (**needed**) for the dinner for the bridegroom's party.

Hamid: Then, what's your idea about this matter?

Jalal: First, I thought of borrowing (**money**) from a relative or friend, so that I wouldn't have to pay interest. But my wife thinks that it isn't proper to be obliged to relatives. Now my idea is to borrow from some money-lender.

Hamid: There's one difficulty in borrowing money from money-lenders. They charge too much interest and are dishonest, too, in their bookkeeping. You are my old friend. My advice is that you try to borrow from the cooperative society.

Jalal: Friend, that I have already done. I met the inspector of the cooperative society. He was my son's classmate and is also a friend of our family. He said money could be borrowed from the society for buying seed or ploughs or animals, but not for weddings. The government regulation does not permit it.

Hamid: This is a bad thing, then. Under these circumstances, you will have to go to a money-lender. Listen to me. A new money-lender has come into our village. He has not been in business long. For this reason, he is still honest. My suggestion is that you should go to him.

Jalal: Brother, thank you very very much. I will certainly go to him. And I had forgotten the most important thing. You are the girl's uncle, aren't you? You must come to the wedding and bring along your wife and children. My wife will be very pleased to meet your wife and children.

Hamid: Why not! I will surely come and bring along my wife and children, too. Now please excuse me. My little girl is sick. I'll take the medicine from the doctor and go home to give it to the patient.

Jalal: I didn't know of your daughter's illness. It's very sad. What's her ailment?

Hamid: Friend, what should I say? First, it was just a common cold, but she slowly began to have a cough. No improvement came of the junior doctor's treatment. Now the senior doctor is giving her treatment.

Jalal: Is the girl's health now better (**than it was before**)?

Hamid: Yes, there is some difference. But not very much. You see, if the patients improve quickly, then how would the doctors earn money? They are also right.

Jalal: In my opinion, the government should open hospitals for the free treatment of all patients.

Hamid: Undoubtedly, you are correct. At election time the government always makes this promise to the people. I think that this time the members of my family and I shall give our votes to some other party.

Jalal: In my opinion, all parties are alike. They are all quick to make promises, but are all slow to fulfill their promise. In one way, the government's position is also right. Where does the government have so much money to open hospitals for everyone immediately? These things will happen slowly.

Hamid: Well, friend, I don't want to waste more of your time. Now excuse me. God willing, we will meet again.

Jalal: Very well. Good-bye.

Hamid: Good-bye.

24.50 [22.6] **The Traveller's Return.**

[Ahmad Ali came to America five years ago to get an education. After finishing his work and obtaining several big and minor degrees, he went back. The journey from New York to Karachi was by air. He boarded the railway train from Karachi to Lahore. Starting at 9:00 in the morning, the train reached Lahore at eight o'clock the next morning. His parents, brothers and sisters, friends and cronies, had all come to the station to receive him. All the people ran towards him when he got off the train. They placed garlands of flowers around his neck. The friends shook hands with him; the brothers embraced him; and his parents kissed him on the forehead.

All these people were very happy over his return. In a little while Ahmad and the rest of the people came out of the station and went home by automobiles. Ahmad Ali was hungry. All took breakfast together. It was the first occasion after many years that Ahmad Ali had sat down for a meal at home with his parents, brothers and sisters.]

Mother: Ahmad Ali, my son! Your daddy and I were restless waiting for you.

Ahmad: Mother dear, I, too, was very restless to see you.

Mother: My son didn't have any difficulties abroad, did he?

Ahmad: No, mother dear. With God's grace, everything was all right.

Younger Sister: Brother dear, what things have you brought me from America?

Baby Boy (Ahmad's nephew): Uncle dear, what have you brought for me?

[**All the children raise a clamor: Brother dear, Uncle dear! What have you brought for us?**]

Mother: Look, kiddies! Don't make noise. Don't bother my son.

Ahmad: Look brothers! Things are very expensive in America. Therefore, I thought I would buy wooden horses and pistols, etc., for you from Lahore.

[**Hearing this, all the children become sad.**]

Ahmad: Look, kids! Don't cry. I was just joking. I have brought many toys for you. They are all coming by boat.

Baby Boy: Uncle dear, you've brought a pistol for me, haven't you?

Ahmad: Yes, sonny.

Baby Boy: And an airplane, too?

Ahmad: Yes.

Baby Girl: Uncle dear, you've brought me a very very big doll, haven't you?

Father: Hey, kids, don't make any more noise, now.

[**All the children quiet down. Everyone is afraid of Grandfather.**]

Father: Ahmad, sonny, you're probably tired after this long journey. I think you should take a rest for a while.

Ahmad: No, Daddy, I'm completely all right. Mother dear, how is your health?

Mother: Son, I'm all right. Sometimes my back begins to ache. You remember that I once fell down the stairs. Since that time, whenever the cold is severe, my back begins to ache.

Ahmad: What do the doctors say?

Mother: Son, old age is the biggest of all diseases.

[**Jamila, Ahmad's (maternal) cousin, comes to see him. Ahmad and Jamila are childhood friends. Jamila is now married.**]

Ahmad: Oh, ho! This is Jamila.

Jamila: Thanks to God, you are hale and hearty.

Ahmad: Well, you're married now, aren't you? Tell me, how's your husband? (**Softly in Jamila's ear: You like him, don't you? Smiling, Jamila says "yes."**)

Jamila: My husband's all right. (**Addressing the mother**) And look at him. He's twenty-seven and is still a bachelor. Arrange his marriage.

Ahmad: Just listen to her! She's ready to arrange my marriage now.

Mother: Well, we won't interfere in this matter. With God's grace, Ahmad is mature and wise. He may marry whenever and whomever he likes. (**Addressing Ahmad's father**) eh! That's right, isn't it?

Father: Undoubtedly, undoubtedly! (**The father dismisses many things with his "undoubtedly."**)

Mother: Please do say something besides "undoubtedly" sometimes.

Father: Wife, you get angry without reason. What I mean is that your idea is right.

[**The doorbell rings. Ahmad's friends have come to see him. Ahmad goes to the living-room to meet his friends.**]

24.51 [23.6] **Remembrance of Times Past.**

[Ikram Ullah is a head-clerk in the commissioner's office. He is a good-looking, middle-aged man. His face has a look of knowledge and experience. The commissioner hasn't come to the office yet, therefore Ikram Ullah has nothing special to do. Sitting in a chair in his room, he is smoking a cigarette. He is reminiscing. He recalls that at one time he was a little boy. His father ran a small-goods shop. The shop had good business. The profit was substantial. Ikram Ullah's parents were well-to-do. They thought a lot about their son's education. When he was five, his father got him admitted to a school. There were several other boys and girls of his age in the school. Ikram Ullah was clever from his childhood. He did his school work industriously. The school-master was kind to him. Passing two grades in one year, he soon reached the sixth grade. Master Narindar Nath taught Geography to the Sixth Grade. This master was very cruel. The boy who didn't memorize his lesson got beaten. The master had a black-colored stick. With that he beat the students. One day Ikram Ullah did not learn his geography-lesson and got a very severe beating. His hands were hurt and his rib began to pain. All the boys who were in the class first became frightened; but when some time passed, they began to get angry. After some time, the bell rang and the Master went out. The school was closed (**for the day**). All the boys ran towards Ikram.]

Mansur: Friend. This master is very cruel. Look, he has inflicted these wounds on Ikram's hands with his beating.

Indar: Friends. I say, damn this master. We should do something about him.

Majid: (**Majid is a very tall, strong boy and takes part in wrestling.**) What "something?" We'll give this master a thrashing. And leave him when he asks forgiveness.

Karim: Yes, yes. You're all like lions when it come to talking. Who will step forward and seize the master?

Majid: Mr. Karim, sir, you specialize in talking. We do the work. Your tongue works and our hand works. If you all stick through with me, then I will give Master Narindar Nath such a thrashing that he'll come to his senses. Now speak out, will you stick through with me?

Zohra: No, brother, We are afraid. If you beat the master, then the report will go to the headmaster. Then, we all will be expelled from school.

Majid: Friends. These girls have placed us in great difficulty. I can't understand why they come to the boys' school. They should have remained in their girls' school. Cowards.

Asiya: Look, Mr. Majid. We aren't cowards. We have as much sympathy for Ikram as you have. We only say, do it legally. Don't do such a thing which harms all (**of us**) and makes us repent.

Majid. All right (**my**) lady. Very well. But your idea is that we do not do anything. Today, Ikram got beaten; tomorrow someone else will get beaten similarly. You are girls, after all. Therefore, no one can do a thing to you. The misery is for us boys.

Asiya: I suggest a plan. Report this to the headmaster. He will fix Master Narindar Nath up.

Indra: Yes, yes. That's right. Oh, Jamil, you are the class-monitor. You take a delegation of four or five boys (**to the headmaster**). Ask him to give us some other master in the place of Master Narindar Nath, otherwise we will go over to the other school. If the headmaster does not take any action, then Ikram's daddy can sue the school.

[All the boys like this suggestion. They selected four boys and two girls to go to the headmaster. These six people, taking Ikram along, went to the headmaster's house. By chance, Master Narindar Nath was also present. The boys and girls told the whole story to the headmaster. As these people told their story the color left Master Narindar Nath's (**face**). The headmaster looked now at the boys and now at Master Narindar Nath. He got very angry when he saw the bruises on Ikram's hands. He promised that he would have Master Narindar Nath transferred to some other place.]

[Remembering this incident, Ikram Ullah smiles. Lying in the ash-tray, his cigarette has burned out. The office-boy comes in and says that the commissioner has come and is asking for Ikram.]

LESSON 25

25.1

jō ādmī khēt-mē̃ kām kar rahā hai, vo kisān hai.	The man, who is working in the field, is a farmer.
jō ādmī khēt-mē̃ kām kar rahē haĩ, vo kisān haĩ.	The men, who are working in the field, are farmers.
jō aurat ghar-kē sāmnē baiṭhī hai, vo mērī mā̃ hai.	The woman, who is seated in front of the house, is my mother.
jō aurtē̃ ghar-kē sāmnē baiṭhī haĩ, vo mērī bahnē̃ haĩ.	The women, who are seated in front of the house, are my sisters.
jō pānī daryā-sē ātā hai, vo maĩ nahī̃ pī saktā.	I cannot drink the water, which comes from the river.
jō tālibilm Sindhī sīkhnā cāhtā hai, us-kō bahot paṛhnā cāhiyē.	The student, who wants to learn Sindhi, should study a lot.
jis gāy-kē pīchē bachṛā dauṛ rahā hai, vo us-kī mā̃ hai.	The cow, behind which the calf is running, is its mother.
jis saṛak-sē ham jā rahē hai, vo bāzār-kō jātī hai.	The road, by which we are going, goes to the bazaar.
jin ādmiyō̃-kā maĩ intazār kar rahā hū̃, vo mērē bhāī haĩ.	The men, for whom I am waiting, are my brothers.
jin ādmīyō̃-kī kitābē̃ maĩ-nē paṛhī thī̃, un-kē sāth maĩ-nē bāt kī.	I talked with the men, whose books I had read.

This section and those following deal with the Urdu equivalents of English relative constructions.

This section is concerned with the relative adjective, **jō**, which has the same forms for the masculine and feminine genders. The subject form, singular and plural, is **jō**; the object form, singular, is **jis**; and the object form, plural, is **jin.**

In the English examples above the relative forms are all pronouns—i.e., **who, whom, which, whose.** (For purpose of facility in recognition the relative clauses have been marked off by commas.) The English noun to which the relative pronoun refers is transferred in the Urdu construction into the relative clause and is modified by the relative adjective. The appropriate form of the personal pronoun, **vo,** represents the noun in the main or independent clause.

Compare the first sentence, **The man, who is working in the field, is a farmer.** and the Urdu, translated literally, **Which man (jō ādmī) is working in the field, he (vo) is a farmer.**; the seventh sentence, **The cow, behind which the calf is running, is its mother.**, and the Urdu, **Behind which cow (jis gāy-) the calf is running, it (vo) is its mother.**; and the tenth sentence, **I talked with the men, whose books I had read.**, and the Urdu, **Which men's books I had read, I spoke with them.**

25.1.1 More examples are:

jō sāhab kal yahā̃ thē, vo mērē vālid haĩ.	The gentleman, who was here yesterday, is my father.
jō k̤hātūn un-kē sāth thī̃, vo mērī mā haĩ.	The woman, who was with them, is my mother.
jō kitāb mēz-par hai, vo mērī hai.	The book, which is on the table, is mine.
jō ādmī ye jāntā hai, vo āp-kō batāēgā.	The man, who knows this, will tell you.
jis ghar-kē sāmnē maĩ khēl rahā hū̃, vo mērē vālid-kā hai.	The house, in front of which I am playing, is my father's.
jis ādmī-nē ye banāyā, vo acchā lōhār hai.	The man, who made this, is a good ironsmith.
jis aurat-nē khānā pakāyā, us-nē usē nahī̃ khāyā.	The woman, who cooked the food, did not eat it.
jis daryā-mē̃ ham tair rahē thē, vo gahrā thā.	The river, in which we were swimming, was deep.
jin ādmiyō̃-nē kitāb paṛhī, kyā unhō̃-nē vo pasand nahī̃ kī?	Didn't the men, who read the book, like it?
jin k̤hanjarō̃-kī mujhē zarūrat hai, vo yahā̃ nahī̃ haĩ.	The daggers, (**which**) I need, are not here.
jis darak̤ht-kē nīcē maĩ baithā hū̃, kyā vo ēk baṛ hai?	Is the tree, under which I am seated, a banyan tree?
jis kuē̃-sē ham pānī lētē haĩ, vo nadī-kē nazdīk hai.	The well, from which we take water, is near the stream.
jō bandūk āp-nē mujhē vapas dī, vo mērī nahī̃ hai.	The gun, which you returned to me, is not mine.
jis ṭōpī-par āp baiṭhē haĩ, kyā vo mērī hai?	Is the cap, upon which you are seated, mine?
jis kursī-par āp baiṭh rahē haĩ, us-mē̃ ēk kīl hai.	There is a nail in the chair, on which you are sitting.
jō miṭhāī halvāī-nē mērē liyē banāyī, vo bahot acchī thī̃.	The sweetmeats, which the sweetmeat-maker made for me, were very good.

REMARKS: (1) **usē** is very often used in place of **us-kō,** and **unhē̃** in place of **un-kō**; similarly, **isē** for **is-kō** and **inhē̃** for **in-kō**

(2) **kīl** (ī) nail, **baṛ** (ā) banyan tree, **baṛhaī** (ā) carpenter, **nazdīk** (adv.) near, **-kē nazdīk** (variant of **-kē pās**) near, **zarūrat** (ī) need, necessity, **k̤hanjar** (ā) dagger, **bandūk** (ī) gun, **halvāī** (ā) sweetmeat-maker.

25.1.2 Exercise 1. **Translate into English.**

1. jō pānī nadī-sē āyā, vo maī pīnā nahī̃ cāhtā. 2. jis ādmī-kā tum intazār kar rahē thē, vo śahar-mē̃ thā. 3. jō mōṭargāṛī ghar-kē sāmnē hai, vo mērī hai. 4. jō saṛak śahar jātī hai, kyā vo lambī hai? 5. jō kapṛē dhōbī vāpas lāyā, vō sāf nahī̃ haī. 6. jis kursī-kī marammat āp-nē kī, vo kahā̃ hai? 7. jin cīzō̃-kī mujhē zarūrat hai, vo sab ghar-mē̃ haī. 8. jis laṛkē-kō lakṛī kāṭnā hai, vo kyū̃ nahī̃ pahō̃cā? 9. jō gāṛī sṭēśan-mē̃ vaḳt-par āyī, vo ḍākgāṛī nahī̃ hai. 10. jis ādmī-nē mujhē ye kitāb dī, us-nē usē likhā thā. 11. jis sāmān-kē pās bairā hai, vo mērā hai. 12. jō mōzē naukar-nē sāf kiyē, vo kahā̃ hai? 13. jis ustarē-kā tum istēmāl kar rahē hō, vo bahot tēz hai. 14. jin aurtō̃-kā āp intazār kar rahē haī, vo vaḳt-par nahī̃ ā saktī̃. 15. jō ādmī kuē̃-kē pās haī, vo kaun haī?

25.1.3 Exercise 2. **Translate into Urdu:**

1. The man, who is plucking flowers from the plants, is our gardener. 2. Where are the shoes, (**which**) the shoemaker repaired? 3. The books, (**which**) I bought, are on the table. 4. Was the man, who was talking with you, speaking in Urdu? 5. Who are the people, for whom you are working? 6. The man, who doesn't have enough money, cannot travel. 7. Farmers, who have small plows, have to work hard. 8. I want the bearer, who can speak Urdu. 9. Who is the man, who was repairing my automobile? 10. Where are the things you need? 11. The man, who has travelled by train, will not want to travel by oxcart. 12. Who is the coolie, who placed my luggage in the train? 13. Which is the bullock, which can carry the largest load? 14. The men, whose help we need, will come tomorrow. 15. Where is the servant, who has to prepare my bed?

25.2

vo ādmī, jō khēt-mē̃ pehrā dē rahē haī, caukidār hai.	The man, who is watching in the field, is a watchman.
vo ādmī, jō khēt-mē̃ pehrā dē rahē haī, caukidār haī.	The men, who are watching in the field, are watchmen.
vo aurat, jō ghar-kē sāmnē baiṭhī hai, mērī mā̃ hai.	The woman, who is seated in front of the house, is my mother.
vo aurtē̃, jō ghar-kē sāmnē baiṭhī haī, mērī bahnē̃ haī.	The women, who are seated in front of the house, are my sisters.
vo sāhab, jō ghar-kē sāmnē kaṛē haī, mērē māmū̃ haī.	The gentleman, who is standing in front of the house, is my (**maternal**) uncle.
vo sāhab, jis-kē sāth maī bāt kar rahā thā, mērē cācā haī.	The gentleman, with whom I was talking, is my (**paternal**) uncle.
vo lōg, jō hamārī taraf ā rahē haī, mērē vāldain haī.	The people, who are coming towards us, are my parents.
vo laṛkī, jis-kē āgē vo cal rahē haī, mērī bahan hai.	The girl, in front of whom they are walking, is my sister.
vo chōṭē laṛkē, jin-kē pīchē vo dauṛ rahē haī, mērē chōṭē bhāī haī.	The little boys, after whom they are running, are my younger brothers.
vo jūtē, jō mērē liyē bahot chōṭē thē, maī-nē bhāī-kō diyē.	I gave the shoes, which were too small for me, to (**my**) cousin.
mērī vo cācī, jō hamē̃ milnē-kō āyī thī, us-kō mērī mā̃-nē lāl jūtē diyē.	My mother gave (**a pair of**) red shoes to my (**paternal**) aunt, who had come to visit us.

vo aurat, jis-nē mujhē ye miṭhāī dī, mērī mumānī hai.	The woman, who gave me this candy, is my (**maternal**) aunt.
vo mēz, jis-kī mujhē zarūrat hai, kōnē-mē̃ hai.	The table, which I need, is in the corner.
vo śāl, jō maī-nē āp-kō diyā, Kaśmir-mē̃ bānā thā.	The shawl, which I gave you, was made in Kashmir.
vo baṅglā, jō daryā-kē kinārē-par hai, bilkul nayā hai.	The bungalow, which is on the bank of the river, is completely new.
vo khēt, jō daryā-kē kinārē-par hai, bahot zarḳhēz hai.	The field, which is on the bank of the river, is very fertile.

This section is concerned with the relative pronoun, **jō,** which has the same forms as the relative adjective, with the exception that **jisē** is often found in the place of **jis-kō** and **jinhē** in the place of **jin-kō.** (See 25.1.1, Remarks 1.) **jinhō̃** is the form which occurs before the postposition **-nē.** Compare the first sentence, **The man, who is working in the field, is a farmer.,** and the literal Urdu translation, **That** (**vo**) **man, who is working in the field, is a farmer.**; the sixth sentence, **The gentleman, with whom I am talking, is my** (paternal) **uncle,** and the Urdu, **That** (**vo**) **man, with whom I am talking, is my uncle.**; the eighth sentence, **The girl, in front of whom they are walking, is my sister.,** and the Urdu, **That** (**vo**) **girl, in front of whom they are walking, is my sister.**

The Urdu construction follows the English closely. The English article **the,** when stressed, is translated into Urdu by the demonstrative adjective **vo,** that.

The difference between this construction and that described in section 25.1 can be ascribed to the place where the emphasis is directed in the English sentence. The construction described here is employed to translate English relative sentences in which emphasis is placed upon the article **the,** modifying the noun to which the relative word refers. (See the sentences at the beginning of this commentary and the underlined words.) The construction of section 25.1 indicates no special stress falling on the article modifying the noun to which the relative refers.

REMARKS: 1) Very often either one of the Urdu constructions described in sections 25.1 and 25.2 will be found translating the English sentences of 25.1 and 25.2.

(2) The children of brothers and sisters, that is cousins, are indicated in Urdu by the words for **brother** and **sister, bhāī** and **bahan.** These are the terms employed by the children of a brother or sister when referring to the children of another brother or sister. For more precise designation the adjectives **cacāzād** (**related through paternal uncle**) and **māmū̃zād** (**related through maternal uncle**) are employed—e.g., **māmū̃zād bhāī, mām-ū̃zād bahan, cacāzād bhāī, cacāzād bahan.**

(3) **khaṛā** (adj.) erect, standing upright, **khaṛā hōnā** to stand, **cācā** (ā) paternal uncle, **cācī** (ī) paternal aunt, **māmū̃** (ā) maternal uncle, **mumānī** (ī) maternal aunt, **tāyāzād** (**adj., n.c.**) related through older brother of father, **pehrā dēnā** to watch, guard, **caukidār** (ā) watchman, **sāhab** (ā) gentleman, **śāl** (ī) shawl, **baṅglā** (ā) bungalow.

25.2.1 Exercise 1. **Translate into English:**

1. kyā vo saṛak, jō śahar jātī hai, lambī hai? 2. vō ādmī, jis-nē mujhē ye kitāb dī, mērē cacā hai. 3. vo lōg, jō hamārē sāmnē cal rahē haī, mērē vāldain haī. 4. vo ādmī, jō daryā-kē kinārē-par ṭhahar rahā hai, kaun hai? 5. vo pānī, jō daryā-sē āyā, maī pīnā nahī̃

cāhtā. 6. vo aurat, jō kuē̃-kē pās hai, mērī mumānī hai. 7. us rīch-kō, jō jañgal-mē̃ bakrē-kō khī̃ctā thā, śikārī-nē mārā. 8. vo naukar, jō bahot acchā thā, gā̃ō̃ vāpas gayā. 9. vo ādmī, jis-kā tum intazār kar rahē thē, śahar-mē̃ thā. 10. us laṛkī-nē, jis-kē sāth maĩ-nē Hindī bōlī, mērī bāt galat samjhī. 11. vo kārīgar, jis-kō mērī mōṭargāṛī-kī marammat karnā paṛā, nahī̃ āyā. 12. vo kursī, jis-kī marammat āp-nē kī, kahā̃ hai? 13. vo khānā, jō āp śahar-sē vāpas lāyā, āp-nē kahā̃ rakhā? 14. us laṛkē-kō, jis-nē mujhē madad dēnī-kī kōśiś kī, maĩ nahī̃ jāntā. 15. vo mōṭargāṛī, jō ghar-kē sāmnē hai, mērī hai.

25.2.2 Exercise 2. **Translate into Urdu:**

1. The man, who is working in the garden, is our gardener. 2. Was the woman, who was talking with you, your (**maternal**) aunt? 3. Who are the people, for whom you are waiting? 4. Can the man, who doesn't have enough money, travel? 5. Where are the shoes, (**which**) the shoemaker repaired? 6. I want the bearer, who can speak Urdu. 7. Who is the coolie, who placed my luggage in the train? 8. The road, by which we will go, goes to the city. 9. The gentleman, for whom I am waiting, is my (**maternal**) uncle. 10. The cow, behind which the calf is running, is its mother. 11. The house, in front of which I am playing, is my (**paternal**) aunt's. 12. Please bring me the things, (**which**) I will need for my journey. 13. Where are the clothes, (**which**) the washerman brought back yesterday? 14. Whose is the fertile field, which is on the bank of the river? 15. The cap, upon which you are seated, is my (**paternal**) uncle's.

25.3. Text 8: **Kahvāḳhānā** [1]

Translate into English. Answer the questions in Urdu:

[dōstō̃[2] āō. āj tumhē̃ Lāhōr-kē ēk maśhūr[3] kahvāḳhānē-kī sair karāē̃. is-kā nām "Pākistān Kāfī Hāus"[4] hai. ye kahvāḳhānā śahar-kī sab-sē ḳhūbsūrat aur bāraunaḳ[5] saṛak, yānī,[6] Māl Rōḍ[7] -par vāḳē[8] hai. in-kā mālik Karācī-kā ēk sēṭh[9] hai. vo bēhad[10] amīr ādmī hai. us-kē kaī kārḳhānē, dukānē̃ aur hōṭal haĩ. is kahvāḳhānē-mē̃ kōī cālīs-kē ḳarīb mēzē̃ haĩ. ām-taur-par[11] kālijō̃-kē tālibilm aur prōfaisar[12] yahā̃ ātē haĩ. in-kē ilāvā kuch vakīl,[13] aḳhbār•navis,[14] musannif[15] aur śāir•lōg[16] -bhī yahā̃ vaḳt kāṭnē[17] -kē liyē ātē haĩ. bāyē̃ kōnē-mē̃ ēk mēz hai. us mēz-par Kurbān Alī,[18] Vahīd Ḳhā̃[18] aur un-kē kuch dōst har rōz śām-kē vaḳt ākar[19] baiṭhtē haĩ. Kurbān Alī yūnivarsiṭī[20] -mē̃ paṛhātā hai. Vahīd Ḳhā-bhī paṛhātā hai. lēkin yūnivarsiṭī-mē̃ nahī̃, balke[21] gavarmeṇṭ[22] ḳālij[23] -mē̃. dōnō̃-kō pā̃c pā̃c[24] sau rūpayē tanḳhāh[25] miltī hai. jab ye lōg śām-kē vaḳt ātē haĩ, tō bairā[26] un-kē pās aurḍar[27] lēnē-kē liyē ātā hai. bairē-kā nām Śahāb Dīn hai. ye lōg kaī sālō̃-sē yahā̃ ātē haĩ aur Śahāb Dīn-bhī kaī sālō̃-sē yahā̃ haĩ. bairē aur in lōgō̃-kē darmiyān[28] is tarāh guftagū[29] hōtī hai.]

Śahāb Dīn: Prōfaisar•Sāhab, sālām•arz kartā[30] hū̃.

Kurbān Alī: sunāō, bhāī, Śahāb Dīn! acchē tō hō na?[31]

Śahāb Dīn: jī,[32] bilkul acchā hū̃. āp-kē jān-ō-māl[33] -kō dūā dētā[34] hū̃. farmāiyē[35] kyā hukam[36] haĩ.

Vahīd Ḳhā̃: bhāī, bas,[37] kahvā[38] pīyē̃gē. cār ādmiyō-kē liyē lē āō.

Śahāb Dīn: ṭhanḍā yā garm?

Kurbān Alī: bhāī, ham tō pīyē̃gē ṭhanḍā. bāḳī sab-lōg garm pīyē̃gē.

Śahāb Dīn: sāhab, āp apnē kahvē-mē̃ dūdh pasand kartē haĩ yā krīm.[40]

[is mez-par is vaḳt ēk Amrīkan laṛkā baiṭhā hai. us-kā nām Ṭhāmsan[41] hai. vo kuch mahīnō̃-sē Pākistān-kī sair karnē-kē liyē safar kartā hai. vo har rōz apnē Pākistānī[42] dōstō̃-sē Urdū bōltā hai. lēkin us-kī Urdū abhī kuch ṭūṭī•phūṭī[43] hai.]

Ṭhāmsan: Śahōb Dīn! dud aur kharīm-mẽ khayā fark hai?

Śahāb Dīn: janāb,[44] maĩ kyā arz karū̃? [45] dūdh dūdh hai aur krīm krīm hai. hã̄, aur krīmvālē kahvē [46] -kī ḳīmat [47] dō ānē zyādā hai.

Vahīd Ḳhã̄:   Śahāb Dīn, sab-kē liyē krīmvālā kahvā lāō. aur, dēkhō, bil [48] hamārē pās lānā.[49]

Śahāb Dīn: bahotbehtar,[50] janāb. (calā jātā [51] hai.)

Vahīd Ḳhã̄:   dēkhō, yār Ṭhamsan! tum-kō bār bār [52] samjhātē [53] haĩ ke [54] krīm-kō tō "kharīm" na kahā kahō.

Ṭhāmsan: Vahīd, bahot śukriyā. maĩ kōśīś kartā hū̃. inśā Allah ēk din [55] ṭhīk sīkh jāū̃gā.

Kurbān Alī: maĩ-nē kahā, yārō, kōī ḳhabar sunāō!

Ṭhāmsan: kyā ḳhabar sunōgē. ham ēk bāt batāē̃.

Vahīd Ḳhã̄:   hã̄, Ṭhāmsan, zarūr.

Ṭhāmsan: hamārā ḳhayāl hai ke [54] ham Pākistān-kē bārē-mẽ ēk kitāb fauran likhẽ.

Kurbān Alī: Ṭhāmsan! tum kitnī dēr-sē Pākistān-mẽ hō?

Ṭhāmsan: dō mahīnē-sē.

Vahīd Ḳhã̄:   kyā tumhārā ḳhayāl hai ke [54] dō mahīnē yahā̃ rahnē-kē bād tum Pākistān-kō acchī tarāh samajhtē hō?

Ṭhāmsan: nahī̃. maĩ Pākistān-kō acchī tarāh tō nahī̃ jāntā. lēkin kaī Amrīkan aur Aṅgrēz [56] siraf ēk haftā Dillī-mẽ rahkar [57] apnē āp-kō Cīn [58] aur Jāpān [59] -kē bārē-mẽ kitābē̃ likhnē-kē ḳābil [60] samajhtē [61] haĩ. maĩ tō Pākistān-kō thōṛā bahot [62] jāntā hū̃ aur kitāb-bhī Pākistān-hī-kē bārē-mẽ likhnā cāhtā hū̃.

Kurbān Alī: tum ṭhīk kahtē hō. lēkin phir-bhī [63] hamārā ḳhāyāl hai ke [54] tumhẽ is mulk-kō thōṛā aur [64] dēkhnā cāhiyē aur us-kē bād kitāb likhnā cāhiyē.

Ṭhāmsan: acchā. maĩ tumhārī bāt-par gaur karū̃gā.[65]

[Śahāb Dīn kahvā lēkar [66] ātā hai. sab dōst apnē pyālō̃-mẽ kahvā ḍālkar [67] pītē haĩ.]

Sarvar Ahmad: (Vahīd-kō mūḳhātib karkē [68]) yār prōfaisar, sunāō. tumhārē kālij-kā kyā hāl hai?

Vahīd Ḳhã̄:   ṭhīk·ṭhāk hai, bhāī. kyū̃? kyā bāt hai?

Sarvar Ahmad: kōī ḳhās bāt nahī̃. mērā chōṭā bhāī vahā̃ paṛhtā hai. zarā us-par nazar rakhā karō.[69]

Vahīd Ḳhã̄:   hã̄, hã̄, zarūr. tum sunāō, tumhārē daftar-kī āj·kal [70] kyā siyāsat [71] hai?

Kurbān Alī: arē,[72] ye kyā tum daftar aur kālij-kī bātē̃ kartē rahtē [73] hō. kōī aur bāt karō. Vahīd Ḳhã̄, yār, tum kōī gazal [74] sunāō.

Vahīd Ḳhã̄:   Kurbān Alī, is vakt tō kōī yād nahī̃ hai.

Sarvar Ahmad: lō,[75] ab ye naḳhrā karē̃gē.[76]

Vahīd Ḳhã̄:   Sarvar·Sāhab, is-mẽ naḳhrē-kī kōī bāt nahī̃. mujhē is vakt vākaī [77] kōī yād nahī̃. śāyad thōṛī dēr-mẽ yād ā jāē.[78] jū̃-hī kōī zehan-mẽ [79] āēgī, āp-kō sunāū̃gā.

savālāt:

1. Śahāb Dīn kaun hai aur vo kitnē sālō̃-sē Kāfī Hāus-mẽ hai? 2. kōnēvālī mēz [80] -par kaun lōg śām-kē vakt baiṭhtē haĩ? 3. Ṭhāmsan-kē bārē-mẽ tum jō kuch jāntē hō batāō! 4. Kurbān Alī aur Vahīd Ḳhã̄ kyā kām kartē haĩ? 5. Kāfī Hāus-mẽ ām-taur-par kaun lōg ātē haĩ?

NOTES: 1. coffee-house (ā); 2. friends (**voc. pl., msc.**); 3. famous (**adj., n.c.**); 4. Pakistan Coffee House (ā); 5. busy (**adj., n.c.**); 6. that is to say; 7. Mall Road (ī); 8. situated (**adj., n.c.**); 9. millionaire (ā); 10. limitless (**adj., n.c.**); 11. usually (**adv.**); 12. professor (ā); 13. lawyer (ā); 14. journalist (ā); 15. author (ā); 16. poet (ā); 17. **vaḳt kāṭnā** to kill time (**tr.**); 18. man's name; 19. having come, see 30.1; 20. university (ī); 21. instead (**conj.**); 22. government (**adj., n.c.**); 23. college (ā); 24. for the repetition see 36.2; 25. salary (ī); 26. waiter (ā); 27. order, request (ā); 28. **-kē darmayān** between (**postpos. phrase**); 29. conversation (ī); 30. **sālām • arz karnā** to greet (**tr.**); 31. = aren't you; 32. sir; 33. well-being (ā); 34. **dūā dēnā** to pray (**tr.**); 35. please tell; 36. order (ā); 37. well (**adv.**); 38. coffee (ā); 39. **lē ānā** to bring (**int.**), cf. **lānā** which is a contraction of this; 40. cream (ī) English loan word; 41. Thompson; 42. Pakistani (**adj., n.c.**); 43. broken (**adj.**); 44. sir; 45. **arz karnā** to grant, yield (**tr.**); 46. **krīmvālā kahvā** coffee with cream, for **vālā** see 31.2; 47. price (ī); 48. bill (ā); 49. bring, the infinitive can function as a polite imperative; 50. very well; 51. **calā jānā** to go away, off (**int.**); 52. time after time, for the repetition see 36.2; 53. **samjhānā** to explain (**tr.**), see 36.1, ff.; 54. see 29.2; 55. **ēk din** some day, one day; 56. Englishman (ā); 57. having stayed, see 30.1; 58. China (ā); 59. Japan (ā) 60. **-kē ḳābil** worthy of (**postpos. phrase**); 61. = consider; 62. **thōṛā bahot** somewhat; 63. still (**adv.**); 64. **thōṛā aur** little more; 65. **g̱aur karnā** to think over, consider (**tr.**); 66. taking, see 30.1; 67. having poured, see 30.1; 68. **muḳhātib karkē** addressing, see 30.1; 69. **nazar rakhā karnā** to keep an eye on (**tr.**); 70. these days, now-a-days (**adv.**); 71. politics (ī); 72. oh!; 73. see 34.3; 74. lyrical poem (ī); 75. look!; 76. **naḳhrā karnā** to elicit insistence, coax, (**tr.**); 77. in fact, in reality (**adv.**); 78. **ā jānā** to come (**int.**), see lesson 28; 79. in mind, to mind; 80. the table in the corner, see 31.2 for **vālā**.

LESSON 26

26.1

jis ādmī-kō maī-nē paisē diyē, ye vo-hī hai.	This is **the** (or **that**) man, to whom I gave the money.
jin ādmiyō̃-kō maī-nē paisē diyē, ye vo-hī haī.	These are **the** (or **those**) men, to whom I gave the money.
jis aurat-kē liyē maī lakṛī lāyī, ye vo-hī hai.	This is **the** (or **that**) woman, for whom I brought the wood.
jin aurtō̃-kē liyē maī lakṛī lāyī, ye vo-hī hai.	These are **the** (or **those**) women, for whom I brought the wood.
jō tālibilm Fārsī sīkhnā cāhtā hai, usī-kō bahot paṛhnā cāhiyē.	**The** student, who wants to learn Persian, should study a lot.
jō tālibilm Paśtō sīkhnā cāhtē haī, un-hī-kō bahot paṛhnā cāhiyē.	**Those** students, who want to learn Pashtu, should study a lot.
jis kitāb-kī mujhē zarūrat hai, vo-hī yahā̃ nahī̃ hai.	**The** (i.e., **that**) book, (which) I need, is not here.
jin kitābō̃-kī mujhē zarūrat hai, vo-hī yahā̃ nahī̃ haī.	**The** (i.e., **those**) books, (which) I need, are not here.
jis kursī-par āp baiṭh rahē haī, usī-mē̃ ēk kīl hai.	There is a nail in **the** (i.e., **that**) chair, on which you are sitting.
jin ādmiyō̃-kī kitābē̃ maī-nē paṛhī thī, un-hī-kē sāth maī-nē bāt kī.	I talked with **those** men, whose books I had read.

The construction illustrated in this section is identical with that of section 25.1 with the exception that in the English sentences of this section the article, **the,** (or the demonstrative adjective, **that, those**) is emphasized. This emphasis is indicated in Urdu by attaching the particle, **-ī,** or **-hī,** to the forms of the demonstrative pronoun **vo.** (**-ī** is attached to the object singular forms, and **-hī** to the subject singular form and to all the plural forms.) Compare the first English sentence, **This is the** (or **that) man, to** whom I gave the money.**, and the literal Urdu translation, **To which man I gave the money, this is that (one).**; the second English sentence, **These are the** (or **those**) **men, to whom I gave the money.**, and the literal Urdu translation, **To which men I gave the money, these are those.**; the fifth English sentence, **The student, who wants to learn Persian, should study a lot.**, and the literal Urdu translation, **Which student wants to learn Persian, he** (or **that one**) **should study a lot.**; and the tenth English sentence, **I talked with those men, whose books I had read.**, and the literal Urdu translation, **Which men's books I had read, with them** (or **those**) **I talked**.

REMARKS: When in the drill exercises, following, this construction is expected, the article or demonstrative adjective will be set in boldface in the English sentence, thus: **the, that, those.**

26.1.1

ye-hī vo ādmī hai, jisē maĩ-nē inām diyā.	**This** is the man, to whom I gave the reward.
ye-hī vo ādmī haĩ, jinhẽ maĩ-nē inām diyā.	**These** are the men, to whom I gave the reward.
ye-hī vo aurat hai, jis-kē liyē maĩ lakṛī lāyā.	**This** is the woman, for whom I brought the wood.
ye-hī vo aurtẽ haĩ, jin-kē liyē maĩ lakṛī lāyā.	**These** are the women, for whom I brought the wood.
ye-hī vo barsātī hai, jis-kē maĩ talāś kar rahā thā.	**This** is the raincoat, for which I was looking.
ye-hī vo bijlī-kī battiyā̃ haĩ, jin-kī āp-kō marammat karnā hōgā.	**These** are the electric lights you will have to fix.

This section illustrates the Urdu consruction for English sentences whose independent clauses contain the demonstrative pronoun **this** (or **these**) which is emphasized (here set in boldface) in utterance.

REMARKS: (1) When in the drill exercises, following, this construction is expected, the demonstrative pronouns will be set in boldface in the English sentences, thus: **this, these.**

(2) **inām** (ā) reward, **talāś** (ī) search, **[-kī] talāś karnā** to search, to look for, **battī** (ī) lamp, wick, **bijlī-kī battī** electric lamp, **bijlī** (ī) electricity, lightning, **barsātī** (ī) raincoat.

26.1.2 Exercise 1. **Translate into English:**

1. jis kuẽ-sē ham pānī lētē haĩ, ye vo-hī hai. 2. jō gāṛī is sṭēśan-mẽ āyī, usī-mẽ bahot lōg nahĩ thē. 3. ye-hī vo saṛak hai, jis-sē ham bāzār jātē haĩ. 4. jō bairā daraḳht-kē nīcē sō rahā hai, usī-kō kām karnā hōgā. 5. jō khānā āp-nē mērē liyē pakāyā, kyā ye vo-hī hai? 6. kyā ye-hī vo khānā hai, jō āp-nē mērē liyē pakāyā? 7. jis ādmī-nē mujhē ye kitāb dī, usī-nē usē likhā thā. 8. ye-hī vo jūtē haĩ, jō maĩ-nē kal bāzār-mẽ ḳharīdē. 9. ye-hī vo khēt haĩ, jō zarḳhēz haĩ. 10. jō kapṛē dhōbī kal vāpas lāyā, vo-hī sāf nahĩ thē.

26.1.3 Exercise 2. **Translate into Urdu:**

1. This is **the** hat I was looking for. 2. Are **these** the people you are waiting for? 3. Is

this the man, who is working on the bank of the river? 4. This is **the** bearer I need. 5. Are **those** people, who are coming towards us, your parents? 6. **These** are the newspapers you should read. 7. Fix **that** automobile which is before my house. 8. Bring me **those** letters which came today. 9. **These** are the people I want to ask questions. 10. Clean **the** shoes which are under the bed.

26.2

jō-bhī aurat kuē̃-kō gayī, apnē sāth pānī lāyī.	Whichever woman went to the well, brought water with her.
jō-bhī aurat pānī lāyī, baṛē daraḵht-kē pās-sē guzrī.	Whichever woman brought water, passed by the large tree.
jō-bhī lōg kamrē-mē̃ āyē, unhō̃-nē phir bāhar jānā cāhā.	Whatever people came into the room, wanted to go out again.
jis-nē-bhī ye kiyā, vo bēvaḵūf hai.	Whoever did this, is a fool.
jō-bhī aisā ḵhayāl kartā hai, vo aur zyādā bēvaḵūf hai.	Whoever thinks so, is a greater fool.
jis-nē-bhī ye sunā, us-nē mujhē batāyā.	Whoever heard this, told (**it**) to me.
jis ādmī-nē-bhī vahā̃ kuch khāyā, vo phir kabhī vahā̃ nahī̃ gayā.	Whichever man ate anything there, never went there again.
jō-bhī pāltū jānvar jaṅgal-mē̃ gayē, phir bāhar nahī̃ āyē.	Whichever pet animals went into the jungle, did not come out again.
jin mazdūrō̃-nē-bhī āp-kē liyē kām kiyā, un-kō inām dījiyē.	Give, whichever laborers worked for you, a reward.
jō-bhī lōg mēlē-mē̃ āyē, unhō̃-nē bahot-sī dilcasp cīzē̃ dēkhī̃.	Whichever people came to the fair, saw many interesting things.
āp jis-kō-bhī jāntē haī, us-kē sāth Panjābī bōlē̃.	Speak Panjabi, with whomever you know.

This section illustrates the Urdu construction for English relative constructions, the relative words of which have **ever** attached to them—e.g., **whoever, whichever, whatever.** This is rendered in Urdu by the particle **-bhī.** The Urdu construction, therefore, is the same as that described in section 25.1, with one addition—the emphatic particle **-bhī** is attached to the subject form of the relative word or to the postposition governing the object form of the relative word.

REMARKS: (1) **apnā** functions as a relative adjective, employed to refer back to the subject of the principal verb. (Compare sentence 1.)

(2) The emphatic particle, **-bhī,** when attached to nouns and pronouns, translates English **too, also.**

(3) **ḵhayāl** (ā) opinion, **bēvaḵūf** (ā) fool, **pāltū jānvar** (ā) pet animal.

26.2.1 More examples of this construction follow:

jis mālī-nē-bhī bāg̠-mē̃ kām kiyā, acchā nahī̃ kiyā.	Whichever gardener worked in the garden, did not do (**the work**) well.
jis tālibilm-nē-bhī javāb diyā, g̠alat diyā.	Whichever student answered, gave the wrong answer.

aurat-nē, jō kuch-bhī numāēś-mẽ dēkhā, ḳharīdnā cāhā.	The woman wanted to buy, whatever she saw in the exhibition.
sāinsdān-nē, jō kuch-bhī kahā, maĩ bilkul nahĩ samajh sakā.	I could not understand at all, whatever the scientist said.
kuttā jis-kō-bhī pasand kartā hai, us-kē sāth ghar jāēgā.	The dog will go home, with whomever he likes.
jis-nē-bhī zehar khāyā, mar gayā.	Whoever ate the poison died.
jis-nē-bhī śarāb dēkhī, us-nē usē pīnā cāhā.	Whoever saw the wine, wanted to drink it.

REMARKS: **numāēś** (ī) exhibition, **sāinsdān** (ā) scientist, **zehar** (ā) poison.

26.2.2 Exercise 1. **Translate into English:**

1. jō-bhī mōṭargāṛī ghar-kē sāmnē hai, vo mērī hai. 2. jin cīzõ-kī-bhī mujhē zarūrat hai, vo sab ghar-mẽ hai. 3. jis daraḳht-kē nīcē-bhī fakīr baiṭhtā hai, vo ēk baṛ hōtā hai. 4. jin mazdūrõ-nē-bhī mujhē madad dī, unhẽ maĩ-nē inām diyā. 5. jis ādmī-nē-bhī ye kiyā, vo acchā lōhār hai. 6. sāinsdān-nē jō kuch-bhī kahā, ham-nē usē ġalat samjhā. 7. jō-bhī bairā mērī Sindhī samajh sakēgā, us-kē sāth maĩ bōlnā cāhtā hũ. 8. jō-bhī gāṛī pās-sē guzrī, us-par chōṭē laṛkē-nē patthar phẽkē. 9. kisān-nē jō kuch-bhī mēlē-mẽ dēkhā, us-nē usē ḳharīdnā cāhā. 10. jō-bhī zyādā bōltā hai, śāyad bēvaḳūf hō.

26.2.3 Exercise 2. **Translate into Urdu:**

1. Whoever brought water was thirsty. 2. Bring out whatever chair is in the room. 3. No one understood whatever the scientist said. 4. Give me whatever you have to eat. 5. Go by which road is the best. 6. The master did not like whatever the servant did. 7. Whoever wrote this letter is a fool. 8. Whoever read this book did not like it. 9. The servant could not understand whatever his master said. 10. Call into the house whichever beggar passes by.

26.3

jab maĩ-nē bail dēkhē, tab vo hal khĩc rahē thē.	When I saw the oxen, they were pulling the plow.
jab āp mērē ghar āyē, ṭhīk usī vaḳt maĩ bāhar jā rahā thā.	When you came to my house, I was at that very moment going out.
jab āg jaltī hai, tab dhuā̃ uṭhtā hai.	When fire burns, smoke rises.
jab havā zōr-sē caltī hai, tab ye śōr macātī hai.	When air travels swiftly, it makes noise.
jab āp śahar-sē vāpas āẽgē, tab kyā āp kisī-kō sāth lāẽgē?	Will you bring anyone along when you return from town?
jab ḳhansāmā bil lāēgā, tab maĩ us-kō paisē dū̃gā.	When the cook brings the bill, I will pay him.
jab bāriś hōtī hai, tab zamīn zarḳhēz hō jātī hai.	When it rains, the earth becomes fertile.
jab gāṛī sṭēśan-mẽ āēgī, tab ham us-mẽ jāẽgē.	When the train will come into the station, we will go into it.
jab kōī ajnabī ghar-mẽ ātā hai, tab kuttā bhõktā hai.	The dog barks, when some stranger comes into the house.
jab kōī tālibilm jamāat-mẽ nahĩ hōtē, tab ustād paṛhtē haĩ.	When there are no students in the class, the teacher reads.

jab sāinsdān tajrabā kar rahā hai, tab usē na satāiyē.	Please do not bother the scientist, when he is doing (an) experiment.
jab śāir kām nahī̃ karnā cāhtā, tab vo gazal sunānē-kē liyē kisī-kō ḍhū̃ṛhtā hai.	When the poet does not want to work, he looks for someone to read his poem to.

This section illustrates the Urdu equivalent for English sentences the relative clauses of which are introduced by the relative adverb **when,** translated by the Urdu **jab,** the correlative of which is **tab.**

REMARKS: (1) **tab** (or **tō**) is frequently not indicated.

(2) See in sentence two **ṭhīk usī vaḳt, at that very moment,** and for the form **usī** see section 26.1.

(3)**jō, when,** is often found in place of **jab,** and **tō, then,** in place of **tab.**

(4) In the fourth sentence **zōr-sē** means, literally, **with force; macānā** of **śōr macānā, make noise,** also means **to stir up, excite, cause, lemp** (ā) lamp, **gazal** (ī) a lyrical poem, **jamāat** (ī) class, **tajrabā** (ā) experiment, **āg** (ī) fire, **klās** (ī) class, **zōr** (ā) strength, force, **tēl** (ā) oil, **dhuā̃** (ā) smoke, **bil** (ā) **śōr** (ā) noise, **havā** (ī) wind, air.

26.3.1 Exercise 1. **Translate into English:**

1. jab āp Hindūstān jāẽgē, tab āp-kō Hindī-mẽ bōlnā cāhiyē. 2. jab baccā ghar-mẽ bahot zyādā śōr macātā hai, tab us-kō bāhar jānā hai. 3. jab kamrē-mẽ bahot dhuā̃ hōtā hai, tab naukar khiṛkiyā̃ khōltā hai. 4. jab lakṛī sūkhī hai, tab āg acchī tarah-sē jaltī hai. 5. jab bairā bil lāyā, mujhē usē paisē dēnā paṛā. 6. jab kuttā bhõkēgā, tab maĩ ghar vāpas ā rahā hū̃gā. 7. jab bāriś huī, usī vaḳt ham daraḳht-kē nīcē ṭhahar rahē thē. 8. jab ajnabī hamārē ghar-kō ātā hai, tab ham us-kō khānā dētē haĩ. 9. jab maĩ ēk sāf ḳamīz cāhtā hū̃, tab mujhē bairē-kō ḍhū̃ṛhnā paṛtā hai. 10. jab tālibilm bahot zyādā paṛhtē haĩ, vo klās-mẽ sōtē haĩ.

26.3.2 Exercise 2. **Translate into Urdu:**

1. When the bullock eats too much, he wants to sleep. 2. When the workman is tired, he cannot work well. 3. When the wind travels swiftly, little birds cannot fly. 4. When you will put dry coal in the fire, it will burn well. 5. You came to my house at the very moment when I was closing the door. 6. When you (**will**) bring oil from the bazaar for your lamps, please bring (**some**) for me, too. 7. When you travel in Pakistan, try to speak Urdu. 8. When rain falls on his dry fields, the farmer becomes happy. 9. When the dog barked, the stranger did not try to come into the house. 10. When the roads are wet, it is dangerous to drive a car swiftly.

26.4

jab-bhī aurat bahot zyādā khātī hai, bīmār hō jātī hai.	Whenever the woman eats too much, she gets sick.
jab-bhī jhagṛālū aurat hamsāī-kē sāth laṛtī hai, galī-kē kuttē cīkhẽ mārtē haĩ.	Whenever the quarrelsome woman fights with her neighbor, the street dogs bark.
jab-bhī tālibilm imtihān-mẽ nākām hūā, us-nē himmat hār dī.	Whenever the student failed the examination, he became dismayed.
jab-bhī ghōṛā sarpaṭ dauṛtā hai, savār ghabrātā hai.	Whenever the horse gallops, the rider is upset.
jab-bhī mērī bīvī bāzār jātī hai, mērā ḳarz baṛhtā hai.	Whenever my wife goes to the bazaar, my debt increases.

jab-bhī ghōṛā bahot dūr jātā haĩ, thak jātā hai.	Whenever the horse goes too far, he gets tired.
jab-bhī tālibilm bahot zyādā paṛhtē haĩ, ustād-kō afsōs hōtā hai.	Whenever the students study too much, the teacher is sorry.
jab-bhī ādmī-nē bahot zyādā pīyā, vo nahĩ khā sakā.	Whenever the man drank too much, he couldn't eat.
jab-bhī āp Pākistān jāẽ, Urdū bōlẽ.	Whenever you go to Pakistan, speak Urdu.
jab-bhī maĩ hiran-kō mārnē-kī kōśiś kartā hũ, mērā niśānā cūk jātā hũ.	Whenever I try to kill a deer, I miss my mark.
jab-bhī imtihān bahot nazdīk ātā hai, tālibilm fiḳr kartā hai.	Whenever the examination is very near, the student worries.

This section illustrates the Urdu construction for English sentences the relative clauses of which are introduced by the relative adverb **whenever** (implying **each time**). The construction is identical with that described in 26.3, with the exception that the emphatic particle **-bhī** is attached to the relative adverb **jab** and the correlative adverb **tab** is not necessarily indicated.

REMARKS: (1) **thak jānā** in the third sentence means **to become tired; cūk jānā** in the tenth sentence means **to miss, fail.**

(2) **afsōs** (ā) sorrow, regret **[-kō] afsōs hōnā** to regret, be sorry, **jhagṛālū** (**adj., n.c.**) quarrelsome, **hamsāī** (ī) neighbor, **cīkhẽ mārnā** to bark, **imtihān** (ā) examination, **nākām** (**adj., n.c.**) unsuccessful, **sarpaṭ dauṛnā** to gallop, **niśānā** (ā) aim.

26.4.1

jab kabhī ustād-nē kuch samjhānē-kī kōśiś kī, tālibilmō̃-nē dūsrē savāl pūchē.	Whenever the teacher tried to explain something, the students asked other questions.
jab kabhī āp-kō mauḳā milē, hamārē yahā̃ āiyē.	Visit us whenever you get the opportunity.
jab kabhī āp-kō vaḳt milē, mujhē ēk lambā-sā ḳhat likhẽ.	Whenever you find time, write me a rather long letter.
jab kabhī bail thak pātē thē, gāṛībān un-kō ārām dēnē-kē liyē ṭhaharā dētā thā.	Whenever the oxen became tired, the driver stopped to give them a rest.

This section illustrates the Urdu construction for English sentences the relative clauses of which are introduced by the relative adverb **whenever** (implying **anytime**).

The construction is identical with that of 26.3 with the exception that the adverb **kabhī, ever,** is placed after the relative adverb **jab** and the correlative adverb **tab** is not necessarily indicated.

REMARKS: (1) English **to get, to find** is rendered into Urdu by putting **the English subject** of **to get** or **to find** into the **object form** before the postposition **-kō** and making **the English object** of **to get, to find** the **subject** of the verb **milnā.**

(2) **gāṛībān** (ā) driver, **mauḳā** (ā) opportunity, **-kē yahā̃** at the place of, **thak jānā** to become tired.

26.4.2 Exercise 1. **Translate into English:**

1. jab-bhī āp śahar-sē kisī-kō apnē sāth lātē haĩ, ghar-mẽ kuch khānā nahĩ hōtā. 2. jab-bhī bairā bil lāēgā, mujhē us-kō paisē dēnā hōgā. 3. jab kabhī ajnabī hamērē ghar-kō āēgā,

ham us-kō pānī dẽgē. 4. jab-bhī naukar mērē liyē kuch kar saktā hai, karnē-kī kōśi kartā hai. 5. jab kabhī bārīś hōtī hai, mērē pās barsātī nahī̃ hōtī. 6. jab kabhī āp cāhẽ mujh-sē milnē-kē liyē āiyē. 7. jab kabhī tumhẽ kisī cīz-kī zarūrat hō, mujhē bulāō 8. jab-bhī aurat bahot dūr caltī hai, us-kō ārām karnē-kē liyē ṭhaharnā hai. 9. jab kabh āp-kō vaḳt milē, ye kitāb paṛhiyē. 10. jab-bhī maĩ ye kitāb paṛhnē-kī kośiś kartā hū̃, kō mujh-sē bāt karnē-kē liyē ātā hai.

26.4.3 Exercise 2. **Translate into Urdu:**

1. Whenever (= **anytime**) the train stops, the traveller goes out for cold water. 2. When ever (= **anytime**) you can, try to see the villages of Pakistan. 3. Whenever (= **each time**) you can, read the Urdu newspapers. 4. Whenever (= **anytime**) it rains, the dog wants to go into the house. 5. Whenever (= **each time**) the student asked a question, the teacher answered it. 6. Whenever (= **each time**) the teacher goes out of the room, the student make noise. 7. Whenever (= **each time**) the ox-cart driver slept, the oxen stopped to rest 8. Whenever (= **anytime**) I got the opportunity, I drank tea. 9. Whenever (=**anytime**) you go to the villages, try to speak Urdu with the farmers. 10. Whenever (= **each time**) he tried to explain something to (**his**) master, the bearer failed.

26.5 Text 9: **Īd.**[1]

Translate into English. Answer questions in Urdu:

Īd Musalmānõ-kā ēk mutabarrik [2] tahvār [3] hai. jis din Ramzān-kā mahīnā ḳhatam hōtā hai, us-sē aglē [4] din Īd hōtī hai. pahilē ham āp lōgõ-kō Ramzān-kē bārē-mẽ kuch batātē haĩ. Musalmānõ-kē liyē ye farz [5] hai ke [6] vo Ramzān-kē mahīnē-mẽ rōzah [7] rakhẽ. rōzē-kā matlab ye hai ke[6] Musalmān sūraj [8] -kē nikalnē [9] -sē sūraj-kē garūb hōnē [10] -tak na kuch khātē haĩ aur na kuch pītē haĩ. rōzē-kā falsafā [11] ye hai ke [6] Musalmānõ-kō sabr [12] -kī ādat rahē.[13] aur, jab mauḳā [14] paṛē, tō vo bhūk aur pyās-kō bardāśt kar [15] sakẽ. is-kē ilāvā [16] ye murād [17] -bhī hai ke [6] lōgõ-kō bhūk aur pyās-kā tajrubā [18] hō, tā-ke [19] unhẽ garībõ-kī musībat-kā ahsās [20] rahē. aur vo ēk dūsrē-kī madad karẽ. is mazhabī [21] farz-kō pūrā karnē-kē liyē saccē [22] Musalmān bahot subah subah [23] uṭhtē haĩ. itnī sūbah ke [6] abhī bilkul andhērā hōtā hai. is vaḳt vo khānā khātē haĩ, aur, jō kuch pīnā hō, pītē haĩ. jab rōśnī [24] hōnē lagē,[25] tō vo khānā pīnā band kar dētē hai. jō lōg zyādā mazhabī haĩ, vo sārā din [26] ibādat kartē [27] haĩ. bāḳī lōg apnā rōz • marrah-kā [28] kām • kāj [29] kartē rahtē [30] haĩ. ye kahnē-kī zarūrat nahī̃ ke [6] Ramzān-mẽ rōz • marrah-kā kām • kāj karnā kuch muśkil hō jātā hai. bahar • hāl,[31] jab śām-kē vaḳt sūraj garūb hōtā hai, tō lōg rōzah khōltē [32] haĩ. khānā khātē haĩ aur śarbat • pānī [33] pītē haĩ. jab Ramzān-kā mahīnā ḳhatam hōtā hai, tō Musalmān Īd manātē [34] haĩ aur bahot ḳhuś hōtē haĩ. ḳhuśī-kī vajah [35] ye hai ke [6] unhõ-nē apnā farz acchī tarāh adā kiyā.[36] jin lōgõ-nē Ramzān-mẽ rōzē na rakhē hõ, vo-bhī ḳhuśī-sē Īd manātē haĩ.

Īd-kē din sab lōg subah subah uṭhtē haĩ, nahātē dhōtē haĩ, aur nayē kapṛē pahantē haĩ. us-kē bād cāy vagairā pītē haĩ. aur ēk dūsrē-kō tohfē [37] dētē haĩ. ām-taur-par baccõ-kō paisē diyē jātē haĩ [38] jin-kō vo jald-hī ḳharc kar dētē [39] haĩ. kōī das bajē-kē ḳarīb [40] sab lōg muḳhtalif [41] masjidõ-mẽ Īd-kī namāz paṛhnē [42] jātē haĩ. kyū̃-kē [6] masjidõ-mẽ sab namāz paṛhnēvālõ [43] -kē liyē kāfī jagah nahī̃ hōtī, is liyē bahot-sē lōg khulē [44] maidānõ-mẽ namāz paṛhtē haĩ. namāz-kē bād maulvī • sāhab taḳrīr kartē haĩ. vō apnī taḳrīr-mẽ Īd aur Ramzān-kē falsafē-par rauśnī ḍāltē [45] haĩ. ye sab kām kōī ēk ḍēṛh ghanṭē-mẽ ḳhatam hō jātā hai. us-kē bād lōg ēk dūsrē-sē galē miltē haĩ aur ēk dūsrē-kō mubārak kahtē [46] haĩ. Īd-kē din bahot paisā ḳhairāt [47] -mẽ diyā jātā hai.[48]

kaī lōg garībō̃-kō muft khānā khilātē[49] haī. Īd-kē din bahot-sī[50] jaghō̃-par mēlā lagtā hai.[51] baccē aur javān laṛkē ām-taur-par in mēlō̃-mē̃ jātē haī.

is Īd-kē ilāvā ēk aur Īd-bhī hai. us-kō Baḳar • Īd[52] kahtē haī. is din-bhī Musalmān mulkō̃-mē̃ bahot ḳhuśī manāyī jātī hai.[48] is Īd-kī ḳhasūsīyat[53] ye hai ke[6] is din[54] Musalmān jānvar • ḳurbān kartē[55] haī aur un-kā gōśt kuch ḳhud khātē haī, lēkin bahot-sā garībō̃-kō dētē haī. jō lōg amīr hō̃, vo kaī bakrē aur dumbē[56] zibah kartē haī. jō bahot garīb hō̃, un-par Īd-kē din ḳurbānī[57] farz nahī̃ hai. ab savāl ye hai ke[6] is Īd-kē din ḳurbānī kyū̃ kī jātē haī[48]? is-kī vajah ye batāyī jātī hai[48] ke[6] ēk dafā Ḳhudā-kē nabī[58] Ibrahīm[59] -nē ḳhāb[60] dēkhā ke[6] vo apnē bēṭē Ismāīl[61] -kō ēk pahāṛ[62] -kī cōṭī-par lē jākar[63] zibah kartē haī. aglī rāt unhō̃-nē phir yehī ḳhāb dēkhā, aur us-sē aglī rāt phir yehī ḳhāb dēkhā. unhō̃-nē ḳhāb-kī tābīr[64] yū̃[65] kī ke[6] Ḳhudā un-sē apnē bēṭē-kī ḳurbānē mā̃gtā hai. cunā-ce unhō̃-nē apnē bēṭē Ismāīl-sē is ḳhāb-kā zikr kiyā.[66] bēṭē-nē-bhī is ḳhāb-kā vo-hī matlab samjhā jō Ibrahīm-nē ḳhud samjhā thā. Ismāīl-nē apnē bāp-sē kahē ke,[6] agar Ḳhudā-kī yehī marzī[67] hai, tō usē ḳurbān hōnē[68] -mē̃ kōī inkār[69] nahī̃. is-kē bād Ibrahīm aur un-kā bēṭā dōnō̃ pahāṛ-par gayē. Ismāīl-nē apnē bāp-sē kahā ke[6] āp mujhē zibah karnē-sē pahilē[70] apnī ā̃khō̃-par paṭṭī[71] bā̃dh lījiyē[72] tā-ke churī cālātē vaḳt[73] āp-kā irādā[74] ṭūṭ na jāē[75] Ibrahīm-nē apnī ā̃khō̃-par paṭṭī bā̃dhī aur Ḳhudā-kā nām lēkar[76] Ismāīl-kē galē-par churī phēr dī.[77] jab unhō̃-nē apnī paṭṭī haṭāyī[78] aur apnī ā̃khē̃ khōlī, tō dēkhā ke[6] Ismāīl tō bilkul ṭhīk • ṭhāk hai aur us-kī jagah[79] ēk dumbā zibah huā huā[80] un-kē sāmnē paṛā hai. unhō̃-nē is mōjzē[81] -kā matlab ye samjhā ke[6] Ḳhudā-nē Ibrahīm-kī apnē sāth muhabbat-kā imtihām[82] -bhī lē liyā aur ye-bhī samjhā diyā[83] kē[6] us-kē bandē[84] us-kī rāh[85] -mē̃ insānō̃[86] -kī nahī̃, balkē[87] jānvarō̃-kī ḳurbānī kiyā karē̃.[88] is vāḳē-kī yād-mē̃ Musalmān Baḳra • Īd manātē haī.

savālāt:

1. Ramzān-kē mahīnē-mē̃ Musalmān kis vaḳt khānā pīnā band kar dētē haī? 2. rōzē-kā falsafā bayān karō.[89] 3. Īd-kē din lōg subah uṭhkar[90] kyā kartē haī? 4. Ibrahīm-nē ḳhāb-mē̃ kyā dēkhā? 5. unhō̃-nē ḳhāb-kā kyā matlab samjhā?

NOTES: 1. Īd (ī), Muslim holiday; 2. holy (**adj., n.c.**); 3. holiday, festival (ā); 4. next (**adj.**); 5. duty (ā); 6. that, see 29.2; 7. fast (ā); 8. sun (ā); 9. to come out (**int.**); 10. setting of sun (ā); 11. philosophy (ā); 12. patience (ā); 13. **ādat rahnā** to be accustomed (**int.**); 14. opportunity (ā); 15. **bardāśt karnā** to endure (**int.**); 16. besides (**postpos. phrase**); 17. object, intention (ī); 18. experience (ā); 19. so that; 20. feeling (ā); 21. religious (**adj.**); 22. = orthodox; 23. early in the morning; 24. light (ī); 25. see 34.1.2; 26. the whole day (adv.); 27. **ibādat karnā** to pray (**tr.**); 28. **rōz • marrah-kā** daily (= **adj.**); 29. chore, task, work (ā); 30. see 34.3; 31. anyway (**conj.**); 32. **rōzah khōlnā** to break a fast (**tr.**); 33. sweet iced drink (ā); 34. to observe (e.g., **holiday**) (**tr.**); 35. reason (ī); 36. **farz adā karnā** to do one's duty; 37. **tohfā** gift (ā); 38. are given, see 37.1; 39. **ḳharc kar dēnā** to spend (**tr.**), see lesson 28; 40. about ten o'clock; 41. different (**adj., n.c.**); 42. = **paṛhnē-kē liyē** see 37.2.2; 43. people who pray, see 31.2 for **vālā;** 44. open (**adj., pst. part.** of **khulnā** to be open (**int.**)); 45. **rauśnī ḍālnā** to elucidate, discuss (**tr.**) (cf. **rōśnī** (ī) light); 46. **mubārak kahnā** to greet (**tr.**); 47. **ḳhairāt** charity (ā); 48. see 37.1; 49. feed, see 36.1, ff.; 50. many, see 38.1 for **-sā;** 51. fair is held; 52. Muslim holiday; 53. particularity, feature (ī); 54. on this day (**adv.**); 55. to sacrifice animals (tr.); 56. **dumbā** ram (ā); 57. **ḳurbānī** sacrifice (ī); 58. prophet (ā); 59. Abraham; 60. dream (ā); 61. Ishmael; 62. mountain (ā); 63. taking, see 30.1 and lesson 28; 64. interpretation (ī); 65. thus (**adv.**); 66. **zikr karnā** to mention (**tr.**); 67. desire (ī); 68. **ḳurbān hōnā** to be sacrificed (**int.**); 69. objection, refusal (ā); 70. cf. **-kē pahilē;** 71. **paṭṭī** strip of cloth (ī); 72. **bā̃dh lēnā** to tie (**tr.**), see lesson 28; 73. = when you move the knife, see 31.4; 74. determination, intention (ā); 75. **ṭūṭ jānā** to break (**int.**), see lesson 28; 76. **nām lēnā** to utter name (**tr.**), see 30.1; 77. **churī phēr dēnā** to pass a knife (**tr.**), see lesson 28; 78. **haṭānā** to remove (**tr.**); 79. in its place; 80. **zibah huā huā** in the state of being slaughtered, for the past participle functioning as an adjective see 33.1, and 33.6 for the repetition; 81. **mōjzā** miracle (ā); 82. test (ā); 83. **samjhā dēnā** to indicate, express (**tr.**), see lesson 28; 84. follower, adherent (ā); 85. way (ī); 86. **insān** human being (ā); 87. but (**conj.**); 88. see 34.5; 89. **bayān karnā** to describe (**tr.**); 90. getting up, see 30.1.

LESSON 27

27.1

jahā̃ gāy car rahī hai, vahā̃ ghās hai.	There is grass, where the cow is grazing.
jahā̃ āp mērē pīchē nahī̃ ā saktē, maĩ vahā̃ jāū̃gā.	I'll go, where you cannot follow me.
jahā̃-sē śōr-kī āvāz ā rahī hai, vahā̃ jahāzī haĩ.	There are sailors, where the noise is coming from.
jahā̃ ghās ugtī hai, vahā̃ śāyad acchī zamīn hai.	Where grass grows, there is probably good land.
jahā̃ kitābē̃ haĩ, vahā̃ dhūl hōtī hai.	Where there are books, there is dust.
kabhī kabhī, jahā̃ mōṭar nahī̃ jā sakē, vahā̃ bailgāṛī jā saktī hai.	Sometimes an ox-cart can go, where an automobile may not be able to go.
jahā̃ rāstā bahot ḍhalvān hōgā, vahā̃ āp-kō bailgāṛī-sē utarnā paṛēgā.	Where the road is too steep, you will have to get out of the ox-cart.

This section illustrates the Urdu construction for English sentences the relative clauses of which are introduced by the relative **adverb,** where, translated by Urdu **jahā̃,** the correlative of which is **vahā̃,** there.

REMARKS: **jahāzī** (ā) sailor, **dhūl** (ī) dust, **ḍhalvān (adj., n.c.)** steep.

27.1.1 Exercise 1. **Translate into English:**

1. jahā̃-sē śōr-kī āvāz ā rahī hai, vahā̃ ēk kārḳhānā hai. 2. jahā̃ daraḳht hō̃gē, vāhā̃ śāyad pānī hōgā. 3. jahā̃-tak āp jā sakē̃gē, vahā̃-tak maĩ jāū̃gā. 4. jahā̃ saṛak tañg hō, vahā̃ mōṭargāṛī āhistā calāō. 5. jahā̃ gāy jātī hai, vahā̃ bachṛā-bhī jātā hai. 6. jahā̃ jahāz jāēgā, vahā jahāzī-bhī jāē̃gē. 7. jahā̃ rāstā bahot ḍhalvān hai, vahā̃ maĩ nahī̃ cal saktā. 8. jahā̃ bahot dhūl hai, vahā̃ rahnā ācchā nahī̃. 9. jahā̃ baṛā jahāz hai, vahā̃ daryā gahrā hai. 10. jahā̃ maĩ jātā hū̃, vahā̃ āp-bhī kyū̃ jānā cāhtē haĩ?

REMARKS: See section 26.2 for remarks on the particle **-bhī.**

27.1.2 Exercise 2. **Translate into Urdu:**

1. There are people working, where the dust is coming from. 2. There is a well, where the ozen are grazing. 3. Where rain falls, grass grows well. 4. I can sometimes go, where my friend cannot go. 5. There is a good restaurant, where I work. 6. There is a house, where you see the light. 7. Stop the automobile, where you can. 8. Please read me the story as far as (= **up to where**) you wish. 9. There is a beautiful garden, where I **(fm.)** am staying. 10. Can you swim as far as (= **up to where**) I can?

27.2

vo jahā̃-bhī gayā, us-nē pānē-kī talāś kī.	Wherever he went, he looked for water.
ghōṛā jahā̃-bhī jāẽgā, vo pyāsā hōgā.	Wherever the horse will go, it will be thirsty.
aurat-nē jahā̃-bhī khāyā, vo bīmār huī.	Wherever the woman ate, she got sick.
mērē safar-mẽ jahā̃-bhī dilcasp jaghē hōgī, maī vahā̃ rukū̃gā.	I will stop, wherever there are interesting spots in my journey.
āp Panjāb-mẽ jahā̃-bhī jāẽ, ām-taur-par gānā • bajānā sunẽgē.	Wherever you go in the Panjab, you generally will hear singing and playing (of musical instruments).

This section illustrates the Urdu construction for English sentences the relative clauses of which are introduced by the relative adverb wherever, translated by the Urdu **jahā̃,** to which is attached the emphatic particle **-bhī.** The correlative **vahā̃** need not be expressed.

27.2.1 Exercise 1. **Translate into English:**

1. jahā̃-bhī dilcasp jaghẽ hõ, vahā̃ mōṭargāṛī rōkiyē. 2. Panjāb-mẽ jahā̃-bhī āp gānā • bajānā sunẽgē, vahā̃ ām-taur-par ēk śādī hōgī. 3. us-nē jahā̃-bhī apnē ghōṛē-kī talāś kī, us-kō nahī̃ pāyā. 4. maī jahā̃-bhī jātā hū̃, vahā̃ āp kyū̃ jānā cāhtē haī? 5. jahā̃-bhī saṛak taṅg hai, tumhẽ gāṛī-sē utarnā paṛēgā. 6. jahā̃-bhī zamīn ḍhalvān hai, hal jōtnā muśkil hai. 7. ghar-mẽ jahā̃-bhī maī kām karnē-kī kōśiś kartā hū̃, vahā̃ bahot śōr-kī āvāz hōtī hai. 8. jahā̃-bhī ghās hōtī hai, vahā̃ bail khānē-kē liyē ṭhahartē haī. 9. jahā̃-bhī rāstā cauṛā hōgā, āp mōṭargāṛī jaldī-sē calā sakẽgē. 10. maī jahā̃-bhī Pākistān-mẽ safar karū̃gā, lōgõ-kē sāth Urdū bōlū̃gā.

27.2.2 Exercise 2. **Translate into Urdu:**

1.Wherever I go in Pakistan, I generally try to talk with people. 2. I'll stop for a while, wherever there is an interesting place. 3. Wherever I run, the little dog will follow me. 4. Wherever the big elephant goes, the others follow him. 5. Wherever you look for the cow, she will not be there. 6. Wherever my automobile will be, my bearer will be nearby. 7. Wherever the master goes, the servant has to follow. 8. Wherever you hear singing, you will see happy people. 9. Wherever I ate in Pakistan, I liked the food. 10. Wherever you go in Pakistan, you should try to understand the people.

27.3

jitna ḳhūbsūrat Bambī hai, utnā-hī Kalkattā hai.	Calcutta is as beautiful as Bombay.
jitnī śakkar ḍālōgē, dahī utnā-hī mīṭhā hōgā.	The curds will be as sweet as the (**amount of**) sugar you put in.
jitnā ṭhaṇḍā pānī piyōgē, utnī-hī pyās lagēgī.	As much cold water (**as**) you drink, you'll be that much thirsty.
jitnē rūpayē mērē pās haī, utnē-hī paisē.	I have as many rupees as I have pice.
jitnē maī usē pasand kartā hū̃, utnē-hī vo mujhē pasand kartā hai.	He likes me as much as I like him.
jitnī laṛkiyā̃ thī̃, utnē-hī vahā̃ laṛkē thē.	There were as many boys as there were girls there.

jitnī mōṭī bīvī thī, utnā-hī dublā ḳhāvind thā.	The husband was as lean as the wife was fat.
jitnē ādmī daftar-sē bāhar āyē, utnē-hī maĩ-nē ginē.	I counted as many men as came out of the office.
klās-mē̃ jitnē tālibilm haĩ, utnī-hī kursiyā̃ haĩ.	There as as many chairs in the class as there are students.

The English sentences, above, contain expressions indicating equality in quantity or quality between one or a group of beings or things or acts. Such sentences are translated into Urdu by constructions with relative forms. The relative clause of the Urdu sentence contains a form of the relative adjective **jitnā, how much,** the correlative of which is **utnā, that much.** To indicate emphasis the particle **-hī** may be attached to **utnā.**

Compare the English sentences with the literal Urdu translations: the first sentence, above, **How much beautiful Bombay is, that much** (beautiful) **Calcutta is.;** the second sentence, **How much sugar you will put** (in), **that much sweet the curds will be.;** the third sentence, **How much cold water you will drink, that much thirsty you will be.;** and the fifth sentence, **How much I like him, that much he likes me.** (Note that in this last example the forms **jitnā** and **utnā** are adverbs.)

REMARKS: (1) **pyās,** of sentence 3, is a feminine noun meaning **thirst.** The noun **pyās** is the subject of the verb, **lagnā** (lit., **to be attached**). The English noun indicating the person in that condition, is translated into **the object form** before **-kō,** e.g., **mujhē pyās lagtī hai. I am thirsty. ghōṛē-kō pyās lagēgī. The horse will become thirsty.**

(2) **dahī** (ā) curds, **śakkar** (ā) sugar, **paisā** (ā) pie (currency).

27.3.1 Exercise 1. **Translate into English:**

1. jitnā āp-kō cāhiyē, utnā lī̃jiyē. 2. jitnī lakṛī kāfī hō, utnī-hī lāiyē. 3. jitnē lōg kamrē-mē̃ hõgē, utnī-hī kursiyā̃ naukar lāēgā. 4. jitnā gahrā kuā̃ hai, utnā-hī gahrā daryā hai. 5. jitnē bakrē mērē pās haĩ, utnē bail us-kē pās haĩ. 6. jitnā baṛā Lahōr hai, utnā baṛā mērā śahar nahī̃ hai. 7. jitnā vo likhtā hai, utnā-hī maĩ paṛhtā hū̃. 8. jitnē lōg bāg-mē̃ thē, utnī-hī kursiyā̃ naukar bāhar lāyā. 9. jitnē mērē pās thē, utnē-hē paisē maĩ-nē ginē. 10. jitnē hiran śikārī-nē dēkhē, utnē sab vo cūk gayā.

27.3.2 Exercise 2. **Translate into Urdu:**

1. Are there as many men as there are women in the village? 2. Why do you need as much coal as you need wood? 3. The teacher will ask as many questions as there are students in the class. 4. The house is not as high as the factory. 5. The workman is not working as hard as the farmer. 6. Place as many dishes on the table as there will be guests. 7. Water the plants as much as you do the trees. 8. The bridge is as wide as the automobile is long. 9. The child threw as many stones at as many monkeys as were on the branch of the tree. 10. The father brought back as many apples from the bazaar as he had children.

27.4

jitnī lakṛī āp-kō cāhiyē, lījiyē.	Take as much wood as you need.
jitnī ghās gāy khā sakī, us-nē khāyī.	The cow ate as much grass as it could (**eat**).
jitnē kitābē̃ āp lē jā sakē̃, lē jāiyē.	Take as many books as you can carry.

jitnē lōgō̃-kē sāth Fārsī bōl sakē̃, bōliyē.	Speak Persian with as many people as you can.
āp jitnī miṭhāī cāhē̃, lījiyē.	Take as much candy as you want.

The construction illustrated in this section is identical with that of 27.3, with the exception that **jitnā** and the correlative **utnā** modify or refer to the same being, thing or act. Here the correlative **utnā** is not necessarily indicated.

REMARKS: **lē jānā**, in sentence three, means **to take (away), to carry.** It is to be considered as functioning as a single verb, the **lē** remaining unchanged and the **jānā** taking the required verbal endings. (See Lesson 28).

27.4.1 Exercise 1. **Translate into English:**

1. jitnī lakṛī āp-kō zarūrat hō, lē jāiyē. 2. jitnā kōēlā tum lā saktē hō, lāō. 3. jitnā ārām maĩ kar sakā, maĩ-nē kiyā. 4. jitnā bail khā saktā hai, kyū̃ nahī̃ khā rahā hai? 5. jitnā pānī āp lā saktē haĩ, kyū̃ nahī̃ lāyē? 6. jitnā kām tum kar saktē hō, kyū̃ nahī̃ kartē? 7. jitnē khānē-kī ādmī-kō zarūrat hai, us-kō dījiyē. 8. jitnī khiṛkiyō̃-kī tum marammat kar sakō, karō. 9. jitnā ṭhaṇḍā pānī āp mujhē dēnā cāhtē haĩ, dījiyē. 10. jitnī mehnat kisān kar saktā hai, vo kartā hai.

27.4.2 Exercise 2. **Translate into Urdu:**

1. Come with as many people as you wish. 2. Bring as much dry wood as you can. 3. Please tell me as much as you have heard. 4. Write to as many people as you know in the Panjab. 5. Read as many Urdu newspapers as you can. 6. Did the hungry man eat as much as he wished? 7. Did the carpenter cut as much wood as he needed? 8. You should work as hard as you can. 9. The man ate as much food as he cooked. 10. The woman cooked as much food as she needed.

27.5

mērā ghar daryā-sē utnā-hī dūr hai, jitnā ke hōṭal.	My house is as far from the river as the hotel is.
jēl bāzār-sē utnī-hī dūr hai, jitnā ke sarkārī daftar.	The jail is as far from the bazaar as the government house is.
rassā utnā-hī lambā hai, jitnā ke kuā̃ gahrā hai.	The rope is as long as the well is deep.
dīvār-par utnī-hī tasvīrē̃ laṭkāiyē, jitnē ke dāġ haĩ.	Hang as many pictures on the wall as there are stains on it.
maĩ us ādmī-kī utnī-hī tārīf karū̃gā, jitnī ke maĩ kar saktā hū̃.	I will praise that man as much as I can.
maĩ us-kē bārē-mē̃ utnā-hī bayān karū̃gā, jitnā ke maĩ jāntā hū̃.	I'll tell as much as I know about him.

The sentences of this section are similar in construction to those of section 27.3. Here the correlative adjective **utnā** is stressed, and the clause in which it appears is placed first. The relative adjective **jitnā** is followed by the particle **ke.** This construction occurs more often in literary than in colloquial language.

Compare the literal translations of the Urdu sentences: the first, **My house is as much far from the river as the hotel is.**; the third, **The rope is as much long, as the well**

is deep.; and the sixth, **I concerning that man will make as much good a description as I can do.**

REMARKS: 1() The postpositional phrase **-kē bārē-mē̃** translates English **about, concerning.**

(2) **dāg** (ā) stain, spot, **bayān** (ā) description, **bayān karnā** to describe, **tārīf** (ī) praise, **tārīf karnā** to praise.

27.5.1 Exercise 1. **Translate into English:**

1. kyā tum utnē-hī bhūkē hō, jitnā ke maĩ hū̃? 2. ye rassā utnā-hī lambā hai, jitnā ke mujhē cāhiyē. 3. utnī-hī kursiyā̃ lāō, jitnē ke lōg haĩ. 4. āp utnē-hī pās kyū̃ nahī̃ ātē, jitnē ke ā saktē haĩ? 5. kyā tumhārā gāȭ śahar-sē utnā-hī dūr hai, jitnā ke mērā hai? 6. kuttā kab utnā-hī khātā hai, jitnā ke vo khā saktā hai? 7. maĩ is mulk-kē bārē-mē̃ utnā-hī acchā bayān karū̃gā, jitnā ke kar saktā hū̃. 8. sarkārī makān utnā-hī ū̃cā hai, jitnā ke cauṛā hai. 9. bāgh utnā-hī śōr kartā hai, jitnā ke ḳhū̃ḳhār hai. 10. jēl-kī dīvār utnī-hī mazbūt hai, jitnī ke mōṭī hai.

27.5.2 Exercise 2. **Translate into Urdu:**

1. Are you (**fm.**) as tired as you are hungry? 2. The well is as far from my house as it is from yours. 3. Please describe your village as well as you can. 4. Is the well as far from here as the river? 5. The field is as long as it is wide. 6. There are as many monkeys in the trees as there are people in the street. 7. There are as many (**pairs of**) shoes before the mosque as there are people inside it. 8. The tree is as far from the hunter as the dreadful animal is. 9. The thirsty traveller is as far from the tank as he is from the well. 10. I have as many clothes as I need.

27.6

laṛkē aur laṛkiyā̃ skūl jātē haĩ.	Boys and girls go to school.
ādmī aur aurtē̃ khēt-mē̃ kām kartē haĩ.	Men and women work in the field.
parindē aur hiran jaṅgal-mē̃ rahtē haĩ.	Birds and deer live in the jungle.
phal aur sabziyā̃ mēz-par haĩ.	Fruits and vegetables are on the table.
kursiyā̃ aur mēzē̃ kamrē-mē̃ haĩ.	There are chairs and tables in the room.
maĩ laṛkō̃ aur laṛkiyō̃-kō dēkhtā hū̃.	I see the boys and girls.
maĩ ādmiyō̃ aur aurtō̃-sē bātcīt kartā hū̃.	I speak with the men and women.
baccā parindō̃ aur hirnō̃-kō pasand kartā hai.	The child likes birds and deer.
aurat rōṭī aur sabziyā̃ pakātī hai.	The woman cooks bread and vegetables.
baṛhaī kursiyā̃ aur mēzē̃ banātā hai.	The carpenter makes chairs and tables.
har ādmī-kē dō hāth aur dō pāȭ hōtē haĩ.	Every man has two hands and two feet.
ādmī-kē dō bēṭē aur dō bēṭiyā̃ haĩ.	The man has two sons and two daughters.
rōśnī aur andhērē-mē̃ fark hai.	There is a difference between light and darkness.
Baṅgal-mē̃ lōg machlī aur cāval khātē haĩ.	In Bengal people eat fish and rice.
Panjāb-mē̃ lōg gōśt aur sabziyā̃ khātē haĩ.	In the Panjab people eat meat and vegetables.

This section illustrates the conjunction **aur,** and. When nouns of different genders linked by **aur** form the subject of a verb, the verb will normally be in the masculine.

When the nouns linked by **aur** occur before a postposition, BOTH forms are placed in the object form.

REMARKS: (1) Sentence 13 illustrates the Urdu equivalent of the English phrase **difference between.** The literal Urdu translation is **In light and darkness there is** (a) **difference.**

(2) **andhērā** (ā) darkness, **gōśt** (ā) meat, flesh, **fark** (ā) difference, distinction, **rōśnī** (ī) light, brightness.

27.7 Text 10: **Jahā̃gīr [1] -kā Adl.[2]**

Translate into English. Answer the questions in Urdu:

Jahā̃gīr-kā aslī [3] nām Nūr-ud-Dīn thā. vo Akbar [1] bādśāh [4] -kā bēṭā, Humāyū̃ [1] -kā pōtā [5] aur Bābar [1] -kā paṛpōtā [6] thā. vo san [7] sōlā sau pā̃c (1605) -mẽ Hindūstān-kē taḳht [8] -par baiṭhā. jab Jahā̃gīr abhī [9] śāhzādā [10] thā ke [11] vo ēk bahot-hī ḳhūbsūrat laṛkī-par āśik hō gayā [12] is laṛkī-kā nām Mehr-un-Nisā thā. ye laṛkī śāhī [13] mahal [14] -mẽ rahtī thī. jab vo javān huī, tō us-kī śādī Bañgāl [15] -kē hākam [16] Alī Ḳulī Ḳhā [17] -sē hō gayī. jab Jahā̃gīr bādśāh banā,[18] tō vo abhī-tak Bañgāl-mẽ thī. lēkin kuch sālõ-kē bād us-kā ḳhāvind, yānī Alī Ḳulī, mar gayā.[19] bādśāh-kō abhī-tak us-sē muhabbat thī. us-nē us-kō śāhī mahal-mẽ vāpas bulvā liyā.[20] kuch sāl guzarnē-kē bād vo bādśāh-sē śādī karnē-par rāzī hō gayī.[21] ab us-kā nām Nūr Jahā̃ hō gayā aur vo Hindūstān-kī malikā [22] ban gayī.[23] ēk dafā-kā zikr hai ke [24] malikā mahal-kī chat [25] -par apnī kanīzõ [26] -kē sāth khaṛī thī aur tīr calā [27] rahī thī. g̱altī-sē ēk tīr ēk dhōbī-kō, jō daryā-kē kinārē kapṛē dhō rahā thā, lagā aur vo mar gayā. dhōban [28] aur us-kē kunbē-nē bādśāh-kē pās śikāyat [29] kī ke [30] kisī-nē dhōbī-kō tīr-sē mār ḍālā [31] hai. taftīś karnē [32] -par mālūm huā ke [30] tīr calānēvālī [33] Hindūstān-kī malikā thī. ab Jahā̃gīr bahot baṛī muśkil-mẽ phā̃s gayā.[34] ēk taraf [35] insāf [36] thā, dūsrī taraf muhabbat thī. kyā karē; kyā na karē. us-kī samajh [37] -mẽ kuch nahī̃ ātā thā. kaī ghanṭē vo is mūāmlē [38] -par sōctā rahā.[39] jab us-kō ye ḳhayāl ātā ke [30] kisī-nē ēk ādmī-kō bēgunah [40] ḳatl [41] kar diyā hai, tō us-kī ā̃khẽ g̱ussē-sē surḳh [42] hō jātī̃. lēkin, jab ye ḳhayāl ātā ke [30] ḳātil [43] malikā hai aur ḳātil-kī sazā [44] ḳānūn-kē mutābiḳ [45] maut hai, tō us-kī ā̃khõ-mẽ ā̃sū ā jātē. us-kō vo zamānā yād ātā thā jab vo ēk javān śāhzādā thā aur malikā ēk naujavān [46] laṛkī thī. usē is zamānē-kā ēk vāḳyā yād āyā, jō baṛā dilcasp hai. ēk din śāhzādā bāg̱-mẽ sair kar rahā thā, us-kē hāthõ-mẽ dō pāltū [47] kabūtar [48] thē. ēk • dam śāhzādē-kō ēk zarūrī kām yād āyā. us-nē apnē kabūtar Mehr-un-Nisā-kō diyē aur kahā, "ḳhūbsūrat laṛkī! zarā hamārē kabūtarõ-kā ḳhayāl rakhō.[49] ham thōṛī dēr-mẽ vāpas ā jāẽgē." jab śāhzādā vāpas āyā, tō laṛkī-nē usē siraf ēk kabūtar vāpas kiyā.[50] śāhzādē-nē kahā, "hamārā dūsrā kabūtar kahā̃ gayā?" Mehr-un-Nisā-nē kahā, "sāhzādē,[51] vo tō uṛ gayā." [52] śāhzādē-nē pūchā, "magar kaisē uṛ gayā?" Mehr-un-Nisā-nē hāth khōlkar [53] dūsrā kabūtar-bhī chōṛ diyā [54] aur kahā, "śāhzādē, aisē!" [55] Jahā̃gīr-kō Nūr-kī ye adā [56] bahot pasand āyī aur vo fauran us-par āśik hō gayā.

ab ye sab bātẽ bādśāh-kō yād ā rahī thī aur us-kō parīśān kartī thī̃.[57] āḳhir, insāf jīt gayā [58] aur muhabbat hār gayī.[59] Jahā̃gīr-nē zanānā pōlīs [60] -kō hukam diyā ke [30] malikā-kō giriftār karkē [61] jēl [62] -mẽ lē jāẽ. cunā̃-ce malikā jēl-mẽ band kar di gayī.[63] lēkin us-kē bād bādśāh bahot g̱amgīn hō gayā. us-nē khānā pīnā chōṛ diyā. jab darbār [64] -kē amīrõ,[65] vazīrõ [66] -nē bādśāh-kā ye hāl dēkhā, tō bahot ghabrāyē. un-kō mālūm thā ke,[30] agar malikā-kō maut [67] -kī sazā hō gayī, tō thōṛē din-kē bād Jahā̃gīr-bhī mar jāēgā. vo malikā-kē bag̱air [68] zindā [69] nahī̃ rah sakēgā. sab darbārī [70] bādśāh-kē pās gayē. unhõ-nē arz kī ke [30] malikā-nē jān • būjhkar [71] dhōbī-kō nahī̃ marā. is liyē usē chōṛ diyā jāē.[72] lēkin Jahā̃gīr-nē un-kī bāt na mānī. thōṛē din-kē bād malikā aur dhōbī-kā muḳadmā darbār-mē̃ pēś hūā.[73] Jahā̃gīr-nē malikā-sē pūchā, "kyā tum apnē jurm [74] -kā iḳrār [75] kartī hō?" malikā-nē javāb diyā, "hā̃, maī apnē jurm-kā iḳrār kartī hū̃." phir bādśāh-nē ḳāziyō̃ [76] -sē pūchā, "ḳānūn-kē mutābiḳ ḳātil-kī kyā sazā hai?" ḳāziyō̃-nē javāb diyā, "ḳānūn kahtā hai ke [30] ḳātil-kī sazā maut hai." Jahā̃gīr-nē faislā [77] sunāyā ke [30] malikā-kō maut-kī sazā dī jāē.[72] jab ye faislā sunāyā gayā.[72] tō sārē darbāriyō̃-kē hōś uṛ gayē.[78] unhō̃-nē dhōbī-kē vārisō̃ [79] -sē kahā ke [30] vo muāvizā [80] lēkar malikā-kō muāf kar dē̃ aur apnā muḳadmā vāpas lē lē̃. dhōban aur us-kē riśtēdār ye mān gayē.[81] unhō̃-nē Jahā̃gīr bādśāh-sē kahā "ham malikā-kē liyē maut-kī sazā nahī̃ cāhtē. ham muāvizā lēkar apnā muḳadmā vāpas lēnē-kō taiyār haī." Jahā̃gīr-nē dō • bārā ḳāziyō̃-sē pūchā "kyā ḳānūn is-kī ijāzat dētā hai?" unhō̃-nē javāb diyā "jī hā̃."

is tarah Hindūstān-kī malikā aur Jahā̃gīr-kī cahētī [82] bīvī-kī jān [83] bacī.[84] muhabbat aur insāf dōnō̃ apnī apnī jagah jīt gayē.

savālāt:

1. Jahā̃gīr-nē bāg-mē̃ kabūtar kis-kō diyē? sārā vāḳyā bayān karō. 2. dhōbī-kō kis-nē mārā? 3. Nūr-Jahā̃-kā pahilā ḳhāvind kaun thā? 4. Jahā̃gīr-nē darbār-mē̃ ḳāziyō̃-sē kyā pūchā aur unhō̃-nē kyā javāb diyā? 5. Jahāgīr-kē bāp, dādā aur pardādā-kā kyā nām thā?

NOTES: 1. name of Mogul emperor; 2. justice (ā); 3. real, actual (**adj., n.c.**); 4. king, emperor (ā); 5. grandson (ā); 6. great-grandson (ā); 7. year (ā); 8. throne (ā); 9. = still, yet; 10. prince (ā); 11. that (**conj.**), see 29.2; 12. **āśik hō jānā** to fall in love (**int.**); 13. royal (**adj., n.c.**); 14. palace (ā); 15. Bengal (ā); 16. governor (ā); 17. name of Nūr Jahān's husband; 18. **bannā** to be made (**int.**); 19. **mar jānā** to die (**int.**), see lesson 28; 20. **bulvā lēnā** to summon (**tr.**), see lesson 28; 21. **rāzī hō jānā** to agree (**int.**); 22. queen (ī); 23. **ban jānā** to be made (**int.**); 24. see fn. 11; 25. roof (ī); 26. **kanīz** hand-maiden (ī); 27. **tīr calānā** to shoot arrow (**tr.**); 28. washerman's wife, washerwoman (ī); 29. complaint (ī); 30. see fn. 11; 31. **mār ḍālnā** to kill (**tr.**), see lesson 28; 32. **taftīś karnā** to investigate (**tr.**); 33. for **vālā** see 31.2; 34. **phãs jānā** to be involved, ensnared (**int.**), see lesson 28; 35. on one side; 36. justice (ā); 37. understanding (ī); 38. **muāmlā** matter (ā); 39. see 34.3; 40. without fault; 41. murder (ā); 42. red (**adj., n.c.**); 43. murderer (ā); 44. punishment (ī); 45. according to (**postpos. phrase**); 46. young; 47. tamed, pet (**adj., n.c.**); 48. pigeon (ā); 49. **ḳhayāl rakhnā** to take care of (**tr.**); 50. **vāpas karnā** to give back (**tr.**); 51. **voc. s. msc.**; 52. **uṛ jānā** to fly off (**int.**), see lesson 28; 53. opening, see 30.1; 54. **chōṛ dēnā** to release (**tr.**), see 30.1 and lesson 28; 55. in this way, thus (**adv.**); 56. charming gesture (ī); 57. upset; 58. **jīt jānā** to win (**int.**), lesson 28; 59. **hār jānā** to lose (**int.**), lesson 28; 60. **zanānā pōlīs** women's police, **zenana police** (ī); 61. **giriftār karnā** to arrest (**tr.**); 62. jail (ī); 63. see 37.1; 64. court (ā); 65. **amīr** nobleman (ā); 66. **vazīr** minister (ā); 67. death (ā); 68. **-kē bagair** without (**postpos. phrase**); 69. alive (**adj.**); 70. courtier (ā); 71. **jān • būjhkar** deliberately (= **adv.**); 72. see 37.1; 73. **pēś hōnā** to present (**int.**) (e.g., a lawsuit); 74. crime (ā); 75. confession (ā); 76. **ḳāzī** Muslim jurist (ā); 77. verdict (ā); 78. **hōś uṛ jānā** to lose presence of mind (**int.**); 79. **vāris** heir (ā); 80. compensation (ā); 81. **mān jānā** to accept, agree to (**int.**); 82. beloved (**adj., n.c.**); 83. life (ī) 84. **bacnā** to be saved (**int.**).

LESSON 28

In the preceding lessons there occurred in several sentences, instead of a single verb, a sequence consisting of **the stem of a verb plus a second verb,** such as **jānā, lēnā, hōnā.** The verbal sequence or cluster functioned as a **single verb** (i.e., the second member assumed the forms required by the different syntactic constructions while the basic meaning of the cluster was conveyed by the first member—that is, the stem form). See in section 18.1.2, **agar khānā ḳharāb hō, tō āp bīmār hō jāẽ. If the food should be bad, you may get sick.**; and in 26.4, **jab-bhī maĩ hiran-kō mārnē-kī kōśiś kartā hū̃, cūk jātā hū̃. Whenever I try to kill a deer, I miss.**

The use of such verbal clusters in the place of single verbs is frequent in Urdu. The second member of the cluster, furthermore, serves to modify the meaning conveyed by the first member or stem form.

REMARKS: (1) The identification of the verbal cluster as transitive or intransitive normally depends upon the second member—i.e., whether it is transitive or intransitive. (Compare section 35.1, Remarks)

(2) In several instances the second member of the verbal cluster has come to be considered an integral part of the first verb. The modification in meaning of the first member is not easily discernible. Compare **hōnā, become** and **hō jānā, become.** It seems that **hō jānā** is more often employed to indicate a single act or event.

(3) The stem form of the cluster can be identified as a gerund (or conjuctive participle). The gerunds will be discussed later.

(4) Not all verbal stems can occur as the first member of these clusters.

28.1

us-kī mā̃ usē samjhā dētī hai.	His mother explains to him.
us-kī mā̃-nē usē samjhā diyā.	His mother explained to him.
us-kī mā̃ usē samjhā dēgī.	His mother will explain to him.
hāthī us ādmī-kō girā dētā hai.	The elephant throws down that man.
hāthī us ādmī-kō girā dēnā cāhtā hai.	The elephant wants to throw down that man.
laṛkā patthar phẽk dētā hai.	The boy throws away the stone.
laṛkē-nē patthar phẽk diyā.	The boy threw away the stone.
laṛkā patthar phẽk dēnē-kī kōśiś kartā hai.	The boy tries to throw away the stone.

klark ḳhat ḍākḳhānē-kō bhēj dētā hai.	The clerk sends the letter to the post office.
klark-nē ḳhat ḍākḳhānē-kō bhēj diyā.	The clerk sent the letter to the post office.
klark-nē ḳhat ḍākḳhānē-kō bhēj diyā hai.	The clerk has sent the letter to the post office.
aurat-nē kām ḳhatam kar diyā.	The woman finished the work.
aurat-nē kām ḳhatam kar diyā hai.	The woman has finished the work.
aurat-nē kām ḳhatam kar diyā thā.	The woman had finished the work.
laṛkī-nē pathik-kō davā pilā dī.	The girl gave the traveller medicine to drink.
us-nē ḳhat āp-kē yahā̃ bhijvā diyā thā.	He had the letter sent to your house.
laṛkē-nē apnē ustād-kō kahānī sunā dī.	The boy told the story to his teacher.
phir us-nē us-kō sac batā diyā.	He then told him the truth.
acchē ādmī-nē faḳīrō̃-kō khānā khilā diyā.	The good man fed the mendicants.
ādmī sigrēṭ phẽk dētā hai.	The man throws away the cigarette.
us-nē usē paisē aur kapṛē dē diyē.	He gave him money and clothing.
laṛkō̃-nē fīs jamā kar dī.	The boys paid the fees.
amīr ādmī-nē apnā sab rupayā dē diyā.	The rich man gave away all his money.
maĩ-nē apnī kitāb apnē dōst-kō dē dī.	I gave my book to my friend.
mērī kitāb mujhē dē dījiyē.	Please give me my book.
us-nē mērī kitāb mujhē dē dī.	He gave me my book.

Here are illustrated verbal clusters with **dēnā.** The use of **dēnā** usually implies that the result or benefit of the action indicated by the stem is **directed away** from the subject (i.e., the English subject) of the verbal cluster towards some other being or thing. Otherwise **dēnā** seems to add emphasis to the action indicated by the stem form.

REMARKS: **ḳhatam** (adj.) finished, **ḳhatam karnā** to finish, **śurū karnā** to begin, **davā** (ī) medicine, **fīs** (ī) fees, **fīs jamā karnā** to pay fees, **faḳīr** (ā) mendicant, beggar, **sac** (ā) truth, **-kē yahā̃** at the place of, **bhijvānā** to cause to send or to send through another person, **phir** then, again, moreover.

28.2

laṛkē-nē baccē-sē miṭhāī chīn lī.	The boy snatched the candy from the child.
us-nē mērī kahānī sun lī.	He overheard my story.
us-nē mērī bāt mān lī.	He agreed to what I said.
sipāhī-nē cōr-kō pakaṛ liyā.	The policeman grabbed the thief.
bāp-nē laṛkē-kō pahcān liyā.	The father recognized the boy.
laṛkē-nē mā̃-kī bāt sun lī.	The boy listened to his mother's story.
musannif-nē afsānā likh liyā.	The author finished writing the short story.
agar āp samajh lē, tō hā̃ kah dījiyē.	If you understand, say 'yes.'
apnī nayī ḳamīz pahan lō.	Put on your new shirt.
is kitāb-par ēk nigāh ḍāl lō!	Take a look at this book!
us-nē mujhē pahcān liyā.	She recognized me.
naukar-nē mēz-sē lālṭain lē lī.	The servant took away the lantern from the table.
nanhē-nē mēz-sē khilaunā lē lēnē-kī kōśiś kī.	The baby tried to take away the toy from the table.

This section illustrates verbal clusters with **lēnā.** The use of **lēnā** usually serves to imply that the result or benefit of the action indicated by the stem form is **directed towards** the subject (i.e., the English subject) of the cluster. Otherwise **lēnā** adds emphasis to the action indicated by the stem form. (Compare the fourth sentence.)

REMARKS: **nigāh** (ī) look, glance, **afsānā** (ā) short story, **musannif** (ā) author, writer, **lālṭain** (ī) lantern.

28.3

vo bīmār hō gayā.	He became sick.
vo bīmār hō gayā hai.	He has become sick.
vo bīmār hō gayā thā.	He had become sick.
vo bīmār paṛ gayī.	She fell sick.
vo bīmār paṛ gayī thī.	She had fallen sick.
vo bīmār hō gāyī.	She became sick.
ādmī sō gayā.	The man went to sleep.
mujhē khānā milnā muśkil hō gayā hai.	It has become difficult for me to obtain food.
billī ṭhīk hō jāẽgī.	The cat will beome well.
us-kā pā̃v phisal gayā.	His foot slipped.
vo apnē bhāī-kē pās pahȭc gayā.	He reached his brother.
vo bahot pānī pī gayā thā.	He had drunk a lot of water.
laṛkā baiṭh gayā.	The boy sat down.
ādmī khaṛā hō gayā.	The man stood up.
baccē jhuk gayē.	The children bowed.
ham lēṭ gayē.	We lay down.
vo mujhē pahcān gayī.	She recognized me.
ye ādmī laṛakpan-mẽ̄-hī fakīr ban gayā.	This man became a beggar while he was still in his youth.
jab maĩ us-kē ghar gayā, vo sō gayā thā.	When I went to his house, he had gone to sleep.
maĩ sārī bāt bhūl gayā thā.	I had forgotten the whole thing.
billī mar gayī.	The cat died.
vo mujh-sē pahilē yahā̃ ā gayā thā.	He had arrived here before me.
maĩ kām karnē baiṭhā-hī thā ke ēk dōst ā gayā.	I was about to start working when a friend came up.

jānā, as the second member of verbal clusters, often indicates that the action indicated by the stem form (especially if it is the stem of an intransitive verb) has been brought to a state of completion. Otherwise the meaning is about the same as that of the stem form when it functions alone.

REMARKS: (1) **bannā,** to become, to be made; **baiṭhnā,** to sit, takes the infinitive of a verb (in the object form) to express **start doing the act indicated by the infinitive;** the conjunction **ke** of that same sentence translates English **that, when.** (See sentence 23, above.)

(2) **-sē pahilē** of sentence twenty-two is identical in function with the postpositional phrase **-kē pahilē, before.**

28.4

tālibilm-nē kitāb phāṛ ḍālī.	The student tore up the book.
ādmī-nē sā̃p-kō lakṛī-sē mār ḍālā.	The man beat the snake (**to death**) with a stick.
us-nē kitāb-mẽ-sē varaḳ phāṛ ḍālē.	He tore the pages out of the book.
us-nē paudē kāṭ dālē.	He cut the plants to pieces.
ādmī sigrēṭ phẽk ḍāltā hai.	The man throws away the cigarette.
naukar-nē macchar mār ḍālā.	The servant killed the mosquito.
baṛhaī-nē daraḳht kāṭ ḍālā.	The carpenter cut down the tree.
ye gandē kapṛē utār ḍālō.	Take off these dirty clothes.
pichlī laṛāī-nē sārī duniyā-kā naḳśā badal ḍālā.	The last war changed the map of the entire world.
ḳarzḳhāhõ-kē taḳāzõ-nē mujhē mār ḍālā hai.	The demands of my creditors have driven me to distraction.

These sentences illustrate verbal clusters with **ḍalnā, to hurl, to throw.** The effect of the use of **ḍālnā** is to add emphasis or force to the action indicated by the stem form.

REMARKS: (1) **duniyā** (ī) world, **naḳśā** (ā) map, **macchar** (ā) mosquito, **laṛāī** (ī) war, **sā̃p** (ā) snake, **varaḳ** (ā) page, **taḳāzā** (ā) demand, **ḳarzḳhāh** (ā) creditor.

(2) Compare sentence five, above, and sentence twenty of section 28.1.

28.5

jab mẽḍak-nē laṛkē-kī āvāz sunī, vo tālāb-mẽ kūd paṛā.	When the frog heard the boy, he jumped into the pond.
jab baccē-nē kahānī-kā anjām sunā, vo ḳhuśī-sē hãs paṛā.	When the child heard the end of the story, he burst out laughing gaily.
chōṭī laṛkī kyũ rō paṛī?	Why did the little girl burst out crying?
laṛkā chat-sē gir paṛā.	The boy fell off the roof.
hamārē ānē-sē pahilē mōṭargāṛī cal paṛī thī.	The automobile had shot off before we arrived.

This section illustrates verbal clusters with **paṛnā. paṛnā** in such clusters indicates the suddenness of the action expressed by the stem form.

REMARKS: **mẽḍak** (ā) frog, **anjām** (ā) end.

28.6

jab maĩ kahānī sunā rahā thā, āp kyũ us-kā anjām bōl uṭhē?	Why did you blurt out the end of the story when I was telling it?
jab hiran-nē śikārī-kō sunā, vo caũk uṭhā.	The deer startled when it heard the hunter.
jab maĩ kamrē-mẽ āyā, naukar jāg uṭhā.	The servant woke up (**suddenly**) when I came into the room.
lakṛī kab jal uṭhī?	When did the wood catch fire?

jab rēlgāṛī rukī, āp kyū̃ ghabrā uṭhē?	Why did you become confused when the train stopped?
jab cōr ghar-mē̃ dāḳhil hūā, caukīdār jāg uṭhā.	The watchman woke up (**suddenly**) when the thief entered the house.

This section illustrates verbal clusters with **uṭhnā. uṭhnā** in such clusters serves to indicate the suddenness of the action expressed by the stem form.

28.7

vo kām kar cukā hai.	He has finished working.
thōṛī dēr-mē̃ maĩ kitāb paṛh cukū̃gā.	In a little while I shall finish reading the book.
maĩ khā cukā hū̃.	I have finished eating.
jab maĩ savāl pūch cukū̃, tab maĩ un-kē javāb pūchū̃gā.	When I am finished asking questions, then I'll ask for the answers to them.
jab us-kī ā̃kh khulī̃, sūraj nikal cukā thā.	When his eyes had opened (= **he woke up**), the sun had (**already**) appeared.
dōpahar-tak pattō̃-sē ōs-kē sab bū̃dē̃ gāyab hō cukī thī̃.	All the dew drops had (**completely**) disappeared from the leaves by noon.
jab-tak āp ye zabān acchī tarah sikhē̃gē, maĩ būṛhā hō cukā hū̃gā.	I will be an old man by the time (**that**) you have learned this language well.
jab mērā bhāī khānā ḳhatam kar cukā, vo sair-kō gayā.	When my brother finished eating, he went out for a walk.
kyā āp vo nāvil paṛhnā ḳhatam kar cukē haĩ?	Have you finished (**reading**) that novel?
jab dādī·ammā kahānī ḳhatam kar cukī̃, baccē sō gayē.	When grandmother finished her story the children went to sleep.

cuknā as the second member of a verbal cluster indicates the completion of the action expressed by the stem form.

REMARKS: **nāvil** (ā) novel, **ōs** (ī) dew, **ōs-kā bū̃d** (ī) dew drop, **gāyab hōnā** to disappear, **pattā** (ā) leaf, **bū̃d** (ī) drop, **zabān** (ī) language, **sūraj** (ā) sun, **sair** (ī) stroll, walk.

28.8 Exercise 1. List the infinitives of the first members (i.e., stem forms) of all the verbal clusters in sections 28.1 to 28.7.

28.8.1 Exercise 2. **Translate into English:**

1. kyā ustād-nē tālibilmō̃-kō kahānī samjhā dī thī? 2. gāṛī dō minaṭ-mē̃ sṭēśan-par pahō̃c jāēgī. 3. naukar-nē apnē mālik-kā huḳam mān liyā. 4. baccē-nē apnē gandē kapṛē utār ḍālē haĩ. 5. mērē savāl pūchnē-sē pahilē tum javāb bōl uṭhnē-kī kyū̃ kōśiś kartē hō? 6. āp apnā kām kab ḳhatam kar dē̃gē? 7. kaun sēb khā gayā? 8. jab kuttē-nē mālik-kō pahcān liyā, tab vo ḳhuś huā. 9. maĩ tairnē-kē liyē daryā-mē̃ kūd paṛū̃gā. 10. cōr-kō ādmī-kō paisē vāpas dē dēnā paṛā. 11. apnī mā̃-kē jānē-par baccā rō uṭhā. 12. ye cīzē̃ lē lījiyē. 13. kyā āp apnā kām ḳhatam kar cukē? 14. bāp-nē laṛkē-kī skūl-kī fīs adā kar dī hai. 15. āp mērī bāt-par kyū̃ hãs paṛē? 16. jab maĩ āp-kē sāth bāt kartī hū̃, āp kyū̃ sō jātē haĩ? 17. naukar āg-kē liyē lakṛī kāṭ ḍālēgā. 18. dō ghanṭē sōnē-kē bād maĩ jāg

uṭhā. 19. tum-nē us-kō sac kyū̃ nahī̃ batā diyā? 20. jab āp ye nāvil paṛhnā k̤hatam kar cukẽgē, maĩ āp-kō ēk dusrī kitāb dū̃gā. 21. agar tum mohtāt na hō, tō tumhārē pā̃v gīlī saṛak-par phisal jāẽgē. 22. āp-nē mērī kitāb-mẽ-sē varak̤ kyū̃ phāṛ ḍālē? 23. chōṭī laṛkī ajnabī-kē pahõcnē-par rō paṛī. 24. burē bandar darak̤ht-sē pakkē phal girā dēnā cāhtē haĩ. 25. jañgal-kē sūkhē darak̤ht jal uṭhē thē. 26. jab musāfir thak gayā, vo ārām karnē-kē liyē darak̤ht-kē nīcē lēṭ gayā. 27. ye purānē jūtē phẽk dō! 28. agar āp kah cukē haĩ, tō maĩ kuch kahū̃gā. 29. dayālū laṛkī-nē pyāsē pathik-kō ṭhaṇḍā pānī pilā diyā. 30. jō ādmī laṛāī karnē-kī kōśiś kartē haĩ, śāyad vo duniyā̃-kā nak̤śā badal ḍālē. 31. laṛkā pēṛ-kī śākh-sē nadī-mẽ gir paṛēgā. 32. kyā naukar-nē āp-kī Hindī samajh lī thī? 33. mērā sigrēṭ kis-nē phẽk diyā? 34. tum mērē kapṛē kab sāf kar cukōgē? 35. mērē jūtē lānē-kē bād naukar baiṭh gayā. 36. aurat-nē bartnõ-par ēk nigāh ḍāl lī, phir dukāndār-sē dō nayī sāṛiyā̃ k̤harīdī̃. 37. jab mẽḍak-nē macherā dēkhā, vo cal paṛā. 38. ādmī bahot zyādā śarāb pī gayā thā. 39. śikārī-kē bandūk uṭhanē-sē pahilē hiran gāyab hō cukẽgē. 40. sipāhī-nē cōr bā̃dhnē-kē liyē us-kī k̤amīz phāṛ ḍālī. 41. jab cōr-nē sipāhī-kō dēkhā, vo ghabrā uṭhā. 42. jab maĩ dōst-kē ghar pahõcā, vo jā cukā thā. 43. agar āp mērī bāt mān lētē haĩ, tō hā̃ kah dījiyē. 44. jab maĩ ye k̤hat paṛh cukū̃gā, maĩ āp-kē sāth bāt karū̃gā. 45. jab hiran-nē śikārī-kā pās-sē calnā sunā, vo caũk uṭhā. 46. lōg pīr-kē sāmnē jhuk jāẽgē. 47. gāy ghās khā cukī thī. 48. hāthī-nē pā̃v-sē k̤hū̃k̤hār bāgh mār ḍālā. 49. jab-tak maĩ bāg-mẽ āyā, bakrā paudõ-sē sab pattē khā cukā thā. 50. baccõ-kō āpnē vāldain-kī bāt sun lēnē-kī kōśiś karnī cāhiyē.

28.8.2 Exercise 3. **Translate into Urdu:**

1. Can you (**msc.**) explain this story to me? 2. Who tore the tenth page out of this book? 3. The man who understood my English tried to answer. 4. What fell off the roof? 5. When had she fallen sick? 6. Please throw down some ripe fruits from the tree to me. 7. If you (**msc.**) become sick, call me. 8. Who blurted out the answers to the questions? 9. Who is the man who glanced at me? 10. The dry branches caught fire. 11. Throw away these old shoes. 12. You should kill all the mosquitoes you can. 13. When you finish this work, I will send you to the post office. 14. You should not try to overhear everything I say. 15. When you have finished this work, I will send you to the post office. 16. Did you send the servant to the post office to buy stamps? 17. Why did the man drink so much cold water? 18. Cut down that big tree which is near the house. 19. When he couldn't understand me, the servant got confused. 20. Did the traveller recognize all the holy places? 21. Have you told me the truth? 22. When the teacher repeated the question, the student blurted out the answer. 23. When the master came out of the house, the servant stood up. 24. After you read this letter, tear it up. 25. Has grandmother finished telling the story? 26. Give this food to the mendicants who are outside. 27. When they heard my Urdu, they burst out laughing. 28. When will the shoemaker finish sewing my shoe? 29. The sick bullock will die. 30. Why did he shoot off when we arrived? 31. Did the automobile reach the station before the train came? 32. Hearing the hunter, the elephants startled. 33. When did you pay your school fees? 34. The hungry traveller will finish eating in a little while. 35. Who tore up the letter I had placed on this table? 36. Upon his leaving, the man's children burst out crying. 37. I (**fm.**) will finish reading this novel tomorrow. 38. Who took the chair away? 39. Take away the chairs after my friends leave. 40. When all my friends arrived, we sat down to talk. 41. It isn't necessary to try to beat to death every snake you see.

42. Have you finished preparing everything for my travel? 43. Why don't you (**fm.**) agree to what I (**msc.**) say? 44. The dish fell off the table. 45. The tiger ran off just before the hunter could kill (**it**) with his gun. 46. Who has finished eating? 47. When I recognized my friend, I called him. 48. You should be careful when you jump into cold water after eating. 49. I (**msc.**) will finish writing these letters after you go. 50. You (**msc.**) must take off your wet shoes.

28.9 Text 11: **Śahar Lāhōr.**[1]

Translate into English. Answer the questions in Urdu:

Lāhōr dunyā[2] -kē sab-sē purānē śahrō̃-mē̃-sē ēk hai. lōg kahtē haī ke[3] āj-sē taḳrīban[4] dō hazār sāl pahilē Rājā Ram Candar[5] -kē ēk bēṭē-nē is śahar-kī bunyād[6] ḍālī thī. agar āp āj • kal Lāhōr jāẽ, tō āp dēkhẽgē ke[3] ye śahar siraf purānā-hī nahī̃, balke bahot ḳhūbsūrat-bhī hai. Lāhōr dō hissō̃-mē̃ munḳasim[7] hai. purānā Lāhōr, jis-kē-gird[8] ēk divār hai, is hissē-mē̃ galiyā̃ tang aur makān purānē faiśan[9] -kē haī. in galiyō̃-mē̃ mōṭargāṛī calānā[10] muśkil hai. kuch galiyā̃ tō itnī tang haī ke[11] un-mē̃ tā̃gā-bhī nahī̃ jā saktā. bāz[12] ghārō̃-mē̃ kamēṭī[13] -kā pānī jātā hai, lēkin kuch lōgō̃-kē gharō̃-mē̃ kuẽ haī. is hissē-mē̃ pānī-kē nikās[14] -kā zyādā acchā intazām[15] nahī̃, is liyē galiyō̃-mē̃ kīcaṛ[16] vagairā hō jātā hai aur safāī rakhnā[17] -bhī muśkil hai. natījā ye hai ke[11] kabhī kabhī vabā[18] phail jātī[19] hai. garmī-kē mausam-mē̃ bahot-sē lōgō̃-kō malēriyā[20] buḳhār[21] hō jātā hai. cū̃-ke Pākistān-mē̃ ḍākṭarō̃ aur narsō̃[22] -kī kamī[23] hai, is liyē har sāl kuch lōg buḳhār-sē mar jātē haī. hā̃,[24] ēk bāt hai. jab-sē Pākistān banā hai Lāhōr-kī kamēṭī purānē śahar-mē̃ safāī rakhnē aur bīmāriyō̃-kī rōk • thām[25] karnē-kī bahot kōśiś kar rahī hai. kaī nayē haspatāl banē haī, jahā̃ bīmārō̃-kā muft ilāj hōtā hai. sarkār-nē Lāhōr-mē̃ ēk nayā mēḍikal kālij[26] khōlā hai. ēk laṛkō̃ aur laṛkiyō̃-kē liyē aur dūsrā siraf laṛkiyō̃-kē liyē. har sāl kōī dō sau laṛkē • laṛkiyā̃ ḍākṭarī pās kartē[27] haī. Lāhōr-kā dusrā hissā nisbatan[28] nayā hai. is ilāḳē[29] -mē̃ bahot-sē bāg aur pārk[30] haī. saṛkẽ cauṛī aur imārtẽ nayī tarz[31] -kī haī. sab-sē maśhūr saṛak-kā nām Māl Rōḍ hai. is saṛak-par lāṭ • sāhab-kī kōṭhī hai. Panjāb Yūnivarsiṭī[32] -kī imārtẽ-bhī isī saṛak-par haī. subah nau bajē-kē ḳarīb[33] is saṛak-par baṛī raunak[34] hōtī hai. saīkrō̃ mard • aurtẽ,[35] sāiklō̃,[36] tā̃gō̃ aur mōṭrō̃-par apnē apnē[37] skūlō̃, kālijō̃ aur daftarō̃-kō jātē haī. har cauk-par ēk sipāhī ṭrēfik-kō kānṭrōl karnē[38] -kē liyē khaṛā hōtā hai. jō lōg ḳānūn-kē ḳhilāf calẽ, un-kā cālān hōtā hai. isī ilāḳē-mē̃ gōrmenṭ kālij[39] hai. ye kālij sārē Pākistān-mē̃ avval • nambar-par hai. is kālij-mē̃ paṛhānēvālē[40] prōfaisrō̃-kī bahot izzat[41] hōtī hai. is kālij-kō śurū huē[42] taḳrīban sau sāl hō gaye haī. yahā̃ kōī bārā sau laṛkē aur laṛkiyā̃ paṛhtē haī. lēkin laṛkiyā̃ muśkil-sē[43] ēk sau hōgī. ām-taur-par laṛkiyā̃ laṛkiyō̃-kē kālijō̃-mē̃ jātī haī. Lahōr-mē̃ laṛkiyō̃-kē liyē kaī kālij haī. āj • kal sab lōg apnē baccō̃-kō tālīm dēnā cāhtē haī.

Lāhōr-kē ird • gird[44] kaī tārīḳhī makāmāt[45] haī. ēk taraf Jahā̃gīr bādśāh-kā maḳbarā[46] hai. is bādśāh-kē bārē-mē̃ ēk kahānī ham āp-kō sunā cukē haī. jō ummid hai āp-kō yād hōgī. is maḳbarē-kē bilkul pās-hī malikā Nūr Jahā̃-kā maḳbarā-bhī hai. dūsrī taraf ēk bēhad[47] ḳhūbsūrat bāg hai jisē Śālīmār[48] kahtē haī. ye bāg mugal bādśāh Śāhjahā̃-kē zamānē-mē̃ banā thā. in imārtō̃-kī dēkh • bhāl[49] mehekmā āsār-e-ḳadīmā[50] -kē zimmē[51] hai. ham-nē abhī Māl Rōḍ-kā zikr kiyā thā. is saṛak-par aḳhbār "Sival enḍ Miliṭērī Gezaṭ"[52] -kā daftar hai. is daftar-mē̃ ēk kamrā hai, jis-mē̃ āj-sē kaī sāl pahilē Ruḍyarḍ Kipling[53] kām kiyā kartā[54] thā. agarce[55] Kipling-nē Hindūstān-kē bārē-mē̃ kaī galat • salat[56] bātẽ likhī haī, phir-bhī[57] bahot-sē Pākistānī us-kē kitābō̃-kō baṛē śauk-sē paṛhtē haī.

Lāhōr-mẽ sab-sē baṛī ḳhūbī [58] ye hai ke [59] yahā̃-kē lōg bahot acchē haĩ. jō ādmī ēk dafā is śahar-mẽ thōṛī dēr rahtā hai, us-kā dil phir isē chōṛnē-kō nahī̃ cāhtā. is śahar-kī āb-ō-havā [60] -bhī acchī hai. lēkin garmī-kē mausam-mẽ yahā̃ rahnā kuch muśkil hō jātā hai. amīr ādmī is mausam-mẽ Marī [61] calē jātē haĩ. lēkin ġarīb lōgõ-kē pās itnā paisā kahā̃, ke [59] vo garmiyõ-mẽ pahāṛõ-par jāẽ. kuch lōgõ-kā ḳhayāl hai ke [59] Karācī Lāhōr-sē zyādā acchā śahar hai. lēkin mērā ḳhayāl hai ke ye lōg ġalat kahtē [62] haĩ. sac pūchō, [63] tō Karācī Lāhōr-kā muḳābilā [64] nahī̃ kar saktā.

savālāt:

1. Lāhōr-kī sab-sē ḳhūbsūrat saṛak kaun-sī hai? 2. Māl Rōḍ-par kaun kaun-sī imārtẽ haĩ? 3. Śālīmār Bāġ kis bādśāh-nē banvāyā thā? 4. purānē Lāhōr-mẽ safāī-kā intazām kaisā hai? 5. Lāhōr-kī kamēṭī aur sarkār-nē bīmāriyõ-kī rōk • thām karnē-kē liyē kyā kiyā hai?

NOTES: 1. city of Lahore (ā); 2. world (ī); 3. that (**conj.**), see 29.2; 4. about, around (**adv.**); 5. name of king; 6. foundation (ī); 7. divided (**adj., n.c.**); 8. **-kē gird** around, about (**postpos. phrase**); 9. fashion, style (ā); 10. to drive (**tr.**), see 36.1, ff.; 11. see fn. 3; 12. some (**indef. adj.**); 13. municipality (ī); 14. drainage (ā); 15. arrangement (ā); 16. mud (ā); 17. **safāī rakhnā** to keep clean (**tr.**); 18. epidemic (ī); 19. **phail jānā** to spread (**int.**); 20. malaria (ā); 21. fever (ā); 22. nurse (ī); 23. lack, deficiency (ī); 24. = but yes; 25. check (ī); 26. medical college (ā); 27. **ḍākṭarī pās karnā** to qualify for medical degree; 28. comparatively (**adv.**); 29. **ilāḳā** area (ā); 30. park (ā); 31. fashion, style (ī); 32. Panjab University (ī); 33. **-kē ḳarīb** about, around (**postpos. phrase**); 34. hub-bub (ī); 35. men and women (ē); 36. **sāikal** bicycle (ī); 37. for the repetition see 36.2, second group of examples; 38. **kāṇṭrōl karnā** to control (**tr.**); 39. Government College (ā); 40. for **vāla** see 31.2; 41. respect (ī); 42. since the beginning (**adv.**); 43. **muśkil-sē** hardly (= **adv.**); 44. **-kē ird • gird** all around, in the vicinity of (**postpos. phrase**); 45. **tārīḳhī makāmāt** historical place (ā); 46. tomb (ā); 47. exceedingly, without limit (**adv.**); 48. Shalimar (Gardens) (ā); 49. care, maintenance (ī); 50. **mehekmā • āsār-e-ḳadīmā** Archaeological Department, **mehekmā** department (ā), **asar** traces, remains (a), **ḳadīmā** old (adj.); 51. **zimmā** concern (ā); 52. Civil and Military Gazette (ā); 53. Rudyard Kipling; 54. see 34.5; 55. even though (**conj.**); 56. erroneous (**adj., n.c.**); 57. nevertheless (**conj.**); 58. merit, virtue (ī); 59. see fn. 3; 60. climate (ī); 61. town of Marree (ī); 62. **ġalat kahnā** to speak wrongly (**tr.**); 63. = if you ask truly; 64. comparison (ā).

LESSON 29

29.1

ādmī-nē kahā, "maĩ āp-kō nahī̃ jāntā."	The man said, "I do not know you."
klark-nē āḳhir musāfir-sē kahā, "hōṭal-mē̃ khānā nahī̃ hai."	The clerk finally told the traveller, "There is no food in the hotel."
naukar-nē batāyā, "ṭaiksī jānē-kō taiyār hai."	The servant reported, "The taxi is ready to go."
us-nē kahā, "maĩ āp-sē āj milū̃gā."	He said, "I will meet you today."
mālī-nē javāb diyā, "maĩ āj bāg-mē̃ kām nahī̃ kar sakū̃gā."	The gardener answered, "I will not be able to work in the garden today."
injinīr-nē mujh-sē kahā, "gāṛī vaḳt-par nahī̃ chūṭēgī."	The engineer told me, "The train will not leave on time."
maĩ-nē us-sē pūchā, "kyā vo Kalkattē vaḳt-par pahõcēgī?"	I asked him, "Will it arrive in Calcutta on time?"
us-nē mujh-sē pūchā, "bas kahā̃ jā rahī hai?"	He asked me, "Where is the bus going?"
maĩ-nē javāb diyā, "mērē ḳhayāl-mē̃ vo Piśāvar jā rahī hai."	I answered, "I think it is going to Peshavar."

This section takes up one method of indicating quoted utterance or speech in Urdu. This construction can be termed "Direct Discourse." When written or printed, the utterance quoted is placed within quotation marks.

REMARKS: (1) **-sē,** in sentence two, functions with the force of **-kō.**

(2) **ḳhayāl** (ā) opinion, **ḳhāsil karnā** to obtain.

29.1.1 Exercise 1. **Translate into English:**

1. kisān-nē mujh-sē kahā, "jahā̃ rāstā bahot ḍhalvān hōgā, vahā̃ āp-kō bailgāṛī-sē utarnā paṛēgā." 2. maĩ-nē javāb diyā, "mērē safar-mē̃ jahā̃-bhī dilcasp jaghē̃ hõgī, maĩ vahā̃ rukū̃gā." 3. maĩ-nē us-sē pūchā, "jitnā maĩ tum-kō pasand kartā hū̃, kyā tum utnā-hī mujhē pasand kartē hō?" 4. klark-nē mujh-sē kahā, "jitnā ḳhūbsūrat Karācī hai, utnē-hī ḳhūbsūrat Lāhōr hai." 5. ustād-nē tālibilm-sē kahā, "jab tum Sindh-mē̃ safar karōgē, tab tumhē̃, jitnē lōgõ-kē sāth Sindhī bōl sakō, bōlnā cāhiyē." 6. dukāndār-nē sipāhī-sē kahā, "maĩ us ādmī-kē bārē-mē̃ utnā-hī acchā bayān karū̃gā, jitnā ke kar saktā hū̃." 7. mālik-kē

naukar-kō hukam diyā, "jin mazdūrō̃-nē-bhī tumhārē liyē kām kiyā, un-kō ināм dō." 8. bīvī-nē khāvind-sē pūchā, "jab āp śahar-sē vāpas āẽgē, tab kyā āp kisī-kō sāth lāẽgē?" 9. musāfir-nē larkē-sē kahā, "jō pānī daryā-sē ātā hai, vo maĩ nahī̃ pī saktā." 10. klark-nē musāfir-sē pūchā, "hōṭal-mē̃ kitnē dinō̃-kē liyē ṭhaharẽgē?"

29.1.2 Exercise 2. **Translate into Urdu:**

1. I asked the ox-cart driver, "How much money will you take to take me to the village?" 2. The servant told his master, "I had to wait a little while in the shops where there were a lot of people." 3. I asked the farmer, "Do you have as many cows as you have bullocks?" 4. The mendicant told the rich man, "It has become difficult for me to obtain food." 5. The mother told her son, "Take off those dirty clothes!" 6. The man asked his friend, "Why did you blurt out the end of the story when I was telling it?" 7. We asked the engineer, "Why did you get confused when the train stopped?" 8. The teacher told his student, "I will be an old man by the time you have learned this lesson well." 9. I told him, "I will go where you cannot follow me." 10. He answered, "I don't have enough money."

29.2

ādmī-nē kahā ke maĩ āp-kō nahī̃ jāntā.	The man said (**that**) he did not know me.
klark-nē musāfir-sē kahē ke hōṭal-mē̃ khānā nahī̃ hai.	The clerk told the traveller (**that**) there was no food in the hotel.
us-nē kahā ke maĩ āp-sē āj milū̃gā.	He said (**that**) he would meet me today.
mālī-nē javāb diyā ke maĩ āj bāg-mē̃ kām nahī̃ kar sakū̃gā.	The gardener answered (**that**) he would not be able to work in the garden that day.
injinīr-nē mujh-sē kahā ke gāṛī vakt-par nahī̃ chūṭēgī.	The engineer told me (**that**) the train would not leave on time.
maĩ-nē us-sē pūchā ke kyā vo Karācī vakt-par pahō̃cēgī?	I asked him if it would arrive in Karachi on time.
us-nē mujh-sē pūchā ke bas kahā̃ jā rahī hai?	He asked me where the bus was going.
maĩ-nē javāb diyā ke mērē khayāl-mē̃ vo Multān jā rahī hai.	I answered (**that**) I thought it was going to Multan.
maĩ nahī̃ jāntā thā ke tumhārē paṛhnē-kā kyā natījā hōgā.	I did not know what the result of your studying would be.
mujhē ummīd thī ke āp Urdū paṛh sakẽgē.	I hoped (**that**) you would be able to read Urdu.
mērē khayāl thā ke āj bāriś hōgī.	I thought (**that**) it would rain today.
mujhē afsōs thā ke maĩ āp-kē sāth daftar nahī̃ ā sakū̃gā.	I regretted (**that**) I would not be able to come with you to the office.

This section presents another method of expressing quoted utterance or speech in Urdu. Here the particle **ke, that,** is placed directly before the utterance which is phrased in exactly the same form as when it was originally spoken or expressed.

The construction is identical with that described in section 29.1 with the exception that the particle **ke** is placed before the quoted utterance and no quotation marks are employed.

REMARKS: (1) It is often not necessary to express the word **that** in such constructions in English; it is therefore placed here in parentheses.

(2) See sentences nine to twelve and observe that words or expressions indicating **knowing, hoping, thinking, regretting,** and the like, participate in this construction.

(3) See the English translation of the sixth sentence for **ke** translating English **if.**

(4) **natījā** (ā) result.

29.2.1 Exercise 1. **Translate into English:**

1. mujhē ummīd hai ke āj bāriś nahī̃ hōgī. 2. kyā āp-kā ḳhayāl hai ke rāstā bahot ḍhalvān hōgā. 3. ham nahī̃ jāntē ke kisān-kē kām karnē-kā kyā natījā hōgā. 4. us-kō afsōs hai ke jitnī miṭhāī vo cāhtā hai, utnī nahī̃ lē saktā. 5. kyā us-nē āp-sē pūchā ke sarkārī makān yahā̃-sē kitnī dūr hai? 6. maī-nē us-sē kahā ke rōśnī aur andhērē-mē̃ fark hai. 7. musāfir-nē hamē̃ batāyā ke Bañgāl-mē̃ lōg machlī aur cāval khātē haī. 8. kyā ajnabī tum-sē pūch rahā hai ke jō rāstā śahar jātā hai, kaun-sā hai? 9. kaun us-kō batāēgā ke ye ṭhīk rāstā nahī̃ hai? 10. kyā āp jāntē haī ke kis-nē ye ḳhat likhā hai?

29.2.2 Exercise 2. **Translate into Urdu:**

1. I hope you will be able to come to see me. 2. Do you know where this road goes? 3. Why does he think I can speak Urdu well? 4. I regret I cannot understand you. 5. Who knew where I could buy rice and fish? 6. Did you ask him when the train would arrive? 7. He told me everything was ready for our departure. 8. Do you know what that man is? 9. Why must you always ask where I have been? 10. The man who knows the road to Multan will tell you.

29.3

māhīgīr-nē kahā ke vo mujhē nahī̃ jāntā thā.	The fisherman said (**that**) he did not know me.
klark-nē musāfir-sē kahā ke hōṭal-mē̃ khānā nahī̃ thā.	The clerk told the traveller (**that**) there was no food in the hotel.
naukar-nē batāyā ke ṭaiksī jānē-kō taiyār thī.	The servant reported (**that**) the taxi was ready to go.
us-nē kahā ke vo āj mujh-sē milēgā.	He said (**that**) he would meet me today.
mālī-nē javāb diyā ke vo us din bāg̱-mē̃ kām nahī̃ kar sakēgā.	The gardener answered (**that**) he would not be able to work in the garden that day.
injinīr-nē mujh-sē kahā ke gāṛī vaḳt-par nahī̃ chū̃ṭēgī.	The engineer told me the train would not leave on time.
maī-nē us-sē pūchā ke kyā vo Ḍhākā vaḳt-par pahõcēgī?	I asked him if it would arrive in Dacca on time.
us-nē mujh-sē pūchā ke bas kahā̃ jā rahī thī.	He asked me where the bus was going.
maī-nē javāb diyā ke mērē ḳhayāl-mē̃ vo Rājśāhī jā rahī thī.	I answered that I thought it was going to Rajshahi.
mujhē nahī̃ mālūm thā ke tumhārē paṛhnē-kā kyā natījā hōgā.	I did not know what the result of your studying would be.
mujhē ummīd thī ke āp Urdū paṛh sakẽgē.	I hoped (**that**) you would be able to read Urdu.
mērā ḳhayāl thā ke āj bādal āẽgē.	I thought (**that**) it would be cloudy today.

kal mujhē afsōs huā ke maĩ āp-kē sāth daftar nahī̃ ā saktā thā. — I regretted yesterday (**that**) I could not come with you to the office.

This section illustrates a third method of expressing quoted utterance or speech in Urdu. Here the tense of the verb of the quoted utterance is the same as that of the English.

Note that in sentences 4 to 7 and 10 to 12 the past of the English future (e.g., **would meet, would be able,** etc.) is translated by the simple future.

Grammarians often term this construction "Indirect Discourse."

29.3.1 Exercise 1. **Translate into English:**

1. dhōbī-nē kahā ke vo kapṛē vāpas nahī̃ layā. 2. mujhē k̤hayāl thā ke maĩ-nē mōṭargāṛī-mē̃ kāfī pānī ḍālā thā. 3. kis-nē āp-sē kahā ke maĩ āp-sē milnē-kē liyē nahī̃ ā saktā thā? 4. kyā naukar-nē batāyā ke us-nē k̤hat ḍākk̤hānē-kō bhēj diyā thā? 5. maĩ-nē samjhā diyā ke vo mōṭargāṛī-kī marammat nahī̃ kar saktā thā. 6. gāṛībān-nē kah diyā ke vo mujhē śahar lē jāēgā. 7. garīb ādmī-nē meharbān aurat-kō javāb diyā ke usē khānā k̤hāsil karnā muśkil hō gayā thā. 8. mā̃-nē baccō̃-sē pūchā ke kaun sab sēbō̃-kō khā gayā thā. 9. mujhē afsōs hai ke jañgal-kē sūkhē darak̤ht jal uṭhē thē. 10. us-nē mujh-sē kahā ke agar maĩ kah cukū̃, tō vo kuch kahēgā.

29.3.2 Exercise 2. **Translate into Urdu:**

1. Who asked me when I would come back? _. Do you know if the servant has killed all the mosquitoes? 3. I told the boy that when he had finished working I would send him to the post office. 4. The servant asked the traveller why he wanted to drink so much cold water. 5. Did you ask the shoemaker when he would finish sewing my shoes? 6. I told my servant that he should give rice to the beggars who were standing in front of the house. 7. He asked me why I didn't agree to everything he said. 8. Aren't you sorry that the answer to the question you blurted out was wrong? 9. The traveller asked who could explain the map to him. 10. Didn't you think it would rain today?

29.4

is baṛē jahāz-par tīn yā cār chōṭī kaśtiyā̃ haĩ. — On this large ship there are three or four little boats.

baṛē jahāz-par tīn yā cār chōṭī kaśtiyā̃ hōtī haĩ. — On a large ship there are three or four little boats.

is mēz-kī tīn ṭā̃gē̃ haĩ. — This table has three legs.

mēzō̃-kī cār ṭā̃gē̃ hōtī haĩ. — Tables have four legs.

ye daryā gahrā hai. — This river is deep.

daryā gahrē hōtē haĩ. — Rivers are deep.

āj • rāt āsmān-par bahot-sē sitārē haĩ. — Tonight there are many stars in the sky.

rāt-kō āsmān-par bahot-sē sitārē hōtē haĩ. — At night there are many stars in the sky.

in kahāniyō̃-mē̃ bahot-sī dilcasp bātē̃ thī̃. — There were many interesting things in these stories.

kahāniyō̃-mē̃ bahot-sī dilcasp bātē̃ hōtī thī̃.	There were many interesting things in stories.
un jhāṛiyō̃-par lambē-sē kā̃ṭē thē.	There were (**rather**) long thorns on those bushes.
jhāṛiyō̃-par lambē-sē kā̃ṭē hōtē thē.	There were (**rather**) long thorns on bushes.
us bāg-mē̃ chōṭē-sē parindē thē.	There were small birds in that garden.
bāgō-mē̃ chōṭē-sē parindē hōtē thē.	There were small birds in gardens.
is bandargāh-mē̃ kaī kaśtiyā̃ thī̃.	There were several boats in this harbor.
bandargāh-mē̃ kaī kaśtiyā̃ hōtī thī̃.	There were several boats in a harbor.
is chōṭē jazīrē-mē̃ bahot-sē jānvar nahī̃ haī.	There are not many animals on this small island.
chōṭē jazīrō̃-mē̃ bahot-sē jānvar nahī̃ hōtē haī.	There are not many animals on small islands.
in nayē jālō̃-mē̃ chēd nahī̃ haī.	There are no holes in these new nets.
nayē jālō̃-mē̃ chēd nahī̃ hōtē haī.	There are no holes in new nets.
in gā̃vō̃-kē pās kīcaṛvālī pagḍanḍiyā̃ thī̃.	There were muddy paths near these villages.
gā̃vō̃-kē pās kīcaṛvālī pagḍanḍiyā̃ hōtī thī̃.	There were muddy paths near villages.
vo saḳht zamīn zarḳhēz nahī̃ hai.	That hard ground is not fertile.
saḳht zamīn zarḳhēz nahī̃ hōtī hai.	Hard ground is not fertile.
ye tañg galī ḳhatarnāk hai.	This narrow street is dangerous.
tañg galī ḳhatarnāk hōtī hai.	A narrow street is dangerous.
is hāthī-kī khāl baṛī khurdarī hai.	This elephant has a very rough hide.
hāthī-kī khāl baṛī khurdarī hōtī hai.	An elephant has a very rough hide.
vo pahāṛ bahot ū̃cē thē.	Those mountains were very high.
pahāṛ ām-taur-par bahot ū̃cē hōtē thē.	The mountains were usually very high.

This section illustrates the difference in function between forms of the verb **hōnā, to be, to become**—i.e., between **hai, thā,** and **hōtā hai, hōtā thā.**

The sentences, above, have been arranged in pairs. The verb in the first sentence of each of these pairs is **hai** or **thā;** that of the second sentence is **hōtā hai** or **hōtā thā.** The use of **hai** or **thā** indicates reference to a specific being, thing or event; the use of **hōtā hai** or **hōtā thā** implies a general statement about a being, thing or event.

Compare the English translations of the following: the first sentence of the first group, **On this** (**specific**) **large ship there are three or four little boats.,** and the second sentence, **On a large ship there are** (**generally**) **three or four little boats.;** the first sentence in the third group, **This (specific) river is deep.**, and the second, **Rivers (generally) are deep.**; the first sentence in the fifth group, **There were many interesting things in these (specific) stories.**, and the second, **There were (generally) many interesting things in stories.**; and the first sentence in the eighth group, **There were several boats in this (specific) harbor.**, and the second sentence, **There were (generally) several boats in a harbor.**

REMARKS: (1) See the fourth, fifth, sixth, seventh and ninth sets of sentences for the function of the particle **-sā.** When this particle is attached to an adjective it gives an allusion of indefiniteness to its meaning. The **-sā** along with the adjective to which it is attached agrees in gender, number and case with the noun modified. **bahot-sē** could be translated **rather many; lambā-sā, rather long; chōṭā-sā, rather small.**

(2) In sentences 15 and 16 **kaī** means **several.**

(3) See **gāvō̃-** of sentences 21 and 22, above, and the singular **gāō** town.

(4) See sentences 27 and 28 for the use of the adjective **baṛā** to mean **very.**

(5) **āsmān** (ā) sky, **kāṭ** (ā) thorn, **khāl** (ā) hide, **galī** (ī) street, **chēd** (ā) hole, **jāl** (ā) net, **jhāṛī** (ī) bush, **ṭā̃g** (ī) leg, **jazīrā** (ā) island, **kaśtī** (ī) boat, **pagḍaṇḍī** (ī) path, **pahāṛ** (ā) mountain, **sitārā** (ā) star.

29.4.1 Exercise 1. **Translate into English:**

1. kyā un gāvō̃-mē̃ bahot-sē lōg thē? 2. mērī haiṭ kahā̃ hai? 3. gāvō̃-kē pās kitnī kīcaṛvālī pagḍaṇḍiyā̃ hōtī haī? 4. daryā-kē kinārē-par bahot-sē māhīgīr thē. 5. kyā saṛkē lambī-sī hōtī thī? 6. baṛē jahāz-par bahot-sē jahāzī hōtē haī. 7. is kuē̃-mē̃ mīṭhā pānī hai. 8. śahar-mē̃ baṛē-sē makān haī. 9. un gāvō̃-kē pās kitnī pagḍaṇḍiyā haī? 10. daryā-kē kinārē-par bahot-sē mahīgīr hōtē thē.

29.4.2 Exercise 2. **Translate into Urdu:**

1. That farmer had a (**rather**) small plow. 2. In a big city there are (**rather**) narrow streets. 3. There were many people in railroad stations. 4. That tree has many flowers and fruits. 5. That automobile has five wheels. 6. Wells are (**rather**) deep. 7. Animals which live in the jungle are dreadful. 8. Moneylenders have a lot of money. 9. That moneylender has many houses. 10. These wells were (**rather**) deep.

29.5 Text 12: **Mērī Āp•bītī.**[1] **(Pahilā Hissā)**

maī san unnīs sau chabbīs-mē̃ disambar [2] -kī satrā tārīkh-kō paidā huā. mērī ammī kahtī haī ke paidā hōṭē-hī[3] maī-nē cīkhnā[4] śurū kar diyā. lēkin kām-ō-bēś[5] maī ēk acchā baccā thā. jab maī tīn sāl-kā thā, mujhē muharikā bukhār [6] huā, jō dō mahīnē rahā. lēkin us-kē bād āj-tak mujhē kōī khatarnāk bīmārī nahī̃ huī. mujhē yād hai ke us zamānē-mē̃ maī kuttō̃-sē bahot ḍartā thā. cār sāl-kī umr-mē̃ maī ēk skūl-mē̃ dākhil hō gayā. jab maī chē sāl-kā thā mērē abbā-nē mujhē ēk chōṭā-sā bāisikal kharīd diyā. maī is bāisikal-par caṛhkar [7] skūl jātā thā. har dafā mujhē rāstē-mē̃ ēk kuttā miltā. ye kuttā bahot baṛā aur khaufnāk [8] thā. jab vo mujhē dēkhtā, bhō̃ktā huā [9] mērē pīchē dauṛtā. maī ḍarkar [10] apnā sāikal tēz calātā, lēkin kuttā-bhī utnī-hī zyādā tēzī-sē mērē pīchē dauṛtā. jab vo mērē pās pahō̃c jātā, tō maī apnī jēb-sē ēk biskuṭ [11] nikālkar [12] us-kī taraf phaīktā. us-kē bād maī apnē sāikal-kō tēz calātā huā [13] skūl pahō̃c jātā. agarce maī ab kuttō̃-sē nahī̃ ḍartā, lēkin phir-bhī maī un-kō zyādā pasand nahī̃ kartā. jab maī das sāl-kā thā, mujhē ghōṛē-kī savārī [14] -kā bahot śauk thā. mērē abbā-kē pās us zamānē-mē̃ dō ghōṛē thē. ēk dafā-kā zikr hai ke maī ghōṛē-par savār hōkar [15] subah subah sair karnē-kē liyē gayā. maī-nē dēkhā ke ēk aur laṛkā, jō umr-mē̃ mujh-sē bahot baṛā thā, apnē ghōṛē-kō tēz dauṛātā [16] thā. maĩ-nē sōcā ke mujhē-bhī apnē ghōṛē-kō tēz dauṛānā cāhiyē. maĩ-nē apnē ghōṛē-kō ēk patlī-sī [17] chaṛī-sē mārā. ghōṛā jō bahot mazbūt thā, fauran sarpaṭ dauṛnē [18] lagā.[19] maĩ-nē ēk hāth-sē lagām [20] aur dūsrē hāth-sē ghōṛē-kī gardan-par, jō lambē bāl thē, un-kō pakṛā. maĩ ḍartā thā ke maĩ nīcē gir paṛũgā. maĩ-nē zōr-sē ghōṛē-kī lagām khaĩcī aur usē ahistā karnē-kī kōśiś kī. lēkin jũ jũ maĩ usē ahistā karnē-kī kōśiś kartā vo aur-bhī tēz dauṛtā. āḵẖir maĩ itnā ghabrāyā ke maĩ-nē cīkhnā śurū kar diyā. mērī cīkhē̃ sunkar [21] ghōṛā-bhī ḍarā aur is dafā itnā tēz dauṛā ke maĩ nīcē gir paṛā. mujhē ḵẖuś·kismatī [22] -sē zyādā cōṭ [23] na lagī.[24] lēkin jab maĩ apnē pãõ-par khaṛā huā, ghōṛā gaib hō cukā thā. maĩ bahot idhar udhar bhāgā, lēkin us-kā kōī niśān na milā. mērē abbā-nē abhī cand [25] din pahilē usē dō hazār rūpayē-mē̃ ḵẖarīdā thā. maĩ ghar vāpas āyā aur maĩ-nē abbā-kō sārā vāḳyā sunāyā. unhõ-nē pōlīs-mē̃ ripōrṭ kī, lēkin ghōṛē-kā kōī patā na calā. bīs sāl hō gayē haĩ, vo āj-tak vāpas nahī̃ āyā. ab tō śayad mar-bhī gayā hōgā. ye kahnē-kī zarūrat nahī̃ ke mērē abbā bahot ḵẖafā huē aur unhõ-nē dō·bārā kabhī mujhē apnē ghōṛē-par caṛhnē na diyā [26] sōlā sāl-kī umr-mē̃ maĩ-nē hāiskūl-kā imtahān pās kiyā aur kālij-mē̃ dāḵẖil hō gayā. cār sāl kālij-mē̃ guzārē. ye zindagī [27] baṛē mazē-kī thī. kālij skūl-sē bahot muḵẖtalif [28] thā. har prōfaisar·sāhab apnē pīryāḍ-mē̃ hāzrī lētē thē. jō klās gair·hāzir [29] hō, usē cār ānē jurmānā hōtā thā. kālij-mē̃ sigraṭ pīnē-kī ijāzat nahī̃ thī. phir-bhī kaī laṛkē cōrī cōrī [30] sigraṭ pītē thē. thōṛī dēr-kē bād maĩ-nē-bhī sigraṭ pīnā śurū kar diyā. tab-sē pī rahā hū̃. agarce paisē fazūl ḵẖarc hōtē haĩ, galā ḵẖarāb hōtā hai, lēkin phir-bhī pītā rahtā hū̃. ēk din-mē̃ bīs sigraṭ. ādat hō gayī hai. ab isē chōṛnā muśkil hai. maĩ kaī dafā kālij-mē̃ sigraṭ pītē huē [31] pakṛā gayā [32] aur mujhē jurmānā huā. lēkin maĩ-nē prōfaisar·sāhab-sē muāf karvā liyā. ye prōfaisar mujh-par bahot meharbān thē. āp-lōg śayad mērī kahānī suntē suntē thak gayē haĩ. bāḳī aglī dafā sunāũgā.

savālāt:

1. jō kuttā mujhē rāstē-mē̃ miltā thā, us-kē bārē-mē̃ tum kyā jāntē hō? 2. maĩ ghōṛē-sē nīcē kyũ gir paṛā? 3. jab maĩ apnē pãõ-par khaṛā huā tō ghōṛā kahā̃ thā? 4. mujhē bacpan-mē̃ kyā bīmārī huī? 5. maĩ-nē sigraṭ pīnā kab śurū kiyā?

NOTES: 1. autobiography (ī); 2. December (ā); 3. as soon as I was born; 4. to scream (tr.); 5. more or less (adv.); 6. typhoid fever (ā); 7. riding, getting on, see 30.1; 8. dreadful (adj., n.c.); 9. barking, see 34.2; 10. becoming frightened, see 30.1; 11. biscuit; 12. taking out, see 30.1; 13. riding, driving, see 34.2; 14. **ghōṛē-kī savārī** horse-riding (ī); 15. **ghōṛē-par savār hōkar** seated on horseback, see 30.1; 16. **dauṛānā** to race, cause to run (tr.), see 36.1, ff.; 17. for -**sā**, see 38.1; 18. **sarpaṭ dauṛnā** to gallop (tr.); 19. see 34.1.2; 20. bridle (ī); 21. hearing, see 30.1; 22. good fortune (ī); 23. hurt (ī); 24. see 34.1.1; 25. few (indef. adj.); 26. see 37.2.3; 27. life (ī); 28. different (adj., n.c.); 29 absent (adj., n.c.); 30. secretly (adv.); 31. see 34.2; 32. see 37.1.

LESSON 30

30.1

apnī kāmyābī-kī ḳhabar sunkar, tālibilm ḳhuśī-sē nācnē lagā.	Hearing the news of his success, the student began to dance with joy.
apnē bēṭē-kā hāth pakaṛkar, bāp-nē śahar--mẽ calnā śurū kiyā.	Taking his son by the hand, the father started to walk through the town.
Rāvalpindī pahõckar, us-nē mujhē ēk lambī-sī ciṭṭhī likhī.	Reaching Rawalpindi, he wrote me a (**rather**) long letter.
ghaṇṭī-kī āvāz sunkar, tālibilm skūl-kī taraf calē.	Hearing the sound of the bell, the students started for school.
apnē naukar-kō sāth lēkar, vo maśhūr jaghẽ dēkhnē-kō gayā.	He went to see the celebrated (or **famous**) places, taking his servant with him.
apnā kamrā sāth lēkar, fōṭōgrāfar tasvīrẽ lēnē-kē liyē bāhar gayā.	The photographer went out to take pictures, taking his camera with him.
dōnõ hisābõ-kō dēkhkar, us-nē tay kiyā ke pahilā ṭhīk thā.	Looking at the two calculations, he decided that the first was correct.
jāgkar, bistar-sē kūd paṛā aur us-nē kapṛē pahanē.	Waking up, he jumped out of bed and dressed.
dhīrē- aur hōśiyārī-sē khiṛkī khōlkar, us-nē bāhar dēkhā.	Having opened the window slowly and carefully, he looked out.
apnē kām-kā natījā dēkhkar, vo himmat hār gayā.	Having seen the result of his work, he became discouraged.
saṛak-par jākar, us-nē ēk ṭaiksī bulāyī aur us-mẽ baiṭh gayā.	Having run into the street, he called a taxi and got into it.
mēz-par kōṭ rakhkar, klark-nē javāb dēnā śurū kiyā.	Having placed (**his**) coat on the table, the clerk began to answer.
pahilī kahānī sunākar, maĩ-nē dūsrī kahānī sunāyī.	Having related the first story, I related the second story.
āp-sē milkar, mujhē baṛī ḳhuśī huī.	I am very glad to meet you. (lit., **Having met you, I became very glad.**)
bāvarcīḳhānē-mẽ jākar, bāvarcī-sē kahō ke āj murg̱ pakāē.	Go into the kitchen and tell the cook to cook a chicken today.

apnē kāgaz baig-mẽ rakhkar, vakīl jānē-kō uṭhā.	The lawyer put his notes into his briefcase and began to leave.
maĩ-nē bāzār jākar, kuch ām ḳharīdē.	I went to the market and bought some mangoes.
vo khānē-kē kamrē-mẽ jākar, ēk mēz-par baiṭh gayā.	He went into the dining-room and sat down at a table.
naukar-kō bulākar, us-nē usē ēk aḳhbār lānē-kō kahā.	He called (**his**) servant and told him to bring a newspaper.

This section deals with the construction involving forms, termed by grammarians the Gerund, Conjunctive Participle, or Absolutive. This form can be identified as comprising **the stem of a verb** to which has been added **-kar.** (See in the first three sentences **sunkar, pakaṛkar, pahõckar.**)

A check of the English translations of these sentences will show the gerund-construction is employed to translate English sentences containing one or more phrases whose principal verbal form ends in **-ing** or is a sequence beginning with the word **having** and **the past principle of a verb.** The first two groups of sentences illustrate these constructions. Note that the verbal form or forms ending in **-ing** and the principal verb must have the **same** subject.

The third group of English sentences, though having the same construction in Urdu, comprise (in English) two independent clauses, linked by the word **and.** Note, again, that the verbs have the **same** subject.

REMARKS: (1) **śurū karnā** of sentences 2 and 12 translates **to begin, to start,** taking the infinitive of the verb which is placed directly before it.

(2) **lagnā** of sentence 1 translates **to begin, to start,** taking the object form of the infinitive which is placed directly before it.

(3) **karnā, to do,** has as its gerund form **karkē** and sometimes **karkar.**

(4) See sentence 4 for the phrase **skūl-kī taraf calnā,** translated **start for school.**

(5) **kāgaz** (ā) paper, notes, **kōṭ** (ā) coat, **ḳhabar** (ī) news, **glās** (ā) glass, **ghanṭī** (ī) bell, **tay (adj.)** decided, **tay karnā** to decide, **baig** (ā) briefcase, satchel, **bistar** (ā) bed, bedding, **bāvarcī** (ā) cook, **vakīl** (ā) lawyer, **kāmyābī** (ī) success, **skūl** (ā) school, **himmat** (ī) courage, **himmat hārnā** to become discouraged, **hisāb** (ā) calculation, account, **hōśiyārī** (ī) intelligence, carefulness.

30.1.1 Exercise 1. **Translate into English:**

1. apnē paṛhnē-kā natījā dēkhkar, vo jānē-kō uṭhā. 2. gadhē-kō mārkar, dhōbī-nē us-kō calāyā. 3. us-kā ḳhat paṛhkar, maĩ himmat hār gayā. 4. hōśiyārī-sē darvāzā khōlkar, us-nē bāhar dēkhā. 5. bāvarcīḳhānē-mẽ jākar, bāvarcī-kō bulāō. 6. gāṛī bulākar, ham us-mē baiṭh gayē. 7. jaldī-sē khiṛkī khōlkar, us-nē ēk ṭaiksī bulāyī. 8. āp-kī kāmyābī-kī ḳhabar sunkar, dōst sab lōgõ-kō batānē lagā. 9. apnī kahānī sunākar, faḳīr-nē ham-sē khānā liyā. 10. tum, bāzār jākar, kyā cīzẽ vāpas lāyē? 11. kisān-kī āvāz sunkar, bail us-kī taraf dauṛnē lagā. 12. apnē mālik-kē pahõcnē-kī ḳhabar sunkar, naukar un-kē sāmnē āyā. 13. ye cīzẽ mōṭargāṛī-mẽ rakhkar, mērā intazār karō. 14. ḳhat likhkar, vo himmat hār gayā. 15. apnā kemrā sāth lēkar, maĩ mandarõ-kī tasvīrẽ lēnē-kē liyē bāhar gayā.

30.1.2 Exercise 2. **Translate into Urdu:**

1. The farmer stopped and fed his bullocks. 2. We (**msc.**) rented a boat and went fish-

ing. 3. Running quickly, he boarded the train and sat down. 4. We went to the villages and spoke with the people. 5. Grab the ox and take him back to the field. 6. Who went to the market and brought back these vegetables? 7. Hearing the news of my success, all my friends came to see me. 8. Waking up, he ran out to see what happened. 9. You shouldn't have gone into the kitchen and told the cook that the food was not good. 10. Who used this plow and broke it? 11. Please place the things on the table and go! 12. Why did you (**fm.**) become happy on reading his letter? 13. Look at the two calculations and tell me which one is correct. 14. Take the child by the hand and go into the garden. 15. Why didn't you (**msc.**) hire a car and go to the celebrated places?

30.2

band karnē-kē bād us-nē ṭēlēfōn-kō phir mēz-par rakh diyā.	After hanging up, he put the telephone back on the table.
ḳhatam karnē-kē bād us-nē kitāb phẽk dī.	After he finished (**reading**) the book, he threw it away.
rēḍiyō sunnē-kē bād us-nē paṛhnā śurū kiyā.	After listening to the radio, he began to study.
masjid-sē ānē-kē bād maĩ-nē apnē jūtē phir pahan liyē.	After coming out of the mosque, I put on my shoes again.
sab kamrõ-mẽ jānē-kē bād āḳhir vo apnē daftar-kō pahõcā.	After going into all the rooms, he finally reached his office.
thōṛī dēr paidal calnē-kē bād maĩ ārām-kē liyē ṭhaharā.	After walking for a while, I stopped for a rest.

This section and the three following illustrate constructions in which the infinitive appears before a postposition or a postpositional phrase. Note that the infinitive is placed in the **object** form.

30.2.1

apnē paisē ginnē-par usē mālūm huā ke vo tohfā nahĩ ḳharīd saktā thā.	On counting his money, he realized he couldn't buy the gift.
daftar vāpas jānē-par, us-nē vahā̃ kisī-kō na pāyā.	On returning to the office, he found no one there.
us-kō milnē-par us-nē kyā kahā?	Upon finding him, what did he say?
ghar pahõcnē-par usē patā calā ke kuch mehmān ayē thē.	On reaching home, he discovered that some guests had arrived.
ghaṇṭī-kī āvāz sunnē-par vo jagā.	He woke up on hearing the bell.

REMARKS: (1) The phrase **mālūm hōnā, to become apparent, to be aware,** of the first sentence and **pātā calnā, to discover, to get indication,** of the fourth sentence take the **ke** construction described in section 29.2.

(2) Both phrases take the English subject in the object form before **-kō** (with the replacment of **usē** for **us-kō**).

(3) **tohfā** (ā) gift.

30.2.2

us-kō milnē-sē usē ciṭṭhī likhnā zyādā āsān hai.	It is easier to write him a letter than to meet him.
us-kō milnē-kē liyē jānē-sē pahilē us-kē javāb-kā intazār karnā zyādā acchā hai.	It is better to wait for his answer before going to see him.
kām karnē-sē bahot-sē lōgō̃-kō daraḳht-kī chā̃ō̃-mē̃ ārām karnā zyādā pasand hai.	Many people prefer to rest in the shade of a tree to working.
maĩ bailgāṛī-par savārī-sē paidal calnā zyādā pasand kartā hū̃.	I prefer walking to riding in an ox-cart.
kyā tum hamārē sāth jānē-sē us-kā intazār karnā zyādā pasand kartē hō?	Do you prefer waiting for him to going with us?

The construction illustrated above is identical with that described in section 20.3.1 and 20.2.2. Here the forms compared are infinitives which, like other nouns, are placed in the object form before postpositions.

REMARKS: chā̃ō̃ (ī) shade.

30.2.3

maĩ sōnē-hī-kō thā ke darvāzē-kī ghanṭī bajī.	I was about to sleep when the doorbell rang.
ham sair-kē liyē bāhar jānē-hī-kō thē ke acānak bāriś hōnē lagī.	We were about to go out for a walk when all of a sudden it began to rain.
pāgal kuttā mujhē kāṭnē-hī-kō thā ke ēk sipāhī-nē usē mār ḍālā.	The mad dog was about to bite me when a policeman killed him.
maĩ kuch kahnē-hī-kō thā ke us-nē ṭōk diyā.	I was about to say something when he interrupted.
sūraj nikalnē-hī-kō thā ke maĩ uṭh baiṭhā.	The sun was about to appear when I got up.
baccā ḍūbnē-hī-kō thā ke mallāh-nē usē bacā liyā.	The child was about to drown when the boatman saved him.
film śurū hōnē-hī-kō thī, lēkin acānak bijlī fēl hō gayī.	The motion picture was about to start, but suddenly the electricity failed.
jab maĩ aḍḍē-par pahō̃cā, mōṭar calnē-hī-kō thī.	When I reached the depot, the car was about to start off.
jab ham ghar pahō̃cē, sab lōg khānā khānē-hī-kō thē.	When we reached home, everybody was about to eat (**supper**).

This section deals with the Urdu construction translating the English phrase consisting of the words **about to plus a verb,** followed by a clause introduced by the conjunction **when.** (See the English sentences, above.)

Urdu translates this with a phrase consisting of the English verb in the **object** form, followed by the emphatic particle, **-hī,** and the postposition, **-kō.** This is followed by a clause introduced by the conjunction **ke, when.**

REMARKS: **acānak** (**adv.**) suddenly, **ṭōk** (ī) hindrance, obstruction, **ṭōk dēnā** to interrupt, **film** (ī) motion picture, **fēl hōnā** to fail, to break down, **mallāh** (ā) sailor.

30.2.4 Exercise 1. **Translate into English:**

1. naukar-kō bulānē-kē bād maĩ bhūl gayā ke maĩ kyā cāhtā thā. 2. apnī kāmyābī-kī k̤habar sunnē-par acānak vo nācnē lagā. 3. masjid-mẽ jānē-sē pahilē apnē jūtē utāriyē. 4. maśhūr jaghẽ dēkhnē-kē bād, kyā āp thōṛī dēr ārām karnā cāhtē haĩ? 5. maĩ ṭēlēfōn-kō band karnē-hī-kō thā ke darvāzē-kī ghanṭī bajī. 6. maśhūr jaghẽ dēkhnē-sē maĩ lōgõ-kē sāth bāt karnā zyādā pasand kartā hū̃. 7. maĩ rēḍiyō sunnē-hī-kō thā ke kuch mehmān āyē. 8. film śurū hōnē-kē bād mujhē ghar vāpas jānā paṛā. 9. ham gāṛī-mẽ jānē-hī-kō thē ke acānak bijlī fēl hō gayī. 10. khiṛkī khōlnē-par us-nē kisī-kō na dēkhā. 11. ham Añgrēzī bōlnē-sē Urdū bōlnā zyādā pasand kartī haĩ. 12. vo paisē dēnē-hī-kō thā ke usē mālūm huā ke vo tohfā nahĩ k̤harīd saktā thā. 13. hamārē sair-kē liyē bāhar jānē-kē bād acānak bāriś hōnē lagī. 14. Bambaī pahõcnē-par vo ārām karnē-kē liyē ṭhaharā. 15. pānī pīnē-sē pahilē tumhē hāth dhōnā cāhiyē. 16. aurat bāzar jānē-hī-kō thī ke us-kī ēk dōst āyī. 17. kāg̲az baig-mẽ rakhnē-kē bād vakīl-nē javāb dēnā śurū kiyā. 18. ustād kahānī sunānē-hī-kō thā ke tālibilm-nē ṭōk diyā. 19. sūraj nikalnē-kē bād parindõ-nē gānā śurū kiyā. 20. mērē sōnē-par naukar hōśiyārī-sē darvāzā khōlkar bāhar gayā.

30.2.5 Exercise 2. **Translate into Urdu:**

1. After I looked at the two calculations I decided that the second was wrong. 2. On seeing the temple the woman wanted to go in. 3. Do you prefer talking to listening? 4. Before you go into a mosque you must take off your shoes. 5. I was about to go out for a walk when you arrived. 6. After I woke up my servant brought tea. 7. The photographer was about to take his picture when the boy ran off. 8. On going into the dining room he saw that his friend (**fm.**) had not arrived. 9. He was about to read the newspaper when the doorbell rang. 10. Your automobile arrived after my servant went out to call a taxi. 11. Before you hang up the telephone ask them when they are coming to see us. 12. He was about to pay the ox-cart driver when he realized he didn't have money. 13. After I reached the depot I saw that the bus had left. 14. Some people prefer giving to taking presents. 15. After I began telling a second story (**my**) friends interrupted. 16. He was about to go home when he realized his automobile had not come. 17. Upon seeing the result of his work he became discouraged. 18. Before you arrived I had decided to go out for a walk. 19. After he bought the gifts he forgot for whom he had bought them. 20. Upon finding the money the poor man began to dance with joy.

30.3. Text 13: **Mērī Āp•bītī (Dūsrā Hissā)**

Translate into English. Answer the questions in Urdu:

jab maĩ-nē kālij-sē bī ē [1] pās kiyā, tō us vak̤t mērī umr unnīs sāl thī. maĩ-nē tay kiyā [2] ke mazīd [3] paṛhnē-kī zarūrat nahĩ. mērā irādā naukrī karnē-kā nahĩ thā, is liyē kē naukrī-mẽ tank̤hāh kāfī nahĩ miltī thī. maĩ-nē sōcā ke, agar maĩ naukrī karū̃gā, tō mērā guzārā nahĩ hōgā.[4] ye sōckar maĩ-nē faislā kiyā [5] kē maĩ biznas [6] karū̃gā. cunā̃ce maĩ-nē jald-hī Amritsar [7] -mẽ ēk chōṭā-sā [8] kārk̤hānā khōl liyā. is kārk̤hānē-mẽ lōhā [9] aur pītal [10] ḍhālā [11] jātā thā aur bartan [12] -bhī banāyē jātē thē. is kārk̤hānē-mẽ siraf bārā kārīgar [13] kām kartē thē. pahilē pahilē tō mujhē kārōbār-mẽ kuch faidā na huā, balke nuksān [14] huā. lēkin maĩ-nē himmat na hārī, balke aur bhī mehnat-sē kām karnā śurū kar diyā. kaī dafā aisā-bhī hōtā thā ke mujhē din• rāt kārk̤hānē-mẽ rahnā paṛtā. K̤hudā-nē jald-hī mērī mehnat-kā bahot acchā natījā diyā aur mujhē nafā hōnā [15] śurū hō gayā. agarce mērā kām ab calnā śurū hō gayā thā, mērā jī [16] is kām-mẽ zyādā nahĩ lagtā thā. mujhē mālūm hōnē lagā [17] ke mērē jaisē śāir • mizāj [18] ādmī-kē liyē kārḳhānā munāsab [19] jagah nahĩ hai. kuch arsē-kē bād hālat-nē kuch aisē paltē khāyā [20] ke mujhē faislā karnē-kē zarūrat-hī na paṛī. san unnīs sau saĩtālīs-mẽ Hindūstān dō hissõ-mẽ taḳsīm hō gayā, aur Pākistān dunyā-kē nakśē [21] -par zāhir huā.[22] jũ-hī [23] ye faislā huā Hindūstān aur Pākistān-mẽ firka • dārānā [24] fisād [25] hōnē lagē.[17] bahot-sē [8] bēgunah [26] ādmī, aurtẽ aur baccē mārē gayē. karōṛõ [27] rūpayē-kī jāēdād [28] barbād hō gayī.[29] lākhõ imārtẽ jal gayĩ. in-hī imārtõ-mẽ mērā chōṭā-sā [8] kārḳhānā-bhī thā. maĩ-bhī un lōgõ-mẽ thā, jō panāh-gazīn [30] hōkar Pākistān gayē. maĩ-nē Lāhōr pahõckar dēkhā ke mērē kunbē-kē dūsrē lōg-bhī vahā̃ maujūd thē. unhõ-nē ēk makān kirāyā [31] -par lē liyā thā. mērī ammī aur abbā, jō apnī sārī jāēdād Hindūstān-mẽ chōṛ āyē thē, kuch dēr tō bahot ġamgīn rahē. lēkin, jab unhõ-nē dēkhā ke lākhõ aur lōg-bhī isī hāl-mẽ haĩ, tō vo apnā ġam [32] bhūl gayā. ab ham sab lōg is kirāyē-kē makān-mẽ rahnā lagē. jald-hī maĩ-nē naukrī-kī talāś karnā śurū kar diyā. abhī thōṛē din-hī guzrē thē ke mujhē ēk acchī-sī [8] naukrī mil gayī. maĩ-nē sōcā taraḳḳī [33] karnē-kē liyē zarūrī [34] hai ke maĩ em ē [35] pās karũ. cunāce maĩ-nē naukrī-kē sāth sāth em ē-kē imtahān-kī taiyārī [36] śurū kar dī. san unnīs sau ikāvan-mẽ maĩ-nē em ē pās kar liyā aur us-kē dō mahīnē bād mujhē Gōmeṇṭ Kālij-mẽ naukrī mil gayī. ab maĩ laṛkõ aur laṛkiyõ-kō iknaumiks [37] paṛhānē lagā.[17] ye zamānā baṛē mazē-kā zamānā thā. mujhē ēk haftē-mẽ taḳrībān sāt ghaṇṭē paṛhānā paṛtā thā. maĩ-nē jald-hī apnē tālibilmõ-kā dil mōh liyā [38] aur vo mujhē bahot pasand karnē lagē.[17] sab tālibilm mehnat-sē ghar-kā kām kartē thē aur mujhē un-kō jurmānā vaġairā karnē-kī zarūrat nahĩ paṛtī thī. isī tarāh din guzartē gayē aur san unnīs sau bāvan ā gayā. is sāl-kē śurū-mẽ mujhē Amrīkā ānē-kē liyē ēk vazīfā [39] mil gayā. maĩ julāī [40] -kī satrā tārīḳh-kō gāṛī-mẽ baiṭhkar Lāhōr-sē Karācī pahõcā aur vahā̃-sē havāī • jahāz-mẽ safar kartā huā Nyū Yārk pahõc gayā. rāstē-mẽ ēk rāt Labnān [41] -kē śahar Bairūt [42] -mẽ ṭhaharnā paṛā kyũ-kē hamārē havāī • jahāz-kī marammat hōnēvālī [43] thī. Bairūt ēk bēhad ḳhūbsūrat śahar hai. us-kē tīn taraf samandar hai. āb-ō-havā bahot acchī hai. sardiyõ-mẽ mausam ḳhuśgavār [44] rahtā hai. Bairūt-kē bād maĩ aur mērē hamsafar [45] ēk din Laṇḍan [46] -bhī ṭhahrē. ab maĩ āp-kō Laṇḍan-kē bārē-mẽ kyā batāũ. mērā ḳhayāl hai ke āp is śahar-kē bārē-mẽ ḳhud-hī sab kuch jāntē haĩ. Nyū Yārk-mẽ kōī das bārā din rahnē-kē bād maĩ Śikāgō [47] calā gayā aur vahā̃ Śikāgō Yūnivarsiṭī-mẽ ēk sāl paṛhā. bāz lōgõ-kā ḳhayāl hai ke Śikāgō bahot gaṇḍā [48] śahar hai. lēkin mērā ḳhayāl hai ke Fileḍalfiyā [49] Śikāgō-sē bahot zyādā gaṇḍā hai. Śikāgō Lēk Miśīgan [50] -kē kinārē-par vāḳyā hai aur yahā̃ sardiyõ-mẽ bēhad sardī paṛtī hai. aktūbar [51] -sē lēkar aprail-tak taḳrībān har rōz barf paṛtī hai aur sārā vaḳt baṛē zōr-kī havā caltī hai. pichlē ēk sāl-sē maĩ Pensalvēniyā [52] Yūnivarsiṭī-mē hũ aur āp lōgõ-kē liyē kahāniyā̃ likhar apnā pēṭ pāltā hũ.[53] lēkin ab mērā jī kuch udās hō rahā hai [54] aur mērā ḳhayāl hai ke maĩ jald-hī Pākistān vāpas calā jāũgā.

savālāt:

1. musannif-kē kārḳhānē-mẽ kyā kām hōtā thā aur vahā̃ kitnē ādmī kām kartē thē? 2. Pākistān bannē-kē bād musannif-nē kyā kām kiyā? 3. maĩ kis kālij-mẽ paṛhātā thā aur kyā? 4. Śikāgō-mẽ mausam kaisā hōtā hai? 5. musannif āj • kal kyā kām kartā hai?

NOTES: 1. B.A. **(degree)** (ī); 2. **tay karnā** to decide **(tr.)**; 3. more, further; 4. **guzārā hōnā** to get along, make both ends meet **(int.)**; 5. **faislā karnā** to decide **(tr.)**; 6. business (ā); 7. city of Amritsar (ā); 8. see 38.1; 9. iron (ā); 10. brass (ā); 11. **ḍhālnā** to melt (**tr.**), see 37.1: 12. utensil (ā); 13. workman (ā); 14. loss (ā); 15. **nafā hōnā** to profit (**int.**); 16. heart (ā); 17. see 34.1.2; 18. poetic tempered (**adj., n.c.**); 19. suitable (**adj., n.c.**); 20. **aisā paltā khāyā** took such a turn; 21. **nakśā** map (ā); 22. **zāhir hōnā** to appear (**tr.**); 23. as soon as (**adv.**); 24. communal (**adj., n.c.**); 25. riot (ā); 26. innocent (**adj., n.c.**); 27. crores, one crore equals ten million (**adv.**); 28. property (ī); 29. **barbād hōnā** to be destroyed (**int.**); 30. refugee (**adj., n.c.**, also = noun); 31. **kirāyā** rent (ā); 32. grief (ā); 33. progress, promotion (ī); 34. necessary (**adj., n.c.**); 35. M.A. (**degree**) (ī); 36. preparation (ī); 37. economics (ī); 38. **mōh lēnā** to captivate (**tr.**); 39. scholarship (ā); 40. July (ī); 41. Lebanon (ā); 42. Beirut (ā); 43. see 31.2 for **vālā;** 44. pleasant (**adj., n.c.**); 45. fellow-traveller (ā); 46. London (ā); 47. Chicago (ā); 48. dirty (adj.); 49. Philadelphia (ā); 50. Lake Michigan (ī); 51. October (ā); 52. Pennsylvania (ī); 53. **apnā pēṭ pāltā hū̃** = I earn a living (lit., **nourish my stomach**); 54. **mērā jī kuch udās hō rahā hai** = I feel homesick.

LESSON 31

31.1

tairtā huā ādmī thak jāẽgā.	The swimming man will become tired.
tairtē huē ādmī thak jāẽgē.	The swimming men will become tired.
chōṭī rōtī huī laṛkī yahā̃ āẽgī.	The little crying girl will come here.
chōṭī rōtī huī laṛkiyā̃ yahā̃ āẽgī.	The little crying girls will come here.
dahārtā huā śēr hamlā karēgā.	The roaring lion will attack.
dahārtā huē śēr hamlā karẽgē.	The roaring lions will attack.
ḍūbtā huā jahāz gāyab hō jāẽgā.	The sinking ship will disappear.
ḍūbtē huē jahāz gāyab hō jāẽgē.	The sinking ships will disappear.
gātā huā pakśī chā̃ō-mẽ ārām karēgā.	The singing bird will rest in the shade.
gātē huē pakśī chā̃ō-mẽ ārām karẽgē.	The singing birds will rest in the shade.
muskarātā huā sūraj nikalēgā.	The smiling sun will appear.
camaktē huē tārē rōśnī dẽgē.	The shining stars will give light.
dauṛtē huē kuttē vāpas āẽgē.	The racing dogs will return.
sōtē huē kisān jāgẽgē.	The sleeping farmers will get up.
uṛtē huī ciṛiyā̃ rukẽgī.	The flying sparrows will stop.

This section takes up the translation into Urdu of English verbal forms ending in **-ing** which function as adjectives.

These are expressed in Urdu by a phrase consisting of **the present participle of the verb and the past participle of hōnā, huā,** both participles agreeing in gender, number, and form with the noun they modify.

The sentences of this section illustrate this participial construction modifying nouns in the subject form. Frequently, the present participle without the past participle of **hōnā** (i.e., **huā**) will perform the same function.

REMARKS: As do many adjectives, this participial phrase will be found functioning as a noun. **tairtā huā,** therefore, will translate **swimming (man)** and **sōtē huē,** sleep**ing (people).**

31.1.1

us-nē sōtē huē naukar-kō jagāyā aur khēt-mẽ bhējā.	He woke up the sleeping servant and sent him into the field.
hamārē darvāzē-par sōtē huē kuttē-kō jagāō.	Wake up the dog sleeping at our door.
vo camaktī huī cīz uṭhāiyē.	Pick up that shining thing.
daraḳht-par kūdtē huē bandarõ-kō bāg̠-sē bāhar nikāl dō.	Drive the monkeys jumping on the tree out of the garden.
śikārī-nē dahārtē huē śēr-kō mār ḍālā.	The hunter killed the roaring lion.
murjhātē huē phalõ-par pānī ḍālō.	Water the fading plants.

These sentences illustrate the participial construction of 31.1 modifying nouns in the object form.

REMARKS: **ibādat** (ī) prayer, **ibādat karnā** to pray, **zarūrī (adj., n.c.)** necessary, **dahārnā** to roar.

31.1.2 Exercise 1. **Translate into English:**

1. dauṛtī huī laṛkī gir paṛēgī. 2. vālid-nē mā̃-kē pās rōtē huī laṛkī-kō bhēj diyā. 3. gātē huē naukarõ-nē āj • subah mujhē jagāyā. 4. laṛkē-nē bhõktē huē kuttõ-kō khilāyā. 5. muskarātē huē ādmī mērī bāt suntē thē. 6. ham-nē paudõ-par pānī ḍāltē huē mālī-kō bulāyā. 7. tairtē huē ādmī-kī taraf rassā phẽk dō! 8. śikārī-nē jaṅgal-mẽ bakrē-kō khĩctē huē śēr mār ḍālā. 9. murjhātē huē paudē mēz-par gir paṛē. 10. tum-nē lakṛī lē jātī huī aurat-kō madad kyũ nahī̃ dī? 11. pānī lē jātē huē ādmī-sē pūchō ke kyā ham us-kō madad dē saktē haĩ? 12. tum-nē dauṛtī huī bhaĩs-kō kahā̃ dēkhā? 13. mālik-nē kamrē-sē nikaltē huē naukar-kō bulāyā. 14. khēt-sē jātī huī gāy kis-nē pakṛī? 15. daryā-kē sāmnē ibādat kartē huē ādmī kaun haĩ?

31.1.3 Exercise 2. **Translate into Urdu:**

1. The smiling man will answer your questions. 2. We saw him performing his prayers every day near the tank. 3. Give some candy to the little girl crying. 4. The farmer awakened the sleeping oxen and began to till the field. 5. The singing birds will awaken you. 6. Must you wake up the sleeping child? 7. We gave the man standing in front of our house food. 8. The barking dog will not bite you. 9. Give the fading plants a little water. 10. We saw him walking in the market. 11. The woman smiling and waving her handkerchief at us is my mother. 12. Did you see him repairing my automobile? 13. Why didn't you stop the man running out of my house? 14. The man walking towards us is my servant. 15. I like to see the stars shining at night.

31.2

Lāhōr-kā rahnēvālā apnā śahar Kalkattē-sē zyādā pasand karēgā.	A Lahore inhabitant will prefer his city to Calcutta.
Amrīkā-sē ānēvālā jahāz kal Bambaī pahõcēgā.	The ship coming from America will reach Bombay tomorrow.
gānēvālē laṛkē kahā̃ haĩ?	Where are the singing boys?

hamārī galī-kē mōṛ-par ēk machlī • bēcnēvālā hai.	There is a fishseller at the corner of our street.
paṛhnē aur likhnēvālē baccē kitābō̃-kī acchī dēkhbāl kartē haĩ.	Children who read and write take good care of books.
Karācī jānēvālī gāṛī ye-hī hai.	This is the train going to Karachi.
Piśāvar Yunivarsiṭī ānēvālē haftē-mē̃ band rahēgī.	The Peshawar University will remain closed during the coming week.
kyā lakṛī kāṭnēvālā ā rahā hai?	Is the woodcutter coming?
kal sab gā̃ō̃vālē pancāet karē̃gē.	All the villagers will go to the Panchayat.
dādī • ammā hamē̃ kalvālī kahānī phir sunāiyē.	Grandmother, please tell us the same story as (**you told us**) yesterday.
maĩ us lambē ṭā̃gō̃vālē ghōṛē-kō k͟harīdnā cāhtā hū̃.	I want to buy that long-legged horse.
vahā̃vālō̃-sē pūchiyē.	Ask the people of that place.
dūdhvālē-kā ghar kahā̃ hai?	Where is the milkman's house?
vo ādmī Karācīvālā hai.	He is a Karachi man.
Īd manānēvālē Musalmān āj gharō̃-mē̃ nahī̃ haĩ.	The Muslims celebrating Id are not in (**their**) homes today.
kyā tum gharvālē hō?	Are you a householder?
maĩ abhī jānēvālā hū̃.	I am about to go now.

This section is concerned with the formation of adjectives and nouns by means of the suffix **-vālā** (= **one who, or something which, performs the act or office described by the verb or nominal form to which it is attached**). The noun or adjective to which it is attached is in the object form. The nominal form, i.e., the adjective or noun thus formed, functions like any other adjective or noun ending in **ā**. (See Lessons 2 and 3)

The last sentence illustrates the addition of **-vālā** to an infinitive to indicate an act about to be carried out.

REMARKS: (1) In the case of two (or more) nouns, linked by **aur, and,** the last alone will take the **-vālā**. See sentence 5.

(2) **mōṛ** (ā) corner, **pancāet** (ī) a deliberative assembly, generally functioning as a court of inquiry.

31.2.1 Exercise 1. **Translate into English:**

1. maĩ nahī̃ jāntā ke is k͟hat-kā likhnēvālā kaun hai. 2. kyā āp-nē Amrikā-sē ānēvālē jahāz-sē kabhī safar kiyā? 3. ānēvālē haftē-mē̃ ham Īd manāē̃gē. 4. vo lambē ṭā̃gō̃vālā ghōṛā tēz-sē dauṛ sakēgā. 5. is gā̃ō̃-mē̃ kitnē gharvālē haĩ? 6. āp kyū̃ jānēvālī haĩ? 7. kyā Piśāvar jānēvālī ḍākgāṛī ye-hī hai? 8. vahā̃vālē lōg āp-kō bāgh batā sakē̃gē. 9. Lāhōr-sē ānēvālī bas dō ghanṭē-mē̃ pahō̃cēgī. 10. āp gā̃ō̃vālō̃-sē bahot sikh sakē̃gē.

31.2.2 Exercise 2. **Translate into Urdu:**

1. The office will remain closed during the coming ten days. 2. Which is the train going to Rawalpindi? 3. How many villagers have gone to the city to work? 4. From where are the singers (= **singing men**) coming? 5. Send in the writer of this letter. 6. Are you a householder? 7. The people of that place sent me here. 8. Ask the fishmonger how much money he will take for this big fish. 9. I was just about to ask a question. 10. How do you know that this man is from a village?

31.3

ıdh pītē pītē us-nē khiṛkī-sē bāhar dēkhā.	He looked out of the window as he was drinking the milk.
ıhāṛ-par caṛhtē caṛhtē vo thak gayā.	He became tired as he climbed up the mountain.
ãstē hãste vo ēk • dam rōnē lagā.	He suddenly began to cry as he was laughing.
ıtē rōtē us-nē apnī sab taklīfẽ mujhē sunāyī̃.	Weeping, he revealed all his troubles to me.
ı ēk jagah rahtē rahtē tañg ā gayā.	He became tired (**of**) living in the same place.
ıtāb paṛhtē paṛhtē vo sō gayā.	He fell asleep reading the book.
ıaī ye fiḳrē likhtē likhtē thak gayā.	I've become tired writing these sentences.
ırat pakātē pakātē bilkul thak gayī.	The woman became completely tired out while cooking.
ımī caltē caltē bilkul thak gayā.	The man became completely tired out while walking.
khtē likhtē mērē hāth bilkul śal hō gayē.	My hands became completely tired while (**I was**) writing.
ıtē rōtē us-kī ā̃khẽ lāl hō gayī̃.	Her eyes became red while (**she was**) crying.
ıtē gātē us-kā galā baiṭh gayā.	His throat became hoarse while (**he was**) singing.
ı apnī chōṭē bahan-kō sulātē sulātē āp-bhī sō gayī.	While putting her little sister to sleep, she too fell asleep.
ıpnā dēkhtē dēkhtē laṛkī-kī ā̃khẽ khul gayī̃.	The girl woke up while (**she was**) dreaming.

The sentences, above, illustrate the function of the present participle in the mascu-ıne object form as an **adverb.** (The participle is repeated, indicating an act in progress ·hile a second act is begun or is going on.)

This construction translates English adverbial phrases containing verbal forms end-ıg in **-ing** (See sentences 4 to 7). Such adverbial phrases can be introduced in English y words such as **while** (See sentences 8 to 14.) or **as** (See sentences 1 to 3), the verbal ırm consisting either of the verb **to be** and a form ending in **-ing** or **-ed,** or of a single erbal form in **-ing.**

REMARKS: (1) **tañg ā jānā** of sentence 5 translates **to become tired of; sapnā ēkhnā** of the fourteenth sentence translates **to dream.**

(2) **gālā** (ā) throat, **fiḳrā** (ā) sentence, **śal hōnā** to become weary.

31.3.1 Exercise 1. **Translate into English:**

. dauṛtē dauṛtē us-kā pāõ phislā aur vo gir paṛā. 2. rōtē rōtē us-kā galā baiṭh gayā. 3. ıujhē kahānī sunātē sunātē vo hãsnē lagā. 4. khātē khātē gāy hamārī taraf dēkhtī thī. . paṛhtē paṛhtē tālibilm-kī ā̃khẽ lāl hō gayī̃. 6. ḍhalvān saṛak-par caṛhtē carhtē ham thak ayē. 7. ḳhat likhtē likhtē laṛkī ēk • dam rōnē lagī. 8. uṛtē uṛtē ciṛiyā̃ pyāsī hō gayī̃. 9. ıālī paudõ-par pānī dētē dētē thak gayā. 10. machliyā̃ pakaṛtē pakaṛtē ādmī pyāsā hō ayā.

31.3.2 Exercise 2. **Translate into Urdu:**

1. The girl became tired as she was bringing water for us. 2. Laughing, he told me th story. 3. The woman saw many things she wanted to buy as she walked in the marke 4. I slipped and fell into the river while walking on the bank. 5. Walking through th jungle, the hunter came to a pond. 6. While reading the book she suddenly jumped u and ran into the kitchen. 7. The washerman became tired while washing the dhoti. { The dog ran barking towards the stranger. 9. As she was talking to me her throat b came hoarse. 10. The woodcutter became tired as he cut up the big tree.

31.4

daraḳht-par caṛhtē vaḳt us-nē ghar-kī taraf dēkhā.	As he climbed up the tree, he looked ove the house.
sīṛhiyō̃-sē utartē vaḳt us-kā pāō̃ phislā aur vo gir paṛā.	As he descended the stairs his foot slippe and he fell.
skūl-sē vāpas ātē vaḳt maĩ-nē apnā ḳalam kahī̃ khō diyā.	As I returned from school I lost my pe somewhere.
gātē vaḳt ēk • dam us-kā galā baiṭh gayā.	His throat suddenly became hoarse as he wa singing.
likhtē vaḳt us-kē ḳalam-kī syāhī ḳhatam hō gayī.	The ink in his pen ran out as he was writ ing.

These sentences illustrate adverbial phrases consisting of the work **vaḳt, time,** modi fied by a present participle of a verb. (Since **vaḳt** is in the object form, the participle i also placed in the object form.)

Compare this construction, keeping in mind the literal translation (i.e., **At the tim (when) he was climbing up the tree . . .; At the time (when) he was descending th stairs . . .; At the time (when) I was returning from school . . .**) with that of sectio 31.3.

This construction designates the time when an act takes place as contrasted wit that of 31.3 which describes an act continuing over a period of time. Very often th same English phrase is employed to translate the two Urdu constructions.

REMARKS: **sīṛhī** (ī) staircase, ladder, stairs, **syāhī** (ī) ink.

31.5. Text 14: **Mohammad Alī.**

Translate into English. Answer the questions in Urdu:

Mohammad Alī Jinnah Hindūstān-kē Musalmānō̃ sab-sē baṛē syāsī [1] līḍar [2] thē. v san aṭhārā sau chiyattar (1876) -mē̃ Karācī-mē̃ paidā huē. un-kē vālid ēk mutavassit darjē-kē [3] tājir [4] thē. un-kā kārōbār-bhī Karācī-mē̃ thā. Misṭar Jinnah-nē apnī ibtadā tālīm [5] Karācī-mē̃ hāsil kī [6] aur us-kē bād mazīd tālīm hāsil karnē-kē liyē Iñglistān calē gayē. vahā̃-sē unhō̃-nē bērisṭrī [8] pās kī aur phir Bambaī-mē̃ rahāiś [9] iḳhtiyār kī.[1 yahā̃ unhō̃-nē kaī sāl vakālat [11] kī. vo bahot mehnat-sē apnā kām kartē thē. jald-hī v Hindūstān-kē cōṭī-kē [12] vakīlō̃ [13] -mē̃ śumār hōnē [14] lagē.[15] isī zamānē-mē̃ unhō̃-n siyāsat [16] -mē̃ hissā lēnā [17] śurū kiyā. apnī ḳābiliyyat,[18] dyānatdārī,[19] aur hubb-e-vatan [2 -kē bāis [21] vo jald-hī Kāñgras Pārṭī [22] -mē̃ bahot ū̃cē ohdō̃ [23] -par pahō̃c gayē. Kāñgras lōgō̃-nē un-kē nām-par ēk hāl [24] -bhī Bambaī-mē̃ banvāyā thā, jisē "Jinnah Hāl" kah jātā hai.[25] lēkin kuch arsē [26] -kē bād Misṭar Jinnah aur dūsrē Kāñgrasī [27] līḍrō̃-k darmiyān iḳhtalāfāt [28] paidā hō gayē. Misṭar Jinnah āzād [29] Hindūstān-mē̃ Musalmānō̃-kē liyē kuch haḳūḳ [30] mā̃gtē thē. lēkin Mahātmā Gā̃dhī [31] aur kuch dūsrē līḍar Misṭar Jinnah-kī bāt mānnē-kō taiyār nahī̃ thē. is-kē ilāvā Hindūstān-kē Musalmān us vaḳt ḳhud-bhī muttahid na thē. in bātō̃-sē bēzār hōkar [32] Misṭar Jinnah-nē Kāñgras Pārṭī-kō chōṛ diyā. kuch sālō̃-kē bād vāpas Iñglistān calē gayē aur Lanḍan-mē̃ apnī vakālat karnē lagē.[15] vo ām-taur-par Prīvī Kaunsal [33] -mē̃ muḳadmē laṛtē [34] thē. san unnīs sau tīs-kē bād Musalmānō̃-kī siyāsī hālat bahot abtar [35] hō gayī aur un-kī rāhnumāī [36] karnēvālā kōī na rahā. tō Allāmā Iḳbāl [37] aur kaī dūsrē Musalmānō̃-kē purzōr [38] darḳhāst karnē-[39] -par Misṭar Jinnah vāpas Hindūstān ā gayē aur dō • bārā Bambaī-mē̃ rahnē lagē.[15] is zamānē-sē Pākistān bannē-tak vo Muslim Līg [40] -kē sadr thē. san unnīs sau cālīs-mē̃ Muslim Līg Pārṭī-nē Misṭar Jinnah-kī rāhnumāī-mē̃ faislā kiyā ke Musalmānō̃-kō apnē liyē ēk alahdā [41] mulk hāsil karnā cāhiyē. ye faislā Muslim Līg-kē sālānā [42] ijlās [43] -mē̃, jō Lāhōr-mē̃ munaḳid huā,[44] kiyā gayā.[45] is faislē-kō ḳarārdād [46] -e-Lāhōr [47] kahtē haī. is ḳarārdād-kē bād Muslim Līg-kā vāhid [48] maḳsad [49] Pākistān-kā hāsil karnā ban gayā. is ḳarārdād-kā matlab ye thā ke Hindūstān-kē jin subō̃ [50] -mē̃ Musalmānō̃-kī aksariyyat [51] hai un-kō Hindūstān-kē bāḳī ilāḳō̃-sē alahdā karkē ēk mulk banā diyā jāē [45] jis-kā nām Pākistān hō.

san unnīs sau saītālīs-mē̃ agast [52] -kī caudā tārīḳh-kō ye maḳsad pūrā [53] hō gayā. Pākistān bannē-kē bād Misṭar Jinnah-nē Muslim Līg-kī sadārat [54] chōṛ dī aur vo Pākistān-kē pahilē Gavarnar • Jenral [55] ban gayē. saccī bāt tō ye hai ke Pākistān-kī jañg Muslim Līg-nē nahī̃ balke Misṭar Jinnah-nē kām-ō-bēś akēlē-hī laṛī. agar vo is muśkil vaḳt-mē̃ Musalmānō̃-kī rāhnumāī karnē-kē liyē na hōtē, tō śāyad Pākistān kabhī vajūd [56] -mē̃ na ātā. vo apnē irādē-kē aisē pakkē [57] thē ke duniyā-kī tāḳat [58] un-kē is irādē-kō tōṛ nahī̃ saktī thī. Hindūstān-kē Musalmān Misṭar Jinnah-kō bēhad pasand kartē thē. un-kō Musalmānō̃-kē dilō̃-par aisā ḳābū [59] thā ke lōg un-kē iśārē-par jānē̃ [60] ḳurbān karnē [61] -kō taiyār thē. hairānī [62] -kī bāt hai ke agarce Misṭar Jinnah Musalmānō̃-kē līḍar thē, un-kā rahnā • sahnā [63] bilkul maġrabī [64] thā. is-kē bāvajūd [65] Musalmānō̃-kō un-par pūrā ētabār [66] thā. Misṭar Jinnah-kē muḳhālif [67] bahot rōyē pītē ke un-kī dāṛhī [68] nahī̃ aur vo namāz nahī̃ paṛhtē (vaġairā), lēkin kisī-nē in lōgō̃-kī parvah [69] na kī. Misṭar Jinnah unnīs sau aṛtālīs (1948) -mē̃ vafāt pā [70] gayē.

savālāt:

1. Misṭar Jinnah kahā̃ paidā huē aur unhō̃-nē kahā̃ hāsil kī? 2. Misṭar Jinnah-kē vālid kyā kām kartē thē? 3. Misṭar Jinnah-nē Kāñgras Pārṭī-kō kyū̃ chōṛ kiyā? 4. Misṭar Jinnah-kā Muslim Līg-sē kyā tālluḳ [71] thā? 5. ḳarārdād-e-Lāhōr-kā kyā matlab thā?

NOTES: 1. political (**adj., n.c.**); 2. leader (ā); 3. **mutavassit • darjē-kā** middle-class (= **adj.**); 4. merchant (ā); 5. **ibtadāī tālīm** early education (ī); 6. obtained, **hāsil karnā** to obtain (**tr.**); 7. England (ā); 8. barristry, legal practice (ī); 9. residence (ī); 10. **iḳhtiyār karnā** to take up, assume; 11. legal practice (ī); 12. **cōṭī-kā** top (= **adj.**); 13. **vakīl** lawyer (ā); 14. **śumār hōnā** to be counted (**int.**); 15. see 34.1.2; 16. politics (ī); 17. to take part (**tr.**); 18. ability (ī); 19. honesty (ī); 20. patriotism (ī); 21. **-kē bāis** for reason of (**postpos. phrase**); 22. Congress Party (ī); 23. **ohdā** rank (ā); 24. hall (ā); 25. see 37.1; 26. **arsā** time, period (ā); 27. Congress (**adj., n.c.**); 28. differences, **pl., s.; iḳhtalāf** (ā); 29. free (**adj. n.c.**); 30. rights, **pl., s.: haḳ** (ā); 31. Mahatma Gandhi; 32. **bēzār hōnā** to become disgusted (**int.**); 33. Privy Council (ī); 34. **muḳaddmā laṛnā** to contest, fight a law suit (**tr.**); 35. bad (**adj., n.c.**); 36. leadership, guidance (ī); 37. Allama Iqbal; 38. vigorous (**adj., n.c.**); 39. **darḳhāst karnā** to request (**tr.**); 40. Muslim League (ī); 41. separate (**adj., n.c.**); 42. annual (**adj., n.c.**); 43. meeting (ā); 44. **munaḳid hōnā** to be held, take place (**int.**); 45. see 37.1; 46. resolution (ī); 47. **ḳarārdād-e-Lāhōr** Lahore Resolution (ī); 48. single (**adj., n.c.**); 49. objective (ā); 50. **subah** province (ā); 51. majority (ī); 52. August (ā); 53. **pūrā hōnā** to be fulfilled (**int.**); 54. presidency (ī); 55. Governor-General (ā); 56. existence (ā); 57. firm (**adj.**); 58. power (ī); 59. control, command (ā); 60. **jān** life (ī); 61. **ḳurbān karnā** to sacrifice (**tr.**); 62. surprise (ī); 63. way of life (ā); 64. western (**adj., n.c.**); 65. in spite of (**postpos. phrase**); 66. confidence (ā); 67. opponents (ā); 68. beard (ī); 69. heed, concern, care (ī); 70. **vafāt pānā** to pass on, die (**tr.**); 71. connection (ā).

LESSON 32

32.1 [25.1.2] **Translate into Urdu:**

1. I do not want to drink the water which came from the stream. 2. The man for whom you were waiting was in the city. 3. The automobile which is in front of the house is mine. 4. Is the road which goes to the city long? 5. The clothes which the washerman brought back are not clean. 6. Where is the chair you repaired? 7. All the things I need are in the house. 8. Why hasn't the boy who has to cut the wood come? 9. The train which arrived in the station on time is not the mail train. 10. The man who gave me this book had written it. 11. The luggage near which the bearer is is mine. 12. Where are the socks the servant cleaned? 13. The razor you are using is very sharp. 14. The women for whom you are waiting cannot come on time. 15. Who are the men near the well?

32.2 [25.1.3] **Translate into English:**

1. jō ādmī paudō̃-sē phūl ṭōr rahā hai, vo hamārā mālī hai. 2. jin jūtō̃-kī mōcī-nē marammat kī, vo kahā̃ haī? 3. jō kitābē̃ maī-nē ḳharīdī̃, vo mēz-par haī. 4. jō ādmī āp-kē sāth bāt kar rahā thā, kyā vo Urdū-mē̃ bōl rahā thā? 5. jin lōgō̃-kē liyē āp kām kar rahē haī, vo kaun haī? 6. jis ādmī-kē pās kāfī paisē nahī, vo safar nahī̃ kar saktā. 7. jin kisānō̃-kē pās chōṭē hal haī, un-kō mehnat karnā hai. 8. jō bairā Urdū bōl saktā hai, maī us-kō cāhtā hū̃. 9. jō ādmī mērī mōṭargāṛī-kī marammat kartā thā, vo kaun hai? 10. jin cīzō̃-kī āp-kō zarūrat hai, vo kahā̃ haī? 11. jis ādmī-nē rēlgāṛī-sē safar kiyā hai, vo bailgāṛī-sē safar karnā nahī̃ cāhēgā. 12. jis ḳūlī-nē mērā sāmān rēlgāṛī-mē̃ rakhā, vo kaun-sā hai? 13. jō bail sab-sē zyādā bōjh lē jā saktā hai, vo kaun-sā hai? 14. jin ādmīyō̃-kī madad-kī ham-kō zarūrat hai, vo kal āē̃gē. 15. jis naukar-kō mērā bistar taiyār karnā hai, vo kahā̃ hai?

32.3 [25.2.1] **Translate into Urdu:**

1. Is the road which goes to the city long? 2. The man who gave me this book is my (**paternal**) uncle. 3. The people who are coming towards us are my parents. 4. Who is the man who is waiting on the bank of the river? 5. I do not want to drink the water which came from the river. 6. The woman who is near the well is my (**maternal**) aunt. 7. The hunter killed the bear which was pulling the goat into the jungle. 8. The servant who was very good returned to the village. 9. The man for whom you were waiting was in the city. 10. The girl with whom I spoke Hindi misunderstood me. 11. The mechanic who had to repair my car did not come. 12. Where is the chair you repaired?

13. Where did you put the food you brought back from the city? 14. I do not know the boy who tried to help me. 15. The automobile which is in front of the house is mine.

32.4 [25.2.2] **Translate into English:**

1. vah ādmī, jō bāg-mẽ kām kar rahā hai, hamārā mālī hai. 2. kyā vo aurat, jō tumhārē sāth bāt kar rahī thī, tumhārī mumānī thī? 3. vo lōg, jin-kā intazār āp kar rahē haĩ, kaun haĩ? 4. kyā vo ādmī, jis-kē pās kāfī paisē nahĩ, safar kar saktā haĩ? 5. vo jūtē, jin-kī marammat mōcī-nē kī, kahā̃ haĩ? 6. maĩ us bairē-kō, jō Urdū bōl saktā hai, cāhtā hū̃. 7. vo ḳūlī, jis-nē mērā sāmān rēlgāṛī-mẽ rakhā, kaun hai? 8. vo saṛak, jis-sē ham jāẽgē, śahar jātī hai. 9. vo sāhab, jis-kā maĩ intazār kar rahā hū̃, mērā māmū̃ hai. 10. vo gāy, jis-kē pīchē bachṛā dauṛ rahā hai, us-kī mā̃ hai. 11. vo ghar, jis-kē sāmnē maĩ khēl rahā hū̃, mērī cacī-kā hai. 12. vo cīzẽ, jin-kī mērē safar-kē liyē zarūrat hōgī, mujhē lāiyē. 13. vo kapṛē, jō dhōbī kal vāpas lāyā, kahā̃ haĩ? 14. vo zarḳhēz khēt, jō daryā-kē kinārē-par hai, kis-kā hai? 15. vo ṭōpī, jis-par āp baiṭhē haĩ, mērē cacā-kī hai.

32.5 [26.1.2] **Translate into Urdu:**

1. This is **the** well from which we take water. 2. There weren't many people in **that** train which came into this station. 3. **This** is the road by which we go to the bazaar. 4. **That** bearer who is sleeping under the tree has to work. 5. Is this **the** food you cooked for me? 6. Is **this** the food you cooked for me? 7. **The** man who gave me the book wrote it. 8. **These** are the shoes which I bought in the market yesterday. 9. **These** are the fields which are fertile. 10. **Those** clothes which the washerman brought back yesterday were not clean.

32.6 [26.1.3] **Translate into English:**

1. jis ṭōpī-kī maĩ talāś kar rahā thā, ye vo-hī hai. 2. kyā yē-hī vo lōg haĩ, jin-kā āp intazār kar rahē haĩ? 3. jō āḍmī daryā-kē kinārē-par kām kar rahā hai, kyā ye vo-hī hai? 4. jis bairē-kī mujhē zarūrat hai, ye vo-hī hai. 5. jō lōg hamārē sāmnē ā rahē haĩ, kyā vo-hī āp-kē mā • bāp haĩ? 6. ye-hī vo aḳhbār haĩ, jō āp-kō paṛhnā cāhiyē. 7. jō mōṭargāṛī mērē makān-kē sāmnē hai, usī-kī marammat karō. 8. jō ḳhat āj āyē, vo-hī mujhē lāiyē. 9. ye-hī vo lōg haĩ, jin-sē maĩ savāl pūchnā cāhtā hū̃. 10. jō jūtē palañg-kē nīcē haĩ, vo-hī sāf karō.

32.7 [26.2.2] **Translate into Urdu:**

1. Whichever automobile is in front of the house is mine. 2. Whichever things I need are in the house. 3. Whichever tree the beggar sits under is a banyan. 4. I rewarded whichever workman helped me. 5. Whichever man did this is a good iron-smith. 6. I misunderstood whatever the scientist said. 7. I want to talk with whichever bearer will be able to understand my Sindhi. 8. The little boy threw stones at whichever train went by. 9. The farmer wanted to buy whatever he saw. 10. Whoever talks too much may be a fool.

32.8 [26.2.3] **Translate into English:**

1. jō-bhī pānī lāyā, vo pyāsā thā. 2. jō-bhī kursī kamrē-mẽ hai, vo bāhar lāiyē. 3. sāinsdān-nē jō kuch-bhī kahā, vo kisī-nē nahĩ samjhā. 4. jō kuch-bhī āp-kē pās hai, vo mujhē khānē-kō dījiyē. 5. jō-bhī saṛak sab-sē acchī hai, us-sē jāiyē. 6. jō kuch-bhī naukar-nē kiyā, usē mālik-nē nahĩ pasand kiyā. 7. jis-nē-bhī ye ciṭṭhī likhē, vah bēvaḳūf hai. 8. jis-nē-bhī ye kitāb paṛhī, us-nē isē nahĩ pasand kī. 9. jō kuch-bhī us-kē mālik-nē kahā, naukar vo nahĩ samajh sakā. 10. jō-bhī faḳīr ghar-kē pās-sē guzrē, usē andar bulāō.

32.9 [26.3.1] **Translate into Urdu:**

You should speak Hindi when you go to India. 2. The child has to go out of the ›use when he makes too much noise. 3. When there is too much smoke in the room the rvant opens the windows. 4. When the wood is dry, the fire burns well. 5. When the :arer brought the bill, I had to pay him the money. 6. I will be returning home when e dog will bark. 7. We were waiting under a tree just when it rained. 8. When a ranger comes to our house, we give him food. 9. When I want a clean shirt I have to ok for the bearer. 10. When students study too much, they sleep in class.

32.10 [26.3.2] **Translate into English:**

jab bail bahot zyādā khātā hai, tab vo sōnā cāhtā hai. 2. jab mazdūr thakā hōtā hai, b vo acchā kām nahī̃ kar saktā. 3. jab havā zōr-sē caltī hai, tab chōṭē parindē nahī̃ uṛ ktē. 4. jab āp āg-mē̃ sūkhā kōēlā rakhẽgē, vo acchī tarah-sē jalēgā. 5. jab maĩ darvāzā nd kar rahā thā, usī vaḳt āp mērē ghar āyē. 6. jab āp bāzār-sē apnē lempō̃-kē liyē tēl ẽgē, tab mērē liyē-bhī lāiyē. 7. jab āp Pākistān-mē̃ safar karẽ, tab Urdū bōlnē-kī ōśiś karẽ. 8. jab sūkhē khētō̃-par pānī girtā hai, tab kisān ḳhuś hōtā hai. 9. jab kuttā ɪō̃kā, tab ajnabī-nē ghar-kē andar ānē-kī kōśiś nahī̃ kī. 10. jab saṛkẽ gīlī haĩ, tab zōr-sē ōtar calānā ḳhatarnāk hai.

32.11 [26.4.2] **Translate into Urdu:**

Whenever (= **each time**) you bring back someone with you from town, there is no od in the house. 2. Whenever (=**each time**) the bearer will bring the bill, I will have pay him. 3. Whenever (= **any time**) a stranger will come to our house, we will give im water. 4. Whenever (= **each time**) he can do something for me, the servant tries. Whenever (= **any time**) it rains, I do not have a raincoat. 6. Whenever (= **any time**) ɔu wish, come to see me. 7. (= **any time**) you need anything call me. 8. Whenever = **each time**) the woman goes too far, she has to stop to rest. 9. Whenever (= **any** **me**) you get the time, read this book. 10. Whenever (= **each time**) I try to read this ook, someone comes to talk with me.

32.12 [26.4.3] **Translate into English:**

jab kabhī rēlgāṛī ruktī hai, musāfir ṭhaṇḍē pānī-kē liyē bāhar jātā hai. 2. jab kabhī āp ar sakẽ, Pakistān-kē gāvō̃ dēkhnē-kī kōśiś karẽ. 3. jab-bhī āp paṛh sakẽ, Urdū aḳhbar aṛhẽ. 4. jab kabhī bāriś hōtī hai, kuttā ghar-kē andar jānā cāhtā hai. 5. jab-bhī ilibilm-nē savāl pūchā, ustād-nē us-kā javāb diyā. 6. jab-bhī ustād kamrē-sē bāhar jātā ai, tālibilm śōr macātē haĩ. 7. jab-bhī gāṛībān sō gayā, bail ārām karnē-kē liyē ṭhaharē. jab kabhī mujhē mauḳā milā, maĩ-nē cāy pī. 9. jab kabhī āp gāvō̃-kō jāẽgē, kisānō̃-kē ith Urdū bōlnē-kī kōśiś karẽ. 10. jab-bhī us-nē mālik-kō kuch samjhānē-kī kōśiś kī, airā nākām rahā.

32.13 [27.1.1] **Translate into Urdu:**

There is a factory where the noise is coming from. 2. There may be water where ıere are trees. 3. I will go as far as you can go. 4. Drive the automobile slowly where ıe road is narrow. 5. Where the cow goes the calf goes too. 6. Where the ship goes, the ailors go too. 7. I cannot walk where the road is too steep. 8. It is not good to live here there is too much dust. 9. The river is deep where the big ship is. 10. Why do ou, too, want to go where I go?

32.14 [27.1.2] **Translate into English:**

jahā̃-sē dhūl ā rahī hai, vahā̃ lōg kām kar rahē haĩ. 2. jahā̃ bail car rahē haĩ, vahā̃ kuā̃ ai. 3. jahā̃ bāriś hōtī hai, vahā̃ ghās acchī tarah-sē ugtī hai. 4. jahā̃ mērā dōst nahī̃ jā ıktā, vahā̃ maĩ kabhī jā saktā hū̃. 5. jahā̃ maĩ kām kartā hū̃, vahā̃ acchā restōraṇṭ hai.

6. jahā̃ āp rōśnī dēkhtē haĩ, vahā̃ ghar hai. 7. jahā̃ āp rōk sakẽ, vahā̃ mōṭargāṛī rōkiy 8. jahā̃-tak āp cāhẽ, vahā̃-tak mujhē kahānī sunāiyē. 9. jahā maĩ rahtī hū̃, vahā̃ ē ḳhūbsūrat bāg hai. 10. jahā̃-tak maĩ tair saktā hū̃, kyā vahā̃-tak tum tair saktē hō?

32.15 [27.2.1] **Translate into Urdu:**

1. Please stop the car wherever there are interesting places. 2. Wherever you hear mus in the Panjāb there generally will be a wedding. 3. Wherever he looked for his horse h didn't find it. 4. Why do you want to go wherever I go? 5. You will have to get out the cart wherever the road is narrow. 6. It is difficult to till wherever the ground steep. 7. Wherever I try to work in the house there is a lot of noise. 8. The oxen sto to eat wherever there is grass. 9. You will be able to drive the automobile fast wher ever the road is wide. 10. I will speak Urdu with people wherever I go in India.

32.16 [27.2.2] **Translate into English:**

1. jahā̃-bhī maĩ Pākistān-mẽ jātā hū̃, vahā̃ maĩ ām-taur-par lōgō̃-sē bāt karnē-kī kōśi kartā hū̃. 2. jahā̃-bhī dilcasp jagah hōgī, vahā̃ maĩ ṭhōṛī dēr-kē liyē ṭhahurū̃gā. 3. jahā̃-bh maĩ dauṛū̃, chōṭā kuttā mērē pīchē jāēgā. 4. jahā̃-bhī baṛā hāthī jātā hai, vahā̃ dūsr hāthī us-kē pīchē jātē haĩ. 5. jahā̃-bhī āp gāy-kī talāś karẽgē, vo vahā̃ nahī̃ hōgī. 6 jahā̃-bhī mērī mōṭar hōgī, mērā bairā pās hōgā. 7. jahā̃-bhī mālik jātā hai, naukar-k pīchē pīchē jānā paṛtā hai. 8. jahā̃-bhī āp gānā sunẽgē, āp ḳhuś lōg dēkhẽgē. 9. jahā̃-bh maĩ-nē Pākistān-mẽ khānā khāyā, maĩ-nē us-kō pasand kiyā. 10. jahā̃-bhī āp Pākistān-m jāẽ, āp-kō lōgō̃-kō samajhnē-kī kōśiś karnā cāhiyē.

32.17 [27.3.1] **Translate into Urdu:**

1. Take as much as you need. 2. Please bring me as much wood as will be sufficient 3. The servant will bring as many chairs as there are people in the room. 4. The rive is as deep as the well. 5. He has as many oxen as I have goats. 6. My city is not as bi as Lahore. 7. I read as much as he writes. 8. The servant brought out as many chair as there were people in the garden. 9. I counted as many pice as I had. 10. The hunte missed as many deer as he saw.

32.18 [27.3.2] **Translate into English:**

1. jitnī aurtẽ gāõ-mẽ rahtī haĩ, kyā us-mē utnē-hī ādmī rahtē haĩ? 2. jitnī lakṛī āp-kē cāhiyē, utnā-hī kōēlā āp-kō kyū̃ cāhiyē? 3. jitnē tālibilm klās-mẽ haĩ, utnē-hī savāl ustā pūchẽgē. 4. jitnā ū̃cā kārḳhānā hai, utnā-hī ū̃cā makān nahī̃. 5. jitnī mehnat kisān ka rahā hai, utnī-hī mazdūr nahī̃ kar rahā hai. 6. jitnē mehmān āẽgē, utnī rakābiyā̃ mēz-pa rakhō. 7. jitnā pānī tum daraḳhtō̃-kō dōgē, utnā-hī paudō̃-kō dō. 8. jitnī lambī mōṭar hai utnā cauṛā pul hai. 9. jitnē bandar daraḳht-kī śāḳh-par thē, utnē-hī patthar baccē-nē phẽkē. 10. jitnē us-kē baccē thē, utnē-hī sēb bāp bāzār-sē vāpas lāyē.

32.19 [27.4.1] **Translate into Urdu:**

1. Carry as much wood as you will need. 2. Bring as much coal as you can carry. 3. I rested as much as I could. 4. Why isn't the ox eating as much as it can? 5. Why didn't you bring as much water as you can? 6. Why don't you do as much work as you can? 7. Give the man as much food as he needs. 8. Repair as many windows as you can. 9. Please give me as much cold water as you wish. 10. The farmer works as hard as he can.

32.20 [27.4.2] **Translate into English:**

1. jitnē lōgō̃-kē sāth āp cāhẽgē, āiyē. 2. jitnī sūkhī lakṛī āp lā sakẽ, lāiyē. 3. jitnā tum-nē sunā, mujhē sunāō. 4. jitnē lōgō̃-kō āp Panjāb-mẽ jāntē haĩ, un-kō khaṭ likhiyē. 5. jitnē

Urdu aḳhbār āp paṛh sakẽ, paṛhiyē. 6. jitnā khānā bhūkē ādmī-nē cāhā, kyā us-nē khāyā? 7. jitnī lakṛī-kī usē zarūrat thī, kyā baṛhaī-nē kāṭī? 8. jitnī mehnat tum kar saktē hō, tum-kō karnā cāhiyē. 9. jitnā khānā us-nē pakāyā, ādmī-nē khāyā. 10. jitnē khānē-kī zarūrat us-kō thī, aurat-nē pakāyā.

32.21 [27.5.1] **Translate into Urdu:**

1. Are you as hungry as I am? 2. This rope is as long as I need. 3. Bring as many chairs as there are people. 4. Why don't you come as near as you can? 5. Is your town as far from the city as mine is? 6. When does a dog eat as much as he can? 7. I will describe this country as well as I can. 8. The government building is as high as it is wide. 9. A tiger makes as much noise as it is dreadful. 10. The wall of the jail is as strong as it is thick.

32.22 [27.5.2] **Translate into English:**

1. kyā āp utnī-hī thakī haĩ, jitnī ke bhūkī haĩ? 2. kuā̃ mērē ghar-sē utnā-hī dūr hai, jitnā ke tumhārē ghar-sē. 3. apnē gā̃õ-kē bārē-mẽ utnā-hī acchā bayān karō, jitnā ke tum kar saktē hō. 4. kyā kuā̃ yahā̃-sē utnā-hī dūr hai, jitnī ke daryā hai? 5. khēt utnā-hī lambā hai, jitnā ke cauṛā. 6. daraḳhtõ-mẽ utnē-hī bandar haĩ, jitnē ke lōg galī-mẽ haĩ. 7. masjid-kē sāmnē utnē-hī jūtē haĩ, jitnē ke us-mẽ lōg haĩ. 8. daraḳht śikārī-sē utnā-hī dūr hai, jitnā ke ḳhũḳhār jānvar hai. 9. pyāsā musāfir tālāb-sē utnā-hī dūr hai, jitnā ke kuẽ-sē. 10. mērē pās utnē-hī kapṛē haĩ, jitnē mujhē cāhiyē.

32.23 [28.8.1] **Translate into Urdu:**

1. Had the teacher explained the story to the students? 2. The train will arrive in the station in two minutes. 3. The servant obeyed his master's order. 4. The child has taken off his dirty clothes. 5. Why do you try to blurt out the answer before I ask the question? 6. When will you finish your work? 7. Who ate up the apples? 8. When the dog recognized (**his**) master, he became happy. 9. I will jump into the river to swim. 10. The thief had to give the man back the money.11. The child burst out crying at his mother's departure. 12. Take away these things. 13. Did you finish your work? 14. The father has paid the boy's school fees. 15. Why did you laugh at my remark? 16. Why do you fall asleep when I (**fm.**) talk with you? 17. The servant will cut up the wood for the fire. 18. I woke up after sleeping two hours. 19. Why didn't you tell him the truth? 20. When you finish reading this novel, I'll give you another book. 21. If you aren't careful, your feet will slip on the wet road. 22. Why did you tear pages out of my book? 23. The little girl broke out crying at the stranger's arrival. 24. The bad monkeys want to throw down the ripe fruits from the tree. 25. The dry trees of the jungle had caught on fire. 26. When the traveller became tired, he lay down under the tree to rest. 27. Throw away these old shoes. 28. If you have finished talking, then I'll say something. 29. The kind girl gave the thirsty traveller cold water to drink. 30. Men, who try to make war, may change the map of the world. 31. The boy will fall from the tree branch into the river. 32. Had the servant understood your Hindi? 33. Who threw away my cigarette? 34. When will you finish cleaning my clothes? 35. The servant sat down after bringing my shoes. 36. The woman glanced at the pots, then bought two new saris from the shop-keeper. 37. When the frog saw the fisherman he shot off. 38. The man had drunk too much wine. 39. The deer will disappear before the hunter raises his gun. 40. The policeman tore up his shirt to tie the thief. 41. When the thief saw the policeman he became confused. 42. When I reached my friend's house, he had gone. 43. If you under-

stand my remarks, say, "Yes." 44. When I finish reading this letter, I'll talk with you. 45. When the deer heard the hunter going by, he startled. 46. The people will bow before the holy man. 47. The cow had finished eating the grass. 48. The elephant killed the dreadful tiger with his foot. 49. By the time I came into the garden, the goat had eaten all the leaves from the plants. 50. Children should try to listen to their parents' remarks.

32.24 [28.8.2] **Translate into English:**

1.kyā āp mujhē ye kahānī samjhā dē saktē haĩ? 2. kis-nē is kitāb-mẽ-sē dasvā̃ varaḳ phāṛ ḍālā? 3. jis ādmī-nē mērī Aṅgrēzī samajh lī, us-nē javāb dēnē-kī kōśiś kī. 4. kaun-sī cīz chat-sē gir paṛī? 5. vo bīmār kab paṛ gayī thī? 6. mujhē daraḳht-sē kuch pakkē phal phẽk dījiyē. 7. agar tum bīmār hō jāō, tō mujhē bulāō. 8. savālõ-kē javāb kaun bōl uṭhā? 9. vo ādmī, jis-nē mujh-par nigāh ḍāl lī, kaun hai? 10. sūkhī śāḳhẽ jal uṭhĩ. 11. ye purānē jūtē phẽk dō! 12. jitnē maccharõ-kō āp mār sakẽ, āp-kō sab mār ḍālnā cāhiyē. 13. jab tum yah kām ḳhatam kar cukō, tab maĩ tum-kō ḍākḳhānē bhējū̃gā. 14. tumhẽ sab kuch, jō maĩ kahū̃, sun lēnē-kē kōśiś karnā nahī̃ cāhiyē. 15. jab tum ye kām ḳhatam kar cukē hōgē, tab maĩ tum-kō ḍākḳhānē bhējū̃gā. 16. kyā āp-nē ṭikiṭ ḳharīdnē-kē liyē naukar-kō ḍākḳānē bhēj diyā? 17. ādmī itnā ṭhanḍā pānī kyū̃ pī gayā? 18. jō baṛā daraḳht ghar-kē pās hai, vo kāṭ ḍālō. 19. jab vo mujhē na samajh sakā, tab naukar ghabrā uṭhā. 20. kyā musāfir-nē sab muḳaddas jaghẽ pahcān lī̃? 21. kyā tum-nē mujhē sac kah diyā? 22. jab phir ustād-nē savāl pūchā, tālibilm us-kā javāb bōl uṭhā. 23. jab mālik ghar-sē bāhar āyā, naukar khaṛā hō gayā. 24. paṛhnē-kē bād ye ḳhat phāṛ ḍālō. 25. kyā dādī • ammā kahānī sunā cukī haĩ? 26. jō faḳīr bāhar haĩ, un-kō yah khānā dē dījiyē. 27. jab unhõ-nē mērī Urdū sunī, vo hās paṛē. 28. mōcī mērā jūtā kab sī cukēgā? 29. bīmār bail mar jāēgā. 30. jab ham pahõcē, vo kyū̃ cal paṛā? 31. kyā rēlgāṛī-kē ānē-sē pahile mōṭar sṭēśan-kō ā pahõcī? 32. śikārī-kī āvāz sunkar hāthī caũk uṭhē. 33. tum-nē skūl-kī fīs kab jamā dī̃? 34. bhūkā musāfir thōṛī dēr-mẽ khā cukēgā. 35. jō ḳhat maĩ-nē is mēz-par rakhā, kis-nē phāṛ ḍālā thā? 36. ādmī-kē jānē-par us-kē baccē rō paṛē. 37. maĩ ye nāvil kal paṛh cukū̃gī. 38. kaun kursī lē gayā? 39. mērē dōstõ-kē jānē-kē bād kursiyā̃ lē jānā. 40. jab mērē sab dōst ā pahõcē, tab ham bāt karnē-kē liyē baiṭh gayē. 41. āp-kō har sā̃p, jisē āp dēkhẽ, mār ḍālnē-kī kōśiś karnē-kī zarūrat nahī̃ hai. 42. kyā tum mērī safar-kē liyē sab kuch taiyār kar cukē hō? 43. jō kuch maĩ kahtā hū̃, āp vo kyū̃ nahī̃ mān lētī? 44. raḳābī mēz-sē gir paṛī. 45. śikārī-kē bandūk-sē mār ḍālnē-kē pahilē-hī bāgh bhāg gayā. 46. kaun khā cukā hai? 47. jab maĩ-nē apnē dōst-kō pahcān liyā, tab maĩ-nē usē bulāyā. 48. jab āp khānē-kē bād ṭhanḍē pānī-mẽ kūd paṛẽ, tab āp-kō mohtāt rahnā cāhiyē. 49. tumhārē jānē-kē bād maĩ ye ḳhat likh cukū̃gā. 50. āp-kō apnē gīlē jūtē utār ḍālnā paṛtā hai.

32.25 [29.1.1] **Translate into Urdu:**

1. The farmer said to me, "You will have to get out of the ox-cart where the road is too steep." 2. I answered, "I will stop in my travel wherever there are interesting places." 3. I asked him, "Do you like me as much as I like you?" 4. The clerk told me, "Lahore is as beautiful as Karaci." 5. The teacher told the student, "When you travel in Sindh, you should speak Sindhī with as many people as you can." 6. The shopkeeper told the policeman, "I will describe the man as well as I can." 7. The master ordered (**his**) servant, "Reward whichever workmen worked for you." 8. The wife asked (**her**) husband, "Will you bring anyone with you, when you return from town?" 9. The

traveller told the boy, "I cannot drink water which comes from the river." 10. The clerk asked the traveller, "How many days will you stay in the hotel?"

32.26 [29.1.2] **Translate into English:**

1. maĩ-nē gāṛībān-sē pūchā, "tum mujhē gāõ lē jānē-kē liyē kitnē paisē lōgē?" 2. naukar-nē mālik-sē kahā, "jin dukānõ-mẽ bahut lōg thē, vahā̃ mujhē thōṛī dēr-kē liyē ṭhaharnā paṛā." 3. maĩ-nē kisān-sē pūchā, "jitnē bail āp-kē pās haĩ, kyā utnī-hī gayẽ haĩ?" 4. faḳīr-nē amīr ādmī-sē kahā, "mērē liyē khānā ḳhāsil karnā muśkil hō gayā." 5. mā̃-nē bēṭē-sē kahā, "vo gandē kapṛē utār ḍālō!" 6. ādmī-nē dōst-sē pūchā, "jab maĩ kahānī sunā rahā thā, tum us-kā anjām kyũ bōl uṭhē?" 7. ham-nē injinīr-sē pūchā, "jab rēlgāṛī rukī, āp kyũ ghabrā uṭhē?" 8. ustād-nē tālibilm-sē kahā, "jab-tak āp ye sabaḳ acchī tarah sikhẽgē, maĩ būṛhā hō cukā hū̃gā." 9. maĩ-nē us-sē kahā, "jahā̃ tum mērē pīchē nahī̃ jā sakō, maĩ vahā̃ jāū̃gā." 10. us-nē javāb diyā, "mērē pās kāfī paisē nahī̃."

32.27 [29.2.1] **Translate into Urdu:**

1. I hope that it will not rain today. 2. Do you think the road will be too steep? 3. We do not know what the result of the farmer's work will be. 4. He is sorry that he cannot take as much candy as he wants. 5. Did he ask you how far the government building is from here? 6. I told him there is a difference between light and darkness. 7. The traveller told us that people in Bengal eat fish and rice. 8. Is the stranger asking you which is the road that goes to the city? 9. Who will tell him that this is not the right road? 10. Do you know who wrote this letter?

32.28 [29.2.2] **Translate into English:**

1. mujhē ummīd hai ke āp mujh-sē milnē-kē liyē ā sakẽgē. 2. kyā āp jāntē haĩ ke ye saṛak kahā̃ jātī hai? 3. vah kyũ ḳhayāl hai ke maĩ Urdū acchī tarah bōl saktā hū̃. 4. mujhē afsōs hi ke maĩ ap-kī bāt nahī̃ samajh saktā. 5. kis-nē jānā ke maĩ cāval aur machlī kahā̃ ḳharīd saktā hū̃? 6. kyā āp-nē us-sē pūchā ke rēlgāṛī kab ā āēgī? 7. us-nē mujh-sē kahā ke hamārē jānē-kē liyē sab kuch taiyār hai. 8. kyā tum jāntē hō ke vo ādmī kaun hai? 9. āp-kō hamēśā kyũ pūchnā paṛtā hai ke āp kahā̃ thē? 10. ādmī, jō jāntā hai ke kaun-sī saṛak Multān jātī hai, āp-kō batāēgā.

32.29 [29.3.1] **Translate into Urdu:**

1. The washerman said he didn't bring the clothes back. 2. I thought that I had put enough water into the automobile. 3. Who told you that I couldn't come to see you? 4. Did the servant report that he had sent the letter to the post office? 5. I explained that he couldn't repair the automobile. 6. The oxcart driver said that he would take me to the city. 7. The poor man answered the kind woman that it had become difficult for him to find food. 8. The mother asked the children who had eaten up all the apples. 9. I am sorry that the dry trees of the jungle had caught on fire. 10. He told me that if I had finished talking he would say something.

32.30 [29.3.2] **Translate into English:**

1. kis-nē mujh-sē pūchā ke maĩ kab vāpas āū̃gā? 2. kyā āp jāntē haĩ ke naukar-nē sab macchar mār ḍālē haĩ? 3. maĩ-nē laṛkē-sē kahā ke jab vo kām kar cukēgā, maĩ us-kō ḍākḳhānē bhēj dū̃gā. 4. naukar-nē musāfir-sē pūchā ke vo itnā ṭhaṇḍā pānī kyũ pīnā cāhtā thā? 5. kyā tum-nē mōcī-sē pūchā ke vo mērē jūtē kab sī cukēgā? 6. maĩ-nē naukar-sē kahā ke jō faḳīr ghar-kē sāmnē khaṛē thē, un-kō vo cāval dē. 7. us-nē mujh-sē pūchā ke maĩ-nē sab kuch, jō us-nē kahā, kyũ nahī̃ mān liyā? 8. kyā tum-kō afsōs

nahī̃ ke jis savāl-kā javāb tum bōl uṭhē, vo ġalat thā? 9. musāfir-nē pūchā ke kaun us-kō naḳśā samjhā dē saktā hai? 10. kyā āp-kō ḳhayāl nahī̃ thā ke āj bāriś hōgī?

32.31 [29.4.1] **Translate into Urdu:**

1. Were there many people in those villages? 2. Where is my hat? 3. How many muddy paths are there near the villages? 4. There were many fishermen on the bank of the river. 5. Were the roads rather long? 6. On a large ship there are rather many sailors. 7. There is sweet water in this well. 8. In a city there are rather big buildings. 9. How many muddy paths are there near those villages? 10. There were many fishermen on the bank of the river.

32.32 [29.4.2] **Translate into English:**

1. us kisān-kē pās chōṭā-sā hal thā. 2. baṛē śahar-mē̃ taṅg-sē rāstē hōtē haĩ. 3. rēlgāṛī-kē sṭēśanō̃-mē̃ bahot-sē lōg hōtē thē. 4. us daraḳht-par bahot-sē phūl aur phal haĩ. 5. us mōṭargāṛī-kē pā̃c pahiyē haĩ. 6. kuē̃ gahrē-sē hōtē haĩ. 7. jānvar, jō jaṅgal-mē̃ rahtē haĩ, ḳhū̃ḳhār haĩ. 8. mahājanō̃-kē pās bahot-sē paisē hōtē haĩ. 9. us mahājan-kē pās bahot-sē makān haĩ. 10. ye kuē̃ gahrē-sē thē.

32.33 [30.1.1] **Translate into Urdu:**

1. Seeing the result of his studying, he rose to go. 2. Beating the donkey, the washerman made him go. 3. Reading his letter, I became discouraged. 4. Opening the door carefully, he looked out. 5. Go into the kitchen and call the cook. 6. We called the carriage and got in. 7. He opened the window quickly and called a taxi. 8. Hearing the news of your success, your friend began to tell all the people. 9. Having told his story, the beggar took food from us. 10. What things did you [**go and**] bring from the market? 11. Hearing the farmer's voice, the ox began to run towards him. 12. Hearing the news of his master's arrival, the servant began to run towards him. 13. Put these things into the automobile and wait for me. 14. Having written the letter, he became discouraged. 15. Taking my camera with me, I went out to take pictures of the temples.

32.34 [30.1.2] **Translate into English:**

1. ṭhaharkar, kisān-nē bailō̃-kō ghās khilāyī. 2. kaśtī kirāyē-par lēkar, ham machliyā̃ pakaṛnē-kō gayē. 3. jaldī-sē dauṛkar, vo ṭrēn-mē̃ gayā aur baiṭhā. 4. gāvō̃-kō jākar, ham-nē lōgō̃-kē sāth bāt kī. 5. bail-kō pakaṛkar, us-kō khēt vāpas lē jāō. 6. kaun, bāzār jākar, ye sabziyā̃ vāpas lāyā? 7. mērī kāmyābī-kī ḳhabar sunkar, sab dōst mujh-sē milnē-kē liyē āyē. 8. jāgkar, jō kūch huā thā, us-kō jānnē-kē liyē vo bāhar dauṛā. 9. bāvarcīḳhānē-mē̃ jākar, āp-kō bāvarcī-sē kahnā na cāhiyē thā ke khānā acchā nahī̃. 10. kis-nē is hal-kā istēmāl karkē tōṛ ḍālā? 11. cīzē̃ mēz-par rakhkar, jāiyē. 12. us-kā ḳhat paṛhkar, āp kyū̃ ḳhuś huī̃? 13. dō hisābō̃-par nigāh ḍālkar, mujhē batāiyē ke kaun-sā ṭhīk hai. 14. baccē-kā hāth pakaṛkar, bāġ-mē̃ jāō! 15. mōṭargāṛī kirāyē-par lēkar, āp maśhūr jaghē̃ kyū̃ nahī̃ gayē?

32.35 [30.2.4] **Translate into Urdu:**

1. After calling the servant I forgot what I wanted. 2. On hearing the news of his success he suddenly began to dance. 3. Before going into the mosque please take off your shoes. 4. Do you want to rest for a little while after you see the celebrated places? 5. I was about to hang up the telephone when the doorbell rang. 6. I prefer talking with people to seeing celebrated places. 7. I was about to listen to the radio when some friends arrived. 8. I had to go home after the movies began. 9. We were about to go into the train when suddenly the electricity failed. 10. On opening the window, he saw no one.

11. We (fm.) prefer speaking Urdu to speaking English. 12. He was about to pay when he realized that he couldn't buy the gift. 13. It suddenly began to rain after we went out for a walk. 14. On reaching Bombay he stopped to rest. 15. You should wash your hands before drinking water. 16. The woman was about to go to the market when a friend of hers arrived. 17. After placing his notes in the briefcase, the lawyer began to answer. 18. The teacher was about to tell a story when the student interrupted. 19. The birds began to sing after the sun came out. 20. On my falling asleep the servant carefully opened the door and went out.

32.36 [30.2.5] **Translate into English:**

1. dō hisābõ-par nigāh ḍālnē-kē bād, maĩ-nē tay kiyā ke dusrā g̠alat thā. 2. mandar dēkhnē-par aurat-nē andar jānā cāhā. 3. kyā āp-kō sunnē-sē bāt karnā zyādā pasand hai? 4. masjid-mẽ jānē-sē pahilē, āp-kō jūtē utārnā paṛtā hai. 5. maĩ sair-kō bāhar jānē-hī-kō thā ke āp ā pahõcē. 6. mērē jāgnē-kē bād naukar cāy lāyā. 7. fōṭōgrāfēr us-kī tasvīr khĩcnē-hī-kō thā ke laṛkā cal paṛā. 8. khānē-kē kamrē-mẽ jānē-par us-nē dēkhā ke us-kī dōst nahĩ pahõcī. 9. vo ak̠hbār paṛhnē-hī-kō thā ke darvāzē-kī ghanṭī bajī. 10. mērē naukar-kē ṭaiksī bulānē-kē liyē bāhar jānē-kē bād tumhārī mōṭargāṛī pahõcī. 11. ṭēlēfōn band karnē-sē pahilē un-sē pūchiyē ke vo ham-sē milnē-kē liyē kab āẽgē? 12. vo g̠arībān-kō paisē dēnē-hī-kō thā ke usē mālūm huā ke us-kē pās paisē nahĩ thē. 13. aḍḍē-par pahõcnē-kē bād maĩ-nē dēkhā ke bas cal gayī thī. 14. kōī lōg tohfē lēnē-sē dēnā zyādā pasand kartē haĩ. 15. mērī dūsrī kahānī śūrū karnē-kē bād, dōstõ-nē ṭōk diyā. 16. vo ghar jānē-hī-kō thā ke usē mālūm huā ke us-kī mōṭargāṛī nahĩ āyī thī. 17. apnē kām-kā natījā dēkhnē-par vo himmat hār gayā. 18. tumhārē ānē-sē pahilē maĩ-nē tay kiyā thā ke sair-kō bāhar jāũgā. 19. tohfē k̠harīdnē-kē bād vo bhūl gayā ke us-nē kin-kē liyē vo k̠harīdē thē. 20. paisē milnē-kē bād, g̠arīb ādmī k̠huśī-sē nācnē lagā.

32.37 [31.1.2] **Translate into Urdu:**

1. The running girl will fall. 2. The father sent the crying daughter to her mother. 3. The singing servants woke me up this morning. 4. The boy fed the barking dogs. 5. The smiling men were listening to me. 6. We called the gardener watering the plants. 7. Throw the swimming man a rope. 8. The hunter killed the lion dragging the goat into the jungle. 9. The fading plants fell on the table. 10. Why didn't you help the woman carrying the wood? 11. Ask the man carrying water if we can help him. 12. Where did you see the ox running? 13. The master called the servant going out of the room. 14. Who caught the cow going out of the field? 15. Who are the men praying before the river?

32.38 [31.1.3] **Translate into English:**

1. muskarātā huā ādmī āp-kē savālõ-kē javāb dēgā. 2. ham-nē us-kō har din tālāb-kē pās ibādat kartē huē dēkhā. 3. rōtī huī chōṭī laṛkī-kō kuch miṭhāī dē dō! 4. sōtē huē bail jagākar kisān khēt-mẽ hal calānē lagā. 5. gātē huē parindē tumhẽ jagāẽgē. 6. kyā āp-kō sōtē huē baccē-kō jagānā zarūrī hai? 7. ham-nē hamārē ghar-kē sāmnē khaṛē huē ādmī-kō khānā diyā. 8. bhõktā huā kuttā tumhẽ nahĩ kāṭēgā. 9. murjhātē huē paudõ-par kuch pānī ḍālō. 10. ham-nē us-kō bāzār-mẽ caltē huē dēkhā. 11. muskarātī aur hamārē sāmnē rūmāl hilātī huī aurat mērī mā̃ hai. 12. kyā āp-nē us-kō mērī mōṭargāṛī-kī marammat kartē huē dēkhā? 13. āp-nē mērē ghar-kē bāhar dauṛtē huē ādmī-kō kyũ nahĩ rōkā? 14. hamārē sāmnē caltē huē ādmī mērē naukar haĩ. 15. maĩ rāt-kō camaktē huē tārē dēkhnā pasand kartā hũ.

32.39 [31.2.1] **Translate into Urdu:**

1. I do not know who the writer of this letter is. 2. Did you ever travel on the ship which comes from America? 3. We will celebrate Id the coming week. 4. That long-legged horse will be able to run quickly. 5. How many householders are there in this village? 6. Why are you about to go? 7. Is this the mail train going to Peshavar? 8. The people of that place will be able to show you the tiger. 9. The bus coming from Lahore will arrive in two hours. 10. You will be able to learn a lot from the villagers.

32.40 [31.2.2] **Translate into English:**

1. daftar ānēvālē das dinõ-mē band rahēgā. 2. Rāvalpindī jānēvālī rēlgāṛī kaun-sī hai? 3. kitnē gāõvālē kām karnē-kē liyē śahar gayē haĩ? 4. gānēvālē ādmī kahā̃-sē ā rahē haĩ? 5. is k̲hat-kē likhnēvālē-kō andar bhēj dījiyē. 6. kyā āp gharvālē haĩ? 7. vahā̃vālē lōgõ-nē mujhē yahā̃ bhējā. 8. machlī bēcnēvālē-sē pūchō ke vo is baṛī machlī-kē liyē kitnē paisē lēgā? 9. maĩ savāl pūchnēvālā-hī thā. 10. āp kaisē jāntē haĩ ke ye ādmī gāõvālā hai?

32.41 [31.3.1] **Translate into Urdu:**

1. His foot slipped as he was running and he fell. 2. She became hoarse while she was crying. 3. As he was telling me the story he began to laugh. 4. The cow looked towards us as she was eating. 5. The student's eyes became red as he was reading. 6. We became tired while we were walking up along the steep road. 7. As she was reading the letter the girl suddenly began to cry. 8. The sparrows became thirsty as they were flying. 9. The gardener became tired as he was watering the plants. 10. The man became thirsty while he was catching fish.

32.42 [31.3.2] **Translate into English:**

1. hamārē liyē pānī lātē lātē laṛkī thak gayī. 2. hãstē hãstē us-nē mujhē kahānī sunāyī. 3. bāzār-mẽ caltē caltē aurat-nē bahot-sī cīzẽ dēkhĩ, jō us-nē k̲harīdnā cāhā. 4. kinārē-par caltē caltē maĩ phislā aur daryā-mẽ gir paṛā. 5. jaṅgal-mẽ caltē caltē śikārī tālāb-par pahõcā. 6. kitāb paṛhtē paṛhtē vo ēk • dam uṭhkar bāvarcīk̲hānē-kī taraf dauṛī. 7. dhōtī dhōtē dhōtē dhōbī thak gayā. 8. bhõktē bhõktē kuttā ajnabī-kī taraf dauṛā. 9. mujh-sē kahtē kahtē us-kā galā baiṭh gayā. 10. baṛā darak̲ht kāṭtē kāṭtē lakṛī kāṭnēvālā thak gayā.

Following are translations of the reading texts given in lessons 25-31. They can be used as exercises in translating English passages into Urdu.

32.43 [25.3] **Coffee-House:**

[Friends, come let us take you today to the most famous Coffee-House in Lahore. Its name is "Pakistan Coffee-House." This coffee-house is located on the most beautiful and busy road, the Mall. Its owner is a Karachi millionaire. He is an exceedingly rich man. He owns many factories, shops and hotels. There are about forty tables in this coffee-house. College students and professors usually come here. Besides them, some lawyers, newspapermen, authors and poets also come here to pass time. There is a table in the left-hand corner. Every evening Kurban Ali, Vahid Khan and their friends come and sit at that table. Kurban Ali teaches at the University. Vahid Khan also teaches, but not at the University. He teaches at the Government College. Both get a salary of five-hundred rupees. When these people come in the evening, the waiter comes to take their order. The waiter's name is Shahab Din. These people have been coming here for several years and Shahab Din has also been here for several years. This kind of conversation takes place between these people and the waiter.]

Shahab: Greetings, Professor.
Kurban: Say, Shahab Din, you're all right—aren't you?
Shahab: Sir, I am very well and pray for your well-being. What can I do for you?
Vahid: Well, we'll just have coffee. Bring (coffee) for four people.
Shahab: Cold or hot?
Kurban: I'll take cold. All the rest will drink hot coffee.
Shahab: Sir, will you like cream or milk in your coffee?

[An American boy is sitting at this table at this time. His name is Thompson. He has been travelling around in Pakistan for some months. He speaks to his Pakistani friends in Urdu every day, but his Urdu is still broken.]

Thompson: Shahab Din! What's the difference between milk and cream?
Shahab: Sir, what shall I say? Milk is milk and cream is cream. And, yes, there's a two-anna extra charge for cream-coffee.
Vahid: Shahab Din, bring coffee with cream for everyone. And, look here, bring the bill to me.
Shahab: Very well, sir. (He goes away.)
Vahid: Look, Friend Thompson. I have advised you so many times not to aspirate your k's.
Thompson: Vahid, thanks. I'm trying. God willing, I'll learn it correctly some day.
Kurban: Friends, what's the news?
Thompson: What will you hear? Shall I tell you something?
Vahid: Yes, sure, Thompson.
Thompson: I think that I should immediately write a book about Pakistan.
Kurban: Thompson! How long have you been in Pakistan?
Thompson: Two months.
Vahid: Do you think you know enough about Pakistan after this two-months' stay?
Thompson: No. I don't know Pakistan well. But many Americans and Englishmen consider themselves competent to write books on China and Japan after they have lived in Delhi for a week. I know Pakistan somewhat and I want to write about Pakistan, too.
Kurban: You are right. But we still think you should see a bit more about this country and then write a book.
Thompson: All right. I'll think about it.

[Shahab Din brings coffee. All the friends pour coffee into their cups and drink.]

Sarvar Ahmad (addressing Vahid): Professor! Tell me how your college is.
Vahid: It's all right, friend. Why? What's the matter?
Sarvar: Nothing special. My younger brother goes there. Just keep an eye on him.
Vahid: Sure. Tell me how are politics in your office these days.
Kurban: Oh! Why do you keep talking about office and college? Say something else. Vahid, sing us a G̱azal.
Vahid: Kurban Ali, I can't recall any, right this minute.
Sarvar: Now he'll fish for insistence!
Vahid: Sarvar, I'm not fishing for more requests. I honesty don't recall any. Perhaps, after a little while, I will. As soon as anything comes to my mind, I'll sing it for you.

32.44 [26.5] **Id:**

Id is a holy occasion for the Muslims. Id falls on the day following the last day of the month of Ramzan. First, let us tell you something about the month of Ramzan. It is a duty for the Muslims to fast during the month of Ramzan. It means that the Muslims (who fast) neither eat nor drink anything between sun-rise and sun-set. The philosophy behind fasting is that the Muslims may keep up their power of endurance and they may be able to bear the shortage of food and drink if circumstances require it. It is also maintained that people may experience hunger and thirst so that they may appreciate the difficulties of the poor, and they may help one another.

To fulfill this religious duty the true Muslims get up early in the morning, so early that it is still completely dark. At this time, they eat food and drink something if they feel like it. When it begins to dawn, they stop eating and drinking. Those who are particularly religious say prayers all day. Other people keep doing their everyday work. Needless to say, it is rather difficult to do everyday work during Ramzan. Anyway, when the sun sets in the evening, people break the fast. They eat dinner and drink things. When the month of Ramzan is over, people celebrate Id and become very gay. The reason for this gaity is that they have done their duty well. Those who have not fasted during Ramzan celebrate, too.

On the day of Id people get up early in the morning, wash and bathe, etc., and put on new clothes. Then they take breakfast and after that give presents to each other. Usually children are given money which they spend quickly. Around ten o'clock people go to different mosques to say Id-prayers. Quite often it happens that there isn't enough space for all the people to say their prayers. Therefore, many people say their prayers in the open. After prayers, the religious leaders deliver speeches. In their speeches they throw light on the philosophy of Id and Ramzan. All this takes about an hour and a half. After that, people embrace and greet one another. Much money is given in charity on the day of Id. Some people give food to the poor.

Fairs are held at many places on the day of Id. Usually, the children and young men go to these fairs. Besides this Id, there is another Id. That is called Bakra Id. On this day, too, there are celebrations in Muslim countries. The particular thing about this Id is that on this day Muslims sacrifice animals and eat some of the meat themselves, but give most of it to the poor. Those who are rich slaughter many goats and rams. Those who are poor are not called upon to make any sacrifice on the day of Id. Now the question is why sacrifice is made on this day of Id. The following is given as the reason. They say that once God's prophet, Abraham, dreamed that he was slaughtering his son Ismael on the top of the mountain. The following night, he had this dream again. And he had it again the night after that. He interpreted this dream to mean that God wanted him to sacrifice his son for His sake. Accordingly, he mentioned this dream to his son, Ismael. The son interpreted this dream just as Abraham himself had done. Ismael told his father that if such was God's will, he had no objection to his being sacrificed. After that both Abraham and his son went over the mountain. Ismael suggested to his father that he cover his eyes with a strip of cloth before sacrificing so that his determination might not be shaken. Abraham put a strip of cloth over his eyes and uttering the name of God passed the knife over Ismael's throat. When he uncovered his eyes and opened them, he saw that Ismael was completely unharmed and in his place a aughtered ram was lying. He interpreted this to mean that God had tested his love for Iim and had also indicated that his men should not offer human sacrifices to Him, but hould sacrifice animals in this way. In memory of this incident the Muslims celebrate his Id.

32.45 [27.7] **The Justice of Jahangir:**

Jahangir's real name was Nur-ud-Din. He was the son of King Akbar, the grand-on of Humayun, and the great-grandson of Babar. He ascended the throne of India in he year 1605. When Jahangir was still a prince, he fell in love with a very pretty girl. 'his girl's name was Mehr-un-Nisā. She lived in the royal palace. When she became of ge, she got married to the governor of Bengal, Ali Kuli Khan. Mehr-un-Nisā was still n Bengal when Jahangir became king. But after a few years her husband, that is to ay, Ali Kuli, died. The king was still in love with Mehr-un-Nisā. He got her to come ack to the royal palace. After seven years passed, she agreed to marry the king. Now ier name was Nur Jahan, and she became the Queen of India. Once upon a time, the ueen was standing on the roof of the palace with her maids shooting arrows. By nistake, an arrow struck a washerman who was washing clothes on the bank of the iver and he died. The washerwoman and her family complained to the king that some-one had shot her husband dead. On making investigations, it transpired that the person vho shot the arrow was the queen of India. Now Jahangir was involved in a great lifficulty. On one side there was the (claim of) justice and on the other side was (the laim of) love. He did not know what to do. For several hours he kept thinking on this natter. When he thought that someone had killed an innocent man, his eyes became ed with anger. But, when he thought that this queen was the murderer and that the entence for the murderer, according to law, was death, then tears came into his eyes. Ie would think of the time when he was a young prince and the queen was a young girl. He remembered an incident of this time which is very charming. One day the rince was strolling in the garden. He had two pet pigeons in his hands. Suddenly, the rince remembered an urgent bit of business. He gave his pigeons to Mehr-un-Nisā nd said, "Beautiful (one)! [just] take care of our pigeons. We'll come back in a little vhile." When the prince came back, Mehr-un-Nisā returned only one pigeon to him. The prince said, "Where did the other pigeon go?" Mehr-un-Nisā said, "Prince he flew way." The prince asked, "But how did it fly away?" Now Mehr-un-Nisā loosened her old and released the other pigeon, too, and said, "Prince, like this." Jahangir liked this harming gesture of Mehr-un-Nisā very much and he, at once, fell in love with her. Now ll these things were coming back to the king and were upsetting him. Finally, justice von and his love lost (the battle). Jahangir ordered the women's police to arrest the queen and take her to the jail. Accordingly, the queen was locked up in jail. But after his the king became very sad. He gave up food and drink. When the councillors and ninisters of the royal court saw this state of the king, they became very upset. They new that, if the queen was sentenced to death, then after a short while Jahangir would lie, too. He would not be able to live without the queen. All the courtiers went to the ing. They proposed that the queen had not killed the washerman deliberately. There-ore, she should be set free. But Jahangir did not heed their plea. After a few days the vasherwoman's suit came up in the court. Jahangir asked the queen, "Do you admit our crime?" The queen replied, "Yes, I plead guilty." Then the king asked the jurists,

"What is the sentence for the murderer, according to the law?" The jurists said, "Th law says that the sentence for a murderer is death." Jahangir gave the verdict that th queen be sentenced to death. When this sentence was announced, all the courtiers lo: their presence of mind. They asked the heirs of the washerman to accept compensatio and to take back their suit against the queen. The washerwoman and her relatives agree to this. They said to King Jahangir, "We do not want a death-sentence for the queer We are ready to accept compensation and take back our claim." Once again the kin asked the jurists, "Does the law permit this?" They replied, "Yes, Sir."

In this way the life of the Indian Queen and Jahangir's beloved wife was savec Love and Justice, both, won their respective claims.

32.46 [28.9] **The City of Lahore:**

Lahore is one of the oldest cities of the world. People say that about two thousan years from today one of Rajah Ram Chandar's sons founded this city. If you go t Lahore, now-a-days, you will see that this city is not only old but is also very beautiful Lahore is divided into two parts: The old city, which has a wall around it, has narrov streets and old-fashioned houses. It is difficult to drive an automobile in these streets Some streets are so narrow that even a tonga cannot go there. Municipal water is sup plied in some houses. But there are wells in some homes. There are no very good ar rangments for drainage in this part. Therefore, streets become muddy and it is difficul to maintain cleanliness. The result is that sometimes epidemics spread. In the summer many people get malaria. Since there is a shortage of doctors and nurses in Pakistan every year some people die of fever. But there is one (significant) thing: the Lahor municipality is trying very hard to maintain cleanliness and check diseases in the ol city. Many new hospitals have been established where patients are treated free of charge The government has opened a new Medical College in Lahore. Now there are two Medi cal Colleges—one for boys and girls and the other for girls only. Every year about two hundred boys and girls qualify to be doctors. The other part of Lahore is comparatively new. In this area there are many gardens and parks. The roads are new and the build ings are modern. The most famous road is called the "Mall Road." The Governmen House is on this road. The Panjab University buildings are also on this road. There is a lo of hub-bub on this road around nine o'clock in the morning. Hundreds of men and womer riding on cycles, in tongas and motor-cars go to their respective schools, colleges and offices. At every crossing, there is a policeman to control the traffic. Those who ride against the law are given a ticket. In this area is the Government College. This college is "Number One" in the whole of Pakistan. The professors who teach in this college are greatly respected. It has been about a hundred years (since) this college was established. About twelve-hundred girls and boys study here. But the girls will hardly number a hundred. Usually, the girls go to girls' colleges. There are several colleges for girls in Lahore. These days all the people want to give an education to their children. There are several places of historical interest around Lahore. On one side there is King Jahangir's tomb. I have told you a story about this king which we hope you remember. Just near this tomb there is also the tomb of Queen Nur Jahan. On the other side, there is an exceedingly beautiful garden which is called the "Shalimar Garden." This garden was built during the reign of the Mogul king Shah Jahan. The care of these buildings is entrusted to the Archaeological Department. We just mentioned the Mall Road. The offices of the "Civil and Military Gazette" are located on this road. There is a room in these offices in which, many years ago, Rudyard Kipling used to work. Even though Kipling has written a lot of erroneous stuff about India, many Pakistanis read his books fondly.

The greatest merit of Lahore is that the people of this city are very nice. Anyone who stays in this town for some time does not want to leave it. The climate of this town is also good. But it becomes rather difficult to live here during the hot weather. The rich people go to Marree during this season, but the poor don't have to go to mountain resorts during the summer. Some people think that Karachi is a better city than Lahore. But I think these people are wrong. To tell you the truth, Karachi does not stand in comparison to Lahore.

32.47 [29.5] **My Autobiography: (Part I)**

I was born on the seventeenth of December in the year 1926. My mother says that as soon as I was born I began to scream. But I was a good baby more or less. When I was three, I got typhoid which lasted two months. But from then up to today I have had no serious illness. I remember that at that time I was very scared of dogs. At the age of four, I got admitted to a school. When I became six, my father bought me a small bicycle. I used to ride this bicycle to school. Every time I would come across a dog in the way. This dog was very big and dreadful. When he would see me, he would bark and run after me. Frightened, I would ride my cycle very fast, but the dog would run after me faster. When he would get near me, I would take a cookie out of my pocket and throw it at him. After that, riding my cycle fast, I would reach school. Even though I am not scared of dogs now, I do not like them very much.

I was very fond of riding horses when I was ten. At that time my daddy had two horses. Once upon a time, I went for an early morning ride. I noticed that another boy who was much older than I rode his horse very fast. I struck my horse with a thin cane. The horse which was very strong at once began to gallop. I held the bridle with one hand and the long hair on the horse's neck with the other. I was afraid that I would fall down. But the more I would try to slow him down, the faster he would run. Finally, I was so upset that I began to scream. Hearing my screams, the horse, also, became scared and this time ran so fast that I fell down. Fortuntely, I did not get hurt too much. When I got on my feet the horse had disappeared. I ran about a lot but found no sign of the horse. My father had bought him for two-thousand rupees only a few days before. I came back home and told my daddy the whole incident. He reported (the matter) to the police but the horse was not traced. It has now been twenty years. He hasn't come back to this day. He is probably dead. Needless to say, my father was very angry, and he never let me ride his horse again. At the age of sixteen, I passed my high-school examination and got admitted to college. This period of life was very pleasant. College was very different from school. Every professor called the roll in his period. Whoever was absent from class got fined four annas. Smoking was not permitted in the college. Still, several boys smoked secretly. After a short while, I, too, began smoking cigarettes. From that time (on) I have smoked. Even though money is spent uselessly and I get a bad throat, (still) I keep on smoking—twenty cigarettes a day. It has become a habit. Now it's difficult to give it up. Several times, I was caught smoking in college and was fined, but I was excused by the professor. This professor was very kind to me. You people are probably bored by my story. I will tell you the rest next time.

32.48 [30.3] **My Autobiography: (Part II)**

I was nineteen when I passed my B.A. from the college. I decided that it was not necessary to study any more. I did not intend to go into service because the jobs didn't offer enough money. I thought that if I took up a job, it would be difficult for me to make both ends meet. Thinking this, I decided that I would go into business. Accordingly, I soon established a small factory in Amritsar. Iron and brass were melted in this factory and utensils made, too. Only twelve workmen worked in this factory. First, I did not make any profit from the business. Instead, I suffered some losses. But I didn't give up. Instead, I started working still harder on it. Sometimes it would happen that I would have to remain at the factory day and night. God rewarded my hard work soon, and I began to make profit. Even though my work had now started paying, I was not much interested in it. I began to realize that the factory was not the suitable place for a man of poetic disposition like myself. After some time circumstances took such a turn that I did not have to make the decision. In 1947, India was divided into two parts and Pakistan appeared on the map of the world. As soon as this decision was made communal riots began in India and Pakistan. Many innocent men, women and children were killed. Property worth tens of millions was destroyed. Hundreds of thousands of buildings were burnt down. Among them was my small factory. I was among those who went over to Pakistan as refugees. On reaching Lahore, I found that my people were also there. They had rented a house. My mother and father who had left all their property in India were very sad for some time. But when they saw that hundreds of thousands of others were in the same circumstances, they overcame their own grief. Now all of us began to live in this rented house. Soon after, I began looking for a job. In but a few days I got a nice job. I felt that to make progress it was necessary that I get an M.A. Accordingly, I started preparing for my M.A. examination and two months after that I got a job in the Government College, Lahore. Now I began to teach economics to boys and girls. This was a very enjoyable period. I had to teach seven hours a week. I won over my students quickly and they began to like me very much. All the students worked hard and did their home-work and I didn't have to fine them. Thus the days passed by. The year 1952 came along. In the beginning of this year I got a scholarship to come to the United States. On July 17, I boarded the train for Karachi in Lahore, and went to New York from there by plane. I had to stop for a night in Beirut, a city in Lebanon, because our plane needed some repairs. Beirut is an exceedingly beautiful city. The sea is on three sides of it. The climate is very good. In winter the climate is delightful. After Beirut I, along with my fellow-travellers, stopped in London. Now, what shall I tell you about London. I think you yourself know everything about this city. After staying in New York for about ten or twelve days, I went to Chicago and studied at the University of Chicago for one year. Some people think Chicago is a very dirty city. But I think that Philadelphia is even dirtier. Chicago is situated on the shores of Lake Michigan. It is exceedingly cold during the winter. It snows here almost every day from October to April and a hard wind blows all the time. For the past year, I have been at the University of Pennsylvania and earn my living by writing stories for you people. But now I am getting homesick and I think I'll go back to Pakistan.

32.49 [31.5] **Mohammad Ali Jinnah:**

Mohammad Ali Jinnah was the greatest political leader of the Indian Muslims. He was born in Karachi in 1876. His father was a middle-class tradesman. His father's) business was also in Karachi. Mr. Jinnah got his early education in Karachi and, after that, went to England for further education. He was admitted to the bar there. Then he came and settled down in Bombay. He practiced law there for many years. He worked very industriously. Soon he began to be considered one of the top-ranking lawyers of India. Around this time he began to take part in politics. Because of his ability, honesty, and patriotism he attained high positions in the (Indian National) Congress. The Congress Party people built a hall in Bombay named after him, which is called "Jinnah Hall." But after some time, differences arose between Mr. Jinnah and the other Congress leaders. Mr. Jinnah pleaded for some rights for the Muslims in a free India. Mr. Gandhi and some other Congress leaders wouldn't accept these demands. Besides, the Indian Muslims were themselves disunited at that time. Disgusted with these things, Mr. Jinnah left the Congress. After some years, he went back to England and established his practice in London. He usually pleaded in the Privy Council. After 1930, the condition of the Indian Muslims became very bad and there was no one to lead them. Allamah Ikbal and some other prominent Muslims strongly urged Mr. Jinah to return to India. He reestablished himself in Bombay. From this time up to the creation of Pakistan, he was the President of the Muslim League. In 1940 the Muslim League, under the lead of Mr. Jinnah, decided that the Muslims ought to have a separate country for themselves. This decision was made at the annual meeting of the Muslim League. It is called the Lahore Resolution. After this the attainment of Pakistan became the single objective of the League. This resolution meant that the Indian provinces with a majority of Muslims in population should be separated from the rest of India so as to form one country which should be named Pakistan. This objective was attained on the fourteenth of August, 1947. Mr. Jinnah gave up the presidency of the League after the birth of Pakistan and he became the country's first Governor-General. To tell you the truth, the battle for Pakistan was fought not by the Muslim League but by Mr. Jinnah single-handed, more or less. If he hadn't been there to lead the Muslims during this difficult time, Pakistan would probably never have come into existence. He was so firm that no power on earth could shake his determination. The Muslims of India liked Mr. Jinnah very much. He had such an appeal to the Muslims that the latter were always ready to even give away their lives at his command. It is surprising that even though Mr. Jinnah was a leader of the Muslims, his way of life was entirely western. In spite of that, the Muslims had complete faith in him. His opponents complained that he did not have a beard and that he didn't say his prayers, but no one listened to them. Mr. Jinnah died in 1947.

LESSON 33

33.1

thakā huā musāfir ārām karnē-kē liyē rukā.	The tired traveller stopped to rest.
is kitāb-sē phāṛā huā varaḳ kahā̃ hai?	Where is the page torn from this book?
bā̃dhī huī gāy śōr macātī hai.	The tied cow makes noise.
jab us-kī mā̃ kamrē-mē̃ āyī, tab sōyī huī laṛkī jāg uṭhī.	When her mother came into the room, the girl (**who had**) fallen asleep woke up.
aurat hamārē ghar-kē sāmnē baiṭhī huī tāzī sabziyā̃ bēc rahī hai.	The woman seated in front of our house is selling fresh vegetables.
kyā tum-nē ye kahānī ēk kitāb-mē̃ likhī huī dēkhī?	Did you see this story written in a book?
maĩ-nē murjhāyē huē paudō̃-kō pānī diyā.	I watered the faded plants.
us-nē rāstē-mē̃ paṛā huā ēk kā̃ṭā uṭhāyā.	She picked up an earring lying in the street.
mujhē pahilē sunāyī huī kahānī na sunāiyē.	Please do not tell me an already-told story.
cōr-nē curāyī huī ghaṛī vāpas kar dī.	The thief returned the stolen watch.
hamārē darvāzē-par sōyē huē kuttē-kō jagāō.	Wake up the dog asleep at our door.
ham-nē daraḳht-kē nīcē bā̃dhē huē ghōṛē-kō pāyā.	We found the horse (**which was**) tied under the tree.

This section illustrates phrases, consisting of the past participle of a verb and **huā** (the past participle of **hōnā**), which function as **adjectives.** (Compare 31.1 to 31.1.1) Both participles agree in gender, number and form with the noun modified. The past participle without the second member (i.e., **huā**) will be found functioning as an adjective.

Note that in sentences 5 and 6 the adjectival phrase follows the noun modified.

33.1.1 Exercise 1. **Translate into English:**

1. kaun is ṭūṭī huī lemp-kī marammat karēgā? 2. sōyā huā naukar ēk • dam jāg uṭhā. 3. kōnē-mē̃ paṛī huī cappal kis-kī hai? 4. darzī-kō ye phaṭā huā kōṭ sīnā paṛēgā. 5. zamin-par lēṭā huā ādmī kaun hai? 6. thakē huē mazdūrō̃-kō kuch pānī dō. 7. kyā ye pānī ubālā huā hai? 8. tumhē̃ zamīn-par girē huē phal khānā nahī̃ cāhiyē. 9. mērī curāyī huī kitāb kis-nē pāyī? 10. daraḳht-kē nīcē bā̃dhī huī gāy-nē śōr macānā śurū kiyā.

33.1.2 Exercise 2. **Translate into Urdu:**

1. Who dragged the dead jackal out of the jungle? 2. Tell the tailor to sew my torn coat.

. Whose is the cow tied near our garden? 4. The tired child began to cry. 5. Can you epair the broken plow? 6. He found his friend asleep in the automobile. 7. Who will ook for the books I lost? 8. When can the carpenter repair this broken chair? 9. Are ou going to tell us again the story you told yesterday? 10. The woman seated in the arden is mending her torn sari.

33.2

ūr-sē pahāṛ bādlō̃ jaisē mālūm hōtē haĩ.	From the distance the hills look like clouds.
uch amīr ādmī akṣar rājkumārō̃ jaisē kapṛē pahantē haĩ.	Some rich men frequently dress like princes.
āt-kō tālāb-kī satah āīnē jaisī mālūm hōtī hai.	At night the surface of the pond looks like a mirror.
e bakrē paisā jānvar kyā hai?	What is this goat-like animal?
e cīz camṛē jaisī mālūm hōtī hai.	This stuff seems like leather.
s-nē ēk mahal jaisā ghar banāyā.	He built a palace-like house.
k bādal jaisā pahāṛ dūr-sē dikhāyī dētā hai.	A cloud-like mountain appears in the distance.
uṛiyā jaisī bhōlī • bhālī laṛkī apnē liyē gā rahī thī.	The doll-like, sweet, little girl was singing to herself.
s kāval jaisē phūl-kō kyā kahtē haĩ?	What do they call this lotus-like flower?
aṛkī-kā cā̃d jaisā cehrā thā.	The girl had a moon-like face.
e cā̃dī jaisē kāgaz śāyad baṛē ḳīmtī haĩ?	This silver-like paper is perhaps very expensive.
Tāj Mahal jaisī kōī imārat duniyā-mẽ nahī̃ hai.	There is no building in the world like the Taj Mahal.

This section illustrates the translation into Urdu of English **like, similar to.** The oun with which the comparison is made is placed in the object form before **jaisā, like, imilar to,** which agrees in gender, number and form with the noun compared.

REMARKS: **āīnā** (ā) mirror, **ḳīmtī (adj., n.c.)** expensive, **kāval** (ā) lotus, **camṛā** (ā) eather, hide, **cā̃d** (ā) moon, **cā̃dī** (ī) silver, **cehrā** (ā) face, **akṣar (adv.)** often, **bhōlā • hālā** (adj.) sweet, innocent, **mahal** (ā) palace, **rājkumār** (ā) prince, **satah** (ī) surface.

33.3

ūdh pīnā mujhē das sāl-sē pasand hai.	I have liked drinking milk for ten years.
naĩ Urdū pandrā sāl-sē paṛh saktā hū̃.	I have been able to read Urdu for fifteen years.
naĩ yahā̃ bīs baras-sē rahtā hū̃.	I have lived here for twenty years.
o ādh ghaṇṭē-sē aisē bōl rahā hai.	He has been speaking like that for half an hour.
o das ghaṇṭō-sē sō rahā hai.	He has been sleeping for ten hours.

This section and the following are concerned with the translation into Urdu of xpressions indicating the period of time **when, during which,** or **over which,** an act was n progress.

This section illustrates the Urdu translation of English time expressions introduced by the preposition **for.** The words denoting time are placed in Urdu before the postposition **-sē** and the verb is placed in the present tense. The construction implies th the act is continuing into the present time. (The literal translation of the first two Urc sentences would be: **I like drinking milk since ten years ago.** and **I am able to read Ur since fifteen years.)**

33.3.1

mujhē pichlē das sāl-sē dūdh pīnā pasand hai.	I have liked drinking milk for the past te years.
maĩ pichlē pandrā sāl-sē Urdū paṛh saktā hū̃.	I have been able to read Urdu for the past fifteen years.
maĩ yahā̃ pichlē bīs baras-sē rahtā hū̃.	I have been living here for the past twen years.
vo pichlē ādh ghaṇṭē-sē aisē bōl rahā hai.	He has been speaking like that for the pa half-hour.
vo pichlē das ghaṇṭō̃-sē sō rahā hai.	He has been sleeping for the past ten hour
maĩ pichlē dō mahinō̃-sē Pākistān-mẽ hū̃.	I have been in Pakistan for the past two months.

This construction is identical with that of 33.3 with one addition, English **the pa** is translated by Urdu **pichlā, last.**

33.3.2

ēk sāl huā maĩ Irān-mẽ thā.	I was in Iran a year ago.
das baras huē maĩ apnī bīvī-kō pahilī dafā milā.	I met my wife for the first time ten year ago.
ēk ghaṇṭā huā is saṛak-par lōgō̃-kī baṛī bhīṛ thī.	An hour ago there was a big crowd of people in this street.
bīs minaṭ huē maĩ ghar-mẽ thā.	I was at home twenty minutes ago.
dō din huē maĩ ēk dūsrī kitāb paṛh rahā thā.	Two days ago I was reading a different book.

Here is illustrated the construction translating English time phrases ending wit the adverb **ago.** The time phrase is translated in Urdu into the object form (which i identical with the subject). The past participle of **hōnā, huā,** which completes the phrase agrees with the noun in gender, number and form.

REMARKS: **bhīṛ** (ā) crowd.

33.3.3

bīs baras pahilē maĩ yahā̃ rahtā thā.	I was living here twenty years ago.
ādh ghaṇṭē pahilē vo is tarah bōlā.	He spoke like this a half-hour ago.
das ghaṇṭē pahilē vo gussē-sē kā̃p rahā thā.	He was trembling with anger ten hours ago
pandrā sāl pahilē maĩ Urdū paṛh saktā thā.	I was able to read Urdu fifteen years ago.

In this construction the time phrase is translated into the object form before **pahilē previously, before.**

33.4

āp us ādmī-sē kahā̃ milē?	Where did you meet that man?

s ādmī-sē miliyē.	Please meet this man.
naī āp-sē phir kab milū̃gā?	When will I meet you again?
:yā tum us ādmī-sē milnā cāhtē hō?	Do you want to meet that man?
ip gavarnar-sē kis liyē milnā cāhtē haī?	Why do you want to meet the governor?
ip-sē milkar maī bahot ḳhuś hū̃.	I am very glad to meet you.

This section and the following, 33.4.1, illustrate constructions with the verb **milnā.**

To denote meeting intentionally or by appointment or visiting, the person "met" s translated into Urdu in the object form before the postposition **-sē** and the person 'doing the meeting" is made the subject of **milnā.**

REMARKS: (1) **kis liyē** of sentence 5 translates **why, wherefore, for what reason.** (2) **gavarnar** (ā) governor.

33.4.1

idmī-kō saṛak-par ēk rupayā milā.	The man found a rupee on the road.
:āstē-mē̃ ādmī-kō us-kā bhāī milā.	The man met his brother on the way.
ālibilm-kō kitāb na milī.	The student did not find the book.
ıs-kō kyā inām milā?	What reward did he get?
ip-kō ye ḍibbē kahā̃-sē milē?	Where did you get these boxes?
ip-kō vo ādmī kahā milā?	Where did you meet (=**run into**) that man?
:isān-kō chuṭṭiyā̃ kab miltī haī?	When does a farmer get a vacation?
:um-kō lōhār-sē kulhāṛī mil sakēgī.	You will be able to get a hatchet from the blacksmith.

Here is illustrated the construction with **milnā,** translating English **meet,** denoting **:o meet, to find, to get by chance, to run into, to come across.** The English subject is ranslated into the object form before **-kō** and the being or thing met or found is made :he subject of **milnā.**

REMARKS: **kulhāṛī** (ā) hatchet, **ḍibbā** (ā) box, **lōhār** (ā) blacksmith.

33.5 Exercise 1. **Translate into English:**

I. kyā āp-kō us jaisī kulhāṛī cāhiyē? 2. maī pandrā sāl-sē is tarah rahtā hū̃. 3. kyā āp :al subah un-sē mil sakē̃gē? 4. rājkumārō̃ jaisē ādmī aḳsar rājā nahī̃ haī. 5. tālibilm pichlē ›ārā sālō̃-sē skūl jātā hai. 6. āp-kō ye kitāb kahā̃-sē milī? 7. ye parindē jaisī aurat kaun ıai? 8. dō sāl huē maī-nē Hindūstān-kō safar kiyā. 9. vo āp-sē kal ḳhūśī-sē milē̃gē. 10. us-kē bāl kōēlē jaisē kālē haī. 11. dō ghanṭē pahilē us-nē mujhē ye bāt batāyī. 12. kyā ›accā bāp jaisā mālūm hōtā hai? 13. āp-kō kitnē mazdūr milē thē? 14. dō mahinē huē naī-nē āp-kō ciṭṭhī likhī. 15. cōr jāntā hai ke vo khēt-kē pās sipāhī-kō milēgā.

33.5.1 Exercise 2. **Translate into Urdu:**

I. Where will I be able to find a good blacksmith like him? 2. What is that snow-like tuff? 3. I have been waiting for you for two hours. 4. My friends can always find ne at home. 5. From the distance that mountain looks like an animal. 6. I have been ooking for the hatchet for the past twenty minutes. 7. Where can I get a strong worker? 3. The boys are like their fathers. 9. You told me this story two weeks ago. 10. I will ›e happy to meet you tomorrow morning. 11. Prince-like men are not always the sons ›f kings. 12. The mechanic fixed your car only a week ago. 13. We found him sleeping n the shade of a banyan tree. 14. Didn't that traveller come here five months ago? 15. A watercarrier like him will be hard to find.

33.6

us-nē gadhē-kō mār mārkar calāyā.	He made the ass go by (**continually**) beating it.
rõ rōkar us-kī ā̃khẽ lāl hō gayī̃.	(**Continually**) crying, her eyes became red.
gā̃ gākar us-kā galā baiṭh gayā.	(**Continually**) singing, his throat became hoarse.
cal calkar maĩ ghāyal hō gayā.	(**Continually**) walking, I became (**utterly**) exhausted.
sō sōkar us-nē apnā bahot-sā vaḳt gãvāyā.	He wasted a lot of his time (**continually**) sleeping.
likh likhkar laṛkē-kē hāth thak gayē.	The boy's hands became tired (**continually**) writing.
pānī pī pīkar us-nē apnī bhūk ḳhatam kar ḍālī.	(**Continually**) drinking water, he killed his appetite.
hās hāskar us-kē pēṭ-mẽ bal paṛ gayē.	(**Continually**) laughing, curves appeared in his belly.

For this construction see section 30.1. To indicate that the act expressed by the gerund is continuing over a period of time the gerund is repeated, with only the second form taking the **kar.**

It can be noted here that what has been previously identified as the stem form of the verb in constructions such as those illustrated in this section, or in verbal clusters, in which the second verb is **saknā, cuknā,** etc. (See also Lesson 28), is a gerund.

REMARKS: **pēṭ** (ā) belly, stomach, **bal** (ā) curve, wrinkle.

33.7 Text 15: **Urdū Zabān [1] -kē Śāir: [2] Mirzā G̱ālib.[3]**

Translate into English. Answer the questions in Urdu:

Mirzā G̱ālib Urdū zabān-kē ēk bahot baṛē śāir thē. un-kā aslī nām Asad Ullah Ḳhā̃ thā. abhī vo chōṭē-kī thē ke mā̃ • bāp mar gayē. un-kē cacā-nē un-kī parvariś kī.[4] abhī vo bārā • caudā sāl-hī-kē thē ke un-kī śādī hō gayē. Mirzā-kā bacpan aur javānī [5] baṛē aiś [6] -ō-ārām-sē guzrē. isī zamānē-mẽ unhō̃-nē apnī tālīm mukammal kī.[7] Mirzā-kō Urdū, Fārsī [8] aur Arabī [9] -par pūrā [10] abūr [11] hāsil thā. bacpan-mẽ-hī unhō̃-nē śēr kahnā [12] śurū kar diyā, lēkin is zamānē-mẽ un-kē kalām [13] -mẽ ēk ḳharābī [14] thī. vo bahot muśkil zabān [15] istēmāl kartē thē. is vajah-sē ām lōgō̃-kō un-kē aśār [16] samajh-mẽ nahī̃ ātē thē. dōstō̃-kē samjhānē-par unhō̃-nē āsān zabān-mẽ śēr kahnā śurū kiyā aur jald-hī vo bahot maśhūr hō gayē. phir-bhī un-kō vo śuhrat [17] hāsil na huī jis-kē vo haḳdār [18] thē. is-kī vajah ye thī ke un-kī śāerī [19] falsafiyānah [20] thī. un-kē zamānē-mẽ ām lōgō̃-kā mazāk [21] bahot ghaṭyā [22] thā. is liyē vo Mirzā-kī śāerī-kō pasand nahī̃ kartē thē. G̱ālib-kō is bāt-kā sārī umr bahot ranj [23] rahā ke māmūlī kism-kē sāir, jō un-kē muḳābilē-mẽ sifar [24] thē, maśhūr hō gayē. lēkin, jō śuhrat Mīrzā-kō apnī zindagī-mẽ hāsil na huī, vo un-kē marnē-kē bād unhẽ hāsil hō gayī. āj har paṛhā? likhā ādmī baṛē śauk-sē un-kē śēr paṛhtā hai aur Mirzā-kī tārīf kartā hai.

Mirzā G̱ālib-kō Añgrēzī sarkār-sē penśan [25] miltī thī. is-kē ilāvā kaī navābō̃ [26] aur rājāō̃ [27] -sē-bhī un-kō tanḳhāh miltī thī. bāz lōgō̃-kā ḳhayāl hai ke Mirzā-kī mahvār [28] āmdanī [29] taḳrīban cār sau rūpayē thī. cār sau rūpayē us zamānē-mẽ bahot baṛī raḳm [30] hōtī thī. lēkin Mirzā bahot aiś-ō-ārām [31] -kī zindagī basar [32] kartē thē. is liyē vo hamēśā paisē-kī kamī-kī śakāyat [33] kartē thē. gadr [34] -kē fauran bād [35] un-kī penšan kuch dēr-kē liyē band hō gayī. is zamānē-mē̃ vaḳaī [36] unhē̃ kuch taṅgī [37] hō gayī lēkin thōṛī dēr-kē bād sarkār-nē un-kī penšan bahāl [38] kar dī. Mirzā kōī kām • kāj nahī̃ kartē thē. bas śarāb [39] pītē thē, dōstō̃-kī dāvat [40] kartē thē aur śer kahtē thē. kabhī kabhī āḳhrī [41] Mugal bādśāh Bahādur Śāh [42] -kē darbār-mē̃ jātē thē. Bahādur Śāh Mirzā-kō paccās rūpayē mahīnā taṅḳhāh dētē thē. ēk dafā unhō̃-nē sōcā ke Aṅgrēzī sarkār-kī naukrī kar lē̃. Dillī-kē kālij-mē̃ Fārsī-kē prōfaisar-kī jagah ḳhālī thī. Aṅgrēz kamiśanar • sāhab-nē Mirzā-sē kahā ke, agar vo cahē̃, tō ye naukrī Mirzā-kō mil saktī hai. kamiśnar Mirzā-kē zātī [43] dōst thē. jab kabhī Mirzā un-kō milnē jātē, kamiśnar • sāhab apnī kōṭhī-sē bāhar ākar un-sē istakbāl [44] kartē. ēk din Mirzā unhē̃ is naukrī-kē bārē-mē̃ milnē gayē. [45] is dafā kamiśnar • sāhab unhē̃ milnē-kē liyē kōṭhī-sē bāhar na āyē. bal-ke apnē daftar-mē̃ baiṭhē Mirzā-kē andar ānē-kā intazār kartē rahē. [46] lēkin Mirzā apnī gāṛī-mē̃ baiṭhē kamiśnar • sāhab-kē bāhar ānē-kā intazār kar rahē thē. jab bahot dēr hō gayī, tō āḳhir kamiśnar • sāhab bāhar āyē. unhō̃-nē Mirzā-sē pūchā, "vel, [47] Mirzā • Sāhab! āp andar kyū̃ nahī̃ āyē?" Mirzā-nē javāb diyā, "maĩ āp-kē bāhar ānē-kā intazār kar rahā thā." kamiśnar • sāhab-nē javāb diyā, "vel, [47] Mirzā jab āp dōst-kī tarah mujhē milnē [45] ātē haĩ, tō maĩ bāhar ākar āp-kā istakbāl kartā hū̃. lēkin, jab naukrī lēnē-kē ātē haĩ, tō phir nahī̃." Mirzā-nē kahā "agar ye bāt hai, tō phir mujhē naukrī-kī zarūrat nahī̃. maĩ Aṅgrēzī sarkār-kī naukrī apnī izzat [48] baṛhānē-kē liyē kartā hū̃, kam karnē [49] -kē liyē nahī̃." ye kahkar Mirzā vāpas ghar calē gayē aur us-kē bād phir kabhī naukrī-kā ḳhayāl na kiyā.

Mirzā bahot ḳhuś • mizāj [50] aur latifagō [51] ādmī thē. unhē̃ ām bahot pasand thē. ēk dafā-kā zikr hai. [52] ke vo apnē ḍrāiṅgrūm-mē̃ apnē dōstō̃-kē sāth baiṭhē thē. bāhar saṛak-par āmō̃-kē kuch chilkē [53] paṛē thē. ittafāk-sē [54] ēk gadhā [55] vahā̃-sē guzrā. us-nē chilkō̃-kō sū̃ghā [56] aur calā gayā. ēk dōst-nē kahā, "dēkhiyē, Mirzā, gadhā-bhī ām nahī̃ khātā." Ġalib-nē javāb diyā, "hā̃, bhāī, jō gadhē hō, vo ām nahī̃ khātē."

savālāt:

1. ām lōg Mirzā-kī śāerī-kō kyū̃ pasand nahī̃ kartē thē? 2. kyā Mirzā garīb thē? 3. āḳhrī Mugal bādśāh-kā nām kyā thā? vo Mirzā-kō kyā taṅḳhāh dētē thē? 4. kamiśnar aur Mirzā-mē̃ kyā guftagū huī? 5. āmō̃-kā latifā bayān karō.

NOTES: 1. language (ī); 2. poet (ā); 3. poet's name; 4. **parvariś karnā** to bring up, nourish (tr.); 5. youth (ī); 6. luxury (ī); 7. **mukammal karnā** to complete (tr.); 8. Persian (adj., n.c.); 9. Arabic (adj., n.c.); 10. full (adj.); 11. command, ability (ā); 12. **śer kahnā** to compose poetry (tr.); 13. writing, composing (ā); 14. weakness, flaw (ī); 15. = vocabulary, language (ī); 16. verse (ā); 17. fame (ī); 18. deserving (adj., n.c.); 19. poetry (ī); 20. philosophic (adj., n.c.); 21. taste (ā); 22. low (adj., n.c.); 23. grief (ā); 24. zero, nothing (ā); 25. pension (ī); 26. navāb = Muslim prince (ā); 27. rājā = Hindu prince (ā); 28. monthly (adj., n.c.); 29. income (ī); 30. sum (ī); 31. luxury (ā); 32. **basar karnā** to spend (tr.); 33. complaint (ī); 34. Mutiny (ā); 35. -kē fauran bād soon after; 36. really (adv.); 37. taṅgī hōnā to be hard up (int.); 38. bahāl karnā to reinstate (tr.); 39. wine (ī); 40. entertainment (ī); 41. last (adj., n.c.); 42. name of Mogul king; 43. personal (adj., n.c.); 44. reception (ā); 45. see 37.2.2; 46. see 34.3; 47. well!; 48. honor, status, prestige (ī); 49. **kam karnā** to decrease, diminish (tr.); 50. even-tempered (adj., n.c.); 51. having sense of humor (adj., n.c.); 52. mention is made of a certain time; 53. **chilkā** peeling skin, peel (ā); 54. by chance (= adv.); 55. donkey (ā); 56. **sū̃ghnā** to smell.

LESSON 34

34.1

yahā̃-sē daryā-tak jānē-mẽ sirf tīn minaṭ lagẽgē.	It will take only three minutes to go from here to the river.
ye kitāb paṛhnā ḳhatam karnē-mẽ mujhē bahot vaḳt lagēgā.	It will take a long time for me to finish reading this book.
buzarīya-e-havāī • jahāz-sē Nyū-Yārk-sē Karācī pahõcnē-mẽ sirf dō din lagtē haĩ.	It takes only two days to reach Karachi by air from New York.
ēk g̱air • mulkī zabān sīkhnē-mē kāfī vaḳt lagtā hai.	It takes quite some time to learn a foreign language.
Urdū sīkhnē-mẽ mujhē bahot bahot vaḳt lagā.	It took me a very long time to learn Urdu.
is ḳhat-kō maśraḳī Pākistān-sē yahā̃ pahõcnē-mẽ sāt din lagē.	It took this letter seven days to reach here from East Pakistan.

This section and the two following are concerned with constructions involving the verb **lagnā**. Here is illustrated the construction with **lagnā** translating **to take** of English time expressions. The phrase denoting time is translated as the subject of **lagnā** and the being or thing expending the time is placed in the object form before the postposition **-kō.**

REMARKS: See the fourth and fifth sentences and the use of **kāfī** and **bahot bahot** to translate **quite some** and **very long.**

34.1.1

mujhē bhūk lagī hai.	I am hungry.
mujhē pyās lagī hai.	I am thirsty.
kyā āp-kō sardī lagī?	Did you catch **(a)** chill?
dukān-kō āg lagī hai.	The store is on fire.
kāg̱az-par syāhī-kē dhabbē lagē haĩ.	There are ink stains on the paper.
cīzõ-par gard lagī hai.	There is dust on the things.
har din dōpahar-kō mujhē bhūk lagtī hai.	I get hungry every day at noon.
dauṛnē-kē bād mujhē pyās lagtī hai.	I get thirsty after running.

Keeping in mind the root meaning of **lagnā (to be attached, applied, or fixed to),** compare the literal translation of the first three Urdu sentences: **Hunger is attached to me.; Thirst is attached to me.;** and **Is a chill attached to you?** This section, then, illustrates the use of **lagnā** in the present perfect tense (See 20.1.2) to indicate a state already in existence. Compare the last two sentences where the present tense indicates a general statement.

REMARKS: **dhabbā** (ā) stain, spot, **gard** (ī) dust, **pyās** (ī) thirst, **bhūk** (ī) hunger, **sardī** (ī) chill, cold, **miṭṭī** (ī) dust (i.e., **from earth**).

34.1.2

rēlgāṛī chūṭnē lagēgī.	The train will begin to leave.
Vazīr-e-Āzām taḳrīr dēnē lagē.	The Prime Minister began to make a speech.
andar śōr sunnē-par, vo darvāzā khōlnē lagā.	On hearing a noise inside, he began to open the door.
jaisē-hī maĩ sṭēśan-par pahō̃cā, gāṛī calnē lagī.	The train began to leave as (**soon as**) I arrived at the station.
jab dhūp nikaltī hai, tab baraf pighalnē lagtī hai.	When the sunlight appears, the snow begins to melt.
ḳarzḳhā-kō dūr-sē dēkhkar, maḳrūz ādmī taṅg galī-mē̃ chupnē lagē.	Seeing the creditor from afar, the debtor began to hide in the alley.
jaisē-hī bādal āyē, mōr nācnē lagē.	As (**soon as**) the clouds appeared, the peacocks began to dance.
śām hōtē-hī sab lōg sair-kō nikalnē lagē.	As (**soon as**) evening came, everyone began to come out for a walk.
jaisē-hī ghanṭī bajī, tālibilm skūl-kē hāl-mē̃ jamā hōnē lagē.	As (**soon as**) the bell rang, the students began to assemble in the schoolhall.
apnā dūdh-kā glās ḳhatam karnē-kē bād, maĩ cāy pīnē lagū̃gā.	After finishing my glass of milk, I will begin to drink tea.
śēr-kī garaj sunkar, baccā cīḳhē̃ mārnē lagā.	Hearing the lion's roar, the child began to scream.
caukidār-kō dēkhkar, cālāk cōr chupnē lagā.	Seeing the watchman, the cunning thief began to hide.

This section illustrates the construction with **lagnā** translating English phrases introduced by **begin** or **start to** followed by a verb. The verb denoting the act begun or started is placed in Urdu in the object form.

REMARKS: **garaj** (ī) roar, **dhūp** (ī) sunlight, **baraf** (ī) snow, **hāl** (ā) hall, **ḳarzḳhā** (ā) creditor, **maḳrūz ādmī** (ā) debtor, **taṅg galī** (ī) alley, **cīḳh** (ī) scream, **cīḳh** (ī) **mārnā** to scream, **Vazīr-e-Āzām** (ā) Prime Minister.

34.1.3 Exercise 1. **Translate into English:**

1. ye kām karnē-mē̃ tumhē̃ kitnā vaḳt lagēgā? 2. jab dhūp niklī, vo darvāzā khōlnē lagā. 3. dō ghanṭē huē unhō̃-nē khānā khāyā. unhē̃ ab kyū̃ bhūk lagī hai? 4. sipāhī-kō dūr-sē dēkhkar cālāk cōr chupnē lagā. 5. āp-kō yahā̃ ānē-mē̃ kyū̃ itnā vaḳt lagā? 6. jaisē-hī ham aḍḍē-par pahō̃cē, bāriś hōnē lagī. 7. apnā dūdh-kā glās ḳhatam karnē-kē bād, baccā rōnē lagā. 8. kyā āp-kō pyās lagī hai? 9. jaisē-hī ghanṭī bajī, ustād savāl pūchnē lagā. 10. din hōtē-hī vo khiṛkiyā̃ khōlnē lagā.

34.1.4 Exercise 2. **Translate into Urdu:**

1. It took me an hour to write this letter. 2. There is too much dust on this road. 3. When will you begin to repair my automobile? 4. (**As soon**) as the Prime Minister began to make a speech the people stopped talking. 5. How long will it take to fly to

India? 6. Why did you start to leave when my friends arrived? 7. Did you become hungry again after you ate at my place? 8. You began to do this work two months ago. 9. When he heard the noise outside, the servant began to open the window. 10. As (**soon as**) I came into the garden, the birds flew off.

34.2

us-nē laṛkī-kō daryā-kē kinārē-par dauṛtē huē dēkhā.	He saw the girl, running along the bank of the river.
laṛkī-nē muskarātē huē rūmāl apnē dōst-kī taraf hilāyā.	The girl, smiling, waved her handkerchief at her friend.
mujhē dēkhkar vo jaldī-sē dauṛtē huē mērē pās āyā.	Seeing me, he came towards me, running quickly.
vo sab gātē aur hãstē huē ēk piknik-kō gayē.	They all went to a picnic, singing and laughing.
vo ḳamīz sītē huē baiṭhī thī.	She was seated sewing the shirt.
us-nē bhaĩs-kō daraḳht-kē nīcē jugālī kartē huē pāyā.	He found the water buffalo, chewing its cud under the tree.
śahar-sē lauṭtē huē vo pul-kē pār jāēgā.	He will cross the bridge on the way back from town.
ham-nē usē ēk ḳhānḳhāh-mẽ akēlē ibādat kartē huē pāyā.	We found him praying alone in the tomb of a Pir.
chōṭī laṛkī rōtē huē mā̃-kē pās dauṛ āyī.	The little girl ran crying to her mother.
faḳīr bhīk mā̃gtē huē din guzārtā thā.	The beggar lived by begging.
kuch lōg ārām•kursiyõ-par lēṭkar paṛhtē huē dhūp saĩk rahē thē.	Some people were sunning themselves, (**while**) lying in easy chairs, reading.

Here is illustrated the participial phrase described in sections 31.1 to 31.1.1 functioning as an adverb. Both forms have the masculine, object singular form (i.e., end in **-ē**). (Sometimes the adverbial participial phrase is placed in the masculine, subject singular form.)

REMARKS: **din guzārnā** of the tenth sentence is translated literally **to pass days; ārām•kursī** (ī) easy chair, **dhūp saĩknā** to bask in sun (lit., to absorb heat, warm up), **jugālī karnā** to chew cud, **ḳhānḳhāh** (ī) tomb of a Pir.

34.2.1 Exercise 1. **Translate into English:**

1. laṛkī dauṛtē huē pānī vāpas lāyī. 2. kuttā bhõktē huē ajnabī-kē pīchē dauṛā. 3. ādmī muskarātē huē mērī bāt suntā thā. 4. laṛkā tairtē huē daryā-kē ēk kinārē-sē dūsrē kinārē-kī taraf calā. 5. aurat lakṛī lātē huē ghar āyī. 6. laṛkī gātē huē bāġ-sē phūl lāyī. 7. us-nē hãstē huē kahānī sunāyī. 8. ādmī rāt-kō ghar lauṭtē huē kuẽ-mẽ gir paṛā. 9. aurat-nē bāzār-mẽ cīzẽ ḳharīdtē huē apnē paisē khō diyē. 10. baccā bāp-kō pahcāntē huē muskarānē lagā.

34.2.2 Exercise 2. **Translate into Urdu:**

1. The farmer, smiling, pointed out the road to the traveller. 2. The little girl sat in the garden, crying. 3. The mother, laughing, gave the children candy. 4. The calf ran after its mother, crying. 5. The servant, running after his master, gave him his coat. 6. Coming out of the house, the woman told the workmen to stop making noise. 7. Did you

find the cow grazing near our field? 8. Who saw the man coming out of my house? 9. The girl saw her mother repairing the saris. 10. The woman, calling to her friends for help, is pulling the child out of the well.

34.3

ādmī suntā rahtā hai.	The man keeps on listening.
ādmī suntē rahtē haĩ.	The men keep on listening.
aurat suntī rahtī hai.	The woman keeps on listening.
aurtē̃ suntī rahtī haĩ.	The women keep on listening.
vo suntē rahtē thē.	They continued listening.
vo suntē rahē.	They continued listening.
vo suntē rahē thē.	They had continued listening.
vo suntē rahē̃gē.	They will continue listening.
ciṛiyā cū̃-cū̃ kartī rahtī hai.	The sparrow keeps on chirping.
ciṛiyā̃ cū̃-cū̃ kartī rahtī haĩ.	The sparrows keep on chirping.
bulbul gātī rahtī hai.	The nightingale keeps on singing.
bulbul gātī rahtī thī̃.	The nightingales kept on singing.
parindā uṛtā rahtā hai.	The bird keeps on flying.
parindē uṛtē rahtē thē.	The birds kept on flying.
bandar lōgō̃-kō tañg kartā rahtā hai.	The monkey keeps on annoying people.
bandar lōgō̃-kō tañg kartē rahtē thē.	The monkeys kept on annoying people.
ciṛiyā • ghar-mē̃ śēr garajtā rahtā hai.	A lion at the zoo continues roaring.
ciṛiyā • ghar-mē̃ dō śēr garajtē rahtē thē.	Two lions at the zoo continued roaring.
vo har vaḳt khātē rahē̃gē.	They will keep on eating all the time.
aurtē̃ bātē̃ kartī rahī̃.	The women kept on talking.
gāṛī caltī rahtī hai.	The train keeps on going.
āg jaltī rahī thī.	The fire had kept on burning.
havā har vaḳt caltī rahtī hai.	The wind keeps on blowing all the time.
bādal āsmān-par chātē rahē̃gē.	The clouds will keep on spreading in the sky.
nadī bahtī rahī.	The stream kept on flowing.
ghōṛā bahot dēr-tak dauṛtā rahēgā.	The horse will keep on running for a long time.
hamsāiyā̃ har vaḳt laṛtī rahtī thī̃.	The neighbors kept on quarreling all the time.

The English verbal phrases, beginning with the word **keep** and a verbal form ending in **-ing** or the words **continue to** and a verb, are translated into Urdu by a phrase consisting of a present participle and **rahnā.** The present participle agrees in gender and number with the subject of **rahnā.** This construction is employed to denote the continuity of an act or state. Compare section 34.4, following.

34.3.1 Exercise 1. **Translate into English:**

1. āp sārī rāt kyũ jāgtē rahē thē? 2. vo kyũ hãstī rahtī haĩ? 3. nadī bahtī rahtī hai. 4. bandar lōgõ-kō tañg kartā rahā. 5. gāy bahot dēr-tak khātī rahtī hai. 6. baṛhaī daraḳht kāṭtā rahtā thā. 7. kyā āg jaltī rahēgī? 8. pattē daraḳht-sē girtē rahē thē. 9. daryā-kā pānī baṛhtā rahēgā. 10. mālī paudõ-par pānī ḍāltā rahtā hai.

34.3.2 Exercise 2. **Translate into Urdu:**

1. How long will you continue working here? 2. The farmer keeps on working in the field. 3. The nightingale had kept on singing for a long time. 4. The girl keeps on drawing water. 5. The rain will continue falling for two weeks. 6. How long will the river keep on rising? 7. The washerman kept on washing the clothes. 8. Will the mechanic continue repairing the automobile? 9. The fire will keep on burning for a long time. 10. The rivers keep on flowing into the ocean.

34.4

ādmī suntā jātā hai.	The man keeps on listening.
ādmī suntē jātē haĩ.	The men keep on listening.
aurat suntī jātī hai.	The woman keeps on listening.
aurtẽ suntī jātī haĩ.	The women keep on listening.
vo suntē jātē thē.	They had continued listening.
vo suntē gayē.	They continued listening.
vo suntē gayē thē.	They had continued listening.
vo suntē jāẽgē.	They will continue listening.
dādī • ammā, kahānī sunātī jāiyē.	Grandma, (**please**) go on telling the story.
kyā ham ṭhahar jāẽ yā caltē jāẽ?	Shall we stop or keep moving?
Ḳisaḳhānī Bāzār-mẽ ham jahā̃-bhī ṭhaharē, tasvīrẽ lētē gayē.	Wherever we stopped in the Kisakhani Bazaar, we went on taking pictures.
jab āp Kalkattē jāẽ, mujhē sāth lētē jāẽ.	Please take me along when you go to Calcutta.
fauj-kē kaptān-nē apnē sipāhiyõ-kō huḳam diyā ke vo baṛhtē jāẽ.	The captain ordered his soldiers to keep on advancing.
ustād-nē ṭālibilmõ-sē kahā, "jab-tak maĩ kām-mẽ lagā hũ, tum apnā kām kartē jāō."	The teacher told the students to go on working while he was busy.
hā̃, hā̃, kahtē jāō.	Yes, yes, keep on talking.
maĩ bōlũgā, āp siraf suntē jāẽ.	I shall speak, you just keep listening.
hãstē jāō, aur mōṭē hō jāō.	Keep laughing and grow fat!

This construction is similar to that of section 34.3 with the exception that the verb jānā is found in the place of **rahnā.** The difference in meaning between this construction and that of 34.3 is that there is implied here the continuation of the act or state, even though there has arisen an occasion for its being checked or altered.

REMARKS: **fauj-kē kaptān** (ā) [army] captain.

34.4.1

daryā bahtā jā rahā hai.	The river continues to flow.
pā̃c havāī • jahāz uṛtē jā rahē haī̃.	Five airplanes continue to fly.
bādal chātē jā rahē haī̃.	The clouds continue to spread.
faujē̃ baṛthī jā rahī thī̃.	The armies were continuing to advance.
duśman pīchē haṭṭā jā rahā thā.	The enemy was continuing to withdraw.
imtehānāt nazdīk ātē jā rahē haī̃.	The examinations continue to come closer.
vaḳt guzartā jā rahā hai.	The time continues to pass.
nayī dulhān ghar-kē liyē udās hōtā jā rahī hai.	The new bride continues to be homesick.
mērā sar • dard baṛhtā jā rahā hai.	My headache continues to grow.
kyā āp vo-hī cīz likhtē jā rahē haī̃?	Do you continue writing the same thing?

These sentences illustrate the participial construction of 34.3 with the **rahnā** construction described in section 23.1 to denote an act or state continuing at a specific time. Compare section 23.1.

REMARKS: **imtehan** (ā) examination (**pl. imtehānāt**).

34.4.2 Exercise 1. **Translate into English:**

1. gāṛībān bailgāṛī calātā calātā gayā. 2. duśmān baṛhtā jātā thā. 3. vo āp-kē sāth Añgrēzī-mē̃ kyū̃ bātē̃ kartē jātē haī̃? 4. daryā baṛhtā jā rahā hai. 5. bādal chātē jā rahē haī̃. 6. kisān khāt-mē̃ mehnat kartā jāēgā. 7. hājī muḳaddas • jaghō̃-kō safar kartā jā rahā thā. 8. āp un-kā intazār kab-tak kartē jāē̃gē? 9. aurat kuē̃-sē pānī khī̃ctī jā rahī hai. 10. ādmī purānē ustarē-sē kyū̃ hajāmat banātā jātā thā?

34.4.3 Exercise 2. **Translate into Urdu:**

1. The bullock keeps on trying to pull the plow. 2. Keep on driving the automobile. 3. I continue to be homesick. 4. The ship kept on coming into the harbor. 5. How long will you continue to wait for them? 6. Time continued to pass. 7. The child kept on asking questions. 8. The monkey keeps on throwing fruit down from the tree. 9. How long will you continue telling me the same story? 10. The villagers kept on going to the city to work.

34.5

musannif hamēśā mehnat kiyā kartā hai.	The author is used to working hard all the time.
kuch lōg hamēśā mehnat kiyā kartē thē.	Some people were used to working hard all the time.
mērā bhāī rōz • subah sair-kē liyē bāhar jāyā kartā hai.	My brother is used to going out for a walk every morning.
kuch vaḳt pahilē ham sab rōz • subah sair-kē liyē bāhar jāyā kartē thē.	Some time ago all of us were used to going out for a walk every morning.

macherā tēz calā kartā hai.	The fisherman is used to walking fast.
sab macherē tēz calā kartē thē.	All fishermen were used to walking fast.
kyā āp masālēdār khānē khāyā kartē haĩ?	Are you used to eating spicy foods?
pahilē ham masālēdār khānē khāyā kartē thē.	Previously we were used to eating spicy foods.
gāṛī Madrās-sē Banglōr jāyā kartī hai.	The train goes from Madras to Bangalore.
gāṛī Madrās-sē Banglōr jāyā kartī thī.	The train used to go from Madras to Bangalore.
ādmī garīb lōgõ-kō paisē diyā kartā hai.	The man goes on giving money to the poor.
aurat garīb lōgõ-kō paisē diyā kartī thī.	The woman used to give money to the poor.
tum har rōz das bajē-tak sōyā kartē hō.	You sleep till ten o'clock every day.
tum har rōz das bajē-tak sōyā kartē thē.	You used to sleep till ten o'clock every day.
vo har rōz subah• savērē uṭhā kartā thā.	He used to get up early every morning.
vo har rōz subah• savērē uṭhā kartī thī.	She used to get up early every morning.
vo hamẽ cīzẽ diyā kartā hai.	He is accustomed to giving us things.
vo kām kiyā karēgā.	He will go on working.
kisān khēt-kō jāyā kartā hai.	The farmer is accustomed to going to the field.
gāy subah-sē śām-tak khāyā karēgī.	The cow will go on eating from morning till night.
vo kām kiyā karẽgī.	They will go on working.
laṛkā akhbār paṛhā kartā thā.	The boy was accustomed to reading the newspaper.
vo har rōz kuch na kuch paṛhā kartī hai.	She is used to reading something or other every day.

This section illustrates the Urdu construction employed to denote a habitual act. A check of the sentences listed above will reveal that this construction consists of what appears to be the subject form, singular, masculine, of a past participle and **karnā.** This participial form remains unchanged, no matter what the gender or number of the subject may be.

REMARKS: (1) **jānā, to go,** has a special form **jāyā** for this construction. See sentences 3, 4, 9, 10.

(2) **kuch na kuch** something or other.

34.5.1 Exercise 1. **Translate into English:**

1. vo har rōz subah• savērē sair-kē liyē bāhar jāyā kartī thī. 2. ādmī tēz calā kartā hai. 3. ye bas hamārē gāõ-sē Dillī jāyā kartī hai. 4. kisān hamēśā mehnat kiyā kartā hai. 5. gāy tēz nahī̃ calā kartī hai. 6. laṛkī har rōz sāt bajē-tak sōyā kartī thī. 7. amīr ādmī garīb lōgõ-kō kuch na kuch diyā kartā hai. 8. kyā āp vo-hī cīz paṛhā kartē haĩ? 9. aurtẽ bātẽ kiyā kartī haĩ. 10. Vazīr-e-Āzām takīr kiyā kartā hai.

34.5.2 Exercise 2. **Translate into Urdu:**

1. Are you accustomed to going out for a walk every morning? 2. Is this the train which goes from Delhi to Calcutta? 3. I am used to eating spicy foods. 4. The woman is not used to walking fast. 5. Farmers are used to getting up early every morning. 6. Are you used to writing to your friend every month? 7. The woman used to chat every evening. 8. Who is in the habit of reading the newspaper every day? 9. The girls used to bring water from the well every morning. 10. The hunter used to hunt at night.

34.6 Text 16: **Urdū Zabān-kē Śāir. Allamah [1] Iḳbāl.[2]**

Translate into English. Answer the questions in Urdu:

Allamah Iḳbāl-kā aslī nām Mohammad Iḳbāl thā. vo Panjāb-kē ēk maśhūr śahar Siālkōṭ-mē̃ paidā huē. abhī vo hāiskūl-mē̃ paṛhtē thē ke unhō̃-nē gazal kahnā śurū kar diyā. us zamānē-mē̃ Urdū-kē bahot maśhūr śāir Navāb Mirzā Ḳhā Dāg [2] thē. vo Dakkan [3] -kē nizām [4] -kē ustād [5] the aur Haydarābād [6] -mē̃ rahtē thē. Iḳbāl-nē apnī gazlē̃ Dāg-kō dēkhnē-kē liyē bhējī. Dāg-nē jald-hī pahcān liyā [7] ke Iḳbāl ēk din bahot baṛē śāir hō jāẽgē. satrā sāl-kī umr-mē̃ Iḳbāl Lāhōr āyē aur Gōrmeṇṭ Kālij-mē̃ dāḳhil hō gayē. yahā̃-sē unhō̃-nē em.ē. pās kiyā aur phir Iṅglistān calē gayē. vahā̃ vo Kembrij Yūnivarsiṭī-mē̃ kuch sāl tālīm hāsil kartē rahē. vahā̃-sē unhō̃-nē pī.ēc.ḍī.[8] -kī ḍigrī lī, aur beristrī-kā imtahān-bhī pās kiyā. tālīm vagairāh-sē fārig [9] hōkar vo vāpas Lāhōr ā gayē aur yahā̃ unhō̃-nē vakālat śurū kar dī. lēkin vakālat-mē̃ un-kā jī na lagā. agar-ce vo kam-ō-bēś sārī umr vakālat kartē rahē, lēkin zyādā mukadmē nahī̃ lētē thē. bas kabhī kabhī [10] adālat-mē̃ calē jātē thē. zyādā vaḳt vo śēr kahtē thē aur kitābē̃ likhtē thē. unhō̃-nē Urdū, Fārsī, aur Aṅgrēzī-mē̃ kaī kitābē̃ likhī haĩ. Iḳbāl-nē zyādā gazlē̃ nahī̃ likhī̃. un-kā kalām Gālib-sē bhī zyādā falsafiyānā [11] hai. un-kī śāerī-kā ēk ḳhās maḳsad thā. un-kō har vaḳt ye fikr rahtā thā ke dunyā-kē Musalmānō̃-kō ḳhāb-sē jagāẽ. un-kā ḳhayāl thā ke Musalmānō̃-kō mutahid hō jānā cāhiyē. unhō̃-nē Hindūstān-kē Musalmānō̃-kō Pākistān-kā tasavvur [12] diyā. kaī sāl vo Misṭar Jinnah aur dusrē līḍrō̃-sē Pākistān-kē bārē-mē̃ ḳhat-ō-kitābat [13] kartē rahē. un-kī rāy ye thī ke Hindūstān-kē Musalmānō̃-kō apnē liyē ēk alehdāh [14] mulk hāsil karnā cāhiyē. Iḳbāl san unnīs sō aṛtīs-mē̃ vafāt pā gayē.

Iḳbāl-kā maḳbarā Lāhōr-mē̃ bādśāhī masjid [15] -kē ḳarīb hai. har sāl aprail [16] -kī ikkīs tāriḳh-kō sārē Pākistān-mē̃ "Iḳbāl • Ḍē" [17] manāyā jātā hai.[18] Iḳbāl-kī yād-mē̃ muśāirē [19] hōtē haĩ, jin-mē śāir apnī apnī nazmē̃ [20] aur gazlē paṛhtē haĩ. un-kē ilāvā dusrē ulamah [21] Iḳbāl-kī śāerī aur un-kē falsafē-par taḳrīrē̃ kartē haĩ. kaī sālō̃-sē Iḳbāl-kē ḳhayālāt [22] -par rīsarc [23] hō rahī hai. har sāl kaī mazmūn [24] un-par likhē jātē haĩ [18] aur śāyā [25] hōtē haĩ. Iḳbāl-kē kalām-kā zyādā hissā Fārsī zabān-mē̃ hai. un-kā ḳhayāl thā ke un-kā paigām [26] siraf Hindūstān-kē Musalmānō̃-kē liyē-hī nahī̃, bal-kē sārī dunyā-kē Musalmānō̃-kē liyē hai. un-kī kuch Fārsī kitābō̃-kā Aṅgrēzī-mē̃ tarjumā [27] hō cukā hai. maslan [28] Iṅglistān-kē ēk maśhūr Prōfaisar Nikalsan [29] -nē, jō Iḳbāl-kē ustād-bhī thē, un-kī ēk kitāb "Israr-e-Ḳhudī" [30] -kā Aṅgrēzī-mē̃ tarjumā kiyā hai. tarjumā • śudā kitāb-kā nām "Sīkriṭs auf ḍī Self" [31] hai. Iḳbāl-nē, jō kitābē̃ Aṅgrēzī-mē̃ likhī haĩ, un-mē̃ sab-sē maśhūr kitāb-kā nām "Siks Lekcarz aun Islām" [32] hai. āp • lōgō̃-kō ye kitābē̃ paṛhnī [33] cāhiyē̃.

Iḳbāl-kē ḳhatūt [34] -kā majmuā [35] bhī śāyā hō cukā hai. ye ḳhatūt bahot dilcasp haĩ. in-mē̃-sē kaī ḳhat Misṭar Jinnah-kē nām haĩ. Iḳbāl dunyā-kē un cand śāirō̃-mē̃-sē haĩ jin-kō apnī zindagī-mē̃-hī bahot śohrat hāsil hō gayī aur marnē-kē bād-bhī vo śohrat kāim rahī.[36] Angrēzī sarkār-nē, jab ye dēkhā ke Iḳbāl sārī dunyā-mẽ apnī śāerī-kī vajah-sē maśhūr hō gayē haĩ, tō us-nē-bhī jhaṭ • paṭ [37] Iḳbāl-kō "sar" [38] -kā ḳhitāb [39] dē diyā. lēkin Iḳbāl-kō is ḳhitāb-kī kabhī kōī ḳhās parvāh na thī.

Iḳbāl-kī sab-sē baṛī ḳhūbī ye thī, ke vo bēhad mutāliyāh [40] kartē thē. un-kō sab maśrakī [41] aur magrabī alūm [42] -par abūr [43] hāsil thā. is tarah un-kī nazar [44] bahot vasī [45] hō gayī thī.

savālāt:

1. Iḳbāl-nē kahã tālīm hāsil kī? 2. Iḳbāl-nē kaun kaun-sī zabānõ-mẽ kitābẽ likhī haĩ? 3. Iḳbāl-kā Hindūstan-kē Musalmānõ-kē bārē-mẽ kyā ḳhayāl thā? 4. Iḳbāl-kī kitāb-kā Angrēzī-mẽ tarjumā kis-nē kiyā? 5. Iḳbāl-kī yād kaisē manāyī jātī hai?

NOTES: 1. term applied to very learned person; 2. name of poet; 3. Deccan (ā); 4. Nizam (ā); 5. teacher, tutor (ā); 6. Hyderabad; 7. **pahcān lēnā** to recognize (**tr.**); 8. Ph.D. (**degree**); 9. **fārig hōnā** to complete (**int.**); 10. = just sometimes; 11. philosophical; 12. idea (ā); 13. correspondence (ī; **pl.**); 14. separate (**adj.**); 15. name of mosque; 16. April; 17. Iqbal-day; 18. see 37.1; 19. **muśāirā** meeting in which poets recite verses (ā); 20. **nazam** poem (ī); 21. scholars, learned people (**s., ālim,** (ā)); 22. thought, ideas (**pl.** of **ḳhayāl,** (ā); 23. research (ī); 24. article, paper (ā); 25. **śāyā hōnā** to be published (**int.**); 26. message (ā); 27. translation (ā); 28. for instance; 29. Nicholson; 30. Search of the Self; 31. Secrets of the Self; 32. Six lectures on Islam; 33. cf. 37.2.1; 34. letters (ā, **pl.**); 35. collection (ā); 36. **ḳāim rahnā** to continue (**int.**); 37. immediately (**adv.**), 38. Sir; 39. title (ā); 40. study (ā); 41. eastern (**adj., n.c.**); 42. field of study (ā, **pl.** of **ilm**); 43. mastery (ā); 44. vision (ī); 45. vast (**adj., n.c.**).

LESSON 35

35.1

āp-kē pahŏ̃ctē-hī vo sō gayā.	He fell asleep immediately after you arrived.
āp-kē pahŏ̃cnē-par vo sō gayā.	He fell asleep upon your arrival.
is k̤hayāl-kē ātē-hī vo cālā gayā.	As soon as this idea came to him, he walked away.
is k̤hayāl-kē ānē-par vo calā gayā.	As this idea came to him, he walked away.
hamārē jātē-hī unhō̃-nē apnē rupayē ginē.	Immediately after we left they counted their money.
hamārē jānē-par unhō̃-nē apnē rupayē ginē.	They counted their money as we left.
ghaṇṭī-kī āvāz suntē-hī vo skūl-kō cal dī.	Immediately after hearing the sound of the bell she went off to school.
ghaṇṭī-kī āvāz sunnē-par vo skūl-kō cal dī.	On hearing the sound of the bell she went off to school.
khānā k̤hatam kartē-hī vo sair-kō gayā.	As soon as he finished eating he went for a walk.
khānā k̤hatam karnē-par vo sair-kō gayā.	After finishing eating he went for a walk.

An examination of the pairs of Urdu sentences above will reveal that they are identical with the exception that the second sentence contains a phrase consisting of an infinitive before the postposition **-par** and the first a present participle in the masculine singular object form to which has been attached the emphatic particle **-hī.** (Compare 30.2.1 for the infinitive construction with **-par.**)

This section illustrates the adverbial use of the present participle in the masculine object form. The construction conveys the idea that the act denoted by the principal verb takes place immediately upon the occurrence of the act denoted by the present participle. Compare the construction with **-par** (30.2.1) which does not stress the immediate sequence of the acts.

Substantives, governed by participles of transitive verbs occurring in this construction, are placed in the object form. (See 9.1.1, Remarks 1.)

REMARKS: See **cal dī** in sentences 7 and 8. In this verbal cluster the first member, **cal,** determines the cluster to be intransitive. (Compare Lesson 28, Introduction, Remarks 1.)

35.1.1 Exercise 1. **Translate into English:**

1. apnē paisē gintē-hī usē mālūm huā ke vo tohfā nahī̃ k̤harīd saktā thā. 2. apnī kāmyābī-kī k̤habar suntē-hī vo nācnē lagā. 3. daftar vāpas ātē-hī us-nē vahā̃ kisī-kō na dēkhā. 4. Bambaī pahõctē-hī vo hōṭal-kō gayā. 5. us-sē miltē-hī us-nē kyā kahā? 6. film-kē śurū hōtē-hī hamẽ ghar vāpas jānā paṛā. 7. hamārē sair-kē liyē bāhar jātē-hī bāriś hōnē lagī. 8. ghanṭī-kī āvāz suntē-hī vo jagā. 9. sūraj nikaltē-hī parindō̃-nē gānā śurū kiyā. 10. ghar pahõctē-hī usē patā calā ke kuch mehmān āyē thē.

35.1.2 Exercise 2. **Translate into Urdu:**

1. As soon as we saw the mosque we wanted to go in. 2. Immediately after looking at the two calculations, I decided that the second was wrong. 3. As soon as I woke up my servant brought me tea. 4. The boy ran off immediately after the photographer took his picture. 5. As soon as I reached the depot I saw that the bus had arrived. 6. As soon as they heard my second story my friends interrupted. 7. As soon as he saw the result of his work he became discouraged. 8. The poor man began to dance with joy as soon as he got the money. 9. Immediately after she put her little sister to sleep she, too, fell asleep. 10. As soon as the train arrived we went in.

35.2

bag̱air ēk-bhī lafz kahē vo apnī ṭōpī uṭhākar cal diyā.	Without saying one word, he picked up his cap and left.
bag̱air lifāfā chā̃k kiyē us-nē k̤hat-kā mazmūn bhā̃p liyā.	Without opening the envelope, he guessed the contents of the letter.
āj maĩ bag̱air rukē das mīl calā.	I walked ten miles today without stopping.
bag̱air dūsrā sabak̤ yād kiyē us-nē tīsrā sabak̤ paṛhnā śurū kiyā.	He started reading the third lesson without memorizing the second.
pā̃c skāuṭ bag̱air apnī vardiyā̃ pahanē kemp-mẽ āyē.	Five boy scouts came to camp without (**wearing**) their uniforms.
tīn tālibilm bag̱air apnī kitābẽ aur k̤alam liyē skūl-kō gayē.	Three students went to school without (**taking**) their books and pens.

This section illustrates the translation into Urdu of English phrases containing a verbal form ending in **-ing,** introduced by the preposition **without.** The Urdu construction consists of a phrase introduced by the word **bag̱air** and ending in a past participle in the masculine singular object form. (The postposition **-kē** will sometimes follow the participle.) Substantives, governed by participles of transitive verbs occurring in this construction, are placed in the object form. (See 9.1.1, Remarks (1).)

REMARKS: (1) The postpositional phrase, **-kē bag̱air, without,** occurs, functioning like other postpositional phrases the first member of which is **-kē.**

(2) **ṭōkṛī** (ī) basket, **vardī** (ī) uniform, **sabak̤** (ā) lesson, **skāuṭ** (ā) boy scout, **chā̃k karnā** to tear open, **mazmūn** (ā) subject, matter, contents, **bhā̃p lēnā** to gues

35.2.1 Exercise 1. **Translate into English:**

1. bag̲air paisē ginē usē mālūm huā ke vo tohfā nahī̃ ḳharīd saktā thā. 2. bag̲air ēk-bhī savāl puchē us-nē bhā̃p liyā ke ajnabī cōr hai. 3. bag̲air ārām karnē-kē liyē rukē vo cār ghaṇṭē calā. 4. bag̲air kitāb paṛhē us-nē tay kiyā ke vo acchī nahī̃. 5. bag̲air ēk-bhī lafz kahē klārk-nē mēz-par bil rakhī. 6. bag̲air apnā kemrā sāth liyē maĩ masjid dēkhnē-kō bāhar gayā. 7. bag̲air kuch kahē bairā mērē liyē pānī lāyā. 8. bag̲air mōṭar-kī talāś kiyē maĩ-nē jān liyā ke vo kahā thā. 9. bag̲air bil dēkhē un-nē paisē diyē. 10. Pākistān-mē̃ safar bag̲air kiyē musannif-nē us-kē bārē-mē̃ kitāb likhī.

35.2.2 Exercise 2. **Translate into Urdu:**

1. Who can write about a country without seeing it? 2. Without reading the book he knew what was in it. 3. He talked an hour without stopping. 4. Without waiting for my answer he left. 5. The tailor showed me the cloth without saying a word. 6. Why did you do the work without trying to understand my order? 7. The automobile came towards us without stopping. 8. How can you learn a foreign language without trying? 9. The horse will not be able to go far without drinking water. 10. How long can a man work without stopping for rest?

35.3

ādmī-kā ēk bēṭā hai, jō paṛhtā hai.	The man has a son who studies.
ādmī-kē dō bēṭē haĩ, jō paṛhtē haĩ.	The man has two sons who study.
ādmī-kī ēk bēṭī hai, jō gātī hai.	The man has a daughter who sings.
ādmī-kī dō bēṭiyā̃ haĩ, jō gātī haĩ.	The man has two daughters who sing.
mērā ēk bhāī hai, jō śahar-mē̃ kām kartā hai.	I have a brother who works in the city.
mērē dō bhāī haĩ, jō śahar-mē̃ kām kartē haĩ.	I have two brothers who work in the city.
mērī ēk bahan hai, jō śādī • śudā hai.	I have a sister who is married.
mērē dō bahnē̃ haĩ, jō śādī • śudā haĩ.	I have two sisters who are married.
hamārā ēk bhāī hai, jō kām nahī̃ kartā.	We have a brother who does not work.
hamārē dō bhāī haĩ, jō kām nahī̃ kartē.	We have two brothers who do not work.

Compare sections 22.5 and 22.5.1 with the possessive construction illustrated in this section.

The construction is identical with that of 22.5.1. It is employed when the person possessed is qualified by a relative clause. Compare the possessive construction of 22.5, which is not qualified by a relative clause.

REMARKS: **śādī • śudā, married,** is an adjective which remains unchanged for gender, number or form.

35.4

ēk aur ēk dō hōtē haĩ.	One and one are two.
pā̃c aur pā̃c das hōtē haĩ.	Five and five are ten.

das-mẽ-sē dō manfī karẽ, tō āṭh hōtē haĩ.	Two from ten are eight.
dō kam das āṭh hōtē haĩ.	Two from ten are eight.
bīs-mẽ-sē pā̃c manfī karẽ, tō pandrā hōtē haĩ.	Five from twenty are fifteen.
pā̃c kam bīs pandrā hōtē haĩ.	Five from twenty are fifteen.
cār-mẽ cār jamā karō.	Add four to four.
che-mẽ-sē ēk ghaṭāō.	Subtract one from six.
chē-mẽ-sē ēk manfī karo.	Subtract one from six.
āṭh-kā che · gunā arṭālīs hōtē haĩ.	Six times eight is forty-eight.
sōlā-kō āṭh-sē taḳsīm karō.	Divide sixteen by eight.
caubīs baṭē tīn āṭh hōtē haĩ.	Twenty-four divided by three is eight.
pā̃c-kō tīn-sē zarab dẽ, tō pandrā hōtē haĩ.	Five multiplied by three is fifteen.
caubīs-kō tīn-sē taḳsim karẽ, tō āṭh hōtē haĩ.	Twenty-four divided by three is eight.

These sentences illustrate the rendition into Urdu of expressions denoting addition, subtraction, multiplication and division. Note the literal translation of the first, third, tenth, twelfth, and fourteenth Urdu sentences: **One and one become two; Two from ten become eight; Six times eight become forty-eight; Twenty-four divided by three become eight;** and **When you divide twenty-four by three, eight becomes.**

REMARKS: **mẽ-sē of sentences** 3, 5, 8, 9, translate **from; baṭnā** of sentence 12 translates **to be divided.**

35.5

āṭh bajē haĩ.	It is eight o'clock.
āṭh baj rahē haĩ.	It is striking eight o'clock.
āṭh baj cukē haĩ.	It has already struck eight o'clock.
āṭh baj gayē haĩ.	It has already struck eight o'clock.
āṭh bajnē-hī-kō haĩ.	It is about to be (= **strike**) eight.
paun bajā hai.	It is 12:45.
savā bārā bajē haĩ.	It is 12:15.
savā bajā hai.	It is 12:15.
ēk bajkar pandrā minaṭ huē haĩ.	It is 1:15.
ḍēṛh bajā hai.	It is 1:30.
paunē dō bajē haĩ.	It is 1:45.
ḍhāī bajē haĩ.	It is 2:30.
sāṛhē tīn bajē haĩ.	It is 3:30.
paunē cār bajē haĩ.	It is 3:45.
āṭh bajnē-mẽ das minaṭ bāḳī haĩ.	It is 7:50.
das minaṭ kam āṭh huē haĩ.	It is ten minutes to eight.
āṭh bajkar das minaṭ huē haĩ.	It is ten minutes after eight.
āṭh bajnē-mẽ das minaṭ (kam) haĩ.	It is ten minutes to eight.
āṭh bajkar das minaṭ-par.	At 8:10.
ṭhīk dōpahar haĩ.	It is exactly noon.
ṭhīk bārā bajē haĩ.	It is exactly noon.
che bajnē-mẽ das minaṭ haĩ.	It is ten minutes to six.
che bajnē-mẽ das minaṭ bāḳī haĩ.	It is ten minutes to six.

āṭh bajnē-mē̃ bis minaṭ haī.	It is twenty minutes to eight.
āṭh bajnē-mē̃ bīs minaṭ bāḳī haī.	It is twenty minutes to eight.
das bajkar pā̃c minaṭ huē haī.	It is five minutes after ten.
gyārā bajkar paccīs minaṭ huē haī.	It is twenty-five minutes after eleven.
gyārā bajkar aṭṭhāīs minaṭ huē haī.	It is twenty-eight minutes after eleven.

This section and the following illustrate the rendition into Urdu of sentences expressing time.

REMARKS: **ḍēṛh (adj.)** one and a half, **ḍhāī (adj.)** two and a half, **paun (adj.)** minus a quarter, **paunē (adj.)** minus a quarter, **bāḳī (adj.)** remaining, **savā (adj.)** plus a quarter, **sāṛhē (adj.)** plus a half.

35.5.1

ye ghaṛī tīn minaṭ āgē hai.	This watch is three minutes fast.
ye ghaṛī tīn minaṭ tēz hai.	This watch is three minutes fast.
ye ghaṛī tīn minaṭ pīchē hai.	This watch is three minutes slow.
ye ghaṛī har rōz tīn minaṭ āgē hō jātī hai.	This watch gains three minutes every day.
ye ghaṛī har rōz tīn minaṭ pīchē hō jātī hai.	This watch loses three minutes every day.
āp pā̃c minaṭ dēr-sē āyē.	You arrived five minutes late.
āp-kē ānē-mē̃ pā̃c minaṭ dēr huī.	There was a delay of five minutes in your arrival.
vo rāt das bajē-kē ḳarīb āyā.	He arrived about ten o'clock at night.

35.7 Text 17. **Syāsī**[1] **Līḍar: Ēk Tanziyā**[2] **Afsānā.**[3]

Translate into English. Answer the questions in Urdu:

(Nōṭ:[4] is afsānē-kē tamām[5] kirdār[6] farzī[7] haī.)

[Ahmad Jalal Ḳhā̃[8] Lāhōr-mē̃ kaī sālō̃-sē rah rahē haī. un-kā pēśā[9] yū̃-tō[10] vakālat hai, lēkin un-kō kisī-nē kabhī adālat-mē̃ muḳadmā laṛtē nahī̃ dēkhā. sac pūchiyē tō un-kō muḳadmē taiyār karnē aur ḳānūnī mūāmlō̃-mē̃ ulajhnē[11] -kī zarūrat-bhī kyā hai. vo ēk bahot baṛē zamindār haī. hazārō̃ ēkaṛ zamin-kē mālik. is zamīn-sē unhē̃ lakhō̃ rūpayē sālānā āmdanī hai. śahar-mē̃ baṛī ālīśān[12] kōṭhī hai. darjanō̃[13] naukar • cākar[14] āgē pīchē phirtē haī. garāj[15] -mē̃ kam-az-kam che mōṭrē̃ hō̃gī. ye sab kuch tō ṭhīk hai, lēkin āḳhir Ḳhā̃ • Sāhab-kē liyē kōī vaḳt kāṭnē-kā sāmān-bhī tō hōnā cāhiyē. is zarūrat-kō pūrā karnē-kē liyē Ḳhā̃ • Sāhab-nē munāsib[16] band-ō-bast kiyā hai. vo Panjāb-kī ḳānūn sāz asemblī[17] -kē membar[18] haī aur vahā̃ apnē ilākē-kē baṛē baṛē zamīndrō̃-kī tarjumānī[19] kartē haī. lēkin Lāhōr-mē̃ vo sōśalisṭ pārṭī-kē sadr haī. āj śām un-kē ghar kuch sōśalisṭ kārkun[20] khānē-par ā rahē haī. khānē-kē bād ēk miṭing[21] hōgī jis-mē̃ sōśalisṭ pārṭī-kā prōgrām banāyā jāēgā.[22] is miṭing-mē Ḳhā̃ • Sāhab baṛī zōr-kī taḳrīr karē̃gē. is vaḳt Ḳhā̃ • Sāhab apnē sekreṭarī[23] -kē sāth taḳrīr taiyār kar rahē haī. un-kī bēṭī Jamīlā-bhī pās baiṭhī hai aur maśvrah dē rahī hai. Jamīlā hāl-hī-mē̃[24] Iṅglistān-sē vāpas āyī hai. vo vahā̃ Kembrij Yūnivarsiṭī-mē̃ paṛh rahī thī.]

Ḳhā̃ • Sāhab: Misṭar Ahmad Alī! (Ahmad Alī sekreṭarī-kā nām hai. vo ēk tīs • sālah javān ādmī hai aur kālij-kā grējūēṭ[25] hai, yānī bī.ē. pās hai. Urdū acchī • ḳhāsī[26] jāntā hai.)

Ahmad Alī: Jī, hazūr.[27] (Ahmad Alī Ḳhā̃ • Sāhab-kī bahot ḳhuśāmad [28] kartā hai. bēcārā [29] kyā karē, Ḳhā̃ • Sāhab baṛē ḳhuśāmad • pasand ādmī haī.)

Ḳhā̃ • Sāhab: hamārī taḳrīr tō tum-nē taiyār kar lī, nā?

Ahmad Alī: jī, Ḳhā̃ • Sāhab. baṛī mehnat-sē taiyār kī hai. lōg sunẽgē tō "vāh, vāh!" karẽgē. bas āp-kī līḍarī [30] āj pakkī hō [31] jāēgī. inśā Allah.

Ḳhā̃ • Sāhab: śābāś! [32] hamārā ḳhayāl hai ke ab tumhārī tanḳhāh baṛhā dẽ. acchā, paṛhkar sunāō.[33]

Ahmad Alī: (taḳrīr paṛhtā hai): ḳhvātīn-ō-hazrāt,[34] āj • śām ham sab lōg is sūbē-kē kuch aham mūāmalāt-par gaur karnē [35] -kē liyē jamā huē haī. āp jāntē haī ke hamārī haḳūmat [36] avām [37] -kī zarūriyāt [38] -kō pūrā karnē-mẽ bilkul nakām [39] rahī hai. jō vādē alekśan-kē vaḳt kiyē gayē thē, un-kō pūrā nahĩ kiyā gayā. garīb bhūkē mar rahē haī. un-kō rōṭī nahī miltī. vo tarah tarah-kī bīmāriyõ-kā śikār hōtē haī, lēkin un-kō ilāj-kē liyē kōī haspatal nahĩ. un-kē baccē anpaṛh [40] haī. un-kī tālīm-kā kōī band-ō-bast nahĩ. jab avām apnē haḳūḳ-kē liyē avāz uṭhātē haī tō unhẽ batāyā jātā hai [22] ke sarkār-kē pās paisā nahĩ hai. agar ye sac hai, ke sarkār-kē pās paisā nahĩ, tō savāl ye hai ke paisā kahā̃-sē āēgā. ḳhvātīn-ō-hazrāt, ham sōśalisṭ ye kahtē haī ke is sūbē-mẽ paisē-kī kōī kamī nahĩ. agar sarmāyādārī [41] -kō ḳhatam kar diyā jāē,[22] tō haḳūmat-kē pās āj itnā paisā hō jāēgā ke garībõ-kī sab zarūriyāt pūrī hō sakẽgī. hamārā ḳhayāl hai ke is sūbē-mẽ zamīn aur sanat [42] -kō sarkārī milkiyyat [43] kar diyā jāē.[22] lēkin ye inḳalābī [44] ḳadam [45] kaun uṭhāēgā. maujūdā haḳumat sarmāyādārõ [46] -kī haḳūmat hai. is haḳūmat-sē aisī ummīd rakhnā bilkul bēkār hai. garībõ-kī imdād karnē-kē liyē aur un-kī hālāt behtar karnē-kē liyē sōśalisṭ inḳalāb [47] zarūrī hai. sōśalisṭ parṭī zindābād! [48]

Ḳhā̃ • Sāhab: Ahmad Alī! śābāś. bahot acchī taḳrīr hai. āj-sē tumhārī tanḳhāh das rūpayē zyādā kartē haī.[49]

Ahmad Alī: hazūr, pā̃c sāl-sē āp-kī naukrī kar rahā hū̃. ye pahilī taraḳḳī hai. mērē ḳhayāl-mẽ tō bīs rūpayē zyādā dījiyē.

Ḳhā̃ • Sāhab: nahĩ, fil • hāl [50] das rūpayē-kī ṭhīk hai.

Jamīlā: abbā • jān, baṛhāiyē is-kī tanḳhāh bīs rūpayē. bēcārā garīb ādmī hai. aur kām-bhī tō bahot mehnat-sē kartā hai.

Ḳhā̃ • Sāhab: acchā, bēṭī, tum kahtī hō, tō is-kī tanḳhāh bīs rūpayē baṛhā dētē haī. ab ḳhuś hō? (Ahmad Alī-sē).

Ahmad Alī: jī, āp-kē jān-ō-māl-kō duā dētā hū̃. (bāhar jātā hai.)

Jamīlā: abbā • jān, taḳrīr tō ṭhīk hai. lēkin agar zamīndrõ-kī zamīnẽ sarkārī milkiyyat hō gayĩ, tō phir āp kyā karẽgē?

Ḳhā̃ • Sāhab: mērī bhōlī [51] bēṭē! kyā tum samajhtī hō ke maī itnā bēvaḳūf hū̃, ke apnī zamīnẽ sarkār-kē havālē [52] kar dū̃gā? asembalī [53] -kē paccās zamīndār membar tō mērī muṭṭhī [54] -mẽ haī. jab kabhī aisā bil asembalī-mẽ pēś hōgā, tō vo us-kē ḳhilāf vōṭ dẽgē. is-kē ilāvā, aglē alekśan-tak tō aisē bil-kē peś hōnē-kā kōī savāl-hī nahĩ. agar nayē alekśan-mẽ hamārī pārṭī jīt gayī, tō phir ham ḳhud-hī aisā bil pēś nahĩ hōnē dẽgē. ye taḳrīr tō vōṭ lēnē-kē liyē hai.

Jamīlā: lēkin, abbā • jān, ye sab tō bēimānī hai.

Khā̃ • Sāhab: bēvakūf larkī, cup rahō. (gussē-mē̃). bāp-kō bēimān kahtī hō! bad • tamīz,[55] gustākh![56]

[Jamīlā rōnē lagtī hai.]

savālāt:

1. Khā̃ • Sāhab-kā pēśā kyā thā? 2. Ahmad Alī-kī tankhāh kaisē barhī? 3. apnē takrīr-mē̃ Khā̃ • Sāhab-nē maujūdā hakūmat-kē bārē-mē̃ kyā kahā? 4. Jamīlā kaun thī? 5. Jamīlā-nē takrīr-kē bārē-mē̃ kyā kahā?

NOTES: 1. political (**adj., n.c.**); 2. satirical (**adj., n.c.**); 3. short story (ā); 4. note (ā); 5. all (**adj., n.c.**); 6. character, person (ā); 7. fictitious (**adj., n.c.**); 8. man's name; 9. profession (ā); 10. **yū̃ tō** in a way; 11. **ulajhnā** to get involved (**int.**); 12. majestic (**adj., n.c.**); 13. dozens (**adv.**); 14. servants (ā, pl.); 15. garage (ā); 16. proper (**adj., n.c.**); 17. legislative assembly (ī); 18. member (ā); 19. representation (ī); 20. worker (ā); 21. meeting (ī); 22. see 37.1; 23. secretary (ā, ī); 24. recently (= **adv.**); 25. graduate (ā); 26. pretty well (**adj.**); 27. yes, sir; 28. flattery (ī); 29. wretch (ā); 30. leadership (ī); 31. **pakkā hōnā** to be assured, become solid (**int.**); 32. very good; 33. read it back; 34. Ladies and Gentlemen; 35. **gaur karnā** to consider (**tr.**); 36. government (ī); 37. common people, masses (ā, **pl.**); 38. need (ī, **pl.**); 39. failed (**adj., n.c.**); 40. illiterate (**adj., n.c.**); 41. capitalism (ī); 42. industry (ī); 43. ownership, property (ī); 44. revolutionary (**adj., n.c.**); 45. step (ā); 46. **sarmāyādār** capitalist (ā); 47. revolution (ā); 48. long live!; 49. increase; 50. for the present; 51. **bhōlā** innocent (**adj.**); 52. **havālā** custody (ā); 53. assembly (ī); 54. fist (ī); 55. ill-mannered (**adj., n.c.**); 56. insolent (**adj., n.c.**).

LESSON 36

36.1

makān lakṛī-kā banā hai.	The house is made of wood.
baṛhaī lakṛī-kā makān banātā hai.	The carpenter makes the house of wood.
ādmī-nē lakṛī-kā makān banvāyā.	The man had the house made of wood.
laṛkā apnē bāp-kī bāt suntā hai.	The boy hears his father.
bāp apnē bēṭē-kō kahānī sunātā hai.	The father tells his son a story.
mā̃-nē māsṭar-sē kahānī sunvāyī.	The mother had the master tell the story (e.g., **to a third person**).
lakṛī jaltī hai.	The wood burns.
ādmī lakṛī-kō jalātā hai.	The man sets fire to the wood.
maĩ-nē naukar-sē lakṛī jalvāyī.	I had the servant burn the wood.
maĩ kām kartā hū̃.	I work.
maĩ kām karātā hū̃.	I get the work done.
maĩ kisān-sē kām karvātā hū̃.	I cause the farmer to have the work done.
sūraj maśrik-sē uṭhtā hai.	The sun rises in the East.
ādmī apnā sāmān uṭhātā hai.	The man picks up his luggage.
ādmī ḳulī-sē apnā sāmān uṭhvātā hai.	The man has the coolie pick up his luggage.
laṛkā apnē bāp-kā hāth pakaṛtā hai.	The boy grasps his father's hand.
maĩ-nē usē rassā pakṛāyā.	I gave him a rope. (lit., **I caused him to seize a rope.**)
sipāhī-nē cōr-kō pakaṛvāyā.	The policeman had the thief caught.
tālibilm sabaḳ samajhtā hai.	The student understands the lesson.
ustād • sāhab tālibilm-kō sabaḳ samjhāẽgē.	The teacher will explain the lesson to the student.
maĩ āp-sē talibilmõ-kō Urdū samjhvā dū̃gī.	I will have you explain Urdu to the students.

is kapṛē-kā rañg badal rahā hai.	The color of this cloth is changing.
is kapṛē-kā rañg badlāiyē.	Please change the color of this cloth.
is kapṛē-kā rañg badalvā dījiyē.	Please have the color of this cloth changed.
bail khēt-kī taraf dauṛ rahē haĩ.	The oxen are running towards the field.
kisān mavēśiyō̃-kō dauṛātā hai.	The farmer hurries the cattle.
maĩ-nē naukar-sē bailō̃-kō dauṛvāyā.	I had the servant hurry the oxen.
laṛkī subah • savērē uṭhtī hai.	The girl wakes up early in the morning.
mā̃ laṛkī-kō subah • savērē uṭhātī hai.	The mother awakens the girl early in the morning.
mā̃ laṛkī-kō bahan-sē uṭhvātī thī.	The mother had the sister wake up the girl.
baccē gānē sun rahē haĩ.	The children are listening to songs.
maĩ unhẽ ēk gānā sunā rahā hū̃.	I am reciting a song to them.
ham āp-kō Chōṭē G̱ulām Alī gānā sunvāẽgē.	We'll have to listen to a song by Choṭe Gulam Ali.

This section and the following are concerned with the changes made in verbal stems to form new stems. These changes may constitute vowel substitutions, suffixation, or combinations of these. (It must be pointed out that all verbal stems do not participate in such formations. The examples given above, and in the sections following, are for purposes of facility in the recognition of the base stem or root of verbs. Such recognitions will aid in the understanding of the meanings of some verbal stems and the constructions in which they participate.)

The sentences have been arranged into groups of three. The verb of the second sentence of each of these groups illustrates what can be termed the **first causative verbal stem**—i.e., the act denoted by the verb of the first sentence is caused to be or made carried out. The verb of the third sentence illustrates the **second causative stem**—i.e., the act denoted by the verb of the second sentence is caused to be carried out. Compare the first three groups of sentences and the literal translation of the Urdu: **The house is made . . . , The carpenter causes the house to be made . . . ,** and **The man caused (someone) to make the house . . . ; The boy hears . . . , The father causes the boy to hear . . . ,** and **The mother caused to hear (through a third person) . . . ; The wood burns, The man causes the wood to burn,** and **I caused the servant to burn the wood.**

This section, 36.1, illustrates the formation of causal stems by the addition of suffixes to the root stem. These suffixes are **-ā** for the first causative and **-vā-** for the second causative. The stems of the first five sets of sentences are, therefore: of the first set, **ban, to be made, bānā, to cause to be made, to make,** and **banvā, to have made, to cause to be made (by someone)**; of the second, **sun, to hear, sunā, to cause to hear, tell, to relate, sunvā, to cause to be heard, told, related**; of the third, **jal, to burn, jalā, to cause to burn, to set afire, jalvā, to cause someone to set afire**; of the fourth, **kar, to do, to make, karā, to cause to do, to make, karvā, to cause someone to do, to make;** and of the fifth, **uṭh, to rise, uṭhā, to cause to rise, to raise, uṭhvā, to cause someone to raise, to pick up.** These stem alternations sometimes serve to form transitive stems from intransitive stems. See the groups of sentences above: of the first, **ban, to be made,** and **banā, to make,** of the third, **jal, to burn, to be afire,** and **jalā, to burn, to set fire to,** and of the fifth, **uṭh, to rise,** and **uṭhā, to cause to rise, to raise.**

REMARKS: Some verbal stems of more than one syllable will drop the short **-a-** in a syllable other than the first when the first causal suffix is added. See in the sixth set above, **pakaṛ** and **pakṛā;** in the seventh set, **samajh** and **samjhā;** and in the eighth, **badal** and **badlā.** For the dropping of the **-a-** in nouns compare Remarks, 3.4.

36.1.1

ādmī naukar-sē pānī mā̃gtā hai.	The man asks the servant for water.
mujhē bāzār-sē ēk guṛiyā mā̃gā dījiyē.	Please have a doll sent to me from the bazaar.
mujhē dukāndār-sē ēk guṛiyā mā̃gvā dījiyē.	Please have the shop keeper send me a doll.
laṭṭū ghūm rahā hai.	The top is spinning.
apnē laṭṭū ghumāō.	Spin your tops.
apnē laṭṭū ghumvāō.	Spin your tops.

The causal stem formation illustrated above consists of the addition of the causal suffixes given in section 36.1 plus a change of vowels—**-ā̃-** is replaced by **-ā-** and **-ū-** by **-u-**. Compare the stems **mā̃g, mā̃gā,** and **mā̃gvā,** and **ghūm, ghumā,** and **ghumvā.**

36.1.2

daraḳht dō hissō̃-mẽ kaṭā hai.	The tree is cut into two pieces.
ādmī daraḳht kāṭtā hai.	The man cuts the tree.
ādmī daraḳht kaṭvātā hai.	The man has the tree cut.
gāy bā̃dhī hai.	The cow is tied.
chōṭā laṛkā apnē jūtē-kē tasmē bā̃dh rahā hai.	The little boy is tying his shoelaces.
chōṭā laṛkā apnē bāp-sē fītē bā̃dhvā rahā hai.	The little boy is having his father tie his shoelaces.
ye lakṛī kab tulī thī?	When was this wood weighed?
lakaṛhārā kā̃ṭē-par lakṛī tōltā hai.	The woodcutter weighs the wood in the scales.
ādmī lakṛī tulvātā hai.	The man has the wood weighed.
khiṛkī khulī thī.	The window was open.
laṛkī-nē khiṛkī khōlī.	The girl opened the window.
mā̃-nē khiṛkī khulvāyī.	The mother had the window opened.

The verbs of these sets of sentences illustrate the formation of the first causal stems by vowel replacement—e.g., **-a-** is replaced by **-ā-** in the first two sets and **-u-** by **-ō-** in the third and fourth sets. The second causative stem is fashioned by adding **-vā-** to the base stem (or root). Compare section 36.1.

REMARKS: **kā̃ṭā** (ā) is a scale for weighing large objects as contrasted with a **tarāzū** (ā) whichis used for small objects; **tasmā** (ā) shoelace, **fītā** (ā) shoelace.

36.1.3

kōṭ phaṭā hai.	The coat is torn.
laṛkē-nē apnā kōṭ phāṛā.	The boy tore his coat.
laṛkī-nē kapṛā phaṛvāyā.	The girl had the cloth torn.
kitābē̃ bāzār-mē̃ biktī haĩ.	Books are sold in the bazaar.
ādmī bāzār-mē̃ kitābē̃ bēc rahā hai.	The man is selling books in the bazaar.
ādmī bāzār-mē̃ apnī kitābē̃ bikvātā hai.	The man is having his books sold in the bazaar.
pyālā ṭūṭā hai.	The cup is broken.
naukar-nē pyālā tōṛā.	The servant broke the cup.
maĩ-nē sandūk tuṛvāyā.	I had the box broken.

The casual stem formation illustrated here consists of both vowel and consonant replacement to form the first causative stem. The second causative stem has consonant alternation before the -vā- suffix. Note that the long **-ū-** of **tūṭnā** is shortened before the -vā-, and that there is no consonant alternation in **bikvānā.**

36.1.4

hamē̃ āj kuch rupayā dē dījiyē.	Please give us some money today.
hamē̃ āj kuch rupayā dilā dījiyā.	Please have some money given to us today.
hamē̃ āj kuch rupayā dilvā dījiyē.	Please cause (**someone else**) to have some money given to us today.
ghōṛā ghās khātā hai.	The horse eats grass.
laṛkā ghōṛē-kō ghās khilātā hai.	The boy feeds the horse grass.
laṛkā naukar-sē ghōṛē-kō ghās khilvātā hai.	The boy has the servant feed the horse grass.
baccā dūdh pītā hai.	The child drinks milk.
mā̃ baccē-kō dūdh pilātī hai.	The mother has the child drink milk.
mā̃ laṛkī-sē baccē-kō dūdh pilvātī hai.	The mother has the girl feed the child milk.
baccē sōtē haĩ.	Children sleep.
mā̃ baccō̃-kō sulātī hai.	The mother puts the children to sleep.
mā̃ laṛkī-sē baccō̃-kō sulvātī hai.	The mother has the girl put the children to sleep.

These sets illustrate the formation of first causative stems by vowel replacement and the addition of the suffix **-lā-**. Compare the stems of the sets given above: **dē, dilā; khā, khilā; pī, pilā;** and **sō, sulā.** Note the vowel-replacement: **-ē-** by **-i-**; **-ā-** by **-i-**; **-ī- by -i-**; and **-ō-** by **-u-**. The stem of the second causative is formed by dropping the **-ā-** of the **-lā-** suffix of the first causative stem and adding **-vā-**.

36.1.5 Exercise 1. **Translate into English:**

1. ye ghar kis-kā banā hai? 2. is kapṛē-kā rang̃ dhōbī-sē badalvāō. 3. ye sāmān uṭhākar gāṛī-mē̃ rakh dō. 4. lakṛī dō hissō̃-mē̃ tūṭī hai. 5. kis-nē ye makān banvāyā? 6. kisī-sē mērā sāmān uṭhvāiyē. 7. kapṛēvālē-kē pās jākar ye kapṛā badlāō. 8. tum mērē liyē kursiyā̃ kab banāōgē? 9. bail rassē-sē darakht-kē nīcē bādhā hai. 10. hamē̃ paṛhnē-kē liyē ēk nayī kitāb māgā dījiyē. 11. ādmī tālāb-mē̃ nahā rahā hai. 12. kyā laṛkē hāthī-kō nahlānā cāhtē haĩ? 13. mālik naukar-sē lakṛī bādhvātā hai. 14. tumhē̃ pyāsē baccē-kō dūdh pilānā hai. 15. agar kisān mavēśiyō̃-kō dauṛāē, tō (śāyad) vo phislē̃. 16. masjid-kē sāmnē phūl biktē haĩ. 17. kamzōr ādmī bhārī lakṛī tulvātā hai. 18. tum-nē skūl-kī fīs kab jamā karvā dī? 19. ye purānē jūtē phē̃k dō! 20. agar pānī garm hō, tō hamē̃ us-kō na pilāiyē.

36.1.6 Exercise 2. **Translate into Urdu:**

1. The bus will stop in front of the temple. 2. Stop the car near the well. 3. The old elephant died in the jungle. 4. The hunter killed the tiger near the field. 5. I saw the jackal running towards the road. 6. He showed me the old building. 7. The ripe fruit dropped from the tree. 8. The monkey threw down the fruits on the boys. 9. I wake up early every morning. 10. You'll have to wake him up. 11. With whom were you speaking outside? 12. Call the bearer! 13. We bathe in the river every day. 14. Sister has to bathe her little brother. 15. What kinds of things are sold in the market? 16. I shall have my books sold next month. 17. Who broke the (**large**) plate? 18. Why did you have the servant break open the closed box? 19. The wheels of the car are spinning. 20. The mechanic makes the wheels spin.

36.2

is kamrē-mē̃ kyā kyā cīzē̃ haĩ?	What (**various**) things are in this room?
kaun kaun āē̃gē?	Who (= **what various persons**) will come?
mulk mulk-kē vazīr yahā̃ āyē.	The ministers of (**various**) countries came here.
un sab-kē pās dō dō rupayē haĩ.	They each have two rupees.
un sab-kō tīn tīn ānē dījiyē.	Give them all three annas each.
vo dō dō karkē andar āē̃gē.	They will enter in two's.
ādmī ādmī-mē̃ fark hōtā hai.	Each man is different.
is kahānī-kā ēk ēk haraf sac hai.	Every letter of this story is true.
ab hamē̃ apnē apnē ghar jānā cāhiyē.	Now we should go, each to his (**own**) home.
kyā āp-kē pās pā̃c pā̃c rupayē-kē dō nōṭ haĩ?	Do you have two five-rupee notes?
tum dōnō̃ ye tarbūz ādhā karkē lē saktē hō.	You can each take half of this melon.

mujhē ṭhīk ṭhīk kahānī sunāiyē.	Please tell me the story exactly.
tūfān-nē baṛē baṛē daraḳht girā diyē.	The storm felled very big trees.
mujhē sac sac batāō ke ye kis-nē kiyā?	Tell me honestly who did it?
holē holē khāō; jaldī kāhā-kī hai?	Eat slowly; what's the hurry?
garm garm khānē-kē bād fauran ṭhanḍā pānī nahī̃ pīnā cāhiyē.	One shouldn't take cold water immediately after a hot meal.
kaisī ṭhanḍī ṭhanḍī havā ā rahī hai.	What a cool breeze is coming!
is kitab-mē̃ kaī acchī acchī kahāniyā̃ haī.	This book has many good stories.
jaldī jaldī na caliyē.	Please do not walk fast.
ḳarīb ḳarīb sab vazīr kebineṭ-kī mīṭīng-mē̃ maujūd thē.	Almost all the ministers were present at the cabinet meeting.
ḳarīb ḳarīb ēk lākh lōg jamā thē.	About one hundred thousand people had gathered.

ḳarīb ḳarīb sau bār us-nē ye dōhrāyā.	He repeated this nearly a hundred times.
ḳarīb ḳarīb sab tālibilm āj bagair pensil-kē āyē haī.	Almost every student has come without a pencil today.

An examination of the sentences given above will reveal that each contains a word which has been repeated. This repetition of words is employed to indicate plurality, distribution in space, and emphasis. The FIRST group of sentences illustrates the use of repetition to indicate plurality, the SECOND illustrates distribution, and the THIRD, emphasis. For the repetition of the past participle, functioning as an adverb, see section 31.3, and section 33.6 for the repetition of a gerund.

REMARKS: (1) See the last sentence for the construction with **bagair** in which the postposition **-kē** follows the noun governed and compare section 35.2. (Compare also 10.1 to 10.4.3 and 11.1 to 11.3)

(2) **haraf** (ā) letter.

36.2.1 Exercise 1. **Translate into English:**

1. āp-nē bāzār-mē̃ kyā kyā cīzē̃ ḳharīdī̃? 2. mōṭargāṛī holē holē calāō! 3. ḳarīb ḳarīb sab phal kaccē thē. 4. ham-nē ghar ghar-mē̃ talāś kī. 5. Kalkattē-sē Dillī safar karnē-mē̃ ham-nē baṛē baṛē gāō̃ dēkhē. 6. har sāl mulk mulk-kē hājī Makkē ātē haī. 7. un paudō̃-par chōṭē chōṭē phūl haī. 8. un sab-kē pās dō dō bail haī. 9. mulk mulk-mē̃ fark hōtā hai. 10. is kitāb-kā ēk ēk lafz likhnā muśkil thā.

36.2.2 Exercise 2. **Translate into Urdu:**

1. Which of all these people do you know? 2. It seems as if I've written about a 100,000 words. 3. What good stories you told yesterday! 4. Give the workmen each two rupees. 5. When we started to swim across the river it did not seem very wide. 6. What (**different**) languages can you speak? 7. Every word of what I say is true. 8. He has a very big field. 9. You should tell me the story exactly. 10. Speak slowly!

36.3

yehī merā ghar hai.	This is my house.
isī-kō dūdh dījiyē.	Give the milk to this (**one**).
yehī lōg mērē sāth āē̃gē.	These people will go with me.

inhī̃-kē sāth jāiyē.	Go with these.
vo-hī mōcī hai.	He is a shoemaker.
usī-kō jūtē dō.	Give him the shoes.
unhī̃-kō pānī dō.	Give them water.
yehī vo ādmī hai jisē maĩ-nē vahā̃ dēkhā.	This is the man whom I had seen there.
vohī ādmī jisē maĩ-nē vahā̃ kal dēkhā thā āj hōṭal-mē̃ āyā.	The (**very**) man whom I had seen there yesterday appeared at the hotel today.
ye ḳalam usī-kē haĩ.	These pens belong to him.
ye ghaṛī usī laṛkī-kī haĩ.	These watches belong to that girl.
maĩ unhī̃-kē sāth thā.	I was with them.
maĩ inhī̃-kē sāth thā.	I was with these.
śurū-sē-hī mujhē ye mālūm thā.	I knew this from the (**very**) beginning.
śurū-sē-hī vo ghabrāyā huē thā.	At the (**very**) beginning he was scared.

This section illustrates the use of the emphatic particle **-hī, -ī, -hī̃,** when occurring with the third person pronoun. **-ī** is added to the singular forms (subject and object) and **-hī** to the subject plural forms. **-hī̃** is added to the plural object forms.

REMARKS: **-hī** can be added to any part of speech to indicate emphasis. See section 30.2.3, and the last two sentences above.

36.4 Text 18. **Mohammad,**[1] **Rasūl • Allah.**[2]

Translate into English. Answer the questions in Urdu.

āj-sē kōī caudā sau sāl pahilē Hazrāt Mohammad, Ḳhudā un-par rahmat karē,[3] Makkē-kē ēk muazziz [4] gharanē [5]-mē̃ paidā huē. un-kē paidā hōnē-sē pahilē-hī un-kē vālid, jin-kā nām Abdullah [6] thā, faut hō [7] gayē thē. cunā̃-ce Hazrat Mohammad-kē dādā Abdul Muttalib [8] -nē un-kī parvariś kī. lēkin thōṛē arsē-kē bād dādā-bhī faut hō gayē aur un-kē cacā Abū Tālib [9] -nē un-kō parvariś kiyā. is zamānē-mē̃ Arabō̃-kī hālat baṛī ḳharāb thī. sārī dunyā-kī burāiyā̃ un-mē̃ maujūd thī̃. vo śarāb pītē thē, juā [10] khēltē thē, zinā [11] kartē thē, jhūṭ bōltē thē. un-kō na cōrī karnē-mē̃ kōī bāk [12] thā na katl-mē̃. us zamānē-kī Arab kaī ḳabīlō̃ [13] -mē̃ taḳsīm thē. aur har ḳabīlā apnē būtō̃ [14] -kī parastiś [15] kartā thā. in ḳabīlō̃-mē̃ har vaḳt laṛāī hōtī rahtī thī. Hazrat Mohammad bacpan-sē-hī apnī ḳom [16] -kī ye hālat dēkhkar udās rahtē thē. vo bahot gaur-ō-fikr [17] kartē aur aksar tanhāī [18] -mē̃ Ḳhudā-kī ibādat kartē thē. un-kō khēl • tamāśē [19] -kā kōī śauk nahī̃ thā. bacpan-mē̃ vo apnē ū̃ṭō̃-kī dēkhbhāl kartē thē. javānī-mē̃ unhō̃-nē tijārat [20] karnā śurū kiyā. vo kapṛā ḳharīdtē aur bēctē thē. kaī dafā vo ḳāflō̃ [21] -kē sāth dūr • drāz [22] jaghō̃-par tijārat-kē silsalē-mē̃ [23] jātē. lēkin is sārē vaḳt-mē̃ un-kā gaur-ō-fikr aur ibādat jārī rahē.[24] makkē-kē pās-hī ēk pahāṛī [25] hai jis-mē ēk gar [26] thā. Hazrat Mohammad us gār-mē̃ jākar kaī kaī ghanṭē Ḳhudā-kī ibādat kartē thē. cālīs sāl-kī umr-mē̃ un-par vahī nazil huī [27] aur Ḳhudā-nē un-kō apnā nabī [28] mukarrar [29] kiyā. us-kē bād unhō̃-nē ghar ākar apnī bīvī-sē is mūāmlē-kē zikr kiyā. un-kī bīvī pahilī aurat thī jō Musalmān huī. phir unhō̃-nē apnē ḳabīlē-kē lōgō̃ aur dōstō̃-kō jamā kiyā. us-sē kahā, "kyā tum • lōg mujhē saccā aur īmāndār ādmī samajhtē hō?" lōgō̃-nē javāb diyā, "bēśak, ai [30] Mohammad! ham-nē tumhē̃ kabhī jhūṭ bōltē yā bēimānī kartē nahī̃ pāyā." Mohammad-nē unsē phir pūchā, "agar maĩ tumhē̃ kahū̃ ke is pahāṛ-kē pīchē duśman [31] -kē ēk fauj [32] jamā hō rahī hai, tō kyā tum yaḳīn [33] karōgē?" lōgō̃-nē kahā, "ai, Abdullah-kē bēṭē, tum jō kuch-bhī kahōgē, ham us-par yaḳīn karẽgē, kyũ-ke tum saccē aur imāndār hō." Mohammad-nē kahā, "tō phir sunō ke Ḳhudā-nē mujhē apnā nabī mukarrar kiyā hai. maĩ tumhẽ saccāī [34] aur nēkī [35] -kā rāstā dikhāũgā. sab-sē pahilī bāt ye hai ke tum butõ-kī parastiś chōṛ dō, kyũ-kē vo tumhārī ibādat-kē ḳābil nahĩ. vo tō mehaz [36] patthar [37] -kē tukṛē haĩ. siraf Ḳhudā-hī ibādat-kē lāyak [38] hai. vo-hī zamīn-aur āsmān-kā paidā karnēvālā hai. tum usī-kī parastiś karō." jab lōgõ-nē ye bāt sunī tō kuch lōg gussē-mẽ āyē. un lōgõ-kō ye ummid na thī ke Mohammad un-kē būtõ-kē ḳhilāf kuch kahẽgē. is vakyā-kē bād hazrat Mohammad-nē Islām-kī tablīg [39] jārī rakhī.[40] lēkin jũ jũ vo tablīg kartē thē Makkēvālē utnē-hī zyādā zōr-sē un-kī muḳhālifat [41] kartē thē. āhistā āhistā lōg musalmān hōnē lagē aur ab hālat-kā ruḳh palatnā [42] śurū huā. jũ jũ Musalmānõ-kī tadād [43] baṛhtī thī, kāfīrõ [44] -kā gussā baṛhtā thā. kāfīr Musalmānõ-par baṛī saḳhtī [45] kartē thē. jab saḳhtī bahot-hī zyādā hō gayī aur kāfīr Hazrat Mohammad-kō katl karnē-kī sāziś [46] karnē lagē tō Musalmānõ-nē Makkā chōṛ diyā. Mohammad aur bāḳī sab Musalmān Madīnē [47] -kō hijrat [48] kar gayē. Rasūl•Allah-kī zindagī-mẽ-hī Musalmānõ-nē Makkā fatah [49] kar liyā. us-kē bād Islām sārē Arab-mẽ phailnā śurū hō gayā. Hazrat Mohammad-kī vafāt [50] -kē vaḳt taḳrīban tamān Arab Musalmān hō cukē thē.

Rasūl• Allah-nē lōgõ-kō jō tālīm dī us-kā khulāsā [51] hasab-ē-zail [52] hai: 1) Ḳhudā jō sārī dunyā-kā paidā karnēvālā hai, vo-hī ibādat-kē ḳābil hai aur us-kē ilāvā aur kōī nahĩ, yānī Ḳhudā ēk hai aur us-kā kōī śarīk [53] nahĩ; 2) Mohammad Ḳhudā-kē rasūl hai. sab Musalmān āpas-mẽ bhāī bhāī haĩ. Ḳhudā-kī nazar-mẽ vo sab barābar haĩ. saccāī, insāf, rahamdilī [54] un ḳhūbiyõ-mẽ-sē haĩ, jō Ḳhudā-kō pasand haĩ. Musalmānõ-kē liyē lāzim [55] hai ke vo Ḳhudā-kī ibādat karẽ, Ramzān-kē mahinē-mẽ rōzā rakhẽ aur Ḳhudā-kī rāh-mẽ rūpayā ḳharc karẽ. in-kē ilāvā aur-bhī kaī bātẽ haĩ, jō āp-kō phir kabhī batāẽgē.

savālāt:

1. Mohammad-nē apnē ḳabīlē-kē lōgõ-sē kyā kahā? 2. kāfīr lōg Musalmānõ-sē kyā salūk kartē [56] thē? 3. Musalmān Makkē-sē hijrat karkē kahā̃ gayē? 4. Mohammad-kī vafāt-kē vaḳt kitnē Arab Musalmān hō cukē thē? 5. Mohammad-nē lōgõ-kō kyā tālīm dī?

NOTES: 1 Mohammed; 2. Prophet of God; 3. = May God give him peace; 4. respectable (**adj.** ,**n.c.**); 5. **gharanā** family (ā); 6. name of Mohammed's father; 7. **faut hōnā** to die (**int.**); 8. name of Mohammed's grandfather; 9. name of Mohammed's paternal-uncle; 10. gambling (ī); 11. fornication (ā); 12. hesitation (ā); 13. **kabīlā** tribe (ā); 14. **būt** idol (ā); 15. worship (ī); 16. nation (ī); 17. contemplation (ā); 18. solitude (ī); 19. amusement (ā); 20. trade, commerce (ī); 21. **kaflah** caravan (ā); 22. distant (**adj., n.c.**); 23. **-kē silsalē-mẽ** in connection with; 24. **jārī rahnā** to continue (**int.**); 25. hill (ī); 26. cave (ā); 27. **vahī nazil huī** divine inspiration descended; 28. prophet (ā); 29. appointed (**adj., n.c.**); 30. oh!; 31. enemy (ā); 32. army (ī); 33. **yaḳīn karnā** to believe (**tr.**); 34. truth (ī); 35. virute, righteousness (ī); 36. just, mere (**adv.**); 37. stone (ā); 38. **-kē lāyak** worthy of (= **postpos. phrase**); 39. preaching (ī); 40. **jārī rakhnā** to continue (**tr.**); 41. opposition (ī); 42. **ruḳh palatnā** to turn face (or attention) towards (**tr.**); 43. number (ī); 44. **kāfīr** heathen; 45. hardship (ī); 46. conspiracy (ī); 47. town of Medina (ā); 48. migration (ā); 49. **fatah karnā** to conquer (**tr.**); 50. death (ī); 51. summary (ā); 52. as follows; 53. partner (ā); 54. kindheartedness (ī); 55. necessary (**adj., n.c.**); 56. **salūk karnā** to behave with, treat (**tr.**).

LESSON 37

37.1

fīs ēk ānā kī gayī.	The fees were made one anna.
darvāzā khōlā gayā.	The door was opened.
lakṛī jalāyī gayī.	The wood was burned.
har cīz-kō kām-mẽ lāyā jātā hai.	Everything is brought into use.
har cīz kām-mẽ lāyī jātī hai.	Everything is brought into use.
zakhmī aurat aspatāl pahõcāyī gayī.	The injured lady was taken to the hospital.
hamẽ ēk havāī • jahāz-mẽ sair karāyī gayī.	We were taken around in an airplane.
ḍākū thānē lē jāyē gayē.	The robbers were taken to the police station.
ḍākūõ-kō thānē lē jāyā gayā.	The robbers were taken to the police station.
kaī lōg bulāyē jāẽgē.	Several people will be invited.
kaī lōgõ-kō bulāyā jāēgā.	Several people will be invited.
yahā̃-par rōz khānā khāyā jātā hai.	Food is eaten here every day.

This section illustrates the Urdu construction employed to translate the English Passive. The construction is a verbal phrase consisting of the past participle of the verb and **jānā,** both forms agreeing in gender and number with the subject. For the impersonal construction the English subject is placed in the object form before **-kō** and the verb takes the masculine singular form. See sentences 4 and 11.

REMARKS: (1) **jānā,** when occurring as the first member of a verbal cluster (See Lesson 28) in this Passive construction, has the form **jāyā** for the past participle. See sentences 8 and 9, above.

(2) **kām-mẽ lānā** of sentences 4 and 5 translates **to put to use; thānē, police station,** illustrates the use of the object form without a postposition to indicate direction towards a place; **ḍākū** (ā) robber, **zakhmī (adj., n.c.)** injured.

37.1.1 Exercise 1. **Translate into English:**

1. hāthī śikāriyõ-sē pakṛā gayā. 2. jānvar śikārī-sē mārā jāēgā. 3. miṭhāī kis-sē khāyī gayī? 4. sāmān rēlgāṛī-mẽ rakhā gayā. 5. phūl masjid-kē sāmnē g̱arīb aurat-sē bēcē gayē thē. 6. ye sūkhī lakṛī aurat-kē liyē lāyī gayī thī. 7. fakīr-kō khānā diyā gayā hai. 8. ye kām kyũ nahī̃ kiyā gayā? 9. ye lakṛī kab kāṭī gayī? 10. āp-kī kitāb kab likhī jāēgī?

37.1.2 Exercise 2. **Translate into Urdu:**

1. Why hasn't my automobile been washed? 2. When had the plants been watered? 3. These clothes will be mended tomorrow. 4. The plow is being dragged by the bullocks

now. 5. How were the vegetables cooked? 6. When was my letter sent to the post office? 7. How many people will be told this story? 8. Wasn't it explained to you that the train wasn't ready to start? 9. Why wasn't my question answered? 10. The thieves were "well taken care of" at the police station.

37.2

aisā karnā acchā nahī̃.	It is not good to do thus.
har vaḳt kām karnā kisī-kē liyā acchā nahī̃.	It is not good for anybody to work all the time.
tālibilm-kē liyē paṛhnā bahot acchā hai.	It is very good for a student to study.
mujhē āj apnī fīs jamā karnā hai.	I am to pay my fees today.
aurat-kō dukān-sē kuch cīzẽ ḳharīdnā cāhiyē.	The woman should buy some things in the shop.
na har vaḳt khēlnā acchā hai na har vaḳt kām karnā.	Neither playing nor working all the time is good.
mā̃•bāp-kā kahnā mānnā har baccē-kā farz hai.	It is the duty of every child to obey his parents.
is bāg-mẽ ṭenis khēlnā manā hai.	Playing tennis is not allowed in this garden.
bagair ijāzat andar ānā manā hai.	"No Entry Without Permission."
sāikilvālō̃-kō idhar-sē guzarnā manā hai.	Cyclists are not allowed to pass this way.
kuch lōgō̃-kō āj-kā kām kal-par chōṛ dēnā pasand hai.	Some people like to put off today's work until tomorrow.
hamẽ apnē baṛō̃-kī bāt mānnā cāhiyē.	We should obey our elders.
maĩ aisā kām karnā nahī̃ pasand kartā hū̃.	I don't like to do such work.

This section and the following illustrate the infinitive in its function as a noun and adjective. (See 2.2 for the noun type.)

37.2 illustrates the infinitive functioning as a noun—i.e., occurring as subject or object of a verb. For examples of the infinitive in the object form before a postposition or postpositional phrase, see section 11.3, 14.2.1, Remarks (2), and 35.1.

37.2.1

mujhē kaī cīzẽ ḳharīdnī haĩ.	I have to buy several things.
abhī mujhē bāzār jākar cāy lānī hai.	I have yet to bring tea from the market.
sārī ḳhat-ō-kitābat eḍiṭar-kē patē-par hōnī cāhiyē.	All correspondence should be addressed to the editor.
laṛkī-kō apnī har kitāb-kī jild bā̃dhvānī cāhiyē.	The girl ought to get each of her books bound.
mujhē Vazīr-e-Āzām kī taḳrīr zarūr sunnī cāhiyē.	I should certainly hear the Prime Minister's speech.
usē apnē chōṭē bhāī-kō āvāz dēnī cāhiyē.	She ought to call her younger brother.
āp lōgō̃-kō Urdū bōlnī cāhiyē.	You people ought to speak Urdu.
dhōbī-kō kapṛē phir sāf karnē haĩ.	The washerman has to wash the clothes again.
mālī-kō paudō̃-par pānī ḍālnā hai.	The gardener has to water the plants.

These sentences illustrate the infinitive functioning as an adjective—i.e., agreeing in gender, number and form with the noun it modifies. (For the adjective type see 3.2, 4.1.2, and 6.1.)

Compare the literal translation of the first two Urdu sentences (the translated infinitive is underlined): **There are for me several things <u>to be bought.</u>** and **Having gone to the market, there is still for me tea <u>to be brought</u>.**

REMARKS: (1) **patā** (ā) address, **jild** (ī) cover, **k̤hat-ō-kitābat** (**fm. pl.**) correspondence, **eḍiṭar** (ā) editor. (2) Compare the constructions described in sections 17.1, 17.1.1, and 17.1.2 and note that this is an alternate construction for these.

37.2.2

vah śikār khēlnē gayā.	He went to hunt.
ham tairnē gayē.	We went swimming.
laṛkiyā̃ pānī lānē jāẽgī.	The girls will go to bring water.
Anvār aur maĩ sair karnē jānā cāhtā haĩ.	Anwar and I want to go for a walk.
mērē bāp apnē afsar-sē milnē daftar-mẽ dauṛē.	My father ran into the office to see one of his officers.
bahnẽ saudā k̤harīdnē gayĩ.	The sisters went shopping.
pandrā laṛkē kaśtī calānē gayē.	Fifteen boys went boating.
ham kal machliyā̃ pakaṛnē jāẽgē.	We'll go fishing tomorrow.
vo mujh-sē milnē āyā.	He came to see me.
Jamīlā mērī bahan-sē milnē āẽgī.	Jamila will come to see my sister.
mērā ēk hamjamāat mujhē kuch batānē āyā.	One of my classmates came to tell me something.
mālanẽ hamārē pās hār bēcnē āẽgī.	The flower sellers will come to sell us garlands.
mehtar galī-kī jhārū dēnē ā rahā hai.	The sweeper is coming to sweep the lane.
ham mēz-par śatranj khēlnē baiṭhē.	We sat down at the table to play chess.
ādmī mēz-par khānā khānē baiṭhēgā.	The man will sit down at the table to eat.

This section illustrates the infinitive occurring in object form without the postpositions **-kō** or **-kē liyē.** Compare section 34.1.2.

REMARKS: **hamjamāat** (ā) classmate, **saudā k̤harīdnā** to go shopping, **kaśtē calānā** to row, go boating, **jhārū dēnā** to sweep.

37.2.3

us-kō jānē dō.	Let him go.
us-kō jānē dījiyē.	(**Please**) let him go.
meharbānī karkē mujhē paṛhnē dījiyē.	(**Please**) let me read.
mujhē apnē pās baiṭhnē dījiyē.	(**Please**) let me sit near you.
baccē-kō patang uṛānē dījiyē.	(**Please**) let the child fly kites.
us-kō paṛhnē dō.	Let him study.
Hāmid aur Nargis-kō khēlnē dō.	Let Hamid and Nargis play.
mujhē pahilē kahnē dō.	Let me speak first.
us-kō andar ānē dō.	Let him (**come**) in.
ab mujhē sitār bajānē dījiyē.	(**Please**) let me play the sitār now.
bōtal ghar-mẽ rahnē dō.	Leave the bottle in the house.

sipāhī-nē riśvat lēkar cōr-kō jānē diyā.	The policeman took the bribe and let the thief go.
mā̃-nē laṛkī-kō bāhar dhūp-mē̃ khēlnē diyā.	The mother let the girl play out in the sun.
laṛkē-nē ḳhat ḍākḳhānē-mē̃ rahnē diyā.	The boy left the letter in the post office.
us-kō mat jānē dō.	Don't let him go.
us-kō andar mat ānē dō.	Don't let him (**come**) in.
us-kō bāhar dhūp-mē̃ mat khēlnē dō.	Don't let her play in the sun.
Hāśim-kō chat-par-sē pataṅg mat uṛānē dō.	Don't let Hashim fly kites from the rooftop.
mērē bāg̠-sē kisī-kō phūl mat tōṛnē dō.	Don't let anyone pick flowers from my garden.
kisī-kō tumhē̃ bēvaḳūf mat banānē dō.	Don't let anyone fool you.

The infinitive in the object form with **dēnā** translates English verbal phrases introduced by the verb **let.**

REMARKS: a **sitār** (ā) is a stringed instrument of the guitar type; **riśvat** (ī) bribe.

37.2.4 Exercise 1. **Translate into English:**

1. maĩ āj-kā kām kal-par chōṛ dēnā pasand kartā hū̃. 2. kyā tum-kō cāy banānī nahī̃ cāhiyē? 3. kaun kal mujh-sē milnē āyā? 4. kis-kō lakṛī jalānā hōgā? 5. āp-kō ye ḳhat-ō-kitābat paṛhnī cāhiyē. 6. mujhē ṭhīk ṭhīk kahānī sunānē dījiyē. 7. ham maśhūr jaghē̃ dēkhnē āyī̃. 8. aisā kām karnā muśkil hai. 9. mujhē is kitāb-kī jild bādhvānī hōgī. 10. kuttē-kō bāg̠-sē bāhar mat jānē dō! 11. afsar hal-kē istēmāl kisānō̃-kō sikhānē āyā. 12. gīlī saṛak-par mōṭar zōr-sē calānā ḳhatarnāk hai. 13. baccē-kō sabziyā̃ khānī cāhiyē̃. 14. un-kō dō dō karkē andar ānē dō. 15. ham-nē un dōnō̃-kō tarbūz ādhā ādhā karkē lēnē diyā. 16. ādmī-kō aurat-kē liyē makān banānā hōgā. 17. kārīgar-kō mōṭar-kī marammat karnī paṛtī hai. 18. maĩ sāthiyō̃-kē sāth śikār khēlnē gayā. 19. kis-nē ḳhat mēz-par rahnē diyā? 20. dōst bātē̃ karnē baiṭhē.

37.2.5 Exercise 2. **Translate into Urdu:**

1. It is not good for bullocks to work too much in the sun. 2. There are many things still to be done. 3. You'll have to go to see him. 4. Please let me sleep. 5. Too much reading is not good for the eyes. 6. You have to answer these letters. 7. He sat down to read the newspaper. 8. Don't let him go without taking the letters. 9. The washerman came to take the clothes. 10. The shoemaker has to mend these shoes. 11. Whose arrival are you waiting for? 12. Let the tired horse rest. 13. The travellers stopped to ask for cold water. 14. Why should I tell you why I came to see the magistrate? 15. I'm tired of doing this type of work. 16. Leave the baggage in the automobile. 17. You'll have to walk faster. 18. Who let the boy go to the river alone? 19. Your weeping will not help you. 20. Who will run out to call me a taxi?

37.3 Text 19. **Ḳhulafā [1] -e-Islām.**

Translate into English. Answer the questions in Urdu:

Islām ēk aisā mazhab [2] hai jis-mē̃ dīn [3] aur syāsat alahdā alahdā nahī̃. ēk acchī hakūmat-kā kāim [4] karnā aur usē jārī rakhnā [5] Musalmānō̃-kē liyē aisā farz hai jaisā ke namāz paṛhnā aur rōzā rakhnā. islāmī [6] hakūmat-kē sadr-kō ḳhalīfā [1] kahtē thē. agar-ce Islām-kī tarīḳh ḳhulafā-kē nāmō̃-sē bharī • parī [7] hai, sahī [8] manō̃-mē̃ Islām-kē ḳhulafā siraf cār thē. ye vo cār ādmī thē, jō Mohammad, Rasūl • Allah-kē bād musalmānõ-kē ḳhalifā banē. sac pūchiyē tō in-kē bād ḳhilāfat[9] ḳhatam hō gayī aur bādśāhat[10] śurū hō gayī.

āiyē, ham āp-kō in ḳhulafā-kē bārē-mẽ kuch batāẽ. jab Rasūl • Allah vafāt pā gayē. tō Musalmānõ-kō fikr huā ke ab un-kī rāhnumāī kaun karēgā. cunā̃-ce kuch Musalmān, jō Rasūl • Allah-kē sahābī[11] thē, ēk jagah jamā huē. unhõ-nē ēk sahābī-kō, jin-kā nām Abū Bakr[12] thā aur jō umr aur tajrubē[13] -mẽ ū̃cā makām[14] rakhtē thē, apnā ḳhalifā cun liyā. is majlis-mẽ bāz lōg maujūd nahī̃ thē. maslan Mohāmmad-kē dāmād[15] Alī vahā̃ na thē. Alī hamēśā Rasūl • Allah-kē dast-e-rāst[16] rahē thē. un-kā ḳhayāl thā ke Musalmān un-kō apnā ḳhalifā cunẽgē. jab un-kō mālūm huā kē un-kī gair • hāzrī-mẽ ḳhalifā cun liyā gayā hai, tō vo kuch ranjidāh[17] huē. pahilē tō unhõ-nē Abū Bakr-kō ḳhalifā mānnē-sē inkār kar diyā. lēkin che mahīnē gazarnē-kē bād unhõ-nē Abū Bakr-kē hāth-par baiat kar[18] lī. Abū Bakr zyādā dēr zindā[19] na rahē. marnē-sē kuch din pahilē unhõ-nē umr-kō apnā jānaśīn[20] mukarrar kar diyā. is dafā kōī alekśan na huā. umr-bhī Rasūl • Allah-kē sahābī thē aur Islām-kī ḳhidmat[21] -mẽ hamēśā pēś • pēś rahē thē. umr-kē zamānē-mẽ Musalmānõ-nē bahot fatūhāt[22] hāsil kī̃ aur Islām-kē jhaṇḍā[23] dūr • darāz mulkõ-mẽ lahrāyā.[24] Umr Musalmānõ-kī ḳhidmat karnā apnā farz samajhtē thē. rāt-kē vaḳt apnē ghar-sē nikalkar vo Madīnē-kī galiyõ-mẽ cakkar lagātē[25] thē. jahā̃ kahī̃[26] kisī-kō musībat-mẽ dēkhtē thē us-kī madad kartē thē. āp-kō ye jānkar śāyad hairānī hō ke us zamānē-mẽ Musalmānõ-kā ḳhalifā bilkul ām ādmiyõ-kī tarah rahtā thā. us-kō rahnē-kē liyē na kōī mahal miltā thā aur nā-hī kōī baṛī tanḳhāh. us zamānē-mẽ sab Musalmānõ-kō jō sarkārī kām kartē thē sarkārī ḳhazānē[27] -sē alauns[28] miltā thā. lēkin Umr-kā alauns ām sarkārī mulāzim[29] -kē alauns-sē zyādā na thā.

Islām-kē ḳhalifā-kē har kām-par Musalmānõ-kī nazar hōtī thī. har Musalmān-kō ye haḳ[30] thā ke ḳhalifā-ke kām • kāj-par nuktā • cinī[31] karē. is-kē ilāvā ḳhalifā-par adālat-mẽ mukaddma-bhī calāyā jā[32] saktā thā. ḳhalifā-kō sarkārī mūāmalõ-mẽ maśvarah dēnē-kē liyē ēk mustaḳil[33] majlis hōtī thī. jisē majlis-e-śūrā[34] kahtē thē.

ēk dafā-kā zikr hai ke ēk śaḳhs-nē Umr-kī adālat-mẽ apnē mālik-kē ḳhilāf mukaddma dāir kiyā.[35] Umr-nē us-kē ḳhilāf faislā sunāyā. ye śaḳhs is faislē-par bahot ḳhafā huā. ēk din ye ādmī subah subah masjid-mẽ gayā. vahā̃ Umr namāz paṛh rahē thē. us-nē ḳhanjar[36] -sē Umr-kō ḳatl kar diyā.

Islām-kē dō aur ḳhalifõ Usmān aur Alī-kā hāl[37] ham āp-kō phir kisī din sunāẽgē.

savālāt:

1. Abū Bakr kaisē ḳhalifā banē? 2. Alī-nē che mahīnē kyū̃ na Abū Bakr-kō ḳhalifā mānā? 3. Abū Bakr-nē marnē-sē pahilē kis-kō ḳhalifā mukarrar kiyā? 4. Umr rāt-kē vaḳt kahā̃ jāyā kartē thē? 5. Umr-kō kis-nē aur kyū̃ ḳatl kiyā?

NOTES: 1. caliphs (**m., pl.**), s. **ḳhalifā;** 2. religion (ā); 3. faith (ā); 4. **kāim karnā** to establish (**tr.**); 5. keep going; 6. Islamic (**adj., n.c.**); 7. full of (**adj., n.c.**); 8. true (**adj., n.c.**); 9. Caliphate (ī); 10. kingship (ā); 11. associate (ā); 12. man's name; 13. **tajrubā** experience (ā); 14. position (ā); 15. son-in-law (ā); 16. right-hand man (ā); 17. sorry (**adj., n.c.**); 18. **baiat karnā** to take allegiance (**tr.**); 19. alive (**adj., n.c.**); 20. successor (ā); 21. service (ī); 22. victories (ī, **pl.**); 23. flag (ā); 24. **lahrānā** to wave, unfurl (**tr.**); 25. **cakkar lagānā** to make rounds of (**tr.**); 26. wherever (**adv.**); 27. **ḳhazānā treasury** (ā); 28. allowance (ā); 29. servant (ā); 30. right (ā); 31. criticism (ī); 32. see 37.1; 33. permanent (**adj., n.c.**); 34. advisory council (ī); 35. presented; 36. daggar (ā); 37. = story (ā).

LESSON 38

38.1

o chōṭā-sā kuttē-kā baccā baṛā ḳhūbsūrat hai.	That (**rather**) small puppy is very pretty.
e chōṭī-sī ghaṛī baṛī ḳimtī hai.	This (**rather**) small watch is very expensive.
k chōṭē-sē pyālē-mẽ thōṛā-sā pānī lāiyē.	Please bring some water in a (**rather**) small cup.
arā-sī madad kāfī hōgī.	Just a little help will do (= **be sufficient**).
ujhē bas ēk zarā-sā ṭukṛā cāhiyē.	All I need is just a (**little**) bit.
hāzī zarā-sē tūfān-sē kabhī nahī̃ ḍartē.	Sailors are never scared of just a little storm.
ujhē thōṛā-sā dūdh, chōṭā-sā ēk rōṭī-kā ṭukṛā aur zarā-sā śahad cāhiyē.	I want some milk, a little piece of bread, and just a little honey.
s baṛē-sē makān-mẽ kaun rahtā hai?	Who lives in that (**rather**) large house?
ūraj-kē g̱arūb hōtē vaḳt zamīn-par lāl-sā raṅg chā gayā.	At sunset a reddish hue spread over the land.
ṭ ēk bhaddā-sā jānvar hai.	The camel is a (**rather**) ugly animal.
ujhē thōṛā-sā pānī dījiyē.	Please give me a little water.
ṛkī-kō thōṛē-sē paisē cāhiyẽ.	The girl needs a little money.
yā āp mērē liyē thōṛā-sā dūdh lā saktē haĩ?	Can you bring some milk for me?

The particle **-sā**, when attached to an adjective, imparts a quality of indefiniteness r vagueness to the description conveyed by the adjective. (Compare the English adjectival uffix **-ish** as in **largish, smallish.**)

38.1.1

e kaun-sā śahar hai?	What (**specific**) town is this?
aĩ kitāb kaun-sī mēz-par rakhū̃?	On which (**specific**) table should I place the book?
o kaun-sē makān-mẽ gayā?	Into which (**specific**) house did he go?
s-nē kaun-sī kitāb paṛhī?	Which (**specific**) book did he read?
p kaun-sī laṛkī-kō jāntē haĩ?	Which of the girls do you know?

vo kaun-sā muammā hai jō ustād-bhī nahī̃ hal kar saktā?	Which is the problem that even the teacher cannot solve?
usē kaun-sē phal pasand haĩ?	Which of the fruits does he like?
maĩ kaun kaun-sē fiḳrē dōhrāū̃?	Exactly which sentences should I repeat?
laṛkī kaun kaun-sē risālē ḳharīdēgī?	Exactly which magazines will the girl buy?
us-kī kaun kaun-sī sahēliyā̃ āẽgī?	Exactly which of her girl-friends will come?
āp-nē Iḳbāl-kī kaun kaun-sī kitābẽ paṛhī haĩ?	Which of Tagore's books have you read?
āp-kō Pākistān-kē kaun kaun-sē śahar zyādā pasand haĩ?	Which of Pakistan's cities do you like most?

The particle **-sā** when attached to the adjective **kaun** (see 18.2, 18.3, and 22.2) imparts a quality of specificity or particularity to its meaning. The **kaun** remains unchanged; only **-sā** agrees in gender, number, and form with the noun modified. For the repetition of **kaun** in sentences 8 to 12 see section 36.2.

Compare the literal translation of these sentences: **āp kaun-sī gāṛī-sē āyē haĩ? By which (specific) train have you come?** and **āp kis gāṛī-sē āyē haĩ? By which train (in general) have you come?**

38.1.2 Exercise 1. **Translate into English:**

1. mērē ḳhayāl-mẽ ye chōṭī-sī sabziyā̃ mahẽgī haĩ. 2. zarā-sā bāriś khētī-kē liyē kabhī kāfī pānī nahī̃ dētā hai. 3. āp-nē kaun-sī kitāb-mẽ ye kahānī likhī? 4. kaun kaun-sē kamrē mērē haĩ? 5. Pākistān-mẽ kaĩ baṛē-sē śahar haĩ. 6. ye ū̃cī-sī imārat kyā hai? 7. āp kaun kaun-sē risālē paṛhtē haĩ? 8. gahrā pānī kālē-sē rañg-kā mālūm paṛtā hai. 9. maĩ kaun-sī saṛak-par jāū̃gā? 10. mujhē kaun kaun-sī jaghẽ pahilē dēkhnā cāhiyẽ?

38.1.3 Exercise 2. **Translate into Urdu:**

1. These rather small vegetables are expensive. 2. Where does this rather narrow street go? 3. Which mechanic fixed this? 4. I need a rather large automobile for travelling. 5. Exactly which places of Pakistan had you seen? 6. Isn't this razor rather sharp? 7. Exactly which letters did you write? 8. Which book of mine did you read? 9. These clothes seem rather dirty. 10. Exactly which things will I need for my journey?

38.2

jaisā vo, vaisā us-kā bhāī.	As he is, so is his brother.
jaisā bāp, vaisā bēṭā.	As is the father, so is the son.
jaisī mā̃, vaisī bēṭī.	As is the mother, so is the daughter.
jaisī mā̃, vaisā bēṭā.	As is the mother, so is the son.
kisān khēt-mẽ jaisā kām kartā hai, vaisā-hī us-sē fāydā uṭhātā hai.	As the farmer works in the field, so he reaps his harvest.
jaisī kahānī us-nē mujhē sunāyī, vaisī-hī maĩ āp-kō sunāū̃gā.	I will tell you the same (**type of**) story he told me.
jaisī kitāb āp-nē pichlē sāl likhī, kyā vaisī-hī āp likh rahē haĩ?	Are you writing the same (**type of**) book as you wrote last year?
jaisī cīzẽ mā̃ bēṭī-kē liyē bāzār-sē lāyī, vaisī-hī bēṭē-kē liyē lāēgī.	The mother will bring back the son the same (**type of**) things from the bazaar as she brought her daughter.

jaisā kām tum-nē mērē dōst-kē liyē kiyā, vaisā-hī mērē liyē karō.	Do the same (**type of**) work for me as you did for my friend.
jaisē kapṛē maĩ-nē kal yahā̃ ḳharīdē, vaisē-hī maĩ cāhtā hū̃.	I want the same (**type of**) clothes as I bought here yesterday.

These sentences illustrate the construction with the relative adjective **jaisā, which sort,** and its correlative **vaisā, that sort.**

Compare, also, sections 25.1 and 27.3.

38.2.1

jaisē us-nē mujhē kahānī sunāyī, vaisē-hī maĩ āp-kō sunāū̃gā.	I will tell you the story just as he told it to me.
jaisā bāp-nē us-sē kahā, vaisā-hī bēṭē-nē kiyā.	The son did exactly as his father told him.
jaisē maĩ-nē baṛhaī-sē kahā, vaisē-hī us-nē kursī-kī marammat kī.	The carpenter fixed the chair just as I told him.
jaisē mā̃ sikhātī hai, vaisē-hī baccē sīkhtē haĩ.	As the mother teaches, so the children learn.
jaisā karōgē, vaisā bharōgē.	As you act, so will you suffer.
jaisā maĩ batāū̃, vaisā kījiyē.	Please do as I say.
jaisē āp-nē batāyā, vaisē-hī us-nē kiyā.	He did as you said.
jaisē tum-nē mērē dōst-kē liyē kām kiyā, vaisē-hī mērē liyē karō.	Work for me exactly as you worked for my friend.

These sentences illustrate the construction with the relative adverb **jaisē, as, according as, in the manner which,** and its correlative **vaise, so, in that manner.** The subject singular masculine forms **jaisā** and **vaisā** often occur as adverbs. (See sentences 2, 5, and 6.) Compare sections 26.3 and 27.1.

38.2.2

āp kaisā kām kartē haĩ?	What work do you do?
ye kaisā risālā hai?	What magazine is this?
us-nē kaisī fazūl bātē̃ sunāyī̃?	What useless things he said!
āp-kē pās kaisī ciṭṭhiyā̃ haĩ?	What letters do you have?

These sentences illustrate the interrogative adjective **kaisā, what sort.**

38.2.3 Exercise 1. **Translate into English:**

1. āp-kī tabīyat kaisī hai? 2. jaisī bāt āp-nē dēkhī, kyā vaisī-hī āp mujhē batā rahē haĩ? 3. us-nē kahā ke jaisē us-nē bāt dēkhī, vaisē-hī vo hamē̃ batāēgā. 4. jaisā kām, vaisā fāydā. 5. āp-kō ghar-sē kaisī ciṭṭhī milī? 6. jaisē maĩ-nē batāyā, vaisē āp-nē kyū̃ nahī̃ kiyā? 7. āp kaisē haĩ? 8. jaisā bāvarcī, vaisā khānā. 9. āp kaisē risālē lāyē? 10. tum kaisā kām kar saktē hō?

38.2.4 Exercise 2. **Translate into Urdu:**

1. How are the people at home? 2. What (**sort of**) building is that? 3. As is the tailor so will the clothes be. 4. Tell me the story just as you heard it. 5. What sort of driver are you? 6. The farmer uses his plow just as the government officer taught him. 7. De-

scribe the building to me just as you saw it. 8. What sort of crop does this field have? 9. Drive the automobile just as I told you. 10. What sort of room did you give me?

38.3

klās-mẽ jitnē tālibīlm thē, sab-kē sab bāhar jānā cāhtē thē.	As many students as were in the class, (**they**) all wanted to go out.
ghar-mẽ jitnē lōg haĩ, sab-kē sab giniyē.	Count as many people as are in the house.
lāibrērī-mẽ jitnī kitābẽ thĩ, sab-kī sab Añgrēzī-mẽ thĩ.	As many books as were in the library, all were in English.
ciṛiyāghar-mẽ jitnē jānvar thē, sab-kē sab lōgõ-par hãsē.	As many animals as were in the zoo, all laughed at the people.

These sentences illustrate English relative constructions the relative clause of which contains the adjective phrase **as many . . . as,** the correlative of which is the word **all.**

Compare sections 27.3, 27.4, and 27.5.

38.4

taḳrīban ēk•sau•paccās ādmī kārḳhānē-mẽ thē.	Nearly one hundred and fifty men were in the factory.
taḳrīban sab mehmān ā cukē haĩ.	Almost all the guests have arrived.
taḳrīban pãc bajē haĩ.	It is almost five o'clock.
taḳrīban sārē Balōcī Musalmān haĩ.	Nearly all Baluchis are Moslems.
vo buṛhiyā taḳrīban āṭh darzan anḍē ḳharīdnā cāhtī hai.	That little old lady wants to buy nearly eight dozen eggs.

These sentences illustrate the translation into Urdu of English phrases introduced by the words, **nearly, almost.**

38.5

kōī ēk sau sāl pahilē ēk faiyāz navāb hamārē mulk-mẽ hakūmat kartā thā.	About a hundred years ago a generous prince ruled over our country.
kōī das minaṭ huē ēk ḳhatūn idhar-sē guzrī thī.	About ten minutes ago a lady had passed this way.
kōī bīs sāl-mẽ duniyā-kā naḳśā-hī badal cukā hōgā.	In about two decades the map of world will have changed.
āj-sē kōī ēk sāl bād maĩ Sindh-mẽ hũgī.	About a year from now I shall be in Sindh.
gāṛī kōī sāt minaṭ-mẽ yahā̃ pahõcēgī.	The train will arrive here in about seven minutes.

These sentences illustrate the translation into Urdu of English phrases introduced by the word **about** (= **approximately**).

38.6 Text 20. **Mērē Dōst.**

Translate into English. Answer the questions in Urdu:

Ḳhudā-kē fazal [1] -sē mujhē dōstō̃-kī kamī kabhī nahī̃ mahsūs [2] huī. bāz lōgō̃-kī ye ḳhāhiś [3] rahtī hai ke kōī un-kā dōst banē, lēkin un-kō kōī dōst nahī̃ miltā. yahā̃ ulṭā [4] mūāmalā hai. kaī dafā kōśiś kartā hū̃ ke dōstō̃-kī tadād kuch ghaṭ jāē.[5] lēkin ye ḳhāhiś kabhī pūrī nahī̃ huī. yā tō mujh-mē̃ kōī aisī ḳhūbī hai ke, jō ēk dafā dōst ban jāē, vo phir pīchā chōṛnē [6] -kā nām nahī̃ lētā. yā phir mērā dōstō̃-mē̃ kōī aisī bāt hai ke maĩ un-sē pīchā chuṛānē-kī ṭhīk tarah kōśiś-hī nahī̃ kartā. bahar • hāl, ab-mē̃ śāyad-hī kōī mulk hōgā jahā̃ mērā kōī dōst nahī̃. āp pūchē̃gē ke agar aisā hai tō rōnā kis bāt-kā hai? dōst tō Ḳhudā-kī ēk nemat [7] hai. muśkil-kē vaḳt kām ātē haĩ. sāhab, maĩ ab āp-kō kaisē samjhāū̃ ke kabhī kabhī zyādā dōst musībat ban jātē haĩ. mērī muśkil-kā sahī andāzā [8] lagānē-kē liyē āp-kō mērē kuch dōstō̃-sē milnā paṛēgā. āiyē, āp-sē un-kā taāruf [9] karvāū̃. in-sē miliyē. ye Jamīl Ḳhā̃ [10] haĩ. ham • lōg in-kō Jē.Kē.[11] kahtē haĩ. ye hazrat baṛē paṛhē • likhē ādmī haĩ. bal-ke sac ye hai ke kuch zarūrat-sē zyādā paṛhē • likhē haĩ. mērē bacpan-kē dōst haĩ. ham dōnō̃ pahilē skūl aur phir kālij-mē̃ ēk sāth paṛhē. Jē.Kē mujhē bahot azīz [12] jāntē haĩ. mērē pās baiṭhkar ḳhuś hōtē haĩ. maĩ-bhī un-kī sohbat [13] -kō pasand kartā hū̃. lēkin is bāt-kā kyā ilāj ke khaṛē khaṛē [14] lōgō̃-kī bēizzatī [15] kar dētē haĩ. andhē [16] -kō andhā aur bēvaḳūf-kō us-kē mū̃h-par bēvaḳūf kah dētē haĩ aur is tarah mahfil-kā raṅg bigaṛ dētē haĩ.[17] kaī dafā samjhāyā hai, lēkin ye hazrat apnī ādat nahī̃ chōṛēgē. ab āp-hī insāf kījiyē ke aisē dōst-kā kyā kiyā jāē.

lījiyē ab in-sē miliyē. in-kā nām Śaukat [10] hai. Śaukat • Sāhab umr-mē̃ mujh-sē kōī dō cār sāl baṛē haĩ. yūnivarsiṭī-mē̃ paṛhātē haĩ. apnē mazmūn-mē̃ baṛē allāmā [18] haĩ. ādmī-kē sīnē [19] -mē̃ bhēṛ [20] -kā dil hai. in-kī tārif kījiyē tō ḳhuś aur agar kabhī in-kī bāt kaṭiyē [21] tō bas phir dō mahīnē-kē liyē in-kī zabān band hō jātī hai. agar in-sē mazāḳ [22] kījiyē tō śarm-sē in-kā mū̃h lāl hō jātā hai. ḳissā muḳhtasar [23] ye, ke cār yārō̃-mē baiṭhē hō, tō kisī kām-kē nahī̃.

ab āp-kō Nasīm • Sāhab [10] -sē milāē̃. ye-bhī ēk kālij-mē̃ paṛhātē haĩ. acchē ḳhuś • śakl ādmī haĩ. dō mahīnē huē inhō̃-nē śādī kī hai. in-kō apnī bīvī-sē bahot muhabbat hai. lēkin vo kabhī ye nahī̃ sōctē ke hamē̃ un-kī bīvī-sē kōī ḳhās dilcaspī nahī̃. jab miltē haĩ tō apnī bīvī-kī tārīf-mē̃ ēk dāstān-e-Aliflailā [24] bayān kartē haĩ. un-sē kaī bātē̃ karnē-kō jī cāhtā hai. lēkin vo apnī bīvī-kī tārīf-sē-hī nahī̃ fārig [25] hōtē. aur agar kabhī bīvī-kā zikr ḳhatam karē̃gē tō apnē hōnēvālē baccē-kā zikr śurū kar dē̃gē.

acchā ab āp-kō Manzūr • Miyā̃ [10] -sē milāē̃. ye baṛē ḳhuś • mizāj ādmī haĩ. kisī-kā dil nahī̃ dukhātē.[26] kisī-kī burāī nahī̃ kartē. in-kī āvāz baṛī surīlī [27] hai. gātē haĩ tō sunnēvālō̃-kā dil mōh lētē [28] haĩ. āp pūchē̃gē ke agar in-mē̃ ye sab ḳhūbiyā̃ haĩ tō phir kam-az-kam in-sē kōī śikāyat nahī̃ hōnī cāhiyē. sāhab, kāś [29] ke aisā hōtā. lēkin yahā̃-bhī ēk baṛī muśkil hai. Ḳhudā-nē in hazrat-kō zarūrtē̃ dī haĩ. zyādā aur paisā diyā hai kam. ab bāz lōgō̃-kā tō ye asūl hōtā hai ke jitnī cādar [30] hō utnē pāvō̃ phailātē haĩ. lēkin in-kā asūl tō ye hai ke pāvō̃, tō phailāō pūrē [31] aur, agar cādar kāfī na hō, tō hamsāyē-sē mā̃g lō. dusrē lafzō̃-mē̃ in-kō ādat hai ḳarz lēnē kī. maĩ ye sāf kar dū̃ ke mērē ḳhayāl-mē̃ ḳarz lēnē-mē̃ kōī ḳharābī nahī̃. sārī dunyā kabhī-na-kabhī [32] ḳarz lētī hai. lēkin hamārē ye dōst ḳarz lēkar phir vāpas karnē-kā kabhī nām nahī̃ lētē. āp pūchē̃gē ke aisī sūrat-mē̃ lōg in-kō̃ ḳarz kyū̃ dētē haĩ. maĩ aur lōgō̃-kē bārē-mē̃ tō kuch nahī̃ kah saktā. lēkin mujh-sē vo aisē ḍrāmāī [33] andāz [34] -mē̃ ḳarz-kī bāt kartē haĩ ke inkār karnā muśkil hō jātā hai. maslan itvār-kē din subah subah darvāzē-kī ghanṭī bajtī hai. maĩ abhī bistar-mē̃-hī hōtā hū̃. vo ātē-hī aisē vaḳt haĩ, jab mērā ghar hōnā yaḳīnī[35] hō. ḳhair naukar ākar mujhē jagātā hai aur us-kē pīchē pīchē Manzūr • Sāhab-bhī namūdār hōtē[36] haĩ. salām duā-kē bād vo mērē pās-hī kursī lēkar baiṭh jātē haĩ. baṛī muhabbat-sē mērā hāl pūchtē haĩ. mērī sehat-kē bārē-mē̃ apnā fikr zāhir kartē haĩ. mujhē kām zyādā karnē-par malāmat kartē[37] haĩ. itnē-mē̃[38] naukar cāy lēkar ātā hai. maĩ cāy pītā hū̃ aur Manzūr • Sāhab-bhī mērē isrār[39] -par ēk pyālā lē lētē haĩ. cāy pītē pītē vo ēk • dam ṭhanḍī āhē̃[40] bharnā[41] śurū kar dētē haĩ. cehrā ġamgīn nazar ātā hai. kabhī vo apnē bāl khē̃ctē haĩ aur kabhī apnē māthē-par hāth phērtē haĩ. agar-ce maĩ un-kī taklīf-kō fauran samajh jātā hū̃, lēkin phir-bhī mujhē un-sē pūchnā paṛtā hai, ke un-kō kyā nayī muśkil paṛī hai. is-kē bād vo ēk lambī taḳrīr kartē haĩ. mērī tārīf kartē haĩ. apnī bad • ḳismatī[42] -kī śikāyat kartē haĩ. apnē baccē-kī bīmārī aur ḍākṭar-kē bil-kā zikr kartē haĩ. ye zikr kartē kartē un-kī ā̃khō̃-mē̃ ā̃sū ā jātē haĩ. ab āp-hī insāf kījiyē ke aisī sūrat-mē maĩ sivāē[43] un-kō karz dēnē-kē aur kyā kar saktā hū̃?

ye mērē dōstō̃-kā ḳissā hai. ye sab lōg mujhē pyārē haĩ. mērē liyē inhē̃ chōṛnā-bhī muśkil hai, lēkin maĩ in-sē taṅg-bhī hū̃.[44] kyā karū̃? kyā na karū̃? śāyad isī tarah un-kī aur mērī umr guzar jāēgī.

savālāt:

1. Jē.Kē.-sē mujhē kyā śikāyat hai? 2. Śaukat • Sāhab kyā kām kartē haĩ? 3. Nasīm • Sāhab apnī bīvī-kē bārē-mē̃ kyā kahtē haĩ? 4. Manzūr • Miyā-mē̃ kyā ḳharābī haĩ? 5. Manzūr • Miyā-kē ḳarz mā̃gnē-kā kyā tarīkā hai? 6. āp-kē ḳhayāl-mē̃ mujh-mē̃ kyā ḳharābī haĩ?

NOTES: 1. grace, kindness (ā); 2. experience (ā); 3. desire (ī); 4. opposite (**adj.**); 5. **ghaṭ jānā** to decrease (**int.**); 6. **pīchā chōṛnā** to abandon, leave (**tr.**); 7. blessing (ī); 8. estimate (ā); 9. introduction (ī); 10. man's name; 11. J.K.; 12. dear (**adj., n.c.**); 13. company (ī); 14. without hesitation, immediately; 15. insult (ī); 16. **andhā** blind (**adj.**); 17. **mahfil-kā raṅg bigaṛ dētā hai** = spoils the party; 18. knowledgeable (**adj., n.c.**); 19. **sīnā** chest, breast (ā); 20. lamb (ā); 21. **bāt kāṭnā** contradict (**tr.**); 22. joke (ā); 23. brief, short (**adj., n.c.**); 24. stories from the Arabian Nights (ī); 25. finished (**adj., n.c.**); 26. hurt (**tr.**); 27. musical (**adj.**); 28. **mōh lēnā** to captivate (**tr.**); 29. = I wish; 30. sheet (ī); 31. fully (**adv.**); 32. somehow or other (**adv.**); 33. dramatic (**adj., n.c.**); 34. manner (ā); 35. sure, certain (**adj., n.c.**); 36 appears; 37. to rebuke (**tr.**); 38. meanwhile; 39. insistence (ā); 40. **āh** sigh (ī); 41. **bharnā** to heave (e.g. sighs) (**tr.**); 42. misfortune (ī); 43. besides, except (**adv.**); 44. = I am annoyed with him.

LESSON 39

RURAL ECONOMIC SURVEY QUESTIONNAIRE:

39.1 Questions Directed to Householder:

is gāō̃-kā nām kyā hai?	What is the name of this village?
kunbē-kē sarbarah-kā nām kyā hai?	What is the name of the head of the family?
āp-kā pēśā kyā hai?	What is your occupation?
āp dūsrā kyā kām kartē haī?	What other work do you do?
agar kām ghar-mē̃ kiyā jātā hai, tō sāl-kē kitnē mahinē lagtē haī?	If the work is done at home, how many months of the year does it take?
jab khētō̃-mē̃ kām nahī̃ rahtā, tab kyā kunbē-kā kōī śaḳhs gāō̃-kē bāhar kamānē-kē liyē jātā hai?	Where there is no work in the field, does any person from the family go out of the village to earn a living?
vo kitnē din bāhar rahtā hai?	How long does he remain away?
agar kunbē-kē kōī ādmī kamānē-kē liyē bāhar jātē haī, tō vo kahā̃ jātē haī?	If any members of the family go out to earn, where do they go?
vo kyā kartē haī?	What are they doing?
vo kitnā kamātē haī?	How much do they earn?

39.2 Family:

is kunbē-mē̃ kitnē śaḳhs haī?	How many persons are there in this family?
kitnē ādmī haī?	How many males?
kitnē aurtē̃ haī?	How many females?
un-kī kyā umr hai?	What is the age of each?
kitnē lōg khēt-mē̃ kām kartē haī?	How many people work in the field?
kitnē ghar-mē̃ rahtē haī?	How many stay at home?
kitnē paṛhnā likhnā jāntē haī?	How many know how to read and write.
kyā kōī hisāb rakh saktā hai?	Can anyone keep accounts?
kātnā kaun jāntā hai?	Who knows how to spin?
dhunnā kaun jāntā hai?	Who knows how to card?

39.3 Land:

kyā āp apnī zamīn-kē mālik haī?	Do you own your land?
kyā āp-kī zamīn kirāyē-par hai?	Do you rent your land?
kyā āp-kī zamīn baṭvārē-par hai?	Is your land on cropshare?

kyā āp-kī zamīn-kē pās rahan hai?	Does anyone hold a mortgage on your land?
kyā āp-nē apnī zamīn kisī-sē kirāyē-par lī hai?	Do you rent your land from anyone?
kyā āp-nē apnī zamīn baṭvārē-par lī hai?	Do you rent your land on cropshare?
kyā kisī-kī zamīn āp-nē girvī̃ rakh rakhī hai?	Do you hold a mortgage on anyone's land?
āp-kī zamīn-kā kaun-sā hissā g̱air·mazrūā hai?	What part of your land is fallow land?
āp-kī zamīn-kā kaun-sā hissā carāgāh hai?	What part of your land is grazing land?
āp-kī zamīn-kā kitnā hissā kāśt-kē ḳabil hai?	How much of your land is fit for cultivation?
kitnī zamīn gā̃õ-mẽ hai?	How much of the land is in the village?
kitnī zamīn gā̃õ-kē bāhar hai?	How much of the land is outside the village?
āp apnī zamīn paṭē-par kyū̃ dētē hai?	Why do you lease your land?
zamīn-par mālguzārī kaun dētā hai?	Who pays the land revenue on the land?
bīj kaun dētā hai?	Who furnishes the seed?
āp bīj kahā̃-sē lētē haĩ?	Where do you get the seeds?
jab fasal bāṭṭī hai, tō kyā pahilē bīj nikāl liyā jātē haĩ?	When the harvest is divided, is a quantity for seed taken out?
kyā kuch aur-bhī nikālā jātā hai?	In anything else taken out?
kyā sirf ḳhās paidāvār-hī bāṭṭī hai?	Are only the main crops divided?
kyā fasal bōnā cāhiyē, ye kaun faislā kartā hai?	Who decides what crops should be sown?
kyā zamīn-kā mālik kisān-kī madad kartā hai?	Does the owner of the land help the cultivator?
āp kis tarah-kī zamīn-par khētī kartē haĩ?	What kind of land do you cultivate?
kyā vo cāval-kī zamīn hai?	Is it rice land?
kyā vo sūkhī zamīn hai?	Is it dry land?
kyā āp-kō pānī-kā ṭaiks alag dēnā paṛtā hai?	Do you have to pay extra water tax?
kyā āp kuẽ-sē zamīn-kī ābpāśī kartē haĩ?	Do you irrigate the land by well?
kyā āp nahar-sē zamīn-kī ābpāśī kartē haĩ?	Do you irrigate the land by canal?
khētī-kī zamīn kitnē hissõ-mẽ bā̃ṭī jātī hai?	Into how many pieces is the land under cultivation divided?
har·ēk hissē-kā kitnā raḳbā hai?	What is the area of each piece?

39.4 Land Revenue and Taccavi:

kyā āp ṭhīk vaḳt-par mālguzārī dētē haĩ?	Do you pay the land revenue punctually?
mālguzārī kis tarah jamā kī jātī hai?	How is the land revenue collected?
mālguzārī-kē liyē rupayā kaisē ātā hai?	How is the money for the land revenue obtained?
kyā bacī huī fasal bēcī jātī hai?	Is surplus produce sold?
kyā āp rupayā udhār lētē haĩ?	Do you borrow money?
kyā āp-nē kabhī-bhī anjumān-e-imdād-e-bāhmī-sē rupayā udhār liyā hai?	Have you ever borrowed money from co-operative societies?

kyā pichlē pā̃c sālō̃-mē̃ jō rupayā āp-nē mālguzārī-kā diyā, vo āp-kō vāpas milā?	During the past five years, have you returned money paid for land revenue?
rupayā kyū̃ vāpas diyā gayā?	Why was the money returned?
pichle pā̃c sālō̃-mē̃ sarkār-sē kitnī takāvī lī gayī?	How much taccavi has been taken from the Government during the past five years?
kab aur kitnī?	When and why?
kyā vo kuē̃ khōdnē-kē liyē lī gayī?	Was it taken for digging wells?
kyā vo mavēśī ḳharīdnē-kē liyē lī gayī?	Was it taken for purchasing cattle?
kyā vo bīj ḳharīdnē-kē liyē lī gayī?	Was it taken for purchasing seeds?
kyā āp-nē takāvī-kī kist barābar adā kī?	Have you paid the installments of taccavi regularly?
āp-nē vo kis tarah cukāyī?	How did you pay them?
kyā āp-kī kōī jāyadād bēcī yā lē lī gayī?	Was any of your property taken and sold?
sarkār-kī kitnī taḳāvī abhī g̱air·adāśudā baḳī hai?	How much of the Government taccavi is remaining (**unpaid**) at present?

39.5 Cattle:

āp-kē pas kitnē tarah-kē mavēśī haī?	How many kinds of cattle do you own?
kitnē bail haī?	How many bullocks?
kitnī gāyē̃ haī?	How many cows?
kitnī bhāisē̃ haī?	How many buffaloes?
in mē̃-sē kitnī āp-nē ḳharīdī̃?	How many of each of these have you bought?
kitnē paidā huē thē?	How many were born?
kitnē bēcē gayē?	How many were sold?
kitnē mar gayē?	How many died?
kitnē uplē banāyē gayē?	How many dung-cakes are made?
kitnē istēmāl kiyē gayē?	How many are used?
kitnē bēcē gayē?	How many are sold?
kitnī gāṛī khād jamā kī gayī?	How many cartloads of manure are collected?
kitnī istēmāl gayī̃?	How many are used?
kitnī bēcī gayī̃?	How many are sold?

39.6 Income and Expenditure:

kyā āp apnī kōī paidāvār bēctē haī?	Do you sell any of your agricultural products?
dūdh bēckar āp kitnī āmdanī paidā kartē haī?	How much income do you get from selling milk?
kyā āp bailgāṛī kirāyē-par lētē haī?	Do you hire bullock-carts?
is-sē āp-kō kitnī āmdanī hōtī hai?	How much income do you get from this?
mazdūrī-sē āp-kō kitnī āmdanī hōtī hai?	How much income do you get from personal labor?
sabziyō̃ āmō̃ aur dūsrē phalō̃-kē bēcnē-sē āp-kō kitnī āmdanī hōtī hai?	How much income do you get from the sale of vegetables, mangoes and other fruits?

daraḳhtō̃-kē bēcnē-sē āp-kō kitnē paisē miltē haĩ?	How much money do you get from the sale of trees?
khād-kē bēcnē-sē āp-kō kitnē paisē miltē haĩ?	How much money do you get from the sale of manure?
jab kunbē-kē sab ādmī kām kartē haĩ, tō kitnā paisā ātā hai?	How much money comes into the family when all the members work?
āp apnē bailō̃-par kitnā paisā ḳharc kartē haĩ?	How much money do you spend on your bullocks?
āp jōtnē, bōnē, rūī jamā karnē, fasal kāṭnē, ghās kāṭnē, mā̃ḍnē, sī̃cnē, vaġairā-kē liyē kyā dētē haĩ?	How much money do you pay for ploughing, sowing, picking cotton, cutting crops, cutting grass, threshing, watering, and so on?
āp bīj-kē liyē kyā dētē haĩ?	How much do you pay for seed?
āp khād-kē liyē kyā dētē haĩ?	How much do you pay for manure?
āp auzārō̃-kī marammat-kē liyē kyā dētē haĩ?	How much do you pay for repairing tools?
āp kitnā kirāyā dētē haĩ?	How much rent do you pay?
āp-kō mālguzārī aur pānī-kē ṭaiks-kē liyē kitnā dēnā paṛtā hai?	How much do you have to pay for land revenue and water tax?
āp dūdh, ghī, tēl, namak, masālē, guṛ, śakkar, cāy, vaġairā-kē liyē kyā dētē haĩ?	How much do you pay for milk, ghee, oil, salt, spices, gur, sugar, tea, and so on?
āp kapṛō̃-kē liyē kyā dētē haĩ?	How much do you pay for clothes?
kyā āp khaddar pahantē haĩ?	Do you use khaddar?
us-kī kyā ḳīmat hai?	How much does it cost?
āp jūtē-kē liyē kyā dētē haĩ?	How much do you pay for shoes?
āp bistar-kē liyē kyā dētē haĩ?	How much do you pay for bedding?
āp-kē miṭṭī-kē bartanō̃-kā kitnā ḳharc hai?	What is the cost of your earthen vessels?
āp-kē ī̃dhan-kā kitnā ḳharc hai?	What is the cost of your fuel?
kyā āp bahot lakṛī istēmāl kartē haĩ?	Do you use much wood?
kyā āp bahot miṭṭī-kā tēl istēmāl kartē haĩ?	Do you use much kerosene?
āp-kē ghar-kī marammat-kā kyā ḳharc hai?	What is the cost of repairs to your house?
davāiyō̃-kā kyā ḳharc hai?	What is the cost of medicine?
kyā āp-nē rupayā udhār liyā hai?	Have you borrowed money?
kisī mahājan-sē?	From a moneylender?
kisī baink-sē?	From a bank?
kisī anjumān-e-imdād-e-bāhmī-sē?	From a cooperative society?
āp har sāl kitnā sūd dētē haĩ?	What interest do you pay per year?
āp karz kis tarah adā kartē haĩ?	How do you pay off the debt?
kyā āp kisī anjumān-e-imdād-e-bāhmī-kē maimbar haĩ?	Are you a member of a cooperative society?
āp-kā kitnā rupayā anjumān-mē̃ jamā hai?	What deposit do you have in the society?
pichlē sāl kyā āp-nē apnī zamīn-kā kuch hissā bēcā?	In the past year have you sold any part of your land?
kyā āp-nē pichlē sāl apnē kōī ghar bēcē?	In the past year have you sold any houses?
kyā kōī ghanē bēcē?	Have you sold any ornaments?

kyā pichlē das sālō̃-mē̃ āp-nē kam zamīn jōtī?	In the past ten years has cultivation of crops decreased?
kyā āp-kō nayē auzārō̃-sē kuch fāidā huā?	Have you found any advantage in the use of new implements?
kyā āp-kō nayē auzārō̃-sē nuksān huā?	Have you found any disadvantage in the use of new implements?
gāõ-mē̃ āp-nē kis tarah-kē bīj istēmāl kiyē haĩ?	What kinds of seeds have been used in the village?
kyā āp-kō Mehekmā-e-zirāat-sē madad miltī hai?	Do you get help from the Agricultural Department?

39.7 Canal and Well Irrigation:

āp-kō apnī fasal-kē liyē pānī kuõ-ya nahrō̃-sē miltā hai?	Do you get water for your crops from wells or canals?
kuõ-sē āp kaun-sī fasal-kī ābpāśī kartē haĩ?	Which crops do you irrigate by wells?
kaun-sī fasal-kī ābpāśī āp nahrō̃-sē kartē haĩ?	Which crops do you irrigate by canals?
kyā āp-kō nahar-kā kāfī pānī miltā hai?	Do you get enough canal water?
āp-kē pās is vaḳt kitnē kuē̃ haĩ?	How many wells do you have now?
āp-kē pās das sāl pahilē kitnē kuē̃ thē?	How many wells did you have ten years ago?

39.8 Market:

kisān apnī paidāvār kis tarah bēctē haĩ?	How do the farmers sell their crops?
kaun is paidāvār-kō ḳharīdtā hai?	Who buys the crops?
kaun is-kē dām muḳarrar kartā hai?	Who fixes the price?
kyā bāzār pās-hī hai?	Is the market nearby?
sab-sē pās-kē bāzār-sē gāõ kitnī dūr hai?	How far is the village from the nearest market?
kyā kisān vahā̃ paidāvār bēcnē jātā hai?	Does the farmer go there to sell his crop?
kyā ḳharīdār gāõ-mē̃ paidāvār ḳharīdnē ātā hai?	Does the buyer come to the village to buy the crop?
kyā kisān-kō kisī-kō kamiśan dēnā paṛtā hai?	Does the farmer have to pay anyone commission?
kisān apnī paidāvār bāzār-mē̃ kaisē lātā hai?	How does the farmer bring his crop to the market?
ṭrak-sē?	By truck?
bail • gāṛī-sē?	By bullock-cart?

39.9 Industry:

gāõ-mē̃ kyā sanatē̃ haĩ?	What industries are there in the village?
kyā kōī kohlū, āṭē-kī cakkiyā̃, cāval-kī maśīn cīnī-kī milē̃ yā bhaṭṭhā haĩ?	Are there any oil mills, flour mills, rice mills, sugar crushing, brick making?
sab-sē purānī sanatē̃ kaun-sī haĩ?	Which are the oldest industries?

kyā kōī sanatē̃ band huī̃.	Have any industries stopped?
kyā gāō̃-mē̃ kōī baṛhaī aur lōhār haī?	Are there any carpenters and blacksmiths in this village?
kyā un-kō paisō̃-mē̃ mazdūrī dī jātī hai?	Are they paid in cash?
kyā kōī camār haī?	Are there any shoe repairmen?
kyā vo murdā jānvārō̃-kī khāl utārtē haī?	Do they skin dead animals?
vo haḍḍiyō̃ aur gośt-kā kyā kartē haī?	What do they do with the bones and flesh?
kyā gāō̃-mē̃ kōī carkhā calāyā jātā hai?	Are any spinning wheels in use in the village?
kitnē?	How many?
kitnē karghē istēmāl kiyē jātē haī?	How many looms are in use?
hāth-kā bunā huā kitnā sūt aur mil-kā bunā huā kitnā sūt banāyā jātā hai?	How much handspun yarn is made and how much millspun yarn?
kapṛā kahā̃ bēcā jātā hai?	Where is the cloth sold?

39.10 Miscellaneous:

pīnē-kē pānī-kē kitnē kuē̃ gāō̃-mē̃ haī?	How many wells for drinking water are there in the village?
kyā kōī tālāb haī?	Are there any tanks?
vo kis-kē haī?	To whom do they belong?
sab-sē nazdīk-kā daryā gāō̃-sē kitnā dūr hai?	How far is the nearest river from the village?
bīmār lōgō̃-kī kaun dēkhbhāl kartā hai?	Who tends to sick people?
kaun-sī bīmāriyā̃ bahot ām haī?	Which diseases are most common?
kyā gāō̃-mē̃ kōī skūl hai?	Is there any school in the village?
vo kis klās-tak hai?	To which grade does it teach?
kitnē ustād haī?	How many teachers are there?
kitnē tālibilm haī?	How many students are there?
skul calānē-kā sālānā ḳharc kyā hai?	What is the cost for conducting the school per year?
rupayā kahā̃-sē ātā hai?	From where does the money come?
skūl kahā̃ lagtā hai?	Where is the school held?
gāō̃-mē̃ kyā kōī śarāb-kī dukān hai?	Is there a liquor shop within the village?
idhar udhar safar karnē-kē jānē-kē kyā zariyē haī?	What are the means of transportation?
gāō̃-sē rēl-kā sṭēśan kitnī dūr hai?	How far is the railway station from the village?
gāō̃-sē pakkī saṛak kitnī dūr hai?	How near is the metalled road to the village?
kyā kōī carāgāhē̃ haī?	Are there any pasture lands?
gāō̃-kā ḍākḳhānā kahā̃ vāḳē hai?	Where is the village post office located?
mavēśiyō̃-kī bīmāriyō̃-kā kaun ilāj kartā hai?	Who treats diseases of cattle?
pichlē pā̃c sālō̃-mē̃ gāō̃-mē̃ kitnī mautē̃ aur paidāiśē̃ huī̃?	How many births and deaths have occurred in the village in the past five years?

ichlē das sālō̃-mē̃ kitnē kunbō̃-nē gā̃ō̃ chōṛā?	During the past ten years how many families have left the village?
o kahā̃ gayē?	Where have they gone?
o kyū̃ gayē?	Why have they left?
ā̃ō̃-mē kitnē mandar haĩ?	How many temples are there in the village?
ā̃ō̃-mē̃ kitnī masjidē̃ haĩ?	How many mosques are there in the village?

LESSON 40

40.1 [33.1.1] **Translate into Urdu:**
1. Who will repair this broken lamp? 2. The sleeping servant suddenly woke up. 3. Whose is the sandal lying in the corner? 4. The tailor will have to sew this torn coat. 5. Who is the man lying on the ground? 6. Give some water to the tired workmen. 7. Is this water boiled? 8. You shouldn't eat fruit (**that has**) fallen on the ground. 9. Who found my stolen book? 10. The cow tied under the tree began to make noise.

40.2 [33.1.2] **Translate into English:**
1. kis-nē marē huē gīḍar-kō jaṅgal-mẽ-sē khĩcā? 2. darzī-kō mērā phaṭā huā kōṭ sīnē-kō kahō. 3. hamārē bāg̠-kē nazdīk bādhī huī gāy kis-kī hai? 4. thakā huā baccā rōnē lagā. 5. kyā āp ṭūṭē huē hal-kī marammat kar saktē haĩ? 6. us-nē apnā dōst mōṭar-mẽ sōyā huā pāyā. 7. mērī khōyī huī kitābẽ kaun ḍhũṛhēgā? 8. baṛhaī is ṭūṭī huī kursī-kī kab marammat kar saktā hai? 9. kyā āp hamẽ kal-kī sunāyī huī kahānī phir sunāẽgē? 10. aurat bāg̠-mẽ baiṭhī huī apnī phaṭī huī sāṛī-kī marammat kar rahī hai.

40.3 [33.5] **Translate into Urdu:**
1. Do you need a hatchet like that? 2. I have been living in this manner for fifteen years. 3. Will you be able to meet him tomorrow morning? 4. Princely men are often not kings. 5. The student has been going to school for the past twelve years. 6. Where did you find this book? 7. Who is this bird-like woman? 8. I travelled to India two years ago. 9. He'll meet you tomorrow gladly. 10. His hair is black like coal. 11. He told me this matter two hours ago. 12. Does the child look like the father? 13. How many workmen did you get? 14. I wrote you a letter two months ago. 15. The thief knows that he will find the policeman near the field.

40.4 [33.5.1] **Translate into English:**
1. mujhe us jaisā acchā lōhār kahā̃ mil sakēgā? 2. vo baraf jaisī cīz kyā hai? 3. maĩ dō ghanṭō̃-sē āp-kā intazār kar rahā hū̃. 4. mērē dōst hamēśā mujh-sē ghar-par mil saktē haĩ. 5. dūr-sē vo pahāṛ jānvar jaisā mālūm hōtā hai. 6. pichlē bīs minaṭō̃-sē maĩ kulhāṛī-kī talāś kartā hū̃. 7. mujhē mazbūt mazdūr kahā̃ mil sakēgā? 8. laṛkī bāp jaisē haĩ. 9. dō haftē huē tum-nē mujhē ye kahānī sunāyī. 10. maĩ āp-sē kal • subah ḳhuśī-sē milū̃gā. 11. rājkumārō̃ jaisē ādmī hamēśā rājāō̃-kē bēṭē nahī̃ hōtē. 12. siraf ēk haftā huā kārīgar-nē āp-kī mōṭar-kī marammat kī. 13. ham-nē us-kō baṛ-kī chāō̃-mẽ sōtē huē pāyā. 14. kyā pā̃c mahinē pahilē vo musāfir yahā̃ na āyā? 15. us jaisā bhiśtī milnā muśkil hōgā.

40.5 [34.1.3] **Translate into Urdu:**

1. How long will it take you to do this work? 2. When the sunlight appeared, he began to open the door. 3. He ate two hours ago. Why is he hungry now? 4. Seeing the policeman from a distance, the clever thief began to hide. 5. Why did it take you so much time to reach here? 6. It began to rain as soon as we reached the depot. 7. After finishing his glass of milk, the child began to cry. 8. Are you thirsty? 9. As soon as the bell rang, the teacher began to ask questions. 10. As soon as it became day he began to open the windows.

40.6 [34.1.4] **Translate into English:**

1. ye ciṭṭhī likhnē-mẽ mujhē ēk ghanṭā lagā. 2. is saṛak-par bahot zyādā miṭṭī lagī hai. 3. tum mērī mōṭar-kī marammat kab karnē lagōgē? 4. jaisē-hī Vazīr-e-Āzām taḳrīr karnē lagē, lōgō-nẽ bāt karnā ḳhatam kar diya. 5. Hindūstān-kō havāī • jahāz-sē jānē-mẽ kitnā vaḳt lagēgā? 6. jab mērē dōst pahõcē, āp kyũ jānē lagē? 7. mērē yahā̃ khānē-kē bād kyā āp-kō phir bhūk lagī hai? 8. dō mahīnē huē āp-nē ye kām karnā śurū kiyā. 9. jab us-nē bāhar śōr sunā, naukar khiṛkī khōlnē lagā. 10. jaisē-hī maĩ bāg-mẽ āyā, parindē uṛ gayē.

40.7 [32.2.1] **Translate into Urdu:**

1. The girl, running, brought back water. 2. The dog, barking, ran after the stranger. 3. The man listened to my conversation, smiling. 4. The boy, swimming, went from one side of the river to the other. 5. The woman came home, bringing the wood. 6. The girl, singing, brought flowers from the garden. 7. He told the story laughing. 8. The man, returning home at night, fell into the well. 9. The woman lost her money, buying things in the market. 10. The child, recognizing his father, began to smile.

40.8 [34.2.2] **Translate into English:**

1. kisān-nē muskarātē huē musāfir-kō saṛak dikhāyī. 2. bāg-mẽ chōṭī laṛkī rōtē huē baiṭhtī thī. 3. baccõ-kō mā̃-nē hāstē huē miṭhāī dī. 4. bachṛā rōtē huē apnī mā̃-kē pīchē dauṛā. 5. naukar-nē apnē mālik-kē pīchē dauṛtē huē us-kō kōṭ diyā. 6. aurat-nē ghar-kē bāhar ātē huē mazdūrõ-kō śōr macānā ḳhatam karnē-kō kahā. 7. kyā āp-nē gāy-kō hamārē khet-kē pās cartē huē pāyā? 8. kis-nē ādmī-kō mērē ghar-sē ātē huē dēkhā? 9. laṛkī-nē apnī mā̃-kō sāṛiyõ-kī marammat kartē huē dēkhā. 10. apnī dōstõ-kō madad dēnē-kē liyē bulātē huē aurat kuẽ-mẽ-sē baccē-kō khĩc rahī hai.

40.9 [34.3.1] **Translate into Urdu:**

1. Why had you kept up all night? 2. Why do they (**fem.**) keep on laughing? 3. The stream continues to flow. 4. The monkey kept on troubling the people. 5. The cow keeps on eating for a long time. 6. The carpenter kept on cutting the tree. 7. Will the fire keep on burning? 8. The leaves kept on falling from the tree. 9. The water of the river will continue to rise. 10. The gardener keeps on watering the plants.

40.10 [34.3.2] **Translate into English:**

1. āp kab-tak yahā̃ kām kartē rahẽgē? 2. kisān khēt-mẽ kām kartā rahtā hai. 3. bulbul bahot dēr-tak gātī rahtī thī. 4. laṛkī pānī khĩctī rahtī hai. 5. pānī dō haftõ-tak girtā rahēgā. 6. daryā kab-tak baṛhtā rahēgā? 7. dhōbī kapṛē dhōtā rahā. 8. kyā kārīgar mōṭar-kī marammat kartā rahēgā? 9. āg bahot dēr-tak jaltī rahēgī. 10. daryā samandar-mẽ girtē rahtē haĩ.

40.11 [34.4.2] **Translate into Urdu:**

1. The cart driver kept on driving the bullock-cart. 2. The enemy kept on advancing. 3. Why do they keep on speaking with you in English? 4. The river continues to rise.

5. The clouds continue to spread. 6. The farmer will keep on working hard in the field. 7. The pilgrim was continuing to make trips to holy places. 8. How long will you keep on waiting for them? 9. The woman continues to draw water from the well. 10. Why was the man continuing to shave with the old razor?

40.12 [34.4.3] **Translate into English:**

1. bail hal khī̃cnē-kī kōśiś kartā jātā hai. 2. mōṭar calātē jāō! 3. maĩ ghar-kē liyē udās hōtā jā rahā hū̃. 4. jahāz bandargāh-mẽ ātā jātā thā. 5. āp kab-tak un-kā intazār kartē jāẽgē? 6. vaḳt guzartā jā rahā thā. 7. baccā savāl pūchtā jātā thā. 8. bandar daraḳht-sē phal girātā jā rahā hai. 9. tum kab-tak ēk-hī kahānī sunātē jāōgē? 10. gāõvālē kām karnē-kē liyē śahar jātē rahē.

40.13 [34.5.1] **Translate into Urdu:**

1. She used to go out for a walk every day early in the morning. 2. The man is accustomed to walking quickly. 3. This bus goes from our town to Delhi. 4. The farmer is always used to working hard. 5. The cow is not used to walking quickly. 6. The girl was accustomed to sleeping until seven o'clock every day. 7. The rich man is accustomed to giving something or other to poor people. 8. Are you used to reading this thing? 9. Women are accustomed to talking. 10. The Prime Minister is accustomed to making speeches.

40.14 [34.5.2] **Translate into English:**

1. kyā āp har rōz subah sair-kē liyē bāhar jāyā kartē haĩ? 2. kyā ye-hī vo gāṛī hai, jō Dillī-sē Kalkattē jāyā kartī hai? 3. maĩ masālēdār khānē khāyā kartā hū̃. 4. aurat tēz nahī̃ calā kartī hai. 5. kisān har rōz subah • savērē jāgā kartē haĩ. 6. kyā āp har mahīnā apnē dōst-kō ciṭṭhī likhā kartē haĩ? 7. aurtẽ har śām bātẽ kiyā kartī thī̃. 8. kaun har rōz aḳhbār paṛhā kartā hai? 9. laṛkiyā̃ har • subah kuẽ-sē pānī lāyā kartī thī̃. 10. śikārī rāt-kō śikār khēlā kartā thā.

40.15 [35.1.1] **Translate into Urdu:**

1. As soon as he counted his money he realized that he could not buy the gift. 2. As soon as he heard the news of his success he began to dance. 3. As soon as he returned to the office he saw no one there. 4. Immediately upon reaching Bombay he went to a hotel. 5. As soon as he met him what did he say? 6. As soon as the film began we had to go home. 7. As soon as we went out for a walk it began to rain. 8. As soon as the bell rang he woke up. 9. As soon as the sun appeared the birds began to sing. 10. Immediately upon reaching home he realized that some guests had arrived.

40.16 [35.1.2] **Translate into English:**

1. masjid-kō dēkhtē-hī ham-nē andar jānā cāhā. 2. dōnõ hisāb-kō dēkhtē-hī maĩ-nē tay kiyā ke dūsrā galat thā. 3. mērē jāgtē-hī naukar mujhē cāy lāyā. 4. fōṭōgrafar-sē us-kī tasvīr khī̃ctē-hī laṛkā cal paṛā. 5. aḍḍē-par pahõctē-hī maĩ-nē dēkhā ke bas ā pahõcī hai. 6. mērī dūsrī kahānī suntē-hī mērē dōstõ-nē ṭōk diyā. 7. apnē kām-kā phal dēkhtē-hī vo himmat hār gayā. 8. paisē miltē-hī garīb ādmī ḳhuśī-sē nācnē lagā. 9. apnī chōṭī bahan-kō sulātē-hī vo-bhī sō gayī. 10. gāṛī pahõctē-hī ham andar gayē.

40.17 [35.2.1] **Translate into Urdu:**

1. Without counting his money he realized that he couldn't buy the gift. 2. Without asking a single question he guessed that the stranger was a thief. 3. He walked for four hours without stopping to rest. 4. Without reading the book he decided it was not good. 5. The clerk placed the book on the table without saying a word. 6. I went out to see

ᵃe temple without taking my camera. 7. The bearer brought me water without saying
ᵃnything. 8. Without looking for the automobile I knew where it was. 9. He paid
ʳithout looking at the bill. 10. The man wrote a book about Pakistan without travelling
ᵃ it.

40.18 [35.2.2] Translate into English:

bagair mulk dēkhē kaun us-kē bārē-mē̃ likh saktā hai? 2. bagair kitāb paṛhē us-nē
ᵉn liyā ke us-mē̃ kyā thā. 3. bagair rūkē vo ēk ghaṇṭē bōlā. 4. bagair mērē javāb-kā
ᵃtazār kiyē vo calā gayā. 5. bagair ēk-bhī lafz kahē darzī-nē mujhē kapṛā dikhāyā. 6.
ᵃgair mērā hukam samajhnē-kī kōśiś kiyē tum-nē kām kyū̃ kiyā? 7. bagair rūkē mōṭar
ᵃmārī taraf āyī. 8. bagair kōśiś kiyē āp gair•mulkī zabān kaisē sīkh saktē haĩ? 9.
ᵃgair pānī piyē ghōṛā bahot dūr nahī̃ jā sakēgā. 10. bagair ārām lēnē-kē liyē rūkē
ᵈmī kab-tak kām kar saktā hai?

40.19 [36.1.5] Translate into Urdu:

What is this house made of? 2. Have the washerman change the color of this cloth.
. Pick up this luggage and place it in the train. 4. The wood is broken into two pieces.
. Who had this house built? 6. Have someone pick up my luggage. 7. Go to the cloth
ᵉaler and change this cloth. 8. When will you make the chairs for me? 9. The bullock
tied with a rope under the tree. 10. Have a new book sent to me to read. 11. The
ᵃan is bathing in the tank. 12. Do the boys want to bathe the elephant? 13. The master
ᵃs the servant tie the wood. 14. You have to feed the thirsty child milk. 15. If the
ᵃrmer makes the cattle run, they may slip. 16. Flowers are sold in front of the mosque.
⁷. The weak man has the heavy wood weighed. 18. When did you have the school
ᵉes paid? 19. Throw these old shoes away. 20. If the water is warm, don't give it to us.

40.20 [36.1.6] Translate into English:

, bas mandar-kē sāmnē rūkēgī. 2. kuē̃-kē pās mōṭar rōkō. 3. būṛhā hāthī jaṅgal-mē̃
ᵃar gayā. 4. śikārī-nē khēt-kē pās bāgh mār ḍālā. 5. maĩ-nē gīdar-kō saṛak-kī taraf
ᵃuṛtē huē dēkhā. 6. us-nē mujhē purānī imārat dikhāyī. 7. pakkā phal darakht-sē gir
ᵃṛā. 8. bandar-nē laṛkō̃-par phal girāyē. 9. maĩ har rōz subah savērē jagtā hū̃. 10.
ᵃmhē̃ usē jagānā paṛēgā. 11. āp kis-kē sāth bāhar bāt kar rahē thē? 12. bairē-kō bulāō!
3. ham har rōz daryā-mē̃ nahātē haĩ. 14. bahan-kō apnē chōṭē bhāī-kō nahlānā hai. 15.
ᵃzār-mē̃ kis tarah-kī cīzē̃ biktī haĩ. 16. maĩ ānēvālē mahīnē-mē̃ apnī kitābē̃ bikvāū̃gā.
⁷. kis-nē thāl tōṛā? 18. āp-nē bãdhē huē sandūk-kō naukar-sē kyū̃ turvāyā? 19. mōṭar-
ᵉ̃ pahiyē ghūm rahē haĩ. 20. kārīgar pahiyō̃-kō ghumātā hai.

40.21 [36.2.1] Translate into Urdu:

. What (**different**) things did you buy in the market? 2. Drive the automobile slowly!
. Nearly all the fruits were raw. 4. We searched in every house. 5. In travelling from
ᶜalcutta to Delhi we saw many large towns. 6. Pilgrims from (**different**) countries
ᵒme to Mecca every year. 7. There are very small flowers on those plants. 8. All of
ᵃem have each two bullocks. 9. There is a difference between each country. 10. It was
ᵈifficult to write each word of this book.

40.22 [36.2.2] Translate into English:

, āp in sab lōgō̃-mē̃ kin kin-kō jāntē haĩ. 2. mujhē mālūm hōtā hai ke maĩ-nē karīb
ᵃarīb ēk lākh lafz likhē haĩ. 3. āp-nē kaisī acchī acchī kahāniyā̃ kal sunāyī̃! 4. mazdūrō̃-
ᵒ dō dō rūpayē dē dō. 5. jab ham tairkar daryā-kē pār jānē lagē, tab (hamē̃) mālūm
ᵃhī̃ thā ke vo bahot cauṛā thā. 6. āp kaun kaun-sī zabānē̃ bōl saktē haĩ? 7. mērī bāt-

kā ēk ēk lafz saccā hai. 8. us-kē pās ēk baṛā baṛā khēt hai. 9. tumhẽ mujhē kahān ṭhīk ṭhīk sunānī cāhiyē. 10. dhīrē dhīrē bōliyē!

40.23 [37.1.1] **Translate into Urdu:**

1. The elephant was caught by the hunters. 2. The animal will be killed by the hunte 3. By whom was the candy eaten? 4. The luggage was placed in the train. 5. Flower had been sold by a poor woman in front of the mosque. 6. This dry wood had bee brought for the woman. 7. Food has been given to the mendicant. 8. Why wasn't thi work done? 9. When was this wood cut? 10. When will your book be written?

40.24 [37.1.2] **Translate into English:**

1. mērī mōṭar kyũ nahĩ dhōyī gayī hai? 2. paudõ-par pānī kab ḍālā gayā thā? 3. i kapṛõ-kī marammat kal kī jāēgī. 4. hal bailõ-sē ab khĩcā jā rahā hai. 5. sabziyā̃ kais pakāyī jātī thĩ? 6. mērī ciṭṭhī ḍākḳhānē kab bhējī gayī? 7. ye kahānī kitnē lōgõ-k sunāyī jāēgī? 8. kyā āp-kō nahĩ samjhā diyā gayā ke gāṛī calnē-kō taiyār nahĩ thī? 9 mērē savāl-kā javāb kyũ nahĩ diyā gayā? 10. cōrõ-kī thānē-mẽ ḳhūb marammat kī gayi

40.25 [37.2.4] **Translate into Urdu:**

1. I like to put off today's work to tomorrow. 2. Shouldn't you make tea? 3. Wh came to see me yesterday? 4. Who will have to burn the wood? 5. You should rea this correspondence. 6. Let me tell the story exactly. 7. We came to see the famou places. 8. It is difficult to do such work. 9. I will have to bind this book. 10. Don't le the dog go out of the garden! 11. The officer came to teach the farmers the use of th plow. 12. It is dangerous to drive a car swiftly on a wet road. 13. The child should ea vegetables. 14. Let them come in in two's. 15. We let [**past tense**] them each take half melon. 16. The man will have to build a house for the woman. 17. The mechanic ha to repair the automobile. 18. I went to hunt with my companions. 19. Who left th note on the table? 20. The friends sat down to talk.

40.26 [37.2.5] **Translate into English:**

1. bailõ-kā dhūp-mẽ bahot zyādā kām karnā acchā nahĩ. 2. abhī bahot cīzẽ karnī hai 3. āp-kō us-sē milnē jānā paṛēgā. 4. mujhē sōnē dījiyē. 5. bahot zyādā paṛhnā ā̃khõ-k liyē acchā nahĩ. 6. āp-kō in ciṭṭhiyõ-kā javāb dēnā hai. 7. vo risālā paṛhnē baiṭhā. 8 bagair ciṭṭhiyā̃ sāth liyē us-kō jānē mat dō! 9. dhōbī kapṛē lēnē āyā. 10. mōcī-kō i jūtõ-kī marammat karnī hai. 11. āp kis-kē ānē-kā intazār kar rahē haĩ? 12. thakē hu ghōṛē-kō ārām lēnē dō! 13. musāfir ṭhanḍā pānī mā̃gnē ṭhaharē. 14. maĩ āp-kō ky batāũ ke maĩ mejisṭrēṭ-sē milnē kyũ āyā? 15. maĩ aisā kām karnē-sē thak gayā hũ. 16 sāmān mōṭar-mẽ rahnē dō! 17. āp-kō tēzī-sē calnā hōgā. 18. kis-nē laṛkē-kō daryā akēl jānē diyā? 19. āp-kā rōnā āp-kō madad nahĩ karēgā. 20. kaun mērē liyē ṭeksī bulān bāhar dauṛēgā?

40.27 [38.1.2] **Translate into Urdu:**

1. I think these rather small vegetables are expensive. 2. A rather small rain never give enough water for agriculture. 3. In what (**specific**) book did you write this story? 4 Which rooms are mine? 5. There are several rather large cities in Pakistan. 6. Wha is this rather high building? 7. Exactly which magazines do you read? 8. Deep wate appears a rather black color. 9. By which (**specific**) road will I go? 10 Exactly whic places should I see first?

40.28 [38.1.3] **Translate into English:**

1. ye chōṭī-sī sabziyā̃ mahẽgī haĩ. 2. ye tañg-sā rāstā kahā̃ jātā hai? 3. kaun-sē kārīga

nē is mōṭar-kī marammat kī? 4. mujhē safar karnē-kē liyē baṛī-sī mōṭargāṛī-kī zarūrat hai. 5. āp-nē Pākistān-kī kaun kaun-sī jaghẽ dēkhī thĩ. 6. kyā ye ustarā tēz-sā nahĩ? 7. āp-nē kaun kaun-sī ciṭṭhiyā̃ likhī haĩ? 8. āp-nē mērī kaun-sī kitāb paṛhī? 9. ye kapṛē gandē-sē mālūm hōtē haĩ. 10. mujhē mērē safar-kē liyē kaun kaun-sī cīzõ-kī zarūrat hōgī?

40.29 [38.2.3] **Translate into Urdu:**

1. How is your health? 2. Are you telling me the same (**type of**) incident you saw? 3. He said that he would tell us the incident just as he saw it. 4. As is the work so is the result. 5. What sort of letter did you get from home? 6. Why didn't you do as I told you? 7. How are you? 8. As is the cook so is the food. 9. What sort of magazines did you bring? 10. What sort of work can you do?

40.30 [38.2.4] **Translate into English:**

1. ghar-mẽ lōg kaisē haĩ? 2. vo kaisī imārat hai? 3. jaisā darzī, vaisē kapṛē. 4. jaisē āp-nē kahānī sunī, vaisē-hī mujhē batāiyē. 5. tum kaisē gāṛībān hō? 6. jaisē sarkārī afsar-nē usē sikhāyā, vaisē-hī kisān apnē hal-kā istēmāl kartā hai. 7. jaisē āp-nē imārat dēkhī, vaisē-hī mujh-sē bayān kījiyē. 8. is khēt-kī kaisī fasal hai? 9. jaisē maĩ-nē tum-kō batāyā, vaisē-hī mōṭar calāō. 10. āp-nē mujhē kaisā kamrā diyā?

Following are translations of the reading texts given in lessons 33 to 38. They can be used in translating English passages into Urdu.

40.31 [33.7] **The Poets of Urdu. (Part One); Mirza Galib.**

Mirza Galib was a very great poet of the Urdu language. His real name was Asad Ullah Khan. He was still young when his parents died. (**After that**) his uncle brought him up. He was about twelve or fourteen when he got married. Mirza's childhood and youth passed luxuriously. Around this time he completed his education. Mirza had a great mastery of the Urdu, Persian and Arabic languages. He started composing poetry around this time. He employed a very difficult vocabulary. For this reason the common man did not understand his poetry. At the advice of his friends, he started using easier language in his verses and quickly became famous. But he still did not attain that fame which he deserved. The reason was that his poetry was philosophic. The taste of the common man in his time was low. Therefore, they did not like Mirza's poetry. Throughout his life Galib lamented the fact that ordinary poets who did not compare to him at all became famous. But the fame which he did not get in his lifetime, he got after his death. Today, every educated man reads his poetry very fondly and praises him.

Mirza Galib got a pension from the British Government. Besides this, he got allowances from several Navobs and Rajahs. Some people think that Mirza's monthly income was about four hundred rupees. Four hundred rupees was a large sum in those days, but Mirza led a life of luxury. Therefore, he always complained of the lack of funds. Immediately after the Mutiny, his pension was stopped for some time. During this time, he was really somewhat short of money. But after a short while the Government reestablished his pension. Mirza had no specific occupation. He drank wine, entertained friends, and composed poetry. Sometimes, he went to the court of the last Mogul king, Bahadur Shah. Bahadur Shah gave Mirza a monthly allowance of fifty rupees. Once he thought of taking a job with the British Government. The post of Professor in Persian was vacant in the Delhi College. The British Commissioner told Mirza he could have the job if he wanted it. The Commissioner was a personal friend of Mirza's.

Whenever Mirza would go to see him, the Commissioner would come out of his bungalow to welcome him. One day, Mirza went to see him about this job. This time the Commissioner didn't come out to welcome him. Instead, he waited in his office for Mirza to come in; but Mirza was waiting in his coach for the Commissioner to come out to receive him. After a long time, the Commissioner finally came out. He asked Mirza, "Well! Mirza! Why didn't you come in?" Mirza replied, "I was waiting for you to come out to meet me." The Commissioner said, "Well, Mirza! When you come to see me as a friend, I come out to receive you; but not when you come for a job." Mirza answered, "If that is so, then I don't care for the job. I seek employment with the British to enhance my prestige and not to lower it." Having said this, Mirza went back home and never thought of taking a job after that.

Mirza was a very even-tempered and humorous man. He liked mangoes a lot. Once upon a time, he was sitting in his drawingroom with his friends. There were some mango-peelings on the street outside. By chance, a donkey passed by. He sniffed around the peelings and went on. A friend remarked, "Look, Mirza! Even a donkey doesn't eat mangoes." Mirza replied, "Yes, brother, those who are asses don't eat mangoes."

40.32 [34.6] **The Poets of Urdu (Part Two); Ikbal.**

Ikbal's real name was Mohammed Ikbal. He was born in Sialkot, a famous city of the Panjab. He started composing lyrical poems when he was still in high school. At that time, the most famous Urdu poet was Mirza Khan Dag. He was a teacher of the Navab of the Deccan and lived in Hyderabad. Ikbal sent his poems to Dag to look them over. Dag soon recognized that Ikbal would one day become a great poet. At the age of seventeen, Ikbal came to Lahore and got admitted to the Government College. He passed his M.A. from here and then went to England. There, he studied at Cambridge for some years. He got his Ph.D. from there and also passed his law examination. He came back to Lahore after finishing his education and started legal practice here. But he didn't have his heart in it. Even though he was in practice of more or less the whole of his life, he didn't take very many cases. He would go to the courts sometimes. Most of the time he composed poetry and wrote books. He has written many books in Urdu, Persian, and English. Ikbal didn't write very much love poetry. In fact, his poetry is even more philosophic than Galib's. There was a specific objective behind his poetry. He was always concerned about waking up the Muslims of the world from their slumber. He felt that the Muslims should unite. He gave the idea of Pakistan to the Indian Muslims. He remained in correspondence with Mr. Jinnah and several other leaders on the subject of Pakistan for several years. His opinion was that the Muslims should get a separate country for themselves. Ikbal died in 1938. Ikbal's tomb is located near the Shahi Mosque in Lahore. Ikbal Day is celebrated all over Pakistan on April 21. Meetings are held in his memory in which poets recite their poems. Besides them, some other learned people deliver speeches on his poetry and philosophy. Research has been conducted on his philosophy for several years. Every year, several articles are written and published on him. The greater part of Ikbal's poetry is in Persian. He thought that his message was addressed not only to the Indian Muslims but to the Muslims all over the world. Some of his Persian books have been translated into English. For instance, a famous English Professor, Nicholson, who was also a teacher of Ikbal, has translated one of his books called, "Isrār-e-Khudī." The English title is "Secrets of the Self." The name of the most famous of Ikbal's writings in English is called "Six Lectures on Islam." You should read these books. A collection of Ikbal's letters has also been published. These letters are very interesting. Several of these letters are addressed to Mr. Jinnah. Ikbal was one of the few poets in the world who became very famous during their (**own**) lifetime and whose fame continued even after their death. When the British Government noted that Ikbal had become world-famous for his poetry, they lost no time in knighting him. But Ikbal never cared too much for this title. Ikbal's strongest point was that he studied a great deal. He had mastery of Western and Eastern fields of knowledge. For that reason he had a vast vision.

40.33 [35.7] **Political Leader.** (**A Satirical Short Story**)

(**Note:** All the characters in this short story are fictitious.)

[Ahmad Jalal Khan has been living in Lahore for many years. His profession is the legal practice, but no one has ever seen him pleading a law-suit in a court. The truth is that he doesn't have to prepare cases and get involved in legal matters. He is a big landlord. He owns thousands of acres of land. He earns hundreds of thousands from this land. He has a majestic palace in the city. Dozens of servants run around him. There would be at least six cars in his garage. All this is very well, but, after all, Khan-Sahab should have something to keep him busy. He has made proper arrangements to satisfy this need. He is a member of the Panjab Legislative Assembly and he represents the big landlords of his area there. But in Lahore, he is the president of the Socialist Party. Tonight some socialist workers are coming to his house for dinner. After the dinner there will be a meeting in which the program of the party will be planned. Khan-Sahab will deliver a forceful speech at this meeting. At this moment he is preparing the speech with his secretary. His daughter, Jamila, is also sitting beside him and is giving advice. Jamila has recently returned from England. She was studying there at Cambridge University.]

Khan-Sahab: Mr. Ahmad Ali! (**Ahmad Ali is the secretary. He is a thirty-year old man and is a college graduate—that is to say, he has a B.A. He knows Urdu well.**)

Ahmad Ali: Yes, your Honor. (**Ahmad Ali flatters Khan-Sahab very much. But what can the poor fellow do? Khan-Sahab likes flattery.**)

Khan-Sahab: You've prepared my speech; haven't you?

Ahmad Ali: Yes, Khan-Sahab. I've worked hard on it. People will applaud when they hear it. God willing, your leadership will be assured tonight.

Khan-Sahab: Very good. I think you deserve a raise in your pay. All right, read it to me.

Ahmad Ali: (**Reads the speech**): Ladies and gentlemen, we have assembled tonight to consider some important problems of this province. You know that our government has failed in providing the common man the necessaries of life. The promises which were made at election time have not been fulfilled. The poor are starving to death; they don't get bread. They fall prey to all sorts of diseases but there are no hospitals for their treatment. Their children are uneducated and there is no arrangement to educate them. When the masses voice their demands they are told that the government doesn't have enough money. If it is true that the government doesn't have enough money, then the question is where is the money going to come from? Ladies and gentlemen, we Socialists maintain that there is no shortage of funds in this province. If capitalism is ended, the government will have enough funds for satisfying the needs of the poor. We think that land and industry should be nationalized in this province. But who will take this revolutionary step? The present government is the government of the capitalists. It is useless to expect such a move from it. The socialist revolution is necessary to help the poor and to improve their lot. Long live the Socialist Party!

Khan-Sahab: Ahmad Ali, very good! It's a very good speech. Your pay is increased by ten rupees from today.

Ahmad Ali: Sir, I have been in your service for five years. This is the first raise. I would suggest a raise of twenty rupees.

Khan-Sahab: No! No! A ten-rupee raise is enough for the present.

Jamila: Daddy! Please give him a twenty-rupee raise. He is a poor man. And he works so hard!

Khan-Sahab: All right dear. I raise his pay by twenty rupees since you recommend that. Are you happy now? (**Addressing Ahmad Ali**).

Ahmad Ali: Sir, God bless you. (**Goes out**).

Jamila: Daddy, the speech is all right. But if the lands of the landlords are nationalized, then what are you going to do?

Khan-Sahab: My innocent daughter! Do you think I am such a fool as to pass my land over to the government? Fifty members of the Assembly are in the palm of my hand. They will oppose it, whenever such a bill comes before the Assembly. Besides, there is no question of such a bill coming up till after the next elections. If our party wins the next elections, then, we ourselves, won't let such a bill be introduced. This speech is only to get votes.

Jamila: But, daddy, this is dishonest!

Khan-Sahab: You silly girl! Shut up! (**Angrily**) You call your daddy dishonest! Ill-mannered, insolent thing!

[Jamila starts crying.]

40.34 [36.4] **Mohammad, The Prophet of God.**

About fourteen-hundred years ago, Mohammad, Peace be on Him, was born in a respectable family of Mecca. His father, whose name was Abdullah, had died before Mohammad was born. He was brought up by his grandfather, Abdul Muttalib. But after a short while his grandfather also passed away, and his uncle Abu Talib brought him up. The condition of the Arabs was very bad in this time. They had all the ills of the world in them. They drank, fornicated, gambled and lied. They hesitated neither to steal nor to murder. The Arabs of that time were divided into many tribes, and each tribe worshipped its (**own**) idols. These tribes fought each other all the time. Mohammad worried about the condition of his nation even in his boyhood. He contemplated a great deal and worshipped God in solitude. He never cared for amusements. As a boy he looked after the camels, and started trading when he grew to manhood. He bought and sold cloth. Several times he went with caravans to distant places in connection with his business. But during all this time his contemplation and worship continued. There is a hill near Mecca in which there used to be a cave. Mohammad used to sit in that cave and worship God for hours. When he was forty he received divine inspiration and God appointed him His Prophet.

After this, he came back home and mentioned the matter to his wife. His wife was the first woman to become a Muslim. Then he gathered together his tribesmen and friends and said to them, "Do you people consider me truthful and honest?" The audience answered "Undoubtedly, O Mohammad. We have never found you telling lies or being dishonest." Mohammad further asked them, "If I tell you that a hostile army is gathering behind this hill, will you believe me?" The people replied, "O Son of Abdullah, we will believe whatever you say because you are truthful and honest." Then Mohammad addressed them as follows, "If that is so, then hear that God has appointed me His Prophet. I will show you the path of truth and righteousness. First of all, you should give up idol-worship, since they do not deserve your worship. They are merely pieces of stone. God, alone, is worthy of praise. He is the creator of the earth and the sky. You should worship him." When the people heard this, some were surprised and others became angry. They did not expect that Mohammad would speak against their idols. Mohammad continued to preach Islam after this incident. But the more he preached the more he was opposed by the people of Mecca. Slowly people began to be converted to Islam and circumstances took a turn. As the number of Muslims increased the anger of the heathens rose. The heathens treated the Muslims very harshly. When the hardship on them became limitless and the heathens began to make plans for murdering Mohammad, the Muslims left Mecca. Mohammad and his associates migrated to Medina.

During the lifetime of the Prophet, the Muslims conquered Mecca. Thereafter Islam began to spread all over Arabia. Around the time of the death of the Prophet nearly all Arabs had become Muslims. The preaching of Mohammad, the Prophet, can be summarized thus: 1) God, who is the Creator of the Universe, is alone worthy of worship and no one else besides Him. In other words, God is One and He had no one to share His power with Him. 2) Mohammad is the Prophet of God. All Muslims are brothers to one another. They are all equal in the eyes of God. Truth, justice and kindheartedness are among those virtues which God likes to see in his men. It is a duty for the Muslims to worship God, fast in the month of Ramzan and spend money in the way of God. There are several other things besides these which we will tell you some other time.

40.35 [37.3] **The Caliphs of Islam.**

Islam is a religion in which politics and faith are not separated. Muslims are duty-bound to establish and maintain a good government just as they are bound to say prayers and fast (**in the month of Ramzan**). (**The man who**) was the head of an Islamic state was called the Caliph. Even though the history of Islam is full of names of Caliphs, there were only four Caliphs of Islam in the real sense of the word. These four were the men who became Caliphs after the death of Prophet Mohammad. To tell you the truth, the Caliphate ended and kingship began after they passed away.

Come, let us tell you something about these Caliphs. When the Prophet died Muslims began to worry about their future leader. Accordingly, some Muslims who had been the associates of the Prophet of God assembled at one place. They elected (**as**) Caliph one of these associates, whose name was Abu Bakr and who occupied a high position because of his age and experience. Some people were absent from this meeting. For instance, Mohammad's son-in-law, Ali was not there. Ali had always been the right-hand man of the Prophet. He was expecting that the Muslims would elect him their Caliph. When he found that a Caliph had been elected in his absence, he was somewhat distressed. For a while, he refused to accept Abu Bakr as the Caliph. But after six months had passed, he (**finally**) gave allegiance to Abu Bakr. Abu Bakr did not live long. A few days before he died he appointed Umr his successor. This time no election was held. Umr had also been an associate of the Prophet and had always been ahead of some of the others in the service of Islam. During his rule, the Muslims gained lots of victories and the banner of Islam waved in places, far and wide. Umr considered it a duty to serve the Muslims. He would come out of his house at night and make a round of the streets of Medina. He would help anyone he would see in trouble. You may be surprised to know that in those days the Caliph of Islam used to live just like an ordinary man. He got neither a palace to live in nor a big salary. In those days, all Muslims who worked for the government got an allowance from the government treasury. But Umr's allowance was not more than that of an ordinary government servant.

The Muslims kept an eye on every action of the Caliph. Every Muslim had the right to criticize the Caliph's action. Besides, the Caliph could be sued in a court of law. There was a Council to advise the Caliph on the affairs of the state. This was called the Advisory Council. Once a man filed a suit against his employer in Umr's court. Umr gave a verdict unfavorable to him. The man was very angry at this decision. Early one morning he went to the mosque where Umr was saying his prayers and murdered him with a dagger.

Some other day we will tell you about the two other Caliphs of Islam—Usman and Ali.

40.36 [38.6] **My Friends.**

With God's grace, I have never felt the lack of friends. Some people want to make friends, but they don't find any. But (**with me**) the case is otherwise. I have tried several times to reduce the number of my friends. But this desire had not been accomplished. Either there is some merit in me which keeps people attached to me after they once become (**my**) friends, or there is something so attractive about my friends that I have never made a real attempt to get rid of them. Anyway, the situation at present is that there is hardly a country in the world where I don't have a friend. You will want to know that if such is the case why do I complain. Friends are a blessing of God. They come to your aid in difficulty. Now, friend, how shall I explain to you that sometimes too many friends become a nuisance. To make a correct estimate of my difficulty, you will have to meet some of my friends. Come, let me introduce them to you.

Meet this one. He is Jamil Khan. We call him "J.K." He is a very educated gentleman. In fact, he is a bit too well-educated. He is a childhood friend. We were together, first in school, and then in college. "J.K." holds me very dear. My company is pleasing to him. I like his company, too. But what can you do about the fact that he would insult a man without the slightest hesitation. He calls attention to people's shortcomings right in their presence and thus spoils the party. I have often advised him against it, but our good friend will not give up this habit of his. Now you tell me what to do with such a friend.

Now meet this man. His name is Shaukat. Shaukat is older than I am by several years. He teaches at the University. He is very knowledgeable in his field. But look at his heart. He is happy when you compliment him, but he will be silent for two months after you have spoken a word of criticism. He blushes red if you joke with him. In short, he is no good in company.

Now let's introduce you to Nasim. He teaches in a college. He is a nice-looking man, just about two months ago, he got married. He loves his wife very much, but he never seems to realize that we do not have any particular interest in his wife. Whenever he meets us, he tells us a long story about the accomplishmnts of his wife. There are several things you want to talk to him about, but he is never through with the account of his wife's merits. And if he is ever through with this topic, then he begins to talk about the expected baby.

Well, now meet Manzur. He is a very even-tempered man. He never hurts anyone. He never gossips about people. He has a very sweet voice. He captures the heart of his audience when he sings. You will say that if he has all these merits then there should be no complaint about him. I wish it were so, but even here there is a great difficulty. He has more needs than he has the money to fulfill (**them**). Now, some people, as a matter of principle, stretch out their legs as far as the blanket extends. But his principle is that one should stretch out his legs full-length, and if the blanket is not (**long**) enough, one should borrow from his neighbor. In other words, he is a habitual borrower. Let me make it clear that there is nothing wrong with borrowing. The whole world does this at one time or other, but this friend never talks of repaying a loan. Well, you might be curious to know why people lend him money at all under these circumstances. I don't know anything about others. But he asks me for a loan in such a dramatic manner that it becomes very difficult to refuse him. For instance, the door rings early one Sunday morning. I am still in bed. He comes at a time when I am sure to be at home. Anyway, the servant comes and wakes me up, with Manzur following him. After an exchange of greetings, he takes a chair and sits beside me. He asks about my health very affectionately, and expresses his concern about it. Then rebukes me for over-working myself. By that time, the servant brings tea. I take tea and Manzur takes a cup on my insistent invitation. Drinking his tea, he begins to heave sighs. His face becomes sad. Sometimes he pulls his hair, and sometimes he runs his hands over his forehead. Even though I understand his trouble, right from the start, I have to ask him what new troubles he has. After that, he makes a long speech. He praises me; complains of his bad luck, mentions his child's illness and the doctor's bill. Tears come to his eyes while he tells all this. Now tell me, what can I do except to loan him money under such conditions.

This is the story of my friends. I hold all these people dear. I am annoyed with them, but at the same time it is difficult for me to give them up. To do or not to do! Maybe our lives will be spent just the way things are now.

Urdu–English Glossary

The letters occur in the following sequence: **a, ā, ã, ā̃, b, c, d, ḍ, ṛ, e, ē, ẽ, ē̃, f, g, g̱, h, , ī, ĩ, ī̃, j, k, ḳ, ḳh, l, m, n, n̄, ṇ, o, ō, õ, ō̃, p, r, s, ś, t, ṭ, u, ū, ũ, ū̃, v, y, z.**

With the exception of **ḳh** (which has a special character in the script) aspirates are onsidered to consist of a consonant plus h and are listed accordingly.

Nouns are marked by gender, i.e., **msc.** and **fm.** Adjectives which do not change heir form for gender, number or case are marked **n.c.** Other adjectives are given in heir masculine form. A list of grammatical abbreviations follows.

List of Abbreviations

adj.	adjective
adv.	adverb
art.	article
aux.	auxiliary
cf.	compare
conj.	conjunction
dem.	demonstrative
e.g.	for example
emph.	emphatic
excl.	exclamation
fm.	feminine
ger.	gerund
hon.	honorific
indef.	indefinite
inf.	infinitive
int.	intransitive
interr.	interrogative
intj.	interjection
msc.	masculine
n.	noun
n.c.	no change (**i.e.,** for gender, number or case)
neg.	negative
obl.	oblique
part.	participle
pers.	personal
pl.	plural
pl. n.	place name
postpos.	postposition
pr. n.	proper noun
prep.	preposition
pron.	pronoun
pst.	past

pt.	particle
refl.	reflexive
rel.	relative
s.	singular
tr.	transitive
vb.	verb

ab: adv., now
ab-tak: adv., still, up to now
abbā: msc., father, daddy
abhī: adv., still, yet, now
abhī-tak: adv., still, up to now
abhī-tō: conj., still, yet
abtar: adj., n.c., worse
abūr: msc., command, ability, mastery
acānak: adv., suddenly
acār: msc., pickle
acchā: adj., good
acchā: adv., well
acchā ḳhāsā: adj., considerable, pretty well
achūt: msc., and **fm., adj., n.c.,** untouchable
adab: msc., respect
adā: fm., charming gesture, blandishment
adā karnā: vb. tr., pay (**e.g.,** fees)
adālat: fm., court of law, courtroom
adheṛ • umar-kā: adj., middle aged
adl: msc., justice
aḍḍā: msc., depot
Afgānistān: pl. n., msc., Afghanistan
Afrīḳā: pl. n., msc., Africa
afsar: msc., officer, official
afsānā: msc., short story
afsānah: msc., short story
afsōs: msc., sorrow, grief.
agar: conj., if
agarce: conj., even though, although
agast: msc., August
aglā: adj., next, forthcoming
aham: adj., n.c., important
ahsān: msc., obligation
ahsās: msc., feeling
aikṭ: msc., act, legislation
aisā: adj., such, of this sort

aisā palṭā khānā: **vb. tr.**, "to take such a turn"
aisē: **adv.**, thus, in this way
aiś: **msc.**, luxury
aiśṭrē: **fm.**, ash-tray
ajī: **excl.**, hey!
ajnabī: **msc.**, stranger
ajnabī: **adj.**, **n.c.**, foreign
Akbār: **pr. n.**, **msc.**, Akbar, name of a Mogul emperor
akēlā: **adj.**, alone
aksar: **adv.**, frequently, usually
aksariyyat: **fm.**, majority
aktūbar: **msc.**, October
akalmand (also **aklmand**): **adj.**, **n.c.**, wise
akhbār: **msc.**, newspaper
akhbār • navīs: **msc.** and **fm.**, newspaperman, journalist
alag: **adj.**, **n.c.**, separate
alahdā: **adj.** separate
alauns: **msc.**, allowance
alāō: **msc.**, bonfire, flame
aleksan: **msc.**, political election
alfāz: **msc. pl.**, words (see **lafz**)
alūm: **msc.**, fields of study
Allah: **msc.**, God, the supreme being of Islam
allāmā: **adj.**, **n.c.**, educated, very learned
aman: **msc.**, peace, safety
Ambēdkar: **pr. n.**, **msc.**, name of Indian political leader
amīr: **msc.**, ruler
amīr: **adj.**, **n.c.**, rich
amīr: **msc.**, nobleman
amīr • vazīr: **msc. pl.**, councillors
ammā̃: **fm.**, mother
ammī: **fm.**, mother
Amritsar: **pl. n.**, **msc.**, Amritsar
Amrīkā: **pl. n.**, **msc.**, America
anāj: **msc.**, grain
anban: **fm.**, quarrel, misunderstanding
andar: **adv.**, in
andar-tak: **adv.**, down to, within
andāzā: **msc.**, estimate
andāzī: **msc.**, archery
andhā: **adj.**, blind
andhērā: **msc.**, darkness
andhērā: **adj.**, dark
anjuman: **fm.**, society
anjuman-e-imdād-e-bāhamī: **fm.**, cooperative society
anpaṛh: **adj.**, **n.c.**, illiterate

anḍā: **msc.,** egg
Añgrēzī: **fm.,** English language
Añgrēzī: **adj., n.c.,** English
añgūṭhī: **fm.,** ring
apīl: **fm.,** appeal
apnā: **refl. adj.,** own
aprail: **msc.,** April
Arab: **msc.,** Arab
Arabī (also **Arbī**): **adj., n.c.,** Arabic
Arabī (also **Arbī**): **fm.,** Arabic language
araz (also **arz**): **fm.,** petition, request
araz karnā (also **arz**): **vb. tr.,** to submit, propose
arz karnā: see **araz karnā**
aṛsaṭh: **adj., n.c.,** sixty-eight
aṛtālīs: **adj., n.c.,** forty-eight
aṛtīs: **adj., n.c.,** thirty-eight
asalām alēkum: hello, expression of greeting
asalām-ō-alēkum: hello, expression of greeting
asar: **msc.,** effect, impression
aslī: **adj., n.c.,** real, actual
aslī nām: **msc.,** real name
aspatāl: **msc.,** see **haspatāl,** hospital
assī: **adj., n.c.,** eighty
aśār: **msc.,** verses
Aśōk Vardhan: **msc.,** Aśoka, ancient ruler of India
aṭh • hattar: **adj., n.c.,** seventy-eight
aṭṭhāis: **adj., n.c.,** twenty-eight
aṭṭhārā, aṭṭhārah: **adj., n.c.,** eighteen
aṭṭhānvē: **adj., n.c.,** ninety-eight
aṭṭhāsī: **adj., n.c.,** eighty-eight
aṭṭhāvan: **adj., n.c.,** fifty-eight
aur: **conj.,** and
aur-bhī kuch: **adj.,** some more, something else
aur-bhī kōī: **pron.,** some one else
aurat: **fm.,** woman
aurḍar: **msc.,** order (request)
auzār: **msc.,** tool, instrument
Avadh: **pl. n., msc.,** Oudh
avval nambar: **adj., n.c.,** "number one"
Ayōdhyā: **pl. n., fm.,** Ayodhya, modern Oudh
azīz: **adj., n.c.,** dear, beloved

āb: **msc.,** water

ābādī: **fm.,** population
āb-ō-havā: **fm.,** climate
ābpāśī: **fm.,** irrigation
ābpāśī karnā: **vb. tr.,** to irrigate
ādat: **fm.,** habit
ādat hōnā: **vb. int.,** to be accustomed
ādābarz: **msc.,** general greeting (**irrespective of time of day**)
ādhā: **adj.,** half
ādmī: **msc.,** man
āg: **fm.,** fire
āgē: **adv.,** ahead, henceforth, in front, in future
āh: **fm.,** sigh
āh karnā: **vb. tr.,** to heave a sigh
āhistā: **adv.,** slowly
āindā: **adj., n.c.,** future, in the future
āīnā: **msc.,** mirror
āj: **adv.,** today
āj • kal: **adv.,** at the present time, nowadays
āj • rāt: **adv.,** tonight
āj • śām: **fm.,** this evening
āḳhir: **adv.,** finally, after all
āḳhrī: **adj., n.c.,** last
ālim: **adj., n.c.,** learned
ālīśān: **adj., n.c.,** majestic
ālū: **msc.,** potato
ām: **msc.,** mango
ām: **adj., n.c.,** common
ām • taur-par: **adv.,** usually, generally
āmdanī: **fm.,** income
āmlā: **msc.,** olive
ānā: **vb. int.,** to come
ānā: **msc.,** anna, a sixteenth of a rupee (**according to older system to coinage**)
ānēvālā: **adj.,** coming, approaching
āp: **pron., hon.,** you
āp • bītī: **fm.,** autobiography
āpas-mẽ: **adv.,** among our—, your—, them—selves, with one another
ārām: **msc.,** rest
ārām karnā: **vb. tr.,** to rest, repose
ārām • kursī: **fm.,** easy chair
āsān: **adj., n.c.,** easy
āsānī: **fm.,** ease
āsānī-sē: **adv.,** easily
āsmān: **msc.,** sky
ās • pās: **adv.,** around
āśik: **msc.** and **fm.,** lover, suitor
āśik hōnā: **vb. int.,** to fall in love

āśram: msc., hermitage, abode
āṭā: msc., flour, ground grain
āṭē-kī cakkī: fm., flour-mill
āṭh: adj., n.c., eight
āṭhvā̃: adj., eighth
āvāz: fm., voice
āzād: adj., n.c., free
āzādī: fm., freedom
ā̃kh: fm., eye
ā̃khē̃ khul jānā: vb. int., to wake up
ā̃sū: msc., tear

bacā lēnā: vb. tr., to save
bacānā: vb. tr., to save
baccā: msc., child
bachṛā: msc., calf
bacnā: vb. int., to be saved
bacpan: msc., childhood
bad: negative prefix and adj., n.c., bad, wicked, mean
badal: msc., change
badal cuknā: vb. int., to change
badalnā: vb. tr., to change
badḳismatī: fm., misfortune
badlā: msc., revenge
badmāś (also badmuāś): msc., rascal
badmāś (also badmuāś): adj., n.c., wicked
badmuāś: see badmāś
badsūrat: adj., n.c., ugly
badtamīz: adj., n.c., ill-mannered
bag̱air (also -kē bag̱air, postpos. phrase): prep., without, apart from
bahan: fm., sister, friend, companion
bahar hāl: adv., anyway, no matter
bahattar: adj., n.c., seventy-two
bahādur: adj., n.c., brave
bahāl karnā: vb. tr., to reinstate
bahānā: msc., excuse, pretence
bahānā banānā: vb. tr., to make excuse
Bahāvalpūr: pl. n.. msc., Bahawalpoor
bahnā: vb. tr., to flow
bahot (also bahut): adv., very, much, many
bahot behtar: adv., very well
bahot din huē: adv., long ago

bahot din pahilē: **adv.,** long ago
bahot kam: **adv.,** rarely
bahot kuch: **adv.,** a lot
bahut: see **bahot**
bahū: **fm.,** daughter-in-law
baiat karnā: **vb. tr.,** to take allegiance
bail: **msc.,** ox
bailgāṛī: **fm.,** oxcart
baink: **msc.,** bank
Bairam K̤hā̃: **pr. n., msc.,** Bairam Khan
bairā: **msc.,** waiter, bearer
Bairut: **pl. n., msc.,** Beirut
baiṭhak: **fm.,** sitting room
baiṭhnā: **vb. int.,** to sit down
bajānā: **vb. tr.,** to sound, strike, play an instrument
bajnā: **vb. int.,** to sound, be struck, be played
bakrā: **msc.,** goat
bakrī: **fm.,** she-goat
Baḳar Īd: **fm.,** Muslim holiday
balke: **conj.,** instead, but, rather
Balucī: **n. and adj., n.c.,** Baluchi
bam: **msc.,** bomb
Bambaī: **pl. n., msc.,** Bombay
ban jānā: **vb. int.,** to be made, **cf.** bannā
banānā: **vb. tr.,** to make
Banāras: **pl. n., msc.,** Banaras
Banārsī: **adj., n.c.,** of Banaras
band: **adj., n.c.,** closed, stopped, shut
band hōnā: **vb. int.,** to be stopped
band karnā: **vb. tr.,** to stop, close, lock up, cut off
bandar: **msc.,** monkey
bandargāh: **fm.,** harbor
bandōbast: **msc.,** arrangement
bandūḳ: **msc.,** gun
bannā: **vb. int.,** to be made, become, rise, prosper
Baṅgāl: **pl. n., msc.,** Bengal
Baṅgālī: **fm., and adj., n.c.,** Bengali
baṅglā: **msc.,** bungalow
barābar: **adj., n.c.,** equal
barāē meharbānī: **adv.,** please
barāt: **fm.,** wedding procession, bridegroom's procession to the home of the bride
barbād: **adj., n.c.,** wasted
barbād hōnā: **vb. int.,** to be destroyed
bardāśt: endurance, patience
bardāśt karnā: **vb. tr.,** to endure

barf: **fm.,** snow, ice

barsānā: **vb. tr.,** to pour down, to shower

barsāt: **fm.,** rainy-season

barsātī: **fm.,** raincoat

bartan: **msc.,** kitchen vessel, utensil

baṛ: **msc.,** banyan tree

baṛā: **adj., adv.,** large, very

baṛā hōnā: **vb. int.,** to grow up

baṛā mazmūn: **msc.,** chief subject

baṛhāī: **msc.,** carpenter

baṛhānā: **vb. tr.,** to increase

baṛhnā: **vb. int.,** advance, increase, rise, flood, grow

baṛī rānī: **fm.,** senior queen

bas: **excl.,** no more, finish, enough, just, in short, only

bas: **fm.,** bus

basar karnā: **vb. tr.,** to spend (time)

basānā: **vb. tr.,** to found, settle, colonize

basāyā: **adj., past pt.,** basānā, founded

basnā: **vb. int.,** to be situated, be populated, be inhabited

bastā: **msc.,** briefcase, bag for schoolbooks

batānā: **vb. tr.,** to tell, point out

battī: **fm.,** lamp, wick

battīs: **adj., n.c.,** thirty-two

baṭvārā: **msc.,** cropshare

bayālīs: **adj., n.c.,** forty-two

bayān: **msc.,** description, account

bayān karnā: **vb. tr.,** to describe

bayāsī: **adj., n.c.,** eighty-two

bazāriyā: **adv.,** by way of, by means of

bazāriyā-e-havāī · jahāz: **adv.,** by airplane

Bābar: **pr. n., msc.,** Babar, name of a Mogul emperor

bābā: **msc.,** father

bābū: **msc.,** clerk, educated man

bād: **adv.,** afterwards

bād-mē̃: **adv.,** afterwards

bādal: **msc.,** cloud

bādšāh: **msc.,** emperor

bādšāhat: **fm.,** kingship.

bāg: **msc.,** garden

bāhar (also bāhir); **adv.,** outside

bāibil: **fm.,** Bible

bāisikal: **fm.,** bicycle

bāīs: **adj., n.c.,** twenty-two

bājā: **msc.,** musical instrument

bāk: **msc.,** hesitation

bāḳī: fm., remaining, remainder
bāl: msc., hair
bāl • baccē: msc. pl., family, children
bālṭī: fm., bucket
bānvē: adj., n.c., ninety-two
Bāṅkūpurā: pl. n., msc., Bankupura
bāp: msc., father
bāpū: msc., father (**form of address**)
bāpū-jī: msc., father (**honorific form of address**)
bāraunāḳ: adj., n.c., busy
bārā (also bārāh): adj., n.c. twelve
bārhvā̃: adj., twelfth
bāriś: fm., rain, rainy season
bāriś hōnā: vb. int., to rain
bāsaṭh: adj., n.c., sixty-two
bāt: fm., matter, account, saying
bāt karnā: vb. tr., to talk together, converse
bāt kāṭnā: vb. tr., to interrupt
bāt samajh-mē̃ ānā: vb. int., to understand
bāt sunnā: vb. tr., to listen
bātcīt: fm., conversation
bātcīt karnā: vb. tr., to discuss, chat
bāvan: adj., n.c., fifty-two
bāvarcī: msc., cook
bāvarcīḳhānā: msc., kitchen
bāyā̃: adj., left (direction)
bāzār: msc., bazaar
Bāgāl: pl. n., msc., Bengal, see **Baṅgāl**
bāṭnā: vb. int., to be divided
bāṭvārā: msc., crop-share
bā̃dh lēnā: vb. tr., to tie
bā̃dhnā: vb. tr., to tie
Bā̃kūpurā: see **Bāṅkupūrā**
bā̃ṭ dēnā: vb. tr., to distribute, divide
bāṭ jānā: vb. int., to be divided
bā̃ṭnā: vb. tr., to divide, distribute
behtar karnā: vb. tr., to improve
beṅk: msc., bank
beristrī: fm., barristry
bēcain: adj., n.c., restless, eager
bēcārā: adj., helpless, wretched
bēcnā: vb. tr., to sell
bēcnēvālā: msc., seller
bēgam: fm., wife, queen, lady
bēgam • sāhibā: fm., madam

bēgunah: adj., n.c., without fault, innocent
bēhad: adv., exceedingly, very, boundless
bēhāthyār: adj., n.c., weaponless
bēhōś: adj., n.c., senseless, stupified
bēīmānī: fm., dishonesty
bēkār: adj., n.c., useless
bēkār: adv., uselessly
bēlbūṭā: msc., embroidery
bēlnā: vb. tr., to roll out, knead
bēōpārī: msc., businessman
bēpanah: adj., n.c., limitless
bēśak: adv., surely
bētāb: adj., n.c., restless, eager
bēṭā: msc., son
bēṭī: fm., daughter
bēvaḳūf: msc., fool
bēzār hōnā: vb. int., to be disgusted
bhaddā: adj., ugly
bhaīs: fm., female buffalo
bhalā: adj., good
bhalā: excl., well!
bhalāyī: (also **bhalāī**): **fm.**, goodness
Bharat: pr. n. msc., Bharat, man's name
bharā huā: adj., full of
bhaṛaknā: vb. int., burst forth, flare out
bhatījā: msc., paternal nephew
bhaūknā: vb. int., to bark
bhayānak: adj., n.c., dreadful
bhāgnā: vb. tr., to flee, run
bhāī: msc., brother, friend, cousin
bhāō: msc., rate
Bhārat: msc., India
bhārī: adj., n.c. heavy
bhāṭ: fm., bard
bhā̃p: fm., steam
bhā̃p lēnā: vb. tr., to guess
bhējnā: vb. tr., to send
bhēṛ: fm., lamb
bhēṛiyā: msc., wolf
bhikh: see **bhīkh**
bhikhmā̃gā: see **bhīkhmaṅgā**
bhiśtī: msc., water-carrier
-bhī: emphatic particle
bhīkh: fm., alms, charity
bhīkhmaṅgā: msc., beggar

bhīkh mā̃gnā: **vb. tr.,** to beg for alms
bhīṛ: **fm.,** crowd
bhōlā: **adj.,** innocent
bhōlī • bhālī: **adj., n.c.,** innocent
bhō̃knā: see **bhaũknā**
bhūk: **fm.,** appetite, hunger
bhūkā: **adj.,** hungry
bhūkē mar jānā: **vb. int.,** to die of hunger
bhūl jānā: **vb. int.,** to forget (**cf.** bhūlnā)
bhūlnā: **vb. int.,** to forget
bhūnnā: **vb. tr.,** to roast
bhūrā: **adj.,** brown
bigaṛnā: **vb. int.,** to be spoiled
bigāṛnā: **vb. tr.,** to spoil
Bihār: **pl. n., msc.,** Bihar
bijlī: **fm.,** electricity
bijlī-kī battī: **fm.,** electric light
biknā: **vb. int.,** to be sold
bil: **msc.,** bill
bilḍing: **fm.,** building
bilkul: **adv.,** completely
bilkul pās-hī: **adv.,** very near, quite near
billī: **fm.,** cat
binā (also **-kē bīnā, postpos. phrase**): **prep.,** without
Birla: **pr. n., msc.,** Birla
biskuṭ: **msc.,** biscuit
bistar: **msc.,** bed, bedding
biznas karnā: **vb. tr.,** to go into business
biznasmain: **msc.,** businessman
bī: **fm.,** lady
bī ē: **msc.,** B.A. (degree)
bīc: **fm.,** beach
bīc: **msc.,** middle
bīc-mẽ: **adv.,** in between
(-kē) bīc-mẽ: **postpost. phrase,** in the middle of
bīj: **msc.,** seed
bīmār: **adj., n.c.,** sick
bīmār: **msc.,** patient, sick person
bimār hō jānā: **vb. int.,** to get sick
bīmārī: **fm.,** illness
Bīrbal: **pr. n., msc.,** Birbal
bīs: **adj., n.c.,** twenty
bītnā: **vb. int.,** to pass by
bīvī: **fm.,** wife
bōjh: **msc.,** burden, weight, load

bōlī: **fm.,** dialect
bōlnā: **vb. int.,** to speak
bōnā: **vb. tr.,** to sow
bōrḍiṅghāus: **msc.,** boarding house
bōṭal: **fm.,** bottle
brāhmaṇ: **msc.,** Brahman
budh: **msc.,** Wednesday
bujhānā: **vb. tr.,** to extinguish
bukhār: **msc.,** fever
bukhār ānā: **vb. int.,** to have fever
bulānā: **vb. tr.,** to call
bulbul: **fm.,** nightingale
bulvā lēnā: **vb. tr.,** to summon, (cf. **bulvānā**)
bulvānā: **vb. tr.,** to summon
bunnā: **vb. tr.,** to knit, weave
bunyād: **fm.,** foundation
bunyād ḍālnā: **vb. tr.,** to lay foundation
burā: **adj.,** bad
burāī: **fm.,** evil, ills, hardship, scandal
buṛhāpā: **msc.,** old age
but: **msc.,** idol
buzdil: **msc.,** coward
buzdilānā: **adj., n.c.,** cowardly
buzurg: **msc.,** respectable old man
bū: **fm.,** smell
būnd: **fm.,** drop
būṛhā: **adj.,** old
būṛhīyā: **fm.,** old woman
bū̃d: **fm.,** drop

cacā: **msc.,** paternal uncle
cacērā: **adj.,** related through paternal uncle
cacī: **fm.,** paternal aunt
cahal • pahal: **msc.,** hubbub, to-do
cahētī: **adj., n.c.,** beloved
cahrā: **msc.,** face
cakkar lagānā: **vb. tr.,** to make the rounds of
cakra: **msc.,** wheel
calā jānā: **vb. int.,** to go away
calānā: **vb. tr.,** to drive
calnā: **vb. int.,** to walk, travel
camaknā: **vb. int.,** to shine
camār: **msc.,** leather-worker

Campāran: **pl. n., msc.,** Champaran, dist. in North Bihar
camṛā: **msc.,** leather, hide, skin
camṛī: **fm.,** leather, hide, skin
canā: **msc.,** grain, chick-pea
cand: **adj., n.c.,** few
candā: **msc.,** subscription, contribution
cappal: **fm.,** sandal
caprāsī: **msc.,** orderly
capṭī: **adj., n.c.,** flat
carāgāh: **fm.,** grazing land, pasture
carḳhā: **msc.,** spinning wheel
carnā: **vb. tr.,** to graze
caṛhānā: **vb. tr.,** to cause to climb
caṛhnā: **vb. int.,** to climb
caubīs: **adj., n.c.,** twenty-four
caudā (also **caudāh**): **adj., n.c.,** fourteen
caudharī: **msc.,** village headman, title of respect of farmers
cauhattar: **adj., n.c.,** seventy-four
cauk: **msc.,** market place, crossing **(of street)**
caukidār: **msc.,** watchman
Caupāṭī: **pl. n., fm.,** seashore in Bombay
caupāyā: **msc.,** cattle
caurānvē: **adj., n.c.,** ninety-four
caurāsī: **adj., n.c.,** eight-four
cauṛā: **adj.,** broad, wide
cauthā: **adj.,** fourth
caũk uṭhnā: **vb. int.,** to wake up suddenly
caũknā: **vb. int.,** to start up from sleep
caũsaṭh: **adj., n.c.,** sixty-four
caũtīs: **adj., n.c.,** thirty-four
cavālīs: **adj., n.c.,** forty-four
cavvan: **adj., n.c.,** fifty-four
cābī: **fm.,** key
cādar: **fm.,** sheet
cāhnā: **vb. tr.,** to want, wish
cāk karnā: **vb. tr.,** to open, tear open
cālāk: **adj., n.c.,** cunning, clever
cālān hōnā: **vb. int.,** to get a summons, ticket
cālīs: **adj., n.c.,** forty
cār: **adj., n.c.,** four
cārō̃ taraf: **adv.,** everywhere, on all sides
cāval: **msc.,** rice
cāy: **fm.,** tea
cā̃d: **msc.,** moon
cā̃dī: **fm.,** silver

Cā̃dnī Cauk: **pl. n.,** msc., name of a bazaar in Delhi
cehrā: **msc.,** face
chabbīs: **adj., n.c.,** twenty-six
chappan: **adj., n.c.,** fifty-six
chaṛī: **fm.,** stick
chat: **fm.,** roof
chatrī: **fm.,** umbrella, pavilion
chattīs: **adj., n.c.,** thirty-six
chaṭā: **adj.,** sixth
chānā: **vb. int.,** to spread
chāōnī: **fm.,** cantonment
chātā: **msc.,** umbrella
chātī: **fm.,** breast
chāyā: **fm.,** shade
chā̃ṭnā: **vb. tr.,** to husk, trim
che: **adj., n.c.,** six
chēd: **msc.,** hole
chihattar: **adj., n.c.,** seventy-six
chilkā: **msc.,** rind, skin of fruit, peeling
chiyālīs: **adj., n.c.,** forty-six
chiyānvē: **adj., n.c.,** ninety-six
chiyāsaṭh: **adj., n.c.,** sixty-six
chiyāsī: **adj., n.c.,** eighty-six
chīnnā: **vb. tr.,** to grab, snatch
chōkrā: **msc.,** child
chōkrō̃: **msc., voc. pl.,** kiddies
chōṛ ānā: **vb. int.,** to abandon, set off
chōṛ dēnā: **vb. tr.,** to release, let go, give up
chōṛkar: **ger. = postpos.** (cf. **chōṛnā**): leaving, with the exception of
chōṛnā: **vb. tr.,** to give up, leave
chōṭā: **adj.,** small
Chōṭā Nāgpur: **pl. n., msc.,** Chota Nagpur
chupānā: **vb. tr.,** to cause to hide
chupnā: **vb. int.,** to hide
churī: **fm.,** knife
chūṭnā: **vb. int.,** to leave
chuṭṭī: **fm.,** vacation, leave
cillānā: **vb. int.,** to scream
ciṛiyā: **fm.,** sparrow, bird
citā: **fm.,** pyre
ciṭṭhī: **fm.,** letter
cīḳhē̃ mārnā: **vb. tr.,** to howl
cīḳhnā: **vb. int.,** to scream
Cīn: **pl. n.,** msc., China

cīnī: fm., sugar
cītā: msc., cheetah
cīz: fm., thing
cīghāṛnā: vb. int., to roar, screech
cōr: msc., thief
cōrī: fm., stealing, theft
cōrī cōrī: adv., secretly
cōrī karnā: vb. tr., to steal
cōṭ: fm., wound, bruise
cōṭī: fm., peak, top
cugnā: vb. tr., to peck and eat (of fowl)
cuhiyā: fm., mouse
cuknā: vb. tr., to be completed
cummā: vb. tr., to kiss (cf. **cūmnā**)
cunā̃ce: adv., accordingly
cunnā: vb. tr., to elect, select, choose
cup: adj., n.c., silent, quiet
cup rahnā: vb. int., to keep quiet
cupcāp: adj., n.c., quiet
cupkē-sē: adv., quietly
curānā: vb. tr., to steal
cūk: fm., error
cūk jānā: vb., int., to miss, fail
cūmnā: vb., tr., to kiss (cf. **cumnā**)
cūṛī: fm., bangle
cū̃ • cū̃ karnā: vb. tr., to chirp
cū̃-ke: conj., since

dabānā: vb. tr., to suppress, put down
dabnā: vb. int., to be suppressed
dafā: fm., time
dafātir: msc. pl., offices (see **daftar**)
daftar: msc., office
dahī: msc., curds, yogurt
daḳhal: msc., interference
daḳhal dēnā: vb. tr., to interfere
daraḳht: msc., tree
darbār: msc., court, audience hall
darbārī: msc., courtier
dard: msc., pain
dard honā: vb. int., to be hurt

dariyā: msc., river
darjan: fm., dozen
darḳhāst: fm., request
darrā: msc., pass (e.g., in mountains)
darust: adj., n.c., correct
darvāzā: msc., door
darvāzē-kī ghaṇṭī: fm., door-bell
darzī: msc., tailor
das: adj., n.c., ten
das lākh: adj., n.c., one million
dast: msc., hand
dast-e-rāst: msc., right-hand man
dasvā̃: adj., tenth
Daśrath: pr. n., msc., King Dashrath
dauṛnā: vb. int., to run
davā: fm., medicine
davāī: fm., medicine
dādā: msc., paternal grandfather
dādā•jān: msc., grandfather
dādī: fm., paternal grandmother
dāir karnā: vb. tr., to present, file (e.g., a lawsuit)
dāḳhil hōnā: vb. int., to enter
dāḳhil karvānā: vb. tr., to cause to be admitted, have enrolled
dāl: fm., pulse, lentils
dām: msc., cost, price
dāmād: msc., son-in-law
dān: msc., grant, gift
dānā: msc., grain, seed, wise man
dāṛhī: fm., beard
dāsī: fm., handmaiden, female slave
dāstān-e-Alaflailā: fm., stories from the Arabian Nights
dāvat: fm., entertainment, feast
dāyā̃: adj., right (i.e., direction)
dā̃t: msc., tooth
dēkhbhāl: fm., care
dēkhbhāl karnā: vb. tr., take care of, to look after
dēkhnā: vb. tr., to see
dēnā: vb. tr., to give
dēr: fm., delay
dēr-sē: adv., late
dēs (also **dēś**): **msc.,** country
dēvtā: msc., divinity, god
dhabbā: msc., stain
dhan: msc., wealth

dhanī: **adj., n.c.,** rich
dharmśālā: **msc.,** almshouse
dhāknā: **vb. tr.,** to cover, conceal
dhiyān: **msc.,** attention, care
dhiyān dēnā: **vb. tr.,** to pay attention
dhīrē: **adv.,** slowly
dhōban: **fm.,** washerwoman
dhōbī: **msc.,** washerman
dhōkar: **ger.,** washing (see **dhōnā**)
dhōnā: **vb. tr.,** to wash
dhōtī: **fm.,** dhōti, a type of trouser
dhunnā: **vb. tr.,** to card (e.g., wool or cotton)
dhūā̃: **msc.,** smoke
dhūl: **fm.,** dust
dhūp: **fm.,** sunlight
dhūp saĩknā: **vb. tr.,** to absorb sun, warm up
dikhānā: **vb. tr.,** to point out, show (cf. dekhnā)
dikhāyī dēnā: **vb. tr.,** to be seen, appear
dil: **msc.,** heart
dilānā: **vb. tr.,** to cause to give, cause to be given
dilcasp: **adj., n.c.,** interesting
dilcaspī: **fm.,** interest
Dillī: **pl. n., msc.,** Delhi
din: **msc.,** morning, day
Disambar: **msc.,** December
diyā: **pst. part.,** see **dēnā**
dīhātī: **msc.,** villager
dījiyē: see **dēnā**
dīn: **msc.** faith, religion
Din-e-Ilāhī: **msc.,** name of Akbar's religion
dīp: **msc.,** lamp
Dīvālī: **fm.,** Festival of Lamps
dīvān: **msc.,** court, tribunal
dīvān-e-ām: **msc.,** General Court, public hall of audience
dīvān-e-ḳhās: **msc.,** Special Court, Privy council chamber
dīvār: **fm.,** wall
dō: **adj., n.c.,** two
dō: see **dēnā**
dō·bārā: **adv.,** once again, a second time, twice
dōhrānā: **vb. tr.,** to repeat
dōnō̃: **adv.,** both
dōpahar: **fm.,** noon
dōst: **msc. and fm.,** friend
dramāī: **adj., n.c.,** dramatic

dublā: **adj.**, lean
dukān: **fm.**, shop
dukān karnā: **vb. tr.**, to run a shop
dukāndār: **msc.**, shop-keeper
dukh: **msc.**, sorrow
dukhānā: **vb. tr.**, to hurt, injure
dukhī: **adj.**, **n.c.**, sad
dulhan: **fm.**, bride
dumbā: **msc.**, ram
duniyā (also **dunyā**); **fm.**, world
duśman: **msc.**, enemy
dūā dēnā: **vb. tr.**, to pray
dūdh: **msc.**, milk
dūdh nikālnā: **vb. tr.**, to milk
dūdhvālā: **msc.**, milkman
dūr: **adj.**, **n.c.**, distant, far
dūr • drāz: **adj.**, **n.c.**, distant
dūsrā: **adj.**, different, other, another, second
dūsrē din subah: **adv.**, on the following day, in the morning
dyanatdārī: **fm.**, honesty

ḍalnā: **vb. tr.**, to drop, throw, put, pour
ḍar: **msc.**, fear
ḍar jānā: **vb. int.**, to be frightened
ḍarānā: **vb. tr.**, to frighten
ḍarnā: **vb. int.**, to fear, be afraid, become frightened
ḍākgārī: **fm.**, mail-train
ḍākḳhānā: **msc.**, post-office
ḍākṭarī: **fm.**, profession of physician
ḍēṛh: **adj.**, **n.c.** one and a half
Ḍhākā: **pl. n.**, **msc.**, Dacca
ḍhālnā: **vb. tr.**, to melt
ḍhālvān: **fm.**, slope
ḍhū̃ḍhnā: see **ḍhū̃ṛhnā**
ḍhūṛhnā (also **ḍhūḍhnā**): **vb. tr.**, to seek, look for, search
ḍigrī: **fm.**, degree
ḍigrī lēnā: **vb. tr.**, to take a degree
Ḍōgrā: **pl. n.**, **msc.**, Dogra
ḍōrā: **msc.**, thread
ḍrāiṅgrūm: **msc.**, drawing room
ḍrāivar: msc., driver
ḍubānā: **vb. tr.**, to sink, drown

ḍūb jānā: vb. int., to sink, drown
ḍūbnā: vb. int., to sink, drown

ehtiyāt: fm., care
ehtiyāt karnā: vb. tr., to take care
ehtiyāt rakhnā: vb. tr., to take care of
Elāhābād: Allahabad, see **Illāhābād**
embaisī: fm., embassy
enjinīr: see **injnīr**
ēk: adj., n.c., one
ēk aur-bhī: adj., n.c., another, one more
ēk dafā-kā zikr hai: once upon a time, it is said, it so happened, it is mentioned
ēk • dam: adv., instantly, forthwith, entirely
ēk-hī: adj., n.c., only one
ēk hōkar: adv., together, as one
ēk jaisā: adv., all alike
ēk-sā: adj., similar, alike
ēk-sāth: adv., together
ēkaṛ: msc., acre
ērōḍrōm: msc., airdrome
Ēśiyā: pl. n., msc., Asia
ētbār: msc., confidence

faislā: msc., decision, decree, verdict
faislā karnā: vb. tr., to decide
faiśan: msc., fashion
faiyāz: adj., n.c., generous
faḳīr: msc., beggar
falsafā: msc., philosophy
falsafiānah: adj., n.c., philosophic, philosophical
falsafiyānā: see **falsafiānah**
fankār: msc., artist
farḳ: msc., difference, distance
farmāiyē: What do you wish? (**lit.**: please command)
farmānā: vb. tr., to order (**respectfully**)
farś: msc., floor, rug
farz: msc., duty
farz adā karnā: vb. tr., to do one's duty
farzī: adj., n.c., fictitious

fasal: **fm.,** harvest, crop, produce
fasād: **msc.,** riot
fatah: **fm.,** conquest, victory
fatūhāt: **fm., pl.,** victories
fauj: **fm.,** army
fauran: **adv.,** immediately
faut hōnā: **vb. int.,** to die
favvārā: **msc.,** fountain
fazal: **msc.,** kindness, grace
fazūl: **adj., n.c.,** useless
fazūl • ḳharc: **adj., n.c.,** extravagant
fāltū: **adj., n.c.,** spare, extra
fārig̱ hōnā: **vb. int.,** to finish, complete
Fārsī: **fm.,** Persian language
fāydā: **msc.,** profit, use, advantage, gain
fāyr karnā: **vb. tr.,** to fire (a gun)
fēl hō jānā: **vb. int.,** to fail
fikr: **msc.,** concern, worry
fikr karnā: **vb. tr.,** to worry
fikrā: **msc.,** sentence
filhāl: **adv.,** for the present
film: **fm.,** motion picture
firḳā (also **firḳah**): **msc.,** party, troop, society, sect
firḳē • dārāna: **adj., n.c.,** communal
fisād: see **fasad**
fīs: **fm.,** fees
fītā: **msc.,** lace, shoe lace
fīt: **msc.,** feet (**in measurement**)
flaiṭ: **msc.,** apartment, flat
fōṭōgrāfar: **msc.,** photographer
friśtā (also **firiśtā**): **msc.,** angel
futūh: **fm. pl.** (of **fatah**), victories, conquests
futūhāt: **fm. pl.** (of **fatah**), victories, conquests

gaddī: **fm.,** throne
gadhā: **msc.,** donkey
gahnā: **msc.,** jewel, jewelry
gahrā: **adj.,** deep
galā: **msc.,** throat
galī: **fm.** street
gandā: **adj.,** dirty
gannā: **msc.,** sugar-cane

Gañgā: **pl. n., fm.,** Ganges River
gap: **fm.,** gossip
gap karnā: **vb. tr.,** to gossip
garāj: **msc.,** garage
gard: **fm.,** dust
gardan: **fm.,** neck
garm: **adj., n.c.,** warm
garmī: **fm.,** summer
Gautam Budh: **msc.,** Gautama Buddha
Gavarmeṇṭ Kālij: **msc.,** Government College
gavarnar: **msc.,** governor
Gavarnar Jenral: **msc.,** Governor General
gayā: **pst. past.,** see **jānā**
gāhak: **msc.** and **fm.,** customer
gājar: **fm.,** carrot
gānā: **vb. tr.,** to sing
gānā: **msc.,** song, saying, music
gānēvālā: **msc.,** singer
gāō̃: **msc.,** village
gaō̃vālā: **msc.,** villager
gāṛī: **fm.,** carriage, train, cart, car
gāṛībān: **msc.,** cart driver
gāy: **fm.,** cow
gãvānā: **vb. tr.,** to waste **(time)**
Gā̃dhī: **pr. n. msc.,** Gandhi, (Mohandas Karamchand)
gēhū̃: **msc.,** wheat
gē̃d: **msc.,** ball
ghabrānā: **vb. int.,** to worry
ghanā: **adj.,** thick, dense
ghaṇṭā: **msc.,** bell
ghaṇṭī: **fm.,** bell
ghar: **msc.,** house, home, family, household
ghar jānā: **vb. int.,** to go home
gharānā: **msc.,** family
gharvālā: **msc.,** householder
ghaṛā: **msc.,** water-pot
ghaṛī: **fm.,** watch
ghaṛīsāz: **msc.,** watch repairman
ghaṭ jānā: **vb. int.,** to decrease
ghaṭānā: **vb. tr.,** to subtract
ghaṭiyā: **adj., n.c.,** low, inferior, cheap
ghāil: **adj., n.c.,** injured, bruised, wounded
ghās: **fm.,** grass
ghāṭ: **msc.,** bank, landing
ghāṭī: **fm.,** valley

ghī: msc., clarified butter
ghōr: adj., n.c., awful, dreadful
ghōṛā: msc., horse
ghōṛī: fm., mare
ghumānā: vb. tr., to cause to spin
ghūmnā: vb. int., to walk, wander, roam, about; turn, revolve
ghūrnā: vb. tr., to stare
ginnā: vb. tr., to count
gir jānā: vb. int., to fall
girānā: vb. tr., to drop (cf. **girnā**)
giriftār hōnā: vb. int., to be imprisoned
girnā: vb. int., to fall
girvī: fm., mortgage
girvī rakhnā: vb. tr., to hold a mortgage
gīdar: msc., jackal
gīdh: msc., vulture
gīlā: adj., wet
gīt: msc., song
Gītā: fm., Bhagavad Gita, a religious poem in the Mahabharata
glās: msc., glass
Gōā: pl. n., msc., Goa
gōbhī: fm., cauliflower
gōd: fm., lap
Gōdāvarī: pl. n., msc., Godavari River
gōl: adj., n.c., round
gōlī: fm., bullet
Gōmatī: pl. n., msc., Gomati River
gōrā: adj., white
gōrī camṛī: fm., white skin
gōśt: msc., meat
grējūeṭ: msc., graduate
grēnaiṭ: msc., granite
grūp: msc., group, faction
guftagū: fm., conversation
Gujarātī: msc., a native of Gujarat
Gujarātī: fm., language of Gujarat
Gujarātī: adj., n.c., pertaining to Gujarat
gulāl: msc., red powder
gum hōnā: vb. int., to be lost
gumbad: msc., dome
gunā: msc. and fm., "times" (end of compound)
gunāh: msc., sin
gunāh karnā: vb. tr., to sin
gurū: msc., Hindu spiritual preceptor, teacher
guṛ: msc., gur (coarse sugar)

guṛiyā: **fm.,** doll
gustāḳh: **adj., n.c.,** insolent
guzarnā: **vb. int.,** to pass, to go, to elapse
gyārā (also **gyārāh):** **adj., n.c.,** eleven
gyārvā̃: **adj.,** eleventh

g̱adar: **msc.,** mutiny
g̱air: **msc.,** stranger, foreigner
g̱air·adāśudā: **adj., n.c.,** unpaid
g̱air·hāzarī: **fm.,** absence
g̱air·hāzir: **adj., n.c.,** absent
g̱air·mazrūā. **adj., n.c.,** fallow
g̱air·mulkī: **adj., n.c.,** foreign
g̱alat: **adj., n.c.,** wrong, incorrect
g̱alat·salat: **adj., n.c.,** erroneous
g̱alatī: **fm.,** error
g̱alatī-sē: **adv.,** in error
g̱am: **msc.,** grief
g̱amgīn: **adj., n.c.,** sad
g̱arārā: **msc.,** trousers for women
g̱arīb: **adj., n.c.,** poor
g̱arūb: **msc.,** setting
g̱arūb hōnā: **vb. int.,** to set (of sun)
g̱aur: **msc.,** deep thought, reflection
g̱aur karnā: **vb. tr.,** to think about, consider
g̱aur-ō-fikr: **msc.** and **fm.,** contemplation
g̱azal: **fm.,** lyrical poem
g̱azal kahnā: **vb. tr.,** to compose lyrical poem
g̱āib: **adj., n.c.,** disappeared, vanished
g̱āib hōnā: **vb. int.,** to disappear
g̱ār: **msc.,** cave
g̱usalḳhānā: **msc.,** bathroom
g̱ussā: **msc.,** anger
g̱ussē-sē kā̃pnā: **vb. int.,** to tremble with anger
g̱ussīlā: **adj.,** angry

haḍḍī: **fm.,** bone
haftā: **msc.,** week
hai: see **hōnā**

Haidarābād: pl. n., msc., Hyderabad
hairānī: fm., surprise, amazement
haī: see **hōnā**
haj: msc., pilgrimage
haj karnā: vb. tr., to go on a pilgrimage
hajāmat: fm., shave
hajāmat banānā: vb. tr., to shave
hakūmat: fm., government
hakūmat karnā: vb. tr., to rule
haḳ: msc., right
haḳdār: adj., n.c., deserving
haḳūḳ: msc. pl., rights
hal: msc., plow
hal jōtnā: vb. tr., to plow, till
halkā: adj., light
halvāī: msc., sweet-meat maker
hamasar: adj., n.c., contemporary
hamārā: adj., our
hamdardī: fm., sympathy
hamēśā: adv., always
hamjamāat: msc., classmate
hamlā: msc., attack
hamlā karnā: vb. tr., to attack
hamsafar: msc., fellow-traveller
hamsāī: fm., neighbor
hamsāyā: msc., neighbor
haṇḍiyā: fm., cooking-pot
har: adj., n.c., each, every
haraf: msc., letter (**of alphabet**)
haram: msc., harem
harā: adj., green
harām-kā: adj., illegal, illegitimate, black-market
harāmḳhōr: msc., grafter
harf: see **haraf**
harījan: msc., untouchable
harrān: adj., n.c., surprised
hasb · zail: adv., as follows
hasb-e-zail: adv., as follows
haspatāl: msc., hospital
haṭ jānā: vb. int., to get out of the way
haṭānā: vb. tr., to remove, keep back
haṭnā: vb. int., to withdraw, get out of the way
havā: fm., wind, climate
havāī · jahāz: msc., airplane
havālā: msc., custody

hazār: adj., n.c., one thousand
hazārõ: adv., thousands
hazrat: msc., title of respect
hāē: excl., alas!
hāiskūl: msc., high school
hājī: msc., pilgrim
hāl: msc., hall
hāl: msc., condition, state, affair, narrative
hālat: fm., condition, state of things, circumstances
hār: msc., necklace, wreath, garland
hār: fm., fatigue, defeat
hār jānā: vb. int., to lose
hāsil karnā: vb. tr., to obtain, get
hāth: msc., hand
hāth khaṛā karnā: vb. tr., to raise hands
hāth milānā: vb. tr., to shake hands
hāthī: msc., elephant
hāus āf pīpal: msc., House of People
hāzrī: fm., roll-call, attendance
hāzrī lēnā: vb. tr., to take roll, make a list
hãsnā: vb. int., to laugh
helō: msc., hello
hēḍ • klark: msc., head clerk
hēḍ • māsṭar: msc., Head Master
hijrat: fm., migration
hilānā: vb. tr., to wave
Himālay: pl. n., msc., Himalaya Mountains
himmat: fm., courage
himmat hārnā: vb. tr., to become discouraged
Hindī: fm., Hindi (language)
Hindū: adj. and msc., Hindu
Hindūstān: pl. n., msc., India
hiran: msc., deer
hisāb: msc., arithmetic, calculation, accounts
hisāb karnā: vb. tr., to keep accounts
hisāb • kitāb: msc., accounts
hissā: msc., part, share
-hī: emphatic particle
hīrā: msc., diamond
holē: adv., softly
holē: adv., softly, slowly
holē bōlnā: vb. int., to speak softly
hō: see **hōnā**
hō jānā: vb. int., to become
Hōlī: fm., Hindu religious festival

hōnā: **vb. int.,** to be, become
hōś: **msc.,** sense, understanding
hōś-mẽ ānā: **vb. int.,** to be sensible, come to one's senses
hōś uṛ jānā: **vb. int.,** to lose presence of mind, become senseless
hōśiyār: **adj., n.c.,** clever
hōśiyārī: **fm.,** sense, cleverness, skill
hōśiyārī-sē: **adj.,** carefully
hōṭal: **msc.,** hotel
hubb-e-vatan: **fm.,** patriotism
hukam: **msc.,** order, command
hukm: see **hukam**
huzūr: **msc.,** "your honor"
hū̃: see **hōnā**

ibādat: **fm.,** prayers
ibādat karnā: **vb. tr.,** perform prayers
ibtadāī talīm: **fm.,** early education, primary education
idhar: **adv.,** hither, here
idhar • udhar: **adv.,** helter skelter, hither and thither
idhar • udhar-kā: **adj.,** irrelevant
ijāzat: **fm.,** permission
ijlās: **msc.,** meeting, assembly
ikatīs: **adj., n.c.,** thirty-one
ikaṭṭhā: **adj.,** collected, accumulated
ikhattar: **adj., n.c.,** seventy-one
ikkānvē: **adj., n.c.,** ninety-one
ikkāsī: **adj., n.c.,** eighty-one
ikkīs: **adj., n.c.,** twenty-one
iknaumiks: **fm.,** economics
iksaṭh: **adj., n.c.,** sixty-one
iktālīs: **adj., n.c.,** forty-one
ikyāvan: **adj., n.c.,** fifty-one
iḳhrājāt: **msc. pl.,** expenses (see **ḳharc**)
iḳhtalāf: **msc.,** difference
iḳhtalāfāt: **msc., pl.,** differences (see **iḳhtalāf**)
iḳhtilāf: **msc.,** difference
iḳhtiyār karnā: **vb. tr.,** to adopt, take up
iḳrār: **msc.,** confession
Ilāhābād: **pl. n., msc.,** Allahabad
ilāj: **msc.,** treatment, remedy
ilāj karnā: **vb.** tr., to treat (e.g., of disease)
ilāḳā: **msc.,** area

ilm: **msc.,** knowledge, learning
Imāmbāṛā: **msc.,** enclosure sacred to Muslim sect, the place where the Muharram is celebrated.
imārat: **fm.,** building
imdād: **fm.,** help
imdādī: **msc.** and **fm.,** assistant
impīryalism: **msc.,** imperialism
imtihān: **msc.,** examination, test
imtēhān: **msc.,** examination, test
in: **obl. pl.,** see **ye**
inām: **msc.,** prize, reward
inc: **msc.,** inch
Indīrā: **pr. n., fm.,** Indira, a woman's name
inhē̃: **obl. pl.,** see **ye**
inhō̃: **obl. pl.,** see **ye**
inkār: **msc.,** refusal, objection
inḳalāb (also **inḳilāb**): **msc.,** revolution, change
inḳalābī: **adj., n.c.,** revolutionary
insāf: **msc.,** justice
insāf karnā: **vb. tr.,** to do justice
insān: **msc.,** human being, mankind
inspekṭar: **msc.** and **fm.,** inspector
inśā Allāh: God willing!
intazām (also **intizām**): **msc.,** arrangement
intazār (also **intizār**): **msc.,** waiting, expectation
intazār karnā: **vb. tr.,** to wait for, expect
intizām: see **intazām**
intizār: see **intazār**
Iñglaind: **pl. n., msc.,** England
Iñglistān: **pl. n., msc.,** England, Great Britain
injinīr: **msc.** and **fm.,** engineer
injīnīring: **fm.,** engineering
irādā: **msc.,** intention, determination, wish, desire
is: **obl. s.,** see **ye**
is liyē: **adv.,** therefore
is-sē: **adv.,** therefore, from this
is vaḳt: **adv.,** now
isē: **obl. s.,** see **yē** (= **is-kō**)
iskūl: **msc.,** school
Islām: **msc.,** Islam
istaḳbāl: **msc.,** welcome
istaḳbāl karnā: **vb. tr.,** to receive (e.g., as guest), welcome
istēmāl: **msc.,** use
istēmāl karnā: **vb. tr.,** to use
iśārā: **msc.,** signal, gesture

itnā: **adj.**, this much, so much
itnā zyādā: **adv.**, too much
itnē pās: **adv.**, so close
ittafāḳ-sē: **adv.**, by chance
ittalā: **fm.**, information
ittalā dēnā: **vb. tr.**, to inform
Itvār: **msc.**, Sunday
izzat: **fm.**, respect, status, honor

-ī: **emphatic particle**
Īd: **fm.**, Muslim festival
īmān: **msc.**, belief, idea, faith, truth, honesty
īmāndār: **adj.**, **n.c.**, honest
Īrān: **pl. n.**, **msc.**, Iran, Persia
Īsā: **pr. n.**, **msc.**, Jesus Christ
Isāī (also **isāyī**): **msc.** and **fm.**, Christian

ĩdhan: **msc.**, fuel

jab: **adv.**, when, as soon as
jab-tak: **adv.**, until
jagah: **fm.**, place
jagānā: **vb. tr.**, to wake up
jahāz: **msc.**, ship
jahāzī: **msc.**, sailor
jahā̃: **adv.**, where
Jahā̃gīr: **pr. n.**, **msc.**, Jahangir, a Mogul emperor
jaisā: **adj.**, like
jaj: **msc.**, judge
jal jānā: **vb. int.**, to burn, burn out (cf. **jalnā**)
jalānā: **vb. tr.**, to cause to burn, light
jald: **adv.**, soon, quickly
jald-hī: **adv.**, soon after
jaldī: **fm.**, quickness, speed
jaldī-sē: **adv.**, quickly
jalnā: **vb. int.**, to burn
jalsā: **msc.**, meeting
jalūs: **msc.**, procession
jamā: **fm.**, accumulation, amount

amā hōnā: vb. int., to collect, be collected, gather, be gathered
amā karnā: vb. tr., to collect, gather, add
amāt (also **jamāat**): **fm.,** class grade (**in school**)
amnā: pl. n., fm., Jumna River
amśēdpur: pl. n., msc., Jamshedpur
anāb: msc., Sir! (**form of address**)
janvarī: fm., January
jan̄g: fm., battle, war
jan̄gal: msc., jungle
jan̄glī: msc. and adj., n.c., savage
jan̄kśan: msc., junction
jaṛā: adj., set, studded
javāb: msc., answer
Javāharlāl Nēhrū: pr. n., msc., Jawaharlal Nehru
javān: adj., n.c., young, mature, of marriageable age
javānī: fm., youth, time of youth
jaziyā: msc., tax on non-Muslims
jazīrā: msc., island
jāēdād: fm., property
jāgnā: vb. int., to get up
jākar: ger., having gone (**cf. jānā**)
jāl: msc., net
jālī: fm., wire gauze
jān: fm., life
jān būjhkar: adv., deliberately
jān-ō-māl: msc., pl., well-being, welfare
jānaśīn: msc., successor
jānā: vb. int., to leave, go
jānēvālā: adj., going, about to go
jānnā: vb. int., to know
jānvar: msc., animal
jānvar • ḳurbān karnā: vb. tr., to sacrifice animals
Jāpān: pl. n., msc., Japan
jārī: adj., n.c., current
jārī rahnā: vb. int., to continue
jārī rakhnā: vb. tr., to continue
Jārj: pr. n., msc., George
jā̃c: fm., investigation
jēb: fm., pocket
jēb • ḳharc: msc., pocket money
jēl: msc., jail
jhagṛā: msc., quarrel
jhagṛālū: adj., n.c., quarrelsome
jhaṇḍā: msc., flag
jhaṭ paṭ: adv., immediately

jhāṛī: fm., bush
jhāṛū: fm., broom
jhāṛū dēnā: vb. tr., to sweep
Jhēlum: pl. n., fm., Jhelum River
jhuk jānā: vb. int., to bend
jhuknā: vb. int., to bend, tilt
jhukānā: vb. tr., to hang, bend, cause to bend
jhūṭ: msc., lie
jhūṭ • mūṭ kahnā: vb. tr., to spoof, kid, tease
jhūṭā: adv., false
jhõpṛī: fm., hut
jild: fm., skin
jin: obl. pl., see **jō**
jinhẽ: obl. pl., see **jō**
jinhõ: obl. pl., see **jō**
Jinnāh: pr. n., msc., Muhammad Ali Jinnah
jis: obl. s., see **jō**
jisē: obl. s., see **jō**
jitnā: adj., as much (as)
jī: msc., heart
jī: adv., yes
-jī: hon. pt.
jī hā̃: adv., yes sir, yes ma'am
jī nahī̃: adv., no sir, no ma'am
jīt: fm., victory
jīt jānā: vb. int., to win, conquer
jītnā: vb. int., to conquer
jō: rel. pron., adj., n.c., which, who
jōṛnā: vb. tr., to join hands, add, save
jōtnā: vb. tr., to yoke, plough, till
jugālī karnā: vb. tr., to chew cud, ruminate
jugrāfiyā: msc., geography
Jumā: msc., Friday
Jumērāt: fm., Thursday
jurābẽ: see **jarābẽ**
jurm: msc., crime, quilt, evil action
jurmānā: msc., fine
jurmānā hōnā: vb. int., to be fined
jurrāb: fm., sock
jurrābẽ: fm. pl., socks
jūā khelnā: vb. tr., to gamble, play at dice
Jūlāī: fm., July
Jūn: msc., June
jūtā: msc., shoe
jū̃ jū̃ . . . aur-bhī: the more . . . the more

jū̃ jū̃ . . . tū̃ tū̃: as . . . as
jū̃-hī: adv., as soon as

kab: adv., when
kabhī: adv., ever
kabhī kabhī: adv., sometimes
kabhī-na-kabhī: adv., one time or another
kabūtar: msc., pigeon
kaccā: adj., raw, uncooked
kahānī: fm., story
kahā̃: adv., where
kahī̃: adv., somewhere
kahlānā: vb. tr., to cause to tell, to be called, to be designated
kahnā: vb. tr., to say
kaibinēṭ: fm., cabinet
kaimp: msc., camp
kaimrā: msc., camera
kaisā: interr. adj., what sort?
kaisē: adv., how?, for what reason
kaī: adj., n.c., several
kal: adv., tomorrow, yesterday
Kaliṅgā: pl. n., msc., Kalinga, an ancient Indian kingdom
Kalkattā: pl. n., msc., Calcutta
kam: adv., less, little
kam karnā: vb. tr., to reduce, decrease
kam-az-kam: adv., at least
kam-ō-bēś: adv., more or less
kam-sē kam: adv., at least
kamal: msc., lotus
kamar: fm., back
kamānā: vb. tr., to earn
kambal: msc., blanket
kambhā: msc., post, pillar
kamētī: fm., municipality
kamiśan: msc., commission
kamiśnar: msc., commissioner
kamī: fm., lack, deficiency
kampanī: fm., company
kamrā: msc., room
kamyūnizm: msc., Communism
kamzōr: adj., n.c., weak, poor
kanīz: fm., maid

kanjūs makkhī cūs: **msc.,** miser of misers
kaṅghā: **msc.,** comb
kaṅghī: **fm.,** comb
kapās: **fm.,** cotton
kapṛā: **msc.,** cloth, clothing
kaptān: **msc.,** captain
Karācī: **pl. n., msc.,** Karaci
karānā: **vb. tr.,** to cause to do (cf. **karnā**)
karīm: **fm.,** cream
karnā: **vb. tr.,** to make, do
karō: see **karnā**
karōṛ: **msc.,** ten million, crore
karvānā: **vb. tr.,** to cause to do
kaṛā: **adj.,** harsh, sharp, hard
kaṛvā: **adj.,** bitter
kasrat: **fm.,** exercise
Kaśmīr: **pl. n., msc.,** Kashmir
kaśtī: **fm.,** boat
kaṭhan: **adj., n.c.,** severe, difficult
kaun: **interr. adj.** and **pron.,** what? which? who?
kaun-sā: **adj.,** which particular
kaunsil cēmbar: **msc.,** Council Chamber
kāfir: **msc.,** heathen
kāfī: **msc.,** coffee
kāfī: **adj., n.c.,** enough
kāfī pās: **adv.,** quite near
kāgaz: **msc.,** note, paper
kālaj: **msc.,** college
kālā: **adj.,** black
kālij: **msc.,** college
kām: **msc.,** work
kām karnā: **vb. tr.,** to work
kām-kā: **adj.,** of use, useful
kām • kāj: **msc.,** chore, duty, occupation
kāmyābī: **fm.,** success
kān: **msc.,** ear
kān: **fm.,** mine
kānṭrōl karnā: **vb. tr.,** to control, direct
Kāṅgras: **fm.,** Indian National Congress Party
Kāṅgrasī: **msc.** and **adj., n.c.,** member of Congress Party
kāpī: **fm.,** copybook
kār: **fm.,** car
kārgah: **fm.,** a weaver's workshop
kārīgar: **msc.,** skilled worker, mechanic
kārkun: **msc.,** worker

kārḳhānā: msc., factory, plant
kārōbār: msc., business, work, labor
kārōbārī: msc., businessman
kārrvāī: fm., action
kāś: conj., "I wish"
Kāśī: pl. n., msc., Banaras
Kāśmīr: pl. n., msc., Kashmir
Kāśmīrī: msc., and **adj., n.c.,** Kashmirian
kāśt: fm., cultivation
kāṭh: msc., wood
kāṭnā: vb. tr., to bite, cut
kãval: msc., lotus
kãvārā: msc., bachelor
kā̃ṭā: msc., earring, thorn, scale
ke: pt. of quotation, that, when
keh: variant of **ke**
-kē āgē: postpos., in front of
-kē āspās: postpos. near, in the neighborhood of
-kē bagair: postpos., without
-kē bād: postpos., after
-kē bāhar: postpos., out of, outside of
-kē bāis: postpos., for reason of
-kē bārē-mē̃: postpos., about, concerning
-kē bāvajūd: postpos., in spite of, in opposition to
-kē binā: postpos., without
-kē darmiyān: postpos., between
-kē gird: postpos., around
-kē ilāvā: postpos., besides
-kē ird • gird: postpos., in the vicinity of
-kē ḳābil: postpos., fit for, worthy of
-kē ḳhilāf: postpos., against
-kē lāiḳ: postpos., worthy of
-kē liyē: postpos., for, in order to
-kē mutābiḳ: postpos., according to
-kē nīcē: postpos., under
-kē pās: postpos., beside, belonging to
-kē pīchē: postpos., behind
-kē sāmnē: postpos., in view of, in front of
-kē sāth: postpos., with
-kē silsilē-mē̃: postpos., in connection with
-kē yahā̃: postpos., at place of
kēlā: msc., banana
Kēnāṭ Sarkal: pl. n., msc., Connaught Circle
khaddar: fm., homespun cloth
khaīcnā: see **khīcnā**

khaṇḍar: msc., ruin
khaṛā hōnā: vb. int., to stand, be standing
khaṭṭā: adj., sour
khād: fm., manure
khādī: fm., coarse cotton stuff
khāl: fm., hide, skin
khānā: vb. tr., to eat
khānā: msc., food, dinner
khā̃sī: fm., cough
khēl • tamāśā: msc., amusement
khēlnā: vb. int., to play
khēt: msc., field
khētī: fm., agriculture
khē̃cnā: see **khī̃cnā**
khilaunā: msc., toy
khilānā: vb. tr., to feed, cause to eat
khiṛkī: fm., window
khīr: fm., dish made of rice and milk
khī̃cnā: vb. tr., to drag, pull, draw
khōdnā: vb. tr., to dig (cf. **khudnā**)
khōlnā: vb. tr., to open (cf. **khulnā**)
khudnā: vb. int., to be cut, be inscribed, be dug
khudvānā: vb. tr., to cause to be dug, inscribed
khulā: adj., open
khulvānā: vb. tr., to cause to be opened
khurdurī: adj., n.c., rough
ki: see **ke**
kidhar: adv., where, whither
kin: obl. pl., see **kaun**
kinārā: msc., bank, shore, edge
kinhō̃: obl. pl., see **kaun**
kirāyā: msc., rent
kirdār: msc., work, deed, occupation, manner, conduct
kis: obl. s., see **kaun**
kis liyē: adv., why? for whom?, for what?
kisān: msc., farmer
kisī: obl. s., see **kōī**
kisī aur: adj., obl. s., some other
kiśtī: fm., boat
kitāb: fm., book
kitnā: interr. adj., how much
kitnē arsē: interr. adv., how long
kiyā: pst. part., see **karnā**
kīcaṛ: msc., mud
kīcaṛvālā: adj., muddy

kījiyē: see **karnā**
kīl: **fm.**, nail
klab: **msc.** and **fm.**, club
klark: **msc.**, clerk
klās: **fm.**, class, grade
-kō: **postpos.**, to
kōāparēṭiv sōsāiṭī: **fm.**, Cooperative Society
kōelā: **msc.**, coal
kōī: **indef. pron.; adj., n.c.**, some, any, something, anything
kōī aur: **pron.**, someone else
kōī na kōī: **pron.**, someone or other
kōlhū: **msc.**, oil-seed crushing machine
kōnā: **msc.**, corner
Kōrōmaṇḍal Kōsṭ: **pl. n., msc.**, Coromandal Coast
Kōryā: **pl. n., msc.**, Korea
kōśiś: **fm.**, attempt
[kī] kōśiś karnā: **vb. tr.**, to attempt, try
kōṭ: **msc.**, coat
kōṭhī: **fm.**, bungalow
kuā̃rā: see **kā̃vārā**
kuch: **indef. pron.**, something, anything, some, several, thing
kuch aur: **pron.**, something else
kuch nahī̃: **pron.**, nothing
kulcē: **msc.**, kind of bread
kulhāṛī: **fm.**, hatchet
kunbā: **msc.**, family
kursī: **fm.**, chair
kuttā: **msc.**, dog
kūā̃: **msc.**, water well
kūdnā: **vb. int.**, jump
kyā: **adj., adv.**, what?
kyū̃ (also **kyō̃**): **adv.**, why?
kyū̃-ke: **conj.**, because

ḳabīlā: **msc.**, tribe
ḳadam: **msc.**, step, gesture
ḳahvā: **msc.**, coffee
ḳahvāḳhānā: **msc.**, coffee house
ḳaid: **fm.**, imprisonment
ḳaid karnā: **vb. tr.**, to imprison, jail
ḳalam: **msc.**, pen
ḳalām: **msc.**, poetic writing

ḳamīz: fm., shirt
Karārdād-e-Lahor: fm., The Lahore Resolution
ḳarīb: adv., near
ḳarīban: adv., almost, about, nearly
ḳarz: msc., loan, debt
ḳarz lēnā: vb. tr., to make a loan, borrow
ḳarz mā̃g lēnā: vb. tr., to borrow money
ḳarzḳhāh: msc., creditor
ḳasūr: msc., fault, error
ḳatl karnā: vb. tr., to murder
ḳaun: fm., nation
ḳayās: msc., guess
ḳābiliyyat: fm., ability
ḳābū: msc., command, control
ḳāflā: msc., caravan
ḳāim karnā: vb. tr., to establish
ḳāim rahnā: vb. int., to continue
ḳānūn: msc., law
ḳānun sāz asemblī: fm., legislative assembly
ḳānūnī: adj., n.c., legal
ḳātil: msc., murderer
ḳāzī: msc., Muslim jurist
ḳāṭā: msc., scale
ḳilā: msc., fort
ḳism: fm., kind, sort
ḳissā: msc., story
ḳīmat: fm., price
ḳīmtī: adj., n.c., expensive, valuable
ḳulī: msc., coolie, laborer
ḳurbān hōnā: vb. int., to be sacrificed
ḳurbān karnā: vb. tr., to sacrifice
ḳurbānī: fm., sacrifice
ḳūlī: msc., coolie, laborer
ḳhabar: fm., news
ḳhabardār: adj., n.c., careful
ḳhafā: adj., n.c., angry
ḳhafā hōnā: vb. intr., to become angry
ḳhairāt: fm., charity
ḳhalīfā: msc., caliph
ḳhanjar: msc., dagger
ḳharāb: adj., n.c., bad
ḳharāb hōnā: vb. int., to break down, to go wrong
ḳharābī: fm., weakness, affliction
ḳharbūzā: msc., melon (cantaloupe)
ḳharc: msc., cost, expense (**pl., iḳhrājāt**)

ḳharīdār: msc., buyer
ḳharīdnā: vb. tr., to buy
ḳharīf: fm., autumn crop
ḳhasūsiyat: fm., feature, particularity
ḳhar: msc., letter
ḳhat-ō-ḳitābat: fm., correspondence
ḳhatam hōnā: vb. int., to be finished, ended
ḳhatam karnā: vb. tr., to finish, end
ḳhatam kar ḍālnā: vb. tr., to put to an end
ḳhatarnāk: adj., n.c., dangerous
ḳhatūt: msc. pl., letters
ḳhaufnāk: adj., n.c., dreadful
ḳhaufzadā: adj., n.c., frightened
ḳhavātīn-ō-hazarāt: msc., Ladies and Gentlemen!
ḳhayāl: msc., opinion, thought, understanding
ḳhayāl rakhnā: vb. tr., to look after, take care
ḳhayālāt: msc. pl., thought (cf. ḳhayāl)
ḳhazānā: msc., treasury
ḳhāb: msc., dream
ḳhābīdā: adj., n.c., sleepy
ḳhāh • maḳhāh: adv., without reason, uselessly
ḳhāhiś: fm., desire
ḳhālī: adj., n.c., empty
ḳhāmōś: excl., keep quiet
ḳhāndān: msc., family
ḳhānḳāh: fm., tomb of Pir
ḳhānsāmā̃: msc., butler
ḳhās: adj., n.c., special
ḳhātūn: fm., lady
ḳhāvind: msc., husband
ḳheriyyat: fm., well-being
ḳhilāfat: fm., caliphate
ḳhitāb: msc., title given in honor
ḳhud: rfl. pt., self
Ḳhudā hāfiz: goodbye (lit.: May God protect you)
Ḳhudā un-par rahmat karē: May God give him peace, May God bless him
Ḳhulāfā: msc., (pl. of ḳhalīfā), Caliphs
ḳhuś: adj., n.c., happy
ḳhuś hōnā: vb. int., to be glad
ḳhuś rahnā: vb. int., to be healthy and happy
ḳhuśāmad: fm., flattery
ḳhuśbūdār: adj., n.c., scented
ḳhuśgavār: adj., n.c., pleasant
ḳhuśhāl: adj., n.c., well off, comfortable
ḳhuśī: fm., gladness

mujhē k̤husī huī: I am glad
k̤husī manānā: **vb. tr.,** to rejoice
k̤husk̤ismatī: **fm.,** good fortune
k̤husk̤ismatī-sē: **adv.,** fortunately
k̤husmizāj: **adj., n.c.,** sweet-tempered
k̤hussakal (also **sakl**): **adj., n.c.,** good-looking
k̤hūb: **adv.,** very, well, nice
k̤hūbī: **fm.,** virtue, merit, pleasantness, goodness
k̤hūbsūrat: **adj., n.c.,** beautiful
k̤hũk̤hār: **adj., n.c.,** dreadful

Labnān: **pl. n., msc.,** Lebanon
lafz: **msc.,** word (**pl.** alfāz)
lagām: **fm.,** rein, bridle
lagnā: **vb. int.,** to be attached to, be fixed to
lagvānā: **vb. tr.,** to cause to be planted
lahar: **fm.,** wave
lahrānā: **vb. tr.,** to wave
Lakhnāū: **pl. n., msc.,** Lucknow
laimp: **msc.,** lamp
lakṛī: **fm.,** wood
Laksmaṇ: **pr. n., msc.,** Lakshman
lambā: **adj.,** long, tall
Lañkā: **pl. n., fm.,** Ceylon
Laṇḍan: **pl. n., msc.,** London
laṛakpan: **msc.,** youth
laṛāī: **fm.,** war, quarrel
laṛkā: **msc.,** boy
laṛkī: **fm.,** girl
laṛnā: **vb. int.,** to fight
latīfagō: **msc.,** jokester
latīfagō: **adj., n.c.,** witty
laṭkānā: **vb. tr.,** to hang
laṭṭū: **msc.,** top
lauḍspīkar: **msc.,** loud-speaker
laumṛī: **fm.,** vixen, she-fox
lauṭnā: **vb. int.,** to retreat, return
Lāhaur: see Lāhōr
Lāhōr: **pl. n., msc.,** Lahore
lāin: **fm.,** line, row

lāisens: msc., license
lākh: msc., one hundred thousand
lāl: adj., n.c., red
Lāl Kilā: pl. n., msc., Red Fort
Lālpur: pl. n., msc., Lalpur
lānā: vb. int., to bring
lāṭ: msc., Lord (term of address)
lāṭ • sāhib: msc., Governor
lāzim: adj., n.c., necessary
lē jānā: vb. int., to take away
lē lēnā: vb. tr., to take
lēkar: ger., = "with"
lēkin: conj., but
lēnā: vb. tr., to take
lēṭnā: vb. int., to lie down
lifāfā: msc., envelope
lifṭ: fm, elevator
likhnā: vb. tr., to write
likhnēvālā: msc., writer
likhvānā: vb. tr., to cause to be inscribed, written
liyā: see lēnā
līḍar: msc., leader
līḍarī: fm., leadership
lījiyē: see lenā
lō: excl., look!
lō: see lēnā
lōg: msc., people
-lōg: pt., people (attached to a noun to form the plural)
lōhā: msc., iron
lōhār: msc., blacksmith
lomṛī: fm., vixen, she-fox
lōṭā: msc., water-pot

macānā: vb. tr., to make noise, stir up, excite
machērā: msc., fisherman
machlī: fm., fish
madad: fm., to help
(-kī) madad dēnā: vb. tr., to help
(-kī) madad karnā: vb. tr., to help
Madīnā: pl. n., msc., Medina

Madrās: **pl. n., msc.,** Madras
magar: **conj.,** but
magrabī: **adj., n.c.,** western
magribī: **adj., n.c.,** western
mah̄aknā: **vb. int.,** to smell pleasant
mahal: **msc.,** palace
mahājan: **msc.,** money lender
mahārājā: **msc.,** Maharajah
mahārāṇī: **fm.,** empress, queen
Mahātmā: **msc.,** honorary title given to M. K. Gandhi
mahãgā: **adj.,** expensive, dear
mahfil: **fm.,** party, company
mahīnā: **msc.,** month
mahsūs hōnā: **vb. int.,** to feel, experience
mahvār: **adj., n.c.,** monthly
maidān: **msc.,** field, plain
maikā: **msc.,** maternal home
mailā: **adj.,** dirty
maimbar: **msc.,** member
mainējar: **msc.,** manager
Maisūr: **pl. n., msc.,** Mysore
maĩ: **pron.,** I
majlis-e-śūrā: **fm.,** advisory council
majmūā: **msc.,** collection
makān: house
makānāt: **msc. pl.,** houses (**cf. makān**)
makenik: **msc.,** mechanic
Makkā: **pl. n., msc.,** Mecca
makkār: **adj., n.c.,** cunning
makkhī: **fm.,** fly
maḳām: **msc.,** position, status
maḳāmāt: **msc. pl.,** places, positions (see maḳām)
maḳāmī: **adj., n.c.,** local
maḳbarā: **msc.,** tomb
maḳsad: **msc.,** objective, purpose, aim
malāmat: **fm.,** reproof, rebuke
malāmat karnā: **vb. tr.** to rebuke, condemn
malēriyā: **msc.,** malaria
malikā: **fm.,** lady, queen
mallāh: **msc.,** boatman
malnā: **vb. tr.,** to rub, smear
mamūlī: **adj., n.c.,** ordinary
mamūzād: **msc.** and **fm.,** maternal cousin
man: **msc.,** mind, heart, interest
man: **msc.,** maund (one maund equals 82 lbs.)

manānā: vb. tr., to observe, celebrate, conciliate
manāyā jānā: vb. int., to be considered, be celebrated
mandar: msc., temple
manfī karnā: vb. tr., to subtract
Manikpur: pl. n., msc., Manikpur
Manōhār: pr. n., msc., Manohar
Manthārā: pr. n., fm., Manthara
manyārī: fm., female bangle-seller
manzil: fm., deck, story
manzūr: msc., acceptance
manzūr hōnā: vb. int., to be acceptable
manzūr karnā: vb. tr., to accept
mar jānā: vb. int., to die
marammat: fm., repairing
(-kī) marammat karnā: vb. tr., to repair
maraz: msc., disease
Marāthī: fm., Marathi (language)
mard: msc., man
marhūm: adj., deceased
Marī: pl. n., fm., Murree
marīz: msc., patient
marīz: adj., n.c., ill
marnā: vb. int., to die
marzī: fm., desire
masālā: msc., spice
masālēdār: adj., n.c. spicy
masjīd: fm., mosque
maslan: adv., for instance, for example
maśgūl: adj., n.c., occupied, busy
maśgūl hōnā: vb. int., to be busy with, engaged in
maśhūr: adj., n.c., famed
maśīn: fm., machine
maśraḳ: see maśriḳ
maśraḳī: adj., n.c., eastern
maśriḳ: msc. and fm., East
maśriḳī: adj., n.c., eastern
maśvarah: see maśvarā
maśvarā: msc., consultation, advice
mat: adv., not
matlab: msc., meaning
maṭar: msc., pea
maujūd: adj., n.c., present
maujūdā: adj., present
mauḳā: msc., occasion, opportunity, situation
mauḳā milnā: vb. int., to have the opportunity

maulvī: msc., Muslim priest, learned man
mauniṭar: msc., monitor
mausam: msc., weather
maut: fm., death
mavēsī: fm., cattle
mazā: msc., pleasure, taste
mazāḵ: msc., joke, wit, pleasantry
mazbūt: adj., n.c., strong
mazdūr: msc., worker, laborer
mazdūrī: fm., wages
mazē karnā: vb. tr., to enjoy oneself
mazē-sē: adv., comfortably
mazēdār: adj., n.c., tasty
mazhab: msc., religion
mazhabī: adj., n.c., religious
mazīd: adj., n.c., more, further
mazmūn: msc., subject, contents, theme (pl. mazāmīn)
māḍarn: adj., n.c., modern
māf: see muāf
māikā: msc., mica
mālan: fm., flowerseller
mālā: fm., garland
Mālābār Kōṣṭ: pl. n., msc., Malabar Coast
mālgūzārī: fm., land-revenue
mālik: msc., master
mālī: msc., gardener
Māltī: pr. n., fm., Malti
mālūm: adj., n.c., known; (e.g., mujhē mālūm nahī̃ I don't know)
mālūm hōnā: vb. int., to seem, appear, know
māmūlī: adj., n.c., ordinary, common
māmū̃:   msc., maternal uncle
mān jānā: vb. int., to accept, agree to
mānā: msc., meaning
Mānikcand: pr. n., msc., Manikchand
mānnā: vb. tr., to assume, obey
Mānsīh: pr. n., msc., Mansinh
mānsūn: fm., monsoon
mār ḍālnā: vb. tr., to kill, drive to distraction
mār paṛnā: vb. int., to beat, thrash
mārc: msc., March
mārnā: vb. tr., to beat, kill
māśā ˙ Allah: excl., with God's grace!
māt karnā: vb. tr., to excell, defeat
māthā: msc., forehead
māgal: msc., Tuesday

mā̃hgā (also **mahā̃gā**): **adj.**, expensive
mā̃: **fm.**, mother
mā̃g: **fm.**, demand
mā̃gnā: **vb. tr.**, to demand, ask for, request
meḍikal kālij: **msc.**, medical college
mehantī: **adj.**, **n.c.**, industrious
meharbān: **adj.**, **n.c.**, kind
meharbānī: **fm.**, kindness
meharbānī:-sē: **adv.**, kindly
mehaz (also **mahz**): **adv.**, just, mere, only
mehekmā: **msc.**, department
mehekmā āsār-e-ḳadīmā: **msc.**, Department of Archaeology, Department for the Preservation of Antiquities
mehekmā-e-zirāat: **msc.**, Department of Agriculture
mehekmā • zarāat: **msc.**, Agricultural Department
mehmān: **msc.** and **fm.**, guest
mehnat: **fm.**, hard work
mehnat karnā: **vb. tr.**, to work hard, toil
mehtar: **msc.**, sweeper
mēlā: **msc.**, a fair, crowd
mēn̄ganīz: **msc.**, manganese
mērā: **adj.**, my, mine
mēz: **fm.**, table
-mē̃: **postpos.**, in
-mē̃-sē: **postpos.**, among
mē̃ḍak: **msc.**, frog
mil: **msc.** and **fm.**, mill
milansār: **adj.**, **n.c.**, friendly, social
milā • julā: **adj.**, friendly, harmonious, mixed
milā lēnā: **vb. tr.**, to incorporate, add
milēṭ: **fm.**, millet
milkiyyat (also **malkiyyat**): **fm.**, ownership
milkīyat: **fm.**, ownership, property
milnā: **vb. int.**, meet, to join
minaṭ: **msc.**, minute
Misar (also **misr**): **pl. n.**, **msc.**, Egypt
mistarī: **msc.**, mechanic
miśan: **msc.**, mission
miṭānā: **vb. tr.**, to abolish, wipe out
miṭhāī: **fm.**, candy
miṭhāyī: see **miṭhāī**
miṭṭī-kā tēl: **msc.**, kerosene
miyā: **msc.**, dear (**term of endearment**), husband
mīyā • bīvī: **msc.**, husband and wife
mojizā: **msc.**, miracle

mōcī: msc., shoemaker
mōh lēnā: vb. tr., to captivate, win (mind)
Mōhan: pr. n., msc., Mohan
mōharikā bukhār: msc., typhoid fever
mōhtāt: adj., n.c., careful
mōr: msc., peacock
mōṛ: msc., turning
mōṭar: fm., motorcar
mōṭarbas: fm., bus
mōṭargāṛī: fm., motorcar
mōṭarsāikal: fm., motorcycle
mōṭarvālā: msc., motorist
mōṭā: adj., fat
mōtī: fm., pearl
mōzā: msc., sock
mōzū: msc., subject, topic
muammā: msc., problem, puzzle
muazzaz (also **muazziz**): adj., n.c., respectable
muāf hōnā: vb. int., to be forgiven
muāf karnā: vb. tr., to forgive, excuse
muāf karvānā: vb. tr., to get forgiveness
muāmalāt: msc. pl., matters
muāvizā: msc., compensation
mubārak: adj., n.c., blessed, happy
mubārak karnā: vb. tr., to greet
mubārakbād: fm., felicitation, congratulation
muft: adj., n.c., free
Mugal: msc., Mogul
muhabbat: fm., love
muhallā: msc., district, division of town
Muharram: msc., first month of the Arabic year, held sacred by the Muslims
muhājir: msc., refugee
mujh: see **maĩ**
mujhē: see **maĩ**
mujhē khuśī huī: I am glad
mukammal: adj., n.c., completed, complete
mukaddas: adj., n.c., hallowed, sacred, holy
mukaddas• jagāh: fm., sacred place
mukadmā: msc., law-suit, case, litigation
mukarrar: adj., n.c., settle, fixed, established
mukābilā: msc., comparison
mukhālif: msc., opponent, enemy
mukhālifat: fm., opposition
mukhātib karnā: vb. tr., to address, speak to

mukhtalif: adj., n.c., different
mukhtasar: adj., n.c., brief, short
mulāhzā: msc., inspection
mulākāt: fm., meeting
mulāzim: msc., servant (**pl. mulāzmīn)**
mulk: msc., country
Mullā: msc., Muslim divine, Mullah
Multān: pl. n., msc., Multan
mumānī: fm., maternal aunt
munakid hōnā: vb. int., to be held, take place
munāfā: msc., profit
munāfā hōnā: vb. int., to profit
mūnāsib: adj., n.c., proper, suitable
Muniyā: pr. n., fm., Muniyan
munī: msc., Hindu sage, ascetic
munkasim: adj., n.c., divided
Munnā: pr. n., msc., Munna
munśī: msc., teacher
murād: fm., object, intention, wish
murdā: adj., n.c. dead
murg: msc., rooster, cock
murgī: fm., hen, chicken
murīd: msc., follower, disciple
murjhānā: vb. int., to fade
murtahan (also **murtahin**): msc., mortgagee
murnā: v. int., to turn
Musalmān: msc., Muslim
musannif: msc., author
musāfir: msc., traveller
musībat: fm., difficulty, misery, misfortune
muskurānā: vb. int., to smile
Muslim Līg: fm., Muslim League
mustakil: adj., n.c., permanent
muśāirā: msc., literary convention where poems are recited by authors
muśkil: adj., n.c., difficult
muśkil-sē: adv., hardly, with difficulty
mutabarrik: adj., n.c., holy, blessed
mutavassit: adj., n.c., intermediate, middle
mustavassit darjē-kā: adj., middle-class
mutālā karnā: vb. tr., to study
muttahid: adj., n.c., united
muttahid hōnā: vb. int., to become united
mutthī: fm., fist
mūāf: msc., pardon, excuse

mūāmlā: msc., matter, incident, affair, business
mūḍ: msc., mood
mũh: msc., face, mouth

na: adv., not (**negative part.**)
nabī: msc., prophet
nadī: fm., river, stream
nafā: msc., profit
nafā hōnā: vb. int., to profit
nahar: fm., canal
nahānā: vb. int., to take a bath
nahī̃: adv., not
nahlānā: vb. tr., to bathe (cf. **nahānā**, give bath)
nakśā: msc., map
naḳad: msc., cash
nal: msc., water-tap
nam: adj., n.c., damp, wet
namak: msc., salt
namāz: fm., prayer
namāz paṛhnā: vb. tr., to offer prayer
namūdār: adj., n.c., apparent, visible
namūdār hōnā: vb. int., to appear
namūnā: msc., example, sample, cross-section
nanhā: msc., child, baby, little son
nanhā: adj., small, tiny
nanhī: fm., child, baby, little daughter
naram: adj., n.c., soft
narm: adj., n.c., soft
nars: fm., nurse
Nastālīḳ: msc., Nastalik (script)
naśā: adj., n.c., intoxicated
naśē-kī dukān: fm., liquor shop
natījā: msc., result
nau: adj., n.c., nine
naujavān: msc., young man
naujavān: adj., n.c., young
naukar: msc., servant
naukar • cākar: msc., pl., servants
naukarānī: fm., maid-servant
naukrī: fm., job, service
naukrī karnā: vb. tr., to take employment
navāb: msc., ruler, prince

navābī: fm., office of the navab
navāsī: adj., n.c., eighty-nine
navā̃: adj., ninth
navvē: adj., n.c., ninety
nayā: adj., new
nazam: fm., poem
nazar: fm., sight, eye, vision
nazar ānā: vb. int., to appear, come in sight
nazar rakhnā: vb. tr., to keep an eye on
nazdīk: adj., n.c., close
nāc: msc., dance
nācnā: vb. int., to dance
Nāgarī: fm., Nagari (script)
nāī: msc., barber
nākām: adj., n.c., failed, fruitless, unsuccessful
nākām hōnā: vb. int., to fail
nām: msc., name
nām lēnā: vb. tr., repeat name (e.g., of a god), call name of, call upon
nānā: msc., maternal grandfather
nānbāī: msc., baker
nānī: fm., maternal grandmother
nāō: fm., boat
nārāz: adj., n.c., displeased
nāśtā karnā: vb. tr., to take breakfast
nāvil: msc., novel
nāzil hōnā: vb. int., to become divinely inspired, to be descended upon
nemat: fm., blessing
-nē: postpos., by
nēkī: fm., virtue, righteousness
nigāh: fm., glance
nigāh ḍālnā: vb. tr., to glance
nikal jānā: vb. int., to come out
nikalnā: vb. int., to come out, appear
nikālnā: vb. tr., to take out, subtract
nikās: msc., drainage, outlet
ninnānvē: adj., n.c., ninety-nine
nisbatan: adv., comparatively
niśān: msc., sign, indication look, mien
niśānā: msc., a mark, goal
nīcē: adv., down
nīl: msc., indigo
nīnd: fm., sleep
nīnd ānā: vb. int., to fall asleep
nōṭ: msc., note
nuksān: msc., disadvantage, loss

nuktā • cīnī: fm., criticism
nuktā • cīnī karnā: vb. tr., to criticize
numāiś: fm., exhibition
numāiśgāh: fm., exhibtion (place of)

ōhadā: see **ōhdā**
ōhdā: msc., rank, position
ōk: fm., oak
ōs: fm., dew
ōs-kī būnd: msc., dewdrops
ōvarkōṭ: msc., overcoat

pacās: adj., n.c., fifty
pacāsī (also **piccāsī**): adj., n.c., eighty-five
paccānvē (also **piccānvē**): adj., n.c., ninety-five
paccīkārī: fm., inlay, mosaic
paccīs: adj., n.c., twenty-five
pachattar (also **pichattar**): adj., n.c., seventy-five
pacpan: adj., n.c., fifty-five
pagḍaṇḍī: fm., path, footpath
pahannā: vb. tr., to dress, put on
pahāṛ: msc., mountain
pahāṛī: fm., hill
pahcān lēnā: vb. tr., to recognize
pahcānnā: vb. tr., to recognize
pahilā: see **pahlā**
pahilē: see **pahlē**
pahinnā: see **pahannā**
pahiyā: msc., wheel
pahlā: adj., first
pahlē: adv., before
pahlvānī: fm., wrestling
pahȏ̃cānā: vb. tr., to cause to arrive, send
pahō̃cnā: vb. int., arrive
pahrā: msc., guard (**cf. pehrā**)
pahū̃cnā: see **pahocnā**
paidal: msc., footsoldier
paidal: adj., n.c., foot
paidal calnā: vb. int., to walk

paidal jānā: vb. int., to walk, go on foot
paidā: adj., n.c., produced, grown, begotten
paidā hōnā: vb. int., to be produced, be grown
paidāiś: fm., birth
paidāvar: fm., crop, produce
paiḡām: msc., message
pair: msc., foot
pairvālā: adj., -legged
paisā: msc., money, price
paisē: msc., pl., money
paisē dēnā: vb. tr., to pay
paĩsāṭh: adj., n.c., sixty-five
paĩtālīs: adj., n.c., forty-five
paĩtīs: adj., n.c., thirty-five
pakaṛnā: vb. tr., to grab, seize, catch
pakānā: vb. tr., to cook
pakkā: adj., ripe, firm
pakkā hō jānā: vb. intr., to be established
pakkā karnā: vb. tr., to establish
pakkī tarāh: adv., for certain
paknā: vb. int., to ripen, be cooked
palañg: msc., bed
panāhgazīn: msc. and **fm.**, refugee
pancāet: fm., Panchayat
pandrā: adj., n.c., fifteen
pandrah: see **pandrā**
Panjāb: pl. n., msc., Panjab
Panjābī: fm. and **adj., n.c.,** Panjabi
pansārī-kī dukān: fm., grocery shop
par: conj., but
parastīś: fm., worship
pardā: msc., purdah
pardādā: msc., great grandfather (**paternal**)
pardēs: msc., foreign country
pardēs-mẽ: adj., abroad
parē dhakēlnā: vb. tr., to push away
parēśān karnā: vb. tr., to upset, bother, annoy
parindā: msc., bird
parīśān karnā: vb. tr., to upset, bother, annoy
parpōtā: msc., great grandson (**paternal**)
parvariś karnā: vb. tr., to bring up, raise, nurture, provide for
parvāh: fm., care, feed, attention
paṛhā likhā: adj., educated
paṛhānā: vb. tr., to teach, make someone read, **(cf. paṛhnā)**
paṛhkar sunānā: vb. tr., to read back

paṛhnā: **vb. tr.**, to read, recite
paṛnā: **vb. int.**, to fall
(-kō) pasand ānā: **vb. int.**, to like, please
paslī: **fm.**, rib
Paśāvar (also **Piśāvar**): **pl. n., msc.**, Peshawar
paśēmān: **adj., n.c.**, repentant
Paśtō: **fm.**, Pashtu language
pataṅg: **msc.** and **fm.**, kite
patā: **msc.**, knowledge, information, direction, hint, signal, sign, indication, whereabouts, address
patā calnā: **vb. int.**, to discover
patlā: **adj.**, thin
patlūnẽ: **fm. pl.**, trousers
patthar: **msc.**, stone
Paṭnā: **pl. n., msc.**, Patna
paṭṭā: **msc.**, lease, rent
paṭṭī: **fm.**, strip of cloth
paudā (also **paudāh**): **msc.**, plant
pāgal: **adj., n.c.**, mad (**insane**)
Pākistān: **pl. n., msc.**, Pakistan
Pākistānī: **msc.** and **fm.**, Pakistani
Pākistānī: **adj., n.c.**, Pakistani
pālak: **fm.**, spinach
pāliś: **fm.**, polish
pāltū: **adj., n.c.**, tame, trained
pāltū jānvar: **msc.**, pet animal
pān: **msc.**, preparation of betal
pānā: **vb. int.**, to get, find
pānī: **msc.**, water
Pānīpat: **pl. n., msc.**, Panipat Plain
pāō̤: **msc.**, quarter seer, half a pound
pāõ: **msc.**, leg, foot
pārk: **msc.**, park
pārlimenṭ: **fm.**, Parliament
pārṭī: **fm.**, party
pās: **adv.**, near
pās honā: **vb. int.**, to graduate, pass
pās karnā: **vb. tr.**, to pass
pās-sē: **adv.**, by
pā̃c: **adj., n.c.**, five
pā̃c • baras-kā plain: **msc.**, five-year plan
pā̃cvā: see **pāncvā**
pehrā: **msc.**, guard (**cf. pahrā**)
pehrā dēnā: **vb. tr.**, to watch
pensil: **fm.**, pencil

Pēpsū: **pl. n., msc.,** abbreviation for Patiala and East Panjab States Union
pēṛ: **msc.,** tree
pēś: **adv.,** before, in front
pēś karnā: **vb. tr.,** to present, put forward
pēś • pēś rahnā: **vb. int.,** be ahead
pēśā: **msc.,** profession, occupation
pēṭ: **msc.,** belly
pēṭrōliyam: **msc.,** petroleum
phail jānā: **vb. int.,** to spread
phailnā: **vb. int.,** to spread
phaïknā: see **phĕknā**
phaïṭā: **msc.,** beating, thrashing
phaïṭā lagānā: **vb. tr.,** to beat up, thrash
phaṭ jānā: **vb. int.,** to be torn
phaṭnā: **vb. int.,** to split, burst, open
phauṛā: **msc.,** spade
phāōṛā: **msc.,** spade
phāṛnā: **vb. tr.,** to tear
phēr dēnā: **vb. tr.,** to return, give back
phĕknā: **vb. tr.,** to throw, cast
phir: **adv.,** again
phir-bhī: **conj.,** still, even, then, nevertheless
phir jānā: **vb. int.,** to turn away
phir kahnā: **vb. tr.,** to repeat, say again
phisalnā: **vb. int.,** to slip
phūl: **msc.,** flower
pichlā: **adj.,** last
pickārī: **fm.,** syringe
pighalnā: **vb. int.,** to melt
piknik: **fm.,** picnic
pilānā: **vb. tr.,** to give to drink, cause to drink **(cf. pīnā)**
piryad: see **pīryaḍ**
pistōl (also **pistaul**): **msc.,** pistol
pī ēc dī: **fm.,** Ph. D. (degree)
pīchē chōṛnā: **vb. tr.,** abandon, leave behind
pīchē: **adv.,** behind
pīlā: **adj.,** yellow
pīnā: **vb. tr.,** to drink, smoke
Pīr: **msc.** holy man
pīr: **msc.** Monday
pīryad: **msc.,** period (**of time**)
pītal: **msc.,** brass
plain: **msc.** and **fm.,** plan
pōlīs: **fm.,** police
Pōrbandar: **pl. n., msc.,** Porbander

pōśak: fm., dress
pōtā: msc., grandson
pōṭlī: fm., bundle
Prahlād: pr. n., msc., Prahlad
Pratāp: pr. n., msc., Pratap
prīvī kaunsal: fm., Privy Council
profaisor: msc. and fm., professor
prōgrām: msc., program
pujārī: msc., (Hindu) priest, worshipper
pul: msc., bridge
purānā: adj., old
purzōr: adj., n.c., vigorous
Puśtū: fm., Pashtu language
pūchnā: vb. tr., to ask
pūjā: fm., worship
pūrā: adj., complete, all
pūrā karnā: vb. tr., to fulfill
pūrē: adv., fully
pyālā: msc., cup
pyār: msc., love, affection
pyār karnā: vb. tr., to love
pyārā: adj., dear, beloved
pyārī: fm., dear, beloved
pyās: fm., thirst
pyāsā: adj., thirsty

rabī: fm., spring-crop
rahamdilī: fm., kind-heartedness
rahāiś (also **rihāiś**): fm., residence
rahāiś iḳhtiyār karnā: vb. tr., to take up residence
rahen: adj., n.c., mortgaged
rahnā: vb. int., to live, remain, stay
rahnā • sahnā: msc., way of life, conduct
rahnē dēnā: vb. tr., to let live, stay
rahnēvālā: msc., inhabitant
rahnumāī: fm., leadership, direction
rakhā jānā: vb. int., to be set
rakhnā: vb. tr., to place
raḳābī: fm., dish
raḳbā: msc., area (in measurement)
raḳm: fm., amount, sum
Ramēś: pr. n., msc., Ramesh

Ramzān: msc., Muslim holiday
rang: msc., color
rang bigāṛnā: vb. tr., to spoil the atmosphere, discolor
rangīn: adj., n.c., colored
ranj: msc., grief
ranjīdāh: adj., n.c., sorry
rassā: msc., rope
rassī: fm., rope, cord
rasūl: msc., prophet, messenger
raunaḳ: fm., hubbub, brightness, splendour
rāh: fm., way
rāj: msc., rule, realm, empire
Rājasthān: pl. n., msc., Rajasthan
rājā: msc., king
rājdhānī: fm., capital
Rājkōṭ: pl. n., msc., state in Kathiawar
rājkumārī: fm., princess
rājpūt: msc., Rajput
rāṇā: msc., rajah, prince
rāṇī: fm., queen
rāstā: msc., way
rāstā dēkhnā: vb. tr., to wait, watch out for
rāt: fm., night
Rāvalpindī: pl. n., msc., Rawalpindi
rāy: fm., advice, opinion
rāzī: adj., n.c., satisfied, pleased
rāzī hōnā: vb. int., to agree, consent
rāzī • khuśī: adj., n.c., comfortable, all right
rejisṭar: msc., registration book, registar
rezarvēśan: fm., reservation
rezarvēśan karnā: vb. tr., to reserve
reziḍēnsī: fm., residency
rēḍiyō: msc., radio
rēgistān: msc., desert
rēl: fm., railway train
rēlgāṛī: fm., train
rēlvē • stēśan: msc., railway station
rēsṭōrānṭ: msc., restaurant
rēśam: msc., silk
rēśmī: adj., n.c., silken
rikśā: fm., rickshaw
ripōrṭ: fm., report
risālā: msc., magazine
riśtēdār: msc. and fm., relative
riśvat: fm., bribe

riyāsat: **fm.**, state, government
rīch: **msc.**, bear
rīsarc: **fm.**, research
rōḍ: **fm.**, road
rōgī: **adj.**, **n.c.** sick, unwell
rōk: **fm.**, restraint, check
rōk thām karnā: **vb. tr.**, to check **(upon)**
rōknā: **vb. tr.**, to stop, hinder, forbid
rōnā: **vb. int.**, to cry
rōnā pīṭnā: **vb. tr.**, to complain, protest
rōśnī: **fm.**, light
rōśnī ḍālnā: **vb. tr.**, to discuss, throw light on
rōṭī: **fm.**, puffed wheaten cake
rōz: **msc.**, day
rōz • marrah-kā: **adj.**, daily
rōz • rōz: **adv.**, every day
rōzah: **msc.**, fast
rōzah rakhnā: **vb. tr.**, to fast
rōzgār: **msc.**, business
rōzī: **fm.**, livelihood
ruk jānā: **vb. intr,** to be stopped
ruknā: **vb. int.**, to stop, be stopped
rukh palaṭnā: **vb. tr.**, to turn, face toward, take a turn
rūī: **fm.**, cotton
rūmāl: **msc.**, handkerchief
rūpayā: **msc.**, rupee

sab: **adj.**, **n.c.**, all
sab kuch: **pron.**, every, everything
sab • lōg: **pron.**, everyone
sab-sē zyādā: **adv.**, most
sabaḳ: **msc.**, lesson
saban: **msc.**, soap, (see **sābun**)
sabkāṇṭineṇṭ: **msc.**, subcontinent
sabr: **msc.**, patience
sabz: **adj.**, **n.c.**, green
sabzī: **fm.**, vegetable
sabzīvālā: **msc.**, vegetable vender
sac: **msc.**, truth
sac: **adj.**, **n.c.**, true
saccā: **adj.**, true
saccāī: **fm.**, truth

saccāyī: see **saccāī**
sadā: **adv.,** always, ever
sadārat: **fm.,** presidency
sadr: **msc.,** president
safar: **msc.,** journey
safar karnā: **vb. tr.,** to travel
safāī: **fm.,** cleanliness
safāī karnā: **vb. tr.,** to clean
safāī rakhnā: **vb. tr.,** to keep clean
safāyī: see **safāī**
safēd: **adj., n.c.,** white
sahābī: **msc.,** religious associate
sahī: **adj., n.c.,** correct
sahī • salāmat: **adj., n.c.,** hale and hearty
sahnā: **vb. tr.,** to endure
sair: **fm.,** walk, stroll
sair karnā: **vb. tr.,** to stroll, walk about
saītālīs: **adj., n.c.,** forty-seven
saītīs: **adj., n.c.,** thirty-seven
sajānā: **vb. tr.,** to adorn, decorate
sajnā: **vb. int.,** to be adorned, be decorated
saknā: **vb. int.,** to be able
sakht: **adj., n.c.,** hard, strict
sakhtī: **fm.,** hardship
salāh: **fm.,** suggestion, plan, advice
salām: **msc.,** hello, term of greeting
salām-ō-alēkum: **msc.,** expression of greeting
salmā: **msc.,** metal thread
salūk karnā: **vb. tr.,** to treat (=handle)
samajh: **fm.,** understanding
samajh-mẽ ānā: **vb. int.,** to understand
samajhdār: **adj., n.c.,** wise
samajhnā: **vb. tr.,** to understand
samandar: **msc.,** ocean
samandrī: **adj., n.c.,** maritime
samandrī • jahāz: **msc.,** ocean liner, ocean-going ship
sambhālnā: **vb. tr.,** to control, take up, maintain, take care of
san: **msc.,** year
sanat: **fm.,** industry
santrī: **msc.,** sentry, policeman
sar: **msc.,** head
sarbarāh: **msc.,** chief
sardār: **msc.,** chief
sardī: **fm.,** cold weather, winter
sarkār: **fm.,** government

sarkārī: **adj., n.c.,** governmental
sarkārī ḳānūn: **msc.,** official law
sarkārī makān: **msc.,** government building
Sarlā: **pr. n., fm.,** Sarla
sarmāyādārī: **fm.,** capitalism
sarpaṭ dauṛnā: **vb. int.,** to gallop
Saryū: **pl. n., fm.,** Saryu River
saṛak: **fm.,** road, street
saṛsaṭh: **adj., n.c.,** sixty-seven
sastā: **adj.,** cheap
sastē-mẽ: **adv.,** cheaply
satah: **fm.,** surface
satattar: **adj., n.c.,** seventy-seven
satāh: see **satah**
satānā: **vb. tr.,** to bother
satrā: **adj., n.c.,** seventeen
satrāh: see **satrā**
satrāvā̃: **adj.,** seventeenth
sattar: **adj., n.c.,** seventy
sattāis: **adj., n.c.,** twenty-seven
sattānvē: **adj., n.c.,** ninety-seven
sattāsī: **adj., n.c.,** eighty-seven
sattāvan: **adj., n.c.,** fifty-seven
sau: **adj., n.c.,** one hundred
saudā: **msc.,** trade, groceries
saudā • sulaf: **msc.,** groceries
savāl: **msc.,** question
savālāt: **msc., pl.** questions
savār: **msc.,** rider, riding
savārī: **fm.,** riding
savērā: **msc.,** dawn, early morning
savēr: **adj., n.c.,** early
savērē: **adv.,** early in morning
sazā: **fm.,** punishment, sentence
sazā dēnā: **vb. tr.,** to punish
sāban: **msc.,** soap
Sābarmatī: **pl. n., fm.,** Sabarmati
sādā: **adj.,** plain
sādgī: **fm.,** simplicity
sādhū: **msc.,** (Hindu) holy man
sāf: **adj., n.c.,** clear, clean
sāf karnā: **vb. tr.,** to clean
sāf sāf: **adv.,** clearly, frankly
sāhib (also **sāhab**): **msc.,** gentleman
sāhūkār: **msc.,** money-lender

sāikal: **fm.,** cycle
sāikalvālā: **msc.,** cyclist
sāins: **fm.,** science
sāinsdān: **msc.,** and **fm.,** scientist
sāl: **msc.,** year
sālām • arz: **msc.,** greetings
sālām • arz karnā: **vb. tr.,** to greet
sālānā: **adj., n.c.,** yearly, annual
sāmān: **msc.,** luggage, arrangements
sāmnē: **adv.,** in front, straight ahead
sārā: **adj.,** whole, entire
Sārnāth **pl. n., msc.,** Sarnath
sāṛhē: **ad:j., n.c.,** half past (**"half more than"**)
sāṛī: **fm.,** sari
sās: **fm.,** mother-in-law
sāt: **adj., n.c.,** seven
sāth: **adv.,** along, along with, with, together with
sāthī: **msc.** and **fm.,** companion
sātvā̃: **adj.,** seventh
sāṭh: **adj.,** sixty
sāziś: **fm.,** conspiracy
sā̃p: **msc.,** snake
sekrēṭarī: **msc.** and **fm.,** secretary
seṭ: **msc.,** set
-sē: **postpos.,** with, from
-sē lēkar: **postpos. phrase,** from
-sē pahlē: **postpos. phrase,** before
sēb: **msc.,** apple
sēhat: **fm.,** health
sēkrēṭēriyaṭ: **msc.,** Secretariat
sēr: **msc.,** seer, a two pound weight
sēṭh: **msc.,** merchant, rich person
sēṭhānī: **fm.,** rich man's wife
sĕkrō̃: **adv.,** hundreds
sifar: **msc.,** zero
sifāriś karnā: **vb. tr.,** to recommend
sigrēt: **msc.** and **fm.,** cigarette
sigrēt pīnā: **vb. tr.,** to smoke a cigarette
sikhānā: **vb. tr.,** to teach
Sindh: **pl. n., msc.,** Sindh
sinēmā: **msc.,** movies
sipāhī: **msc.,** policeman
siraf: see **sirf**
sirf: **adv.,** only
Sitambar: **msc.,** September

sitār: **msc.,** guitar, zither
sivāē: **prep., postpos.,** except, besides
Sivil Eṇḍ Miliṭērī Gezaṭ: **msc.,** "Civil and Military Gazette"
siyāsat (also **syāsat**): **fm.,** politics
siyāsī (also **syāsī**): **adj., n.c.,** political
siyāsīyāt (also **syāsiyāt**): **fm.,** political science
siāhī: see **sīyāhī**
sīdhā: **adj.,** straight
Sīkh: **msc.,** Sikh
sīnā: **vb. tr.,** to sew
sīnā: **msc.,** chest, breast
sīṛhī: **fm.,** step, stair, stairs
Sītā: **pr. n., fm.,** Sita, wife of Ram
sīṭ: **fm.,** seat
sīṭī bajānā: **vb. tr.,** to blow, whistle
sīyāhī: **fm.,** ink
sī̃cnā: **vb. tr.,** to water
sī̃g: **msc.,** horn
skāūṭ: **msc.,** boy scout
skūl: **msc.,** school
sohbat: **fm.,** company
sō jānā: **vb. int.,** to go to sleep (cf. **sōnā**)
sōcnā: **vb. tr.,** to think, consider
sōlā: **adj., n.c.,** sixteen
sōlāh: see **sōlā**
sōnā: **vb. tr.,** to sleep
sōnā: **msc.,** gold
Sōśalisṭ Pārṭī: **fm.,** Socialist Party
Srīnagar: **pl. n., msc.,** Śrinagar
sṭāp: **msc.,** stop, bus stop
sṭēśan: **msc.,** station
sṭīl: **msc.,** steel
subah: **fm.,** morning
subah • savērē: **adv.,** early in the morning
subah • subah: **adv.,** early in the morning
sudhār: **msc.,** improvement
sudhārnā: **vb. tr.,** to improve
sukhī: **adj., n.c.,** happy
sulānā: **vb. tr.,** to put to sleep
Sumitrā: **pr. n., fm.,** Sumitra
sunānā: **vb. tr.,** to tell
sundar: **adj., n.c.,** beautiful
sunnā: **vb. tr.,** to hear, listen to
surākh: **msc.,** hole
surīlā: **adj., n.c.,** musical

surk̤h: **adj., n.c.,** red
susar: **msc.,** father-in-law
sust: **adj., n.c.,** lazy
Suśīlā: **pr. n., fm.,** Sushila
sūbā: **msc.,** province
sūd: **msc.,** interest, usury, profit
sūeṭar: **msc.,** sweater
sūkh jānā: **vb. int.,** to be dried up
sūkhā: **adj.,** dried out, dry
sūkhnā: **vb. int.,** to be dried up
sūraj: **msc.,** sun
Sūrajmal: **pr. n., msc.,** Surajmal
sūrat: **fm.,** condition, form
Sūrdās: **pr. n., msc.,** Surdas, a poet
sūt: **msc.,** yarn
sū̃ghnā: **vb. tr.,** to smell
syāhī: see **siyāhī**
Syāmū: **pr. n., msc.,** Syamu
syānā: **adj.,** wise, mature

śahad: **msc.,** honey
śahar: **msc.,** city
śakal: **fm.,** form
śakkar: **msc.,** sugar
śak̤hs: **msc.,** person
śarāb: **fm.,** wine, liquor
śarārat: **fm.,** mischief
śarārtī: **adj., n.c.,** mischievous
śarbat: **msc.,** sweet, cold beverage
śarbat • pānī: **msc.,** sweet, iced drink
śarīk: **msc.,** partner
śarmindā: **adj., n.c.,** repentent, ashamed
śart: **fm.,** agreement, stipulation
Śatrahan: **pr. n., msc.,** Shatrahan, a prince
śatranj: **fm.,** chess
śauk: **msc.,** interest, fondness
śābāś: **excl.,** well done!
śādī: **fm.,** wedding, marriage
śādī • śūdā: **adj., n.c.,** married
śāerī: see **śāirī**
Śāh • Jahā̃: **pr. n., msc.,** Shah Jahan
śāhī: **adj., n.c.,** royal

śāhzādā (also śehzādā): msc., prince
śāir: msc., poet
śāir • mizāj: adj., n.c., poetic, poetic tempered
śāirī: fm., poetry
śāḳh: fm., branch
śāl: msc., shawl
śāl hōnā: vb. int., to become tired
Śālīmār: pl. n., msc., Shalimar Garden
śām: fm., evening
śāmat: fm., misery
śāmil: adj., n.c., counted, included
śān: fm., glory, pomp
śāyad: adv., perhaps
śāyē: adj., n.c., published, revealed
śāyē hōnā: vb. int., to be published
śēr: msc., lion, tiger
Śēr • Śāh: pr. n., msc., Sher Shah
Śikāgō: pl. n., msc., Chicago
śikār: msc., hunt, prey
śikār karnā: vb. tr., to hunt
śikārī: msc., hunter
śikāyat: fm., complaint
Śimlā: pl. n., msc., Simla
śohrat: fm., fame
śōhar: msc., husband
śōr: msc., noise
śugal mēlā: msc., entertainment
śuhrat: fm., fame
śukr: msc., thanks
śukriyā: msc., thank you
śumāl: msc., north
śumār hōnā: vb. int., to be counted, reckoned
śurū: msc., beginning
śurū karnā: vb. tr., to begin
śurū-sē-hī: adv., from the very beginning

tab: conj., adv., then
tabdīl karnā: vb. tr., to transfer
tabiyyat: fm., health, condition, disposition
tablīg: fm., proselytizing
taftīś: fm., investigation
tahvār: msc., holiday, festival, occasion

tairnā: **vb. int.**, to swim
taiyār: **adj., n.c.**, ready
taiyār karnā: **vb. tr.**, to prepare
taiyārī: **fm.**, preparation
taĩtālīs: **adj., n.c.**, forty-three
taĩtīs: **adj., n.c.**, thirty-three
tajrabā (also **tajarbā, tajrubā**): **msc.**, experiment, experience
tajvīz: **fm.**, suggestion
takkar: **fm.**, accident, collision
taklīf: **fm.**, trouble
Taksilā: **pl. n., fm.**, Taxila
taḳāvī: **fm.**, taccavi, money advanced to cultivators
taḳāzā: **msc.**, demand
taḳht: **msc.**, throne
taḳrīban: **adv.**, about, almost
taḳrīr: **fm.**, sermon, speech
taḳsīm: **fm.**, division
taḳsīm: **adj., n.c.**, divided
taḳsīm hōnā: **vb. int.**, to be divided
taḳsīm karnā: **vb. tr.**, to divide
talāḳ: **fm.**, divorce
talāś: **fm.**, search
talāś karnā: **vb. tr.**, to look for
talvār: **fm.**, sword
tamām: **adj., n.c.**, entire
tan: **msc.**, body
tandrūstī: **fm.**, health, condition
tanhāī: **fm.**, solitude
tanḳhāh: **fm.**, salary
tanz-sē: **adv.**, ironically
tanziyā: **adj., n.c.**, satirical
tañg: **adj., n.c.**, narrow, tight
tañg galī: **fm.**, alley
tañg karnā: **vb. tr.**, to annoy
tañgī: **fm.**, tightness, discomfort
taraf: **fm.**, direction
tarah: **fm.**, kind, manner (also **tarāh**)
taraḳḳī: **fm.**, increase, raise, progress
taraḳḳī karnā: **vb. tr.**, to make progress
tarāh: (see **tarah**)
tarāzū: **fm.**, scales
tarbūz: **msc.**, melon
tarīḳ: **msc.**, method, technique, device
tarjumā: **msc.**, translation
tarjumā śudā: **adj., n.c.**, translated

tarjumānī: fm., representation

tarkīb: fm., scheme, plan

tarz: fm., fashion, style

tasavvur: msc., idea

tasmā: msc., shoe-lace, leather strap

tasvīr: fm., picture

taśrīf lānā: vb. intr., to come

taśrīf rakhiyē: excl., Please sit down!

taubā karnā (also tobā karnā): vb. tr., to ask forgiveness

tauliyā: msc., towel

tay karnā: vb. tr., to decide, arrange

tābīr: fm., interpretation

tādā: fm., number, quantity

Tāj Mahal: msc., Taj Mahal

tājir: msc., merchant

tāḳat: fm., power

tāḳatvar: adj., n.c., powerful

tā-ke: conj., so that

tāl dēnā: vb. tr., to dispose, dismiss (e.g., problem)

tālāb: msc., tank

tālib-e-ilm: msc., student (pl. tulabā)

tālibilm: msc., s. and pl. (colloq.) student

tālīm: fm., education

tālluḳ: msc., connection

Tān Sēn: pr. n., msc., Tansen, musician at the court of Akbar

tārā: msc., star

tārghar: msc., telegraph-office

tārīf: fm., praise

tārīḳh: fm., date, history

tārīḳhī: adj., n.c., historical

tāruf: msc., introduction

tāyāzād: adj., n.c., cousin (related through elder paternal uncle)

tāzā: adj., fresh

tā̃gā: msc., tonga, two-wheeled horse-drawn vehicle

tā̃gēvālā: msc., tonga driver

tēīs: adj., n.c., twenty-three

tēl: msc., oil

tērā: adj., your

tērā (also tērāh): adj., n.c., thirteen

tēz: adj., n.c., fast, sharp, hot, high (e.g., in price)

tēz: adv., quickly

tēzī: fm., swiftness

tēzī-sē: adv., fast, quickly

thailā: msc., bag

thak jānā: vb. intr., to become tired

thakā: adj., tired
thakān: fm., fatigue
thakā huā: adj., tired
thā: see **hōnā**
thālī: fm., dish, plate, flat dish
thānā: msc., police-station
thōṛā: adj., little
thōṛī dēr: fm., little while
Tibbat: pl. n., msc., Tibet
tihattar: adj., n.c., seventy-three
tijārat: fm., trade, commerce
tikōnā: adj., triangular, three-cornered
tilak: msc., mark on forehead
tirānvē: adj., n.c., ninety-three
tirāsī: adj., n.c., eighty-three
tīn: adj., n.c., three
tīr: msc., arrow
tīr calānā: vb. tr., to shoot arrows
tīs: adj., n.c., thirty
tīsrā: adj., third
tohfā: msc., gift
tō: conj., moreover, then
tōbā karnā: vb. tr., to ask forgiveness
tōlnā: vb. tr., to weigh
tōṛnā: vb. tr., to pluck, break
tōtā: msc., parrot
trēpan: adj., n.c., fifty-three
trēsaṭh: adj., n.c., sixty-three
tukṛā: msc., piece
tulabā: msc. and fm. pl., students (pl. of **tālibilm**)
tulnā: vb. int., to be weighed
Tulsī Dās: pr. n., msc., Tulsi Das
tum: pron., you
tumhārā: poss. adj., your
tumhẽ: see **tum**
tūfān: msc., storm

ṭaiks: msc., tax
(-kō) ṭakkar lagnā: vb. int., to collide
ṭakrānā: vb. tr., to strike against
ṭamāṭar: msc., tomato
ṭāṅg: fm., leg

ṭēksī: fm., taxi
ṭēlīfōn: msc., telephone
ṭēnis: fm., tennis
ṭhaharnā: vb. int., to stop
ṭhaṇḍ: fm., cold, coldness
ṭhaṇḍā: adj., cold
ṭhēkēdār: msc., contractor
ṭhīk: adv., all right, exactly
ṭhīk karnā: vb. tr., to have or get fixed
ṭhīk ṭhāk: adv., completely all right, perfectly, exactly
ṭīlā: msc., mound
Ṭōḍarmal: p. n., msc., Todarmal
ṭōk: fm., hindrance
ṭōkṛī: fm., basket
ṭōpī: fm., cap, hat
ṭraifik: fm., traffic
ṭraifik kānṭrol karnā: vb. tr., to direct, traffic
ṭraifik pōlīs: fm., traffic police
ṭrak: msc., truck
ṭrām: fm., trolley
Ṭrāvankōr-Kōcin: pl. n., fm., Travancore-Cochin
ṭrēn: fm., train
ṭukṛā: msc., piece, scrap
ṭūṭ jānā: vb. int., to break, be broken
ṭūṭā: adj., broken, destroyed
ṭūṭā • phūṭā: adj., broken
ṭūṭnā: vb. int., to break

ubalnā: vb. int., to boil
ubālnā: vb. tr., to boil
uchalnā: vb. int., to jump
Udaypur: pl. n., msc., Udaipur
udās: adj., n.c., sad
udās hōnā: vb. int., to be sad
udāsī: fm., loneliness
udhar: adv., there, towards there
udhār: msc., loan, debt
udhār lēnā: vb. tr., to borrow
ugānā: vb. tr., to grow
ugnā: vb. int., to grow
ulajhnā: vb. int., to get involved
ulāmā: msc., pl., learned people

ulṭā: **adj.**, opposite
ummīd: **fm.**, hope
umr guzar jānā: **vb. int.**, to spend life
umar (also **umr**): **fm.**, life, age
un: **obl. pl.**, see **vo**
unattīs: **adj.**, **n.c.**, twenty-nine
unāsī: **adj.**, **n.c.**, seventy-nine
uncās: **adj.**, **n.c.**, forty-nine
unhattar: **adj.**, **n.c.**, sixty-nine
unhē̃: **obl. pl.**, see **vo**
unhō̃: **obl. pl.**, see **vo**
unnīs: **adj.**, **n.c.**, nineteen
unsaṭh: **adj.**, **n.c.**, fifty-nine
untālīs: **adj.**, **n.c.**, thirty-nine
uplā: **msc.**, dung-cake
Urdū: **fm.**, Urdu (**language**)
uṛ jānā: **vb. int.**, to fly off (cf. **uṛnā**)
Uṛīsā: **pl. n.**, **msc.**, Orissa
uṛnā: **vb. int.**, to fly
us: **obl. s.**, see **vo**
us vaḳt: **adv.**, then
usē: **obl. sing.**, see **vo**
usī: **obl. sing.**, **emphat.**, see **vo**
ustarā: **msc.**, razor
ustād: **msc.**, instructor
ustād • sāhib (also **ustād • sāhab**): **msc. hon.**, teacher
ustānī: **fm.**, female instructor
utarnā: **vb. int.**, to descend, get out of
utnā: **adj.**, that much
uṭh baiṭhnā: **vb. int.**, to get up suddenly (**cf. uṭhnā**)
uṭhānā: **vb. tr.**, to pick up, lift up, reap (**cf. uṭhnā**)
uṭhnā: **vb. int.**, to get up
ūpar: **adv.**, up, upwards
ū̃cā: **adj.**, high, loud
ū̃glī: **fm.**, finger
ū̃ṭ: **msc.**, camel
ū̃ṭgāṛī: **fm.**, camel-cart

vabā: **fm.**, epidemic
vafad: **msc.**, delegation
vafāt: **fm.**, death
vafāt pā jānā: **vb. int.**, to die

vafāt pānā: vb. tr., to die, pass away
vag̱airā: adv., etc., and so forth
vahā̃: adv., there
vahī: fm., divine inspiration
vahī̃: adv., there
vaidik: adj., n.c., Vedic
vaisā: adj., of that kind
vaisā: adv., just so, thus, in that way
vajah: fm., reason
vajūd: msc., existence
vakālat: fm., legal practice
vakīl: msc., lawyer
vaḳt: msc., time
vaḳt kāṭnā: vb. tr., to kill time
vaḳt-par: adv., in time, on time
valēkum assalām: msc., answer to **assalām alekum** (q.v.), (**lit:** and peace be on you)
varaḳ: msc., leaf (**of paper**)
Vardhā: pl. n., msc., Wardha
vardī: fm., uniform
varnā: conj., lest, otherwise
vasī: adj., n.c., extensive, vast
vaz: msc., sermon
vaz karnā: vb. tr., to preach
vazīfā: msc., scholarship
vazīr: msc., state minister
vazīr-e-azam: msc., Prime Minister
vādā: msc., promise
vāh vāh!: excl.,
vāhid: adj., n.c., single
vāisrāy: msc., Viceroy
vāḳaī: adv., really, in fact
vāḳeā (cf. **vāḳyā**)**: msc.,** happening
vāḳif: adj., n.c., acquainted with, informed about
vāḳyā (cf. **vāḳeā**)**: msc.,** incident
vāldain: msc. pl., parents
vālid: msc., father
vālid • sāhab: msc., father
vāpas: adv., back
vāpas dēnā: vb. tr., to give back
vāris: msc., heir
vāstā: msc., connection
vāz: msc., sermon
vel: excl., well!
Vēd: msc., Veda
vikālat: fm., legal practice

Vilāyat: fm., England, Europe, America
vo: pron., that, he, she, it
vōṭ: msc., vote

yahā̃: adv., here
yahī̃: adv., here, in this place
yaḳīn: msc., certainly
yaḳīn karnā: vb. tr., to believe, trust
yaḳīnī: adj., n.c., sure, certain
yā: conj., or
yād: fm., memory, remembrance
yād ānā: vb. intr., to remember
yād dilānā: vb. tr., to remind
yād karnā: vb. tr., to memorize
yād rakhnā: vb. tr., to remember
yānī: conj., that is to say
yār: term of friendship
ye: pron., dem adj., he, she, it, this
Yōrap: pl. n., msc., Europe
Yūnān: pl. n., msc., Greece
yūnivarsiṭī: fm., university
yū̃: adv., thus
yū̃ tō: conj., in a way, somehow

zabān: fm., language, tongue
zaḳhmī: adj., n.c., wounded, hurt, injured
zamānā: msc., time, occasion
zamīn: fm., earth, ground
zanānā pōlīs: fm., female police
zarab: fm., blow, stroke, wound
zarab dēnā: vb. tr., to multiply (arithmetic)
zarā: adv., a little
zarāē: msc., means (pl. of zariyā)
zariyā: msc., means (pl. zariyē, zarāē)
zarḳhēz: adj., n.c., fertile
zarūr: adv., certainly
zarūrat: fm., need, necessity
(-kō) zarūrat hōnā: vb. int., to need
zarūrī: adj., n.c., necessary, important, urgent

zāē karnā: **vb. tr.,** to waste
zāhir: **adj., n.c.,** manifest
zāhir hōnā: **vb. int.,** to appear
zālim: **adj., n.c.,** cruel
zātī: **adj., n.c.,** personal
zehan: **msc.,** mind
zehar: **msc.,** poison
zēvar: **msc.,** ornaments, jewelry
zibah karnā: **vb. tr.,** to slaughter
zikr: **msc.,** reference, mention
zilā: **msc.,** district
zimmā: **msc.,** concern
zimmēdār: **adj., n.c.,** responsible
zinā: **msc.,** fornication
zinā karnā: **vb. tr.,** to fornicate
zindagī: **fm.,** life
zindā: **adj., n.c.,** alive
zindābād: **adv.,** long live . . . !
zindgī: see **zindagī**
zōr: **msc.,** force
zōr-ṣē: **adv.,** forcefully
zubān: see **zabān**
zukām: **msc.,** cold
zyādā: **adv.,** too much, more
zyādātar: **adv.,** greater, for the most part, generally

English–Urdu Glossary

bandon: **chōṛnā, vb., tr.; chōṛ ānā, vb., int.; pīchē chōṛnā,** (leave behind), **vb., tr.**
bility: **ḳābiliyyat, fm; abūr, msc.**
be) able: **saknā, vb., int.**
bode: **āśram, msc.**
bolish: **miṭānā, vb., tr.**
bout (approximately): **ḳarīban, taḳrīban, adv.; -kē bāre-mē̃** (= concerning), **postpos.**
bout (= near): **-kē nazdīk, -kē ḳarīb, postpos.**
bout (approximately): **taḳrīban, adv.**
bove: **ūpar, adv.** and **-kē ūpar, postpos.**
broad: **pardēs-mē̃, adv.**
bsent: **g̱air • hāzir, g̱air • hāzar, adj., n.c.**
ccept: **mān jānā, vb., int.; manzūr karnā, vb., tr.; manzūr hōnā, vb., int.**
cceptance: **manzūr, msc.**
ccident: **ṭakkar, fm.**
ccidentally: **ittafāḳ-sē, adv.; ittifāḳ-sē, adv.**
ccording to: **-kē mutābiḳ, postpos.**
ccordingly: **cunā̃ce, adv.**
ccount: **bayān, msc.**
to give an) account of: **bayān karnā, vb., tr.**
ccounts: **hisāb, msc., hisāb • kitāb, fm.**
keep) accounts: **hisāb karnā, vb., tr.**
ccumulated: **ikaṭṭhā, adj.**
be) accustomed to: **ādat hōnā, vb., int.**
cre: **ēkaṛ, msc.**
ct: **ēkṭ, msc**
ction: **kārravāī, fm.**
ctual: **aslī, adj., n.c.**
dd: **jōṛnā, milā lēnā, vb., tr.**
ddress (domicile): **patā, msc.**
ddress (speak to): **muḳhātib karnā, vb., tr.**
dmit (= enroll, accept, register): **dāḳhil karnā, vb., tr.**
dorn: **sajānā, vb., tr.; sajnā, vb., int.**

advance: **baṛhnā, vb., int.**
advantage: **fāydā, msc.,**
advice: **maśvarā, msc.;** opinion: **rāy, salāh, fm.**
affair: **muāmlā, hāl,** (condition), **msc.**
affection: **pyār, msc.**
(be) afraid: **ḍarnā, vb., int.**
after: **-kē bād, postpos.**
after (= behind): **-kē pīchē, postpos.**
after all: **āḳhir, adv.**
afterwards: **bād, bād-mẽ, us-kē bād-sē,** adv.
again: **phir, adv.**
against: **-kē ḳhilāf, postpos.**
age: **umar, fm.** (also **umr**)
(age of) youth: **javānī, fm.**
agree: **rāzī hōnā, mān jānā, vb., int.**
agreement: **śart, fm.**
Agricultural Department: **mehekmā-e-zirāat, msc.**
agriculture: **khētī, zirāat, fm.**
ahead: **āgē, adv.**
aim: **maḳsad, msc.**
air: **havā, fm.**
airdrome: **ērōḍrōm, havāī • aḍḍā, msc.**
airplane: **havāī • jahāz, msc.**
(by) airplane: **bazariyā-e-havāī • jahāz, adv.**
Akbar: **Akbar, msc.**
alas!: **hāyē, excl.**
alike: **ēk-sā adj.**
alive: **zindā, adj., n.c.**
all: **sab, adj., n.c.; sārā, adj.; tamām, adj., n.c.; pūrā, adj.**
all alike: **ēk jaisā, adj.**
all right: **rāzī ḳhuśī, adj., n.c.; ṭhīk, ṭhīk ṭhāk, adj.**
Allahabad: **Ilāhābād, pl. n.** and **msc.**
allegiance: **baiat, fm.**
(take) allegiance: **baiat karnā, vb., tr.**
alley: **tang galī, galī. fm.**
allowance: **alauns, msc.**
almost: **ḳarīban, taḳrīban, adv.**
alms: **bhīkh, ḳhairāt, fm.**
almshouse: **dharmśālā, ġarīb • ḳhānā, msc.**
alone: **akēlā, adj.**
along: **sāth, adv.**
along with: **sāth sāth, adv.**
although: **agarce, conj.**
always: **hamēśā, sadā, adv.**
amazement: **hairānī, fm.**

merica: Amērikā, Amrīkā, pl. n., msc.
mong: -mẽ-sē, postpos.; -kē bīc-mẽ (= middle), postpos.
mong (our)selves: āpas-mẽ.
mong (them)selves: āpas-mẽ
mong (your)selves: āpas-mẽ
mount: raḳm, raḳam, fm.
mritsar: Amritsar, pl. n., msc.
musement: khēl • tamāśā, msc.
nd: aur, conj.
nd so forth (= etc.): vag̱airā
ngel: friśtā, firiśtā, msc.
nger: g̱ussā, msc.
ngry: g̱ussīlā, adj., ḳhafā, adj., n.c.
get) angry: ḳhafā hōnā, vb., int.
nimal: jānvar, msc.
nna: ānā, msc.
nnoy: tañg karnā, parēśān karnā, satānā, vb., tr.
nother: dūsrā, aur kōī, ēk aur-bhī, pron., adj.
nswer: javāb, msc.
ny: kōī, kuch, indef. pron., adj.
nyone else: kōī aur, indef. pron.
nything: kōī, indef. pron., adj.; kuch, indef. pron., adj.
nyway: bahar hāl, adv.
part: alag, adv.
partment: flaiṭ, msc.
pparent: namūdār, adj., n.c.
pparently: bazāhiē, adv.
ppeal: apīl, fm.
ppear: nikalnā, nikal jānā, mālūm hōnā, mālūm paṛnā, nazar ānā, vb., int.; dikhāyī dēnā, vb., tr.; namūdār hōnā, zāhir ānā, zāhir hōnā, int., vb.
ppetite (= hunger): bhūk; fm.
pple: sēb, msc.
ppoint muḳarrar karnā, vb., tr.
pproaching (= coming): ānēvālā, adj.
April: aprail, msc.
Arab: Arab, msc.
Arabian Nights: dāstān-e-Aliflailā, fm.
Arabic: arabī, arbī, adj., n.c.
Arabic language: Arabī, Arbī, fm.
rchery: tīr andāzī, fm.
rea: ilāḳā, raḳbā, msc.
rithmetic: hisāb, msc.
rmy: fauj, fm.
round: ās • pās, adv.; -kē gird, -kē ās • pās, postpos.
rrange: tay karnā, intazam karnā, vb., tr.

arrangement: **bandōbast, intazām, msc.**
arrive: **pahõcnā, ā jānā, vb. int.**
cause to arrive: **pahõcānā, vb. tr.**
arrow: **tīr, msc.**
article (subject): **mazūm, msc.**
artisan: **kārīgar, msc.**
as: **jaisā, postpos.; jaisā, relative adj.; jis tarah, relative adv.**
as . . . as: **jũ jũ . . . tũ tũ**
as follows: **hasb-e-zail**
ascertain: **yaḳīn karnā, vb. tr.**
ascetic: **darvēś, msc.**
ashamed: **śarmindā, adj., n.c.**
ash-tray: **aiśṭrē, fm.**
Asia: **ēśiyā, msc.**
ask: **pūchnā, vb., tr.**
ask for: **mā̃gnā, vb., tr.**
ask forgiveness: **taubā karnā, vb., tr.**
assembly: **ijlās, msc.; majlis, fm.**
assistant: **imdādī, msc.** and **fm.**
associate: **bandā, msc.; suhābī, msc.** and **fm.**
assume: **mānnā, farz karnā, vb., tr.**
assuredly: **bēśak, adv.**
attach: **lagānā, vb., tr.**
(be) attached to: **lagnā, vb., int.**
attack: **hamlā, msc.; hamlā karnā, vb., tr.**
attempt: **kōśiś, fm.; kōśiś karnā, vb., tr.**
attend: **hāzir hōnā, maujūd hōnā, vb., int.**
attend to (keep mind): **khayāē rakhnā, vb., tr.**
attendance: **hāzrī, fm.**
attendant: **mulāzim (pl., mulāzmīn), msc.**
attention: **dhiyān, msc.; parvāh, fm.**
(pay) attention to: **dhiyān dēnā, vb., tr.**
audience-hall (king's court): **darbār, dīvān-e-ām, msc.**
August: **agast, msc.**
aunt: **ḳhālā** (blood) mother's sister, **fm.**
  maternal: **mamānī, fm., mumānī, fm., pl.;** (in-law)
  paternal: **cacī, fm.**
author: **musannaf, musannif, msc.**
autobiography: **āpbītī, fm.**
autumn crop: **ḳharīf, fm.**
awful: **bahut ḳharāb, adj., n.c.**

B.A.: **bī ē, msc.**

bachelor: **kū̃vārā, msc.** (pronounced **kū̃ārā)**
back: **kamar, fm.; vāpas, adv.**
bad: **ḳharāb, adj., n.c.; burā, adj.,; bād-, prefix**
bag: **thailā, msc.; thailī, fm.**
bag for school-books: **bastā, msc.**
baker: **nānbāī, msc.**
ball: **gẽ̄d, msc.**
Baluchī: **Balūchī, Balōchī, adj., n.c.,** and **n., msc.,** and **fm.**
banana: **kēlā, msc.**
bangle: **cūṛī, fm.**
bangleseller: **manyārī, fm.**
bank: **baink, msc.**
bank (of river): **kinārā, ghāṭ, msc.**
banyan tree: **baṛ, msc.**
barber: **nāī, msc.**
bard: **bhāṭ, bhā̃ḍ, gavayyā śāir, msc.**
bark: **bhaunknā, bhaũkna, bhȭknā, vb., int.**
barristry: **beristṛī, fm.**
basket: **ṭōkrī, fm.**
bath: **g̱usal, msc.**
bathe: **nahlānā, vb., tr.; nahānā, vb.,** int.
bathroom: **g̱usalḳhānā, msc.**
battle: **laṛāī, jang, fm.**
bazaar: **bāzār, msc.**
be, become: **hōnā, vb., int.**
beach: **bīc, fm.**
bear: **rīch, msc.**
beard: **dāṛhī, fm.**
bearer: **bairā, msc.**
beat: **mārnā, tr.;** (to be beaten), **mār paṛnā, int.**
beating: **mār, fm.;** (get beating), **mār khānā, vb., tr.**
beautiful: **ḳhūbsūrat, sundar, adj., n.c.**
because: **kyū̃-ke, conj.**
because of: **-kē bāis, postpos.**
become: **hōnā, hō jānā, bannā** (= be made), **vb., int.**
bed (= bedding): **bistar, msc.**
bed (= bedstead): **palang, msc.**
bedding: **bistar, msc.**
between: **-kē darmiyān, -kē darmayān, -kē bīc-mẽ̄, postpos.**
before: **pahlē, pahilē, -sē pahlē, āge** (= ahead), **sāmnē** (= in front, facing), **adv.; -kē āgē, postpos.**
beg: **mā̃gnā, vb., tr.**
beg alms: **bhīk mā̃gnā, vb., tr.**
beg pardon: **taubā karnā, tauba mā̃gnā, vb., tr.**
beggar: **faḳīr, bhīkmā̃gā, msc.**
begin: **lagnā, vb., int.; śurū karnā, vb., tr.**

beginning: **śurū, msc.**
behind: **pīchē, adv.; -kē pīchē, postpos.**
belief: **īmān, msc.**
believe: **īmān rakhnā, yaḳīn karnā, vb., tr.**
bell: **ghaṇṭā, msc.; ghaṇṭī, fm.**
belly: **pēṭ, msc.**
belonging to: **-kē pās, postpos.**
beloved: **pyārā, msc.; pyārī, fm.; cahēṭ, adj.; azīz, adj., n.c.**
bend: **jhuknā, jhuk jānā, vb. int.; jhukānā, vb., tr.**
Bengal: **Bañgāl, pl. n., msc.**
Bengali: **bañgālī, n., msc. and fm.; adj., n.c.**
beside (= near): **-kē pās, postpos.**
besides: **sivāē, prep., postpos.; -kē alāva, postpos.**
betel preparation: **pān, msc.**
between: **-kē darmayān** (also, **darmiyān), -kē bīc-mẽ, postpos.; bīc-mẽ, adv.**
Bhagavad Gita: **Gītā, fm.**
Bharat: **Bhārat, pr. n., msc.**
Bible: **bāibil, fm.**
bicycle: **bāisikal, fm.**
Bihar: **Bihār, pl. n., msc.**
bill: **bil, msc.**
bird: **parindā, msc.**
birth (origin): **paidāiś, fm.**
biscuit: **biskuṭ, msc.**
bite: **kāṭnā, vb., tr.**
bitter: **karvā, khaṭṭā, adj.**
black: **kālā, adj.**
blacksmith: **lōhār, msc.**
blandishment: **ādā, fm.**
blanket: **kambal, msc.**
blessed: **mubārak̤, mutabarrik̤, adj., n.c.**
blessing: **nemat, fm.**
blind: **andhā, adj.**
blow: **zarab, fm.**
blow (whistle): **sīṭī bajānā, vb., tr.**
blow (wind): **calnā, vb., int.**
boarding-house: **bōrḍiñghāus, msc.**
boat: **kiśtī, nāō, fm.**
boatman: **mallāh, msc.**
body: **tan, jism, msc.**
boil: **ubālnā, vb., tr.; ubalnā, vb., int.**
bomb: **bam, msc.**
Bombay: **Bambaī, pl. n., fm., (msc.)**
bone: **haḍḍī, fm.**
bonfire: **alāō, msc.**

book: **kitāb, fm.**
borrow: **ḳarz lēnā, udhār lēnā, udhār mā̃gnā, vb., tr.**
borrow money: **ḳarz mā̃g lēnā, vb., tr.**
both: **dōnō̃, adv.**
bother: **satānā, parēśān karnā, vb., tr.**
bottle: **bōtal, msc.**
boundless: **bēhad, adv.**
boy: **laṛkā, chōkrā, msc.**
boy scout: **skauṭ, msc.**
Brahman: **Brāhman, msc.**
branch: **śāḳh, fm.**
brass: **pītal, msc.** and **fm.**
brave: **bahādur, adj., n.c.**
bread: **rōṭī, fm.**
break: **tōṛnā, vb., tr.; ṭūṭnā, vb., int.; ṭūṭ jānā, vb. int.**
breast: **sīnā, msc.**
bribe: **riśvat, fm.**
bride: **dulhan, fm.**
bridle: **lagām, fm.**
brief: **muḳhtasar, adj., n.c.**
briefcase: **bastā, msc.**
bright: **rōśan, adj., n.c.**
brightness: **rōśnī, raunaḳ, fm.**
bring: **lānā, lē ānā, vb., int.**
bring up (e.g., child): **parvariś karnā, vb., tr.**
broad: **cauṛā, adj.**
broken: **ṭūṭā, ṭūṭā phūṭā, adj.**
(be) broken: **ṭūṭnā, ṭūṭ jānā, vb., int.**
broom: **jhāṛū, fm.**
brother: **bhāī, msc.**
brother-in-law (wife's brother): **sālā, msc.**
brown: **bhūrā, adj.**
browse (i.e., graze): **carnā, vb., tr.**
bruise: **cōṭ lagnā, kucalnā, vb., tr.**
bruised: **ghāyal, zaḳhmē, adj., n.c.**
bucket: **bālṭī, fm.**
buffalo: **bhaĩs, fm.; bhaĩsā, msc.**
building: **imārat, bilḍiṅg, fm.; makān, msc.**
bullet: **gōlī, fm.**
bundle: **pōṭlī, fm.**
bungalow: **baṅglā, msc.; kōṭhī, fm.**
burden: **bōjh, msc.**
burn: **jal jānā, jalnā, vb., int.; jalānā, vb., tr.**
burst: **phaṭnā, vb., int.; phāṛnā** (to tear), **vb., tr.**
burst forth: **bhaṛaknā, vb., int.**

bus: **bas, mōṭarbas, fm.**
bush: **jhāṛī, fm.**
business: **kārōbār, rōzgār, kām, msc.**
business man: **bēōpārī, biznasmain, kārōbārī, msc.**
busy: **bāraunaḳ, maśg̣ūl, adj., n.c.**
(be) busy: **maśg̣ūl hōnā, vb., int.**
but: **lēkin, magar, balke, par, conj.**
butler: **ḳhānsāmā̃, msc.**
butter: **makkhan, msc.**
(clarified) butter: **ghī, msc.**
buy: **ḳharīdnā, vb., tr.**
buyer: **ḳharīdār, msc.**
by: **-nē, postpos.; pās-sē, adv.**

cabinet: **kēbinēṭ, fm.**
calculation: **hisāb, msc.**
Calcutta: **Kalkattā, pl. n., msc.**
calf: **bachṛā, msc.**
caliph: **Khalīfā, msc.**
Caliphate: **Khilāfat, fm.**
caliphs: **Khulafā, msc., pl. of Khalīfā.**
call: **bulānā, vb., tr.**
(be) called: **kahlānā, vb., int.**
camel: **ū̃ṭ, msc.; ū̃ṭnī, fm.**
camel-cart: **ū̃ṭgāṛī, fm.**
camera: **kēmrā, msc.**
camp: **kemp, msc.**
canal: **nahar, fm.**
candy: **miṭhāī, fm.**
cantonment: **chāōnī, fm.**
cap: **ṭōpī, fm.**
capital (city): **dār-ul-ḳhilāfā, msc.**
capital (money): **sarmāyā, msc.**
capital (letter): **baṛā haraf, msc.**
capitalist: **sarmāyādār, msc.**
captain: **kaptān, msc.**
captivate: **mōhnā, mōh lēnā, vb., tr.**
car: **kār, fm.**
caravan: **ḳaflah, msc.**
card (**i.e.,** cotton): **dhunnā, vb., tr.**
care: **dēkhbhāl, fm.**
care (anxiety): **parvā, fm.**

care (attention): dhiyān, msc.
care (caution): ehtiyāt, ḳhabardārī, fm.
careful: ḳhabardār, mōhtāt, adj., n.c.
careful (prudent): hōśyār, hōśiyār, adj., n.c.
carefully: hōśiyārī-sē, adv.
carpenter: baṛhāī, msc.
carriage: gāṛī, fm.
carrot: gājar, fm. and msc.
cart: gāṛī, fm.
case (at law): muḳadmā, msc.
case (box): sandūḳ, msc.
cash: naḳad, msc.
cast: phẽknā, vb., tr.
cat: billī, fm.
catch: pakaṛnā, pakaṛ lēnā, vb., tr.
cattle: caupāyā, msc.; mavēśī, fm.
cauliflower: gōbhī, fm.
cave: gār, msc.
celebrate (observe): manānā, vb., tr.
(be) celebrated: manāyā jānā, vb., int.
celebrated (famous): maśhūr, adj., n.c.
certain: yaḳīn, yaḳīnī, adj., n.c.
(for) certain: pakkī tarāh, adv.
certainly: pakkī tarāh, beśak, zarūr, adv.
certainty: yaḳīnī, fm.
Ceylon: Lãkā, fm. and msc.
cigarette: sigrēṭ, fm.
chair: kursī, fm.
chance: ittafāḳ, ittifāḳ, msc.
by chance: ittafāḳ-sē, adv.
(get a) chance: mauḳā milnā, vb., int.
change: badal, inḳalāb, msc.
change: badalnā, tabdīl karnā, vb., tr.
character (alphabet): haraf, harf, msc.
character (manner, conduct): kirdār, msc.
character (nature): ḳhaslat, fm.
charity: ḳhairāt, fm.
charm: dil kaśī, fm.
chat: bātcīt, fm.; bātcīt karnā, bāt karnā, vb., tr.
cheap: sastā, adj.
cheaply: sastē-mẽ, adv.
check: rōk, fm.
(place) check upon: rōk thām karnā, vb., tr.
checkmate (i.e., chess): māt karnā, vb., tr.
cheetah: cītā, msc.

chess: **śatranj, fm.**
chest (breast): **sīnā, msc.**
chest (box): **sandūḳ, msc.**
chew: **cabānā, vb., tr.**
chew cud: **jugālī karnā, vb., tr.**
chicken: **murg̠, msc.; murg̠ī, fm.**
chickpea: **canā, msc.**
chief: **sardār, buzurg, msc.**
chief (person): **sarbarāh, msc.**
child: **baccā, msc.**
childhood: **bacpan, msc.**
children: **bāl • baccē, msc. pl.**
China: **Cīn, pl. n., msc.**
chirp: **cū̃ • cū̃ karnā, vb., tr.**
choose: **cunnā, vb., tr.**
chore: **kām, msc.**
Christian: **Īsāī, msc.** and **fm.**
circumstances: **hālat, fm.**
city: **śahar, msc.**
class: **jamāt, jamāat, klās, fm.**
classmate: **hamjamāt, msc.** and **fm.**
clean: **sāf, adj., n.c.; sāf karnā, vb., tr.**
(keep) clean: **safāī rakhnā, vb., tr.**
cleanliness: **safāī, fm.**
clear (clean): **sāf, adj., n.c.**
clear (of sky): **khulā, adj.**
clear (evident): **zāhir, adj., n.c.**
clear (free): **āzād, adj., n.c.**
(be) cleared: **chaṭnā, vb., int.**
clearly: **sāf sāf, adv.**
clerk: **klark, msc.** and **fm.; bābū, msc.**
clever: **cālāk, hōśiyār, adj., n.c.**
climate: **ābōhavā, fm.; havā, fm.**
climb: **caṛhnā, vb., int.**
(make) climb: **caṛhānā, vb., tr.**
close: **nazdīk: adj.; adv.**
close: **band karnā, vb., tr.**
closed: **band: adj., n.c.**
be closed: **band hōnā, adj., n.c.**
cloth: **kapṛā, msc.**
clothe, put on clothes: **kapṛē pahannā, vb., tr.**
clothing: **kapṛē, msc. pl.**
cloud: **bādal, msc.**
club: **klab, fm.**
coal: **kōelā, msc.**

coat: kōṭ, msc.
cock: murḡā, msc.
coffee: ḳahvā, msc.; kāfī, fm.
coffeehouse: ḳahvā ḳhānā, kāfī haus, msc.
cold: sardī, ṭhaṇḍ, fm.; (illness) zukām, msc.; ṭhaṇḍā, adj.
sard, adj., n.c.
collect: jamā karnā, vb., tr., jamā hōnā, vb., int.
(be) collected: jamā hōnā, vb., int.
collected (gathered) ikaṭṭhā, adj.
collection: majmuā, msc.
college: kālij, msc.
collision: ṭakkar, fm.
colonize: kālōnī banānā, vb., tr.
color: raṅg, msc.
colored: raṅgīn, msc.
comb: kaṅghī, fm.; kaṅghā, msc.
come: ānā, ā jānā, vb., int.
come into view: nazar ānā, vb., int.
come out: nikalnā, nikal jānā, vb., int.
comfortable: rāzī ḳhuśī, ḳhuś • hāl, adj., n.c.
comfortably: mazē-sē, adv.
coming: ānēvālā, adj.
command: abūr, huḳm, huḳam, msc.
commerce: tijārat, fm.
commission: kamiśan, msc.
commissioner: kamiśnor, msc.
common: ām, adj., n.c.
communism: kamyūnizm, msc.
companion: sāthī, msc. and fm.
company: sohbat, kampanī, fm.
comparatively: nisbatan, adv.
comparison: muḳābalā, msc.
compensation: muāvizā, msc.
complain: śikāyat karnā, vb., tr.
complaint (accusation): śikāyat, fm.
complaint (illness): bīmārī, fm.
complete: pūrā, adj.; tamām, mukammal, adj., n.c.;
pūrā karnā, ḳhatam karnā, vb., tr.
(be) completed: cuknā, ḳhatam hōnā, vb., int.
completed: mukammal, adj., n.c.
completely: bilkul, adv.
completely, all right: ṭhik ṭhāk, adj.
compose (write): tasnīf karna, vb., tr.
compose lyric poems: ḡazal kahnā, vb., tr.
conceal: chipānā, chūpānā, vb., tr.

concern (thought): **fikr, msc. and fm.**
concerning: **-kē bārē-mẽ, postpos.**
conciliate: **manānā, vb., tr.**
condemn: **malāmat karnā, vb., tr.**
condition (state): **hāl, msc.; hālat, fm.**
condition (term): **śart, fm.**
condition (form): **sūart, fm.**
condition (health): **tabiyat, tandrūstī, fm.**
conduct: **rahnā • sahnā, kirdār, msc.**
confession: **iḳrār, msc.**
confidence: **ētbār, msc.**
congratulation: **mubārakbād, fm.**
Congress Party: **Kāṅgrēs, fm.**
(pertaining to) Congress Party: **kāṅgrēsī, adj., n.c.**
connection (matter, relation): **tālluḳ, vāstā, msc.**
(in) connection with: **-kē silsilē-mẽ, postpos.**
conquer: **jītnā, vb., tr.; jīt jānā, vb., int.**
conquest: **fatah, fm.**
conquests: **futūh, fm., pl.** (of **fatah**); **futūhāt, fm., pl.** (of **fatah**)
consent: **rāzī hōnā, vb., int.**
consider: **gōr karnā, sōcnā, fikr karnā, vb., tr.**
(be) considered: **gōr kujā jānā, vb., int.**
considerable: **acchā • ḳhāsā, adj.**
conspiracy: **sāziś, fm.**
consultation: **maśvarā, msc.**
contemplation: **gaurōfikr, msc.; fikr** (= concern), **msc.**
contemporary: **hamasar, msc.**
contents: **mazmūn, msc.**
continue: **jārī rakhnā, vb., tr.; jārī rahnā, ḳāim rahnā, vb., int.**
continually: **hamēśā, adv.**
contractor: **ṭhēkēdār, msc.**
contradict: **bāt kāṭnā, vb., tr.**
contribution (assessment): **candā, msc.**
control: **ḳabū, msc.; kānṭrōl karnā, sambhālnā, vb., tr.**
convention (literary): **muśāirā, msc.**
conversation: **bātcīt, guftagū, fm.**
converse: **bātcīt karnā, bāt karnā, vb., tr.**
conversing: **muḳhātib, bātcit karnavālā, adj., n.c.**
conviction, punishment: **sazā, msc.**
cook: **bāvarcī, msc.; pakānā, vb., tr.**
(be) cooked: **paknā, vb., int.**
cooking-pot: **haṇḍiyā, fm.**
coolie: **ḳulī, msc.**
cooperative society: **anjuman-e-imdād-e-bāhmī, kōāparētiv sōsāiṭī, fm.**
copybook: **kāpī, fm.**

cord: **rassī, fm.**
corner: **kōnā, mōṛ, msc.**
correct: **durust, sahī, ṭhīk, adj., n.c.**
correspondence: **ḳhat-ō-kitābat, fm.**
cost: **dām, msc., pl.; ḳharc, msc.**
cotton: **kapās, rūī, fm.**
(coarse) cotton stuff: **khādī, fm.**
cough: **khā̃sī, fm.**
Council Chamber: **Kauncil Cēmbar, msc.**
advisory council: **majlis-e-śūrā, fm.**
councillors: **amīr • vazīr, kaunslers, msc.**
count: **ginnā,** (calculate) **hisāb karnā, vb., tr.**
(be) counted: **śumār hōnā, vb., int.**
counted (= included): **śāmil, adj., n.c.**
country: **mulk, dēs, msc.**
courage: **himmat, fm.**
(muster) courage: **himmat karnā, vb., tr.**
(hope) courage: **himmat karnā, vb., tr.**
court: **darbār, dīvān, msc.**
court of law: **adālat, fm.**
courtroom: **adālat-kā kamrā, msc.**
courtier: **darbārī, msc.**
cousin: (—) **bahan, fm.;** (—)**bhāī, msc.**
cousin by father's brother: **cacērī bahan, fm.; cacērā bhāī, msc.**
cousin by father's older brother: **tāyāzād bhāī, msc.; tāyāzād bahan, fm.**
cousin by father's sister: **phūphērī bahan, phāpizād bahan, fm.; phūphērā bhāī, phūpizad bhāī, msc.**
cousin by mother's brother: **mamērī bahan, mamū̃zād bahan, fm.; mamērā bhāī, mamū̃zād bhāī, msc.**
cousin by mother's sister: **khālizād bahan, fm.; khālizād bhāī, msc.**
cover: **ḍhā̃knā, vb., tr.**
cow: **gāy, fm.**
coward: **buzdil, msc.**
cowardly: **buzdilī, adv.**
cream: **karīm, fm.**
creditor: **ḳarzḳhāh, msc.**
crime: **jurm, msc.**
criticism: **nuktā • cīnī, fm.**
criticize: **nuktā • cīnī karnā, vb., tr.**
crop: **fasal, paidāvār, fm.**
cropshare: **baṭvārā, msc.**
crore (10 million): **karōṛ, msc.**
crossing: **cauk, caurahā, msc.**
cross section: **namūnā, msc.,** (= example, sample)
crowd: **bhīṛ, fm.; mēlā, msc.**

cruel: **zālim, adj., n.c.**
cry: **rōnā, vb., int.**
cultivation: **kāśt, khētī, fm.**
cunning: **cālāk, makkār, adj., n.c.**
cup: **pyālā, msc.**
current: **jārī, adj., n.c.**
custody: **havālā, msc.**
customer: **gāhak, msc.**
cut: **kāṭnā, vb., tr.**
cut off (impede, block): **band karnā, vb., tr.**
cycle: **sāikal, fm.**
cyclist: **sāikalvālā, msc.**

Dacca: **Ḍhākā, pl. n., msc.**
daddy: **abbā, msc.**
dagger: **ḳhanjar, msc.**
daily: **rōz rōz, har rōz, adv.; rōz marrāh-kā, adj.**
damp: **nam, adj., n.c.**
dance: **nāc, msc., nācnā, vb., tr.**
dangerous: **ḳhatarnāk, adj., n.c.**
dark: **andhērā, adj.**
darkness: **andhērā, msc.**
date: **tārīḳh, fm.**
daughter: **bēṭī, fm.**
daughter-in-law: **bahū, fm.**
dawn: **savērā, msc.**
day: **din, rōz, msc.**
dead: **murdā, adj.**
deaf: **bahrā, adj.**
dear (expensive): **mahãgā, adj.**
dear (beloved): **azīz, adj., n.c.; pyārā, adj.**
dear (n.): **pyārī, fm.; pyārā, msc.; mehbūb (fm.); mehbūbā (fm.)**
death: **maut, vafāt, fm.**
deceased: **marhūm, adj.**
debt: **ḳarz, udhār, msc.**
December: **ḍisambar, msc.**
decide: **faislā karnā, tay karnā, vb., tr.**
decision: **faislā, msc.**
deck: **arśā, msc.**
decorate: **sajānā, vb., tr.**
(be) decorated: **sajnā, vb., int.**
decrease: **ghaṭ jānā, vb., int.; kam karnā, vb., tr.**

decree: **faislā, msc.**
deep: **gahrā, adj.**
deer: **hiran, msc.**
defeat: **hār, fm.; hārnā, vb., int.; māt karnā,** (in chess), **vb., tr.; māt dēnā, vb., tr.**
deficiency: **kamī, fm.**
degree: **ḍigrī, fm.**
(take a) degree: **ḍigrī lēnā, vb., tr.**
delay: **dēr, fm.; dēr karnā, vb., tr.**
delegation: **vafad, msc.**
Delhi: **Dillī, msc.**
deliberately: **jān būjhkar, = adv.**
deliver (= save): **bacānā, vb., tr.**
deliver (hand over): **sõpnā, saũpnā, dēnā, vb., tr.**
demand: **mãg, fm.; taḳāzā, msc.; mãgnā, vb., tr.**
dense: **ghanā, adj.**
deny: **inkār karnā, vb., tr.**
Department of Agriculture: **mehekmā-e-zirāat, msc.**
Department of Antiquities: **mehekmā āsār-e-ḳadīmā, msc.**
depot (= stop): **aḍḍā, msc.**
descend: **utarnā, nāzil hōnā, vb., int.**
describe: **bayān karnā, vb., tr.**
description: **bayān, msc.**
desert: **rēgistān, msc.**
deserving: **mustaujib, mastōjib, adj., n.c.**
desire: **ḳhāhiś, fm.; irādā, msc.**
despite (in spite of): **-kē bāvajūd, postpos.**
destroy: **barbād karnā, nābūd karnā,** (murder) **katl karnā, vb., tr.**
destroyed (= ruined): **barbād huā, adj.**
(be) destroyed: **barbād hōnā, vb., int.**
determination: **azm, irādā, msc.**
device: **tarkīb, fm.**
dew: **ōs, śabnam, fm.**
dewdrop: **ōs-kī bũd, fm.**
dhotī: **dhōtī, fm.**
dialect: **bōlī, fm.**
diamond: **hīrā, msc.**
die: **marnā, mar jānā, intiḳāl hōnā, intiḳāl hō jānā, intiḳāl kar jānā, vafāt pā jānā, vb., int.; intiḳāl karnā, vafāt pānā, vb., tr.**
die of hunger: **bhūkē mar jānā, vb., int.**
difference: **farḳ, iḳhtalāf, msc.**
different (other): **muḳhtalif, adj., n.c.; dūsrā, adj.**
difficult: **muśkil, kaṭhan, adj., n.c.**
difficulty: **musībat, muśkil, fm.**
(with) difficulty: **muśkil-sē, adv.**
dig: **khōdnā, vb., tr.**

dinner: **khānā, msc.**
direct traffic: **ṭrēfik kāṇṭrōl karnā, vb., tr.**
direction (hint): **patā, msc.**
direction (guidance): **rahnumāī, fm.**
direction (locale): **taraf, fm.**
dirty: **gandā, mailā, adj.**
disadvantage (= loss): **nuḳsān, msc.**
disappear: **g̠āib hōnā, vb., int.**
disciple: **murīd, msc.**
discolor: **rañg bigāṛnā, vb., tr.**
discomfort: **tañgī, fm.**
discourse: **taḳrīr, fm.**
discover: **(-kō) patā calnā, vb., int.**
discretion (= understanding): **samajh, fm.**
discriminate (= recognize): **pahcānnā, vb., tr.**
discuss: **bātcīt karnā, vb., tr.**
disease: **maraz, marz, msc.; bīmārī, fm.**
(be) disgusted (angry, dissatisfied): **bēzār hōnā, vb., int.**
dish: **bartan, msc., raḳābī, thālī, fm.**
dishonesty: **bēīmānī, fm.**
dismiss: **tāl dēnā, vb., tr.**
displeased (angry): **nārāz, adj., n.c.**
dispose: **tāl dēnā, vb., tr.**
disposition: (condition, health): **tabiyyat, fm.**
distant: **dūr, dūr•drāz, adj., n.c.**
distress (difficulty): **musībat, fm.**
distribute: **bā̃ṭnā, vb., tr.**
district: **muhallā, zilā, msc.**
divide: **taḳsīm karnā, bā̃ṭnā, bā̃ṭ dēnā, vb., tr.**
(be) divided: **taḳsīm hōnā, bāṭnā, vb., int.**
divided: **taḳsīm, munḳasim, adj., n.c.**
divinity: **dēvtā, msc.**
division: **taḳsīm, fm.**
division (district): **muhallā, msc.**
divorce: **talāḳ, fm.**
do: **karnā, vb., tr.**
(cause to) do: **karānā, karvānā, vb., tr.**
dog: **kuttā, msc.**
Dogra: **Dōgṛā, pr. n. and n., msc.**
doll: **guṛiyā, guṛyā, fm.**
dome: **gumbad, msc.**
donkey: **gadhā, msc.**
don't: **mat, adv.**
door: **darvāzā, msc.**
doorbell: **darvāzē-kī ghaṇṭī, fm.**

down: **nīcē, adv.**
down into: **(andar)-tak, adv.**
dozen: **darjan, fm.**
drag: **khĩcnā, vb., intr.; khĩcnā, vb., tr.**
drainage: **nakās, nikās, msc.**
dramatic: **dramāī, adj., n.c.**
drawing room: **ḍrāiṅg • rūm, msc.**
dreadful: **bhayānak, ḳhaufnāk, ḳhũḳhār, adj., n.c.**
dream: **ḳhāb, msc.**
dress: **libās, msc.; pōśāk, fm.; pahannā, vb., tr.**
dried out: **sūkhā, adj.**
(be) dried up: **sūkh jānā, vb., int.**
drink: **pīnā, vb., tr.**
(cause to) drink: **pilānā, vb., tr.**
(cold) drink: **śarbat, msc.**
drive: **calānā, vb., tr.**
driver: **gāṛībān, msc.**
drop: **bũd, fm.; ḍālnā, girānā, vb., tr.**
drown: **ḍubnā, ḍub jānā, vb., int.**
dry: **sūkhā, adj.**
dry up: **sūkh jānā, vb., int.**
dung-cake: **uplā, msc.**
dust: **dhūl, gard, fm.**
duty: **farz, kām • kāj, msc.**
(do one's) duty: **farz adā karnā, vb., tr.**

each: **har, adj., n.c.**
eager: **bēcain, bētāb, adj., n.c.**
ear: **kān, msc.**
early: **jaldī, savēr, adj., n.c.**
early in the morning: **subah savērē, subah subah, adv.**
earn: **kamānā, vb., tr.**
earring: **kā̃ṭā, bundā, msc.; bālī, fm.**
earth: **zamīn, fm.**
ease: **āsānī, fm.**
easily: **āsānī-sē, adv.**
east: **maśraḳ, maśrik, msc.**
eastern: **maśraḳī, maśriḳī, adj., n.c.**
easy: **āsān, adj., n.c.**
easy chair: **ārām • kursī, fm.**
economics: **iknaumiks, māśiyāt, iḳtasādiyāt, fm.**
edge: **kinārā, msc.**

educate: **sikhānā, vb., tr.**
educated: **paṛhā • likhā, adj.**
education: **tālīm, fm.**
effect: **asar, msc.**
egg: **aṇḍā, msc.**
Egypt: **Misar, Misr, msc.**
eight: **āṭh, adj., n.c.**
eighteen: **aṭṭhārā, adj., n.c.**
eighth: **āṭhvā̃, adj.**
eighty: **assī, adj., n.c.**
eighty-one: **ikkāsī, adj., n.c.**
eighty-two: **bayāsī, adj., n.c.**
eighty-three: **tirāsī, adj., n.c.**
eighty-four: **caurāsī, adj., n.c.**
eighty-five: **picāsī, adj., n.c.**
eighty-six: **chiyāsī, adj., n.c.**
eighty-seven: **sattāsī, adj., n.c.**
eighty-eight: **aṭṭhāsī, adj., n.c.**
eighty-nine: **navāsī, adj., n.c.**
elapse: **guzarnā, vb., tr.**
elect: **cunnā, vb., tr.**
election: **alēkśān, msc.**
electric light: **bijlī-kī battī, fm.**
electric plant: **bijlī-kā kārḳhānā, msc.**
electricity: **bijlī, fm.**
elephant: **hāthī, msc.**
elevator: **lifṭ, fm.**
eleven: **gyārā, adj., n.c.**
eleventh: **gyārvā̃, adj.**
embassy: **ēmbasī, fm.**
embrace: **galē milnā, galē lagnā, vb., int.; galē lagānā, vb., tr.**
embroidery: **bēlbūṭā, msc.; kaśīdākārī, fm.**
emperor: **bādśāh, śāhanśāh, msc.**
empire: **rāj, msc.; saltanat, fm.**
employment: **kārōbār, msc.; naukrī, fm., mulāzimat, fm.**
(take) employment: **naukrī karnā, vb., tr.**
empress: **mahārāṇī, malikā, fm.**
empty: **ḳhālī, adj., n.c**
end: **ḳhatam karnā, vb., tr.; ḳhatam hōnā, vb., int.**
(be) ended: **ḳhatam hōnā, vb., int.**
endurance: **bardāśt, fm.**
endure: **bardāśt karnā, vb., tr., sahnā, vb., int.**
enemy: **duśman, (opponent) mukhālif, msc. and fm.**
engineer: **injinīr, msc. and fm.**
engineering: **injīnīring, fm.**

England: **Iñglaind, Iñglistān, msc.; vilāyat, fm.**
English: **Añgrēzī, adj., n.c.**
English language: **Añgrēzī, fm.**
enjoy: **ḳhuśī manānā, mazē karnā, vb., tr.**
enjoyment: **mazā, msc.**
enough: **bas, adv.; kāfī, adj., n.c.**
enroll: **dāḳhil hōnā, vb., int.;** (have someone enrolled) **dāḳhil karvānā, vb., tr.**
ensnare: **phā̃s lēnā, vb., int.**
enter: **dāḳhil hōnā, vb., int.**
entertainment: **dāvat, fm.; mēlā, msc.**
entire: **sārā, adj.; tamām, adj., n.c.**
entirely: **ēk • dam, sab, adv.**
envelope: **lifāfā, msc.**
epidemic: **vabā, fm.**
equal: **barābar, adj., n.c.**
era: **daur, msc.**
erect: **khaṛā, adj.**
erroneous: **g̱alat • śalat, adj., n.c.**
error: **g̱alatī, cūk, g̱altī, fm.; ḳasūr, msc.**
(in) error: **g̱alatī-sē, adv.**
escape: **bacnā, vb., int.**
establish: **ḳāim karnā, vb., tr.**
established: **ḳāim • śudā, adj., n.c.**
estimate: **andāzā, msc.**
et cetera: **vag̱airā, adv.**
Europe: **Yūrup, msc.**
even: **hī, bhī, emph.; phir-bhī, adv.**
even though: **agarce, conj.**
evening: **śām, fm.**
(this) evening: **āj • śām, fm.**
ever: **kabhī, sadā, hamēśā, adv.**
every: **har, adj.**
every day: **rōz • rōz, adv.**
everyone: **sab lōg, harēk, msc.**
everything: **sab kuch, pron.**
everywhere: **har taraf, cārō̃ taraf, har jagah, har kahī̃, adv.**
evil: **burāī, fm.; burā, adj.; ḳharāb, adj., n.c.**
evil action: **burī bāt, fm.**
ewe: **bhēṛ, fm.**
exactly: **ṭhīk, ṭhīk ṭhīk, adv.**
examination: **imtihān, imtehān, msc.**
examine: **imtihān lēnā, imtehān lēnā, vb., tr.**
example: **namūnā, msc.**
(for) example: **maslan, adv.**
exceedingly: **bēhad, adv.**

excell: **māt karnā, vb., tr.**
except: **chōṛkar, ger.; sivāē, prep.** and **postpos.; magar, conj.**
exception: **istisnā, msc.**
(with the) exception of: **chōṛkar, ger.**
exchange: **badlā, msc.; badalnā, vb., tr.**
excite: **macānā, uksānā, ubhārnā, vb., tr.**
excuse: **bahānā, msc.; muāf karnā, māf karnā, vb., tr.**
exercise: **maśk, fm.;** (physical) **kasrat, fm.**
exhibition: **numāeś, fm.**
exhibition place: **numāeśgāh, fm.**
exist: **hōtā hōnā, maujūd hōnā, vb., int.**
existence: **vajūd, msc.; zindagī, fm.**
expect: **intazār karnā, vb., tr.**
expectation: **intazār, msc.**
expel: **nikāl dēnā, vb., tr.**
expend: **ḳharc dēnā, vb., tr.**
expense: **ḳharc, msc.**
expensive: **ḳimtī, adj., n.c.; mahãgā, adj.**
experience: **mahsūs hōnā, vb., int.; tajrabā, tajarbā, msc.**
experiment: **tajrabā, tajarbā, msc.**
explain: **bayān karnā, vb., tr.**
explanation: **bayān, msc.**
extend: **baṛhānā, vb., tr.**
extensive: **vasī, adj., n.c.**
extinguish: **bujhānā, vb., tr.**
extra: **fāltū, adj.**
extract: **nikālnā, vb., tr.**
extravagant: **fazūl ḳharc, adj., n.c.**
extremely: **bēhad, adv.**
eye: **ā̃kh, fm.**
eye (of needle): **nākā, msc.**

face: **cahrā, cehrā, mū̃h, msc.**
face (to turn): **rukh palaṭnā, vb., tr.**
fact: **vāḳiā, msc.**
in fact: **vāḳayī, sacmuc, adv.**
faction: **grūp, msc.**
factory: **kārḳhānā, msc.; faikṭōrī, fm.**
fade: **murjhānā, vb., int.**
fail: **cūk jānā, fēl hō jānā, vb., int.**
failed: **nākām, adj., n.c.**
fail (in examination): **nākām hōnā, fail hōnā, vb., int.**

fair (crowd): **mēlā, msc.**
faith (religion): **dīn, msc.**
faith (trust): **īmān, msc.**
fall: **girnā, paṛnā, vb., int.**
fall dead: **markar gir jānā, vb., int.**
fall in love: **āśik hōnā, vb., int.**
fallow: **gair • mazrūā, adj.**
false: **jhūṭ, adj.; galat, adj., n.c.**
fame: **śōhrat, śuhrat, fm.**
famed: **maśhūr, adj., n.c.**
family: **bāl • baccē, msc. pl.; ghar, gharānā, kunbā, ḳhāndān, msc.**
famous: **maśhūr, adj., n.c.**
far: **dūr, adj., n.c.**
farmer: **kisān, msc.**
far-fetched: **dūr-kā, adj.**
far-sighted: **dūr bīn, adj., n.c.**
fashion: **faiśan, msc.; tarz, fm.**
fast: **tēz, adj., n.c.; tēzī-sē, adv.**
fast (religious): **rōzāh, msc.; rōzāh rakhnā, vb., tr.**
fat: **mōṭā,** adj.
father: **vālid • sāhib, vālid • sāhab, vālid, abbā, bāp, msc.**
father-in-law: **susar, msc.**
fatigue: **thakān, fm.**
fault: **ḳasūr, msc.**
faultless: **bēgunah, adj., n.c.**
fear: **ḍar, msc.; ḍarnā vb., int.**
feast: **dāvat, fm.**
feature: **ḳhasūsiyat, haiat, fm.**
feed: **khilānā, vb., tr.**
feel: **mahsūs karnā, vb., tr.;** (be felt) **mahsūs hōnā, vb., int.**
feeling: **ahsās, msc.**
fees: **fīs, fm.**
feet: **pair, pāõ, msc.;** (measurement) **fīṭ, msc.**
felicitation: **mubāraḳbād, fm.**
female: **mādā, fm.**
female slave: **dāsī, laundī, fm.**
fertile: **zarḳhēz, adj., n.c.**
festival: **tahvār, msc.**
Festival of Lamps: **Dīvālī, fm.**
fever: **buḳhār, msc.**
(have) fever: **buḳhār ānā, vb., int.**
few: **cand, adj., n.c.;** (a little bit) **ṭhōrā-sā, adj.**
fictitious: **farzī, adj., n.c.**
field (farming): **khēt, msc.**
field (of endeavor): **mazmūn, msc.**

fifteen: paṇdrā, adj., n.c.
fifth: pācvā̃, adj.
fifty: pacās, adj., n.c.
fifty-one: ikyāvan, adj., n.c.
fifty-two: bāvan, adj., n.c.
fifty-three: trēpan, adj., n.c.
fifty-four: cavan, adj., n.c.
fifty-five: pacpan, adj., n.c.
fifty-six: chappan, adj., n.c.
fifty-seven: sattāvan, adj., n.c.
fifty-eight: aṭṭhāvan, adj., n.c.
fifty-nine: unsaṭh, adj., n.c.
fight: laṛnā, vb., int.
file: dāir karnā, vb., tr.
film: film, fm. and msc.
finally: āḳhir, adv.
find: pānā, vb., tr.
fine: jurmānā, msc.; jurmānā karnā, vb., tr.
(be) fined: jurmānā hōnā, vb., int.
finger: ũglī, fm.
finish: bas, adv.; ḳhatam karnā, vb., tr.; fārig̱ hōnā, vb., int.
(be) finished: ḳhatam hōnā, vb., int.
fire: āg, fm.; (to shoot) fāyr karnā, vb., tr.
firm: pakkā, adj.
first: pahlā, pahilā, adj.; avval, adj., n.c.
fish: machlī, fm.
fisherman: machērā, msc.
fist: muṭṭhī, fm.
fit for: -kē ḳābil, postpos.
five: pā̃c, adj., n.c.
five-year-plan: pā̃c • sāl plain, pā̃c • sāl mansūbā, msc.
fix: muḳarrar karnā, vb., tr.
(have/get) fixed: ṭhīk karānā, vb., tr.
fixed: muḳarrar, adj., n.c.
(be) fixed/attached to: lagnā, vb., int.
flag: jhaṇḍā, msc.
flame: śōlā, msc.
flare out: bhaṛaknā, vb., int.
flat: capṭā, adj.
flat (apartment): flaiṭ, msc.
flattery: ḳhuśāmad, fm.
flavor: mazā, msc.; ḳhuśbū, fm.
flee: bhāgnā, vb., int.
fling: phẽknā, vb., tr.
flood: baṛhnā, vb., int.

floor: **farś, msc.**
flour: **āṭā, msc.**
flourmill: **āṭē-kī cakkī, fm.**
flow: **bahnā, vb., int.**
flower: **phūl, msc.**
flowerseller: **mālan, fm.**
fly: **makkhī, fm.; uṛnā, vb., int.**
fly off: **uṛ jānā, vb., int.**
follow (= to go/come after): **pīchē ānā, vb., int.; pīchē jānā, vb., int.**
(as) follows: **hasab-e-zail, adv.**
follower: **murīd, msc.**
fondness: **śauk, msc.**
food: **khānā, msc.**
fool: **bēvakūf, msc.**
foot: **pair, pāõ, msc.;** (measurement) **fuṭ, msc.**
footpath: **pagḍaṇḍī, fuṭpāṭh, fm.**
for: **-kē liyē, -liyē, -kē vāste, postpos.; kyũke, conj.**
forbid: **rōknā, vb., tr.**
force: **zōr, msc.**
forcefully: **zōr-sē, adv.**
forehead: **māthā, msc.; pēśānī, fm.**
foreign: **ajnabī, gair • mulkī, adj., n.c.**
foreign country: **pardēs, gair • mulk, msc.**
foreigner: **gair • mulkī, msc.** and **fm.**
forget: **bhūl jānā, vb., int.; bhūlnā, vb., int.**
forgive: **muāf karnā, vb., tr.**
forgiven: **muāf • śudā, adj., n.c.**
(be) forgiven: **muāf kar dēnā,** vb., tr.
forgiveness: **muāfī, fm.**
(get) forgiveness: **muāf karvānā, vb., tr.**
form: **śakal, sūrat, fm.**
fornicate: **zinā karnā, vb., tr.**
fornication: **zinā, msc.**
fort: **kilā, msc.**
forthcoming: **aglā, adj.**
forthwith: **ēk • dam, adv.**
fortunately: **khuś • kismatī-sē, adv.**
fortune (wealth): **daulat, fm.**
forty: **cālīs, adj., n.c.**
forty-one: **iktālīs, adj., n.c.**
forty-two: **bayālīs, adj., n.c.**
forty-three: **tētālīs, adj., n.c.**
forty-four: **cavālīs, adj., n.c.**
forty-five: **paĩtālīs, adj., n.c.**
forty-six: **chiyālīs, adj., n.c.**

forty-seven: **saitālīs, adj., n.c.**
forty-eight: **aṛtālīs, adj., n.c.**
forty-nine: **uncās, adj., n.c.**
found: **bunyād ḍālnā, basānā, vb., tr.**
foundation: **bunyād, fm.**
founded: **basāyā, adj.**
fountain: **favvārā, msc.**
four: **cār, adj., n.c.**
fourteen: **caudā, adj., n.c.**
fourth: **cauthā, adj.**
fowl: **murg̱, msc.**
fox: **laumaṛ, msc.; laumṛī, fm.**
frankly: **sāf sāf, adv.**
free: **āzād, muft, adj., n.c.**
freedom: **āzādī, fm.**
frequently: **aksar, adv.**
fresh: **tāzā, adj.**
Friday: **jumā, msc.**
friend: **dōst, msc.** and **fm.**
friendly: **milansār, adj., n.c.**
fright: **ḍar, msc.**
frighten: **ḍarānā, vb., tr.**
(be) frightened: **ḍar jānā, ḍarnā, vb., int.**
frog: **mēḍak, msc.**
from: **-sē, postpos.**
(in) front: **pēś, sāmnē, adv.**
(in) front of: **-kē āgē, -kē sāmnē, postpos.**
fuel: **īdhan, msc.**
fulfill: **pūrā karnā, vb., tr.**
full: **pūrā, adj.**
full of: **bharā • parā, bharā huā, adj.**
fun (have) fun: **mazē karnā, vb., tr.**
further: **mazīd, adj., n.c.; āgē baṛhānā, vb., tr.**
future: **āindā, adj., n.c.**

gain: **fāydā, msc.**
gallop: **sarpat dauṛnā, vb., int.**
gamble: **jūā khēlnā, vb., int.** and **tr.**
Gandhi: **Gā̃dhī, Mōhandās Karmcand Gā̃dhī, pr. n., msc.**
Ganges River: **Gangā, fm.**
garage: **garāj, msc.**
garden: **bāg̱, msc.**

ardener: **mālī, msc.**
arland: **hār, msc.; mālā, fm.**
ather: **jamā hōnā, vb., int.; jamā karnā, vb., tr.**
be) gathered: **jamā hōnā, vb., int.**
General Court: **dīvān-e-ām, msc.**
enerally: **zyādātar, adv.**
enerous: **faiyāz, adj., n.c.**
entleman: **sāhib, sāhab, śharīf ādmī, msc.**
eography: **jugrāfiyā, msc.**
George: **Jārj, msc.**
esture: **iśārā, msc.; harkat, fm.**
et: **hāsil karnā, pānā, vb., tr.**
et along: **guzārā karnā, vb., tr.**
et involved: **ulajhnā, vb., int.**
et out of: **utarnā, vb., int.**
et out of the way: **haṭ jānā, haṭnā, vb., int.**
et up: **jāgnā, uṭh baiṭhnā, vb., int.**
hee: **ghī, msc.**
ift: **tōhfā, msc.**
irl: **laṛkī, fm.**
ive: **dēnā, vb., tr.**
(cause to) give: **dilānā, vb., tr.**
give away: **ḳurbān karnā, vb., tr.**
give back: **vāpas dēnā, vāpas karnā, vb., tr.**
give to drink: **pilānā, vb., tr.**
give up: **chōṛ dēnā, chōṛnā, ḳurbān karnā, vb., tr.**
glad: **ḳhuś, adj., n.c.**
(be) glad: **ḳhuś hōnā, vb., int.**
(I am) glad: **mujhē khuśī huī**
gladness: **ḳhuśī, fm.**
glance: **nigāh, fm.; nigāh ḍālnā, vb., tr.**
glass: **glās, msc.**
glory: **śān, fm.**
go: **jānā, vb., int.**
go away: **calā jānā, vb., int.**
go on foot: **paidal jānā, vb., int.**
Goa: **Gōā, pl. n., msc.**
goal: **maḳsad,** (target) **niśānā, msc.**
goat: **bakrā, msc.**
God: **Ḳhudā, Allah, msc.**
God willing: **Inśāllah, adv.**
Godavari River: **Gōdāvarī, msc .**
gold: **sōnā, msc.**
golden: **sōnē-kā, adj.**
Gomati River: **Gōmtī, msc.**

good: acchā, bhalā, adj.
good fortune: ḳhuś•ḳismatī, fm.
goodbye: Ḳhudā hāfiz (lit., may God protect you.)
good-looking: ḳhuś•śakal, adj., n.c.
goodness: bhalāyī, ḳhūbī, fm.
gossip: gap, fm.
gossip: gap karnā, gap mārnā, vb., tr.
govern: hakūmat karnā, vb., tr.
government: hakūmat, hukūmat, sarkār, fm.
government building: sarkārī imārat, fm.
Government College: gavarmeṇṭ kālij, msc.
governmental: sakārī, adj., n.c.
governor: gavarnar, lāṭ•sāhib, msc.
Governor General: gavarnar jenral, msc.
grab: chīnnā, pakaṛnā, vb., tr.
grace: adā, ān, fm.
grade: jamāt, klās, fm.
graduate: grējūeṭ, msc. and fm.; pās hōnā, vb., int.
grafter: harāmḳhōr, msc. and fm.
grain: anāj, msc.
grand: ālīśān, adj., n.c.
grandfather (paternal): dādā, msc.
grandfather (maternal): nānā, msc.
(great) grandfather (paternal): pardādā, msc.
grandmother: dādī, fm.
grandmother (paternal): dādī, fm.
grandmother (maternal): nānī, fm.
grandson: pōtā, msc.
(great) grandson (paternal): parpōtā, msc.
granite: grēnaiṭ, msc.
grass: ghās, fm. and msc.
graze: carnā, vb., int. and tr.
to (keep) grazing: cartā rahnā, vb., int.
grazing land: carāgāh, msc.
great: baṛā, adj.
Great Britain: Iṅglistān, msc.
greater: baṛā, adj.
Greece: Yūnan, msc.
green: harā, adj.; sabz, adj., n.c.
greet: mubārak bād dēnā, sālām arz karnā, vb., tr.
greetings: sālām, msc.
grief: afsōs, ġam, ranj, msc.
groceries: saudā sulaf, saudā sulf, msc.
grocery shop: pansārū-kī dukān, fm.
ground: zamīn, fm.

group: **grūp, msc.**
grow: **baṛhnā, vb., int.; ugānā, vb., tr.**
grow up: **baṛā hōnā, vb., int.**
grown: **ugā huā, adj.**
(be) grown: **ugnā, vb., int.**
guard: **pahrā, msc.**
guess: **andāzā, ḳiyās, msc.; bhā̃p lēnā, vb., tr.; andāzā karnā, ḳiyās karnā, vb., tr.**
guest: **mehmān,** msc. and **fm.**
guilt: **jurm, ḳasūr, msc.**
guitar: **sitār, msc.**
Gujarati: **Gujrātī, msc.** and **fm.**
Gujarati language: **Gujrātī, fm.**
gun: **bandūḳ, fm.**

haberdashery shop: **bisātī-kī dukān, fm.**
habit: **ādat, fm.**
haggling: **jhagṛā, msc.**
hair: **bāl, msc.**
hale and hearty: **sahī • salāmat, adj., n.c.**
half: **ādhā, adj.**
plus one half: **sāṛhē,** (= prefix)
hall: **hāl, msc.**
hallowed: **muḳaddas, adj., n.c.**
hand: **dast, hāth, msc.**
(raise) hands: **hāth ḳharā karnā, vb., tr.**
(shake) hands: **hāth milānā, vb., tr.**
handkerchief: **rūmāl, msc.**
handmaiden: **kanīz, fm.**
hang: **laṭkānā, vb., tr.;** (be hung) **laṭaknā, vb., int.**
(bend): **jhukānā, vb., tr.**
(be bent): **jhuknā, vb., int.**
Hanuman: **Hanūmān, pr. n., msc.**
happen: **guzarnā, ā paṛnā, vb., int.**
(it so) happened: **aisā huā**
happening: **vāḳeā, msc.**
happy: **ḳhuś, mubāraḳ, sukhī, adj., n.c.**
(be) happy: **ḳhuṣ hōnā, vb., int.**
harbor: **bandargāh, fm.**
hard: **saḳht, adj., n.c.**
hard (difficult): **muśkil, adj., n.c.; kaṛā, adj.**
hardly: **muśkil-sē, adv.**
hardship: **burāī, saḳhtī, fm.**

harem: **haram, msc.**
harsh: **kaṛā, adj.; saḳht, adj., n.c.**
harshness: **saḳhtī, fm.**
harvest: **fasal, fm.**
haste: **jaldī, fm.**
hat: **ṭōpī, fm.; haiṭ, msc.**
hatchet: **kulhāṛī, fm.**
have: **-kē pās hōnā, postpos.** and **vb., int.**
have (keep): **rakhnā, vb., tr.**
have to: **hōnā, paṛnā, vb., int.**
having gone: **jākar, ger.**
he: **vo, pron.**
head: **sar, msc.**
head (chief): **sarbarah, msc.**
head clerk: **hēḍ•klark, hēḍ•māsṭar, msc.**
health: **sēhat, tandrūstī, fm.**
healthy: **tandrūst, adj., n.c.**
(be) healthy and happy: **ḳhuś hōnā, vb., int.**
hear: **sunnā, vb., tr.**
(be) heard: **sunāī paṛnā, sunā jānā, sunāī dēnā, vb., int.**
heart: **dil, jī, msc.**
heathen: **kāfir, adj.** and **n. msc.**
heave: **phẽknā, vb., tr.**
heave a sigh: **āh karnā, vb. tr.**
heavy: **bhārī, adj., n.c.**
heir: **vāris, msc.**
hello: **hēlō, salām, ādāb arz, asalām alēkum** (also **asalām-ō-alēkum), valēkum asalām** (answer to **asalām alēkum)**
help: **imdād, madad, fm.; madad karnā, madad dēnā, vb., tr.**
helpless: **bēcārā, adj.**
hen: **murgī, fm.**
henceforth: **āgē, adv.**
here: **idhar, yahā̃, yahī̃, adv.**
hermitage: **āśram, ḳhānḳā, fm.**
hesitate: **pas-ō-pēś karnā, vb., tr.**
hesitation: **bāk, pas-ō-pēś, fm.**
(without) hesitation: **khaṛē khaṛē, binā pas-ō-pēś, adv.**
hey!: **ajī, excl.**
hidden: **chipā huā, chupā huā, adj.**
hide: **chipnā, chupnā, vb., int.; chupānā, vb., tr.**
(be) hidden: **chipā hōnā, vb., int.**
hide (skin): **camṛī, khāl, fm.;** (leather) **camṛā, msc.**
hideous: **badsūrat, adj., n.c.**
high: **ū̃cā, adj.**
high (expensive): **mahãgā, adj.**

high (sharp): tēz, adj., n.c.
hill: pahāṛī, fm.
Himalaya Mountains: Himālay, msc.
hinder: rōknā, rukāvat ḍālnā, vb., tr.
Hindi: Hindī, fm.
hindrance: rōk, rukāvat, fm.
Hindu: Hindū, adj. and n., msc.
hint: patā, msc.
historical: tārīḳhī, adj., n.c.
(get) hit (collision): [-kō] ṭakkar lagnā, vb., int.
hither: idhar, adv.
(became) hoarse: galā baiṭhā huā, adj., n.c.
(become) hoarse: galā baiṭh jānā, galā baiṭhnā, vb., tr.
hold: rakhnā, pakaṛ lēnā, vb., tr.; (be) held munaḳid hōnā, vb., int.
hole: chēd, surāḳh, msc.
Holi: Hōlī, fm.
holiday: tahvār, msc.
holy: muḳaddas, mutabarrik, adj., n.c.
holy man: pīr, sādhū, msc.
home: ghar, msc.
(go) home: ghar jānā, vb., int.
homesickness: ghar-kī yād, fm.
(be) homesick: ghar • yād ānā, vb., int.
homespun cloth: khaddar, fm.
honest: īmāndār, adj., n.c.
honesty: dyānatdārī, fm.; īmān, msc.
honey: śehad, msc.
honor: izzat, fm.
hope: ummīd, fm.
horn: sī̃g, msc.
horse: ghōṛā, msc.
horse (mare): ghōṛī, fm.
hospital: haspatāl, msc.
hot: garm, tēz, adj., n.c.
hotel: hōṭal, msc.
house: ghar, makān, msc.
House of the People: hāus āv pīpal, msc.; ḳaumī asemblī, fm.
household: ghar, msc.
householder: gharvālā, msc.
how: kaisē, adv.
how much: kitnā, int., adj.
howl: cīkhē̃ mārnā, vb., int.
hubbub: cahal • pahal, raunaḳ, fm.
human: insānī, adj.
human beings: insān, msc.

Humayun: **Humāyū̃, pr. n., msc.**
humor: **mazāh, msc.**
humorous: **latīfagō, pur mazāh, adj.**
hundred: **sau, adj., n.c.**
hundreds: **sēkrō̃, adj., n.c.**
hunger: **bhūk, fm.**
hungry: **bhūkā, adj.**
hunt: **śikār, msc.**
hunter: **śikārī, msc.**
hurt: **cōṭ, fm.; zaḳham, msc.**
(be) hurt: **cōṭ khānā, vb., tr.**
husband: **ḳhāvind, śōhar, msc.**
husband and wife: **miyā̃ • bīvī, msc., pl.**
hut: **jhōpṛī, fm.**
Hyderabad: **Hāiderābād, pl. n.** and **msc.**

I: **maĩ, pron.**
I am glad: **mujhē khūśī huī**
I don't know: **mujhē mālūm nahī̃**
"I wish": **kāś, excl.**
ice: **barf, baraf, fm.**
idea: **īmān, tasavvur, ḳhayāl, msc.**
idol: **būt, msc.**
if: **agar, conj.**
ill: **bīmār, marīz, adj., n.c.**
illegal: **gair • ḳānūnī, adj., n.c.**
illegitimate: **harām-kā, adj.**
illiterate: **an • paṛh, adj., n.c.**
ill-mannered: **bad • tamīz, adj., n.c.**
illness: **bīmārī, fm.**
ills: **burāī, fm.**
immediately: **fauran, adv.**
imperialism: **impīryalism, msc.**
important: **aham, eham, adj., n.c.**
impression: **asar, msc.**
imprison: **ḳaid karnā, vb., tr.**
imprisoned: **muḳayyad, adj., n.c.**
(be) imprisoned: **giriftār hōnā, vb., int.**
imprisonment: **ḳaid, fm.**
improve: **behtar karnā, sudhārnā, vb., tr.**

improvement: **sudhār, msc.; behtarī, fm.**
in: **andar, adv.; -mẽ, postpos.**
in short: **bas, mukhtasaran, adv.**
incense: **lōbān, agar, msc.**
inch: **inc, msc.**
incident: **muāmlā, vākeā, msc.**
included: **śāmil, adj., n.c.**
income: **āmdanī, fm.**
incorporate: **milā lēnā, vb., tr.**
incorrect: **galat, adj., n.c.**
increase (development): **tarakkī, fm.**
increase: **baṛhānā, vb., tr.; baṛhnā, vb., int.**
India: **Bhārat, Hindūstān, msc.**
indication: **niśān, patā, msc.**
indigo: **nīl, msc.**
Indira: **Indīrā, pr. n., fm.**
industrious: **mehantī, adj., n.c.**
industry: **sanat, fm.**
inferior: **ghaṭiyā, adj.**
infinite: **bēpanāh, lāintahā, adj., n.c.**
inform: **ittalā dēnā, vb., tr.**
information: **ittalā, fm.**
informed about: **vākif, adj., n.c.**
inhabit: **basnā, vb., int.**
inhabitant: **rahnēvālā, msc.**
inhabited: **ābād huā, adj.**
(be) inhabited: **basānā, vb., tr.**
injure: **coṭ lagānā, vb., tr.**
injured: **ghāyal, zakhmī, adj., n.c.**
ink: **siyāhī, fm.**
inlay: **paccīkārī, fm.**
innocent: **bēgunah, māsūm, adj., n.c.; bhōlā, adj.**
innocent girl: **bhōlī • bhālī laṛkī, fm.**
inquire: **pūchnā, vb., tr.**
inscribe: **likhnā, khōdnā, vb., tr.**
(be) inscribed: **khudnā, vb., int.**
(cause to) inscribe: **likhvānā, khudvānā, vb., tr.**
insist: **isrār karnā, vb., tr.**
insolent: **gustākh, adj., n.c.**
inspect: **mulāhzā karnā, vb., tr.**
inspection: **mulāhzā, msc.**
inspector: **inspekṭār, msc.**
inspiration: **vahī, fm.**
(divine) inspiration: **vahī, fm.**
instance: **misāl, fm.**

(for) instance: **maslan**
instantly: **ek · dam, adv.**
instead: **balke, conj.**
instructor: **ustād, msc.**
instructress: **ustānī, fm.**
instrument (tool): **auzār, msc.**
intend: **irādā karnā, vb., tr.**
intention: **irādā, msc.**
interest: **dilcaspī, fm.; śauk, msc.**
interest (on money): **sūd, msc.**
interesting: **dilcasp, adj., n.c.**
interfere: **daḳhal dēnā, vb., tr.**
interference: **daḳhal, msc.**
intermediate: **mutavassit, adj., n.c.; bīc-kā, adj.**
interpretation: **tābīr, fm.**
intoxication: **naśā, msc.**
introduction: **taāruf, msc.**
investigation: **jā̃c, taftīś, fm.**
invitation: **dāvat, fm.**
Iran: **Īrān, pl. n., msc.**
iron: **lōhā, msc.; lōhē-kā, adj.**
ironically: **tanz-sē, adv.**
irrelevant: **idhar · udhar-kī, adj.**
irrigate: **ābpāśī karnā, sī̃cnā, vb., tr.**
irrigation: **ābpāśī, fm.**
Islam: **Islām, msc.**
island: **jazīrā, msc.**
it: **ye, vo, pron.**

jackal: **gīdaṛ, msc.**
Jahangir: **Jahā̃gir, pr. n., msc.**
jail: **jēl, msc.** and **fm.**
Jamshedpur: **Jamśēdpur, pl. n., msc.**
Janak: **Janak, pr. n., msc.**
January: **janvarī, fm.**
Japan: **Jāpān, pl. n., msc.**
Javaharlal Nehru: **Javāharlāl Nēhrū, pr. n., msc.**
Jesus: **Īsā, pr. n., msc.**
jewel: **javāhir, msc.**
jewelry: **javāhirāt, zēvar, msc.**
Jhelum River: **Jhelum, pl. n., msc.**
Jinnah: **Jinnā, pr. n., msc.**

job: **naukrī, fm.; kām, msc.**
join: **milnā, vb., int.**
join hands: **hāth jōṛnā, vb., tr.**
joke: **mazāḳ, msc.**
journalist: **aḳhbār•navīs, msc.**
journey: **safar, msc.**
judge: **jaj, msc.**
July: **jōlāī, jaulāī, fm.**
Jumna River: **Jammā, pl. n., fm.**
jump: **kūdnā, uchalnā, vb., int.**
junction: **jankśan, msc.**
June: **jūn, msc.**
jungle: **jañgal, msc.**
Jurist: **ālim-e-ḳanūn, msc.**
(Muslim) jurist: **ḳāzī, msc.**
just: **bas, mehaz, adv.**
just so: **vaisā, adv.**
justice: **adl, insāf, msc.**
(do) justice: **insāf karnā, vb., tr.**

Kalinga: **Kaliñg, pl. n., msc.**
Kamla: **Kamlā, pr. n., fm.**
Kashmir: **Kaśmīr, pl. n., msc.**
Kashmirian: **kaśmīrī, msc.** and **fm.**
keep: **rakhnā, vb., tr.**
keep back: **haṭnā, vb., int.; haṭānā, vb., tr.**
keep going: **caltā rakhnā, vb., int.**
kerosene: **miṭṭī-kā tēl, msc.**
key: **cābī, fm.**
kid: **jhūṭ•mūṭ kahnā, mazāḳ karnā, vb., tr.**
kill: **mār ḍālnā, mārnā, vb., tr.**
"kill time": **vaḳt kāṭnā, vaḳt guzarnā, vb., tr.**
kind (sort): **ḳism, tarah, tarāh, fm.**
kind: **meharbān, adj., n.c.**
kind-heartedness: **rahamdilī, fm.**
kindly: **meharbānī-sē, adv.**
kindness: **fazal, meharbānī, fm.**
king: **bādśāh, rājā, msc.**
kingship: **bādśāhat, fm.**
kiss: **cūmnā, pyār karnā, vb., tr.**
kitchen: **bāvarcīḳhānā, msc.**
kitchen vessel: **bartan, msc.**

kite: **pataṅg, msc. and fm.**
knead: **bēlnā, vb., tr.**
knife: **chūrī, fm.; cāḳū, msc.**
knit: **bunnā, vb., tr.**
know: **jānnā, vb., tr.**
knowledge: **ilm, patā, msc.**
known: **mālūm, adj., n.c.**
Korea: **Kōryā, pl. n., msc.**
Kuran: **Kurān, msc.**

labor: **kām, kārōbār, msc.; mehnat, fm.**
laborer: **mazdūr, msc.**
lack: **kamī, fm.**
Ladies and Gentlemen!: **ḳhavātīn-ō-hazarāt, msc.**
lady: **bēgam, ḳhātūn, fm.**
Lahore: **Lāhōr, pl. n., msc.**
The Lahore Resolution: **Karārdād-e-Lahōr, fm.**
lake: **jhīl, fm.**
Lake Michigan: **Lēk Miśegan, fm.**
Lakshman: **Lakśmaṇ, pr. n., msc.**
Lalitāditya: **Lālitāditya, pr. n., msc.**
Lalpur: **Lālpur, pl. n., msc.**
lamb: **bhēṛ, fm.**
lame: **laṅgṛā, adj.**
lamp: **battī, fm.; laimp, lemp, dīp, msc.**
land: **zamīn, fm.**
land (country): **mulk, msc.**
land-revenue: **mālguzārī, fm.**
lane: **galī, fm.**
language: **zabān, bōlī, fm.**
lap: **gōd, fm.**
large: **baṛā, (fat) mōṭā, adj.**
last: **āḳhrī, pichlā, adj.**
late: **dēr-sē, adv.**
laugh: **hãsnā, vb., int.**
law: **ḳānūn, msc.**
(official) law: **sarkārī ḳānūn, msc.**
law-suit: **muḳadmā, msc.**
lawn: **maidān, ghās-kā maidān, msc.**
lawyer: **vakīl, msc.**
lay: **lagānā, rakhnā, vb., tr.**
lay before: **sāmnē rakhnā, vb., tr.**

lazy: **sust, adj., n.c.**
lead: **lē calnā, vb., int.; rāh dikhānā, vb., tr.**
leader: **līḍar, msc.** and **fm.**
leadership: **līḍarī, ḳayādat, fm.**
leaf: **pattā,** (of book) **varaḳ, varḳ, msc.**
lean: **dublā, adj.**
learn: **sīkhnā, vb., tr.**
learned: **allāmā, adj.; ālim, adj., n.c.**
learned Muslim: **maulvī, msc.**
learned people: **ulamā, paṛhē • likhē ādmī, msc. pl.**
learning: **ilm, msc.**
lease: **paṭṭā, msc.**
least: **sab-sē kam, sab-sē chōṭā, adj.**
(at) least: **kam-az-kam, kam-sē kam, adv.**
leather: **camṛā, msc.**
leather strap: **tasmā, msc.**
leatherworker (shoemaker): **camār, msc.**
leave: **chōṛnā, vb., tr.**
leave (go): **jānā, vb., int.**
leave behind: **pīchē chōṛnā, vb., tr.**
leave (vacation): **chuṭṭī, fm.**
leaving out: **chōṛkar, ger.**
Lebanon: **Labnān, pl. n., msc.**
left (not right): **bāyā̃, adj.**
leg: **ṭā̃g, fm.;** (of furniture) **pair, pāyā, msc.**
legged: **pairvālā, adj.**
legal: **ḳānūnī, adj., n.c.**
legal practice: **vikālat, vakālat, fm.**
legislation: **ēkṭ, ḳānūn, msc.**
Legislative Assembly: **ḳānūn-sāz asemblī, fm.**
lentils: **dāl, fm.**
less: **kam, adj., n.c.**
lessen: **ghaṭnā, vb., int.; ghaṭānā, vb., tr.**
lesson: **sabaḳ, msc.**
lest: **varnā, aisā na hō ke, conj.**
let: **dēnā, vb., tr.**
let go: **chōṛ dēnā, vb., tr.**
let live: **rahnē dēnā, vb., tr.**
letter: **ḳhat, msc.; ciṭṭhī, fm.**
letter (of alphabet): **haraf, harf, msc.**
letters: **ḳhatūt, msc. pl.**
library: **laibrārī, fm.; kutubḳhānā, msc.**
licence: **lāisens, msc.**
lie: **jhūṭ, msc.; jhūṭ bōlnā, vb., tr.**
lie down: **lēṭnā, vb., int.**

life: zindagī, jān, umar, fm.
(spend one's) life: umar guzar jānā, vb., int.
lift: uṭhānā, vb., tr.
lift up: uṭhānā, vb., tr.
light: halkā, adj.; rōśnī, fm.
light: bijlī jalānā, vb., tr.
like: jaisā, adj.; pasand ānā, vb., tr.
limitless: bēpanāh, adj., n.c.
line: lāin, fm.
lion: śēr, msc.
liquor: śarāb, fm.
list: fehrist, fm.
(make a) list: fehrist banānā, vb., tr.
listen: sunnā, bāt sunnā, vb., tr.
litigation: muḳadmē bāzī, muḳadmā bāzī, fm.
little: kām, adv.; zarā, adv., n.c.; chōṭā, adj.; thōṛā, adj.
little while: thōṛī dēr, fm.
live (exist): jīnā, vb., int.
live (dwell): rahnā, vb., int.
live (pass life): guzārnā, vb., tr.
livelihood: rōzī, fm.
load: bōjh, msc.
load: lādnā, vb., tr.
loan: ḳarz, udhār,
local: maḳāmī, adj., n.c.
located: vāḳē, adj.
lock up: band karnā, vb., tr.
loiter: bēkār ghumnā, vb., int.
Lokmanya Tilak: Lōkmānya Tilak, pr. n., msc.
loneliness: akēlāpan, msc.
long: lambā, adj.
(how) long: kitnē arsē, adv.
long ago: bahot din pahlē, bahot din huē, adv.
long live!: zindābād, excl.
look!: lō, dēkhō, excl.
look: niśān, msc.; nigāh, śakal • surat, fm.; dēkhnā, vb., tr.
look after: dēkhbhāl karnā, vb., tr.
look for: ḍhū̃ḍhnā, talāś karnā, vb., tr.
lord: lāṭ, lārḍ, msc.
lose: hār jānā, vb., int.; hārnā, vb., int.
loss: nuḳsān, msc.
lost: khōyā huā, adj.
(be) lost: gum hōnā, vb., int.
lotus: kamal, kāval, msc.
loud: ū̃cā, adj.

loudspeaker: **lauḍspīkar, msc.**
love: **muhabbat, fm.; pyār, msc.; pyār karnā, vb., tr.**
lover: **āśik, msc.** and **fm.**
low: **nīcā, adj.**
Lucknow: **Lakhnāu, pl. n., msc.**
luggage: **sāmān, msc.**
luxury: **aiś, msc.**
lyric poem: **g̱azal, fm.**

machine: **maśīn, fm.**
mad: (insane): **pāgal, adj., n.c.**
madam: **bēgam • sāhibā, bēgam • sāhabā, fm.**
made: see **make**
Madras: **Madrās, pl. n., msc.**
magazine: **risālā, msc.**
Maharajah: **mahārājā, msc.**
maid: **kanīz, fm.**
maidservant: **naukarānī, fm.**
maintain: **sambhālnā, vb., tr.**
majestic: **ālīśān, adj., n.c.**
majority: **aksariyyat, fm.**
make: **banānā, karnā, vb., tr.**
make excuses: **bahānā banānā, vb., tr.**
make progress: **taraḳḳī karnā, vb., tr.**
make the rounds of: **cakkar lagānā, vb., tr.**
(be) made: **ban jānā, bannā, vb., int.**
malaria: **malēriyā, msc.**
man: **ādmī, mard, msc.**
man (servant): **naukar, msc.**
manager: **mainējar, manījar, msc.**
manganese: **mēnganīz, fm.**
mango: **ām, msc.**
manifest: **zāhir, adj., n.c.**
mankind: **insān, msc.**
manner: **andāz, msc.; tarah, tarāh, fm.**
manure: **khād, fm.**
many: **bahot, adj., n.c.**
many things: **bahot kuch, adj., n.c.**
map: **nakśā, msc.**
Marathi language: **Marāṭhī, fm.**
March: **mārc, msc.**
mare: **ghōṛī, fm.**

maritime: **samandrī, adj., n.c.**
mark: **niśānā, msc.**
mark on forehead: **tilak, msc.**
market: **bāzār, msc.**
marketplace: **bāzār, msc.**
marriage: **śādī, fm.**
marriageable: **śādī-kē ḳābil, adj., n.c.**
married: **śādī • śūdā, adj., n.c.**
married couple: **mīyā̃ • bīvī, msc.**
master: **mālik, msc.**
mastery: **abūr, msc.**
maternal home: **maikā, msc.**
matter: **bāt, fm.; mūāmlā, muāmlā, msc.**
matters: **muāmlāt, msc. pl.**
(no) matter: **bahar ṃāl, ḳhāh, adv.**
mature: **javān, puḳhtā, adj., i.c.; syānā, adj.**
maund: **man, msc.**
meal: **khānā, msc.**
mean: **bad, prefix** and **adj., n.c.**
meaning: **matlab, mānā, msc.**
means: **zariyā (pl. zariyē, zarāē), msc.**
meat: **gōśt, msc.**
Mecca: **Makkā, pl. n., msc.**
mechanic: **kārīgar, mikenik, mistarī, msc.**
medical: **tibbi, adj., n.c.**
medical college: **meḍikal kālij, msc.**
medicine: **davā, davāī, fm.**
Medina: **Medīnā, pl. n., msc.**
meet: **milnā, vb., int.**
(make both ends) meet: **guzarā hōnā, vb., int.; guzarā karnā, vb., tr.**
meeting: **ijlās, jalsā, msc.; mulāḳāt, fm.**
melon: **ḳharbūzā, tarbūz, msc.**
melt: **pighālnā, vb., tr.; (be melted) pighalnā, vb., int.**
member: **maimbar, msc. and fm.**
memorize: **yād karnā, vb., tr.**
memory: **yād, fm.**
mention: **zikr, msc.; zikr karnā, vb., tr.**
(it is) mentioned: **ēk dafā-kā zikr hai**
merchant: **dukāndār, mercaṇṭ, msc.**
mere: **mehaz, adv.**
merit: **ḳhūbī, fm.**
message: **paigām, msc.**
messenger: **caprāsī, msc.; (of God) rasūl, msc.**
method: **tarīḳā, msc.**
mica: **māikā, msc.**

middle: bīc, msc.; -kē bīc-mẽ, postpos.; mutvassat, mutavassit, adj., n.c.
middle-aged: aḍhēr umar-kā, adj.
middle class: mutavassit darjē-kā, adj.
(in the) midst of: -kē bīc-mẽ, postpos.
mien: niśān, cahrā, andāz, msc.
migration: hijrat, fm.
milk: dūdh, msc.
milk: dūdh nikālnā, vb., tr.
milkman: dūdhvālā, msc.
mill: mil, fm. and msc.
millet: mileṭ, bājrāh, msc.
million: das lākh, milyan, adj., n.c.
mind: zehan, dimāg̲, man, msc.
mine: kān, fm.
mine: mērā, poss. adj.
minister: vazīr, msc.
minute: minaṭ, msc.
miracle: moyizā, msc.
mirror: āīnā, śīśā, msc.
mischief: śarārat, fm.
mischievous: śarārtī, adj., n.c.
miser: kanjūs, msc.
miser of misers: kanjūs • makkhīcūs, adj., n.c.
misery: musībat, śāmat, fm.
misfortune: bad • ḳismatī, musībat, fm.
miss: cūk jānā, vb., int.
mission: miśan, msc.
misunderstanding: anban, g̲alat • fehmī, fm.
modern: māḍarn, adj., n.c.; nayā, adj.
Mogul: Mug̲al, msc.
Mohan: Mōhan, pr. n., msc.
Monday: pīr, msc.
money: paisā, msc.; paisē, msc. pl.
money advance to cultivators: taḳāvi, fm.
moneylender: mahājan, sāhūkār, msc.
monitor: mauniṭar, msc. and fm.
monkey: bandar, msc.
monsoon: mānsūn, fm.
month: mahīnā, msc.
monthly: mahvār, adj., n.c.
mood: mūḍ, fm.
moon: cā̃d, msc.
more: zyādā, adj., n.c. and adv.; mazīd̲, adj., n.c.
the more . . . the more: jū̃ jū̃ . . . tū̃ tū̃
more or less: kam-ō-bēś, adv.

moreover: **to, conj.; is-kē alāvā**
morning: **subah, fm.; saverā, din, msc.**
(in the) morning: **subah-kō, adv.**
(next) morning: **aglī subah, adv.**
mortgage: **girvī, fm.**
(hold a) mortgage: **girvī rakhnā, vb., tr.**
mortgaged: **rahan, adj., n.c.**
mortgagee: **murtahan, msc.**
mosaic: **paccīkārī, fm.**
mosque: **masjid, fm.**
most: **sab-sē zyādā, adv.**
mostly: **zyādātar, adv.**
mother: **mā̃, ammā̃, ammī, vālidā, fm.**
mother-in-law: **sās, fm.**
Motilal Nehru: **Mōtīlāl Nēhrū, pr., n., msc.**
motion picture: **film, fm.** and **msc.**
motorcar: **mōṭar, msc.** and **fm.; mōṭargāṛī, fm.**
motorcycle: **mōṭarsāikil, fm.** and **msc.**
motorist: **mōṭarvālā, msc.**
mound: **ṭīlā, msc.**
mountain: **pahāṛ, msc.**
mouse: **cūhā, msc.**
mouth: **mũh, msc.**
movies: **film, fm.; sinēmā, msc.**
much: **bahot, adv.**
(as) much as: **jitnā, adj.**
(how) much: **kitnā, int. adj.**
(so) much: **itnā, adj.**
(this) much: **itnā, adj.**
(too) much: **itnā zyādā, adj.; bahot zyādā, adj., n.c.**
(that) much: **utnā, adv.**
mud: **kīcaṛ, msc.**
muddy: **kīcaṛvālā, adj.**
Muharram: **Muharram, msc.**
mullah: **mullā, msc.**
Multan: **Multān, pl. n., msc.**
multiplication: **zarab, msc.**
multiply: **zarab dēnā, vb., tr.**
municipality: **kamēṭī, fm.**
Muniyan: **Muniyā, pr. n., fm.**
Munna: **Munnā, pr. n., msc.**
murder: **ḳatl karnā, vb., tr.**
murderer: **ḳātil, msc.**
Murree: **Marī, pl. n., fm.**
music: **gānā, msc.; mausīḳī, fm.**

musical: **surīlā, adj.**
musical instrument: **bājā, msc.**
Muslim: **Musalmān, Muslim, msc.** and **fm.**
Muslim League: **Muslīm Līg, fm.**
Muslim priest: **Maulvī, msc.**
mutiny: **g̱adar, msc.**
my: **mērā, poss. adj.**
Mysore: **Maisūr, pl. n., msc.**

Nagari: **nagrī, fm.**
nail: **kīl, fm.**
name: **nām, msc.**
narrow: **tañg, adj., n.c.**
nastalik: **nastalīḳ, msc.**
nation: **ḳom, ḳaum, fm.**
near: **-kē nazdīk, -kē ird gird, -kē ās • pās, postpos.; pās, adv.**
near enough (= quite near): **kāfī pās, adv.**
near to: **bilkul pās-hī, adv.**
nearly: **ḳarīban, adv.**
necessary: **lāzim, zarūrī, adj., n.c.**
necessity: **zarūrat, fm.**
neck: **gardan, fm.**
necklace: **hār, neklis, msc.**
need: **zarūrat, fm.**
neighbor: **hamsāyā, paṛausī, msc.; hamsāī, paṛausan, fm.**
nephew: (paternal) **bhatījā;** (maternal) **bhanjā, msc.**
net: **jāl, msc.**
nevertheless: **phir-bhī, tāham, adv.**
new: **nayā, adj.**
news: **ḳhabar, fm.**
newspaper: **aḳhbār, fm.**
newspaperman: **aḳhbār • navīs, msc.**
newspaperwoman: **aḳhbār • navīs, fm.**
next: **aglā, adj.**
nice: **acchā, adj.; ḳhūb, adj., n.c.**
nicely: **ḳhūb, acchī tarah, adv.**
night: **rāt, fm.**
nightingale: **bulbul, fm.**
nine: **nau, adj., n.c.**
nineteen: **unnīs, adj., n.c.**
ninety: **navvē, adj., n.c.**
ninety-one: **ikkānvē, adj., n.c.**

ninety-two: **bānvē, adj., n.c.**
ninety-three: **tirānvē, adj., n.c.**
ninety-four: **caurānvē, cūrānvē, adj., n.c.**
ninety-five: **piccānvē, paccānvē, adj., n.c.**
ninety-six: **chiyānvē, adj., n.c.**
ninety-seven: **sattānvē, adj., n.c.**
ninety-eight: **aṭṭhānvē, adj., n.c.**
ninety-nine: **ninnānvē, adj., n.c.**
ninth: **navā̃, adj.**
no: **nahī̃, adv.**
no matter: **bahar hāl, ḳhāh**
no more: **bas**
noise: **śōr, msc.**
(make) noise: **śōr macānā, vb., tr.**
noon: **dōpahar, msc.**
north: **śumāl, msc.**
not: **mat, na, nahī̃, adv.**
note: **nōṭ, msc.**
nothing: **kuch nahī̃**
novel: **nāval, nāvil, msc.**
now: **ab, abhī, is vaḳt, adv.**
(up to) now: **ab-tak, adv.**
nowadays: **āj • kal**
number: **nambar, msc.; tādād, fm.**
Nurjahan: **Nūrjahā̃, pr. n., fm.**
nurse: **nars, fm.**
nurture: **parvariś karnā, vb., tr.**

oak: **ōk, fm.** and **msc.**
obey: **mānnā, vb., tr.** and **int.**
object: **murād, fm.; mafūl, msc.**
objection: **etrāz, msc.**
objective: **maḳad, msc.**
obligation: **ahsān, msc.**
observe: **manānā, vb., tr.**
obtain: **hāsil karnā, vb., tr.**
occasion: **mauḳā, msc.**
occupation: **kām • kāj, pēśā, msc.**
occupied: **maśġūl, adj., n.c.**
ocean: **samandar, msc.**
ocean liner: **samandrī jahāz, msc.**
October: **akṭūbar, msc.**

offering: **ḳurbāni, fm.**
office: **daftar (pl., dafātir), msc.**
officer: **afsar, msc.**
official: **afsar, sarkārī ādmī, msc.**
oil: **tēl, msc.**
oil seed crusher: **kōlhū, msc.**
old: **buṛhā, purānā, adj.**
old age: **buṛhāpā, msc.**
old woman: **būṛhīyā, fm.**
olive: **āmlā, msc.**
once: **ēk bār, adv.**
once again: **dō bārā, adv.**
one: **ēk, adj., n.c.**
one and a half: **ḍēṛh, adj., n.c.**
only: **sirf, bas, mehaz, adv.**
only one: **ēk-hī, adv.**
open: **khulā, adj.; khōlnā, vb., tr.**
(be) open: **khulnā, vb., int.**
(have) opened: **khulānā, vb., tr.; khulvānā, vb., tr.**
open up: **khulnā, vb., int.**
opinion: **ḳhayāl, msc.; rāy, fm.**
opponent: **muḳhālif, msc.** and **fm.**
opportunity: **mauḳā, msc.**
(have the) opportunity: **mauḳā milnā, vb., int.**
opposite: **ulṭā, adj.**
opposition: **muḳhālifat, fm.**
or: **yā, conj.**
order: **hukam, hukm, msc.; aurḍar, msc.**
(in) order to: **-kē liyē, postpos.**
order (respectfully): **farmānā, vb., tr.**
orderly: **arḍalī, msc.**
ordinary: **māmūlī, adj., n.c.**
Orissa: **Uṛīsā, pl. n., msc.**
ornaments: **zēvar, msc.**
other: **dūsrā, adj.**
otherwise: **varnā, adv.**
Oudh: **Avadh, pl. n., msc.**
our: **hamārā, adj.**
out: **bāhar, adv.**
out of: **-kē bāhar, postpos.**
outside: **bāhar, adv.**
outside of: **-kē bāhar, postpos.**
overcoat: **ōvarkōṭ, msc.**
own: **apnā, adj.**
ownership: **milkīyat, fm.**

ox: **bail, msc.**
oxcart: **bailgāṛī, fm.**

pain: **dard, msc.**
Pakistan: **Pākistān, pl. n., msc.**
Pakistan Coffee House: **Pākistān Kāfī Hāus, msc.**
Pakistani: **Pākistānī, msc.** and **fm.; adj., n.c.**
palace: **mahal, msc.**
panchayat: **pancāet, pancāyat, fm.**
Panipat Plain: **Pānīpat, pl. n., msc.**
paper: **kāgaz, msc.**
pardon: **muāfī, māfī, fm.**
pardon: **muāf karnā, vb., tr.**
parents: **vāldain, msc. pl.**
park: **pārk, msc.**
parliament: **pārlīmeṇṭ, fm.**
parrot: **tōtā, msc.**
part: **hissā, msc.**
particularity: **ḳhasūsīyat, fm.**
partner: **śarīk, msc.** and **fm.**
party: **firḳa, msc.; mehfil, pārṭī, fm.**
Pashtu Language: **Paśtō, Paśtū, fm.**
pass: **bītnā, vb., tr.; guzarnā, vb., int.; guzārnā, vb., tr.**
pass (examination): **pās hōnā, vb., int.; pās kārnā, vb., tr.**
pass away: **vafāt pānā, vb., tr.**
pass: **darrā, msc.**
pasture: **carāgāh, fm.**
path: **pagḍaṇḍī, fm.**
patience: **bardāśt, fm.; sabr, sabar, msc.**
patient: **bīmār, msc.** and **fm.; marīz, msc.**
Patna: **Paṭnā, pl. n.**
patriotism: **hubb-e-vatna, msc.**
pavilion: **paivēliyan, msc.**
pay: **adā karnā, paisē dēnā, vb., tr.**
pea: **maṭar, msc.**
peace: **aman, msc.**
peacock: **mōr, msc.**
peak: **cōṭī, fm.**
pearl: **mōtī, msc.**
peck: **cōnc mārnā, vb., tr.**
peck and eat: **cugnā, vb., tr.**
peeling: **chilkā, msc.**
pen: **ḳalam, msc.**
pencil: **pensil, fm.**
pension: **penśan, fm.**

people: **lōg, msc.**
perfectly: **ṭhīk ṭhīk, adv.**
perhaps: **śāyad, adv.**
period: **pīryaḍ, msc.**
permanent: **mustaḳil, adj., n.c.**
permission: **ijāzat, fm.**
Persia: **Īran, msc.**
Persian language: **Fārsī, fm.**
person: **śaḳhs, msc.**
personal: **zātī, adj., n.c.**
Peshawar: **Piśāvar, pl. n., msc.**
petroleum: **pēṭroliyam, msc.**
pet animal: **pāltū jānvar, msc.**
Ph.D.: **pī ēc ḍī, fm.**
philosophic: **falsafiānah, adj., n.c.**
philosophy: **falsafā, msc.**
photographer: **fōṭōgrafar, msc.** and **fm.**
pick up: **uṭhānā, vb., tr.**
pickle: **acār, msc.**
picnic: **piknik, fm.**
picture: **tasvīr, fm.**
pie: (S. Asian currency): **pāī, fm.**
piece: **tukṛā, msc.**
pigeon: **kabūtar, msc.**
pilgrim: **hājī, msc.**
pilgrimage: **haj, msc.**
(make the) pilgrimage: **haj karnā, vb., tr.**
pillar: **setūn, sitūn, msc.**
pink: **gulābī, adj., n.c.**
pink powder: **gulābī pāūḍar, msc.**
Pir's tomb: **ḳhānḳāh, fm.**
pistol: **pistōl, msc.**
place: **jagah, fm.**
place: **rakhnā, vb., tr.**
(at) place of: **-kē yahā̃, postpos.**
places: **maḳāmāt, msc. pl.**
plain: **sādā, adj.; maidān, msc.; plain, msc.** and **fm.**
plan: **salāh, fm.**
plant: **paudā, msc.**
plant: **lagānā, vb., tr.**
plate: **thālī, raḳābī, plaiṭ, fm.**
play: **khēlnā, vb., tr.**
pleasant: **ḳhuś·gavār, adj., n.c.**
pleasantness: **ḳhūbī, latāfat, fm.**
pleasantry: **mazāḳ, msc.**

please: **pasand ānā, vb., int.**
please: **meharbānī-sē, barāē meharbānī, adv.**
pleased: **rāzī, adj., n.c.**
plow: **hal, msc.**
plow: **hal jōtnā, hal calānā, vb., tr.**
pluck: **tōṛnā, vb., tr.**
pocket: **jēb, fm.**
pocket money: **jēb • ḳharc, msc.**
poem: **nazam, nazm, fm.**
poet: **śāir, msc.**
poetic: **śāir • mizāj, adj., n.c.**
poetry: **śāirī, fm.**
point: **nuḳtā, msc.**
point out: **batānā, dikhānā, vb., tr.**
poison: **zehar, msc.**
police: **pōlīs, fm.**
policeman: **sipāhī, sanṭrī, msc.**
police station: **thānā, msc.**
polish: **pāliś, fm.**
political: **syāsī, siyāsī, adj., n.c.**
political science: **syāsiyāt, fm.**
politics: **syāsat, siyāsat, fm.**
pomp: **śān, fm.**
poor: **g̲arīb, (in strength) kamzōr, adj., n.c.**
populate: **ābād karnā, vb., tr.**
(be) populated: **basnā, vb., int.**
population: **ābādī, fm.**
Porbandar: **Porbandar, pl. n., msc.**
position: **ōhdā, maḳām, msc.**
post (pole): **khambhā, msc.**
post: **ḳhat ḍālnā, vb., tr.**
post office: **ḍākḳhānā, msc.**
potato: **ālū, msc.**
pound: **pāūṇḍ, msc.**
half a pound: **ādhā • pāūṇḍ, msc.**
pour: **ḍālnā, vb., tr.**
pour down (rain): **barasnā, vb., int.**
power: **tāḳat, fm.**
powerful: **tāḳatvar, adj., n.c.**
practice of law: **vikālat, fm.**
praise: **tārīf, fm.**
pray: **dūā dēnā, vb., tr.**
prayer: **namāz, ibādat, fm.**
(perform) prayers: **ibādat karnā, vb., tr.**
prefer: **zyādā pasand karnā, vb., tr.**

preparation: **taiyārī, fm.**
prepare: **taiyār karnā, vb., tr.**
presence: **maujūdgī, fm.**
(lose) presence of mind: **hōś uṛ jānā, vb., int.**
present: **maujūdā, maujūd, adj., n.c.**
present (gift): **tohfā, msc.; pēś karnā, vb., tr.**
(for the) present: **filhāl, adv.**
presidency: **safārat, fm.**
president: **sadr, sadar, msc.**
pretense: **bahānā, msc.**
prey: **śikār, msc.**
price: **ḳīmat, fm.; bhāō, msc.; dām, msc., pl.**
priest: **maulvī (Muslim), pujārī (Hindū), msc.**
primary: **ibtadāī, adj., n.c.**
primary education: **ibtadāī talīm, fm.**
Prime Minister: **vazīr-e-āzām, msc.**
prince: **śāhzādā, śahzādā, msc.; rājkumār**
princess: **śāhzādī, śahzādī, fm.; rājkumārī**
Privy Council: **prīvī kaunsal, fm.**
Privy Council Chamber: **prīvī kaunsal caimbar, msc.**
prize: **inām, msc.**
problem: **maslā, msc.; muśkil, fm.; (a puzzle) muammā, msc.**
procession: **jalūs, msc.**
produce: **fasal, paidāvār, fm.**
produced: **paidā • śudā, adj., n.c.**
(be) produced: **paidā hōnā, vb., int.**
profession: **pēśā, msc.**
professor: **prōfaisar, msc.** and **fm.**
profit: **fāydā, munāfā, nafā, sūd, msc.**
profit (usury): **munāfā hōnā, nafā hōnā, vb., tr.**
program: **prōgrām, msc.**
progress: **taraḳḳī, fm.**
promise: **vādā, msc.**
proper: **munāsib, adj., n.c.**
property: **jāēdād, milkiyyat, fm.**
prophet: **nabī, rasūl, msc.**
propose: **araz karnā, tajvīz karnā, vb., tr.**
proselytizing: **tablīg̱, fm.**
prosper: **khuś • hāl hōnā, vb., int.**
protest: **ehtajāj karnā, vb., tr.**
provide: **mohiyā karnā, vb., tr.**
provide for: **parvariś karnā, vb., tr.**
province: **sūbā, msc.**
published: **śāē, adj., n.c.**
(be) published: **śāē hōnā, vb., int.**

pull: **khaĩcnā, khẽcnā, khĩcnā, vb., tr.**
pulse: **dāl, fm.**
punish: **sazā dēnā, vb., tr.**
punishment: **sazā, fm.**
Punjab: **Panjāb, pl. n., msc.**
Punjabi: **Panjābī, adj., n.c.**
Punjabi (language): **Panjābī, fm.**
purdah: **pardā, msc.**
pure: **ḳhālis, adj., n.c.**
purpose: **maḳsad, msc.**
push: **dhakēlnā, vb., tr.**
put: **rakhnā, ḍālnā, vb., tr.**
put down: **nīcē rakhnā, (by force, suppress) dabānā, vb., tr.**
put forward: **sāmnē rakhnā, (present) pēś karnā, vb., tr.**
put on (clothes): **pahannā, vb., tr.**
put to an end: **ḳhatam kar ḍālnā, vb., tr.**
puzzle: **muammā, msc.**
pyr : **citā, fm.**

quantity: **tādād, fm.**
quarrel: **laṛāī, fm.; jhagṛā, msc.**
quarrelsome: **jhagṛālū, adj., n.c.**
quarter (one fourth): **cauthāī, fm.**
quarter of an anna (old currency): **paisā, msc.**
quarter seer: **pāō, msc.**
queen: **malikā, ranī, mahārānī, bēgam, fm.**
question: **savāl (pl., savālāt,), msc.**
quickly: **jaldī, jaldī-sē, tēzī-sē, tēz, adv.**
quickness: **jaldī, fm.**
quiet: **cup, cupcāp, adj., n.c.**
(keep) quiet: **cup rahnā, vb., int.**
(keep) quiet!: **ḳhāmōś, excl.**
quietly: **cupkē-sē, adv.**

radio: **rēdiyō, msc.**
rag: **cīthṛā, msc.**
railway station: **rēlvē • stēśan, msc.**
railway train: **rēl, fm.**
rain: **bāriś, fm.**

rain: **bāriś hōnā, vb., int.**
raincoat: **barsātī, fm.**
rainy season: **barsāt, fm.**
raise: **taraḳḳī, fm.**
rajah: **rājāh, msc.**
Rajastan: **Rājasthān, pl. n., msc.**
Rajput: **rājpūt, msc.**
ram: **dumbā, msc.**
Ramesh: **Ramēś, pr. n., msc.**
rank: **ōhdā, msc.**
rarely: **bahot kam, adv.**
rascal: **badmāś, msc.**
raw: **kaccā, adj.**
Rawalpindi: **Rāvalpiṇḍī, pl. n., msc.**
razor: **ustarā, msc.**
read: **paṛhnā, vb., tr.**
(make someone) read: **paṛhānā, vb., tr.**
read black: **paṛhkar sunānā, vb., tr.**
ready: **taiyār, adv.**
real: **aslī, adj., n.c.**
real name: **aslī nām, msc.**
really: **vāḳayī, adv.**
realm: **rāj, msc.**
reap: **fasal kāṭnā, vb., tr.**
reason: **vajāh, fm.; sabab, msc.**
rebuke: **malāmat, fm.**
rebuke: **malāmat karnā, vb., tr.**
receive: **istaḳbāl karnā, vb., tr.**
recite: **paṛhnā, vb., int.**
recite prayer: **namāz paṛhnā, vb., tr.**
recognize: **pahcānnā, pahcān lēnā, vb., tr.**
recommend: **sifāriś karnā, vb., tr.**
reconquer: **vāpas jītnā, vb., tr.**
recover from grief: **sambhālnā, simbhālnā, vb., tr.,** and **int.**
red: **lāl, surḳh, adj., n.c.**
Red Fort: **lāl ḳilā, pl. n., msc.**
reduce: **kam karnā, vb., tr.**
reference: **zikr, msc.**
reflection: **gaur, msc.**
refreshments: **śarbat pánī, msc.**
refugee: **panāhgazīn, muhājir, msc.**
refusal: **inkār, msc.**
register: **rejisṭar, msc.**
rein: **lagām, fm.**
reinstate: **bahāl karnā, vb., tr.**

rejoice: ḳhuśī manānā, vb., int.
related through paternal uncle: cacērā, adj.
relative: riśtēdār, msc. and fm.
religion: mazhab, dīn, msc.
religious: mazhabī, adj., n.c.
relish: mazā, śauḳ, msc.
remain: rahnā, vb., int.
remainder: bāḳī, adj., n.c. and fm. n.
remedy: ilāj, msc.
remember: yād ānā, vb., int.; yād rakhnā, vb., tr.; yad karnā, vb., tr.
remembrance: yād, fm.
remind: yād dilānā, vb., tr.
remove: haṭānā, vb., tr.
rent: kirāyā, msc.
repair: marammat karnā, vb., tr.
repairing: marammat, fm.
repeat: dōhrānā, phir kahnā, vb., tr.
repentant: paśēmān, adj., n.c.; śarmindā, adj., n.c.
report: ripōrṭ, fm.
repose: ārām, msc.
representation: tarjumānī, fm.
reproof: malāmat, fm.
request: darḳhāst, fm.
request: mā̃gnā, darḳhāst karnā, vb., tr.
research: rīsarc, fm.
reservation: rizarvēśan, fm.
reserve: rizarvēśan karnā, vb., tr.
reserve (cause to): rizarvēśan karānā, vb., tr.
residence: rahāiś, rihāiś, fm.
residency: rēzīḍēnsī, sukūnat, fm.
respect: adab, msc.; izzat, fm.
respectable: muazziz, adj., n.c.
responsible: zimmēdār, adj., n.c.
rest: ārām, msc.; ārām karnā, vb., tr.
restaurant: rēsṭōrāṇṭ, hōṭal, msc.
restless: bēcain, bētāb, adj., n.c.
restraint: rōk, fm.
result: natījā, msc.
retire to sleep: sō jānā, vb., int.
retreat: pīchē haṭnā, vb., int.
return: vāpas jānā, vāpas ānā, lauṭnā, vb., int.
return something: vāpas karnā, vb., tr.
revealed: munkaśif, (religious) ilhāmē, adj., n.c.
revenge: badlā, msc.

revolution: **inḳilāb, msc.**
revolutionary: **inḳilābī, adj., n.c.**
revolve: **ghūmnā, vb., int.**
reward: **inām, msc.**
rib: **paslī, fm.**
rice: **cāval, msc.**
rich: **amīr, adj., n.c.**
rich man: **sēṭh, amīr ādmī, msc.**
rich man's wife: **sēṭhānī, fm.**
rickshaw: **rikśā, fm.**
rider: **savār, msc.**
riding: **savārī, fm.**
right: **dāyā̃, fm.; haḳ, msc.**
righteousness: **nēkī, fm.**
righthand man: **dast-e-rāst, msc.**
rights: **haḳūḳ, msc. pl.**
rind: **chilkā, msc.**
ring: **angūṭhī, fm.**
riot: **fisād, msc.**
ripe: **pakkā, adj.**
ripen: **paknā, vb., int.**
rise: **uṭhnā, baṛhnā, vb., int.**
river: **dariyā, msc.; nadī, fm.**
road: **saṛak, rōḍ, fm.**
roam about: **ghūmnā, vb., int.**
roar: **dahāṛnā, vb., int.**
roast: **bhūnnā, vb., tr.**
roll: **lapēṭnā, vb., tr.**
(take) roll: **hāzrī lēnā, vb., tr.**
roll out: **bēlnā, vb., tr.**
roll call: **hāzrī, fm.**
roof: **chat, fm.**
room: **kamrā, msc.**
rope: **rassā, msc.; rassī, fm.**
rough: **khurdurā, adj.**
round: **gōl, adj., n.c.**
row: **lāin, ḳatār, fm.**
royal: **śāhī, adj., n.c.**
rub: **malnā, ragaṛnā, vb., tr.**
ruin: **khanḍar, msc.**
rule: **rāj, msc.**
rule: **hakūmat karnā, rāj karnā, vb., tr.**
ruler: **hākim, rājāh, navāb, amīr, msc.**
ruminate: **jugālī karnā, vb., tr.**

run: **dauṛnā, (run away) bhāgnā, vb., int.**
run a shop: **dukān karnā, vb., tr.**
rupee: **rūpayā, msc.**

sacred: **muḳaddas, adj., n.c.**
sacred place: **muḳaddas • jagāh, fm.**
sacrifice: **ḳurbānī, fm.**
sacrifice: **ḳurbān karnā, vb., tr.**
(be) sacrificed: **ḳurbān hōnā, vb., int.**
sad: **udās, g̱amgīn, adj., n.c.**
safety: **hifāzat, fm.**
sage: **pīr** (Muslim); **gurū, munī, sādhū** (Hindu), **msc.**
sailor: **jahāzī, msc.**
saint: **pīr, msc.**
salary: **tanḳhāh, fm.**
salt: **namak, msc.**
sample: **namūnā, msc.**
sandal: **cappal, fm.; saindil, msc.** and **fm.**
sari: **sāṛī, fm.**
Sarla: **Sarlā, pr. n., fm.**
satirical: **tanziyā, adj., n.c.**
satisfied: **rāzī, mutmāin, adj., n.c.**
savage: **jañglī, msc.** and **adj., n.c.**
save: **bacā lēnā, bacānā, vb., tr.**
(be) saved: **bacnā, vb., int.**
say: **kahnā, vb., tr.**
say again: **phir kahnā, vb., tr.**
(it is) said: **ye kahā jātā hai**
saying: **kahāvat, fm.**
scale: **tarāzū, fm.; kāṇṭā, skail, msc.**
scandal: **badnāmī, fm.**
scent: **ḳhuśbū, fm.**
scented: **ḳhuśbūdār, adj., n.c.**
scheme: **tarkīb, tajvīz, fm.**
scholarship: **vazīfā, msc.**
school: **skūl, iskūl, msc.**
science: **sāins, fm.**
scientist: **sāinsdān, msc.** and **fm.**
scrap: **ṭukṛā, msc.**
scream: **cillānā, vb., int.**
scribe: **likhnēvālā, msc.**
sea: **samandar, msc.**

search: talāś, fm.
search: ḍhū̃ḍhnā, talāś karnā, vb., tr.
seashore: sāhil, msc.
season: mausam, msc.
seat: sīṭ, fm.
second: dūsrā, adj.
Secretariat: saikrīṭēriyaṭ, msc.
secretary: saikrēṭarī, msc. and fm.
secretly: cōrī cōrī, adv.
see: dēkhnā, vb., tr.
seed: bīj, msc.
seek: ḍhū̃ḍhnā, vb., tr.
seem: mālūm paṛnā, mālūm hōnā, vb., int.
seen: dēkhā huā, adj.
(be) seen: dikhāyī dēnā, vb., int.
seer (weight): sēr, msc.
seize: pakaṛnā, giriftār karnā, vb., tr.
select: cunnā, vb., tr.
self: ḳhud, refl.
sell: bēcnā, vb., tr.
seller: bēcnēvālā, msc.
send: bhējnā, pahō̃cānā, vb., tr.
senior queen: baṛī rānī, fm.
sense: hōśiyārī, fm.
senseless: behōś, adj., n.c.
senses: hōś, havās, msc.
(come to one's) senses: hōś-mē̃ ānā, vb., int.
sentence: fiḳrā, msc.; (punishment) sazā, fm.
sentry: santarī, msc.
separate: alehdā, alag, adj., n.c.
September: sitambar, msc.
sermon: taḳrīr, fm.; (religious) vāaz, msc.
servant: naukar, msc.; mulāzim (pl. mulāzmīn) msc.
servants: naukar • cākar, msc., pl.
set: (appoint) muḳarrar karnā, vb., tr.
(be) set: rakhā jānā, vb., int.
set off (release, abandon): chōṛ dēnā, vb., tr.
settle (inhabit): basānā, vb., tr.
settled (certain): muḳarrar, adj., n.c.
seven: sāt, adj., n.c.
seventeen: satrā, adj., n.c.
seventeenth: satrāvā̃, adj.
seventh: sātvā̃, adj.
seventy: sattar, adj., n.c.
seventy-one: ikhattar, adj., n.c.

seventy-two: **bahattar, adj., n.c.**
seventy-three: **tihattar, adj., n.c.**
seventy-four: **cauhattar, adj., n.c.**
seventy-five: **pichattar, adj., n.c.**
seventy-six: **chihattar, adj., n.c.**
seventy-seven: **satattar, adj., n.c.**
seventy-eight: **aṭhattar, adj., n.c.**
seventy-nine: **unāsī, adj., n.c.**
several: **kaī, adj., n.c.; kuch, pron.**
severe (hard, difficult): **kaṭhan, saḳht, adj., n.c.**
sew: **sīnā, vb., tr.**
shade: **sāyā, chāyā, fm.**
Shah Jahan: **Śāhjahā̃, msc.**
Shalimar Garden: **Śālīmār, pl. n., msc.**
share: **hissā, msc.**
sharpness (splendor): **tēz, adj., n.c.**
Shatrahan: **Śatrahan, pr. n., msc.**
shave: **hajāmat banānā, vb., tr.**
shawl: **śāl, fm.** and **msc.**
she: **vo, ye, pron.**
sheet: **cādar, fm.**
she-fox: **laumṛī, fm.**
she-goat: **bakrī, fm.**
sherbet: **śārbat, msc.**
Sher Shah: **Śērśāh, msc.**
shine: **camaknā, vb., int.**
ship: **jahāz, samāndrī jahāz, msc.**
shirt: **ḳamīs, fm.**
shoe: **jūtā, msc.**
shoelace: **fītā, tasmā, msc.**
shoemaker: **mōcī, camār, msc.**
shoot: **gōlī mārnā, vb., tr.**
shoot arrows: **tīr calānā, vb., tr.**
shop: **dukān, fm.**
shopkeeper: **dukāndār, msc.**
shore: **kinārā, msc.**
short: **thōṛā, adj.; kam, muḳhtasar, adj., n.c.**
(in) short: **bas, adv.**
short story: **afsānā, msc.**
show: **dikhānā, vb., tr.**
shower: **barsānā, vb., tr.**
shrine: **mazār, msc.**
shut: **band, adj., n.c.**
sick: **bīmār, adj., n.c.**
(get) sick: **bīmār hō jānā, vb., int.**

sick person: **bīmār, msc. and fm.**
sigh: **āh, fm.**
sight: **nazar, fm.**
sign: **niśān, patā, msc.**
signal: **iśārā, patā, msc.**
Sikh: **Sīkh, msc.**
silent: **cup, ḳhāmōś, adj., n.c.**
silk: **rēśam, msc.**
silken: **rēśmī, adj., n.c.**
silver: **c̃ādī, fm.**
similar: **ēk-sā, adj.**
Simla: **Śimlā, pl. n., msc.**
simplicity: **sādgī, fm.**
sin: **gunāh, msc.**
sin: **gunāh karnā, vb., tr.**
since: **c̃ū-kē, jab-sē, conj.**
Sindh: **Sindh, pl. n., msc.**
sing: **gānā, vb., tr.**
singer: **gānēvālā, msc.**
singing: **gānēvālā, adj.**
single: **akēlā, adj.; vāhid, adj., n.c.**
sink: **ḍubnā, vb., int.; ḍub jānā, vb., int.**
sir!: **janāb, form of address to a man**
sister: **bahan, fm.**
sit down: **baiṭhnā, vb., int.**
(please) sit down: **taśrīf rakhiyē**
sitting room: **baiṭhak, fm.**
situation: **mauḳā, msc.**
six: **che, adj., n.c.**
sixteen: **sōlā, adj., n.c.**
sixth: **chaṭā, adj.**
sixty: **sāṭh, adj., n.c.**
sixty-one: **iksaṭh, adj., n.c.**
sixty-two: **bāsaṭh, adj., n.c.**
sixty-three: **trēsaṭh, adj., n.c.**
sixty-four: **caũsaṭh, adj., n.c.**
sixty-five: **saĩsaṭh, adj., n.c.**
sixty-six: **chiyāsaṭh, adj., n.c.**
sixty-seven: **saṛsaṭh, adj., n.c.**
sixty-eight: **aṛsaṭh, adj., n.c.**
sixty-nine: **unhattar, adj., n.c.**
skin: **khāl, jild, camṛī, fm.**
sky: **āsmān, msc.**
slaughter: **zibah karnā, vb., tr.**
slave: **g̠ulām, msc.**

(female) slave: **lauṇḍī, fm.**
sleep: **nīnd, fm.; nīnd ānā, sōnā, vb., int.**
(go to) sleep; fall asleep: **sō jānā, vb., int.**
(put to) sleep: **sulānā, vb., tr.**
sleepy: **k͟hābīdā, adj., n.c.**
slip: **phisalnā, vb., int.**
slope: **ḍhalvān, fm.**
slowly: **āhistā, dhīrē, hōlē, adv.**
small: **chōṭā, adj.**
small-goods shop: **bisātī-kī dukān, fm.**
smear: **malnā, phailānā, vb., tr.**
smell: **bū, fm.**
smell: **sūͫghnā, vb., tr.**
smell pleasant: **mahaknā, vb., int.**
smile: **muskurānā, vb., int.**
smoke: **dhuāͫ, msc.**
smoke a cigarette: **sigrēṭ pīnā, vb., tr.**
snake: **sāͫp, msc.**
snatch: **chīnnā, vb., tr.**
snow: **barf, baraf, fm.**
so: **aisā, is tarah, adv.**
so that: **tā-ke, conj.**
soap: **sābun, msc.**
sociable: **milansār, adj., n.c.**
Socialist Party: **sōśalisṭ pārṭī, fm.**
society: **anjuman, fm.**
sock: **jurrāb, fm.; mōzā (pl. mōzē), msc.**
soft: **naram, adj., n.c.**
(speak) softly: **hōlē hōlē bōlnā, vb., int.** and **tr.**
sold: **bēcā huā, adj.**
(be) sold: **biknā, vb., int.**
solidify: **pakkā hō jānā, vb., int.**
solitude: **tanhāī, fm.**
some: **kuch, adj., ind. pron.**
some more: **aur-bhī kuch**
some one else: **aur-bhī kōī**
some other: **kōī aur**
somehow: **kisī na kisī tarah, adv.**
somehow: **kisī na kisī tarah-sē, adv.**
somehow or other: **kisī na kisī tarah-sē, adv.**
someone: **kōī ēk śak͟hs; kōī, pron.**
someone or another: **kōī na kōī**
something: **kuch, adj., ind. pron.**
something else: **kuch aur**
sometimes: **kabhī kabhī, adv.**

somewhere: kahī̃, adv.
son: bēṭā, msc.
song: gānā, gīt, msc.
son-in-law: dāmād, msc.
soon: jald, adv.
soon after: jald-hī, adv.
sorrow: afsōs, dukh, ranj, msc.
sorry: ranjīdāh, adj., n.c.
sort: ḳism, tarah, tarāh, fm.
sound: bajānā, vb., tr.; bajnā, vb., int.
sour: khaṭṭā, adj.
sow: bōnā, vb., tr.
spade: phāuṛā, phāvṛā, msc.
spare: fāltū, adj., n.c.
sparrow: ciṛiyā, fm.
speak: bōlnā, vb., int.
speak softly: hōlē hōlē bōlnā, vb., int.
speak to: bōlnā, (address) muḳhātib karnā, vb., tr.
special: ḳhās, adj., n.c.
Special Court: dīvān-e-ḳhās, msc.; adālat-e-ḳhusūsī, fm.
speed: raftār, fm.
spend (time): basar karnā, vaḳt guzārnā, vb., tr.
spice: masālā, msc.
spicy: masālēdār, adj., n.c.
spin: ghūmnā, vb., int.
(cause to) spin: ghumānā, vb., tr.
spinach: pālak, msc.
spinning wheel: carḳhā, msc.
splendor: śān-ō-śaukat, fm.
split: phaṭnā, alag alag hōnā, vb., int.
spoil: bigāṛnā, vb., tr.; bigaṛnā, vb., int.
spoof: jhūṭ • mūṭ kahnā, vb., tr.
spread: phailnā, chānā, vb., int.; phailānā, vb., tr.
spring: bahār, msc.
spring-crop: rabī, fm.
square (in city): maidān, msc.
Srinagar: Srīnagar, Śrīnagar, pl. n., msc.
stain: dāg, dhabbā, msc.
stairs: sīṛhī, fm.
stand: khaṛā hōnā, vb., int.
(be) standing: khaṛā hōnā, vb., int.
star: tārā, sitārā, msc.
stare: ghūrnā, vb., tr.
start: calnē lagnā, vb., int.
start up from sleep: caũknā, vb., int.

state: **hāl, msc.**
state (country): **riyāsat, saltanat, fm.**
state of affairs: **hālat, msc.**
station: **stēśan, msc.**
status: **maḳām, martabā, msc.; izzat, fm.**
stay: **rahnā, vb., int.**
steal: **cōrī karnā, curānā, vb., tr.**
steam: **bhā̃p, fm.**
steel: **farlād, sṭīl, msc.**
step: **ḳadam, msc.; sīṛhī, fm.**
stick: **chaṛī, fm.**
still: **abhī, abhī-tak, abhī-tō, phir-bhī, adv.**
stipulation: **śart, fm.**
stir: **calānā, vb., tr.**
stir up: **macānā, bhaṛkānā, vb., tr.**
stone: **patthar, msc.**
stop (= bus or trolley stop): **sṭāp, msc.**
stop: **band karnā, rōknā, vb., tr.**
(be) stopped: **band hōnā, ruk jānā, ruknā, vb., int.**
stopping place: **sṭāp, msc.**
storey: **manzil, fm.**
storm: **tūfān, msc.**
story: **kahānī, dāstān, fm.**
(short) story: **afsānā, afsānah, msc.**
stories from the Arabian Nights: **dāstān-e-alaflailā, fm.**
straight: **sīdhā, adj.**
straight ahead: **sāmnē, sīdhē āgē-kō, adv.**
stranger: **ajnabī, msc.** and **fm.**
stream: **nadī, fm.; caśmā, msc.**
street: **galī, saṛak, fm.**
strict: **saḳht, adj.**
strike: **bajānā, vb., tr.**
(be) struck: **bajnā, vb., int.**
strike against: **ṭakrānā, vb., int.**
strip (= take off): **utārnā, vb., tr.**
strip of cloth: **paṭṭī, fm.**
stroke: **zarab, zarb, fm.**
stroll: **sair, fm.**
stroll: **sair karnā, vb., tr.**
strong: **mazbūt, adj., n.c.**
studded: **jaṛā, adj.**
student: **tālibilm, talīb-e-ilm, (pl., tulabā), msc.** and **fm.**
study: **mutālā karnā, vb., tr.**
stupefied: **madhōś, adj., n.c.**
style: **tarz, fm.** and **msc.**
subcontinent: **sabkāṇṭineṇṭ, msc.**

subject: **mazmūn (pl., mazāmīn), msc.; mōzū, msc.**
submit (= present, offer petition): **araz karnā, arz karnā, vb., tr.**
subscription: **candā, msc.**
subtract: **bhatānā, manfī karnā, nikālnā, vb., tr.**
success: **kāmyābī, fm.**
successor: **jānaśīn, msc.** and **fm.**
such: **aisā, is ḳism-kā, adj.**
suddenly: **acānak, adv.**
sugar: **cīnī, śakkar, fm.**
suggestion: **salāh, tajvīz, fm.**
suitable: **munāsab, munāsib, adj., n.c.**
suitor: **āśiḳ, msc.** and **fm.**
sum: **raḳm, fm.**
Sumitra: **Sumitra, pr. n., fm.**
summer: **garmī, fm.**
summon: **bulvā lēnā, bulvānā, vb., tr.**
(be) summoned: **bulvāyā jānā, vb., int.**
(get a) summons: **sāman milnā, vb., int.**
sun: **sūraj,** msc.
Sunday: **itvār, msc.**
sunlight: **dhūp, fm.**
(absorb) sunlight: **dhūp saīknā, dhūp khānā, vb., tr.**
supress: **dabānā, vb., tr.**
(be) suppressed: **dabnā, vb., int.**
Surajmal: **Sūrajmal, pr. n., msc.**
Surdas: **Sūrdās, pr. n., msc.**
sure: **yaḳīnī, adj., n.c.**
surely: **bēśak, adv.**
surface: **satah, satāh, fm.**
surprise: **hairānī, fm.**
surprized: **hairān, adj., n.c.**
sweep: **jhāṛū dēnā, vb., tr.**
sweet: **mīṭhā, adj.**
sweetmeat maker: **halvāī, msc.**
swiftness: **tēzī, fm.**
swim: **tairnā, vb., int.**
sword: **talvār, fm.**
sympathy: **hamdardī, fm.**
syringe: **pickārī, fm.**

table: **mēz, fm.**
taccavī (loans to farmers): **taḳāvī, fm.**
tailor: **darzī, msc.**

Taj Mahal: **Tāj Mahal, pr. n., msc.**
take: **lēnā, lē lēnā, vb., tr.**
take (time): **lagnā, vb., int.**
take away: **lē jānā, vb., tr.**
take care: **ehtiyāt karnā, ehtiyāt rakhnā, ḳhayāl rakhnā, vb., tr.**
take out: **nikālnā, vb., tr.**
take place: **munaḳad hōnā, munaḳid hōnā, vb., int.**
take up: **sambhālnā, iḳhtayār karnā, vb., tr.**
talk: **bōlnā, vb., int.; bātcīt karnā ,vb., tr.**
talk together: **bāt karnā, vb., tr.**
tall: **lambā, adj.**
tank: **tālāb, msc.**
taste: **mazā, msc.**
tasty: **mazēdār, adj., n.c.**
tatter: **paṭṭī, fm.**
tax: **ṭēks, msc.**
tax on non-Muslims: **jaziyā, msc.**
taxi: **ṭēksī, fm.**
Taxila: **Takslā, pl. n., fm.**
tea: **cāy, fm.**
teach: **paṛhānā, sikhānā, vb., tr.**
teacher: **ustād, ustād • sāhab msc.**
tear: **ā̃sū, msc.**
tear: **phāṛnā, vb., tr.**
tear open: **cāk karnā, vb., tr.**
tease: **jhūṭ • mūṭ kahnā, chaiṛnā, vb., tr.**
technique: **tarīḳā, msc.; ṭeknīḳ, fm.**
teeth: **dā̃t, msc. pl.**
telegraph: **tār dēnā, vb., tr.**
telegraph office: **tārghar, msc.**
telephone: **ṭēlīfōn, msc.**
tell: **batānā, sunānā, vb., tr.**
temple: **mandar, msc.**
ten: **das, adj., n.c.**
tennis: **ṭēnis, fm.**
tenth: **dasvā̃, adj.**
test: **imtihān, imtehān, msc.**
thank you, thanks: **śukriyā, msc.**
that: **ke, keh** (particle of quotation), **conj.**
that: **vo, pron.**
that is (i.e.): **yānī, conj.**
theft: **cōrī, fm.**
theme: **mazmūn, msc.**
then: **phir-bhī, us vaḳt, adv.; tab, adv., conj.; to, conj.**
there: **vahā̃, vahī̃, udhar, adv.**

therefore: **is liyē, is-se, adv.**
thick: **ghanā, adj.**
thief: **cōr, msc.**
thin: **patlā, adj.**
thing: **cīz, fm.**
think: **sōcnā, vb., tr.**
think about: **gaur karnā, vb., tr.**
third: **tīsrā, adj.**
thirst: **pyās, fm.**
thirsty: **pyāsā, adj.**
thirty: **tīs, adj., n.c.**
thirty-one: **ikattīs, adj., n.c.**
thirty-two: **battīs, adj., n.c.**
thirty-three: **tẽtīs, adj., n.c.**
thirty-four: **caũtīs, adj., n.c.**
thirty-five: **paĩtīs, adj., n.c.**
thirty-six: **chattīs, adj., n.c.**
thirty-seven: **saĩtīs, adj., n.c.**
thirty-eight: **aṛtīs, adj., n.c.**
thirty-nine: **untālīs, adj., n.c.**
this: **ye, pron., adj.**
thither: **udhar, adv.**
thorn: **kā̃ṭā, msc.**
thought: **k̲hayāl (pl., k̲havālat), gaur, msc.**
thousand: **hazār, msc.** and **adj., n.c.**
(hundred) thousand: **lākh, msc.** and **adj., n.c.**
thousands: **hazārõ, = adv.**
thrash: **mār paṛnā, vb., tr.**
thrashing: **ṭhukāī, fm.**
thread: **ḍōrā, dhāgā, msc.**
(metal) thread: **salmā, msc.**
three: **tīn, adj., n.c.**
three-cornered: **tikōnā, adj.**
throat: **galā, msc.**
throne: **tak̲ht, msc.; gaddī, fm.**
throw: **phẽknā, ḍālnā, vb., tr.**
Thursday: **jumērāt, fm.**
thus: **aisē, vaisē, yū̃, adv.**
Tibet: **Tibbat, pl. n., msc.**
ticket: **ṭikiṭ, msc.; (from a policeman), cālān, msc.**
(get a) ticket: **cālān hōnā, vb., int.**
tie: **bā̃dhnā, vb., tr.**
tiger: **śēr, msc.**
tight: **tang, adj., n.c.**
tightness: **tangī, fm.**

till: **jōtnā, khētī karnā, hal jōtnā, vb., tr.**
tilt: **jhuknā, vb., int.**
time: **dafā, fm.; vaḳt, zamānā, msc.**
(in) time: **vaḳt-par, adv.**
tiny: **nanhā, adj.**
tipsy: **matvālā, adj.; mast, maḳhmūr, adj., n.c.**
tired: **thakā, adj.**
(become) tired: **thak jānā, vb., int.**
title: **ḳhitāb, ḳhatāb, msc.**
to: **-kō, postpos.**
today: **āj, adv.**
to-do: **cahal • pahal, fm.**
together: **ek-sāth, ek hōkar, adv.**
together with: **sāth, adv.**
tomato: **ṭamāṭar, msc.**
tomb: **maḳbarā, msc.**
tomorrow: **kal, adv.**
tonga: **tā̃gā, msc.**
tonga-driver: **tā̃gēvālā, msc.**
tongue: **zabān, fm.**
tonight: **āj • rāt, āj • śām, fm.**
too: **bhī, adv.**
too much: **zyādā, adj.,** and **adv.**
tool: **auzār, msc.**
top: **cōṭī, fm.;** (toy) **laṭṭū, msc.**
topic: **mōzū, msc.**
tot (child): **nanhā, msc.**
towel: **tauliyā, msc.**
toy: **khilaunā, msc.**
trade: **tijārat, fm.**
trade: **tājir, msc.**
traffic: **ṭraifik, fm.**
traffic police: **ṭraifik pōlīs, fm.**
train: **rēlgāṛī, ṭrēn, gāṛī, fm.**
trained: **tarbiyat śudā, adj., n.c.**
transfer: **tabdīl karnā, vb., tr.**
translated: **tarjumā śudā, adj., n.c.**
translation: **tarjumā, msc.**
Travancore-Cochin: **Trāvankōr-Kōcin, pl. n., msc.**
travel: **safar karnā, vb., tr.**
traveler: **musāfir, msc.** and **fm.**
(fellow) traveler: **ham • safar, msc.** and **fm.**
treasury: **ḳhazānā, msc.**
treat: **ilāj karnā, salūk karnā, vb., tr.**
treatment: **ilāj, msc.**

tree: **daraḳht, pēṛ, msc.**
tremble: **kā̃pnā, vb., int.**
tremble with anger: **gussē-sē kā̃pnā, vb., int.**
trianglar: **tikōnā, adj.**
tribe: **ḳabīlā, msc.**
tribunal: **adālat, fm.; ṭrībūnal, msc.**
trolley: **ṭrām, fm.**
troop: **dastā, msc.**
trouble: **taklīf, fm.**
trousers: **garārā, msc.; patlūn, śalvār, fm.; pājāmā, msc.**
truck: **ṭrak, msc.**
true: **sac, adj., n.c.**
trust: **īmān, bharōsā, msc.**
trust: **yaḳīn karnā, bharōsā karnā, vb., tr.**
truth: **sac, msc.; saccāī, fm.**
Tuesday: **māgal, msc.**
Tulsi Das: **Tulsī Dās, pr. n., msc.**
turn: **muṛnā, palaṭnā, ghūmnā, vb., int.**
twelfth: **bārhvā̃, adj.**
twelve: **bārā, adj., n.c.**
twenty: **bīs, adj., n.c.**
twenty-one: **ikkīs, adj., n.c.**
twenty-two: **bāīs, adj., n.c.**
twenty-three: **tēīs, adj., n.c.**
twenty-four: **caubīs**
twenty-five: **paccīs, adj., n.c.**
twenty-six: **chabbīs, adj., n.c.**
twenty-seven: **sattāīs, adj., n.c.**
twenty-eight: **aṭṭhāīs, adj., n.c.**
twenty-nine: **unattīs, adj., n.c.**
two: **dō, adj., n.c.**

ugly: **badsūrat, adj., n.c.**
umbrella: **chatrī, fm.; chātā, msc.**
unarmed: **bēhathyār, adj., n.c.**
uncle (paternal): **cacā, msc.**
uncle (maternal): **māmū̃, msc.**
uncle (mother's sister's husband): **ḳhālū, msc.**
uncooked: **kaccā, adj.**
under: **-kē nīcē, postpos.**
understand: **samajhnā, samajh-mẽ ānā, vb., tr.**
understanding: **samajh, fm.**

unemployed: **bēkār, adj., n.c.**
uniform: **vardī, fm.**
unimportant: **māmūlī, adj., n.c.**
united: **muttahid, adj., n.c.**
(be) united: **muttahid hōnā, vb., int.**
university: **yūnivarsiṭī, fm.**
unpaid: **g̱air • adā śudā, adj., n.c.**
unsuccessful: **nākām, adj., n.c.**
until: **jab-tak, adv.**
untouchable: **achūt, harijan, msc.** and **fm.**
up, upwards: **ūpar, adv.**
upon (above): **-kē ūpar, postpos.**
upset: **parēśān karnā, vb., tr.**
Urdu (language): **Urdū, fm.**
urgent: **zarūrī, adj., n.c.**
use: **istēmāl, fāydā, msc.**
use: **istēmāl karnā, vb., tr.**
useful: **kām-kā, adj.; kārāmad, adj., n.c.**
useless: **bēkār, fazūl, adj., n.c.**
uselessly: **bēkār, adv.**
usually: **aḳsar, ām • taur-par, adv.**
usury: **sūd, msc.**
utensil: **bartan, msc.**

valuable: **ḳīmtī, adj., n.c.**
vanished: **g̱āib, adj., n.c.**
vast: **vasī, adj., n.c.**
Veda: **Vēd, msc.**
Vedic: **Vēdī, adj., n.c.**
vegetable: **sabzī, fm.**
vegetable vender: **sabzīvālā, msc.**
verdict: **faislā, msc.**
verses: **aśār, msc.**
very: **bahot, bēhad, ḳhūb, adv.; baṛā, adj.**
viceroy: **vāisrāy, msc.**
victim: **śikār, msc.** and **fm.**
victory: **fatah, jīt, fm.**
victories: **fatūhāt, futūh, fm., pl.**
view: **nazar, fm.**
(in) view of: **nazar-kē sāmnē, -kī vajah-sē, postpos.**
vigorous: **purzōr, adj., n.c.**
village: **gāõ, msc.**

village headman: **caudharī, caudhrī, msc.**
villager: **gā̃ōvālā, msc.; dīhātī, msc.** and **fm.**
virtue: **k̤hūbī, nēkī, fm.**
visible: **namū̃dār, adj., n.c.**
vision: **nazar, fm.**
vixen: **lumṛī, laumṛī, fm.**
vote: **vōṭ, msc.**
vulture: **gīdh, msc.**

wages: **mazdūrī, fm.**
wait: **intazār karnā, vb., tr.**
waiter: **bairā, msc.**
waiting: **intazār, msc.**
wake: **jāgnā, vb., int.: jagānā, vb., tr.**
wake up: **ā̃khẽ khul jānā, caũk uṭhnā, vb., int.; jagānā, vb., tr.**
walk: **sair, fm.**
walk: **calnā, paidal jānā, paidal calnā, vb., int.; sair karnā, vb., tr.**
wall: **dīvār, fm.**
wander about: **ghūmnā, vb., int.**
want: **zarūrat, fm.**
want: **cāhnā, vb., tr.**
war: **jang, laṛāī, fm.**
warm: **garm, garam, adj., n.c.**
warm up: **garm karnā, vb., tr.**
wash: **dhōnā, vb., tr.**
washerman: **dhōbī, msc.**
washerwoman: **dhōban, fm.**
waste: **barbād karnā, zāē karnā, vb., tr.**
waste (time): **gãvānā, vb., tr.**
wasted: **barbād śudā, adj., n.c.**
watch: **ghaṛī, fm.**
watch: **k̤hayāl rakhnā, pehrā dēnā, vb., tr.**
watch out for: **rāstā dēkhnā, vb., tr.**
watchman: **caukidār, msc.**
watchrepairman: **ghaṛīsāz, msc.**
water: **pānī, āb, msc.**
water-carrier: **bhiśtī, sak̤kā, msc.**
water-pot: **ghaṛā, lōṭā, msc.**
water-tap: **nal, msc.**
wave: **lahar, fm.**
wave: **hilānā, vb., tr.; lahrānā, vb., tr.,** and **int.**
way: **rāh, fm.; rāstā, msc.**

(by) way of: **bazariyā, adv.**
(in a) way: **yū̃ tō, adv.**
way of life: **rahnā • sahnā, msc.**
weak: **kamzōr, adj., n.c.**
weakness: **ḳharābī, kamzōrī, fm.**
wealth: **daulat, fm.**
weapon: **hathyār, msc.**
weaponless: **bēhathyār, adj., n.c.**
weather: **mausam, msc.**
weave: **bunnā, vb., tr.**
wedding: **śādī, fm.**
wedding procession: **barāt, fm.**
Wednesday: **budh, msc.**
week: **haftā, msc.**
weigh: **tōlnā, vb., tr.**
(be) weighed: **tulnā, vb., int.**
weight: **bōjh, msc.**
welcome: **istaḳbāl, msc.**
welfare: **ḳheriyat, falāh, fm.**
well: **acchā, adj.; ḳhūb, adv.**
well done: **śābāś, excl.**
well off: **ḳhuś • hāl, adv.**
well (for water): **kūā̃, msc.**
well-being: **jān-ō-māl, msc., pl.; falāh-ō-behbūd, fm.; ḳheriyat, fm.**
western: **magrabī, adj., n.c.**
wet: **gīlā, adj.; nam, adj., n.c.**
what: **kyā, int. adv.**
what sort: **kaisā, int. adj.**
wheat: **gēhū̃, msc.**
wheel: **pahiyā, msc.**
when: **jab, rel. adv.; kab, int. adv.; ke, conj.**
where: **kahā̃, adv.**
where (whither): **kidhar, adv.**
whereabouts: **patā, msc.**
wherefore: **kis liyē, adv.**
which: **jō, adj.; kaun, int. adj.**
which particular: **kaun-sā, adj.**
whistle: **sīṭī bajānā, vb., tr.**
white: **safēd, adj., n.c.; gōrā, adj.**
white skin: **gōrī camrī, fm.**
whither: **kidhar, adv.**
who: **jō rel., adj.; kaun, int. adj.**
whole: **sārā, adj., tamām, adj., n.c.**
wicked: **bad, prefix; badaimāl, adj., n.c.**
why: **kaisē, kis liyē, adv.; kyū̃, kyō̃, int. adv.**

wide: caṛā, adj.
wife: bīvī, bēgam, fm.
win: jīt jānā, vb., int.; jītnā, mōh lēnā, vb., tr.
wind: havā, fm.
window: khiṛkī, fm.
wine: śarāb, fm.
winter: sardī, fm.
wipe: pȫcnā, vb., tr.
wipe out: miṭānā, vb., tr.
wire: tār, msc.
wire gauze: jālī, fm.
wise: aḳalmand, adj., n.c.; syānā, adj.
wish: murād, fm.; irādā, msc.
wish: cāhnā, vb., tr.
wit: mazāḳ, msc.
with: sāth, adv.; -kē sāth, -sē, postpos.; lēkar, ger.
withdraw: haṭnā, vb., int.
within: andar-tak, adv.
without: bag̲air, prep.; -kē bag̲air, -kē binā, postpos.
without: binā, adv.; prep.; -kē binā, postpos.
without reason: ḳhāh • maḳhāh
wolf: bhēṛiyā, msc.
woman: aurat, fm.
wood: lakṛī, kāṭh, fm.
woodcutter: lakaṛhārā, msc.
word: lafz (pl., alfāz), msc.
work: kām, kārōbār, msc.
work: kām karnā, vb., tr.
work hard: mehnat karnā, vb., tr.
(hard) work: mehnat, fm.
worker: mazdūr, kām karnēvālā, kārkun, msc.
world: jahā̃, msc.; dunyā, fm.
worry: fikr, msc.
worry: fikr karnā, vb., tr.
worship: parastiś, pūjā, fm.
worshipper (Hindu): pujārī, msc.
worthy: lāiḳ, ḳābil, msc. and fm.
worthy of: -kē lāiḳ, -kē ḳābil, postpos.
wound: zaḳham, msc.
wounded: zaḳhmī, adj., n.c.
wreath: phūlȫ-kī cādar, fm.
wrestling: pahlvānī, fm.
wretched: bēcārā, adj.
write: likhnā, vb., tr.
writer: likhnēvālā, msc.

writing: **tasnīf, fm.**
written: **likhā huā, adj.**
(cause to be) written: **likhvānā, vb., tr.**
wrong: **g̱alat, adj., n.c.;** (injustice) **bēinsāf, fm.**

yarn: **sūt, msc.**
year: **sāl, baras, san, msc.**
yearly: **sālānā, adj.**
yellow: **pīlā, adj.; zard, adj., n.c.**
yes: **hā̃, jī, adv.**
yes (sir): **jī hā̃, adv.**
yesterday: **kal, adv.**
yet: **abhī, abhī-tak, abhī-tō, adv.**
yoke: **jōtnā, vb., tr.**
you: **āp, hon, pron.; tum, pron.**
young: **javān, naujavān, adj., n.c.**
young man: **naujavān, msc.**
your: **tērā, tumhārā, āp-kā, poss. adj.**
your honor: **huzūr, msc.**
youth (childhood): **laṛakpan, msc.**

zero: **sifar, msc.**
zither: **sitār, chētārā, msc.**
Zoroaster: **Zarduśt, pr. n., msc.**

INDEX

[Note: Numbers refer to paragraphs.]
"Absolutive." 28 (Remark 3), 30.1.
Addition. 35.4.
Adjective. **Agreement**—3.2, 4.3, 6.1, 11.4–11.4.1; **Predicate Adjective**—12.5; **Demonstrative Adjective**—6.2–6.3.5; **Interrogative Adjective**—18.2–18.4.2, 22.2, 38.2.2; **Indefinite Adjective**—17.3–17.3.4; **Relative Adjective**—25.1, 26.1–26.2.3, 27.3–27.5.2, 38.2–38.2.1, 38.3.
Adverb. 4.4, 10.1, 12.6, 14.3, 31.3; **Interrogative Adverb**—12.1–12.1.2, 13.3; **Relative Adverb**—26.3 and Remark 4, 26.4–26.4.1, 27.1, 27.2, 38.2.1; **Negative Adverb**—12.3–12.6, 13.1–13.4, 23.2–23.4.2; **Sequence**—9.1.1 (Remark 3).
agar. 18.1–18.1.4, 19.4
Agreement. **Subject with verb**—2.1, 2.2, 2.3; **Adjective**—3.2, 4.3, 6.1, 6.2, 9.1.1 (Remark 2); **Postposition**—14.1–14.2, 14.3
Animate vs. Inanimate. 7.1.1 (Remarks).
apnā (Reflexive Adjective). 17.5 (fn. 9), 26.2 (Remark 1).
Aspirates. 1.9, 1.13.
aur. 27.6, 30.1, 35.4.

baṛā. 29.4 (Remark 4).
bhī. 26.2, 26.4, 27.2, 35.2.
binā. 35.2.

cāhiyẽ. 17.1, 19.2, 19.3, 23.2.2.
cāhnā. 3.1, 12.4
Causative Stems. 36.1–36.1.4.
Comparative. 20.3–20.3.6.
Conditional Constructions. 18.1–18.1.4, 19.4, 23.2.1, 23.2.4.
"Conjunctive Participle." 28 (Remark 3), 30.1.
Consonants. 1.2–1.3, 1.5–1.13.
"Contrary to Fact" Condition. 19.4, 23.2.4.
cuknā. 28.7

ḍālnā. 28.4.
Days of Week, 14.4.1 (Remark 1).
Demonstratives. Pronouns—6.2–6.3.3; Adjectives—6.2–6.3.3.
dẽnā. 28.1, 37.2.3; **Imperative**—18.1.1 (Remarks); **Future**—15.2.1; **Past Participle**—22.1.2.
Diphthongs. 1.4.1.
"Direct Discourse." 29.1, 29.2.
Direct Object. **Noun**—5.2–5.6, 6.1, 21.1.1–21.1.4; **Personal Pronouns**—5.1–5.1.1.

Division. 35.4.
Double Consonants. 1.2.9.

Future. 15.1–15.1.1, 15.2–15.2.2, 18.1.3–18.1.4, 23.2–23.2.1; of **hōnā**—15.2, 20.1.4, 21.1.4, 21.2.3.
"Future Perfect." 20.1.4, 21.1.4, 21.2.3.

"Genitive" Construction. 14.1–14.2, 22.5–22.5.5.
Gerund. 28 (Remark 3), 30.1, 33.6.
gunā (= "times"). 35.4.

hamārā. 13.5–13.5.3, 14.3, 33.2 (Remarks).
hī (Emphatic Particle). 26.1–26.1.1, 27.3, 27.5, 35.1, 36.3, 38.2–38.2.1.
hōnā. **Present**—2.1; **Past**—19.1, 19.1.2, 22.1.1; **Future (and Subjunctive)**—15.2, 20.1.4, 22.4.2; **Construction with hōnā**—17.1.1, 29.4.
huā (Past Participle of hōnā). 31.1–31.1.2, 33.1, 33.3.2, 34.2.

ī (Emphatic Particle). 26.1–26.1.1, 26.3 (Remark 2), 36.3.
Imperative. 7.1–7.1.1, 18.1.1.
"Imperfect" Tense. 19.1.
"Impersonal Construction" (= Passive). 37.1.
Indefinite Adjective. 17.3–17.3.2.
Indefinite Pronoun. 17.3–17.3.1.
"Indirect Discourse." 29.3.
"Indirect Object." 9.2.
Infinitive. 3.1, 12.4, 17.1–17.1.2, 30.2–30.2.3, 35.1, 37.2.2–37.2.3; as **Noun**—11.3, 14.2.1 (Remark 2), 37..2; as **Adjective**—37.2.1.
inhẽ. 25.1.1 (Remark 1).
inhõ. 21.1 (Remarks), 22.2.1.
Interrogative Adjective. 18.2–18.2.1, 18.3, 18.4, 22.2 (See also under **"Adjective"**).
Interrogative Pronoun. 18.2–18.2.1, 22.2 (See also under **"Pronoun"**).
Intransitive Verb. 20.1, 28 (Remark 1).
isē. 25.1.1 (Remark 1).

jab (Relative Adverb). 26.3, 26.4–26.4.1.
jānā 20.1 (Remarks), 28 (Remark 2), 28.3, 34.4, 37.1; **Past Participle**—20.1.1 (Remarks), 22.1.
jahā̃ (Relative Adverb). 27.1, 27.2.
jaisā (Relative Adjective and Pronoun). 38.2.
jaisā (Postposition). 33.2.
jaisē (Relative Adverb). 38.2.1.
jāyā. 34.5 (Remark 1), 37.1 (Remark 1). (See **jānā**).
jinhẽ. 25.2.
jinhõ. 25.2.
jisē. 25.2.
jitnā (Relative Adjective). 27.3, 27.4, 27.5, 38.3.
jō (Relative Adjective). 25.1, 26.1, 26.2–26.2.1; **Relative Pronoun**—25.2, 26.1.1, 35.3.
jō (Relative Adverb). 26.3 (Remark 4).

kā (Postposition). 14.1–14.2, 35.3.
kab (Interrogative Adverb). 12.1.2.
kabhī (Interrogative Adverb). 26.4.1.
kahā̃ (Interrogative Adverb). 12.1.
kaī (Indefinite Adjective). 29.4 (Remark 2).
kaisā (Interrogative Adjective). 38.2.
kam. 20.3.5–20.3.6.

ḳarīb ("about"). 38.4.
karkar. 30.1 (Remark 3).
karkē (See **karnā**). Cf. **karkar.**
karnā. 15.3–15.3.2, 34.5, **Imperative**—18.1.1 (Remarks); **Past Participle**—22.1.4; **Gerund**—30.1 (Remark 3).
kaun (Interrogative Adjective and **Pronoun).** 18.2, 38.1.1.
kē (See **Possession**). 22.5, 35.2 (Remark 1).
kē binā. 35.2 (Remark 1).
kē liyē. 11.3.
kē nīcē. 10.2–10.2.1.
kē pās. 11.1–11.2.1.
kē pichē. 10.1–10.1.1.
kē sāmnē. 10.4–10.4.1.
kē sāth. 10.3–10.3.1.
ki, kē. 27.5, 28.3 (Remark 1), 29.2 and Remark 3, 29.3, 30.2.1 (Remark 1), 30.2.3.
kinhõ (See **kaun**). 21.1 (Remarks), 22.2.
kitnā (Interrogative Adjective). 18.4.
kō (Postposition). 9.1.1 (Remark 1), 9.2, 10.3 (Remarks), 17.1–17.1.2, 17.2, 33.4.1, 34.1.
kōī (Indefinite Adjective and **Pronoun).** 17.3–17.3.4.
kuch (Indefinite Adjective and **Pronoun).** 17.4.
kyā (Interrogative Adjective and **Pronoun).** 18.2.1.
kyā (Interrogative Particle). 11.5–11.5.2, 13.2.
kyõ, kyũ (Interrogative Adverb). 12.1.1, 13.3.

lagnā. 27.3 (Remark 1), 30.1 (Remark 2), 34.1–34.1.2.
lēnā. 28.2; Future—15.2.2; **Imperative**—18.1.1 (Remarks); **Past Participle**—22.1.3.
lōg (= **Plural Particle).**
Long Consonants. 1.2.9.

mālūm hōnā. 30.2.1 (Remark 1).
mat (Negative Particle).
mẽ (Postposition). 9.1–9.1.1.
mērā. 33.2 (Remarks).
milnā. 26.4.1 (Remark 1), 33.4–33.4.1.
Multiplication. 35.4.

na (Negative Particle). 23.2.1, 23.2.4.
nahī̃ (Negative Adverb). 12.3–12.6, 13.1–13.4, 23.2–23.2.1, 23.2.5–23.4.2.
Nasal Consonants. 1.2.2, 1.10.
Nasalized Diphthong. 1.8.
Nasalized Vowel. 1.8.
nē (Postposition). 21.1–21.2.4.
Negation. 23.2–23.4.2.
Negative Particle. 12.3–12.6, 13.1–13.4.
Non-Aspirates. 1.2.1, 1.5.
Noun. Masculine: ending in ā—2.2; ending in **a**—9.1.1 (Remark 4); **other nouns**—3.3; **Feminine:** ending in ī—2.3; **others**—3.4, 4.1, 4.2; **Direct Object**—5.1, 5.2, 5.3, 5.4, 5.5, 5.6; **Indirect Object**—9.2.
Noun + Verb. 23.1.1 (Remark 1); **Noun + karnā**—22.1.5 (Remark 1).
Numerals. 2.4, 3.5, 4.6, 5.7, 6.4, 7.3.

Object Form. 21.1.1, 21.2.
Ordinal numbers. 19.5.

pahilē. 33.3.3.
par (Postposition). 9.3, 35.1.
paṛnā. 17.1.2, 22.4–22.4.1, 28.5.
pasand. with **hōnā**—20.2–20.2.2; with **karnā**—15.3–15.3.2.
Passive. 37.1.
"Past Continuative." 19.1, 23.1.
Past Participle. 20.1–20.1.4, 21.1–21.2.3, 35.2, 37.1; as **Adjective**—33.1.
"Past Participle." (with **karnā** = **gerund**). 34.5.
"Past Perfect." 20.1.3, 21.1.3, 21.2.2, 23.3.2, 23.4.2.
"Past Progressive." 23.1.
Past Tense. 19.1, 23.2.6, 26.5 (fn. 39).
(Simple) Perfect. 20.1, 23.3, 23.4.
pichlē. 33.3.1.
"Possession." 11.2–11.2.1, 22.5–22.5.5, 35.3.
Possessive Pronominal Adjective. 13.5–13.5.3, 14.3.
Postpositional Compounds. 10.1–10.4.1, 11.1–11.3.1, 33.2, 35.2 (Remark 1).
Postpositions. 5.1–5.6, 9.1–9.4.1, 14.1–14.3, 21.1–21.2.4, 22.5–22.5.5, 30.2–30.2.3.
Predicate-Adjective Construction. 3.2, 20.3–20.3.8.
Present Participle. 2.1, 19.1, 34.3–34.4.1; as **Adjective**—31.1–31.1.1, 31.4; as **Adverb**—31.3, 34.2, 35.1, as **Noun**—31.1 (Remarks).
"Present Perfect." 20.1.2, 21.1.2, 21.2.1, 23.3.1, 23.4.1.
"Present Progressive." 23.1.
Present Tense. 2.1, 12.3, 18.1–18.1.1.
Pronoun. **Personal**—2.1, 5.1, 9.4.1 (Remark 1), 10.1 (Remarks), 14.1–14.1.1; **Demonstrative**—6.2–6.3.3; **Interrogative**—18.2–18.2.1; **Relative**—25.2, 26.1.1; **Indefinite**—17.3–17.3.3.

rahnā. 27.7 (fn. 109), 34.3, 34.4.1; **Past Participle Construction**—23.1.
Reflexive Adjective. 26.2 (Remark 1).
Relative Adjective. 25.1, 26.1, 26.2–26.2.1.
Relative Construction. 25.1, 25.2, 26.1–26.4.1, 27.1–27.5, 38.2, 38.3.
Relative Pronoun. 25.2, 26.1.1.
Repetition. 4.4 (Remark 2), 31.3, 33.6, 36.2, 33.6.
Retroflex Consonant. 1.7.

sā. 18.3, 25.3 (fn. 92), 29.4 (Remark 1), 38.1–38.1.1.
sab-kē sab. 38.3.
saknā. 12.2, 13.4.
śāyad. 14.4.
sē (Postposition). 9.4, 29.1 (Remark 1), 33.3–33.3.1, 33.4.
sē pahilē. 28.3 (Remark 2).
Sequence of Adverbs. 9.1.1 (Remark 3).
Sibilants. 1.11.
"Simple Perfect." 20.1, 21.1–21.1.1.
śrī. 28.9 (fn. 3), 30.3 (fn. 17).
Stem (Verbal). 2.1 (Remark 2), 12.2, 13.4 (Remarks), 20.1, 23.1, 28 and Remark 3—28.7, 30.1, 36.1–36.1.4; = **Gerund**—33.6.
Subject Form. 21.2.
Subjunctive. 14.4–14.4.1, 18.1.2–18.1.3, 23.2.1; of **pīnā**—18.1.2 (Remark 2).
Subtraction. 35.4.
Superlative. 20.3.2.

tab (Correlative). 26.3, 26.4–26.4.1.
tērā. 26.5 (fn. 48).
thā (See **hōnā**). 19.1–19.1.1, 20.1.3, 21.1.3, 21.2.2.

Time Phrase. 7.2, 33.3–33.3.3, 35.5–35.5.1.
tõ. 17.5 (fn. 18), 18.1–18.1.4; **Correlative**—26.3 (Remark 4).
Transitive Verb. 21.1–21.2.4, 28 (Remark 1).
tumhārā. 13.5–13.5.3, 14.3 33.2 (Remarks).

unhẽ̆. 25.1.1 (Remark 1).
unhõ̆. 21.1 (Remarks), 22.2.2.
"Unreal Subjunctive." 19.4.
usē. 25.1.1 (Remark 1).
uṭhnā. 28.6.
utnā. 27.3–27.5.

vo. (See **Pronouns**)
vahā̃ **(Correlative Adverb).** 27.1, 27.2.
vaisā **(Correlative).** 38.2.
vaisē **(Correlative Adverb).** 38.2.1.
vālā. 31.2.
Verbal Clusters. Lesson 28.
Verbal Stem. 2.1 (Remark 2), 20.1, 23.1, 36.1–36.1.4.
Vowel Replacement. 36.1.1–36.1.4.
Vowels. 1.1, 1.4, 1.8.

ye. (See **Pronouns**).

zyādā. 20.2.1–20.2.2, 20.3.1.